INTERVIEWING

Principles and Practices

THIRTEENTH EDITION

Charles J. Stewart
Purdue University

William B. Cash, Jr.

Mc Graw Hill
Connect Learn Succeed™

The McGraw-Hill Companies

INTERVIEWING: PRINCIPLES AND PRACTICES, THIRTEENTH EDITION

Published by McGraw-Hill, a business unit of The McGraw-Hill Companies, Inc., 1221 Avenue of the Americas, New York, NY 10020.

This book is printed on acid-free paper.

1 2 3 4 5 6 7 8 9 0 DOC/DOC 1 0 9 8 7 6 5 4 3 2 1 0

ISBN 978-0-07-340681-7
MHID 0-07-340681-3

Vice President & Editor-in-Chief: Michael Ryan
Vice President EDP/Central Publishing Services: Kimberly Meriwether David
Executive Sponsoring Editor: Susan Gouijnstook
Executive Marketing Manager: Pamela Cooper
Project Manager: Melissa Leick
Design Coordinator: Brenda A. Rowles
Cover Designer: Studio Montage, St. Louis, Missouri
Photo Research Coordinator: Brian Pecko
Cover Image: © Getty Images/RF
Buyer: Susan K. Culbertson
Media Project Manager: Sridevi Palani
Compositor: MPS Limited, A Macmillan Company
Typeface: 10/12 Times Roman
Printer: R. R. Donnelley

Library of Congress Cataloging-in-Publication Data

Stewart, Charles J.
Interviewing : principles and practices / Charles J. Stewart, William B.
Cash, Jr.—13th ed.
p. cm.
ISBN 978-0-07-340681-7
1. Interviewing—Textbooks. 2. Employment interviewing—Textbooks.
3. Counseling—Textbooks. I. Cash, William B. II. Title.
BF637.I5S75 2010
158'.39—dc22

2010028050

www.mhhe.com

To the memory of William "Bill" Cash, Jr., student, co-author, and friend

ABOUT THE AUTHORS

Charles J. Stewart

Charles J. Stewart is the former Margaret Church Distinguished Professor of Communication at Purdue University where he taught from 1961 to 2009. He taught undergraduate courses in interviewing and persuasion and graduate courses in such areas as persuasion and social protest, apologetic rhetoric, and extremist rhetoric on the Internet. He received the Charles B. Murphy Award for Outstanding Undergraduate Teaching from Purdue University and the Donald H. Ecroyd Award for Outstanding Teaching in Higher Education from the National Communication Association. He has written articles, chapters, and books on interviewing, persuasion, and social movements.

He has been a consultant with organizations such as the Internal Revenue Service, the American Electric Power Company, Libby Foods, the Indiana University School of Dentistry, and the United Association of Plumbers and Pipefitters. He was recently sworn in as a Court Appointed Special Advocate (CASA) for children.

William B. Cash, Jr.

The late William "Bill" Cash began his work life in his father's shoe and clothing store in northern Ohio. While still in high school, he began to work in broadcasting and advertising, and this led to bachelor's and master's degrees in broadcasting and speech communication at Kent State University. After completing his academic work at Kent State, he joined the speech communication faculty at Eastern Illinois University and began to consult with dozens of companies such as Blaw-Knox, IBM, and Hewitt Associates. Bill took a leave from Eastern Illinois and pursued a PhD in organizational communication under W. Charles Redding. He returned to the faculty at Eastern Illinois and created and taught a course in interviewing.

Bill Cash left college teaching and held positions with Ralston Purina, Detroit Edison, Baxter, and Curtis Mathis, often at the vice president level. After several years in industry, he returned to teaching and took a faculty position at National-Louis University in Chicago. He became the first chair of the College of Management and Business and developed courses in human resources, management, and marketing.

BRIEF CONTENTS

CONTENTS

PREFACE

This thirteenth edition of *Interviewing: Principles and Practices* continues to reflect the growing sophistication with which interviewing is being approached, the ever-expanding body of research in all types of interview settings, recent interpersonal communication theory, and the importance of equal opportunity laws on interviewing practices. We have included the latest research findings and developments throughout the text while continuing to maintain the emphasis on building interviewing skills for both interviewers and interviewees. The increasing diversification within the United States and the influences of the global village receive treatment in most chapters.

We made this edition more student-friendly by eliminating unnecessary words, materials, and dated models, offering precise explanations, providing fewer lists, and using bold print to call attention to important terms. Guidelines, observations, principles, and cautions appear in the margins. A list of key terms is provided at the end of each chapter, and there is a glossary of important terms and theories at the end of the text.

Changes in the Thirteenth Edition

Each chapter includes new or revised examples and illustrations, student activities, suggested readings, research findings, and an interview that challenges students to apply theory and principles to a realistic interview. In each interview, the parties do some things well and others poorly. We want students to be able to identify strengths and weaknesses and to offer alternatives that would have made the interview more effective for each party. We have restructured some chapters to take readers through them in a more natural progression of concepts and interview stages.

Major changes include:

- Chapter 1 focuses more concisely on what an interview is and is not, with added emphasis on the interview as a collaborative effort between two parties. It includes new material on the focus group interview, the e-mail interview, and the virtual interview.
- Chapter 2 now includes an expanded and refined treatment of the importance of relationship in the interview, including relational history; intimate, casual, distant, formal, and functional relationships; relational memory; dialectical tensions; global relationships; and the influence of gender in relationships.
- Chapter 3 includes new materials on question types and question pitfalls and the influence of demographic characteristics and culture in questioning and responding.
- Chapter 4 is restructured with a thorough discussion of the body of the interview before opening and closing, reflecting with this change how one should prepare for an interview.

- Chapter 5 has a new title, "The Informational Interview," to reflect more accurately the essential purpose of this interview. A strong emphasis remains on the journalistic interview. There is new material on laws pertaining to recording interviews, detecting dishonesty in interviews, and three types of informational interviews: broadcast, oral history, and videoconference.
- Chapter 6 contains new materials on openings, culture and the global setting, probing questions in surveys, face-to-face and telephone interviews, and survey interviews over the Internet.
- Chapter 7 includes a revised and updated treatment of EEO laws, cross-cultural interviews, behaviorally based recruiting, and assessing the honesty of applicants.
- Chapter 8 includes a revised and expanded treatment of applicant self-analysis, the growing problem of dishonesty in the employment process, and new materials on face-to-face and virtual job/career fairs.
- Chapter 9 discusses the strengths and weaknesses of the 360-degree approach to performance review and focuses on four performance models: behaviorally anchored rating scale, management by objectives, universal performance interviewing model, and the 360-degree approach.
- Chapter 10 is restructured to make it a more natural progression of stages in the persuasion process and includes new materials on the ethics of persuasion, prospecting for interviewees, and selecting interviewees.
- Chapter 11 includes more material on the ethics of the interviewee in the persuasive interview and new materials on language strategies.
- Chapter 12 has some restructuring and additional materials on counselor self-analysis and cross-cultural counseling.
- Chapter 13 includes new materials on the health care interview as a collaborative effort between provider and patient, an expanded emphasis on the relationship of provider and patient, and material on patients turning increasingly to the Internet for medical information and how this may affect the provider-patient relationship.

Chapter-by-Chapter Overview

Chapter 1 develops a definition of interviewing and contrasts interviewing with other forms of interpersonal communication, including social conversations and small groups. It introduces students to six traditional types of interviews and to nontraditional types such as focus group, videoconference, e-mail, and virtual interviews.

Chapter 2 takes students through a step-by-step development of the Cash–Stewart model of interviewing as it treats the interview as a complex interpersonal communication process. This chapter emphasizes the importance of the interview as a relational form of communication (emphasizing relational dimensions, global relationships, and gender in relationships) and of how self-concept in interviews (addressing concepts such as self-image, self-esteem, and self-reliance differ in non-Western cultures that are collectivist rather than individualist). The discussion of the importance of self-disclosure in interviews incorporates politeness theory and notes how self-disclosure differs between sexes and among cultures. The nature and uses of verbal and nonverbal communication are highlighted and so are language use and space according to age, sex, culture, and ethnicity. Students are introduced to four types of listening: for empathy, for comprehension, for evaluation, and for resolution. And students become aware of the potential influences of "outside forces" on each interview party.

Chapter 3 introduces students to the many types and uses of questions in interviews, literally the tools of the trade. It contains an identification and illustration of common question pitfalls that plague both parties in interviews. This chapter discusses the apparent relevance of questions to interviewers and interviewees from other cultures. It also addresses responses to questions that require personal disclosure and discusses how men and women and those of differing cultures may disclose information differently.

Chapter 4 focuses on the structure of interviews, including openings, bodies, and closings. It emphasizes how verbal and nonverbal communication in openings and closings differs between males and females and how cultures other than Western ones regard handshaking, touching, and eye contact. This chapter contains a discussion of question sequences as well as outline sequences in discussions of interview guides and schedules to help students develop the bodies of interviews.

Chapter 5, on the informational interview, focuses on ways to enhance the effectiveness of information gathering in a wide variety of situations, including journalistic ones. It applies principles to interviews conducted by attorneys, police officers, recruiters, health care professionals, insurance claims investigators, and teachers, as well as journalists. There is strong emphasis on preparation, relationship, and motivation.

Chapter 6, on the survey interview, stresses the importance of meticulous preparation, structure, question development, and conducting interviews when replicability and reliability are essential to successful outcomes. Special attention is given to question strategies and scales and to methods of sampling the target population.

Chapter 7, on the recruiting interview, reflects the employer's roles of attracting and selecting new employees. It contains a lengthy identification and discussion of relevant EEO laws that pertain to the employee selection process. It assesses what applicants want in positions and careers, use of computers and the Internet to attract and inform applicants, and job fairs. This chapter continues to refine its discussion of electronic systems for scanning resumes, quantitative tests to assess applicants, videotaping and videoconferencing, the behavior-based interview, nontraditional interviewing approaches, and on-the-job questions.

Chapter 8 addresses the selection interview from the applicant's perspective. It contains discussions of the reality of cultural diversity, databases and Internet resources for searching for positions and learning about organizations, positions, and careers or job fairs. There are guidelines for preparing resumes and cover letters and sample resumes, including one designed for electronic scanning. Although this chapter places strong emphasis on responding to questions effectively, including those that violate EEO laws, there is corresponding emphasis on asking questions effectively.

Chapter 9, on performance review interviews, contains discussions of the balanced scoreboard approach and preparing for the review. This chapter continues to introduce students to a variety of models for conducting performance reviews, while emphasizing the interview as a coaching rather than judgmental opportunity and process. It also introduces students to the "performance problem interview," which avoids the negative connotation and implication of guilt associated with the old "discipline interview."

Chapter 10, which focuses on the *persuader* in the persuasive interview, emphasizes the ethical responsibilities of the persuader. It incorporates discussions of persuasion theories, including identification, balance or consistency, inoculation, forced or induced compliance, and psychological reactance. Its focus is on persuasion in everyday life, not merely in sales situations. This chapter also addresses values, differences in cultures, and how cultures view time, bargaining, and relationship building. There is strong emphasis on structuring the persuasive interview.

Chapter 11 focuses on the *persuadee* in the persuasive interview. It emphasizes the ethical responsibilities of the persuadee and the need to be an informed participant. Students are introduced to common psychological and language strategies persuaders employ. The chapter focuses on the persuadee as an active and critical participant who understands how to identify and assess logical strategies and the evidence that supports them.

Chapter 12 focuses on preparing, structuring, and conducting counseling interviews by lay counselors who have minimal training in counseling. It emphasizes the need for self-analysis as well as analysis of the interviewee, selection of appropriate interviewing approaches, listening, observing, and responding in appropriate and effective ways to interviewees from widely different cultures and backgrounds. The interviewer must be people-oriented rather than task-oriented. Students are introduced to a sequential phase model and a client-centered approach to counseling.

Chapter 13 focuses on the health care interview as a collaborative effort between provider and patient and addresses the relationships and interactions of the two parties. It discusses the effect of gender, age, ethnic group, and culture on the provider-patient relationship and treats information getting, information giving, counseling, and persuading as joint efforts of patient and provider. This chapter notes differences in information seeking, nonverbal interactions, and preference for verbal communication among differing cultures.

Some of the principles and guidelines presented in these thirteen chapters may seem simple or obvious. However, in our experiences as professors, managers, practitioners, and consultants of interviewing in academic, professional, industrial, business, and social settings, we have found again and again that overlooking the simple and the obvious creates problems in real-life interviews.

Chapter Pedagogy

We have included a **sample interview at the end of each chapter,** not as a perfect example of interviewing but to illustrate interviewing types, situations, approaches, and mistakes and to challenge students to distinguish between effective and ineffective interviewing practices. We believe that students learn by applying the research and principles discussed in each chapter to a realistic interview that allows them to detect when interview parties are right on target as well as when they miss the target completely. The **role-playing cases** at the ends of Chapters 5 through 13 provide students with opportunities to design and conduct practice interviews and to observe others' efforts to employ the principles discussed. **Student activities** at the end of each chapter provide ideas for in- and out-of-class exercises, experiences, and information gathering. We have made many of these less complex and time-consuming. The **up-to-date readings** at the end of each chapter will help students and instructors who are interested in delving more deeply into specific topics, theories, and types of interviews. The glossary provides students with definitions of key words and concepts introduced throughout the text.

Intended Courses

This book is designed for courses in such departments as speech, communication, journalism, business, supervision, education, political science, nursing, criminology, and social work. It is also useful in workshops in various fields. We believe this book is of value to beginning students as well as to seasoned veterans because the principles, research, and techniques are changing rapidly in many fields. We have treated theory and research findings where applicable, but our primary concern is with principles and techniques that can be translated into immediate practice in and out of the classroom.

Ancillary Materials

For the Student

Student's Online Learning Center (OLC)

The Student's Online Learning Center Web site that accompanies this text offers a variety of resources for students, including—for each chapter—a chapter summary; an interactive quiz with multiple-choice, fill-in, and/or true/false questions; and flashcards of key terms. Please visit the *Interviewing* OLC at www.mhhe.com/Stewart13e.

For the Instructor

The Instructor's Manual, written by Charles Stewart, Test Bank, and PowerPoint slides are available to instructors on the password-protected Instructor's section of the Online Learning Center Web site.

Acknowledgments

We wish to express our gratitude to students at Purdue University and National-Louis University College of Management, and to past and present colleagues and clients for their inspiration, suggestions, exercises, theories, criticism, and encouragement. We thank Suzanne Collins, Ellen Phelps, Rebecca Parker, Mary Alice Baker, Kasie Roberson, Vernon Miller, Dana Olen, Kathleen Powell, Garold Markle, and Patrice Buzzanell for their resources, interest, and suggestions.

We are very grateful to the following reviewers for the many helpful comments and suggestions they provided us:

Rosalind Baty, Baylor University

Karen Beck, University of Houston–Downtown

Rita Rahoi-Gilchrest, Winona State University
Alberta Gloria, University of Wisconsin–Madison
Kathleen Golden, Edinboro University of Pennsylvania
Patricia Holmes, University of Louisiana at Lafayette
Debi Iba, Texas Christian University
Vivi McEuen, California State University, Chico
Patricia Mellon, Purdue University Calumet
Vernon Miller, Michigan State University
Cindy Ridle, Western Illinois University
Diana Sibberson, University of Akron
Vicky Verano, Florida State University
Cory Young, Ithaca College

CHAPTER 1 An Introduction to Interviewing

Interviews are daily occurrences.

If you were to walk into an interviewing classroom on the first day of the semester and ask classmates why they were there, you might be surprised at their responses. A senior might reply that she was hoping to discover how to prepare more effectively for job interviews. A student majoring in journalism might explain that interviewing skills are critical to his future career as a television reporter. A person planning to enter sales might comment that her adviser recommended the course to get an introduction to persuasion principles necessary for working one-on-one with clients. A sociology student might explain that interviewing, particularly conducting surveys, is essential in his research. A nursing student might remark that she will need effective interviewing skills when working with patients. A management major might point to chapters and units on employment, performance review, and counseling interviews that are essential to her planned career. You would learn quickly why interviewing is the most common form of purposeful, planned communication. Interviews may be formal or informal, unstructured or structured, simplistic or sophisticated, supportive or threatening. They may last for a few minutes to hours and be intimate or highly functional.

Interviews share characteristics with intimate interactions, social conversations, small groups, and presentations, but they are significantly different. This chapter identifies the essential elements of interviewing, distinguishes interviewing from other types of communication, and discusses traditional and nontraditional forms of interviewing.

The Essential Elements of Interviews

Interactional

Interviews involve exchanging and sharing.

Roles may switch from moment to moment.

An interview is **interactional** because there is an **exchanging,** or sharing, of roles, responsibilities, feelings, beliefs, motives, and information. If one person does all of the talking and the other all of the listening, a speech to an audience of one, not an interview, is taking place. Although you may identify the interviewer and interviewee in interviews, you interchange these roles as interviews progress. For instance, if as an interviewee you ask questions about Internet security with one of your school's Web specialists, make a counteroffer for a hybrid automobile, talk to an academic counselor about a summer internship in Kenya, or request a nurse practitioner to explain the possible side effects of a prescribed drug, you assume the role of interviewer for the moment and the interviewer takes on the role of interviewee. As the other person responds, makes a counteroffer, answers questions, or gives explanations, the roles switch back to traditional ones.

Interactional does not mean equal. In some interviews, such as journalistic and counseling, an ideal division of speaking time might be 70 percent to 30 percent, with the interviewee doing most of the talking. In others, such as information giving and sales, the ratio might be reversed with the interviewer doing most of the talking and questioning. Both parties must determine an appropriate ratio. For instance, in an employment interview, each party will dominate specific segments such as when recruiters and applicants ask or answer questions, give or get information.

Interactional also means a sharing of responsibilities. When thinking of interviews such as recruiting, journalistic, health care, and persuasive, you may focus on the responsibilities of one party—the applicant in the recruiting interview, the investigator in the journalistic or police interview, the health care professional in the medical interview, and the persuader in the persuasive interview. In the real world, however, both parties are responsible for the success or failure of each interview. The interview is a mutual activity and will not work if either party fails to appreciate the collaborative nature of the effort. For example, the recruiter is responsible for studying the applicant's credentials, preparing insightful and challenging questions, being up-to-date on information about the organization, and replying honestly and fully to the applicant's questions. On the other hand, the applicant is responsible for doing a careful self-analysis, preparing thorough and honest credentials, researching the organization and position, replying honestly and fully to questions, and asking carefully phrased questions about the position and organization. It takes two parties to make an interview a success. That is why we address the roles of both interviewer and interviewee throughout this book.

It takes two to make an interview a success.

Few interviews are successful if either party is unwilling to share feelings, beliefs, motives, and information. Before an interview begins, be aware of your **feelings** (pride, fear, anger, sympathy), **motives** (security, belonging, freedom, ambition), **beliefs** (social, political, historic, economic, religious), and **information** (facts, data, opinions) and those of the other party. John Stewart writes that communication is a "continuous, complex collaborative process of verbal and nonverbal meaning-making."[1] When discussing the nature of the interview, we should place a strong emphasis on the word **collaborative.** Creating and sharing comes from words and nonverbal signals—touches, hugs, handshakes, and facial looks—that express interest, concerns, and reactions. Close interpersonal interchanges such as interviews involve risk that can be minimized but never eliminated, and if either party "plays it safe," the interview is likely to fail.

All interviews involve risk.

Process

A **process** is a dynamic, continuing, ongoing, ever-changing interaction of variables with a degree of **system** or **structure.** The parties in each interaction generate energy through their desires to achieve specific goals. Communication interactions are not static. Role changes, exchanges of information, and revelations of feelings and motives produce reactions and insights that lead to new and unexpected areas. "Human communicators are always sending and receiving simultaneously. As a result each communicator has the opportunity to change how things are going at any time in the process."[2] Although each interview is unique, each involves an interaction of perceptions, verbal and nonverbal messages, levels of disclosure, feedback, listening, motivation, expectations, and assumptions. Both parties bring knowledge, experiences,

An interview is a complex, ever-changing process.

No interview occurs in a vacuum.

© Digital Vision

More than two people may be involved in an interview, but never more than two parties—an interviewer party and an interviewee party.

expectations, pressures, and personal limitations to the interaction. Every interview occurs at a specific time, on a specific date, at a specific location surrounded by objects, persons, and sounds, and precedes or follows events that may impact it for good or ill. Theorists agree that all communication takes place in a **cultural context,** a context that is increasingly critical in our twenty-first-century global village.[3]

Like other processes, once an interview begins, we "cannot not communicate."[4] We may communicate effectively or poorly, but we will communicate something as long as we are within sight or sound of one another. The result may be success or failure. Chapter 2 develops a general summary model that discusses and illustrates the many communication variables that interact in the interviewing process.

Parties

A dyadic process involves two parties.

The interview is a **dyadic—two-party**—process. We typically think of it as involving two people—a sales representative and a buyer, a physician and a patient, a reporter and an eyewitness, but many interviews include more than two people but never more than two parties. For instance, two recruiters from Macy's may be interviewing a college senior, two detectives may be interviewing a crime victim, and three friends (planning to room together next semester) may be interviewing an apartment manager. In each of these situations, there are two distinct parties—an interviewer party and an interviewee party.

If there are more than two parties involved (three different investment firms bidding on lakeside acreage or four designers from Ford discussing a new hybrid vehicle), a small group interaction is occurring, not an interview. There are four parties in the first interaction and one party in the second.

Purpose

All interviews have a degree of structure.

At least one of the two parties must come to an interview with an important goal—other than mere enjoyment—and intention to focus on specific subject matter. This **predetermined** and **serious** purpose distinguishes the interview from social **conversation** or informal, unplanned interactions such as meeting a friend on the street. While conversations are rarely organized in advance, interviews must have a degree of advanced planning and structure, even if little more than a purpose and topics. In most effective interviews, the interviewer plans the opening, selects topics, prepares questions, gathers

An interview is a conversation and much more.

information, and determines how to close the interview. Chapter 4 deals with the principles and techniques of opening, developing, and closing interviews.

Although good conversations and interviews share many characteristics such as exchanging speaking and listening, mutual concern that each party finds the interaction pleasant and rewarding, and effective sharing of verbal and nonverbal messages, they are very different. Imagine going to an employer to ask for a raise or to a recruiter for a summer internship without giving thought to how you will begin, the case you will present, information you might provide, questions you will ask, answers you will give, or what you will say if your request or application is rejected. On the other hand, imagine a friend or co-worker who always plans conversations in detail. Most of us would seek to avoid this person either face-to-face or on the telephone, perhaps resorting to e-mails for necessary interactions, because there is little enjoyment in carefully structured or scripted conversations.

Questions

Asking and answering **questions** are important in all interviews. Some interviews, such as market surveys and journalistic interviews, consist entirely of questions and answers. Others, such as recruiting, counseling, and health care, include a mixture of questions and information sharing. And still others, such as sales, training, and performance review, involve strategic questions from both parties designed to obtain or clarify information and to change another person's way of thinking, feeling, or acting.

Questions play multiple roles in interviews.

Without either party asking and answering questions, how could you discuss a grade with a professor, counsel a student who is skipping too many lectures, interview for an internship, take part in a performance review, or explain a difficult psychological theory? Questions are the tools interview parties employ to obtain information, check the accuracy of messages sent and received, verify impressions and assumptions, and provoke feeling or thought. Chapter 3 introduces you to a variety of question types and their uses and misuses.

An interview, then, is an interactional communication process between two parties, at least one of whom has a predetermined and serious purpose, that involves the asking and answering of questions.

With this definition as a guide, determine which of the following interactions constitutes an interview and which does not.

Exercise #1—What Is and Is Not an Interview?

1. A student is meeting with her doctor and nurse practitioner to determine when she might be able to resume practice with the gymnastics team.
2. Three supervisors are discussing ways they might alter performance reviews in the second quarter of the year.
3. An academic counselor is discussing possible class schedules with a student.
4. A representative from a large construction management firm is meeting with a group of students during an on-campus job fair.
5. A Navy recruiter is meeting with a potential recruit at an Armed Forces Recruiting Center in a shopping mall.

no **6.** A professor is asking questions about an assigned case study and its practical applications in computer software design.

yes **7.** Two members of an architectural consulting firm are discussing a building proposal with a school superintendent.

yes **8.** A college student is talking on the telephone with an alumnus about contributing to the annual scholarship fund campaign.

yes **9.** A television reporter is meeting with the vice president for student affairs and dean of students to discuss a recent series of assaults on campus.

yes **10.** A sales representative is attempting to sell furnishings to two brothers who are planning to open a quality men's clothing store.

Traditional Forms of Interviewing

Our definition of interviewing encompasses a wide variety of interview types, many of which require specialized training and specific abilities. Nearly 25 years ago, Charles Redding, a professor at Purdue University, developed a situational schema of traditional forms of interviewing according to their functions. Let's use Redding's schema as a way of introducing the many types and uses of interviewing, both formal and informal.

Information-Giving Interviews
Purpose: exchange information Accurately, effectively, and efficiently

> **Information giving is common but difficult.**

Whenever two parties take part in orienting, training, coaching, instructing, and briefing sessions, they are involved in information-giving interviews, the primary purpose of which is to exchange information as accurately, effectively, and efficiently as possible. These sessions may appear, at first glance, not to be interviews because questions and answers may play minor roles in them. Information-giving interviews may also seem simple when compared to others—merely transferring facts, data, reports, and opinions from one party to another, but they are deceptively difficult encounters. Because this type is so common and critical in health care interviews, Chapter 13 will discuss the principles, problems, and techniques of information giving in the health care interviews.

Information-Gathering Interviews
– use of skillful questions

> **Information gathering is pervasive in our world.**

Whenever two parties take part in surveys, exit interviews, research sessions, investigations, diagnostic sessions, journalistic interviews, and brief requests for information, the interviewer's primary purpose is to gather accurate, insightful, and useful information through the skillful use of questions, many created and phrased carefully prior to the interview and others created on the spot to probe carefully into interviewee responses, attitudes, and feelings. Chapter 5 discusses the principles and practices of moderately structured informational interviews such as journalistic interviews and investigations. Chapter 6 introduces you to the principles and practices of highly structured surveys and polls. And Chapter 13 discusses information gathering in the health care setting.

Selection Interviews
: Recruiter vs. Applicant For AND Placement of a worker

The most common form of the selection interview takes place between a recruiter attempting to select the best qualified applicant for a position in an organization and

Selection is critical in the lives of people and organizations.

an applicant attempting to attain this position. Another form, the placement interview, occurs when an interviewer is trying to determine the ideal placement of a staff member already a part of the organization. This interview may involve a promotion, a restructuring of an organization, or a reassignment such as from sales to management. Because the selection or employment interview plays such a major role in all of our personal and professional lives, we will focus in detail on the recruiter in Chapter 7 and the applicant in Chapter 8.

Reviewing the Interviewee's Behavior

; To make interviewee continue doing a good job!

Performance review is essential to employee and employer.

When two parties focus on the interviewee's skills, performance, abilities, or behavior, they are taking part in scheduled or nonscheduled performance reviews (what once were referred to commonly as the annual or semiannual appraisal interview). The emphasis is on coaching a student, employee, or team member to continue that which is good and to set goals for future performance. If an interviewee has a personal or organizational problem, the parties are likely to be involved in a counseling interview in which the interviewer is striving to help the interviewee attain insights into a problem and possible ways of dealing with the problem. If the personal or organizational problem is severe, the interview may move from an emphasis on counseling to a reprimand, disciplinary action, or dismissal. Chapter 9 focuses on models for conducting performance reviews and the principles essential for the performance problem interview. Chapter 12 addresses the principles and practices of conducting and taking part in counseling interviews.

Reviewing the Interviewer's Behavior

Interviewer behavior is vital in consumer and employee relations.

In this form of interviewing, the emphasis is on the interviewer's behavior, performance, or attitudes. Common settings involve receipt of complaints about grades, services, products, or reactions. Others involve formal or informal grievances against an organization or staff member. These settings are often interviewee-initiated, such as filing a grievance, while others are interviewer-initiated in which the goal is to receive suggestions for improving a service, correcting an action, or upgrading a product. Chapter 9 on the performance review and Chapter 12 on the counseling interview offer suggestions for reviewing the interviewer's behavior.

Persuasion

Persuasion is more than selling a product or service.

The persuasive interview occurs whenever one party attempts to alter or reinforce the thinking, feeling, or acting of another party. The sales interview comes immediately to mind in which one person is trying to sell a product (guitar) or a service (guitar lessons) to another person. In the real world, however, we are involved in one-on-one persuasive interactions on a daily basis. The persuasive interview may be as informal as one friend trying to persuade another friend to attend a concert or as formal as a developer trying to persuade a couple to purchase a log home in the Pocono Mountains of Pennsylvania. Innumerable charities call us, ring our doorbells, and encounter us on the street and at malls making their cases for donations. After you graduate, the development, music, and athletic offices of your alma mater will not forget you or let you forget them. Chapters 10 and 11 address the highly complex nature of the persuasive interview.

Nontraditional Forms of Interviewing

There are a growing number of nontraditional interviewing forms, some of them face-to-face and others using electronic means of interacting. Many are included in the Charles Redding schema but with unique twists and means of communicating.

The Focus Group Interview

The focus group interview, introduced in the 1930s and employed in the 1940s to analyze Army training and morale films during World War II, has been developed and refined over the last 20 years to collect qualitative information in areas such as marketing, advertising, political campaigns, management, publishing, and academic research.[5] It consists of a small group of people (usually 6 or 12) as an interviewee party and a highly skilled interviewer (moderator or facilitator) who asks a carefully selected, small set of questions that focus on a specific topic. The emphasis in focus group interviews is on opinions, insights, and responses gleaned from careful listening and recording that may generate research hypotheses, stimulate new ideas and creativity, analyze potential problems, and generate impressions of new products, services, advertisements, and campaign strategies.

This form of "group" interviewing is unique in that it involves interactions among interviewees as well as with the interviewer and these enhanced interactions generate a range of information and opinions different from an interview with a single interviewee. Melinda Lewis writes that the focus group interview "taps into human tendencies where attitudes and perceptions are developed through interaction with other people. During a group discussion, individuals may shift due to the influence of other comments."[6] The interviewer must be skilled not only in listening insightfully to interactions and asking open-ended, probing questions but in drawing out group members who may be hesitant to express or defend opinions or inhibited by the give-and-take of a free-flowing interaction among 8 or 10 interviewees. Some sources warn against using focus group interviews when "the environment is emotionally charged and more information of any type is likely to intensify the conflict," "statistical projections are needed," and when the interviewer "cannot ensure the confidentiality of sensitive information."[7]

The Telephone Interview

When we hear the word *interview,* we tend to think of a face-to-face meeting between two parties. With the invention of the telephone, however, interviews no longer had to be face-to-face encounters; they could be ear-to-ear. Telephone interviews became so commonplace and irritating that many states and the federal government created "Don't Call" lists to protect our privacy and sanity.

Organizations have turned to the telephone to conduct initial employment screening interviews, fund-raising campaigns, and opinion polls to save time, reduce monetary expenses, and eliminate the time necessary to send staff to numerous locations. They use conference calls to enable several members of an organization to ask questions and hear replies from staff and clients in multiple locations scattered over a wide geographical area. Interviewers and interviewees can talk to several people at one time, answer or clarify questions directly, be heard while responding, and receive immediate feedback.

The telephone interview is convenient and inexpensive.

A major problem with telephone interviews is the lack of "presence" of parties. Hearing a voice is not the same as being able to observe an interviewer's or interviewee's appearance, dress, manner, eye contact, face, gestures, and posture. Some studies comparing telephone and face-to-face interviews suggest that the two methods produce similar communicative results, with respondents giving fewer socially acceptable answers over the telephone and preferring the anonymity it provides.[8] Other studies urge caution in turning too quickly to the telephone. One study found that interviewers do not like telephone interviews, and this attitude may affect how interviewees reply. Another study discovered that fewer interviewees (particularly older ones) prefer the telephone, and this may lower degree of cooperation.[9] People may feel uneasy about discussing sensitive issues with strangers they cannot see, and it is difficult to make convincing confidentiality guarantees when not face-to-face. On the other hand, interviewees such as job applicants may take the telephone interview, what one source refers to as the "fuzzy slipper" interview, less seriously than a face-to-face interview, perhaps not as an interview at all.[10] These attitudes may lead to casual dress, speaking manner, and choice of words, including slang and vocal fillers such as "you know," "know what I mean," and "you betcha."

The widespread use of the cell phone has created a new world of "talking," and we assume some listening, that seemingly takes place everywhere, from dorm rooms, kitchens, and backyards to restrooms, parks, and classrooms. When we walk through our campuses at 7:00 in the morning and see, and hear, students on their cell phones, we wonder whom they are talking to so early in the morning.

The growing sophistication of two-way video technology may reduce the problems and concerns caused by critical nonverbal cues missing from the telephone interview. Cell phone technology that allows parties to send visual images of one another while they are talking is an important development. Tiny headshots, of course, are far from the presence of face-to-face interviews, but they are a step forward in the electronic interview process.

Not many years ago, we would seek the privacy of a telephone booth when making a personal or business call and take precautions that would prevent us from being overheard. Times have changed, and today there is a growing concern for the **privacy** not only of the interview parties but of those who cannot avoid being part of the interviewing process. Cell phone users, apparently feeling they must talk loud enough for all of us within 75 feet to hear, shout to the person on the other end. You can go to any restaurant, lounge area, or airport boarding area today and hear complete conversations that otherwise would be held behind closed doors to ensure confidentiality. We have heard executives discussing mergers, profit margins, and personnel changes; patients discussing their diagnoses and prescriptions with medical practitioners; and students requesting help with assignments, grade adjustments, and personal problems.

There are ways to avoid irritating the 81 percent of adults in the United States who are bothered by cell phone use in public places.[11] Suggestions include speaking quietly, keeping calls brief, turning away from others, finding a more appropriate location such as a booth, or taking calls without a central focus such as stores or sidewalks. Taking calls in theaters, churches, classrooms, restaurants, and crowded waiting areas such as airports are most irritating.

The Videoconference Interview

By the late 1990s, surveys indicated that 82 percent of companies were using or planning to use **videoconference** technology to conduct recruiting interviews because it was less expensive, enabled parties to see one another, and could be conducted globally.[12] Some 10 years later, videoconferencing had expanded well beyond this figure to include many types of interviews. Although this technology would seem to be as good as "being there in person," there are significant differences from face-to-face interviews.

Both parties must focus attention on the interaction.

Since visual cues are limited to the top half or faces of participants, or group shots in the case of multiple-person interview parties, there are fewer nonverbal cues. One result is fewer interruptions that lead to longer and fewer turns by participants. It is more difficult to interact freely and naturally with people on a screen. Perhaps this is why participants provide more negative evaluations of others in the interview who may appear to dominate the process. One study showed that interviewers liked the videoconference because they could "unobtrusively take more notes, check their watches, or refer to resumes without disrupting the flow of the interview" or, perhaps, being noticed by the other party. On the other hand, they had trouble "reading nonverbal behaviors such as facial expression, eye contact, and fidgeting" and telling "whether a pause was due to the technology, or the applicant being stumped." Although a significant majority of interviewers (88%) indicated that they would be willing to use videoconferencing for interviews, a significant majority (76%) said they preferred face-to-face interviews.[13]

Interviewees in teleconference interviews should be aware of the length of their answers to enhance turn-taking and avoid the appearance of trying to dominate the interview. They, too, can check their lists of questions, take notes, and watch their time without being noticed. Above all, interviewees should be aware of the importance of upper-body movement, gestures, eye contact, and facial expressions that will attract favorable and unfavorable attention. With technology, there is no traditional handshake and the interviewee is alone in a room, and these factors may generate tension for some. Follow these suggestions for a more effective and enjoyable interview: speak up so you can be heard easily, dress conservatively in solid colors, look at the camera full-face, limit movements, try to forget about the camera, expect some lag time between questions and responses.[14] One study indicated that applicants in recruiting interviews were more satisfied with their performance in face-to-face interviews when the interviews were less structured and more satisfied with their performance in videoconference interviews when the interviews were highly structured.[15] Since questions in highly structured interviews tend to require shorter answers, interviewees may have felt less pressured to determine length and content of answers and turn-taking.

The E-Mail Interview

The Internet lacks the nonverbal cues critical in interviews.

With the introduction of the Internet, many interviews went from face-to-face and ear-to-ear to finger-to-finger. It has enabled large numbers of people to make inquiries, send and receive information, and discuss problems at any time of the day or night and nearly anywhere in the world. But are these multiple-party interactions literally electronic mail rather than interviews? If two parties use the Internet to interact in real time

The Internet can provide important information on positions and organizations and background on interviewers and interviewees.

so it is truly an interaction, it meets our definition of an interview. Small video cameras mounted on the computer that send live pictures and sound between interview parties may make electronic interactions superior to the telephone and ever closer to the face-to-face interview. One obstacle to overcome is the reluctance of parties to type lengthy answers to questions that they can provide easily in person or over the telephone. The Internet's potential seems unlimited and, as it becomes more visually interactive, it will take on more of the properties of the traditional interview in which both parties not only ask and answer questions but communicate nonverbally through appearance, face, voice, and gesture. Unfortunately, the small screen will continue to limit the visibility and effectiveness of nonverbal communication.

Although much emphasis has centered on using e-mail in the employment selection process, the e-mail interview is gaining use in other fields. For instance, physicians are finding the Internet efficient, timely, and effective when interacting with patients; it is a modern-day e-house call.[16] The American Medical Association recently issued guidelines for physician-patient electronic communications, warning that technology must not replace face-to-face interactions with patients. To ensure privacy and security, some physicians are using voice recognition software.

A number of studies have focused on the use of e-mail in conducting sophisticated research interviews. The authors indicate that disadvantages such as difficulty in opening interviews (frequent false starts), establishing rapport with interviewees, determining emotional reactions, and translating unusual symbols and acronyms interviewees may

ON THE WEB

Learn more about the growing uses of electronic interviews in a variety of settings. Search at least two databases under headings such as telephone interviews, conference calls, and video talk-back. Try search engines such as ComAbstracts (http://www.cios.org), Yahoo (http://www.yahoo.com), Infoseek (http://www.infoseek.com), and ERIC (http://www.indiana.edu/~eric_rec). In which interview settings are electronic interviews most common? What are the advantages and disadvantages of electronic interviews? How will new developments affect electronic interviews in the future? How will the growing use of electronic interviews affect the ways we conduct traditional face-to-face interviews?

use are outweighed by reduced cost and time, wider geographical and individual diversity, enhanced self-disclosure due to a greater degree of anonymity, elimination of interviewer interruptions, ease of probing into answers, ease of transcription of responses, and streamlined data analysis.[17] One researcher concluded, "While a mixed mode interviewing strategy should always be considered when possible, semi-structured e-mail interviewing can be a viable alternative to the face-to-face and telephone interviews, especially when time, financial constraints, or geographical boundaries are barriers to an investigation."[18]

The Virtual Interview

The "virtual" interview is gaining a great deal of attention, but its meanings and uses vary according to the person or organization using the term. Regardless of meaning, most virtual interviews employ some form of electronic means. Some sources use the term to mean practice or simulated interviews.[19] They emphasize that "applicants" must take the interview as seriously as if it were the real thing and pay careful attention to dress, body language, posture, manners, and eye contact, and respond to questions correctly, smoothly, and confidently. Applicants proceed to answer a series of typical employment interview questions by picking the correct answer from a series provided for each. They are informed if they chose the incorrect answer and why it was incorrect.

Some organizations are conducting virtual job fairs because they are cheaper and recruiters need not spend time traveling to locations around the country.[20] In the mode of the electronic game, interviewers and applicants may attend in the form of avatars. Some organizations report that applicants seem to relax when appearing in the form of an avatar, but they warn that applicants still need to know how to dress, act, and respond. Interviews are conducted in the form of instant-messaging chats.

It is not surprising, then, that some organizations are using virtual job interviews in place of face-to-face interactions, at least in the screening process that may involve hundreds of interviews. One source warns that in this age of the video game, virtual interviews may not be taken 100 percent seriously by one or both parties; it seems like a game instead of reality.[21] Important suggestions for applicants include: carry yourself with your voice much as you would during a telephone interview, avoid slang and chatspeak, do not try to show off your gaming skills or use tricks, and act professionally even if you are dressed in your underwear. Some sources use an innovative "asynchronous" approach in which the interviewer need not be present in real time. One recommends this approach for marketing, sales, customer service, and other positions that require excellent communication and presentation skills and you need to see them.[22]

Wake Forest University has experimented with virtual admissions interviews in which applicants may sit in their living rooms with a webcam, microphone, and Internet and have a distant face-to-face interview with an admissions officer. An admissions officer reports that they can interview students who cannot travel to the Winston-Salem, North Carolina, campus, and "This allows us to have personal contact with every applicant. We can get a sense of who the applicant is beyond academic credentials. The interview helps decide if the student is a good fit for Wake Forest."[23] Applicants have responded positively, and Wake Forest plans to extend the virtual interview offer to a wider variety of prospective students.

The virtual interview most similar to gaming is being experimented with in the medical profession in which interviews can take place in simulated operating rooms and other selected venues. In one application of this software in London, "most students were positively surprised at the level of realism" achieved for "specific objects."[24] The emphasis at present is on the teaching possibilities of virtual interviews for training physicians and nurses.

Summary

Interviewing is an interactional communication process between two parties, at least one of whom has a predetermined and serious purpose, that involves the asking and answering of questions. This definition encompasses a wide variety of interview settings that require training, preparation, interpersonal skills, flexibility, and a willingness to face risks involved in intimate, person-to-person interactions. Interviewing is a learned skill and art, and perhaps the first hurdle to overcome is the assumption that we do it well because we do it so often. The increasing flexibility of the telephone and the Internet is resulting in significant numbers of interviews no longer occurring face-to-face, and this is posing new challenges and concerns.

There is a vast difference between skilled and unskilled interviewers and interviewees, and the skilled ones know that practice makes perfect only if you know what you are practicing. Studies in health care, for example, have revealed that medical students, physicians, and nurses who do not receive formal training in interviewing patients actually become less effective interviewers over time, not more effective.

The first essential step in developing and improving interviewing skills is to understand the deceptively complex interviewing process and its many interacting variables. Successful interviewing requires you to understand both parties and their relationship, the exchanging of roles, perceptions of self and other, communication interactions, feedback, situation, and the influence of outside forces. Chapter 2 explains and illustrates the interviewing process by developing a model step-by-step that contains all of the fundamental elements that interact in each interview.

Key Terms and Concepts

The online learning center for this text features FLASHCARDS and CROSSWORD PUZZLES for studying based on these terms and concepts.

Beliefs
Collaborative
Conversation
Cultural context
Dyadic
Electronic interviews
E-mail interviews
Exchanging
Feelings
Focus group interviews
Formal
Information
Information-gathering interviews
Information-giving interviews
Interactional
Internet
Interpersonal
Interview
Intimate

Involvement
Meaning making
Motives
Nontraditional forms
Parties
Persuasion
Predetermined purpose
Privacy
Process
Purpose
Questions
Reviewing interviewee behavior
Reviewing interviewer behavior
Selection interview
Serious purpose
Structure
System
Telephone interview
Traditional forms
Two-party process
Videoconference interview
Virtual interview

An Interview for Review and Analysis

As a severe economic recession affected states across the country, funding for community schools has dwindled as local and state tax revenues have plummeted. School boards have had to make difficult decisions no one wanted to make such as eliminating courses, laying off teachers, cutting support staff, and deferring new construction and plans to implement full-day kindergarten. Inevitably, they have turned to the arts and extracurricular activities such as bands, orchestras, and choral groups. The Westview School Corporation is now considering a proposal to make all musical programs "pay-as-you-play" with no public funding. Joshua Stevens, Marie Chavez, and Drew Chan, recent graduates of Westview High School and now juniors in college, have decided to meet with as many citizens as possible in Westview to see if they can generate support for the music program. Their first meeting is with Eric and Sarah Mudd in their home at 7:00 p.m.

As you read through this interaction, answer the following questions: Is this an interview or a small group discussion? How is this interaction similar to and different from a speech or social conversation? If this is, in fact, an interview, what traditional form does it take? What is the predetermined purpose of this interaction? What is the approximate ratio of listening and speaking between the parties, and how appropriate is it? When, if ever, do the principal roles of interviewer and interviewee switch from one party to the other? What makes this interaction a collaborative process? What roles do questions play?

1. **Joshua:** Hi Mrs. Mudd, I'm Joshua Stevens who graduated from Westview two years ago.
2. **Marie:** I'm Marie Chavez, and I graduated with Joshua and am now a junior at Temple.
3. **Drew:** And I'm Drew Chan, a classmate of Joshua and Marie.
4. **Mrs. Mudd:** I believe I remember a couple of you from the Westview Christmas Show. My niece goes to Westview. What can I do for you this evening?
5. **Drew:** Well . . . we're contacting homeowners in Westview to discuss the economic situation facing our former high school and wonder if we might meet with you and Mr. Mudd for a few minutes this evening.
6. **Mrs. Mudd:** I'm free for a while, but my husband is working in the study. He may join us when he hears voices. Come in and sit down.

7. **Marie:** Thanks Mrs. Mudd. I'm sure you have been reading and hearing about how the severe economic recession is affecting the Westview schools.
8. **Mrs. Mudd:** Yes; it sounds like there are going to be some painful cuts in staff and programs at all levels. What are your specific concerns as recent graduates?
9. **Drew:** As you recall, we were all actively involved in the music programs while at Westview. I played the trumpet in the marching band and the orchestra.
10. **Joshua:** I played the violin in the orchestra and in the chamber music program.
11. **Marie:** I was in the choir and the glee club.
12. **Drew:** We all believe that the music program was important to us not only artistically but in our academics. It made us well-rounded and, we think, helped us to earn scholarships to Temple, Villanova, and Penn State.
13. **Joshua:** I know it played an important role in my being admitted to Penn State in computer engineering. Admissions officers are looking for more than narrow academic preparation.
14. **Mr. Mudd:** What's this big meeting all about? I could hear you from the study.
15. **Marie:** We hope we didn't bother you. We're recent graduates of Westview and are meeting with residents of Westview to discuss the economic impact on the school system. I'm Marie; this is Drew; and this is Joshua.
16. **Mr. Mudd:** It's good to meet grads of our schools. You are all juniors in college now?
17. **Drew:** That's correct, at Temple, Villanova, and Penn State.
18. **Mrs. Mudd:** Very impressive. So what is your purpose in visiting residents like us? You must have one.
19. **Joshua:** Yes, we were all active in music while at all levels in the Westview schools, and we're very concerned about the negative impacts the proposed "pay-as-you-play" policy would have on future graduates.
20. **Mrs. Mudd:** We know this policy could pose some financial problems for a few students, but it seems better than eliminating programs altogether.
21. **Mr. Mudd:** I agree.
22. **Marie:** Music lessons can be very expensive when you add them on top of the cost of instruments, not to mention the added cost of textbooks under the new policy that ended book rental. Several of my friends did not join the band or orchestra because they could not afford instruments; now they would face expensive music lessons.
23. **Drew:** This might keep them out of the choral groups as well.
24. **Mrs. Mudd:** Can't most of our families afford instruments or a few lessons?
25. **Mr. Mudd:** Well, if the school board must make a decision between cutting courses, particularly small advanced courses in English, science, and mathematics that are so important in college admissions, and music, which would you choose?
26. **Joshua:** That's a tough call, we know. But are you aware that football, basketball, and baseball will be exempt from the "pay-as-you-play" policy? Only so-called minor

sports such as tennis, swimming, gymnastics, and soccer will be affected, and of course music.

27. Mr. Mudd: No, I don't think we were aware of that.

28. Mrs. Mudd: No, we weren't. They do bring in revenue, of course. What are the coaches and players saying?

29. Marie: Nothing; there's a lot of silence right now. That's why we're talking to residents. We believe many are unaware of the ramifications and limitations of this policy or the values of programs such as music.

30. Mrs. Mudd: What about a policy that would provide a sliding scale for those with the most severe economic needs?

31. Drew: Other school systems have tried something like that in the past, but it is both costly and time-consuming to do thorough income reviews. Some students would rather drop music than subject their parents to these reviews.

32. Mr. Mudd: If they truly value music as you say, this would seem to be a small price to pay, so to speak.

33. Joshua: We're also concerned about a stigma being placed on those who pay less for whatever reason and hard feelings between those who get help and those who miss a cutoff by a few dollars and must drop music.

34. Mrs. Mudd: You're making some good points. What are you asking residents like us to do at this time? We certainly cannot afford to pay more taxes, particularly with unemployment rising in this area with the auto layoffs and plant closings. Something has to give in the school system because it is by far the largest city expenditure we have.

35. Drew: First, we would like residents to ask for details of the proposed policy, what is included and what is excluded from the "pay-as-you-play" plan.

36. Joshua: We would also urge you to attend school board meetings and to make sure they are open to everyone. We plan to attend public meetings when possible and devote our weekends to meeting with residents such as you.

37. Mr. Mudd: We will pay attention to what is going on and try to attend some school board meetings, but we can't make any promises. If the economy gets worse, music may not be the only programs that will suffer.

38. Marie: We understand your concerns, and we really appreciate your taking the time to talk with us this evening.

39. Mrs. Mudd: Good luck in your studies.

40. Joshua: Do you have any more questions?

41. Mr. Mudd: No . . . not at this time. How can we get in touch if we do have questions or concerns?

42. Drew: Here is a flier that explains our concerns and lists our e-mail addresses. It's easier to get in touch with us on our campuses.

43. Marie: Thanks again for meeting with us.

Student Activities

1. Take part in three seven-minute information-gathering interviews: one face-to-face, one over the telephone, and one through e-mail. How were the three interviews similar and different? How did interactions vary? How did lack of presence, eye contact, appearance, facial expressions, and gestures affect the interviews? How did you and the other party attempt to compensate for these? Which interview resulted in the most information exchange?
2. Watch three televised interviews: one with a sports figure, one with a government official, and one with a person who survived a harrowing experience. After each interview, write down what you liked most and least about the interview. Now, compare your likes and dislikes. Which were due to interviewing skills of the two parties? Which were due to the situation and topic: sports, government, or life experience? Which were due to the interviewer and which to the interviewee?
3. Keep a log of all the interviews you take part in over a three-day period. How many were traditional and how many were nontraditional forms? How many did you initiate and why? What characteristics made some the most memorable, some the most enjoyable, and some the most important? What did you learn about interviewing from keeping careful track of your interviewing experiences?
4. Interviews are interactional, and this often means sharing interviewer and interviewee roles as an interview progresses. Watch a selection of interviews on C-SPAN that last at least 15 minutes. Note how often roles switch and how often attempted switches fail because one party blocks the exchange in some way. What are the most common and effective means of exchanging roles? How long do these exchanges last before another exchange takes place? How do parties react when an attempted exchange fails?

Notes

1. John Stewart, ed., *Bridges Not Walls,* 7th ed. (New York: McGraw-Hill, 2009), p. 16.
2. Stewart, p. 20.
3. Sarah Trenholm and Arthur Jensen, *Interpersonal Communication* (New York: Oxford University Press, 2008), p. 9; Stewart, pp. 8, 25–27.
4. Michael T. Motley, "Communication as Interaction: A Reply to Beach and Bavelas," *Western Journal of Speech Communication* 54 (Fall 1990), pp. 613–623.
5. "Effective Interviewing: The Focus Group Interview," Virtual Interviewing Assistant, http://www2.ku/~coms/virtual_assistant/via/focus.html, accessed October 12, 2006; Program Development and Evaluation, *Focus Group Interviews, Quick Tips #5,* University of Wisconsin-Extension, Madison, WI, 2002; "Focus Group Approach to Needs Assessment," Iowa State University Extension, 2001, http://www.extension.iastate.edu/communities/tools/assess/focus.html, accessed December 2, 2008.
6. M. Lewis, "Focus Group Interviews in Qualitative Research: A Review of the Literature," *Action Research E-Reports,* 2 (2000). Available at http://www.fhs.usyd.edu.au/arow/arer/002.htm.

7. "When to Use Focus Group Interviews," Community Engagement, Minnesota Department of Health, updated January 16, 2008, http://www.health.state.mn.us/community_eng/needs/focus.html, accessed December 2, 2008.

8. Theresa F. Rogers, "Interviews by Telephone and in Person: Quality of Responses and Field Performance," *Public Opinion Quarterly* 39 (1976), pp. 51–65; Stephen Kegeles, Clifton F. Frank, and John P. Kirscht, "Interviewing a National Sample by Long-Distance Telephone," *Public Opinion Quarterly* 33 (1969–1970), pp. 412–419.

9. Lawrence A. Jordan, Alfred C. Marcus, and Leo G. Reeder, "Response Style in Telephone and Household Interviewing," *Public Opinion Quarterly* 44 (1980), pp. 210–222; Peter V. Miller and Charles F. Cannell, "A Study of Experimental Techniques in Telephone Interviewing," *Public Opinion Quarterly* 46 (1982), pp. 250–269.

10. Martin E. Murphy, "The Interview Series: (1) Interviews Defined," The Jacobson Group, http://www.jacobsononline.com.

11. Scott Campbell, "Perceptions of Mobile Phone Use in Public: The Roles of Individualism, Collectivism, and Focus of the Setting," *Communication Reports* 21 (2008), pp. 70–81.

12. Derek S. Chapman and Patricia M. Rowe, "The Impact of Videoconference Technology, Interview Structure, and Interviewer Gender on Interviewer Evaluations in the Employment Interview: A Field Experiment," *Journal of Occupational and Organizational Psychology* (2001), p. 279.

13. Chapman and Rowe, pp. 279–298.

14. Carole Martin, "Smile, You're on Camera," Interview Center, http://www.interview.monster.com/articles/video, accessed September 30, 2006.

15. Derek S. Chapman and Patricia M. Rowe, "The Influence of Video Conference Technology and Interview Structure on the Recruiting Function of the Employment Interview: A Field Experiment," *International Journal of Selection and Assessment* (September 2002), p. 185.

16. Susan Jenks, *Florida Today,* "Forget the Office, the Doctor Will 'e' You Now," Lafayette, Indiana *Journal & Courier,* January 6, 2009, pp. D1–2.

17. Kay A. Persichitte, Suzanne Young, and Donald D. Tharp, "Conducting Research on the Internet: Strategies for Electronic Interviewing," U.S. Department of Education, Educational Resources Information Center (ERIC), ED 409 860.

18. Lokman I. Meho, "E-Mail Interviewing in Qualitative Research: A Methodological Discussion," *Journal of the American Society for Information Science and Technology* 57(10) (2006), pp. 1284–1295.

19. "Interview Preparation: The Virtual Interview," Western State College of Colorado Career Services, http://www.western.edu/career/Interview_virtual/Virtual_interview.htm, accessed December 11, 2008; "Virtual Interview," 3M Careers: Virtual Interview, http://solutions.3m.com/wps/portal/3M/en_US/Careers/Home/Students/VirtualInterview/, accessed December 16, 2008.

20. Eric Chabrow, "Second Life: The Virtual Job Interview," posted June 20, 2007, http://blogs.cioinsight.com/parallax_view/content/workplace/second_life_the_virtual_job, accessed December 16, 2008.

21. "Virtual Interviews Less Serious?" http://blog.recruitv.com/2008/09/virtual-interviews-less-serious/, accessed December 16, 2008.

22. "Interview Connect: The Virtual Interview Management Solution," http://www.interviewconnect.com/, accessed December 15, 2008.

23. "Wake Forest University offers virtual interviews for admissions," Wake Forest University New Service, December 1, 2008, http://www.wfu.edu/news/release/2008.12.01.i.php, accessed December 11, 2008.

24. Bertalan Mesko, "Interview with Dr. James Kinross: Simulation in Second Life," *Medicine Meets Virtual Reality* 17, November 27, 2008, http://mmvr17.wordpress.com/2008/11/27/interview-with-dr-james-kinross-simulation-in . . . , accessed December 16, 2008.

Resources

Holstein, James A., and Jaber F. Gubrium, eds. *Inside Interviewing: New Lenses, New Concerns*. Thousand Oaks, CA: Sage, 2003.

Lancaster, Lynne C., and David Stillman. *When Generations Collide*. New York: HarperBusiness, 2002.

Martin, Judith N., and Thomas K. Nakayama. *Intercultural Communication Experiences and Contexts*. New York: McGraw-Hill, 2007.

Stewart, John. *Bridges Not Walls: A Book about Interpersonal Communication*. New York: McGraw-Hill, 2009.

Trenholm, Sarah, and Arthur Jensen. *Interpersonal Communication*. New York: Oxford University Press, 2008.

CHAPTER 2 An Interpersonal Communication Process

Interviewing is more than asking and answering questions.

Every interview is a **complex communication process.** If you are to be a successful interviewer or interviewee, you must understand and appreciate the total process, not merely the questions and answers that are its most obvious characteristics. This chapter delves into this intricate and sometimes puzzling process by developing part-by-part a model that portrays its many elements and interactive nature.

Two Parties in the Interview

Each party consists of unique and complex individuals.

The two circles in Figure 2.1 represent the two parties that are the heart and soul of the interviewing process. Each is a unique product of culture, environment, education, training, and experiences. Each is a mixture of personality traits. A person may be optimistic or pessimistic, trusting or suspicious, flexible or inflexible, sociable or unsociable. And each adheres to specific beliefs, attitudes, and values and is motivated by an ever-changing variety of expectations, desires, needs, and interests. In a very real sense, the whole person speaks and the whole person listens in interactions we call interviews.[1]

Each interview contributes to a relational history.

Although each party consists of unique individuals, both must collaborate to produce a successful interview. Neither party can **go it alone.** The overlapping circles in Figure 2.1 symbolize the relational nature of the interview process in which two parties do something **with, not to** one another. The parties are connected interpersonally because each has a stake in the outcome of the interview. Their relationship may commence with this interview or have a **relational history** that goes back hours, days, weeks, months, or years. For instance, you may interact with a professional mentor for the first time or you may have established a long-standing and long-lasting relationship. Interactions between parties with no prior history may be difficult because neither party may know what to expect from the other, how to get the interaction started, when to speak and when to listen, and what information may and may not be shared. In some cultures, "all strangers are viewed as sources of potential relationships; in others, relationships develop only after long and careful scrutiny."[2] Stereotypes such as age, gender, race, and ethnicity may play significant negative roles in zero-history situations, particularly during the anxious opening minutes of an interaction.[3] On the other hand, negative expectations and attitudes may exist because previous interactions between the parties did not go well.

A relationship may be **intimate** with a close friend, **casual** with a co-worker, **distant** with a sales associate, **formal** with a college dean, or **functional** with a physician. This

Figure 2.1 *The interview parties*

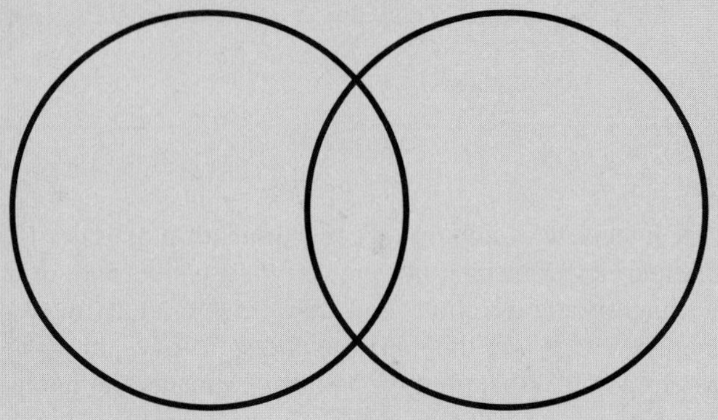

relationship may change over time, including during an interaction. What may start out as a purely functional relationship between a student and a professor may evolve into a close, personal friendship for a lifetime. John Stewart and Carole Logan write that "each time they communicate, relational partners construct and modify patterns that define who they are for and with each other."[4]

A situation may alter a relationship.

Your relationships change as situations change. For instance, you may have a pleasant, supportive relationship with a co-worker until that person becomes your supervisor. You may be skilled at dealing with routine and simple situations but become "unglued" when new and unexpected crises or demands materialize. Sarah Trenholm and Arthur Jensen claim that you must acquire **role competence** to know "the parts you and your partner will play in the relationship" and to develop "workable rules and norms." Competence also requires flexibility to know "when to adapt and when not to."[5]

Relational Dimensions

All of your relationships are multidimensional, and five dimensions are particularly relevant to interviews: similarity, inclusion, liking, control, and trust.

Similarity

A few similarities do not equal relational peers.

Relationships are fostered when both parties share cultural norms and values, education, experiences, personality traits, beliefs, and expectations. For instance, you may come from the same city, share ethnic heritage, have the same major, like the same music, and espouse the same political views. You may find it easier to interact with persons of your age, gender, and race. Awareness of such similarities enables interview parties to understand one another and establish common ground—literally to expand the overlap of the circles until perceived similarities overcome perceived dissimilarities. Be cautious in your perceptions, however, because surface similarities such as age, dress, and ethnicity may be all that you have in common. Judith Martin and Thomas Nakayama write that "similarity is based not on whether people actually are similar but on the perception of a similar trait."[6]

Inclusion

Wanting to take part leads to collaboration.

Relationships are enhanced when both parties desire to take part and to be active speakers and listeners, questioners, and respondents. The more you are involved and share, the more satisfied you will be with the relationship and look forward to future interactions. Degree of satisfaction may be apparent in each party's words, gestures, face, eyes, and actions. Effective relationships develop when interviewer and interviewee become interdependent, when "Each becomes aware that what" they do and not do "will have an impact on the other" and each begins to act with the "other party's interests" in mind. Their behaviors are no longer individual actions but instead are what John Shotter calls "**joint actions.**"[7] Neither party should come to an interview with expectations that are either too high, and thus unattainable, or too low, and thus unrewarding and unfulfilling.

Liking

We interact more freely with persons we like.

Interview relationships are cultivated when the parties like and respect one another and there is a marked degree of warmth or friendship. Liking occurs when there is a "we" instead of a "me-you" feeling and you communicate in a way the other party finds pleasant, productive, and fair. Signals for liking and disliking are inconsistent, however. In one study, parties lowered their loudness to express disliking as well as liking for one another. In others, decreased talk time seemed to indicate liking by showing greater attentiveness or disliking by exhibiting disengagement from the interaction.[8] Some of us find showing affection to be difficult, particularly in formal or public settings, and prefer to keep acquaintances as well as strangers at a safe distance.

You may come to an interview with an ambivalent or hostile attitude toward the other party, perhaps due to relational history or what James Honeycutt calls **relational memory.** He writes that "even though relationships are in constant motion, relationship memory structures provide a perceptual anchor [so that] individuals can determine where they are in a relationship."[9] Relational memory may aid parties in dealing with what researchers call **dialectical tensions** that result from conflicts between "important but opposing needs or desires," or "between opposing" or contrasting "'voices,' each expressing a different or contradictory impulse."[10] Kory Floyd writes that such dialectical tensions are not necessarily bad because "researchers believe they are a normal part of any close, interdependent relationship, and they become a problem only when people fail to manage them properly."[11]

Control

Because each party in an interview participates in a continuous process, each is responsible for its success or failure. John Stewart introduced us to the concept of "nexting" that he labels, "The most important single communication skill" because whenever "you face a communication challenge or problem, the most useful question you can ask yourself is, 'What can I help to happen next?'"[12] He claims that "since no one person determines all the outcomes of a communication event, you can help determine some outcomes, even if you feel almost powerless. Since no one person is 100 percent to blame or at fault, and all parties share response-ability, your next contribution can affect what's happening."[13]

Who controls what and when often poses problems in interviews because they frequently involve organizational hierarchies or chains of command: president over vice president, dean over assistant dean, manager over associate, supervisor over intern. This **upward** and **downward** communication may encumber each party, perhaps in different ways. Edward Hall observes, "One's status in a social system also affects what must be attended. People at the top pay attention to different things from those in the middle or the bottom of the system."[14] As a student, you have undoubtedly experienced this when dealing with professors about teams, projects, papers, grades, and education itself. What you look for and value are likely to be quite different from what your professor looks for and values.

Hierarchy may hinder the flow of information and self-disclosure.

Trust

Fisher and Brown claim that trust is the "single most important element of a good working relationship."[15] Trust is essential because how interviews are conducted, with whom, when, the climate of the encounter, and potential outcomes affect each party directly—your income, your career, your purchase, your profits, your health, and your understanding. Relationships are cultivated when parties trust one another to be honest, sincere, reliable, truthful, fair, even-tempered, and of high ethical standards—in other words **safe.** William Gudykunst and Young Kim write, "When we trust others, we expect positive outcomes from our interactions with them; when we have anxiety about interacting with others, we fear negative outcomes from our interactions with them."[16]

Creating trust is a delicate process and may take months or years to develop with another party, but it can be destroyed in an instant if you feel betrayed by a friend, colleague, or co-worker.[17] During World War II, workers in shipyards and on docks were warned with giant posters that "A slip of the lip can sink a ship." This is good advice to all of us, because a secret or confidence that is "leaked" to another, for instance, can literally sink a relationship. "Trust provides a context in which interaction can be more honest, spontaneous, direct, and open."[18] As we will emphasize shortly when discussing levels of interactions, disclosure is critical to the success of interviews, and uninhibited disclosure requires trust. Unpredictable persons and outcomes lead to cautious questions and responses and sharing of information and attitudes—risk is too high.

Trust is essential in every interview.

Global Relationships

Since your social, political, and work worlds will be global in nature, you must understand how relationships come about and are fostered in different countries and cultures. Martin, Nakayama, and Flores warn, for instance, that "in intercultural conflict situations, when we are experiencing high anxieties with unfamiliar behavior (for example, accents, gestures, facial expressions), we may automatically withhold trust."[19] "Some anxiety is present in the early stages of any relationship, but anxiety is greater in intercultural relationships. It arises from concern about possible negative consequences. We may be afraid that we'll look stupid or that we'll offend someone because we're unfamiliar with that person's language or culture."[20]

Persons in the United States tend to have numerous friendly, informal relationships and to place considerable importance on how a person looks, particularly early in relationships.[21] Americans create and discard relationships frequently, while Australians make deeper and longer-lasting commitments. Arabs, like Americans, develop relationships quickly but, unlike Americans who dislike taking advantage of relationships by asking for favors, Arabs believe friends have a duty to help one another.

Relationships develop differently in different cultures.

The Chinese develop very strong, long-term relationships and, like Arabs, see them as involving obligations.[22] In Mexico, trust in relationships develops slowly, is given sparingly, and must be earned. Betrayal of trust will result in the greatest harm possible to a relationship.[23] Like Mexicans, Germans develop relationships slowly because they see them as very important, and using first names before a relationship is well-established is considered rude behavior. Japanese prefer not to interact with strangers, want background information on parties before establishing relationships, prefer doing business with people they have known for years, and take lots of time establishing relationships.

Gender in Relationships

Researchers have generally concluded that men and women are more similar than different in their forms of communication and relationships, and Kathryn Dindia argues that rather than men being from Mars and women from Venus, as a recent best-selling book proclaimed, a more accurate metaphor is "Men are from North Dakota, and women are from South Dakota."[24] Brant Burleson and Adrienne Kunkel found, for instance, "substantial similarity—not difference—in the values both sexes place on supportive communication skills, such as comforting and listening."[25] Similarities have certainly increased since women have taken on a wide variety of roles in contemporary society.

Gender differences have evolved but not disappeared.

Regardless of similarities, however, gender differences of interview participants may be critical in establishing and refining relationships because they are influenced by what you say and how you say it, how you see communication functioning in relationships, and your notions of the nature of relationships. Men's talk tends to be directive and goal-oriented with statements that "tend to press compliance, agreement, or belief." Women's talk, in contrast, may be more polite and expressive, containing less intense words, qualifiers (perhaps, maybe), and disclaimers ("Maybe I'm wrong but . . ." "I may not fully understand the situation, but . . .").[26] Women, for instance, tend to use communication as a primary way of establishing relationships, while men tend to communicate "to exert control, preserve independence, and enhance status."[27] Women tend to give more praise and compliments and are reluctant to criticize directly in the workplace while men tend to remain silent when a co-worker is doing something well and to take criticism straight.[28] It is not surprising, then, that researchers have discovered that women report "greater satisfaction with their interactions than do men.[29] On the other hand, researchers have also found that "women are more likely to betray and be betrayed by other women." Men, on the other hand, report they are more often betrayed by other men with whom they are competing.[30] Each of these differences may impact the critical interview relationship.

Interchanging Roles during Interviews

> **A single party cannot make an interview a success but can ensure its failure.**

> **A directive approach allows the interviewer to maintain control.**

Both parties speak and listen from time to time, are likely to ask and answer questions, and may take on the roles and responsibilities of interviewer and interviewee. Neither party can sit back and expect the other to make the interview a success single-handedly. Some claim that "human communicators are always sending and receiving simultaneously. As a result, each communicator has the opportunity to change how things are going at any time in the process."[31] The small circles within the party circles in Figure 2.2 portray the interchange of roles in interviews. John Stewart's "nexting" consists of the verbal and nonverbal signals parties send to keep interactions progressing.

The degree to which roles are exchanged and control is shared is often affected by the status or expertise of the parties who initiated the interview, type of interview, situations, and atmosphere of the interaction—supportive or defensive, friendly or hostile, warm or cool, formal or informal. These factors determine which of two fundamental approaches an interviewer selects—**directive** or **nondirective**—and this choice affects the exchanging of interviewer and interviewee roles.

Directive Approach

When selecting a directive approach, an **interviewer** establishes the purpose of the interview and attempts to control the pacing, climate, formality, and drift of the interview. Questions are likely to be closed with brief, direct answers. Although an aggressive interviewee may assume some control as the interview progresses, the interviewer intends to control the interview. Typical directive interviews include information giving, surveys and opinion polls, employee recruiting, and disciplinary and persuasive interviews (particularly sales). The directive approach is easy to learn, takes less time, enables you to maintain control, and is easy to replicate from one interview to the next.

Figure 2.2 *The switching of roles*

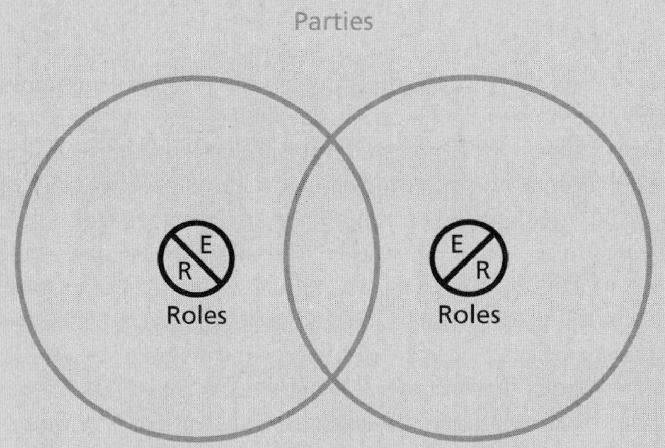

The following exchange illustrates a directive interviewing approach:

1. **Interviewer:** When did you arrive in town?
2. **Interviewee:** About 2:30 yesterday afternoon.
3. **Interviewer:** Have you had a chance to see much of our campus?
4. **Interviewee:** Mainly just the area around the Memorial Union.
5. **Interviewer:** I'll arrange for some students to give you a guided tour after your lecture.
6. **Interviewee:** That sounds great.

Nondirective Approach

In a nondirective approach, **interviewees** have significant control over subject matter, length of answers, interview climate, and formality. Questions are likely to be open-ended and neutral to give the interviewee maximum opportunity and freedom to respond. Typical nondirective interviews are journalistic, oral history, investigations, counseling, performance review, and problem solving. The nondirective approach allows for greater flexibility and adaptability, encourages probing questions, and invites the interviewee to volunteer information.

A nondirective approach enables the interviewee to share control.

The following is a nondirective interview exchange:

1. **Interviewer:** How was your trip down?
2. **Interviewee:** It was a bit scary with ice on the roads, but I got here about 2:30 in the afternoon, pretty much on schedule.
3. **Interviewer:** I'm glad you got here okay. What have you seen of campus so far?
4. **Interviewee:** Mainly the area around the Memorial Union. I got to see the new virtual lab in McMasters Hall, try out the reproduction of Plato's Academy Park north of the Union, and see the room where I will be lecturing tomorrow.
5. **Interviewer:** What would you like to see after your lecture?
6. **Interviewee:** I'm very interested in seeing your new visual and performing arts center and visiting some computer graphics facilities, maybe visit a class or two.

Combination of Approaches

You may select a combination of directive and nondirective approaches. For instance, as an academic counselor you might use a nondirective approach to get a student talking about recurring academic issues and then change to a directive approach when referring to university regulations pertaining to incompletes or dropping courses. As a recruiter you may use a nondirective approach at the start of an interview to relax an applicant, then switch to a directive approach when giving information about the organization and position, and return to a nondirective approach when answering the applicant's questions.

Be flexible and adaptable when selecting approaches.

Be flexible in choosing the most appropriate approach and when to switch from one approach to another. Too often the choice of an interviewing approach is governed by societal roles and expectations. You tend to behave as prescribed by the roles you

The roles we play should guide but not dictate approaches.

play in life. For instance, an employee, applicant, client, or patient "enters an interview expecting that the interviewer will direct and influence one's conversational behaviors much more extensively than one will influence the interviewer's behavior. You both make it happen that way."[32] Adherence to societal roles and expectations may produce an ineffective interview.

Perceptions of Interviewer and Interviewee

Each party comes to an interview with perceptions of self and of the other party, and these perceptions may change positively or negatively as the interview progresses. Theorists claim that relationships are largely due to these perceptions and determine how we communicate. Be aware of four critical perceptions portrayed by the double-ended arrows in Figure 2.3.

Four perceptions drive most of our interactions.

- Your self-perception.
- Your perception of the other party.
- How the other party perceives you.
- How the other party perceives self.

Perceptions of Self

Your self-perceptions, or **self-concept,** come from your physical, social, and psychological perceptions derived from your experiences, activities, attitudes, accomplishments, possessions, and interactions with others, particularly your superior and subordinate roles and relationships. Self-concept is a dual creation of interpretations and how you perceive others to have interpreted who you have been, are, and will be—**self-identity.** These others include groups to which you belong or desire to belong and so-called significant others.

Figure 2.3 *Perceptions of self and others*

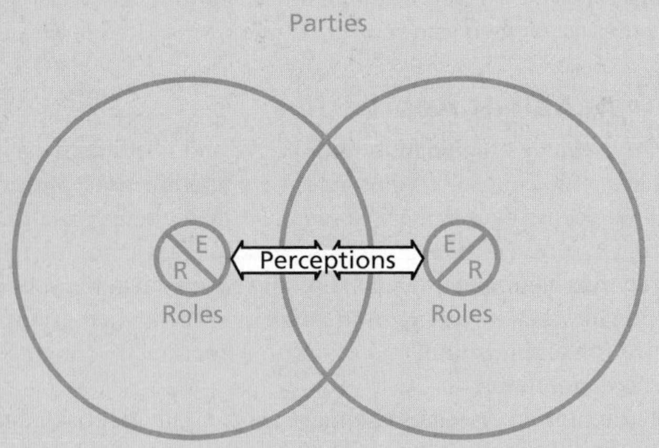

What we perceive ourselves to be may be more important than what we are.

Your self-concept and self-identity are affected by the expectations family, society, professions, and organizations place upon you. You may experience different self-concepts as you move from one situation or role to another, from a situation in which you feel comfortable and in charge to one in which you feel inexperienced, inept, or fearful.

We see ourselves differently under different circumstances.

Self-esteem, the positive or negative feelings you have of yourself, is an important element of self-concept. Theorists claim that a person with high self-esteem is more perceptive, confident, and likely to express attitudes that are popular or unpopular. Persons with low self-esteem, who see themselves having little value or significance, may want the approval of others but are so self-critical that they cannot interpret accurately the behavior and communication of others.[33] You must understand how you perceive yourself and how other parties perceive themselves, because self-concept (particularly self-esteem) may determine whether an interview takes place and its ultimate success or failure. You may succeed or fail in an interview because you are convinced you will—a **self-fulfilling prophecy.** Self-perceptions influence messages sent and received, risks taken, confidence, and degree of self-disclosure.

Self-esteem is closely related to self-worth.

Culture and Gender Differences

Many citizens of the global village are less concerned with self than with group.

Concepts such as self-image, self-identity, self-esteem, self-reliance, and self-awareness are central in American and Western cultures because they emphasize the individual. They are not central in Eastern cultures and South American countries. Japanese, Chinese, and Indians, for example, are collectivist rather than individualist cultures and are more concerned with the image, esteem, and achievement of the group. Attributing successful negotiations to an individual in China would be considered egotistical, self-advancing, and disrespectful. Success is attributed to the group or team. Failure to appreciate cultural differences causes many communication problems for American interviewers and interviewees.

Kory Floyd reminds us that gender matters in self-concept because "gender roles are socially constructed ideas about how women and men should think and behave."[34] Men are expected to be more assertive, in charge, and self-sufficient while women are taught to be "feminine," submissive, and to show empathy and emotional expressiveness. Not all men and women act this way, of course, but you cannot easily ignore the role of society on gender and self-concept and its potential impact on an interview.

Perceptions of the Other Party

How you perceive the other affects how you approach the interview and how you react during the interview. For instance, you may be in awe of the other's reputation or position—a leading biochemist, the CEO of your company, the college president. Previous encounters with a party may lead you to look forward to or dread an interview. Your **perceptions** may be influenced by the other's age, gender, race, ethnic group, size, and physical attractiveness—particularly if the person differs significantly from you. A positive endorsement of a third party may alter the way

Perceptions are a two-way process.

Allow interactions to alter or reinforce perceptions.

you perceive a person. If you are flexible and adaptable, perceptions of the other party may change as an interview progresses by:

- The way an interview begins or ends.
- The other party's manner and attitudes.
- The other party's dress and appearance.
- The other party's listening and feedback.
- Verbal and nonverbal interactions.
- Questions asked and answers given.

Interview exchanges may alter your perceptions. For instance, they may become positive when questions are followed by information requested rather than refusals or evasions, when requests are followed by discussion or agreement rather than demands followed by compliance, and when constructive criticism is followed by understanding rather than by fear or resentment. You may be pleasantly surprised by the warmth, understanding, and cooperation of the other party, particularly when you have been anxious and defensive about what you anticipated as an unpleasant encounter.

Communication Interactions

The curved arrows in Figure 2.4 that link the two parties symbolize the communication levels of verbal and nonverbal interactions that occur during interviews. The three numbered levels differ in relational distance, self-disclosure, risk encountered, perceived meanings, and amount and type of content exchanged.

Levels of Interactions

Level 1 interactions avoid judgments, attitudes, and feelings.

Level 1 interactions are relatively safe, nonthreatening exchanges about such topics as hometowns, professions, sporting events, college courses, and families. They generate answers that are safe, socially acceptable, comfortable, and ambiguous. When you respond with phrases such as "Pretty good," "Not bad," and "Can't complain," they are Level 1 interactions that do not reveal judgments, attitudes, or feelings.

Level 1 interactions are safe and superficial.

Each level is a metaphorical door, with the door being slightly open in Level 1 interactions. General ideas, surface feelings, and simple information pass through, but either party may close the door quickly and safely if necessary. The thickness of the arrow indicates that Level 1 communication exchanges are most common in interviews, and the length of the arrow symbolizes **relational distance.** Level 1 interactions dominate interviews in which there is no relational history, trust is low because of previous encounters between the parties, the issue is controversial, or the role relationship is between superior and subordinate or a high-status and low-status party. The following interaction illustrates typical Level 1 communication:

1. **Interviewer:** How do you feel about the proposal to reduce staff through resignations and retirements?
2. **Interviewee:** It probably makes sense under these circumstances.
3. **Interviewer:** And the budget cuts in your department?
4. **Interviewee:** I'm okay with them.

Figure 2.4 *Communication interactions*

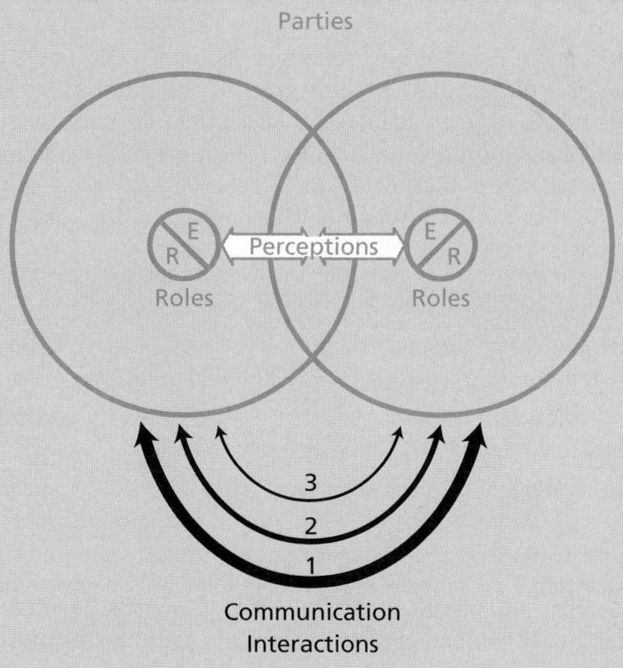

Parties play it safe during these interchanges. The topics are not threatening, and neither party reveals feelings or attitudes.

> **Level 2 interactions require trust and risk-taking.**

Level 2 interactions deal with personal, controversial, or threatening topics and probe into beliefs, attitudes, values, and positions. Responses tend to be half-safe, half-revealing as parties seek to cooperate without revealing too much. The metaphorical door is half open (the optimist's view) or half closed (the pessimist's view) as more specific and revealing ideas, feelings, and information pass through. Though willing to take more risk, parties retain the opportunity to close the door quickly. The thickness of the arrow signifies that Level 2 interactions are less common than Level 1, and the length of the arrow indicates that a closer relationship between parties is necessary to move from superficial to more revealing exchanges. This interaction illustrates Level 2 communication.

1. **Interviewer:** How do you feel about the proposal to reduce staff by 50 through resignations and retirements during the next 12 months?
2. **Interviewee:** It may be the best under the circumstances, but I am concerned about losing some of our best people.
3. **Interviewer:** I appreciate that concern. How about the budget cuts in your department?
4. **Interviewee:** I know we must cut our budget, but I wonder about the long-term repercussions to our competitiveness.

The parties, though cautious, are more specific and revealing.

Level 3 interactions involve full disclosure.

Level 3 interactions deal with more personal and controversial areas of inquiry. Respondents fully disclose their feelings, beliefs, attitudes, and perceptions. Little is withheld, and sometimes questioners get more than they bargained for. The metaphorical door is wide open. The risk is great to both parties, but so are the benefits. The arrow is thin to indicate that Level 3 interactions are uncommon in interviews and may be unattainable during initial contacts. The arrow is short to indicate that the relationship between parties must be trusting, that each party wants to be included in the interaction, and that they share control. This interaction illustrates Level 3 communication.

A positive relationship is essential for Level 3 interactions.

1. **Interviewer:** How do you feel about **my** proposal to reduce staff by 50 through resignations and retirements during the next 12 months?
2. **Interviewee:** I can understand why you might choose this plan, but it dodges the hard decision to cut unproductive staff and to retain some of our best employees.
3. **Interviewer:** I can see why you might feel that way, but this prevents us, actually me, from having to lay off or fire our colleagues.
4. **Interviewee:** Hey, I've been in your place before and understand how distasteful it is to lay off or fire people. Unfortunately, that goes with your position. Some of these retirements and resignations will come in critical areas that will deter us from getting back on our economic feet for years, probably until we can hire their replacements.

We are on the line in many interview settings.

Relationships, perceptions, responses, and the **situation** make communication levels unpredictable and difficult to change. It is essential in most interviews to get beyond Level 1 to Level 2 or Level 3 to obtain information, detect feelings, attain self-disclosure, discover insights, and achieve necessary commitments. Unlike small groups or audiences into which you can blend or hide, the intimate, interpersonal nature of the interview is often threatening because it places your ego and sometimes your social, financial, professional, psychological, or physical welfare on the line. Interviews deal with *your* behavior, *your* performance, *your* reputation, *your* decisions, *your* weaknesses, *your* feelings, *your* money, or *your* future. David Johnson writes:

> Yet self-disclosure does carry a degree of risk. For just as knowing you better is likely to result in a closer relationship, sometimes it could result in people liking you less. "Familiarity breeds contempt" means that some people may learn something about you that detracts from the relationship. . . . "Nothing ventured, nothing gained," means that some risk is vital to achieving any worthwhile goal. To build a meaningful relationship you have to disclose yourself to the other person and take the risk that the other person may reject rather than like you.[35]

Because of the risks associated with self-disclosure, communication theorists have offered suggestions for reducing risk. For instance, be aware of the nature of your relationship with the other party; begin with a safe level of disclosure; be sure the disclosure is relevant and appropriate for this interview; be sensitive to the effect your disclosure will have on the other party and persons not involved in the interview; continue to disclose at a level at which the other party reciprocates; and be particularly cautious when communicating online.[36] People tend to have fewer inhibitions when interacting online and may disclose too much information, what some refer to as "hyperpersonal" revelations, and this information may come earlier ("fast-tracked") in online interactions.[37] Most of us have experienced others (students, professors, associates, acquaintances, clients) using antagonistic words and accusations online they would never make face-to-face or on the telephone with us.

Gender, Culture, and Self-Disclosure

Women disclose more freely than men.

Gender and **culture** of interview participants may influence the levels of **communication interactions** and the **self-disclosure** that takes place during an interview.

Gender

Generally speaking women disclose more than men and, except for anger, are allowed to express emotions (fear, sadness, sympathy) more than men. Because women are perceived to be better listeners and more responsive than men, disclosure is often highest between woman-to-woman parties (perhaps because talk is at the very heart of women's relationships), about equal in woman-to-man parties, and lowest among man-to-man parties.[38]

Culture

Culture may dictate what we disclose and to whom.

Culture may determine what is disclosed to whom and how. For example, Americans of European descent may disclose a wider range of topics, including very personal information, than Japanese and Chinese, disclose more about their careers and less about their families than Ghanians, and disclose to more different types of people than Asians. Asians tend to disclose more to those with expertise and ability to exhibit honest and positive attitudes than to those who like to talk and show more emotional feelings. Research suggests that people in high-context, collectivist cultures, such as Japan and China, in which they are expected to work for the good of the group and to know and follow cultural norms, disclose less than those in low-context, individualist cultures, such as the United States and Great Britain, in which they strive to succeed as individuals and cultural norms are less well known and more flexible. Conflict may result if we overdisclose, underdisclose, or disclose to the wrong person in differing cultures. Regardless of culture, however, important ingredients may determine degree of self-disclosure, including perceived similarity, competence, involvement, and self-disclosures that may take the relationship to a higher level.[39]

While cultures vary in how, when, and to whom self-disclosure is appropriate, some theorists claim that the notion of politeness—maintaining positive rather than negative face—is universal. According to **"politeness theory,"** all humans want to be appreciated and protected. Littlejohn writes:

Positive and negative face are universal motives.

> *Positive face* is the desire to be appreciated and approved, to be liked and honored, and *positive politeness* is designed to meet these desires. Showing concern, complimenting, and using respectful forms of address are examples. *Negative face* is the desire to be free from imposition or intrusion, and *negative politeness* is designed to protect the other person when negative face needs are threatened. Acknowledging the imposition when making a request is a common example.[40]

You encounter situations in which politeness is essential not only when dealing with persons from other cultures but whenever you are involved in challenging, complaining, evaluating, disciplining, advising, and counseling. Guerrero, Andersen, and Afifi write that "people face a constant struggle between wanting to do whatever they want (which satisfies their negative face needs) and wanting to do what makes them look good to others (which satisfies their positive face needs)."[41] They identify several severe "face threatening acts," such as behavior that violates an important cultural, social, or professional rule (missing an anniversary date or failure to follow the chain-of-command); behavior that produces significant harm (damaged relationship or lost income); behavior for which the party is directly responsible (an accident or poor hiring decision); and the more power or authority the other party has over the offending party (professor, supervisor, or military officer). The desire to be polite—to avoid hurting or upsetting another and to show appreciation, understanding, or agreement—is one of the most common causes of deception.[42] A simple misleading statement or answer to a question may seem warranted to sustain politeness and harmony in an interview.

Verbal Interactions

Communication interactions in interviews are intricate and inseparable combinations of verbal and nonverbal symbols, some intentional and some not. Although inseparable on many occasions, we will separate them for instructional purposes only.

Never assume communication is taking place.

Verbal interactions, words, are merely arbitrary connections of letters that serve as symbols for people, animals, things, places, events, ideas, beliefs, and feelings. Their imperfect nature is brought home to you nearly every day in misunderstandings, confusions, embarrassments, antagonisms, and hurt feelings over what you assume to be perfectly clear, common, and neutral words. Perhaps *the greatest single problem with human communication is the assumption of it,* and the use and misuse of words cause many problems in interviews. Journalism professor Michael Skube has written about the lack of familiarity many college students have with what he has *assumed* to be commonly understood words, including impetus, lucid, advocate, derelict, and brevity.[43]

We've all thought at times that if others would use words properly, there would be few communication problems. In fact, the arbitrary nature of language, not improper use, causes most problems.

Multiple Meanings

A word rarely has a single meaning.

Simple words have many meanings. Those for *argue* range from giving reasons or evidence to disagreeing in words and persuading. *Game* may refer to a basketball game, a wild animal, or a person willing to try new things. To *reveal* may mean to tell, disclose, make known through divine inspiration, or violate a confidence.

Ambiguities

Words may be so ambiguous that any two parties may assign very different meanings to them. What are a "nice" apartment, an "affordable" education, a "simple" set of instructions, a "small" college, and a "living" wage? When is a person "young," "middle-aged," or "old"? How do you know that something is "one of the best" or "one of the rarest"? Have you ever met a U.S. citizen who was not "middle class" regardless of income?

Beware of words that sound alike.

Sound Alikes

Similar sounding words may lead to confusion in interviews because you usually hear, not see, words. Examples include see and sea, do and due, sail and sale, and to, too, and two. You may be startled by a word only to realize that you had misinterpreted what was meant. Pronunciation or enunciation may add to this problem. A banker in Los Angeles related an incident in which she was talking to a banking associate in Chicago and thought she heard the other say, "We're axing John." The associate had meant "asking John," not firing him.

Connotations

Words are rarely neutral.

Many words have positive and negative connotations. You may describe a suit as "expensive" or "cheap," a car as "used" or "preowned," or the purchase of a condo as a "cost" or an "investment." Persuasion can mean to inspire or to contrive; execution can mean to perform or to hang; politician can mean leader or schemer. The exact meaning may be in the eye of the beholder at a given moment in a given situation.

Jargon

Either party may cause communication problems by altering or creating words. For instance, every profession has its own specialized jargon. "Vehicular control devices" are stoplights. "Spin doctoring" is explaining or defending issues. A hammer, according to the military, is a "manually powered fastener-driving impact device." Try to use the simplest, clearest, most appropriate words in each situation and for each interview party. Be aware of your own personal, cultural, or professional jargon.

Slang

Slang comes and goes and often determines who's in and who's out.

Each generation has a kind of unofficial jargon we call *slang*. Fast, powerful cars went from "keen" and "neat" in the 1940s and 1950s, to "hot," "cool," "groovy," and "far out" in the 1960s and 1970s, to "decent," "tough," and "mean" in the 1980s, to "awesome," "way cool," "outrageous," and "white hot" in the 1990s. In the twenty-first century, these cars are "hot," "rockin'," "slammin'," "jammin'," "poppin'," and "kickin'." Using slang properly places you in the in-group, and you may ridicule those who do not understand slang or use it incorrectly.

Euphemisms

You use a euphemism when you substitute a better-sounding word for a common word. For instance, you are likely to purchase a lifelike Christmas tree rather than an artificial or fake one, inquire about the location of the powder room or facility rather than the toilet, purchase an appliance from an associate rather than a clerk, and experience discomfort rather than pain from an invasive procedure rather than surgery. All of these substitutions merely sound better and seem more social.

Naming is an effort to alter social reality.

Naming

You may label a person, place, or thing not to make it sound better but to alter how you and the other party see reality. You may purchase a diet cola but not a diet beer, experience a downturn rather than a recession, and order a quarter-pound hamburger but not a four-ounce hamburger. When substituting woman for girl, flight attendant for stewardess, firefighter for fireman, you are not being merely "politically" correct but are addressing the reality that men and women perform professional roles, not girls and boys. Words matter, and they may alter or reinforce perceptions of reality.

Power Words

Words may be powerful or not.

There are power and powerless speech forms.[44] Power word forms include certainty, challenges, orders, verbal aggression, leading questions, metaphors, and memorable phrases such as "Read my lips!" "Make my day!" "Take your best shot!" "Live with it!" "Let's roll!" and "Get a life!" Powerless forms include apologies, disclaimers, excuses, indirect questions, and nonfluencies such as "Uh" and "Umm." "Know what I mean" and "You know" have become all too common in everyday and professional communications and seem to dominate many broadcast interviews. They are powerless, meaningless distractions that communicate the inability of a person to articulate thoughts and sentences. Few people are impressed with opening phrases such as "I didn't mean to . . . ," "It's not my fault that . . . ," and "Do you think maybe . . . ?"

Regional and Role Differences

You may assume all Americans speak "English," but there are regional and role differences. People in New Jersey go to the shore, while those in California go to the beach. A person in New England is likely to ask for a soda, a person in New York may order pop, while a person in the Midwest is likely to ask for a coke. A government entitlement program such as Social Security has different meanings for 24-year-old and 64-year-old interview parties. Employees and management view downsizing and outsourcing very differently.

Gender Differences

Gender differences may lead to power differences.

Studies of gender and communication have noted a variety of differences in language use among men and women. For example, men tend to be socialized into developing and using power speech forms and to dominate interactions, while women tend to be socialized into developing powerless speech forms and to foster relationships and exchanges during interactions. Research indicates that women's talk is more polite and expressive, contains more qualifiers and disclaimers, includes more second- and third-person pronouns (such as we and they rather than I or me), makes more color distinctions, includes fewer mechanical and technical terms, and is more tentative than men's talk.[45] Men not only can use more intense language than women, but they are often expected to do so because it is considered masculine. If a woman uses the same language, she may be termed bitchy, pushy, or opinionated or accused of trying to be a man. Speaking styles, ingrained in us since childhood, explain why many women find it difficult to operate equally and effectively in a male-dominated society.

Stereotypes are dangerous assumptions.

Be cautious when stereotyping language and interaction differences among genders. Julia Wood writes that "despite jokes about women's talkativeness, research indicates that in most contexts, men not only hold their own but dominate the conversation."[46] In addition, men tend to interrupt women more than other men and do so to state opinions; women tend to interrupt to ask questions. Recent studies also indicate, however, that both men and women use tentative forms of speech. Several factors may affect how men and women use language, including context of the interview, subject matter, length of the interaction (affecting how much parties become comfortable with one another), status differences between the parties, and roles being played.[47]

Global Differences

Global use of words may be more significant than foreign words.

Language differences are magnified in the global village, even when people are speaking the same language. North Americans tend to value precision, directness, explicit words, power speech forms, and use of "I" to begin sentences. We value tough or straight talk.[48] Other cultures value the group or collective rather than the individual and rarely begin with "I" or call attention to themselves. Chinese children are taught to downplay self-expression. Japanese tend to be implicit rather than explicit and employ ambiguous words and qualifiers. Koreans prefer not to give negative or "no" responses but to imply disagreements to maintain group harmony. And Arab-speaking peoples tend to employ what is referred to as "sweet talk" or accommodating language with elaborate metaphors and similes.

Idioms such as "bought the farm," "get your feet wet," "wild goose chase," "stud muffin," and "hit a home run" are unique expressions in every country and may pose serious problems for those with varying degrees of expertise in a language or culture. Wen-Shu Lee writes of her experiences as a new graduate student in the United States. Although she was fluent in English, she was taken aback when a fellow student looked at her notes in Chinese and remarked, "That's Greek to me." When she said that it was Chinese, not Greek, the student thought this was really funny. Only then did Lee realize that she had misunderstood a common idiom in the United States. She warns that some people will remain silent when hearing an idiom rather than risk appearing stupid, and recommends that "speakers need to work together to establish a conversational decorum in which it is all right or socially acceptable to bring up problems."[49]

Guidelines for Reducing Language Problems

Famous linguist Irving Lee wrote years ago that we often "talk past" one another instead of with one another.[50] These guidelines can enhance effective use of language during interviews.

Language problems are avoidable.

- Choose words and phrases carefully.
- Expand your vocabulary.
- Be aware that slight changes in words can alter meanings.
- Order words carefully in sentences and thoughts.
- Listen to the context in which words are used.
- Learn the jargon of professions and groups.
- Keep up to date with changing uses of language.
- Know how the meaning of words may be affected by gender, age, race, culture, ethnic group, and situation.

Nonverbal Interactions

Nonverbal signals send many different messages.

The oral, face-to-face nature of most interviews means that successful communication relies heavily upon nonverbal signals such as physical appearance, dress, eye contact, voice, touches, head nods, pauses, handshakes, winks, glances, silence, posture, and proximity of the two parties. Nonverbal communication is important because both parties are likely to detect what the other does and does not do. Your facial expressions may be your most effective nonverbal channel. The interactive nature of the interview depends upon nonverbal signals to regulate the flow of communication and turn taking. Research shows that you rely on nonverbal cues to express yourself and interpret the expressions of others and to know when it is your time to talk or listen.[51]

A single behavioral act may convey a message. Poor eye contact may tell the other party that you have something to hide, a limp handshake that you are timid, a serious facial expression that you are sincere, the touch of a hand or arm that you are sympathetic or understanding, or a puzzled expression that you are confused. Your speaking rate may communicate urgency (fast speed), the gravity of the situation (slow speed), lack of interest (fast speed), lack of preparation (slow speed), nervousness (fast speed and breathless voice), or indecision (halting voice). **Silence** may encourage the other to talk, signal that you are not in a hurry, express agreement with what is being said, and keep the other party talking, but it can also signal apathy, boredom, fear, or intimidation.[52]

You send and receive messages with a combination of nonverbal acts that enhances the impact of the message. For instance, you may show interest by leaning forward, maintaining good eye contact, nodding your head, and having a serious facial expression. On the other hand, when you fidget, cross and uncross arms and legs, sit rigid, look down, furrow brows, and speak in a high-pitched voice, you may reveal a high level of anxiety, fear, or agitation. A drooping body, frown, and slow speaking rate may reveal sadness or resignation to anticipated failure or discipline. Leaning backward, staring at the other party, raising an eyebrow, and shaking your head may signal disagreement, anger, or disgust. The way you shake hands and look the other in the eye may signal trustworthiness. Body movements, gestures, and posture may show dynamism or lack of it. Positions of power are exhibited through physical appearance, spatial behavior, eye behavior, body movements, and touch. Any behavioral act may be interpreted in a meaningful way by the other party. Your message may be intentional or unintentional, accurate or inaccurate, but it will be interpreted.

Any behavioral act, or its absence, can convey a message.

Physical appearance and dress are particularly important during the first few minutes of interviews as you get to know and respect one another. This critical first impression often begins before words are exchanged. You may respond more favorably to attractive persons who are neither too fat nor too thin, tall rather than short, shapely rather than unshapely, pretty and handsome rather than plain or ugly. Parties see attractive persons to be more poised, outgoing, interesting, and sociable. How you dress and prepare yourself physically for an interview reveals how you view yourself, the other party, the situation, and the nature and importance of the interview.[53]

In mixed messages, the *how* may overcome the *what*.

Nonverbal communication may be more important than words. Research indicates that nonverbal actions exchange feelings and emotions more accurately; convey meanings and intentions relatively free of deception, distortion, and confusion; are more efficient; and are more suitable for suggesting or imparting ideas and emotions indirectly. Nonverbal behaviors are assumed to be more truthful than words and, if verbal and nonverbal messages conflict—sending mixed messages—you are likely to believe the nonverbal. *How* tends to dominate the *what.*

Verbal and nonverbal messages are intricately intertwined.

Theorists claim, however, that it is nearly impossible to isolate the verbal from the nonverbal because they are so intertwined during interviews. For example, the nonverbal may **complement** the verbal. Vocal stress may call attention to an important word (like underlining or italicizing in print):"I'm planning to change programs in *May*," "My *net* income last year was *slightly* over $152,000," or "I'm *not* thinking of leaving." You may complement words with a sincere tone of voice and deliberate speaking rate. A serious facial expression and direct eye contact may help words communicate sympathy and understanding. The nonverbal accentuates and verifies your words. Nonverbal actions may **reinforce** verbal messages: a head nod while saying yes, a head shake while saying no. A nonverbal action may act as a **substitute** for words when you point to a chair without saying, "Sit here," or smile to express recognition or friendship. Nonverbal substitutes, a kind of everyday sign language, may be more effective and less disruptive than words. Silence, for instance, can signal agreement or disagreement tactfully.

Gender

Women are more adept at nonverbal communication.

Gender differences may affect interviews because women seem to be more skilled at and rely more on nonverbal communication than men. For instance, facial expressions, pauses, and bodily gestures are more important in women's interactions than men's, perhaps because women are more expressive than men. Women tend to gaze more and are less uncomfortable when eye contact is broken. Men's lower-pitched voices are viewed as more credible and dynamic than women's higher-pitched voices. Female parties stand or sit closer than opposite-sex parties, and males maintain more distance than opposite-sex or female parties.

Culture

Differing cultures share many nonverbal signals. For instance, around the world people nod their heads in agreement, shake their heads in disagreement, give thumbs down for disapproval, shake fists in anger, and clap hands to show approval. On the other hand, nonverbal communication differs significantly among cultures.

In the United States, African-American participants tend to maintain eye contact more when speaking than when listening. They give more nonverbal feedback when listening than European-Americans. In general, African-Americans are more animated and personal, while European-Americans are more subdued. They tend to avoid eye contact with superiors out of respect,

Stock4B–RF/Getty Images

Be aware of cultural differences in nonverbal communication.

a trait that is often misinterpreted by European-American superiors who see lack of eye contact as a sign of disinterest, lack of confidence, or dishonesty. And African-Americans tend to touch more and stand closer together when communicating than do European-Americans.[54]

Black and white Americans use different nonverbal signals.

On the global scene, Americans are taught to look others in the eye when speaking, while Africans are taught to avoid eye contact when listening to others. An honest "look me in the eye" for a Westerner may express a lack of respect to an Asian. An American widens his or her eyes to show wonder or surprise, while the Chinese do so to express anger, the French to express disbelief, and Hispanics to show lack of understanding. Americans are taught to smile in response to a smile, but this is not so in Israel. Japanese are taught to mask negative feelings with smiles and laughter. Americans are taught to have little direct physical contact with others while communicating, but Mediterranean and Latin countries encourage direct contact. On a loudness scale of 1 to 10, with 10 being high, Arabs would be near 10, Americans would be near the middle, and Europeans would be near 1. Arabs perceive loudness as signs of strength and sincerity and softness as signs of weakness and deviousness. Not surprisingly, many Americans and Europeans see Arabs as pushy and rude. A firm handshake is important in American society but signals nothing in Japan.

Be aware of the diversity of nonverbal messages in different parts of the world.

Many gestures you observe in different cultures and countries may have very different meanings. For instance, a simple wave means "hello" in the United States and "come here" in Algeria. Some uses may be positive or negative. A finger to the forehead means smart in the United States and stupid in many European cultures. A thumb up means "way to go" in the United States and "screw you" in Iran. A circular motion of a finger around the ear means crazy in the United States and "you have a telephone call" in the Netherlands. Fingers in a circle means "okay" in the United States but is an obscene gesture in Brazil.[55]

Feedback

Feedback is immediate and pervasive in interviews, and meaningful feedback, sent and received, is essential to verify what is being communicated and how it is being communicated. The large, double-ended arrow that links the top of the party circles in Figure 2.5 symbolizes the heavy stream of feedback between interview parties. Feedback is both verbal (questions and answers, arguments and counterarguments, agreements and disagreements, challenges and compliances) and nonverbal (facial expressions, gestures, raised eyebrows, eye contact, vocal utterances, and posture).

You can detect critical feedback and assess how an interview is progressing by observing and listening carefully to what is and is not taking place.

Be perceptive, sensitive, and receptive.

- Does the other party move closer or farther away?
- Does the other party select a power position from which to take part?
- How does the tone of the interaction change?
- How do eye contact, posture, voice, and manner change?

Figure 2.5 *Feedback*

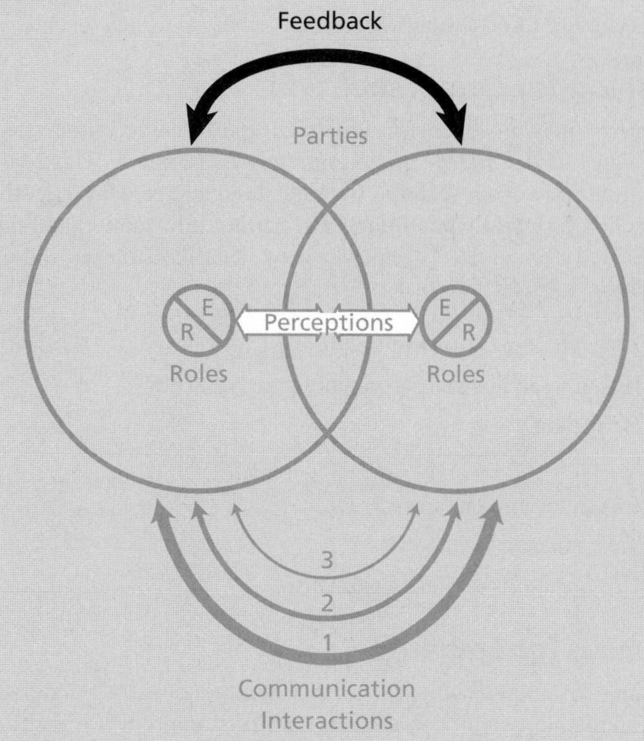

- Does attentiveness grow or lessen?
- Does the other party become more or less willing to disclose information, feelings, and attitudes?

Be careful of reading too much into small nonverbal actions and changes. A person may be fidgeting because a chair is hard, not because of questions or answers. A person may be paying less attention because of noise and interruptions, not disinterest. A person may speak loudly because of habit, not because of a hearing impairment. Poor eye contact may indicate shyness or culture, not deceptiveness or mistrust.

It is difficult to listen with your mouth open and your ears closed.

Listening skills are essential to obtaining information, detecting clues, and generating Level 2 and Level 3 responses. Few people listen well. Surveys of hundreds of corporations in the United States reveal that poor listening skills create barriers in all positions from entry level to CEO.

An interviewer may not listen carefully to answers received, while an interviewee may not listen carefully to questions asked. Both may lead a friendly critic to remark, "Did you hear what you just asked?" or "Did you hear what you just said?" Often you may be so concerned about your primary role as questioner or respondent that you do not listen. Most of your training has prepared you for talking, not listening.

Be flexible in selecting listening approaches.

There are four approaches to listening: for comprehension, for empathy, for evaluation, and for resolution. Each is designed to play a specific role in giving, receiving, and processing information during interviews.

Listening for Comprehension

The intent of listening for comprehension is to understand content.

Listening for comprehension is designed to receive, understand, and remember an interchange as accurately and completely as possible. The goal is to concentrate on a question, answer, or reaction to understand and remain objective, not to judge. This approach is essential when giving and getting information and during the first minutes of interviews when determining how to react. Use these guidelines for listening for comprehension:

- Listen to a question before phrasing an answer.
- Listen to an answer before phrasing a question.
- Be patient.
- Listen to tone of voice and vocal emphasis.
- Listen for content and ideas.
- Take notes.
- Use questions to clarify and verify.

Listening for Empathy

The intent of empathic listening is to understand the other party.

Listening for empathy communicates genuine concern, understanding, and involvement. Empathic listening reassures, comforts, expresses warmth, and shows regard. It is not expressing sympathy or feeling sorry for someone but the ability to place one's self in another's situation. Follow these guidelines for listening with empathy:

- Show interest and concern.
- Do not interrupt.
- Be comfortable with displays of emotion.
- Remain nonjudgmental.
- Listen to give options and guidelines.
- Reply with tact and understanding.

Listening for Evaluation

The intent of evaluative listening is to judge content and actions.

Listening for evaluation, or *critical listening,* judges what you hear and observe. It often follows comprehension and empathy because you are not ready to judge until you comprehend the verbal and nonverbal elements of interactions. Openly expressing criticism may diminish cooperation and levels of disclosure. Follow these guidelines for evaluative listening:

- Listen carefully to questions and answers.
- Listen to content.

- Observe nonverbal clues.
- Ask for clarification.
- Avoid defensive reactions.

Listening for Resolution

John Stewart has developed a fourth type of listening called **dialogic listening.**[56] Dialogic listening focuses on *ours* rather than *mine* or *yours* and believes the agenda for resolving a problem or task supersedes the individual. Dialogic listening is most appropriate for problem-solving interviews when the goal is the joint resolution of a problem or task. Stewart likens dialogic listening to adding clay to a mold together, to see how the other person will react, what the person will add, and how this will affect the shape and content of the product. Follow these guidelines when listening for resolution:

The intent of dialogic listening is to resolve problems.

- Encourage interaction.
- Trust the other party to make contributions.
- Focus on the communication, not the psychology, of the interview.
- Focus on the present rather than past or future.
- Paraphrase and add to the other party's responses and ideas.

Although active and insightful listening is critical to both parties, listening is difficult. It is an invisible skill, so it is difficult to learn by observing. You learn to be a passive listener as a child, student, employee, and subordinate. A few years ago, a charity called the home of one of the authors. He was interested in giving to the charity but wanted written information on the charity and the opportunity to send a donation through the mail. The fund-raiser was determined to get an immediate commitment of a specific dollar donation over the telephone that evening and commented that it cost money to send out information. When the author commented that he would add a donation to defray this expense, the caller commented sarcastically, "Sure you will!" That ended the interview.

You can become an effective listener. First, strive to be as satisfied when listening as you are when talking. Second, overcome the expectation that you must be entertained at all times. Third, be an active listener by attending carefully and critically to content and nonverbal signals. Fourth, concentrate on listening despite distractions such as physical surroundings, interruptions, and appearance. Fifth, use the most appropriate listening approach.

Listening, like speaking, is a learned skill.

The Interview Situation

No interview takes place in a vacuum. Each occurs at a given *time,* in a given *place,* with given *surroundings.* Either party may initiate the process and each comes with perceptions of what is about to take place in this setting and why. The many situational variables that influence interviews are symbolized by the imploding arrows in Figure 2.6.

Figure 2.6 *Situational variables*

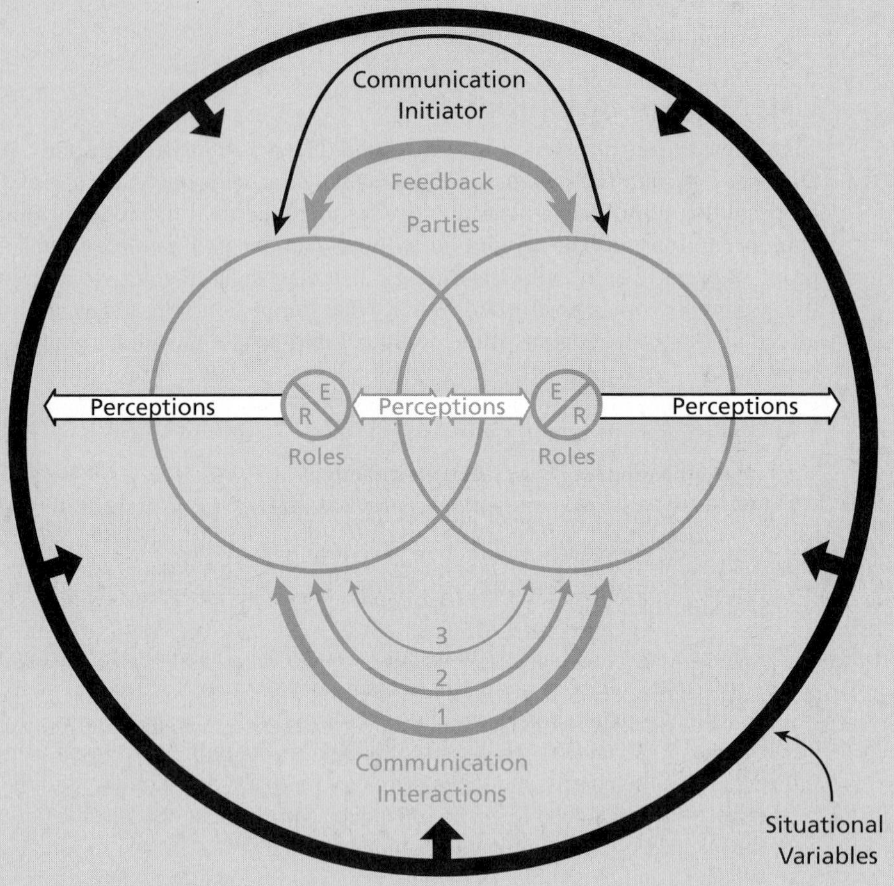

Initiating the Interview

Either party may initiate an interview, as shown by the arrows in Figure 2.6 that emerge from the top of the circle and touch each party. For example, you may initiate an interview with a supervisor to discuss a proposal you have developed, or your supervisor may initiate an interview to discuss a problem in your division that you need to address.

Who initiates an interview and how may affect control, roles, and atmosphere.

The situation often determines who initiates an interview and who must be interviewed. For instance, a fender-bender in a parking lot may require you to contact the police, and the investigating officer will ask questions to determine the cause and fault of the accident. Conversely, the person who initiates the interview affects the situation by determining how the contact is initiated and where and when an interview will take place.

You can enhance the climate of the interview by initiating the interview directly rather than through a secretary, staff member, or friend. Inform the other party about the nature, purpose, and use of the interview and begin in a positive and informative manner.

Perceptions

A party may see the interview as routine or an event.

Each party comes to an interview with unique perceptions of the situation, including purpose, need, urgency, timing, place, and setting. Figure 2.6 symbolizes these perceptions by the arrows that run from each party to the situational circle. The interviewer may see the interview as a routine, everyday activity, nothing special or exciting, while the interviewee may see the interview as an extraordinary, once-in-a-lifetime event likely to affect career, advancement, marriage, financial plans, health, or social status.

Settings are seldom neutral.

Interview parties may see the setting quite differently. Supervisors may perceive their offices to be simple business locations, while their subordinates may see them as alien, off-limits environments, particularly if workers feel few of them ever come out as "happy campers." A professor may feel very relaxed sitting behind a desk, but a student may feel threatened when sitting in front of the desk.

Both parties have vested interests in the nature and outcome of an interview, but their goals may be quite different. A reporter may want you to reveal your personal feelings about a recent conflict within an organization, but you may be determined to keep these private.

Perceptions are critical in moving beyond Level 1 interactions.

Parties are most likely to communicate beyond Level 1 if they perceive the situation to be familiar rather than strange, informal rather than formal, warm rather than cold, private rather than open, and close rather than distant physically, socially, and psychologically. Organizations attempt to enhance concentration and motivation with well-lighted, pleasantly painted, moderate-sized rooms with comfortable furniture, temperature, and ventilation. Some attempt to create business and professional settings that resemble living rooms, dining rooms, family rooms, and studies to make interview parties feel more at home and more willing and able to communicate at Levels 2 and 3.

Time of Day, Week, and Year

Each of us has optimum times for interactions.

You tend to interact best at certain times of the day, week, and year. For instance, you may be a morning, afternoon, or evening person, meaning this is the optimum time for performance, production, communication, thinking, creativity, handling of conflicts, and dealing with important matters. It is unwise to address difficult issues or exchange important or extensive information just before lunch or late in the day or work shift when people are mentally and physically tired. Moods may be dark and motivation low on Monday mornings and Friday afternoons. Holidays are good times for some interviews (sales, employment selection, journalistic) but bad for others (dismissals, reprimands, investigations, health care). Counselors note marked increases in crisis interviews with lonely people during family-oriented and happy seasons such as Thanksgiving, Christmas, and Passover. Police officers claim that full moons bring out strange behaviors in people.

Take into account events before and after interviews.

Be aware of events that precede or follow interviews. Wednesday morning may ordinarily be a good time for a professor, but not *this* one. A student facing a major examination may find it difficult to concentrate and answer questions. A possible layoff or personal problem may affect mood, expectations, concentration, and listening.

Place

Don't underestimate the importance of place.

Consider whose turf is best for the interview. For instance, you may feel more comfortable and less threatened in your home, room, office, or business. On the other hand, a neutral place such as a lounge area or restaurant might work best. We protect our turf. Think of your reactions when you walked into your room or office and found another person in your chair or at your desk. When one of the authors was head of a large academic department, he discovered that faculty often preferred to interact in their offices unless privacy was important or the issue was departmental rather than personal. When possible, select the location most conducive to effective communication.

Surroundings

Surroundings help create a productive climate.

Objects and decorations may create an appropriate atmosphere and interview climate. Trophies, awards, degrees, and licenses attractively displayed communicate achievements, professional credibility, and stature in a field. Pictures, statues, and busts of leaders or famous persons communicate organizational and personal history, success, recognition, endorsement, and contacts. Models or samples may display state-of-the-art products and services. Colors of walls, types of carpeting, wall hangings, wallpaper, and curtains can provide a warm, attractive atmosphere conducive to effective communication.

Control noise to focus attention on the interaction.

Noise in an interview is anything that interferes with the communication process, including background noise, doors opening and closing, music, others talking, objects being dropped, and traffic. The interview may be interrupted by a cell phone, arrival of a faxed letter, or an e-mail message. People coming in and out of the room, walking by an open door, or asking for assistance are common distractions. The authors are surprised by the number of students who walk into their offices and interrupt conferences with students, as if their fellow students were invisible.

You generate a different kind of noise by coming to an interview fatigued, angry, overwhelmed with personal problems, or thinking about the next interview. You may be distracted by a headache, upset stomach, or cold. It is tempting to look out a window at traffic, building construction, or scenery, or to concentrate on pictures, objects, furniture in the room, or the other party's mannerisms.

Come to each interview ready to communicate.

Eliminate negative influences of noise by selecting locations free of background noise or taking simple precautions: close a door, window, or curtain; turn off a cell phone, television, or CD player. Inform others you do not wish to be disturbed. Limit self-generated noise by coming to each interview physically and psychologically ready to concentrate. During the interview, strive to blot out noise by focusing your attention on the other party, questions, answers, and nonverbal signals.

Territoriality

You may select a seat, arrange books and papers, and place coats and hats strategically around you to stake out your physical and psychological space. You may resent those who invade this carefully crafted space with their choice of seating, possessions, eyes, voices, or bodies. Think of how you have reacted to common invasions of territory:

- Other students walking into a professor's office while you were discussing a problem.

Maintain an arm's length of distance between parties.

- Diners at another table listening to your conversation with a prospective employer.
- Colleagues talking loudly at the next workstation when you were giving information to a client.
- Persons who seated themselves at the same table while you were talking with a mentor.

Relationship affects territorial comfort zones.

Proximity of interview parties affects comfort level. You may feel uncomfortable with persons who insist on talking nose-to-nose, and may react by backing up, placing furniture between you, or terminating the interview. Trenholm and Jensen write about "**territorial markers**" and use the term "**personal space**" to describe an "imaginary bubble" around us that we consider to be "almost as private as the body itself."[57] Researchers have identified intimate distance (touching to 18 inches), personal distance (1½ to 4 feet), and social distance (4 to 12 feet).[58] Two to four feet—approximately an arm's length or on opposite sides of a table or desk—is an optimum distance for most interviews.

Relationship, particularly status, situation, and feelings of parties toward one another, influences the size of the bubble with which you are comfortable. High-status people stand or sit closer to low-status people, while low-status people prefer greater distances when dealing with superiors. We maintain a greater distance with a stranger than with close associates, peers, and friends. Some people want to "get in your face" when angry, while others widen the space because their anger is translated into distancing themselves from you physically, socially, and psychologically.

Age, gender, and culture influence territorial preferences.

Age, gender, and culture determine space preferences. For instance, people of the same age stand or sit closer together than those of mixed ages, particularly when the age difference is significant. All-male parties tend to arrange themselves farther apart than all-female or mixed-sex parties. North Americans prefer greater personal distances than do Middle Eastern and Latin American peoples. Many Arabs and Latin Americans see us as distant and cold, while we see them as intruding into our space. Northern Europeans tend to prefer greater personal distance than Southern Europeans.[59]

Where you sit and on what you sit is often determined by status, gender, furnishings, cultural norms, relationship between parties, and personal preferences. For example, a superior and a subordinate may sit across a desk from one another, arrangement A in Figure 2.7, with one sitting in a large leather swivel chair while the other sits on a simple chair. This provides distance in a formal setting in which one party desires to maintain a superior position. Two chairs at right angles near the corner of a desk or table, arrangement B, creates a less formal atmosphere and a greater feeling of equality between parties. Students and staff often prefer this arrangement with college professors and department heads or supervisors.

Seating may equalize control and enhance the interview climate.

You may remove physical obstacles and reduce the superior-subordinate atmosphere further by placing chairs at opposite sides of a small coffee table or by omitting the table altogether, arrangements C and D. A circular table, arrangement E, is growing in popularity, especially in counseling interviews or interviews involving more than two people, because it avoids a head-of-the-table position, allows participants to pass out materials, and provides a surface on which to write, review printed items, and place refreshments.

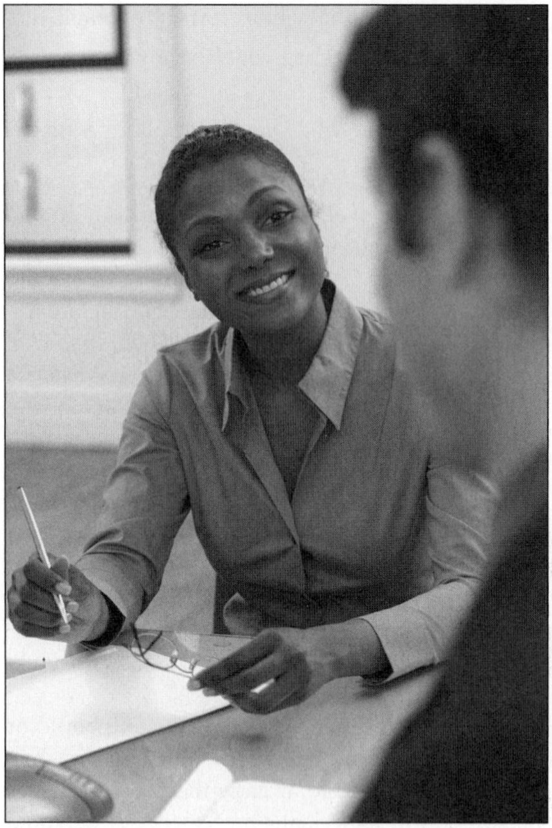
Comstock Images/Getty Images

A corner seating arrangement is preferred by many interviewers and interviewees.

The circular table or chairs around a small table works well for panel interviews. Arrangement F is most suitable when one or both parties consist of several persons such as a focus group.

Outside Forces

Although your primary concern is likely to be the parties in a situation, you must be aware of possible **outside forces** that may influence one or both parties before, during, and after the interview. Figure 2.8 indicates that common outside forces are family, associates, friends, employers, government agencies, and professional associations.

Outside forces may have input before the interview by providing guidelines for taking part in or conducting the interview, including topics to cover, structure to follow, questions to ask, answers to give, demands to make, or attitudes to assume. Some union contracts and corporate policies, for example, prescribe what questions can be asked and how they are to be phrased during employment interviews. No deviations or probing questions are permitted. In Chapters 7 and 8, we discuss how Equal Employment Opportunity (EEO) laws influence questions recruiters can ask and how applicants might respond in employment interviews.

We are not really alone with the other party.

Outside forces impact the interview when parties try to follow views and guidelines from organizations, supervisors, and peers. For example, organizational policies may place restraints on the opening of the interview, the parties, perceptions, level of interactions, self-disclosure, nature of messages, feedback, and interviewing approach. Policies often prescribe how to structure and conduct surveys, recruiting, performance review, counseling, and health care interviews.

Outside forces determine roles in many interviews.

Both parties may be concerned about post-interview reactions of outside forces. How will you report what took place, particularly answers, topics covered, demands, and agreements? For instance, interviewers may take hard lines in a negotiation or ask pressure questions during selection interviews because that is what their organizations demand. Interviewees may respond as outside forces have suggested or according to how they want the interview reported afterward. You may need to report that you "drove a hard bargain" and "got a real deal" when purchasing a new car, told a boss "where to get off," asked the questions you were told to ask, and demanded your money back. You may be cautious in interchanges because of possible lawsuits, grievances, or negative reactions of friends, colleagues, or supervisors.

Figure 2.7 *Seating arrangements*

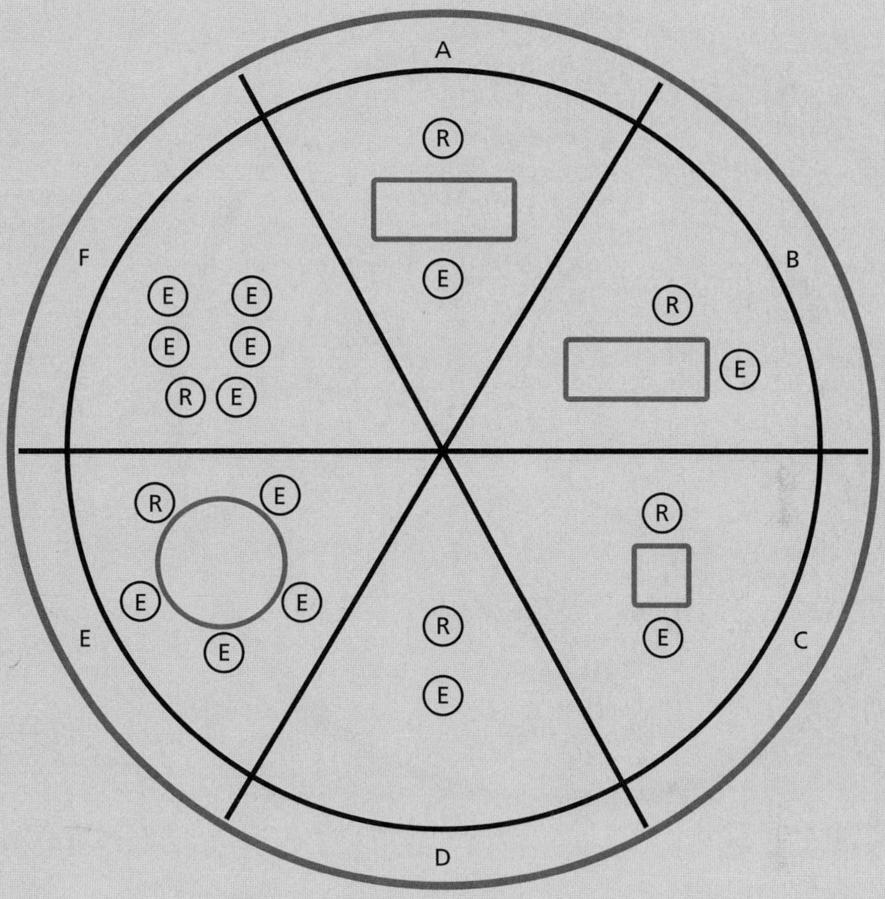

For instance:

Know what advice you must take.

- What advice is wise to take?
- Which advice is appropriate for you, your position, and the situation?
- What advice must you take?
- How might your inclination to "satisfy the group" following an interview negatively affect the interview?

Be aware of outside forces impinging on the other party to understand attitudes, responses, and behavior and avoid questions and topics that are off limits or demands that are impossible to grant. You may make demands and "let off steam" to organizational representatives on the telephone who have no authority to grant your wishes

Figure 2.8 *Outside forces*

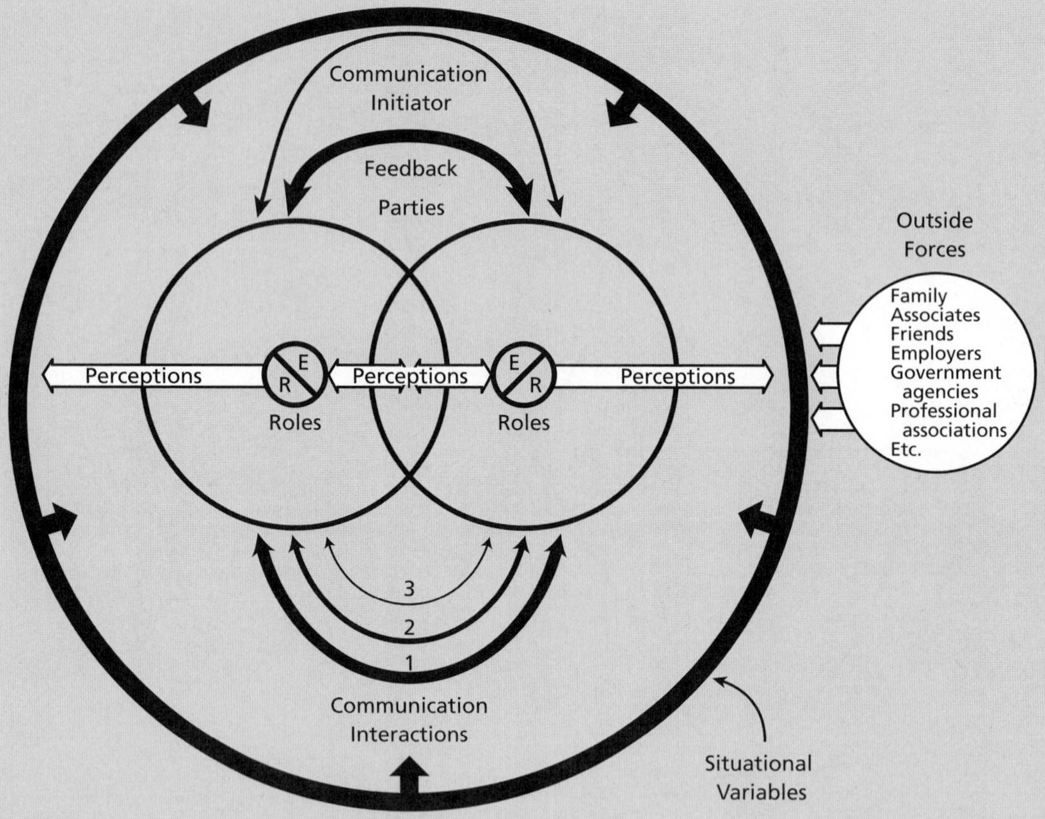

and who are not responsible for the problem. As bearers of bad news, representatives become the organization's scapegoats and our targets.

Summary

This chapter developed a summary model of the process that contains the many interacting variables present in each interview: two parties, exchanging of roles, perceptions, levels of exchanges, verbal and nonverbal messages, relationships, feedback, listening, situation, and outside forces. Interviewing is a dynamic, complicated process between two complex parties operating with imperfect verbal and nonverbal symbols guided and controlled by perceptions and the situation. The ability to listen (for comprehension, empathy, evaluation, and resolution) and to employ silence strategically are often more important than what you have to say.

A thorough understanding of the process is a prerequisite for successful interviewing. Be aware that perceptions of self, the other party, how the other party sees you, and the situation are critical in determining how interviews progress and whether desired outcomes are achieved. Acknowledge and adapt to the influence of outside forces.

Interviewer and interviewee must be flexible and adaptable in choosing which approach to take (directive, nondirective, or a combination) not only because each party is unique and each situation is different, but because each party is molded and affected by demographics such as age, gender, race, and culture. This chapter has tried to enhance your awareness of how demographics and culture affect self-esteem, disclosure, levels of communication, language, nonverbal communication, and territoriality. In the global village of the twenty-first century, be aware of how different people and different cultures communicate.

Key Terms and Concepts

The online learning center for this text features FLASHCARDS and CROSSWORD PUZZLES for studying based on these terms and concepts

Communication interactions
Complement
Complex communication process
Control
Culture
Defensive climate
Dialectical tensions
Dialogic listening
Directive
Downward communication
Feedback
Focus groups
Gender
Global relationships
Hyperpersonal revelations
Idioms
Initiating
Interpersonal
Joint actions
Levels of interactions
Listening
Nexting
Noise
Nondirective
Nonverbal interactions
Observing
Outside forces
Perceptions
Personal space
Politeness theory
Process
Proximity
Reinforce
Relational dimensions
Relational distance
Relational history
Relational memory
Role competence
Self-concept
Self-disclosure
Self-esteem
Self-fulfilling prophecy
Self-identity
Silence
Situation
Substitute
Supportive climate
Territorial markers
Territoriality
Upward communication
Verbal interactions

An Interview for Review and Analysis

This interview is designed to incorporate all of the principles and theories presented in this chapter and to provide you with an opportunity to analyze them and determine how they affect the interview and the relationship between the two parties.[60] Begin by reading carefully the description of the two parties and the situation. Note the goal of this interview. Then, as you read carefully each interaction, think about the questions posed for review and analysis. Finally, what suggestions would you offer to the manager and Joe for handling such situations and for improving their interviewing skills?

Joe is a production supervisor with 20 years of experience and a good record. The plant manager is considering him for promotion and this interview is a first step in that process. It is exploratory rather than decision making. Company policy stipulates that employees are *not* to be informed when being actively considered for promotion, so Joe is unaware that a promotion may be in the offing. Company policy does allow mentioning overall considerations related to the current workforce situation and to established company criteria for promotions. Two hours prior to the interview, Joe received a call from the manager's secretary asking him to report to the manager. No reason is given. Joe enters the manager's office at 4:30 p.m. (his shift ends at 5:00 p.m.) and is seated across the desk from the manager.

What *perceptions* do Joe and the manager have of themselves, of one another, and of the situation? How would you assess the relationship between Joe and the manager? When, if ever, do the parties *exchange roles* of interviewer and interviewee? At which *communication levels* do most interactions occur? How do *words* influence the interview? How does *nonverbal behavior* affect the interview? Which *listening approaches* do Joe and the manager employ most often and with what effect? Which *interviewing approach* does the manager employ? How do *situational variables* influence this interview? What role do *outside forces* play in this interview?

1. **Manager:** Joe, come in. (smiling) Have a seat. It's been awhile since we've had time for a chat.
2. **Joe:** (sitting facing the manager) Thank you, sir. (soft voice)
3. **Manager:** (serious facial expression and tone of voice) How are things moving along these days, Joe? *Everything* under control in your section?
4. **Joe:** Fine sir. No complaints. (fast speaking rate)
5. **Manager:** I'm *glad* to hear there are no *complaints*. (pause) You think you're doing okay?
6. **Joe:** As good as I know how, sir. (shifts weight in chair)
7. **Manager:** Good. (pause; looks Joe directly in the eyes) By the way, have you ever thought of uh, (pause) doing *something else?*
8. **Joe:** (pause; speaks slowly) Well (pause) uh, yes and no. I do like my job a lot. (rapidly)
9. **Manager:** Hmmm, I see. You don't want to change your job?
10. **Joe:** Uh (pause) no. (pause) I don't think so.
11. **Manager:** (looking closely at Joe; measuring his words) I see. Why do you want to stay on this job?
12. **Joe:** Well, I know the work real well. And everybody seems to like me.
13. **Manager:** Seems to like you? (looks Joe directly in the eyes)
14. **Joe:** Oh (pause) there may be one or two people who don't like me. But we manage to get along.
15. **Manager:** Some people don't like you, then? (sounds accusatory)
16. **Joe:** Well, I wouldn't exactly say *that*. Occasionally someone gets sore because I won't give him overtime.
17. **Manager:** That's the *only* reason?
18. **Joe:** Yes, sir! That's the only thing of importance I can think of. (firm voice, direct eye contact)

19. **Manager:** I see. (pause) Uh, Joe, do you ever think of (pause) *bettering* yourself?
20. **Joe:** Everyone wants to do better. Know what I mean?
21. **Manager:** What do you mean?
22. **Joe:** Well, I mean, almost anyone can find ways to improve. (looks down)
23. **Manager:** You think, then, you could handle your job better?
24. **Joe:** Oh, there's always room for improvement.
25. **Manager:** Joe, have you ever thought of bettering yourself on (pause) *another* job?
26. **Joe:** I like this job and company very much, sir! I know this job well, and you and the company have been very good to me.
27. **Manager:** I don't think you listened *carefully* to my question, Joe. Have you ever thought of *bettering* yourself on *another* job?
28. **Joe:** Well, everybody daydreams about how things might be at another company or even owning your own business. But I haven't given it much serious thought, really.
29. **Manager:** I take it, then, that you prefer definitely to stay on your *present job*.
30. **Joe:** Yes, sir. (pause) Do you have something specific in mind, sir? (rapid speaking voice)
31. **Manager:** Oh, don't worry about that, Joe. I'm glad we had time for this little chat. We'll have to get together again soon. Good luck. (shakes Joe's hand firmly without meeting his eyes)

Student Activities

1. Observe three face-to-face interactions that last at least 10 minutes each. One is a male-to-male interaction, one a female-to-female interaction, and one a female-to-male interaction. Look for similarities and differences in length of interchanges, degree of self-disclosure, and nonverbal elements such as eye contact, voice, and body movements such as gestures, leaning forward, and proximity.
2. Record three broadcast interviews in which one interviewee is an elected official, one a professional athlete, and one a person who recently survived a life-threatening accident. Focus on uses of language: ambiguities, jargon, slang, and power words. How, when, and why were these used by interviewees? Which were unique because of the interviewee's position or experiences?
3. Watch a televised interview that lasts at least 15 minutes and determine which communication levels dominated portions of the interview: Level 1, Level 2, or Level 3. How do you believe the relationship of the parties affected these levels and when they occurred?
4. Interview four students on your campus from different parts of the world about their experiences in communicating with students who have lived in the United States for all their lives. Ask them about communication problems that have occurred while on campus, language uses that have led to confusions, differences in meanings of nonverbal actions and reactions, and relationship differences.

Notes

1. Robert S. Goyer, W. Charles Redding, and John T. Rickey, *Interviewing Principles and Techniques: A Project Text* (Dubuque, IA: Wm. C. Brown, 1968), p. 23.
2. Judith N. Martin and Thomas K. Nakayama, *Intercultural Communication in Contexts* (New York: McGraw-Hill, 2007), p. 371.
3. Martin and Nakayama, pp. 367–368.
4. John Stewart and Carole Logan, *Together: Communicating Interpersonally* (New York: McGraw-Hill, 1998), p. 277.
5. Sarah Trenholm and Arthur Jensen, *Interpersonal Communication* (New York: Oxford University Press, 2008), p. 44.
6. Judith N. Martin and Thomas K. Nakayama, *Intercultural Communication in Contexts* (New York: McGraw-Hill, 2004), p. 345.
7. Trenholm and Jensen, p. 32.
8. George B. Ray and Kory Floyd, "Nonverbal Expressions of Liking and Disliking in Initial Interaction: Encoding and Decoding Perspectives," *Southern Communication Journal* 71 (March 2006), p. 60.
9. Trenholm and Jensen, p. 33.
10. Kory Floyd, *Interpersonal Communication: The Whole Story* (New York: McGraw-Hill, 2009), p. 336; Trenholm and Jensen, p. 31.
11. Floyd, p. 337.
12. John Stewart, *Bridges Not Walls: A Book about Interpersonal Communication* (New York: McGraw-Hill, 2009), p. 18.
13. Stewart, p. 31.
14. Edward T. Hall, "Context and Meaning," in Larry A. Samovar and Richard E. Porter, eds., *Intercultural Communication: A Reader* (Belmont, CA: Wadsworth, 2000), p. 35.
15. R. Fisher and S. Brown in Judith N. Martin, Thomas K. Nakayama, and Lisa Flores, *Intercultural Communication: Experiences and Contexts* (New York: McGraw-Hill, 2002), p. 334.
16. William B. Gudykunst and Young Yun Kim, *Communication with Strangers* (New York: McGraw-Hill, 2003), p. 339.
17. Trenholm and Jensen, p. 309.
18. Larry A. Samovar, Richard E. Porter, and Edwin R. McDaniel, *Intercultural Communication: A Reader* (Boston, MA: Wadsworth CENGAGE Learning, 2009), p. 391.
19. Judith N. Martin, Thomas K. Nakayama, and Lisa A. Flores, *Intercultural Communication Experiences and Contexts* (New York: McGraw-Hill, 2004), p. 334.
20. Martin and Nakayama, 2007, p. 367.
21. Donald W. Klopf, *Intercultural Encounters* (Englewood, CO: Morton, 1998), pp. 176–193; Carley H. Dodd, *Dynamics of Intercultural Communication* (New York: McGraw-Hill, 1995), pp. 21–24.

22. Martin and Nakayama, 2007, p. 371.

23. Samovar, Porter, and McDaniel, p. 261.

24. K. Dindia and D. J. Canary, eds., *Sex Differences and Similarities in Communication* (Mahwah, NJ: Lawrence Erlbaum, 2006), pp. 3–20.

25. Brant Burleson and Adrienne Kunkel, "Revisiting the Different Cultures Thesis: An Assessment of Sex Differences and Similarities in Supportive Communication," in K. Dindia and D. J. Canary, eds., *Sex Differences and Similarities in Communication* (Mahwah, NJ: Lawrence Erlbaum, 2006), pp. 137–159.

26. Trenholm and Jensen, pp. 106–108.

27. Stewart and Logan, p. 84.

28. Trenholm and Jensen, p. 361.

29. Stewart, p. 345.

30. Stewart, p. 384.

31. Stewart, p. 20.

32. Stewart and Logan, p. 277.

33. Trenholm and Jensen, pp. 14 and 201; Stewart, p. 321; Floyd, pp. 83–87.

34. Floyd, p. 87.

35. David W. Johnson, "Being Open with and to Other People," in Stewart, p. 254.

36. Stewart, p. 258; Trenholm and Jensen, pp. 218–219; Floyd, pp. 114–115.

37. Floyd, pp. 115–116; Trenholm and Jensen, p. 298.

38. Diana K. Ivy and Phil Backlund, *Exploring Gender Speak: Personal Effectiveness in Gender Communication* (New York: McGraw-Hill, 1994), p. 219; Stewart, p. 344; Floyd, pp. 112–113.

39. Martin and Nakayama, 2007, p. 377.

40. Stephen W. Littlejohn, *Theories of Human Communication* (Belmont, CA: Wadsworth, 1996), p. 262.

41. Laura K. Guerrero, Peter A. Andersen, and Walid A. Afifi, *Close Encounters in Relationships* (New York: McGraw-Hill, 2001), p. 46.

42. Floyd, pp. 413–414.

43. Michael Skube, "College Students Lack Familiarity with Language, Ideas," Lafayette, IN, *Journal & Courier,* August 30, 2006, p. A5.

44. Sik Hung Ng and James J. Bradac, *Power in Language: Verbal Communication and Social Influence* (Newbury Park, CA: Sage, 1993), pp. 45–51.

45. Guerrero, Andersen, and Afifi, pp. 297–298; Ivy and Backlund, pp. 163–165; Trenholm and Jensen, p. 106; Floyd, p. 71.

46. Julia T. Wood, "Gendered Interaction: Masculine and Feminine Styles of Verbal Communication," reprinted in Kathleen S. Verderber, ed., *Voices: A Selection of Multicultural Readings* (Belmont, CA: Wadsworth, 1995), p. 24.

47. Trenholm and Jensen, p. 107.

48. William B. Gudykunst, *Bridging Differences: Effective Intergroup Communication* (Newbury Park, CA: Sage, 1991), pp. 42–59.
49. Wen-Shu Lee, "That's Greek to Me: Between a Rock and a Hard Place in Intercultural Encounters," in Larry A. Samovar and Richard E. Porter, eds., *Intercultural Communication: A Reader* (Belmont, CA: Wadsworth, 2000), pp. 217–219.
50. Irving J. Lee, *How to Talk with People* (New York: Harper & Row, 1952), pp. 11–26.
51. Stewart, p. 186.
52. Stewart, p. 146.
53. Floyd, pp. 230–233; Stewart, pp. 186–186.
54. Trenholm and Jensen, pp. 381–383; Donald W. Klopf, *Intercultural Encounters* (Englewood, CO: Morton, 1998), pp. 232–233.
55. Martin and Nakayama, 2007, pp. 254–262.
56. Stewart, p. 233–242.
57. Trenholm and Jensen, pp. 60–61.
58. Trenholm and Jensen, p. 60.
59. Martin and Nakayama, 2007, pp. 259–260.
60. This interview is loosely based on pp. 24–25 in *The Executive Interview* by Benjamin Balinsky and Ruth Burger. Copyright 1959 by Benjamin Balinsky and Ruth Burger. It is reprinted by permission of HarperCollins.

Resources

Martin, Judith N., and Thomas K. Nakayama. *Intercultural Communication in Contexts.* New York: McGraw-Hill, 2007.

Samovar, Larry A., Richard E. Porter, and Edwin R. McDaniel. *Intercultural Communication: A Reader.* Belmont, CA: Wadsworth CENGAGE Learning, 2009.

Stewart, John, ed. *Bridges Not Walls: A Book about Interpersonal Communication*. New York: McGraw-Hill, 2009.

Trenholm, Sarah, and Arthur Jensen. *Interpersonal Communication*. New York: Oxford University Press, 2008.

Wood, Julia T. *But I Thought You Meant . . . Misunderstandings in Human Communication*. Mountain View, CA: Mayfield, 1998.

CHAPTER 3 Questions and Their Uses

Questions are tools.

A question is any action that solicits an answer.

Questions are literally tools of the trade in interviews, and it is difficult to imagine an interview in which they do not play significant roles for both parties. Technology editor Jamie McKenzie writes, "Questions may be the most powerful technology we have ever created" because "they allow us to control our lives and allow us to make sense of a confusing world" by leading "to insight and understanding."[1] A question need not be a complete sentence with a question mark affixed to the end but *any phrase, statement, or nonverbal act that invites an answer or response.* Like all tools (hammers, screwdrivers, wrenches, golf clubs, knives, paintbrushes), each type of question has a name, unique characteristics, performs specific functions for which it was crafted, and enables us to perform tasks effectively and efficiently.

This chapter deals with types of questions available to interview parties, their specific uses, and question pitfalls into which unwary parties may tumble. We will begin by identifying the most fundamental types of questions: open and closed.

Open and Closed Questions

Open and closed questions vary in the amount of information they solicit and degree of interviewer control. The amount of information may range from a single word to lengthy descriptions, narratives, and reports of statistical data.

Open Questions

Open questions invite open answers.

Open questions vary in degree of openness ranging from a topic or area of inquiry to more specified subject matter. Regardless, respondents have considerable freedom to determine the amount and kind of information to give.

Highly Open Questions

Highly open questions have virtually no restrictions, such as:

Tell me about your mission trip to Haiti.

What do you remember about the tornado?

What was it like growing up during the Great Depression in the 1930s?

Moderately Open Questions

Moderately open questions are more restrictive but give respondents considerable latitude in answers. The questions above might be narrowed to:

What are living conditions like in Haiti?

What were your first thoughts after you emerged from your basement when the tornado had passed?

Tell me about losing your job at the Ford factory during the Great Depression.

Public opinion pollsters often hand a statement, picture, advertisement, or product offer to a person and then ask:

What comes to mind when you see this picture of a large housing development on former ranch land?

If this political ad were sent to your home, how might it affect your attitude toward the candidate who sent it?

Here are several reasons given for passing antismoking ordinances in communities. Tell me how you feel about them.

Interviewees can volunteer and elaborate.

Open Questions Have Advantages

Open questions encourage respondents to talk, determine the nature and amount of information to give, and volunteer information you might not think to ask for. Lengthy answers reveal what respondents think is important and motivate them to provide details and description. Open questions communicate interest and trust in the respondent's judgment, are usually easier to answer, and pose less threat. Longer answers reveal a respondent's level of knowledge, uncertainty, intensity of feelings, perceptions, and prejudices.

Steve Mason/Getty Images

Open questions let the respondent do the talking and allow the interviewer to listen and observe.

Open Questions Have Disadvantages

A single answer may consume a significant portion of interview time because the respondent determines the length and nature of each answer. On the one hand, respondents may give unimportant or irrelevant information, and on the other may withhold important information they feel is irrelevant

Interviewees can pick and choose, reveal and hide.

or too obvious, sensitive, or dangerous. Keep respondents on track and maintain control by tactfully intervening to move on. Lengthy, rambling answers are difficult to record and process.

Closed Questions

Closed questions are narrow in focus and restrict the interviewee's freedom to determine the amount and kind of information to provide.

Moderately Closed Questions

Restricted questions lead to restricted answers.

Moderately closed questions ask for specific, limited pieces of information, such as:

Who are your favorite NFL quarterbacks?
Which soft drinks do you purchase most often?
What did you do first when your plane landed in the Hudson River?
Which college courses do you feel have prepared you best for a career in sales?

Highly Closed Questions

Highly closed questions may ask interviewees to pick an answer.

Highly closed questions are very restrictive and may ask respondents to identify a single bit of information, such as:

What time was it when you first smelled smoke in your apartment?
How many credit hours are you taking this semester?
Which presidential candidate did you vote for in the last election?

Some highly closed questions ask respondents to select answers from options provided, such as:

Which of these domestic airlines have you flown on most often?

_____ U.S. Airways
_____ Delta
_____ American
_____ United
_____ Air Tran
_____ Southwest

How do you feel about the billions of dollars the government has loaned to the auto industry?

_____ Strongly approve
_____ Approve
_____ Undecided
_____ Disapprove
_____ Strongly disapprove

Bipolar Questions

Bipolar questions offer polar opposites for answers.

Closed questions may be **bipolar** because they limit respondents to two polar choices. Some ask you to select an answer from polar opposites. For example:

Do you plan to attend the press briefing or the press conference?

Are you a conservative or a liberal?

Are you a morning or afternoon person?

Other bipolar questions ask for an evaluation or attitude. For example:

Do you approve or disapprove of the proposed smoking ban in bars and restaurants?

Do you like or dislike the new bus routes on campus?

Are you for or against a sales tax on grocery items?

A yes or no question is likely to generate a yes or no answer.

The most common bipolar questions ask for yes or no responses. For example:

Are you going to the game on Sunday?

Do you have a car on campus?

Have you heard about the proposed merger with GM?

Closed Questions Have Advantages

Closed questions provide control and direction.

Closed questions permit interviewers to control the length of answers and guide respondents to specific information needed. Closed questions require little effort from either party and allow you to ask more questions, in more areas, in less time. And answers are easy to replicate, tabulate, and analyze from one interview to another. This is why surveys employ closed questions.

Closed Questions Have Disadvantages

Closed questions stifle volunteering.

Answers to closed questions often contain too little information, requiring you to ask several questions when one open question would do the job. And they do not reveal why a person has a particular attitude, the person's degree of feeling or commitment, or why this person typically makes choices. For instance, an interviewee may not know which Hondas are American-made and which are Japanese-made. Interviewers talk more than interviewees when asking closed questions, so less information is exchanged. Interviewees have no opportunity to volunteer or explain information and can rate, rank, select an answer, or say yes or no without knowing anything about a topic.

Figure 3.1 illustrates the major advantages and disadvantages of open and closed questions. As you narrow a question, the amount of data decreases. As the amount of data decreases, your control increases, less time and skill are required, and the degree of precision, reliability, and reproducibility increases. On the other hand, as you open up a question, the amount of data increases and interviewees may reveal knowledge level, understanding, reasons for feeling or acting, attitudes, and hidden motives.

Combinations often lead to the best results.

Interviews often include open and closed questions with varying degrees of constraint to get the information desired. For instance, an interviewer might follow up a bipolar question such as "Are you familiar with the president's economic stimulus plan?" with an open-ended question such as "What do you know about this plan?" An open-ended

Figure 3.1 *Question options*

Advantages and Disadvantages of Question Types	Type of Questions			
	Highly Open	Moderately Open	Moderately Closed	Highly Closed
Breadth and depth of potential information				
Degree of precision, reproducibility, reliability				
R's control over question and response				
Interviewer skill required				
Reliability of data				
Economic use of time				
Opportunity for E to reveal feelings and information				

☐ High ☐ Medium ═ Low

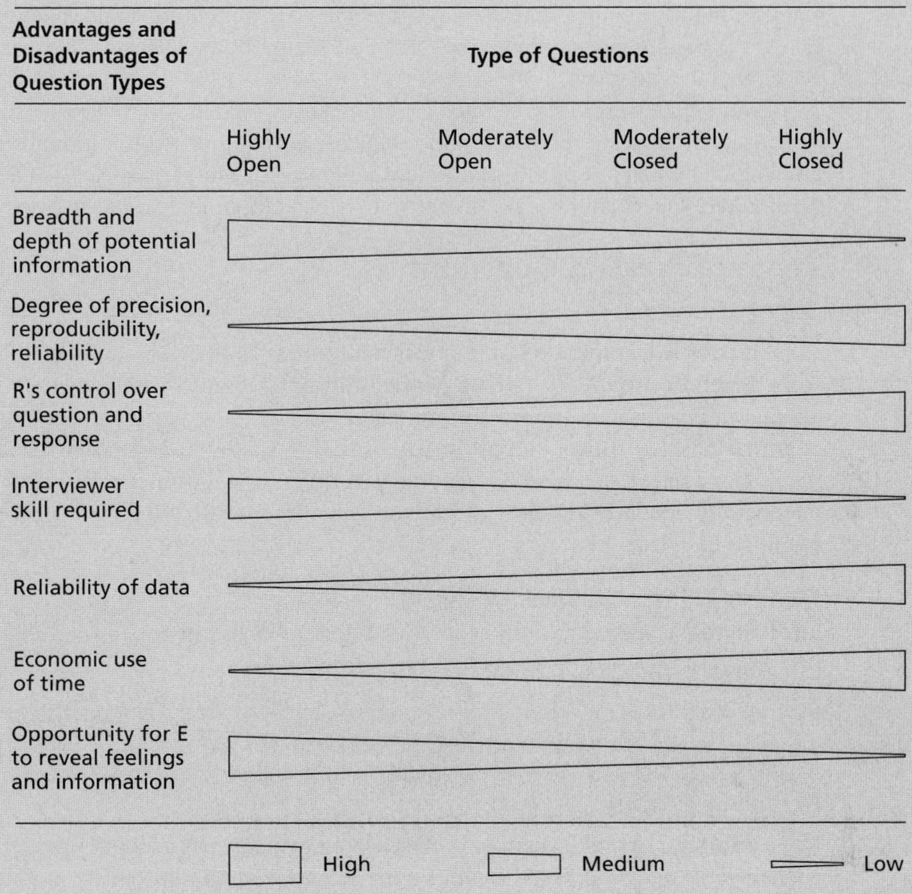

question such as "Tell me about your study abroad semester in Poland" may be followed up with a more closed question such as, "What was your major research project?"

Primary and Probing Questions

Primary questions make sense out of context.

Primary questions introduce topics or new areas within a topic and can stand alone even when taken out of context.

How did you become interested in politics?

Tell me about your business trip to China.

What was your training regimen in preparing to cycle across the country?

All examples of open and closed questions presented earlier are primary questions.

Probing questions make sense only in context.

Questions that seek to discover additional information following a primary question, are called **probing** or follow-up questions. They make no sense if asked without connection to a previous question. Imagine someone beginning an interview or topic by asking "What's your best estimate?" or "Tell me more about that" when you have not yet replied to a question.

Probing questions may be open or closed. They enable you to dig deeper into areas and discover what an interview party may be implying or avoiding in answers. They are essential when a respondent does not reply to a question or appears to be giving an incomplete, superficial, vague, suggestible, irrelevant, or inaccurate answer.

Types of Probing Questions

Silent Probes

Be patient and be quiet.

If an answer is incomplete or the respondent seems hesitant to continue, remain silent for a few moments, use a **silent probe**, appropriate nonverbal signals such as eye contact, a head nod, sitting back in a chair, or a gesture to encourage the person to continue. Silence shows interest in what is being said and respect for the answer and the respondent. A person may become less defensive if you communicate disbelief, uncertainty, or confusion through a tactful, silent probe rather than words. An exchange might go like this:

Interviewer: What did you think of the play?

Interviewee: It was okay, and the student actors were very good.

Interviewer: (silence and smiling)

Interviewee: On Friday night after a long week of classes and assignments, I prefer a more lighthearted play, not one that is so deep and depressing.

Nudging Probes

A nudge replaces silence with a word or phrase.

Use a **nudging probe** if a silent probe fails or words seem necessary to get at what is needed. This question literally nudges the interviewee to reply or to continue with an answer. The nudging probe is usually simple and brief, such as the following:

I see.	And?
Go on.	So?
Yes?	Uh-huh?

A common mistake is the assumption that all questions must be multiple-word sentences. Instead of urging the respondent to continue through a simple verbal nudge, you may ask a lengthy probing question that stifles the interchange or a primary question that may open up a new area or topic, the opposite of what is needed. Valuable information may remain undetected.

Clearinghouse Probes

Ask rather than assume.

A **clearinghouse probe** is an essential tool for discovering whether a series of questions has uncovered everything of importance on a topic or issue. Clearinghouse questions encourage respondents to volunteer information you might not think to ask about and to fill in gaps your questions have missed. This probing tool literally clears out an area or topic, such as the following:

What else did Officer Jacobs have to say about the incident?

Is there anything else I need to know before taking the exam?

What have I not asked that you think is important when considering an intern position at the governor's office?

A good clearinghouse probe enables you to proceed to the next topic or series of questions, confident that you have gotten all important information. You cannot anticipate or plan for all information a party might be willing to reveal. What you do not ask may be more important than what you do ask.

Informational Probes

Pry open vague, superficial, and suggestive answers.

Informational probing questions are used to get additional information or explanations. For example, if an answer appears to be superficial, begin a probing question with a phrase such as:

Tell me why you think he said that?

And what are these downsides to accepting an early offer of a graduate assistantship?

How did she explain that?

An answer may be vague or ambiguous, perhaps inviting a number of interpretations. Ask an informational probe such as:

When you ask for a "little more time" with your paper, what do you mean by "little"?

Exactly how did your supervisor threaten you?

You say you graduated from a small college; how many students were enrolled at the time?

An answer may suggest a feeling or attitude in addition to factual material, so ask an informational probe such as:

Tell me about your anger toward the perpetrator of this Ponzi scheme that cost you all of your investments.

You say that you have a fear of heights; tell me more about this fear.

Explain your negative attitude toward recent immigrants into the United States.

Restatement Probes

Restate or rephrase to get complete answers.

Respondents often do not answer the question that is asked or answer only a portion of it. Rather than create a new probing question, restate all or part of the original question, perhaps using vocal emphasis to draw attention to the original concern. Rephrasing an original question tactfully may avoid embarrassing an interviewee. The following is a **restatement probe:**

Interviewer: Tell me how you feel about the government's efforts to bail out failing automobile companies.

Interviewee: I'm certainly not in favor of offering more bailouts to big banks, I can tell you that!

Interviewer: I can understand that, but how do you feel about bailouts for the auto companies?

If a person seems hesitant to answer a question or answers only part of it, the question may be unclear or seem to demand what is not easy to provide. Restate the question in a clearer, easier to answer fashion. For example:

Interviewer: What is your ethical stance on placing state workers on furloughs to help balance the state budget?

Interviewee: Well, I'm not sure I have an ethical stance on this.

Interviewer: Let me rephrase the question. How fair is this to state workers?

If you ask a question with more than one part, a respondent may answer only one part. Restate the portion or portions left unanswered. For instance:

Interviewer: Tell me about your first thoughts when you saw the plane land in the river and how you felt.

Interviewee: Well, at first, I had trouble believing I had just seen a large aircraft land in the water only a few yards from the ferry I was riding on.

Interviewer: And how did this make you feel?

Reflective Probes

Reflective questions verify and clarify.

A **reflective probe** literally reflects the answer just received to *verify* or to *clarify* it so you know you have interpreted it as the respondent intended. Make it obvious that you are seeking verification and clarification, not attempting to lead or trap the interviewee into giving a desired answer or to question honesty or intelligence. Be tactful verbally and nonverbally. If an answer seems inaccurate (wrong date or figure, inaccurate quotation, mix-up in words), ask a reflective probing question such as the following:

That was *after* the fire was first detected?

That was *gross* profits from the fund-raiser?

By former President Bush, you are referring to President George H. W. Bush?

If unsure about what a respondent has said or implied, ask a reflective question to resolve uncertainty, such as the following:

You're saying, then, that it would be best if a number of construction companies went out of business?

You're still considering this move to the Northwest?

Am I understanding you correctly that you believe all stem cell research, without exception, is immoral?

A reflective probe differs from a restatement probe in that the first seeks to clarify or verify an answer while the second seeks to obtain more information following a primary question.

Mirror Probes

Mirror questions summarize to ensure accuracy.

The **mirror question** ensures that you have understood a series of answers or have retained information accurately. The mirror question is closely related to the reflective question, but the mirror question, rather than reflecting an answer just received, *summarizes* a series of answers or interchanges to ensure accurate understanding and retention. It may mirror or summarize a large portion or an entire interview. For example, a person may ask a mirror question to be certain of instructions, elements of a proposal, prescribed regimens, agreed-upon procedures, and so on. For instance, a physician might use the following mirror question to verify understanding of a patient's symptoms.

> Okay. You first experienced this lower back pain when you were helping your father build a garden shed. It seemed to get better until you were doing your regular workouts at the gym. There are times when your right leg feels numb and others when there are shooting pains down the inside of your leg. The pain seems to subside when you lie down for an hour or so or at night. Am I correct?

If asked properly, reflective and mirror questions can help you avoid errors caused by faulty assumptions, poor memory, or misinterpretations.

Skillful Interviewing with Probing Questions

Skillful probing leads to insightful answers.

The use of probing questions separates skilled from unskilled interviewers. The unskilled person sticks with a prepared list of questions, thinks ahead to the next question, anticipates questions prematurely, or is impatient. The skilled person listens carefully to each response to determine if the answer is satisfactory. If it is not, the questioner determines the probable cause within seconds and phrases an appropriate probing question. Skillful probing not only discovers more relevant, accurate, and complete information but may heighten the other party's motivation because the questioner is obviously interested and listening.

Be patient and be persistent.

Probing questions may cause problems, however. Sometimes when a person does not respond immediately, you may jump in with a probing question when none is needed. Phrase probing questions carefully and be aware of vocal emphasis. Stanley Payne illustrates how the meaning of a simple "Why" question can be altered by stressing different words.[2]

Why do you say that?

Why ***do*** you say that?

Why do ***you*** say that?

Why do you ***say*** that?

Why do you say ***that?***

The "simple" why question may unintentionally communicate disapproval, disbelief, mistrust, or make the other party defensive and more reluctant to answer fully. A poorly phrased probing question may alter the meaning of the primary question or bias the reply. Be tactful and not demanding. When using reflective or mirror questions, try not to misquote or put words into the person's mouth.

Exercise #1—Supply the Probing Question

Supply an appropriate probing question for each of the following interactions. Be sure the question probes into the answer and is not a primary question introducing a new facet of the topic. Watch assumptions about answers, and phrase probing questions tactfully.

1. **Interviewer:** What did you do in your internship?

   Interviewee: Oh, I worked on press releases and stuff like that.

   Interviewer:
2. **Interviewer:** Why did you major in history?

   Interviewee: My mother.

   Interviewer:
3. **Interviewer:** How did you like *Dracula* produced by the university theater last weekend?

   Interviewee: The technical part was amazing.

   Interviewer:
4. **Interviewer:** What is your philosophy of life?

   Interviewee: (silence)

   Interviewer:
5. **Interviewer:** In your opinion, who do you think was the greatest playwright of the twentieth century?

   Interviewee: John Wayne.

   Interviewer:
6. **Interviewer:** Whom do you plan to vote for in the primaries?

   Interviewee: I don't know.

   Interviewer:
7. **Interviewer:** How was your trip to Spain?

   Interviewee: It was awesome.

   Interviewer:
8. **Interviewer:** What did you think of the lecture on global warming?

   Interviewee: It was okay.

   Interviewer:
9. **Interviewer:** How large was your hometown?

   Interviewee: It was not very big.

   Interviewer:

10. **Interviewer:** Are you going to graduate school?
Interviewee: That depends.
Interviewer:

Neutral and Leading Questions

Neutral questions encourage honest answers.

Leading questions direct interviewees to specific answers.

Neutral questions allow respondents to decide upon answers without direction or pressure from questioners. For example, in open, neutral questions, the interviewee determines the length, details, and nature of the answers. In closed, neutral questions such as bipolar questions, a person may choose between two equal choices: yes-no, approve-disapprove, agree-disagree. All questions discussed and illustrated so far have been neutral questions.

Leading questions suggest the answer expected or desired because the questioner leads the respondent toward a particular answer by making "it easier or more tempting for the respondent to give one answer than another."[3] A person merely agrees with the interviewer.

Interviewer bias occurs whenever respondents provide answers they ***feel*** interviewers prefer to hear. Such bias may be *intentional* or *unintentional*. Leading questions are a major source of interviewer bias, but others are status difference between the parties, an interviewee's perceptions or assumptions, the climate of the interview situation, word choice, dress, symbols such as political buttons, and nonverbal actions such as voice, eye contact, gestures, or a raised eyebrow.

The varying degrees of leading and the distinction between neutral and leading questions are illustrated in the following questions.

Neutral Questions	Leading Questions
1. Do you like to hunt?	1. I assume you like to hunt.
2. Are you walking to the game?	2. You're walking to the game, aren't you?
3. How did this 007 movie compare to the last one?	3. Didn't you like the last 007 movie better than this one?
4. How do you feel about dieting?	4. Do you dislike dieting like most people?
5. What was your reaction to the memo on use of our computers?	5. What was your reaction to the insulting memo on the use of our computers?
6. Have you ever smoked cigarettes?	6. When was the last time you smoked a cigarette?
7. Have you ever cheated on your taxes?	7. Have you stopped cheating on your taxes?
8. Would you call yourself a conservative or liberal?	8. Would you call yourself a conservative or a socialist?

9. How do you feel about gun control laws that would restrict the sale of assault-style rifles?	**9.** How do you feel about gun control laws that would violate the second amendment by restricting the sale of rifles?
10. Do you want a lite beer?	**10.** I assume you want a lite beer.

Interviewer bias leads to dictated responses.

All 10 leading questions make it easier for a person to reply in a particular way. The potential for **interviewer bias** is obvious. The situation, tone of the interview, manner in which the question is asked, and relationship with the interviewer may influence the respondent's ability or willingness to ignore the direction provided. For instance, if you were in a nonthreatening, informal, pleasant situation with a friend or equal in an organizational or social situation, you might ignore or even object to a leading question. However, if you were in a threatening, formal situation with a superior, you might feel obligated to answer as the interviewer prefers. At other times, you might go along with the direction because you want to be cooperative, avoid upsetting a person, or "not make a scene." If that's the answer a person wants, you give it, particularly when you do not care one way or the other.

An apparent bipolar question may in reality have only one pole.

The first four and the last two leading questions are mild in direction. Each appears to be bipolar, to ask for a yes or no, agree or disagree response. However, the phrasing of each guides the respondent toward one pole; they are actually *unipolar* questions. You can avoid many leading questions by limiting the use of closed questions because open questions are less likely to be leading questions.

Respondents could ignore the direction of questions 1, 2, 3, 9, and 10 if their relationship did not seem to depend on yes answers. Question 4 uses a bandwagon (follow-the-crowd) technique, and a respondent's answer might depend on past experiences with this interviewer and whether the respondent wants to follow the majority. Question 10 suggests that the respondent will want a lite beer. A person with ambivalent or apathetic feelings might just go along with the answer the interviewer seems to want.

Loaded questions dictate answers through language or entrapment.

Loaded Questions

Loaded questions are extreme leading questions. Questions 5 to 8 provide strong direction, virtual dictation of the correct answer; that's why they are called *loaded* questions. Questions 5 and 8 are loaded because of name-calling and emotionally charged words. In response to question 8, a person is likely to choose the least onerous of the choices provided, conservative, because few Americans see themselves as socialists. Questions 6 and 7 entrap the respondent. Question 6 implies that the respondent has smoked cigarettes. Question 7 charges the person with cheating on taxes. A yes or no may get the person in trouble.

Leading questions have legitimate functions.

Since leading questions, particularly loaded ones, have potential for severe interviewer bias, avoid them unless you know what you are doing! Introductory phrases such as "According to the law," "As we all know," "As witnesses have testified," and "As the doctor warned" may lead respondents to give acceptable answers rather than true feelings or beliefs. You can turn a neutral question into a leading question by the nonverbal manner in which you ask it. For example, you might

Figure 3.2 *Types of questions*

	Neutral		Leading	
	Open	**Closed**	**Open**	**Closed**
Primary	How do you feel about the new IRS requirement?	Do you approve or disapprove of the new IRS requirement?	Most top accountants favor the new IRS requirement; how do you feel about it?	Do you favor the new IRS requirement like most top accountants I've talked to?
Probing	Why do you feel that way?	Is your approval moderate or strong?	If you favor the new requirement, why did you initially oppose it?	I assume you favor the new requirement because you're retiring in two weeks.

appear to demand a certain answer by leaning toward the respondent, looking the person directly in the eyes, or raising an eyebrow. You might place vocal emphasis on a key word, such as:

Did you *like* that concert?

When did you *show up* at the meeting?

You're going to select *her* for this position?

Regardless of their potential for mischief, leading questions have important uses. Recruiters use them to see how interviewees respond under stress. Sales representatives use leading questions to close sales. Police officers ask loaded questions to provoke witnesses. Journalists ask leading questions to prod reluctant interviewees into responding. Counselors have discovered that a loaded question such as "When was the last time you got drunk?" shows that a range of answers is acceptable and that none will shock the interviewer.

Do not confuse neutral mirror and reflective probing questions with leading questions. Mirrors and reflectives may appear to direct respondents toward particular answers, but their purposes are clarification and verification, not leading or direction. If they lead by accident, they are failures.

Figure 3.2 compares types of questions available to interviewers and interviewees, including open and closed, primary and probing, and neutral and leading questions.

Exercise #2—Identification of Questions

Identify each of the following questions in four ways: (1) open or closed, (2) primary or probing, (3) neutral or leading, and (4) whether it is a special type of question tool: bipolar, loaded, nudging probe, clearinghouse probe, informational probe, restatement probe, reflective probe, or mirror probe.

1. Did you take the MCAT last week?
2. What else did you do on your camping trip?
3. Let's see if I understand this deal correctly. If I get laid off while I'm still paying on this car, you will give me two months without payments. If by that time I am still laid off and cannot make further payments, you will take the car back without penalty and I can apply the payments I have already made to a used car on your lot. Is this correct?
4. Which computer games do you like best?
5. What did you see when you approached the intersection?
6. **Interviewer:** How are your classes going?

   Interviewee: It's been a good semester with the internship at Lilly and all.

   Interviewer: How are your classes going?
7. On a 1 to 10 scale with 10 being high, how would you rate this spring break?
8. You're saying, then, that the recession may change your mind about going to graduate school?
9. Uh huh.
10. That was pretty dumb, wasn't it?
11. When did you switch majors from science to engineering?
12. Tell me about your bicycle trip across the country.
13. Do you take I-75 or I-65 when going to Atlanta?
14. Don't you think you should start writing the paper now instead of the night before it's due?
15. Have you stopped cheating on your diet?

Common Question Pitfalls

Awareness of question tools and their uses is the first step in learning to interview effectively and efficiently. The second step is knowing how to create and use questions to obtain accurate, honest, insightful, and thorough answers. A slight alteration in wording can change a question from open to closed, primary to probing, and neutral to leading.

Phrase questions carefully to avoid common pitfalls.

Because you often must create questions on the spot during the heat of an interview, it is easy to stumble into common **question pitfalls** without knowing it. These pitfalls include the bipolar trap, the tell me everything, the open-to-closed switch, the double-barreled inquisition, the leading push, the guessing game, the yes (no) response, the curious probe, the quiz show, and the don't ask, don't tell question.

The Bipolar Trap

You fall into a **bipolar trap** when you ask a bipolar question designed to elicit a yes or no answer when you really want a detailed answer or specific information. This pitfall

Avoid unintentional bipolar questions.

is obvious in questions that begin with words such as do you, did you, are you, have you, were you, can you, is there, would you, and was it. If all you want is a yes or no, each may be satisfactory, but a yes or no tells you little. Notice how little information is exchanged in this interaction:

Interviewer: Have you experienced any unusual pains?

Interviewee: No.

Interviewer: Do you think you are in good health?

Interviewee: Yes.

Interviewer: Any concerns about your health?

Interviewee: No.

Bipolar questions assume there are only two possible answers and that the answers are poles apart: conservative–liberal, like–dislike, approve–disapprove, agree–disagree, high–low, yes–no. They do not allow for degrees of awareness, liking, feeling, using, or knowing. The health care interviewer in the preceding example may assume that the patient has an accurate and insightful understanding of his or her health. Studies indicate the opposite, that most of us prefer to give positive answers to physicians and do not report important symptoms.

Eliminate bipolar traps by reserving bipolar questions for situations in which only a yes or no or a single word is desired. Begin questions with words and phrases such as *what, why, how, explain,* and *tell me about* that ask for detailed information, feelings, or attitudes.

The Tell Me Everything

The **tell me everything** question is at the opposite end of the scale from the bipolar trap. Instead of a simple yes–no or agree–disagree, this question trap occurs when the interviewer asks an extremely open question with no restrictions or guidelines for the interviewee. The interviewee may have a difficult time determining where to begin, what to include, what to exclude, and when to end. The tell me everything pitfall occurs in an employment interview when a recruiter asks "Tell me about yourself," in a journalistic interview when a reporter asks "What was it like in Afghanistan," a friend asks "Tell me all about your safari in Kenya," or a health care provider asks "Tell me about your medical history."

Ask open-ended questions rather than closed and bipolar questions, but don't make them too open. In the examples above, for instance, let the interviewee know what part of self, the Afghanistan deployment, the safari, and the medical history you are most interested in. If an interviewee were to respond as first directed, the answer could take an hour and you might have difficulty shutting the person off tactfully.

Think before asking and know when to stop asking.

The Open-to-Closed Switch

The **open-to-closed switch** question occurs when you ask an open question but, before the interviewee can respond, you rephrase it into a closed or bipolar question. This trap is readily apparent in interviews, such as:

Tell me about your trip to China. Did you have problems with the language?

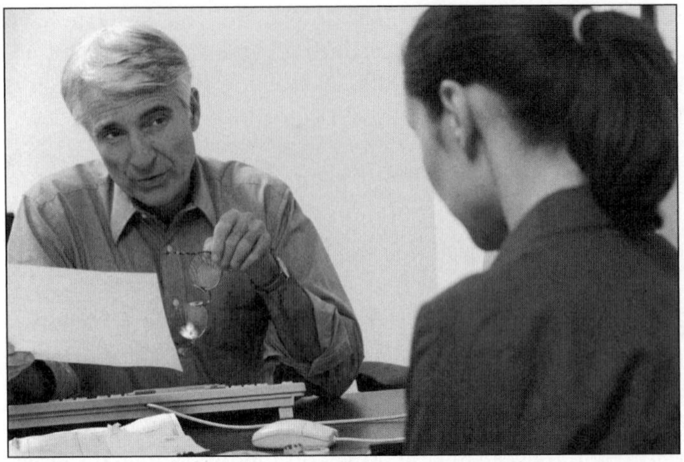

© Brand X Pictures/PunchStock

How you ask a question may bias the answer you receive.

What did you do during your student teaching at Central High School? Was it about what you expected?

Why did you purchase a crossover vehicle? Was it because you don't like minivans?

The open-to-closed switch occurs when you are still phrasing a question in your mind. This rummaging about for the right phrasing often changes a perfectly good open question into a narrow, closed question. The respondent is likely to address only the second question and perhaps with a simple yes or no. Avoid the open-to-closed switch by preparing questions prior to the interview and thinking through questions before asking them.

The Double-Barreled Inquisition

Ask one question at a time.

The **double-barreled inquisition** question occurs when you ask two (or more) questions at the same time instead of a single, precise question. Double-barreled questions are common in interactions:

How was your flight to Alaska and how did you like Denali National Park?

What interests you in fashion design and what type of career do you want to pursue?

Tell me about your hobbies and how these help you unwind after a busy day.

Respondents are unlikely to remember or address both parts of double-barreled questions and will answer what they remember. Some will select the portion they want to answer and ignore the rest. Others will answer both parts but provide few details in either. Respondents may feel they are being subjected to a third-degree inquisition when asked a double-barreled question. You may find it necessary to repeat a portion of the initial question to get all of the information wanted. At worst, you may be unaware of missing information and go to another primary question prematurely.

Avoid the double-barreled trap and its dangers by asking one question at a time. If you ask a double-barreled question, repeat the part the interviewee does not answer.

The Leading Push

Push only when there is a need to push.

The **leading push** occurs when you ask a question that suggests how a person ought to respond. The push may be intentional (you want to influence an answer) or unintentional (you are not aware of the push). It is easy to interject feelings or attitudes in questions through language and nonverbal signals, such as the following:

That was a great game, wasn't it?

I'm going to the exam help session, aren't you?

You haven't had a physical for over *six years*?

You may not realize you have asked a leading question and remain unaware that the interviewee may have given you a skewed answer to please you or to avoid a confrontation. The interviewee may go along with whatever answers you seem to want, particularly if you are in a superior role. Avoid the leading push trap and its dangers by phrasing questions neutrally and listening to each question you ask.

The Guessing Game

Don't guess; ask!

The **guessing game** pitfall occurs when you try to guess information instead of asking for it. Guessing is common in most interview settings: journalism, health care, recruiting, and investigations. Strings of closed, guessing questions fail to accomplish what a single open-ended question could do. Observe the failure of this guessing spree to gain detailed information.

Interviewer: Was the scene pretty terrible?

Interviewee: Yes.

Interviewer: Was the car on fire when you got there?

Interviewee: Not yet.

Interviewer: Were all of the occupants out of the car?

Interviewee: I don't think so.

Interviewer: Was there a lot of fuel on the ground?

Interviewee: No.

Interviewer: Was the car mangled?

Interviewee: Yes.

Interviewer: What did you see?

Guessing wastes time and energy when a single open question, such as the last one, will get information quickly and efficiently. Avoid the guessing game pitfall by *asking* rather than *guessing* and relying on open-ended questions.

The Yes (No) Response

The **yes (no) response** pitfall occurs when you ask a question that has only one obvious answer, a yes or a no. Each of the following questions is likely to get a predictable response:

An obvious question will generate an obvious answer.

(asked of a student) Did you study for this exam?

(asked of a sales representative for Ford) Do you think this Ford truck is superior to the Toyota Tundra?

(asked of an applicant) Do you think you're qualified for this position?

Avoid the yes (no) question pitfall by opening up your questions and avoiding the obvious.

The Curious Probe

If every question you ask is relevant to your predetermined purpose, you will avoid **curious probes.** Do not ask for information you do not need and will not use. If an interviewee may perceive a question to be irrelevant, explain why it is important. The order of questions may result in perceived irrelevance. For example, ask for demographic data such as age, income, educational level, and marital status only if this information is clearly **necessary** and **relevant** and at the **end** of the interview after you have established trust and asked a series of relevant questions. Ask for personal information at the **beginning** only when it is being used to **qualify** interviewees.

Curiosity may be fatal to interviewers.

As an interviewee, do not assume a question is irrelevant; the interviewer may have a legitimate and important reason for asking. Other cultures ask questions that might appear irrelevant to you but not to them. For instance, Japanese often ask personal questions early in interactions so they can learn important characteristics about the interviewee, including personality, knowledge, skills, and background. A Japanese party might ask where you were born, where you went to school, how you feel about Japanese food, what Japanese you speak, and what hobbies you have.

The Quiz Show

Interviews are not **quiz shows** with applicants, subjects, clients, employees, or patients serving as contestants. The parties you interview must have a store of knowledge that enables them to answer comfortably and intelligently. *Information level* is critical in interviews. Questions above a respondent's information level may cause embarrassment or resentment because no one wants to appear uninformed, ill-informed, uneducated, or unintelligent. On the other hand, questions beneath a respondent's level of information may be insulting. Respondents may fake answers or give vague answers rather than admit ignorance.

What does the interviewee know of relevance to this topic?

Avoid the quiz show pitfall by asking for information in common categories or frames of reference such as pounds rather than ounces, cups rather than pots of coffee, or number of hours watching television per day rather than month or year. Determine if a respondent is a layperson, novice, or expert on the topic to avoid overly simple or overly complex words, explanations, and requests.

Complexity vs. Simplicity

Questions should be simple, clear requests for reasonable amounts of information. Avoid overly complex questions that challenge respondents to figure out what you want. The following is a common type of survey question asked over the telephone:

> Now, I would like your opinion on some leading brands of beer. I would like you to rate these brands by using the numbers from plus five to minus five. If you like the brand, give it a number from plus one to plus five. The more you like it, the bigger the plus number you should give it. If you dislike the brand, give it a number from minus one to minus five. The more you dislike it, the bigger the minus number you should give it. If you neither like nor dislike the brand, give it a zero.

If you must ask such a complicated question, use sample answers to explain the scale and give interviewees opportunities to try out the scale on nonbeer items to determine if they understand both the question and how to answer it correctly. If the interview is face-to-face, provide a small card containing the scale or answer options.

Phrase questions carefully to avoid a mixture of negatives, maybes, and positives. The following question illustrates this problem:

> Pick the most appropriate response. You feel that you understand each other, but you have never told them this.
>
> 1. You have never felt this way, or you have felt this way and never told them this.
> 2. You occasionally have felt this way, but you have never told them this.
> 3. You frequently have felt this way, but you have never told them this.

Imagine trying to answer this complex question over the telephone.

The Don't Ask, Don't Tell

Don't ask, don't tell questions delve into informational and emotional areas that many respondents may be incapable of addressing because of social, psychological, or situational constraints. You learn from an early age, for instance, that it is more socially acceptable to be humble than boastful. If an interviewer asks you to assess your beauty, intelligence, creativity, generosity, or bravery, you are likely to pose an "Aw shucks" attitude or say "Yes" with a flourish that treats your answer as a joke. You also learn that "there is a time and a place for everything," so you do not discuss certain topics in mixed groups, in public, or in political, religious, or social settings. Some areas are taboo in most situations: sex, personal income, religious convictions, and certain illnesses.

Delve into inaccessible areas only when necessary.

As an interviewer, explain why a question is essential to ask, and delay "touchy" or "taboo" questions until you have established a comfortable climate and positive relationship. Avoid the don't ask, don't tell pitfall by phrasing questions carefully to lessen social and psychological constraints and to avoid offending an interviewee.

Sex and cultural differences among respondents may affect social and psychological *accessibility*. Research indicates that women disclose more information about themselves, use more psychological or emotional verbs, discuss their personal lives more in business interactions, have less difficulty expressing intimate feelings, talk more about other people's accomplishments and minimize their own, and appear to be more comfortable when hearing accolades about themselves.[4] Cultures also differ in readily accessible areas. Always learn as much as you can about an interviewee prior to an interview to determine what can and cannot be asked and how it should be asked.

Avoid common question pitfalls by planning questions prior to the interview so you do not have to create each on the spot in the give-and-take of the interaction. Think before uttering a question, stop when you have asked a good open question instead of rephrasing it, use bipolar questions sparingly, avoid questions that are too open-ended, ask only necessary questions, ask for information at the interviewee's level, avoid complex questions, and be aware of the accessibility factor in questions and answers. Above all, know the common question pitfalls well enough that you can catch yourself before tumbling into one.

Avoid pitfalls by preparing and thinking.

Exercise #3—What Are the Pitfalls in These Questions?

Each of the following questions illustrates one or more of the common question pitfalls: bipolar trap, open-to-closed switch, double-barreled inquisition, leading push, guessing game, yes (no) response, tell me everything, curious probe, complexity vs. simplicity, quiz show, and don't ask, don't tell. Identify the pitfall(s) of each question and rephrase it to make it a good question. Avoid a new pitfall in your revised question.

1. (asked of a patient) Do you want to have a heart attack?
2. Tell me about eastern Europe.
3. You're concerned about your investments, aren't you?
4. Did you join the Army for the bonus?
5. Tell me about your position at KMG; is it high tech?
6. Tell me about your flight to Amsterdam and the family you stayed with.
7. Are you the prettiest of the cheerleaders?
8. (asked of an investment counselor) Are your investments sound?
9. Do you approve or disapprove of the job Congress is doing?
10. (asked in an employment interview) What does your father do?

Summary

Questions are the tools of the trade in interviews. If you know question types, unique uses, and advantages and disadvantages, you can develop considerable interviewing skill and enjoy the experiences.

You have a limitless variety of question tools to choose from, and each tool has unique characteristics, capabilities, and pitfalls. Knowing which question to select and how to use it is essential for interviewing effectively and efficiently. Each question has three characteristics: (1) open or closed, (2) primary or probing, and (3) neutral or leading. Open questions are designed to discover large amounts of information, while closed questions are designed to gain specific bits of information. Primary questions open up topics and

ON THE WEB

Browse an Internet site to locate a variety of question–answer interactions that vary in intensity from happy to sad, cooperative to uncooperative, friendly to hostile, and understanding to patronizing. Identify the different types of primary and probing questions in these interactions. Which question pitfalls can you identify? Which of these pitfalls were accidental and which purposeful? Use search engines such as the Knight Ridder Newspapers (http://www.kri.com), CNBC (http://www.cnbc.com), and CNN (http://cnn.com).

subtopics, while probing questions probe into answers for more information, explanations, clarifications, and verifications. Neutral questions give respondents freedom to answer as they wish, while leading questions nudge or shove respondents toward specific answers.

Phrasing questions is essential to get the information needed. If you phrase questions carefully and think before asking, you can avoid common question pitfalls such as the bipolar trap, tell me everything, open-to-closed switch, double-barreled inquisition, leading push, guessing game, yes (no) response, curious probe, quiz show, complexity vs. simplicity, and don't ask, don't tell.

Key Terms and Concepts

OLC

The online learning center for this text features FLASHCARDS and CROSSWORD PUZZLES for studying based on these terms and concepts.

Bipolar question
Bipolar trap
Clearinghouse probe
Closed question
Complexity vs. simplicity
Curious probe
Don't ask, don't tell
Double-barreled inquisition
Guessing game
Informational probe
Interviewer bias
Leading push
Leading question
Loaded question
Mirror probe
Neutral question
Nudging probe
Open question
Open-to-closed switch
Primary question
Probing question
Question
Question pitfalls
Quiz show
Reflective probe
Restatement probe
Silent probe
Tell me everything
Yes (no) response

An Interview for Review and Analysis

A student has decided to interview some of his professors about their military experiences for a field project in an interviewing course. The goal is to learn about their experiences and how these experiences might have affected their attitudes toward the military in general and military personnel in particular. Professor Al Harrison once mentioned in class that he had been in the Air Force, so he is one of three selected for this project.

As you read through this interview, identify the questions as open or closed, primary or probing, and neutral or leading. Look for specific types of questions such as bipolar, loaded, silent probe, nudging probe, clearinghouse probe, informational probe, restatement probe, reflective probe, and mirror probe. Does the student stumble into common question pitfalls such as leading push, bipolar trap, yes or no response, tell me everything, open-to-closed switch, guessing game, double-barreled inquisition, curious probe, quiz show, complexity vs. simplicity, and don't ask, don't tell?

1. **Interviewer:** Hi Professor Harrison. As I told you after class a few days ago, I'm conducting interviews with three faculty members who have served in the military.
2. **Interviewee:** Good morning Melissa. Why have you selected this project?
3. **Interviewer:** Well, I've often thought that most faculty are antimilitary, and I'm an Army ROTC member, so . . .
4. **Interviewee:** So you want to see if I'm "one of those"?

5. **Interviewer:** Well, not quite. I'm interested in your military experiences and how these experiences might have affected your views of the military and military people.
6. **Interviewee:** Okay, where do we start?
7. **Interviewer:** Well, I understand you were in the Air Force.
8. **Interviewee:** Yes, I was.
9. **Interviewer:** How long were you in the Air Force?
10. **Interviewee:** About 11 months.
11. **Interviewer:** Did you have an accident or a physical problem that caused you to leave so soon?
12. **Interviewee:** No.
13. **Interviewer:** Why was your service so short?
14. **Interviewee:** We did our job and returned to our reserve units.
15. **Interviewer:** Then, you were in a reserve unit during most of your military experience.
16. **Interviewee:** That's correct.
17. **Interviewer:** What reserve unit were you in?
18. **Interviewee:** The 122nd Tactical Fighter Squadron of the Indiana Air National Guard.
19. **Interviewer:** You said you "Got your job done," in 11 months.
20. **Interviewee:** That's correct.
21. **Interviewer:** What job was that?
22. **Interviewee:** We were called up in 1961 during the Berlin Crisis to prevent the Soviet Union from turning over all access routes to West Berlin to the East Germans.
23. **Interviewer:** That's when the United States flew around-the-clock missions to resupply Berlin.
24. **Interviewee:** No, wrong Berlin crisis.
25. **Interviewer:** Oh. What did you do when you were on active duty; were you a pilot?
26. **Interviewee:** No.
27. **Interviewer:** I assume you were an officer.
28. **Interviewee:** No.
29. **Interviewer:** What rank were you and what did you do?
30. **Interviewee:** I was a staff sergeant.
31. **Interviewer:** I see. And what were your duties?
32. **Interviewee:** I was a weapons specialist and, while on active duty, served as a nuclear weapons instructor for pilots.
33. **Interviewer:** That sounds interesting. Tell me all about it.
34. **Interviewee:** Well, we took care of the weapons on our fighter planes, loaded and downloaded ordnance. Things like that.
35. **Interviewer:** What about the nuclear weapons?

36. Interviewee: I was a certified member of a nuclear loading team and taught the pilots how to arm and drop the nuclear weapons our fighters could carry.

37. Interviewer: Why were you chosen to do this?

38. Interviewee: Well, I had a top-secret clearance and had worked with nuclear weapons and cockpit controls for some time. But mostly I was picked because I was a college professor in "real life" and could lecture.

39. Interviewer: I see. Tell me how your military experiences have affected your attitudes toward the military.

40. Interviewee: When my unit was called up, my wife was eight months pregnant with our first child and I had just started my first faculty position. It was very traumatic for all of us because we had no idea how long I would be on active duty or where I might be sent. We have had a lot of empathy with the thousands of reservists who have been called up to serve in Iraq and Afghanistan.

41. Interviewer: Was it a scary time?

42. Interviewee: It was for the 165,000 of us who were called up, but not very scary for the civilians who continued their lives as usual.

43. Interviewer: Uh huh.

44. Interviewee: We thought we would soon be in a nuclear war with the Soviet Union and practiced each day how to react to an all-out nuclear war, including how to evacuate our base within a few hours if necessary. When we went home in the evening, no one wanted to talk about it. The American public became much more alarmed a year later during the Cuban Missile Crisis because it got so much television and press coverage.

45. Interviewer: How did this affect your attitudes toward the military?

46. Interviewee: As an enlisted NCO, I grew to have little faith in many of our officers, mainly those who were not pilots, and their decisions, no offense intended because you are in ROTC.

47. Interviewer: No offense taken. Go on.

48. Interviewee: Well, there was a great deal of wasted time and materiel and decisions that made no sense, such as loading ordnance on aircraft when the weather was too bad to fly any sort of training mission. It was dangerous downloading bombs and rockets with fuses already set.

49. Interviewer: Would you join the Guard and choose to be a weapons specialist if you had to do it all over again?

50. Interviewee: Oh yes. I've always been interested in guns of all types, and my squadron was a great outfit. I'm proud that I served in the military and wish more young people did so now.

51. Interviewer: Well, that's all of the questions I have. What advice do you have for a future Army officer?

52. Interviewee: Learn how to communicate with those under you and show them the respect they deserve.

53. **Interviewer:** Thanks Professor Harrison for that good advice. I promise I will remember it.

54. **Interviewee:** You're welcome, and good luck with your project and ROTC.

Student Activities

1. Prepare two sets of 10 questions—one with all neutral questions and one with at least four leading questions. Interview six people, three with each list of questions. How did the answers vary to the neutral and leading questions? How did different people (age, gender, education, and occupation) react to leading and neutral questions?
2. Select a current local or national controversial issue and conduct two 8- to 10-minute interviews. Use only primary, open-ended questions in the first, and in the second, ask the same primary, open-ended questions plus probing questions. Compare and contrast the amount and nature of the information you attain in each interview.
3. Create a list of closed questions, including a number of bipolar questions, on a controversial issue. Interview four people, a friend, a family member, an acquaintance, and a stranger. Which ones gave you closed, bipolar answers and which elaborated regardless of question types used? How can you explain the differences in the responses? What does this tell you about asking closed questions?
4. Record a series of investigative interviews during a program such as *Larry King Live, 60 Minutes,* or *Dateline* and see if you can detect common question pitfalls. Which were intentional and which were unintentional? How did these affect the answers received? How did they appear to affect the climate of the interview?

Notes

1. Joyce Kasman Valenza, "For the best answers, ask tough questions," *The Philadelphia Inquirer,* April 20, 2000, http://www.joycevalenza.com/questions.html, accessed September 26, 2006.
2. Stanley L. Payne, *The Art of Asking Questions* (Princeton, NJ: Princeton University Press, 1980), p. 204.
3. Robert L. Kahn and Charles F. Cannell, *The Dynamics of Interviewing* (New York: John Wiley, 1964), p. 205.
4. Lillian Glass, *He Says, She Says: Closing the Communication Gap between the Sexes* (New York: Putnam, 1993), pp. 45–59.

Resources

"A questioning toolkit," *The Educational Technology Journal* 7, November–December 1997, http://www.fno.org/nov97/toolkit.html, accessed September 26, 2006.

Payne, Stanley L. *The Art of Asking Questions*. Princeton, NJ: Princeton University Press, 1980.

Stone, Florence. "Six types of interview questions and when to use them," http://www.amanet.org/editorials/eprint.cjm?ED=85, accessed March 20, 2009.

"Types of questions," http://www2.warwick.ac.uk/services/careers/undergrad/hunting/inttestass/interview/plan/, accessed September 26, 2006.

"What are the basic types of questions you can ask during an interview?" http://scism.sbu.ac.uk/inmandw/tutorials/kaqa/qu7.htm, accessed September 26, 2006.

Wood, Julia T. *But I Thought You Meant . . . Misunderstandings in Human Communication.* Mountain View, CA: Mayfield, 1998.

CHAPTER 4 Structuring the Interview

Since every interview has a predetermined and serious purpose, each has a degree of structure, the extent and nature of which are determined by purpose, length, and complexity. Different types of interviews may require a somewhat different structure, but fundamental principles and techniques apply to all. This chapter focuses on these principles and techniques and how they apply to the three major interview parts: body, opening, and closing. It is organized according to the order in which you should proceed when preparing for an interview, starting with developing the body of the interview.

The Body of the Interview

Once you have determined a clear purpose, you are ready to structure the interview. If it will be brief and informal, such as asking for a simple clarification of a procedure or a few instructions, you may prepare little more than a few topic areas or questions and operate from memory or a piece of notepaper. For a longer, more formal interview, prepare a detailed outline of topics or carefully phrased questions. For formal interviews, such as surveys, prepare a schedule for the interview containing all questions and answer options.

Interview Guide

An interview guide contains topics, not questions.

The temptation, once you have a purpose in mind, is to start jotting down some questions. It's much wiser to start with an **interview guide,** a carefully structured outline of topics and subtopics to be covered during an interview. A guide helps you develop specific areas of inquiry, not a list of questions. This structure ensures coverage of all important topics and prevents forgetting important items during the heat of an interview. The guide may suggest probing questions and distinguish relevant from irrelevant information. It will assist in **recording** answers and **recall** at a later date.

Outline Sequences

Since the interview guide is an outline, review the fundamentals of outlining learned over the years to impose a clear, systematic structure on your interview. **Outline sequences** are quite useful for interviews.

A **topical sequence** follows natural divisions of a topic or issue. For example, an interview during a search for a graduate school might include admissions criteria, areas of study, degree requirements, faculty, funding sources, and information on the school and university. The traditional **journalist's guide** consisting of six key words—who, what, when, where, how, and why—is useful in many different interview settings.

Sequences help organize topics and impose a degree of structure on interviews.

A **time sequence** treats topics or parts of topics in chronological order. For instance, an interviewer explaining a workshop on "Searching for a Job" may start with registration at 8:30 a.m., and then proceed to the 9:00 a.m. session on networking, the 9:30 a.m. session on locating open positions, the 10:00 a.m. session on preparing resumes, the 10:30 a.m. session on taking part in interviews, and the 11:00 a.m. open session for personal consultations.

A **space sequence** arranges topics according to spatial divisions: left to right, top to bottom, north to south, or neighborhood to neighborhood. A person conducting tours of a new airport facility might begin with access to the airport, and proceed to parking, curbside check-in, airline check-in areas, restaurants, commercial shops, and concourses.

A **cause-to-effect sequence** explores causes and effects. For instance, you may be interested in what caused a power outage on campus, a drop in income for intercollegiate athletics in the northeast, increased enrollment in history courses, or a multiple-car accident on the interstate. An interviewer might begin with a cause or causes and then proceed to effect, or discuss an apparent effect and then move to possible causes.

A **problem-solution sequence** consists of a problem phase and a solution phase. You might discuss your grade with a professor first by identifying what you consider to be a serious problem and then by looking for solutions to improve exam scores. You might discuss a weight problem with a physician and then ways to address the problem.

Developing an Interview Guide

Let's assume you are thinking about a tour of Europe before starting graduate school in the fall. You have never traveled outside the United States and have many questions and concerns. Your graduate teaching assistant in a political science course mentioned in class that she had toured Europe for several weeks prior to starting her graduate studies. She has agreed to an interview about her experiences. First, decide on the major areas of information you want, such as the following topical sequence.

I. Cost
II. Possible European countries
III. Nature of a tour
IV. Requirements

Second, place possible subtopics under each major topic, such as the following:

A guide ensures the consideration of all important topics and subtopics.

I. Cost
   A. Round-trip air travel from the United States to Europe
   B. Travel while in Europe
   C. Hotels
   D. Food
   E. Tips
   F. Souvenirs
   G. Entry fees to sights

II. Europe
   A. Countries to visit
   B. Safety
   C. Climate
   D. Topography
   E. Language barriers
III. Nature of the tour
   A. Number of days
   B. Transportation
   C. Housing
   D. Food
   E. Friendliness of the people
   F. Sights to see
IV. Requirements
   A. Language
   B. Immunizations
   C. Physical condition
   D. Clothing
   E. Access to ATMs

Third, determine if there are subtopics of subtopics. For instance, you might want to know average temperature, typical breakfasts, safety from pickpockets, dress-up clothes, background of people on the tour, and specific types of clothing such as shoes, raingear, and hats. You may not know enough to develop subdivisions under some headings, or may discover additional subtopics as the interview progresses.

Interviews may include more than one sequence or none at all.

It is not unusual to employ more than one outline sequence in an interview. The sample outline is a topical sequence of major divisions, but a spatial sequence might be appropriate for subdivisions under housing, sightseeing, and countries.

Interview Schedules

A Nonscheduled Interview

After completing an interview guide, decide if additional structuring and preparation are needed. The guide may be sufficient, or you may transform all or part of it into questions. If you settle on a guide, you will conduct a **nonscheduled interview** with no questions prepared in advance. The nonscheduled interview is most appropriate when an interview will be brief, interviewees and information levels differ significantly, interviewees are reluctant to respond or have poor memories, or there is little preparation time.

A nonscheduled interview is merely an interview guide.

A nonscheduled interview gives you unlimited freedom to probe into answers and adapt to different interviewees and situations because it is the most flexible of interview schedules. However, nonscheduled interviews require considerable skill and are difficult to replicate from one interview to another. You may have difficulty controlling for time limits. And interviewer bias may creep into unplanned questions.

A Moderately Scheduled Interview

A **moderately scheduled interview** contains all major questions with possible probing questions under each. The sentences and phrases in a guide become questions. The moderate schedule, like the nonscheduled interview, allows freedom to probe into answers and adapt to different interviewees, but it also imposes a greater degree of structure, aids in recording answers, and is easier to conduct and replicate. You need not create every question on the spot but have them thought out and carefully worded in advance. This lessens pressures during the interview. Since interview parties tend to wander during unstructured interviews, listing questions makes it easier to keep on track and return to a structure when desired. Journalists, medical personnel, recruiters, lawyers, police officers, and insurance investigators, to name a few, use moderately scheduled interviews. A moderately scheduled interview would look like this:

A moderately scheduled interview lessens the need for instant question creation.

I. Why did you choose to live in an apartment above a business downtown?
   A. When did you decide to do this?
   B. What influenced you most in this decision?
   C. Who influenced you most in this decision?

II. Why did you choose this apartment?
   A. How did it compare in cost to others you considered?
   B. What role did location play?
   C. How important was space?
   D. How important were the lease stipulations?

III. What bothers you most about living downtown?
   A. What about noise from traffic?
   B. What about parking during business hours?
   C. What about transportation to and from your job?
   D. What about shopping?

A Highly Scheduled Interview

A **highly scheduled interview** includes all questions worded exactly as they will be used in an interview. It permits no unplanned probing, word changes, or deviation from the schedule. Questions may be closed in nature so respondents can give brief, specific answers. Highly scheduled interviews are easy to replicate and conduct, take less time than nonscheduled and moderately scheduled interviews, and prevent parties from wandering into irrelevant areas or spending too much time on one or two topics. Flexibility and adaptation are not options, however. Probing questions must be planned. Researchers and survey takers use highly scheduled interviews such as the following:

Highly scheduled interviews sacrifice flexibility and adaptability for control.

I. Which problem caused by this deep economic recession concerns you the most?
   A. Why does this problem concern you the most?
   B. When did you become highly concerned about this problem?
   C. How do you think the state government should address this problem?
   D. How do you think the federal government should address this problem?

II. Do you believe this problem will be better or worse within the next 12 months?
    A. (If better): Why do you feel it will be better within a year?
    B. (If worse): Why do you feel it will be worse within a year?

III. Which of the many solutions being offered by the government, economists, and political parties do you favor?
    A. Why do you feel this way?
    B. How has your attitude toward this solution changed during the past three months?
    C. What would change your mind about this solution?

A Highly Scheduled Standardized Interview

Highly scheduled standardized interviews provide precision, replicability, and reliability.

The **highly scheduled standardized interview** is the most thoroughly planned and structured. All questions and answer options are stated in identical words to each interviewee who then picks answers from those provided. There is no straying from the schedule by either party. Highly scheduled standardized interviews are the easiest to conduct, record, tabulate, and replicate, so even novice interviewers can handle them. However, the breadth of information is restricted, and probing into answers, explaining questions, and adapting to different interviewees are not permitted. Respondents have no chance to explain, amplify, qualify, or question answer options. **Built-in interviewer bias** may be worse than **accidental bias** encountered in nonscheduled and moderately scheduled interviews.

Researchers and survey takers use highly scheduled standardized interviews because their procedures must produce the same results in repeated interviews by several interviewers. The following is a highly scheduled standardized interview:

I. Which of the following solutions to our energy dependence problem do you feel has the best potential for making an immediate impact?
    A. Biofuels
    B. Wind
    C. Nuclear energy
    D. Drilling in the wilderness areas of Alaska
    E. Solar

II. How likely do you feel this solution will be implemented within the next five years?
    A. Highly likely
    B. Likely
    C. Unsure
    D. Unlikely
    E. Highly unlikely

III. Who do you think is most likely to implement this solution?
    A. The government
    B. Petroleum companies
    C. Private investments
    D. Power companies
    E. Combination

IV. How do you believe this solution should be funded?
   A. User fees
   B. Taxes
   C. Private investment
   D. Profits of producers
   E. Combination

Each interviewing schedule has unique advantages and disadvantages. Your task is to choose the schedule best suited to your needs, skills, type of information desired, and situation. One type of schedule does not fit all interview types and situations. A schedule designed for a survey would be a terrible schedule for an employment interview. Be aware of the options available and which one or ones seem most appropriate for each interview. Figure 4.1 summarizes the advantages and disadvantages of each schedule.

Combination of Schedules

Combined schedules enable interviewers to satisfy multiple needs.

Consider strategic combinations of schedules. For example, use a nonscheduled approach during the opening minutes, a moderately scheduled approach when it is necessary to probe and adapt to interviewees, and a highly scheduled standardized approach for easily quantifiable information such as demographic data on age, gender, religion, formal education, marital status, and organizational memberships. Although schedules are usually lists of questions, they may range from a topic outline to a manuscript. For instance, you might write major arguments for a persuasive interview, instructions for an information-giving interview, and the opening and closing for a survey interview.

Exercise #1—Interview Schedules

Which schedule would be most appropriate for each of the situations below: nonscheduled, moderately scheduled, highly scheduled, highly scheduled standardized? Explain why you would select this schedule.

1. You are attempting to persuade the EEO of a large construction management firm to hold the annual golf outing for district vice presidents at your resort.
2. You are a police officer who is interviewing an eyewitness to a shooting at a shopping mall.
3. As an assistant admissions officer at your college, you are preparing a survey of high school seniors to discover the five most important criteria they are using to select a college for next fall.
4. You are a recruiter for your law firm and are conducting initial employment interviews with third-year law students.
5. You are interviewing a professor to determine your grade standing prior to the final exam.

Question Sequences

In Chapter 3, we discussed a variety of question tools, and in this chapter we have introduced you to a variety of question schedules. It is now time to identify strategic use of

Figure 4.1 *Structural options*

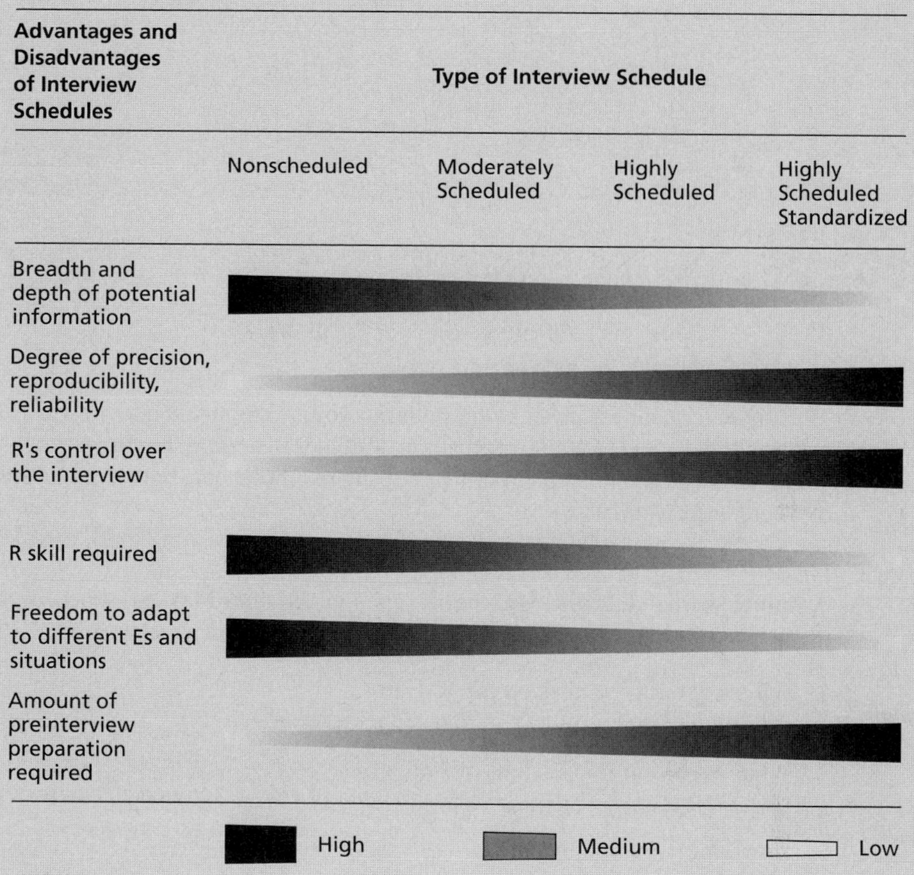

question sequences. Common **question sequences** are tunnel, funnel, inverted funnel, hourglass, diamond, and quintamensional design.

Tunnel Sequence

A tunnel sequence works well with informal and simple interviews.

The **tunnel sequence,** sometimes called a *string of beads,* is a series of similar questions, either open or closed. Each question may cover a different topic, ask for a specific bit of information, or assess a different attitude or feeling. See Figure 4.2. This is a tunnel sequence.

I understand that you took part in the "Tea Party" to protest state and federal taxes.

1. When did this protest occur?
2. Who organized this protest?
3. Where did you hold your protest?

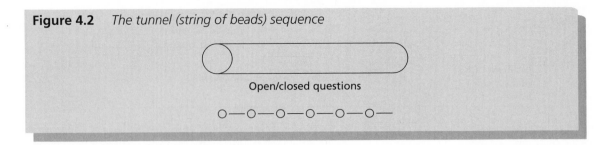

Figure 4.2 *The tunnel (string of beads) sequence*

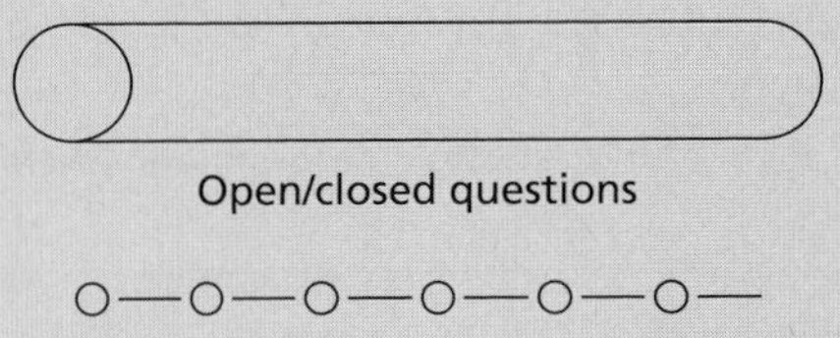

4. How many people were at the protest?
5. What was the featured event of the protest?
6. Will this become an annual event?

The tunnel sequence is common in polls, surveys, journalistic interviews, and medical interviews designed to elicit information, attitudes, reactions, and intentions. When the questions are closed in nature (perhaps a string of bipolar questions), information is easy to record and quantify.

Funnel Sequence

A funnel sequence works well with motivated interviewees.

A **funnel sequence** begins with broad, open-ended questions and proceeds with more restricted questions. See Figure 4.3. The following is a funnel sequence.

1. Tell me about your mission trip to Haiti.
2. What were your most memorable experiences?
3. What were your impressions of Haitians?
4. Where were you in Haiti?
5. How long were you there?
6. Do you plan to go on another mission trip?

Figure 4.3 *The funnel sequence*

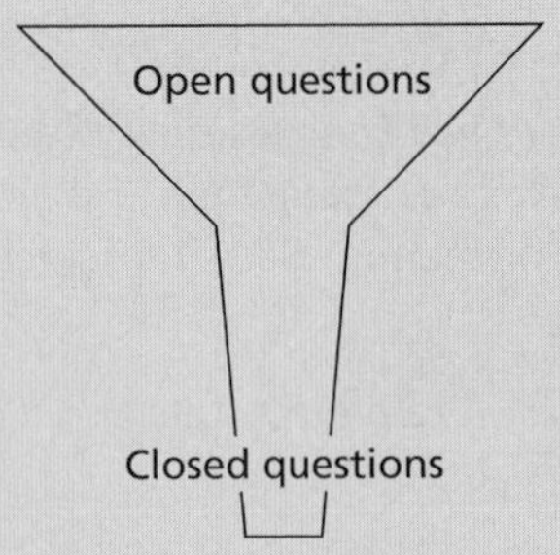

A funnel sequence begins with an open-ended question and is most appropriate when respondents are familiar with a topic, feel free to talk about it, want to express their feelings, and are motivated to reveal and explain attitudes. Open questions are easier to answer, pose less threat to respondents, and get people talking, so the funnel sequence is a good way to begin interviews.

The funnel sequence avoids possible conditioning or biasing of later responses. For example, if you begin an interview with a closed question such as "Do you think we should bail out large banks?" you force a respondent to take a polar position that may affect the remainder of the interview and make the

Figure 4.4 *The inverted funnel sequence*

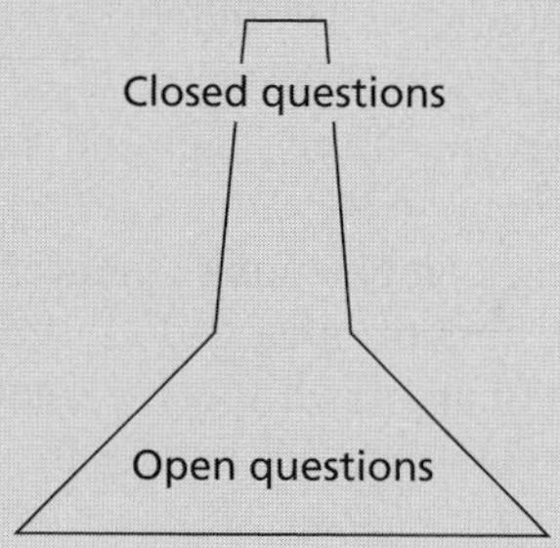

person defensive. An open question such as "How do you feel about the bailout of large banks?" does not force respondents to take polarized positions and enables them to explain and qualify positions.

Inverted Funnel Sequence

The **inverted funnel sequence** begins with closed questions and proceeds toward open questions. It is most useful when you need to motivate an interviewee to respond or an interviewee is emotionally involved in an issue or situation and cannot readily reply to an open question. See Figure 4.4. The following is an inverted funnel sequence.

1. **Interviewer:** When did you emerge from the tornado shelter?
2. **Interviewee:** It was about 5:15, some 10 or 15 minutes after the tornado hit.
3. **Interviewer:** What was the first thing you remember seeing when you came out of the tornado shelter?
4. **Interviewee:** It was the total destruction of homes and trees in our neighborhood.
5. **Interviewer:** What did you do then?
6. **Interviewee:** We started looking for people we knew to be in the area to see if we could help.
7. **Interviewer:** Tell me about the people you found.
8. **Interviewee:** Well, the Jacobs next door were all bloody from flying glass in their home, and . . .

An inverted funnel sequence provides a warm-up time for those reluctant to talk.

The inverted funnel sequence is useful when interviewees feel they do not know much about a topic or they do not want to talk. A respondent's memory or thought processes may need assistance, and closed questions can serve as warm-ups and may work when open-ended ones might overwhelm a person or result in disorganized and confused answers. This sequence may end with a clearinghouse question such as "Is there anything else you would like to say?"

Figure 4.5 *The hourglass sequence*

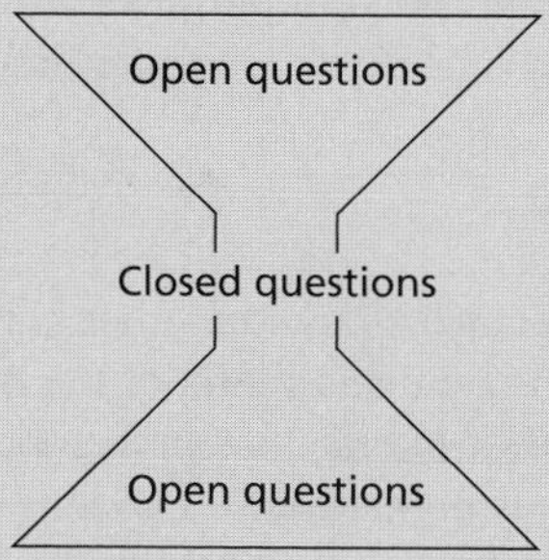

Combination Sequences

Sometimes a situation calls for a combination of question sequences. For instance, the **hourglass sequence** begins with open questions, proceeds to one or more closed questions, and ends with open questions. It is employed when you wish to begin with a funnel sequence and then proceed in your line of questioning to an inverted funnel sequence. It is a combination that enables you to narrow your focus and then proceed to open it up once more when the interviewee or topic warrants it. See Figure 4.5.

Figure 4.6 *The diamond sequence*

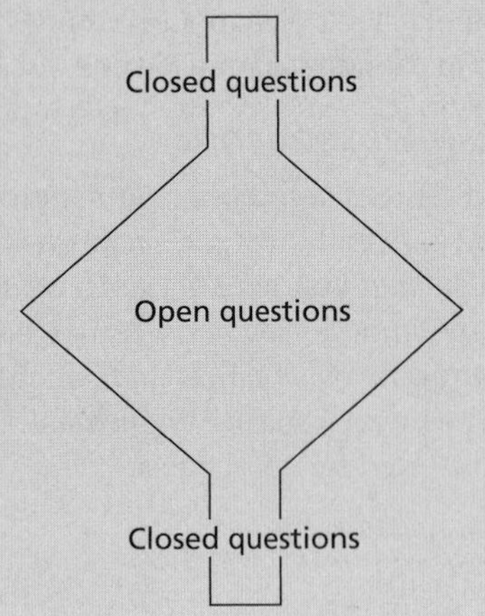

There is a second combination sequence that places funnel sequences top-to-top, what some writers call a **diamond sequence.**[1] This sequence enables interviewers to begin with closed questions, proceed to open questions, and end with closed questions. See Figure 4.6.

Each of these combination sequences offers different arrangements of open and closed questions that enable you to approach specific interview situations and interviewees with greater flexibility and adaptability.

Quintamensional Design Sequence

George Gallup, the famous poll designer, developed the **quintamensional design sequence** to assess the intensity of opinions and attitudes.[2] This five-step approach proceeds from an interviewee's awareness of the issue to attitudes uninfluenced by the interviewer, specific attitudes, reasons for these attitudes, and intensity of attitude. For example:

The quintamensional design is effective at assessing attitudes and beliefs.

1. *Awareness:* What do you know about the proposal to allow students to carry concealed weapons on campus?
2. *Uninfluenced attitudes:* How might this proposal affect you?
3. *Specific attitude:* Do you approve or disapprove of students carrying concealed weapons on campus?
4. *Reason why:* Why do you feel this way?
5. *Intensity of attitude:* How strongly do you feel about this—strongly, very strongly, not something you will change your mind on?

You can use this sequence, or modify it by creating questions most suitable for specific interview situations.

Once you have determined a specific purpose for your interview and developed a structure appropriate for your interview, you are now ready to create an opening that is adapted to the parties in the interview, the situation, and your purpose. The few seconds or minutes spent in the opening are critical to the success of your interview.

Opening the Interview

It takes two parties to launch an interview successfully.

What you do and say, or fail to do and say, influences how the other party perceives self, you, and the situation. The **opening** sets the tone and mood of the interview and affects willingness and ability to go beyond Level 1 interactions in the opening. It may determine whether an interview continues or ends prematurely. The tone may be serious or lighthearted, optimistic or pessimistic, professional or nonprofessional, formal or informal, threatening or nonthreatening, relaxed or tense. A poor opening may lead to a **defensive climate** with superficial, vague, and inaccurate responses. If dissatisfied with the opening, a party may say no, walk away, close the door, or hang up the phone.

The primary function of the opening is to **motivate** both parties to participate willingly and to communicate freely and accurately. Motivation is a **mutual product** of interviewer and interviewee, so every opening must be a **dialogue,** not a **monologue.** It is *done with* the other party, not *to* the other party. Too often the interviewee is given little opportunity to say anything beyond single-word responses to opening questions such as "How are you this morning?" "Nice day, isn't it?" and "Got a minute?" Do not interrupt an interviewee. A study of physicians interacting with patients, for instance, revealed that physicians did not permit patients to complete their opening statements 69 percent of the time. And when this happened, fewer than 2 percent of patients attempted to complete their statements.[3]

The Two-Step Process

The opening is a two-step process of establishing rapport and orienting the other party that encourages active participation and willingness to continue into the body of the interview. What is included and how content is shared depends upon interview type, situation, relationship, and preference.

Establish Rapport

Rapport is a process of establishing and sustaining a relationship between interviewer and interviewee by creating feelings of goodwill and trust. You may begin with a self-introduction ("I'm Martha Dodge from accounting") or a simple greeting if the relationship is established and positive ("Good morning, Jim") accompanied by appropriate nonverbal actions such as a firm handshake, eye contact, a smile, a nod, and a pleasant, friendly voice. The rapport step may include personal inquiries or small talk about the weather, mutual acquaintances, families, sports, or news events. Consider flavoring a personal inquiry and small talk with tasteful and appropriate humor. Do not prolong the rapport stage; know when enough is enough.

Do not overdo small talk or compliments.

Customs of a geographical area, organizational traditions or policies, culture, status differences, relationship, formality of the occasion, interview type, and situation may determine the appropriate verbal and nonverbal rapport-building techniques of each interview. Do not refer to strangers, superiors, or high-status persons by first names unless asked to do so. Limit humor or small talk when a party is busy or the situation is highly formal or serious. Overdoing sweet talk such as congratulations, praise, and expressions of admiration can turn off an interview party. Be sincere.

Orient the Other Party

Orientation is an essential second step in the opening. You may explain the purpose, length, nature of the interview, how the information will be used, and why and how you selected this party to interview. Study each situation carefully to determine the extent and nature of orientation.

Be careful of assuming too much or too little about the other party.

Do not assume that because you and the other party appear to be similar (gender, age, appearance, language, educational background, or culture) that you are similar in ways critical to the success of the interview. LaRay Barna warns that "The aura of

photoAlto/AGE foto stock

What you do and say in the opening seconds sets the tone for the remainder of the interview.

similarity is a serious stumbling block to successful intercultural communication. A look-alike facade is deceiving when representatives from contrasting cultures meet, each wearing Western dress, speaking English, and using similar greeting rituals."[4] You may assume that you share similar nonverbal codes, beliefs, attitudes, or values. "Unless there is overt reporting of assumptions made by each party, which seldom happens, there is no chance of comparing impressions and correcting misinterpretations." Be sure orientation is mutual so each party knows what to expect during the interview.

Rapport and orientation are often intermixed and reduce **relational uncertainty.** By the end of the opening, both parties should be aware of important similarities, the desire of each to take part in the interview, degree of warmth or friendliness, how control will be shared, and level of trust. A poor opening may mislead a party and create problems during an interview. Recall how angry you became when you discovered that an appeal for assistance from a person at your door turned out to be a ruse to sell you magazine subscriptions.

The rapport and orientation steps are illustrated in the following opening.

1. **Interviewer:** Hi Jane, I see you're getting ready to go to class.
2. **Interviewee:** Yes; this is my busy class day.
3. **Interviewer:** How's your semester going so far?
4. **Interviewee:** Okay, but I'm carrying 18 hours with some really tough classes.
5. **Interviewer:** That's a lot. I'd like to talk to you about moving from the residence hall to an apartment with Sara and me next fall. We've found some really good deals and think the three of us would be great roommates.
6. **Interviewee:** Well, I have been thinking about an apartment for next year, but I only have a few minutes right now. Can we make this short?
7. **Interviewer:** Sure. Let me ask a couple of quick questions about what you're looking for in an apartment.

Verbal Opening Techniques

Be creative when opening interviews, and adapt to the interviewee and the situation. Don't fall into the habit of using an "all occasions" opening for all interviews or interviews of a specific type, such as employment interviews or information-gathering interviews. The following **verbal opening techniques** may build rapport, orient the other party, or serve as complete openings.

State the Purpose

This technique explains *why* you are conducting the interview.

Adapt the opening to each interviewee and situation.

> **Example:** (a professor to a student) I've asked you to meet with me because I'm chairing a committee whose purpose is to get more of our students interested in graduate teaching assistantships when they complete their B.S. degrees, and you have expressed an interest in going on to graduate school next fall.

There are occasions when stating a detailed purpose would make its achievement difficult. This is the case in some research, survey, and sales interviews. You may need to withhold a specific purpose until later in the interview to get honest, unguarded answers, to motivate the interviewee to take part, or to avoid defensiveness.

> **Example:** (a research study by a politically conservative think tank) I'm conducting a study of how people on Main Street feel about President Obama's multibillion-dollar bailouts of financial institutions.

Summarize a Problem

This technique is appropriate when an interviewee is unaware of a problem, vaguely aware of it, or unaware of details. Be sure the summary **informs** the interviewee but does not spill into the body of the interview.

Know when to end the opening and move on.

> **Example:** As you know, it's become customary for presidents of the United States to declare wars on illegal drugs. Unfortunately, the problem has grown more severe each year. I'd like to get your reactions to the proposal being discussed by some drug enforcement agencies that would make the growing and selling of marijuana legal.

Explain How a Problem Was Discovered

This technique explains *how* a problem was detected and perhaps *by whom*. Be honest and specific in revealing sources of information without placing the interviewee on the defensive because of overt or implied accusations.

> **Example:** I was checking my grades on the course Web site last night and discovered that my exam grade that was 87 is now listed as 72. I'm trying to discover how it could have changed more than three weeks after the exam.

Offer an Incentive or Reward

An incentive may be effective if it appeals to the interviewee, and it must be significant enough to make a difference and appropriate for the interview and situation. Because many sales pitches include a gift to motivate people to participate, it may become difficult to convince a respondent that you are conducting a research, journalistic, or survey interview if you offer an incentive.

> **Example:** We're conducting a market survey here at Chalmers Mall, and anyone who takes the survey will get a coupon worth 10 percent off any item at any store in the mall, including sale items.

Request Advice or Assistance

Be sincere in offering incentives or requesting advice.

This interview opening is common because help is often what an interviewer needs. Be sure the need is clear, precise, and one the interviewee can satisfy. Be sincere in asking for advice. Do not use this opening as a technique for another purpose such as networking, climbing the ladder, or boosting one's ego.

> **Example:** I'm considering changes in some of my investments in this bear market, and Merriam Kang said you gave her some excellent advice. I was wondering if we might talk about my situation.

Refer to the Known Position of the Interviewee

This technique identifies the interviewee's position on an issue or problem. A tactless or seemingly hostile reference to a known position may create a defensive attitude or antagonize the other party. A common problem is an inaccurate or incomplete interpretation of the position.

> **Example:** Dave, I know your position on overtime when we're laying off staff, but we really need some of our accountants to work extra time to meet the April 15 tax deadline.

Refer to the Person Who Sent You

A referral is an excellent means of connecting positively with another party. Never use a person's name without permission to do so, and be sure the person you name did send you. Discover if the interviewee knows, respects, and likes the person you intend to name. It can be embarrassing or disastrous to discover after using a name that the interviewee does not recall or dislikes the reference.

> **Example:** I'm preparing a history of the College of Liberal Arts for our special edition of *Alumni News* that focuses on the 50th anniversary of the college. Dean Montovani suggested that I talk with you because you came to campus when the college was the School of Science and Humanities.

Know what to do if references to an organization generate negative reactions.

Refer to Your Organization

Often you must refer to an organization you represent (company, hospital, government agency, religious group) to give you your identity and legitimacy as an interviewer. Your position with an organization may dictate whom you interview, when, where, and why. Realize that some interview parties will not be fans of your organization, particularly if you represent possible negative publicity, lawsuits, regulatory enforcement, or legal investigations.

> **Example:** (over the telephone) Good evening. Is this Richard Truit? . . . I'm Jason Gilbert from FEMA and understand your home was severely damaged during the recent flood on the Red River.

Request a Specific Amount of Time

Make an appointment for interviews of more than 5 or 10 minutes.

You may ask for a specific amount of time. Be realistic in your request and, by the end of this period, either complete the task or begin to close the interview. Give the interviewee an opportunity to continue the interview or to terminate it, perhaps arranging for another meeting. "Got a second?" is probably the most overused and misused interview opening. You can't get seated in one second, let alone conduct an interview.

> **Example:** I'm concerned about my grade in your class and wonder if you have about 15 minutes to go over the first two exams with me.

Ask a Question

An open-ended, easy to answer question may establish rapport or begin to orient the interviewee. Common opening questions include:

> **Examples:** What are you looking for in replacement for your SUV?
> How can I help with the Mother's Day brunch?
> Tell me about your graduation plans.

Be careful of employing closed questions that can be answered with a quick no or rejection. Common closed, dead-end questions are:

> **Examples:** Can I help you?
> Do you need assistance?
> How are you?

Many interviewees are turned off by a single, obvious answer, yes-no question.

> **Examples:** Do you like my class?
> Are we going to do anything important in class today?
> Are you busy?

These 10 verbal opening techniques provide a variety of ways to open interviews effectively.

Use a Combination

Make the opening a dialogue between two parties.

Most openings include a strategic combination of techniques. Create an opening that is most appropriate for each interview and situation and avoid the temptation to use a standard or stock opening. We are all creatures of habit, and if a technique works well once, we may assume it is appropriate for a variety of situations. **Above all, involve the interviewee in the opening.** As an interviewee, insist on playing an active role from the beginning. Don't be a mere bystander.

Nonverbal Communication in Openings

First impressions often determine the tone and flow of communication.

Verbal opening techniques are accompanied by appropriate **nonverbal communication.** An effective opening depends upon *how* you look, act, and say *what* you say. Nonverbal communication is critical in creating a good first impression and establishing your legitimacy. It signals sincerity, trust and trustworthiness, warmth, interest, the seriousness of the interview, and the emotions being experienced.

Territoriality

Always knock before entering a room, even if the door is open, you are a superior, or you are in your own home, building, or organization. You are entering another's *space,* and any perceived violation of this territory is likely to begin an interview poorly. Wait until the other party signals to enter with a smile, head nod, wave, or by pointing to a chair. Maintain good eye contact without staring because it shows trust and allows you to pick up nonverbal signals that say "come in," "be seated," "sit there," and "I'm interested/willing to talk to you," or "Not now," "You're interrupting," or "I'm very busy."

Face, Appearance, and Dress

Appearance and dress should send appropriate opening signals.

Your appearance and dress contribute a great deal to first impressions. They may communicate interest, sincerity, warmth, urgency, attractiveness, neatness, maturity, professionalism, and knowledge of what is appropriate dress for this interview and setting. Do not signal catastrophe when the interview will be routine, friendliness when you are about to discipline a person, warmth when you are angry, happiness when a major problem needs urgent attention, or closeness when you have never met.

Touch

Know when and with whom touch is appropriate.

If shaking hands is appropriate for the relationship and the situation, give a firm but not crushing handshake. Be careful of overdoing handshaking with acquaintances and colleagues or during informal interviews. Touching another is generally appropriate only when both parties have an established and close relationship.

Reading Nonverbal Communication

Sex and culture regulate nonverbal communication in openings.

Do not underestimate the importance of verbal and nonverbal communication in openings, but do not read too much into simple words and nonverbal acts or try to read everyone the same. Even people of apparently similar backgrounds may differ significantly in communicative behavior.

Interpersonal communication theorists emphasize the importance we place on nonverbal clues. For instance, Trenholm and Jensen write, "People read a lot in our facial expressions. They infer some personality traits and attitudes, judge reactions to their own messages, regard facial expressions as verbal replacements, and, primarily, use them to determine our emotional state."[5] Regarding first impressions, Floyd notes that "the quality of a person's clothing is a relatively reliable cue to his or her socioeconomic status" and type or style of clothing may enable us, often quite accurately, to identify an interview party with a particular cultural or political group.[6] Stewart warns us, however, that we "tend to *notice* those behaviors [and possibly appearance and dress] that are consistent with the beliefs we have about another and ignore those that are inconsistent."[7]

Lillian Glass has catalogued 105 "talk differences" between American men and women in basic areas of communication: body language, facial language, speech and voice patterns, language content, and behavioral patterns. She has found that men touch others more often, tend to avoid eye contact and not look directly at the other person, sound more abrupt and less approachable, make direct accusations, and give fewer compliments.[8]

Americans share rules for greeting others, but these rules may not be shared with other cultures. Shaking hands, for instance, is a Western custom, particularly in the United States, so do not ascribe meaning to firmness or lack of firmness when interviewing persons from other cultures. They may see handshaking as merely a quaint Western custom of little importance. While Americans expect persons to look them in the eyes to exhibit trust, openness, and sincerity, other cultures consider such eye contact to be impolite and insulting. The United States is not a touching society, but do not be shocked if a party from Italy or Latin America touches you during an opening.

Exercise #2—Interview Openings

How satisfactory is each of the following openings? Consider the interviewing situation and type, the techniques used, and what is omitted. How might each be improved? Do not assume that each opening is unsatisfactory.

1. This is an interview taking place in the office area of a large trucking firm. The interviewer is a recruiter for the company.

   Interviewer: Are you busy, Bob?

   Interviewee: Of course I am.

   Interviewer: Oh, I'm sorry to interrupt, but I wanted to talk to you about my interviews for the five openings we have.

2. This is an interview between Brad Wilkins, the union representative, and Cheryl Beaupre, the plant manager of an automotive assembly plant.

   Interviewer: I was just watching CNN on my lunch hour, and it was reporting a plan to shut down all of our assembly plants during July and August. What do you know about this?

   Interviewee: Not much.

   Interviewer: The union needs to know what's going on.

3. This is an interview taking place between a student and a professor in the professor's office.

   Interviewer: Hi Professor Adair. Got a second?

   Interviewee: A second yes.

   Interviewer: Uh, well, I really need a few minutes.

4. This is a recruiting interview for a flight instructor at a small training facility outside Baltimore.

   Interviewer: Hi. I'm Shaun Steinberg. (shakes hands) How was your flight from Pittsburgh?

Interviewee: It was really smooth with clear skies all the way.

Interviewer: Awesome! Well, let's get to the important stuff. Tell me about yourself.

5. This interview is taking place in the hallway near the U.S. Senate chamber between an NBC Capitol Hill correspondent and a senator. The senator is leaving a committee meeting to attend a Senate meeting on the economy.

   Interviewer: Senator Dirks! (waving and shouting) Would you comment on the bailout bill for Amtrak?

   Interviewee: We'll be discussing that today.

   Interviewer: Are you leaning toward supporting it because a major Amtrak facility is in your state?

Closing the Interview

Take your time and be tactful in what you say and do in the closing.

The closing is a critical stage in every interview because it not only affects this interview but also your relationship with a party and the nature, atmosphere, cooperation, and expectations of future contacts. Each interview creates or alters a relational history. An abrupt closing may make the other party feel used, important only as long as needed. The closing is not something tacked onto the end of an interview, an escape mechanization to end an interaction.

It is natural to relax and let your guard down when an interview seems completed and to get on to your next task or appointment. Be attentive to everything you do and say and don't do and say during these final seconds or minutes of an interaction because the other party will be watching and listening for important signals about your relationship, appreciation, interest, and sincerity. Both parties should be aware that a closing is commencing.

Closings tend to be signaled nonverbally before any words are exchanged. Mark Knapp and his colleagues, in their classic study of "leave-taking" in interpersonal interactions, identified a variety of nonverbal closing actions, some of them rather subtle.[9] For instance, you may straighten up in your seat, lean forward, uncross your legs, place your hands on your knees as if preparing to rise, look at your watch, pause briefly, or break eye contact. Other more obvious actions are standing up, moving away from the other party, or offering to shake hands. Whether subtle or not, these nonverbal actions enable you to signal that you want to close the interview. As an interviewee, watch for such subtle signals to detect when a closing is commencing so you are not taken by surprise or experience an awkward ending to the interaction. At the same time, be aware that a person may be checking a watch to see that there is adequate time remaining for additional questions or information sharing, uncrossing legs to get more comfortable, or breaking eye contact to think of a new question. Years ago the authors placed small clocks inconspicuously on their desks because they discovered that every time they checked their watches, students started into leave-taking, assuming this was a signal for them to leave.

Both parties make closings successful.

Guidelines for Closing Interviews

Follow a number of simple rules for conducting effective closings. First, the closing, like the opening, is a **dialogue,** not a **monologue.** When you are the interviewer, encourage the interviewee to take part by employing verbal and nonverbal signals, including silence. When you are the interviewee, take an active part in the closing by responding to questions, adding a few important comments or facts not covered, and expressing appreciation when appropriate. Second, be sincere and honest in the closing and make no promises you cannot or will not keep. Third, pace the interview carefully so you do not have to rush the closing. The **law of recency** suggests that people recall the last thing said or done during an interview, so being rushed or dismissed with an ill-chosen nonverbal action or phrase may jeopardize the effects of the interview, your relationship, and future contacts with this party. Fourth, be aware that the other party will be observing and interpreting everything you say and do, and everything you don't say and don't do, until you are out of sight and sound of one another. A slip of the lip or an inappropriate nonverbal act may negate all that you accomplished during the interview. Fifth, leave the door open, and perhaps set the groundwork, for future contacts. If an additional contact is planned (quite common in health care, employment, counseling, and sales interviews), explain what will happen next, where it will happen, when it will happen, and why it will happen. When possible, make a specific appointment before leaving rather than playing phone or e-mail tag later. Sixth, don't introduce new topics or ideas or make inquiries when the interview has in fact or psychologically come to a close. A **false closing** occurs when your verbal and nonverbal messages signal that the interview is coming to a close only for you to open it back up. This may be awkward for both parties and such after-the-fact interactions are likely to be superficial and add little to the interview.

Be careful of what you do and say.

Avoid what Erving Goffman has called **failed departures** that occur when you have brought an interview to a successful close and taken leave from the other party. Then a short time later you run into the party in the hall, parking lot, or restaurant.[10] The result is awkward because both of you have said your good-byes (after interviewing for a position, talking to a counselor, purchasing a product), and now you try to think of something appropriate to say when there is nothing to say. Practice situations to determine what you might say when this happens to avoid awkward and embarrassing moments.

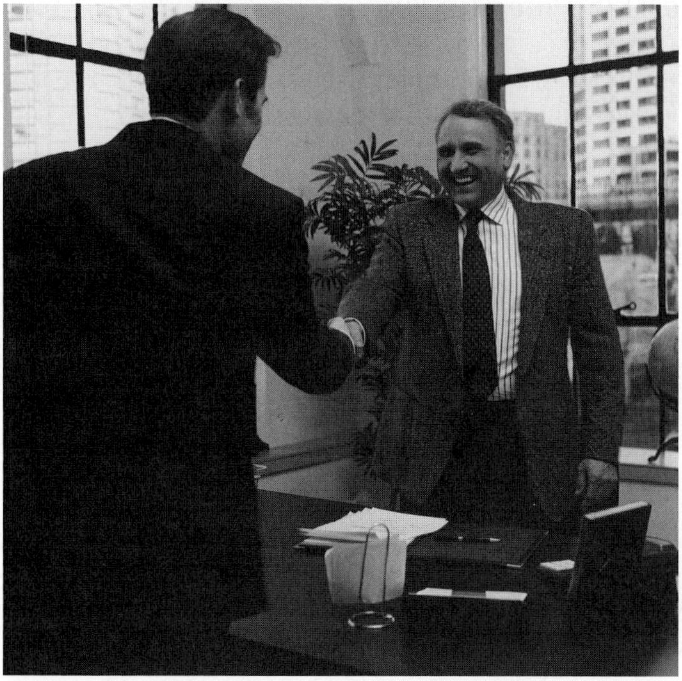

Keith Bropsky/Getty Images

Remember that the interview is not completed until the interviewer and interviewee are out of sight and sound of one another.

Closing Techniques

Be creative and imaginative in closing interviews. Adapt each closing to the interviewee and the situation. The following techniques may serve as entire closings, begin the closing process, or complete the closing.

Offer to Answer Questions

Regardless of technique, involve the interviewee in the closing.

Be sincere in your desire to answer questions and give the other party adequate time to ask them. Do not give a brief answer to one question and then end the interview.

What questions have I not answered for you?

Do you have any questions for me?

Do you have any further questions before we bring the videoconference to a close?

Use Clearinghouse Questions

Questions, intentions, and inquiries allow you to close effectively.

A clearinghouse question allows you to determine if you have covered all topics, answered all questions, or resolved all concerns. Be sure the request is communicated as an honest and sincere effort to ferret out unaddressed questions, information, or areas of concern.

Is there anything else you would like to add before we close?

Are there questions I have not addressed?

What information have I not asked for that you feel is important to know?

Declare Completion of the Intended Purpose

State that the task is completed. The word *well* probably signals more closings than any other word or phrase. When we hear it, we automatically assume that leave-taking is commencing and begin to wind things up. Is this what you want to happen?

Well, that's all the questions I have.

Okay, that should do it.

That answers all of my concerns.

Make Personal Inquiries

Be genuinely interested in the other party.

Personal inquiries are pleasant ways to end interviews and to enhance relationships. They must be sincere and give the interviewee adequate time to address an inquiry or concern. Be sincerely interested.

When do you start your vacation in China?

How's your brother doing in the Army?

Are you still planning to enter law school in the fall?

Make Professional Inquiries

Professional inquiries are more formal than personal ones, and they must be sincere and show genuine interest. We appreciate interest in our careers.

How is your internship going at Lockeed?

When do you start the new office complex?

What are your plans for the fall semester?

Signal That Time Is Up

Do not rush the closing but end the interview when most appropriate.

This technique is most effective when a time limit has been agreed to in advance or during the opening. Be tactful, and avoid the impression that you are running an interview assembly line.

I'm sorry, but I have a class in a few minutes.

Well, I see our time's up for today. How about meeting again this time next Wednesday?

You were kind enough to meet with me for a half-hour, and I've used up my time.

Explain the Reason for the Closing

Explain honestly why the interview must end. A phony-sounding reason can harm the interview and relationship.

I must close the interview because I have another appointment.

I'm sorry, but I have another client waiting to see me.

We must bring this to a close because the office closes at 5:00.

Express Appreciation or Satisfaction

A statement of appreciation or satisfaction is a common closing because you have usually received something—information, assistance, evaluation, a story, a sale, a position, a recruit, time. Be sincere.

It has been great talking to you, and I really appreciate your help.

Thanks for your help with this survey.

I appreciate your willingness to listen to my problem.

Arrange for the Next Meeting

If a subsequent interview is necessary, arrange it now.

If appropriate, set up the next meeting or reveal what will happen next, including date, time, place, topic, content, or purpose.

I have some additional questions to ask; could we meet at the same time on Friday?

This has been a good start on this issue. How about getting together again on the 5th?

Could you come for a daylong interview at our regional office in Memphis on the 14th or 15th?

When it is unnecessary to set a specific time for another interview, simple phrases may communicate a likely time between interactions. For instance, "See you," or "Until next time" signal short intervals. "Let's stay in touch" and "Don't be a stranger" signal moderate intervals. "Good-bye" and "So long" tend to signal lengthy or forever intervals. "We'll be in touch" and "Don't call us; we'll call you" may signal the traditional "brush-off" that means never. Be aware of cultural differences and expectations between parties that may lead to confusion when using such "subtle" phrases. Interviewees from other cultures not familiar with the "Don't call us; we'll call you" phrase have been known to quit their current positions in anticipation of immediate job offers that never came.

Summarize the Interview

A summary closing is common for informational, performance, counseling, and sales interviews. It may repeat important information, stages, and agreements or verify accuracy and agreement. Be sure the summary is accurate and addresses the major areas of information, analysis, or agreement.

> Well, it's been a pleasure working with you on this project. It's agreed, then, that we will begin the annual meeting with an overview for the year, move to a discussion of special projects, a report on progress of the new stadium, and finally the outlook for the next 12 months.

Nonverbal Closing Actions

Plan the closing as carefully as you do the opening and body of the interview.

Understand what words and actions are *saying* to the other party. Decide which closing techniques are most suitable. Your role in an interview and your relationship with the other party may require some techniques, rule out others, and determine who will initiate the closing and when. Usually you will combine several verbal and nonverbal techniques into effective closings. For example:

> Well (closing a notebook), I think that answers all of my questions. (leaning forward and smiling) You've given me a lot of exciting information for my field project. (rising from the chair) I really appreciate your help. (shakes hands and looks the interviewee directly in the eyes)

Exercise #3—Interview Closings

How satisfactory is each of the following closings? Consider the interviewing situation and type, relationship, the techniques used, nonverbal communication, and what is omitted. How might each be improved? Do not assume each closing is unsatisfactory.

1. This is a performance review of Alicia McRobbins who has been doing an excellent job in HR.

   Interviewer: You've been doing a great job in HR this quarter Alicia (glancing at his watch). How's your husband been doing after his knee surgery?

   Interviewee: Thanks Bob. He's still in a lot of pain and sees his surgeon tomorrow.

   Interviewer: That right? See you.

2. This is a journalistic interview between a television news reporter and a couple who have just been rescued from their flooded home.

   Interviewer: Were you really frightened when the water rose to the second floor of your home?

   Interviewee: Yeah. We thought we were going to die.

   Interviewer: Okay. (turning to the mayor of the town)

3. This is a sales interview between Brian and Kasie who are looking for two desktop computers for their study at home.

ON THE WEB

This chapter has presented guidelines and techniques for developing effective openings and closings. Use the Internet to locate sample interviews on issues such as education, the economy, foreign affairs, and medicine. Critique the openings and closings used in these interviews. Two useful Internet resources for locating interviews are CNN (http://cnn.com) and C-SPAN (http://indycable.com/cabletv/comastindyupgrade/ch24.htm).

Interviewer: This is really a bargain for this model of desktop that includes all of the software and a printer.

Interviewee: Yes, they are about what we had in mind, but we're still looking around.

Interviewer: Okay. Let me know if I can help.

Interviewee: Thanks.

4. This is a recruiting interview for a position as a flight instructor at a small airport. The applicant is a recent graduate of a university professional flight program with limited experience as an instructor.

Interviewer: Oh, I see my time's up. Thanks for your interest in our position.

Interviewee: Thank you for talking to me. This is a nice airport.

Interviewer: I'm glad you like it. (does not look the applicant in the eye) We'll call you in a week or so. Good luck with your job search.

5. This is an interview between a consultant and a client involved in finance. The economy has taken a major hit during the previous 10 months, and the client is trying to assess the strength of the regional building market.

Interviewer: Well, (leaning forward) that's my best estimate of housing trends for the coming year. I have a meeting in about an hour with another client concerned about the same situation.

Interviewee: Thanks. I appreciate your realistic assessment of the situation.

Interviewer: (leaning back) What are your thoughts on refinancing the commercial and condominium development near the university sports complex?

Summary

All three parts of each interview—opening, body, and closing—are vital to its success. Do not underestimate the importance of both words and nonverbal actions and reactions during all three stages. Be conscious of cultural differences that affect the meaning of actions such as handshaking, eye contact, voice, touch, and gestures.

The opening influences how both parties perceive themselves and one another. It sets the tone for the remainder of the interview, orients the interviewee, and influences the willingness of both parties to communicate beyond Level 1. The opening often determines whether the interview will continue or end prematurely. Select opening techniques most appropriate for each interview.

The body of the interview must be carefully structured with an appropriate sequence that guides the interviewer's questions, areas of information, or points systematically and allows the interviewee to understand where the interview is going and why. A nonscheduled interview is simply an interview guide with topics and subtopics an interviewer wants to cover. A moderately scheduled interview contains all major questions and possible probing questions under each. A highly scheduled interview includes all questions to be asked during an interview. A highly scheduled standardized interview contains all questions to be asked with prescribed answer options under each. Question sequences allow strategic structuring of questions within scheduled interviews.

The closing not only brings the interview to an end but may summarize information, verify agreements, arrange future contacts, and enhance relationships. A good closing should make both parties glad they took part and pleased with the results. Be sincere and honest. Do not rush the closing. Both sides should be actively involved in the closing.

Key Terms and Concepts

The online learning center for this text features FLASHCARDS and CROSSWORD PUZZLES for studying based on these terms and concepts.

Accidental bias
Built-in interviewer bias
Cause-to-effect sequence
Closing
Closing techniques
Combination schedule
Culture
Defensive climate
Diamond sequence
Failed departures
False closings
Funnel sequence
Highly scheduled interview
Highly scheduled standardized interview
Hourglass sequence
Interview guide
Interview schedules
Inverted funnel sequence
Journalist's guide
Law of recency
Moderately scheduled interview
Nonscheduled interview
Nonverbal closing actions
Nonverbal communication
Opening
Orientation
Outline sequences
Problem-solution sequence
Question sequences
Quintamensional design sequence
Rapport
Relational uncertainty
Space sequence
Territoriality
Time sequence
Topical sequence
Tunnel sequence
Verbal opening techniques

An Interview for Review and Analysis

This interview is taking place between a student who is majoring in hospitality and tourism management and a faculty member in communication who recently returned from a two-week safari in Kenya. The student is conducting this interview as part of a field project on hospitality and tourism in several African nations. The student is currently taking a course in persuasion with the interviewee.

How satisfactory is the opening? Which type of schedule does the interviewer appear to be using? Which structural sequence(s) can you detect? Which question sequence(s) can you detect? How satisfactory is the closing? How does nonverbal communication affect this interview?

1. **Interviewer:** Good morning Professor Lopez. Got a minute or two?
2. **Interviewee:** I do have some time, yes. (smiling) My office hour goes on for another 25 minutes.
3. **Interviewer:** (sits down) Good. (smiles but appears nervous)
4. **Interviewee:** Please sit down. (grins)
5. **Interviewer:** Oh, I'm sorry, I didn't mean to barge in. (looks down) I mentioned in our persuasion class the other afternoon that I'm doing a project in my hospitality and tourism course on destinations in Africa.
6. **Interviewee:** I remember you mentioning that.
7. **Interviewer:** Well, you told us a bit about your recent safari in Kenya, and I'd like to talk to you about your trip for my project.
8. **Interviewee:** Okay. What would you like to know?
9. **Interviewer:** How long was your trip?
10. **Interviewee:** Counting travel time from Chicago to Nairobi, it was 15 days.
11. **Interviewer:** Your first stop in Kenya, then, was the capital of Nairobi?
12. **Interviewee:** Yes, we stayed overnight in Nairobi before heading north to the Samburu area.
13. **Interviewer:** Where was your hotel?
14. **Interviewee:** In the center of the city.
15. **Interviewer:** Was it safe?
16. **Interviewee:** Oh yes. We entered through a gate that was manned by armed guards who checked us out and used mirrors to check under our safari van.
17. **Interviewer:** How would you rate the hotel?
18. **Interviewee:** I think it was definitely a five star hotel.
19. **Interviewer:** Tell me about it.
20. **Interviewee:** It was the Nairobi Serena Hotel, part of the Serena chain of hotels in Kenya. It was surrounded by a beautiful garden, and the lobby and restaurant/bar complex was very impressive, all decorated in an African motif. Our room was large, beautifully decorated, and looked out on our own patio. Fresh roses were in the bedroom and bathroom areas. The food was outstanding, as was all service in the hotel.
21. **Interviewer:** Tell me about the typical accommodations while you were out in the bush.
22. **Interviewee:** They tended to be in heavily forested and secure compounds. The lobby, restaurant, bar, and swimming pool areas were all open air. Yes, there were swimming pools in each compound. The living areas tended to be off a short distance

down beautifully landscaped pathways. Most often the rooms were in units of 2 to 10, sort of motel like. All were very nice, clean, and roomy. Each bed was surrounded by a floor-to-ceiling mosquito screen.

23. **Interviewer:** Tell me about the most unusual accommodation.

24. **Interviewee:** Oh, that was the Sweetwaters Tented Camp, South of the Samburu area. Each of us had a large tent on a raised platform with a thatch roof over the top. The sleeping area was typical for a tent, but the back part of the tent was a very modern bathroom with shower and dressing area. Hot water came from outdoor wood fired boilers that served several tents. They placed hot water bottles in the beds each evening to warm them up for us. Some of our group who were unaware of this practice got into their beds and thought a wild animal was under the covers. The first morning we came out of our tent, several zebras were grazing a few yards away and a giraffe was getting a drink from a small pond about 50 yards away.

25. **Interviewer:** It certainly sounds like you had a wonderful trip and that the hotel accommodations were excellent.

26. **Interviewee:** Yes we did, and yes they were.

27. **Interviewer:** Is there anything else you would like to tell me?

28. **Interviewee:** Well, the roads in Kenya were terrible, and it took us hours to travel rather short distances. On the other hand, we saw a large variety of animals in their world in a beautiful high plains country.

29. **Interviewer:** Well . . . that's about it. Oh, by the way, did you get to see how the natives live in the outlying areas and the bush?

30. **Interviewee:** Yes, we did.

31. **Interviewer:** Tell me about that.

32. **Interviewee:** You have to understand that Kenya is a very poor country and relies heavily on tourism. The people in the countryside and small villages live in what we can only describe as shacks. Unemployment is very high and income is very small.

33. **Interviewer:** What about natives in the bush?

34. **Interviewee:** One of our most memorable experiences was a visit to a Maasai village in southern Kenya just a short distance from the Tanzanian border.

35. **Interviewer:** What was that like?

36. **Interviewee:** They live in circular compounds with small huts made of a lattice work of small saplings covered in dried cow dung. The roof is thatched. There are no windows and only one small door. Of course, the floor is dirt.

37. **Interviewer:** Tell me about the interior.

38. **Interviewee:** As you enter, there is a small walled-off area for the shelter of young cows and sheep. The main area has a fire pit in the center with an animal hide bed on each side, one for the mother and one for the young children. Men have several wives and move from hut to hut, usually sleeping on the ground. The smoky, dark interior keeps out the bugs. The only modern item we saw was a very old iron frying pan.

39. **Interviewer:** Are they safe from the wild animals around them?

40. **Interviewee:** Yes, generally so. They have thicket barriers between each hut and only a small gate or two that are closed up after dark. Their traditional red clothing and smoky smell warns animals to stay away when they are tending their herds in the bush during the day.

41. **Interviewer:** Well, I think that's it. Thanks for your help with this project. If I have some additional questions, may I call or e-mail you?

42. **Interviewee**: Of course. Good luck with your project, and I hope you can get to Kenya sometime.

Student Activities

1. Select an interview topic of particular interest to you. It may be, for instance, historical, economic, political, technical, or career-based. First, phrase a carefully worded purpose. Second, create an interview guide, determining which outline sequence or sequences to use. Third, turn the guide into an appropriate moderately scheduled, highly scheduled, or highly scheduled standardized format. Fourth, determine which question sequence or sequences you might use. Pay particular attention to why you have made each of these decisions.
2. Watch several television interviews, and observe how they are opened. Which techniques are most common? How are these techniques related to relationships, interview types, situations, and length of interviews? Which nonverbal actions did you observe, and how did these affect the openings? How effective were rapport-building and orientation?
3. Watch several television interviews, and observe how they are closed. Which techniques are most common? How are these techniques related to relationships, interview types, situations, and length of interviews? Which nonverbal actions did you observe, and how did these affect the closings? Were there any false closings and, if so, how did the parties handle them and bring interviews to a close?
4. Record a televised interview of at least 10 to 15 minutes in length. Construct an interview guide from it. Which structural sequences did the interviewer use? Which type of question schedule do you think the interviewer used? Which question sequences did the interviewer employ? How do you think interview type, situation, relationship between parties, and issue affected the interviewer's choices?
5. Conduct one interview over the Internet and one face-to-face in which you focus on interview structure. How did the Internet affect interactions, particularly during the opening and closing? What did you do differently when preparing for these two interviews? Which mode of interviewing did you find most appealing and most difficult?

Notes

1. http://scit.ac.uk/university/scit/modules/cp4414/lectures/week3interview/sid021, accessed September 28, 2006.
2. George Gallup, "The Quintamensional Plan for Question Design," *Public Opinion Quarterly* 11 (1947), p. 385.

3. H. B. Beckman and R. M. Frankel, "The Effect of Physician Behavior on the Collection of Data," *Annals of Internal Medicine* (1984), pp. 692–696.
4. LaRay M. Barna, "Stumbling Blocks in Intercultural Communication," in Larry A. Samovar and Richard E. Porter, eds., *Intercultural Communication: A Reader* (Belmont, CA: Wadsworth, 1988), pp. 323–324.
5. Sarah Trenholm and Arthur Jensen, *Interpersonal Communication* (New York: Oxford University Press, 2008), p. 66.
6. Kory Floyd, *Interpersonal Communication: The Whole Story* (New York: McGraw-Hill, 2009), p. 241.
7. John Stewart, *Bridges Not Walls: A Book about Interpersonal Communication* (New York: McGraw-Hill, 2009), p. 186.
8. Lillian Glass, *He Says, She Says: Closing the Communication Gap between the Sexes* (New York: Putnam, 1993), pp. 45–59.
9. Mark L. Knapp, Roderick P. Hart, Gustav W. Friedrich, and Gary M. Shulman, "The Rhetoric of Goodbye: Verbal and Nonverbal Correlates of Human Leave-Taking," *Speech Monographs* 40 (1973), pp. 182–198.
10. Erving Goffman, *Relations in Public* (New York: Basic Books, 1971), p. 88.

Resources

Adler, Ronald B., and Jeanne Marquardt Elmhorst. *Communicating at Work: Principles and Practices for Business and the Professions*. New York: McGraw-Hill, 2008.

"Conducting the Information Interview: Module 5: Conducting the Interview," http://www.rogue.com/interview/module5.html, accessed April 21, 2009.

Knapp, Mark L., Roderick P. Hart, Gustav W. Friedrich, and Gary M. Shulman. "The Rhetoric of Goodbye: Verbal and Nonverbal Correlates of Human Leave-Taking," *Speech Monographs* 40 (1973), pp. 182–198.

Krivonos, Paul D., and Mark L. Knapp. "Initiating Communication: What Do You Say When You Say Hello?" *Central States Speech Journal* 26 (1975), pp. 115–125.

Sandberg, Anne. "Build an Interview: Interview Questions and Structured Interviewing," http://www.buildaninterview.com/interviewing_opening_and_closingremarks:asp, accessed April 21, 2009.

Zunin, Leonard, and Natalie Zunin. *Contact: The First Four Minutes*. London: Random House, 1986.

CHAPTER 5 The Informational Interview

The informational interview is the most common of interviews.

The **informational interview** is perhaps the most common form of interviewing because you participate in or observe informational interviews nearly every day. Journalists, recruiters, police officers, attorneys, counselors, supervisors, consumers, professors, and students, to name only a few, rely on them to obtain or transmit an infinite variety of facts, opinions, attitudes, feelings, and observations. The informational interview may be as brief and informal as a student asking a professor for clarification of a project's due date or as lengthy and formal as a journalist talking to a governor about a state's finances.

Regardless of length, formality, or setting, the **purpose** of the informational interview is to get relevant and timely information as accurately and completely as possible in the shortest amount of time. Gathering this information requires careful preparation questioning, insightful listening and observing, and skillful probing into answers to dig beneath surface information for facts, examples, stories, explanations, attitudes, and reactions. Unfortunately, few of us are trained in interviewing. Chip Scanlan (author of *Reporting and Writing: Basics for the 21st Century*) writes that even "journalists get little or no training in this vital aspect of their job. Most learn by painful trial and error."[1] This is the case in spite of the claim by many leading journalists that the interview "is quite possibly the most important step in the entire development and production of the article."[2]

Preparing the Interview

Thorough preparation is essential if you hope to conduct or take part effectively in an informational interview. There is no typical informational interview to serve as a model to follow because, as Eric Nalder the Pulitzer Prize winning chief investigative reporter for the *Seattle Times* writes, they are as varied as the conversations we have and the people we talk to.[3] Preparation consists of determining your goal, researching the topic, and structuring the interview. Scanlan describes interviewing as "a process, like writing, that involves a series of decisions and actions designed to get the best possible information."[4] The first step in this process is to determine your goal.

Your purpose controls how you prepare and what you do in informational interviews.

Determining Your Goal

Begin by deciding exactly *why* you are going to conduct an interview. What kinds of information do you want: facts, opinions, feelings, expert testimony, eyewitness accounts? A clear goal is essential in determining the length of an interview, selecting an interviewee, and deciding when and where to conduct the interview. Ken Metzler, a long-time professor of journalism at the University of Oregon, claims that when you know exactly what you want, "you're halfway there."[5]

The **situation** might constrict your goal. For instance, if the setting is a news conference or briefing, the interviewee party may dictate the types and numbers of questions you can ask, information available, whether some topics will be off the record, quotations you can attribute to the interviewee, and when you may report certain facts and opinions. Situational factors such as seriousness of a problem, availability of sources, and recency of an incident may determine the urgency of your interview, how long you will have to conduct it, and what you can ask ethically and legally.

The **product** of your interview (or series of interviews in some cases) may also affect your goal. If, for instance, you are preparing a field project for an interviewing course, a feature story for the 6:00 p.m. news, an investigative report on a shooting at a local factory, or a report on how employees feel about a new flexible work policy, this product may determine the number of interviews you conduct, the length of each interview, the persons you will interview, the types of information you will need, and the questions you will ask.

Researching the Topic

A thorough research of the topic serves five major functions in the informational interview. First, research enables you to determine what information is readily available from other sources so you do not waste valuable interview time. Why, for instance, would you ask simple biographical questions when such information is readily available on a Web site or in organizational literature? Helpful sources may include a course syllabus, journal or newspaper articles, the Internet, databases, annual reports, instructional manuals, court documents, archives, reference works, organizational records, and previous interviews. Some journalists claim that research time should be 10 times the actual interview time.[6]

The Internet and databases are essential resources for interviews.

Second, research may reveal areas of the topic that remain unaddressed and of particular interest to you, such as explanations, personal experiences, interpretations of data, the many sides of an issue, attitudes, and feelings. Research enables you to ask insightful questions and avoid **false assumptions** about events, causes and effects, and the willingness and ability of an interviewee to give accurate information.

Paying attention to omissions, dates, and interim events may help you focus the interview.

Third, be perceptive and critical about the pre-interview information you discover. Not everything in print, particularly on the Internet, is accurate and truthful. Many sources have hidden agendas that lead to shoddy data. Is the information you have the most recent available? Have sources changed their minds because of changing circumstances or experiences? Are newer studies available? What anecdotes or quotations might be important for your study, report, or story? Are quotations cited in sources taken out of context? Are there apparent inaccuracies, even in usually reliable sources?

Show interest in me, and I'll show interest in you.

Fourth, it is important during the interview that your questions reveal that you have done your homework to establish credibility with the interviewee. Eric Raymond and Rick Moen recommend that "when you ask your question, display the fact that you have done these things first; this will help establish that you're not being a lazy sponge and wasting people's time. Better yet, display what you have *learned* from doing these

ON THE WEB

Use the Internet to research your college or one that you might select as a graduate or professional school. Focus first on the college or university, then on the school or college within this larger structure, and finally on the department. What kinds of information are readily available? How up-to-date is the information? What kinds of information are not included that you would have to discover through interviews with faculty or students?

things."[7] Failure to do your homework and a show of ignorance on a topic or issue during an interview can destroy your credibility and embarrass you and your organization. Don't try to impress a person with your knowledge; let your knowledge and understanding of a topic reveal itself in your questions and reactions. You may phrase initial questions to reveal your familiarity with an area such as medicine, technology, the economy, military affairs, or history.

Fifth, evidence of your research shows you cannot be easily fooled and motivates interviewees to respond honestly, insightfully, and in depth. We tend to be flattered when others take the time to learn about us, our interests, fields, accomplishments, and opinions. We take pride in what we do and who we are. Know appropriate jargon and technical terms and use and pronounce them correctly. Know the respondent's name (and how it is pronounced), title, and organization. You should know if a person is a professor or an instructor, an editor or a reporter, a pilot or a navigator, a CEO or CFO,and a doctor with a PhD, MD, DVM, DDS, DO, or EdD degree.

Structuring the Interview

Interview Guide

As you research a topic, jot down areas and subareas that might evolve into an **interview guide.** The guide may be an elaborate outline, major aspects of a topic, key words in a notebook, or the traditional journalistic interview guide.

- *Who* was involved?
- *What* happened?
- *When* did it happen?
- *Where* did it happen?
- *How* did it happen?
- *Why* did it happen?

Length, sophistication, and importance of the interview will dictate the nature and details of the guide.

Plan a structural sequence but remain flexible.

Refer to the structural sequences discussed in Chapter 4. Chronological sequences are particularly effective in moving through stories or happenings because they have occurred in time sequences. A logical sequence such as cause-to-effect or problem-to-solution is appropriate for dealing with issues and crises. A space sequence is helpful when an interview will deal with places. Remain flexible because few informational interviews go exactly as planned.

Interview Schedule

A moderate schedule is a useful tool for long interviews.

If the interview will be brief or you are highly skilled in conducting informational interviews and phrasing questions, you may prepare only a guide and conduct a non-scheduled interview. If not, develop a moderate schedule that turns topics and subtopics into primary questions and provides possible probing questions under each.

A moderate schedule eliminates the necessity of creating each question at the moment of utterance and allows you to phrase questions carefully and precisely. At the same time, the moderate schedule allows **flexibility** to delete questions or create new ones as the need or opportunity arises. For instance, you may accidentally discover an issue or topic not detected during research or planning that warrants a detour.

You may fear that if you digress from the planned schedule or guide, you will lose your train of thought and control of the interview. These risks are worth taking, and the moderate schedule minimizes them. You can return to your schedule and pick up where you left off. Thomas Berner recommends that if a good question comes up in answer to another question, jot it down in the margin of your schedule and return to it when most appropriate.[8] The freedom to adapt and improvise makes the moderate schedule ideal for informational interviews.

Selecting Interviewees and Interviewers

Once you have determined a goal, conducted the necessary research, and structured a guide and schedule, select interviewees and decide who should conduct the interviews.

Selecting Interviewees

Your goal and the situation will determine the party or parties you will interview: an injured police officer, a witness to a fire at an oil refinery, a member of the state legislature, or a cancer survivor. In other situations, you may need to select from several police officers injured while on duty, a number of witnesses to an oil refinery fire, members of a state legislative committee, or several cancer survivors. It may be essential to interview experts on a subject or your goal may be to discover the differing points of view or experiences of laypersons. Use the following four criteria when selecting interviewees: level of information, availability, willingness, and ability.

Level of Information

Make sure your interviewee possesses the information you need.

The most important criterion is whether or not a party has the information you need. If so, what is the party's level of expertise through experiences, education, training, and positions? For instance, primary sources are those directly involved with the information you want, support sources are those with important connections to primary sources, and expert sources are those with superior knowledge or skills relating to the information you need.[9] Sometimes a goal is to assess a person's level of expertise. As an oral historian, you may want to interview a person who was actively involved in organizing a political

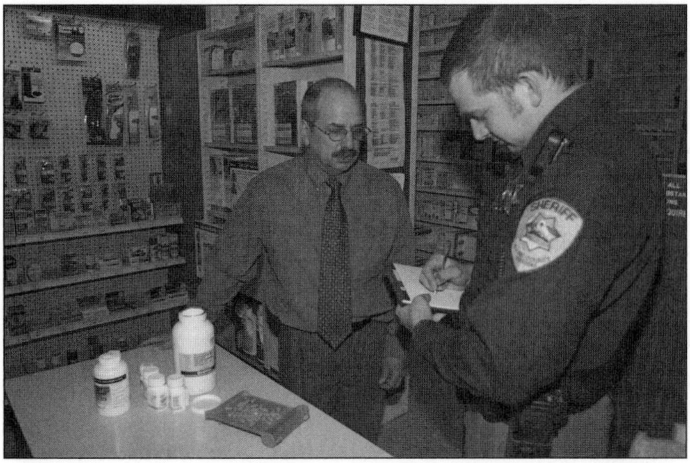

© Mikael Karlsson

Select interviewees with several criteria in mind.

rally for President John Kennedy, not merely a person who attended the rally. As a journalist, you may need to interview a CEO about a proposed merger, not an employee.

Raymond Gorden writes about **key informants** who can supply information on local situations, assist in selecting and contacting knowledgeable interviewees, and aid in securing their cooperation.[10] Discover who these people are and how they might assist in selecting respondents. A key informant might be a family member, friend, fellow member of a student organization, employer, or aide.

Availability

Do not assume a potential interviewee is unavailable; ask.

A source might be too far away, available only for a few minutes when you need an in-depth interview, or unavailable until after a deadline. Consider the telephone, videoconference, or e-mail before giving up on a source. And never assume a person is unavailable. Stories abound among journalists and researchers about famous interviews that occurred merely because interviewers asked for interviews or were persistent in asking. You may talk yourself out of an interview by being certain the person will not talk—a self-fulfilling prophecy: "You don't have time to talk, do you?"

Consider a possible go-between, Gorden's key informant, such as a mutual friend or associate, an aide, or the public relations department. You might go to where a person works, lives, or plays rather than expect the person to come to you. Sometimes an interviewee will ask to see some or all of your questions in advance. Be careful of excessive demands about topics, questions, off-limit subjects, and off-the-record comments that may make the person no longer a viable party. Meeting such demands may destroy the spontaneity of the interview.

Willingness

Fear of what may be revealed in an interview might make participants reluctant.

Potential respondents may be unwilling to meet with you for a variety of reasons. They may mistrust you or your organization, profession, or position. They may fear that information they give will harm them, their organizations, or significant others, particularly because of inaccurate reporting, hidden agendas, or sensationalism prevalent in many news sources. They may feel the information you want is no one else's business or that it is unimportant and therefore a waste of time.[11] In short, a respondent may feel there is nothing in the interview that warrants the time and risks involved. Lawsuits materialize today over almost anything a person might say or not say, and organizations are particularly fearful of being sued for millions. They control persons who can speak for them. Those who have dealt with the press and investigators recall times when they were misquoted, taken out of context, had information reported erroneously, or ended up being the focus of a report they thought would involve many people.

You may have to convince interviewees that you can be trusted for confidentiality, accuracy, thoroughness, and fair reporting. Parties are likely to cooperate if they have an interest in you, the topic, or the outcome of the interview. Point out why their interests will be better served if information and attitudes are known. Sometimes you may have to employ a bit of arm-twisting such as "If you don't talk to us, we'll have to rely on other sources" or "The other parties involved have already told their sides of the incident. Are you certain you do not want us to hear yours?" Be careful of threats. They can ruin an interview, damage a relationship, and preclude future contacts. Be wary of persons who are too eager to be interviewed. Consider their motivations and reputations.

Resort to arm-twisting as a last resort.

Ability

Is the potential interviewee able to transmit information freely and accurately? Several problems may make a person unacceptable: poor memory, failing health, state of shock, biases or prejudices, habitual lying, proneness to exaggeration or oversimplification, and repression of horrific memories. Elderly witnesses may remember events very differently than they really were. A father or mother grieving over the loss of a child (and confronted with recorders, interviewers, lights, and cameras) may be unable to focus on details. Interviewers often expect persons to relate minute details and exact timing of events that took place months or years before, when most of us have trouble recalling what we did yesterday.

Many potential interviewees are willing but unable.

If time permits, get to know each interviewee ahead of time. Learn about the person's accomplishments, personality, reputation, biases, interests, and interviewing traits. How skilled is the person at responding to (and evading) questions? Many persons are interviewed daily, and a growing number have taken intensive courses in which they have learned how to confront interviewers, use humor to evade questions, and phrase ambiguous answers that reveal little or nothing. Eugene Webb and Jerry Salancik write that the interviewer "in time, should know" a "source well enough to be able to know when a distortion is occurring, from a facial expression that doesn't correspond to a certain reply."[12]

Some interviewees study how to respond, evade, and confront.

Selecting Interviewers

Eric Nalder claims that the number one trait of an ideal journalist, or any informational interviewer, is curiosity about everyone and everything. Similarly, Ken Metzler claims "the best interviewers are those who enjoy people and are eager to learn more about the people they meet—and who are eternally curious about darned near everything."[13] Along with curiosity, the interviewer should be friendly, courteous, organized, observant, patient, persistent, and skillful.

A situation may require an interviewer of a certain age, gender, race, ethnic group, religion, political party, or educational level. A 70-year-old interviewer might find it as difficult to relate to a teenager as a teenager would to the 70-year-old. A woman might confide more readily to a female interviewer than to a male interviewer. An interviewer of Haitian ancestry might be more effective with Hatian immigrants because of common culture, traditions, and communication customs.

Status difference and similarity affect motivation, freedom to respond, control, and rapport.

Status difference or **similarity** between interviewer and interviewee may offer unique advantages for the interviewer. When an interviewer is *subordinate* to an interviewee (student to professor, hourly worker to manager, vice president to president):

- The interviewer does not have to be an expert.
- The interviewee will not feel threatened.
- The interviewee will feel freer to speak.
- The interviewee might want to help the interviewer.

Famous NBC news correspondent, anchor, and host David Brinkley remarked in a PBS interview that he welcomed the opportunity to meet with journalism students and young reporters in his office, to show them around the studio, and to discuss the academic background needed to be effective reporters.

When an interviewer is *superior* to the interviewee (captain to sergeant, CEO to division head, physician to nurse practitioner):

- The interviewer can control the interview.
- The interviewer can reward the interviewee.
- The interviewee may feel motivated to please the interviewer.
- The interviewee may feel honored to be a participant.

Some organizations give high-status-sounding titles to representatives to enhance their superior aura: chief correspondent rather than correspondent, vice president instead of sales director, editor rather than reporter, executive rather than supervisor.

Status is a critical criterion for some interviewees.

When the interviewer is *equal* to the interviewee (student to student, associate to associate, researcher to researcher):

- Rapport is easily established.
- There are fewer communication barriers.
- There are fewer pressures.
- A high degree of empathy is possible.

In many situations, we prefer to be interviewed by people similar to us in a variety of ways, including gender, age, education level, and professional field. Some interviewees will not grant interviews to organizations or people they perceive to be of lower status. If they are senior U.S. senators, for instance, they expect the newspaper or network to send its senior correspondent.

Relationship of Interviewer and Interviewee

Be aware of the relational history of the parties.

By the time you have researched and selected interviewees and interviewers, you should have an accurate picture of the **relationship** that will exist during the interview. Robert Ogles and other journalism professors note, for example, that journalistic interviews rely on "secondary relationships" that are nonintimate and limited to one or very few relational dimensions.[14] These dimensions tend to be more functional than emotional and rely on surface cues such as obvious similarities, appearance, and nonverbal behavior.

Many informational interviews involve all of the relational dimensions discussed in Chapter 2. Be aware of perceived similarities and differences of both parties.

- To what extent does each want to be *included and involved* in this interview?
- To what degree do the parties *like and respect* one another?
- How much *control or dominance* is each party likely to exert or try to exert during the interview?
- What is the level of *trust between the parties?*

A positive relationship is critical to the success of the simplest interviews because they tend to delve into beliefs, attitudes, values, feelings, and inner secrets.

Opening the Interview

Having completed your research, developed a guide and schedule of questions, selected an interviewee and an interviewer (presumably you), and determined the relationship that exists between the parties, you are now ready to create an effective opening. Plan the opening with great care because the level of trust between and your interviewee begins immediately with the way you look, the way you act, how you sound, the words you use, the comments you make, and the questions you ask.[15] Be respectful. Metzler and others comment on the importance of small talk, icebreaker questions, and friendly comments that enable both parties to establish rapport and to get ready for the body of the interview.

A solid opening is essential in motivating an interviewee.

You may not be good at such "informalities" so you might overprepare so they sound trite, mechanical, or staged. Do not be too familiar with the interviewee. Are you really on a first name or nickname basis? If you are a stranger, identify yourself, your position, and the organization you represent. Even if you are well known to another, explain *what* you wish to discuss and *why,* reveal how the information will be *employed,* and state *how long* the interview will take. Don't pull out a notebook or produce a recorder immediately because these can threaten an interviewee.

Consider an icebreaker question about something you have noticed in the interviewee's office or about hobbies, interests, or a news item. Congratulate the person on a recent recognition or accomplishment. Insert something humorous that you discovered in your research or encountered in planning the interview. Refer tactfully to the interviewee's position on an issue. Icebreaker questions and comments create interest in the interview and get people talking and ready to discuss substantive questions and issues. Don't begin with difficult or potentially embarrassing questions. Raymond and Moen warn, "Beware of asking the wrong question." Prepare the opening question carefully: "Think it through. Hasty sounding questions get hasty answers, or none at all. The more you do to demonstrate that having put thought and effort into solving your problem before seeking help, the more likely you are to actually get help."

Review the opening techniques discussed in Chapter 4 and select one or a combination best suited for this interview. Don't fall into the habit of using the same opening for every occasion.

Design the opening to fit each occasion and interviewee.[16] A casual compliment, friendly remark about a topic or mutual friend, or a bit of small talk might create a friendly, relaxed atmosphere with one person and produce the opposite effect with a busy, hassled interviewee who neither likes nor has time for small talk. As we discussed in Chapter 2, establishing a positive relationship between interviewer and interviewee is critical to the success of every interview. Try to establish a "friendly conversational rapport, like old friends talking" without seeming to be too friendly or close. Enhance the relationship, but don't try to leap beyond it.[17] Avoid any semblance of artificiality in the opening.

Know what "off the record" means to both parties.

Be sure both parties have a mutual understanding of **ground rules** governing the interaction before proceeding past the opening. This is particularly important in investigative interviews conducted by police officers, journalists, and supervisors. If everything of importance is **off the record,** why conduct the interview? Make it clear there can be no retroactive off-the-record demands. Be sure both parties understand what "off the record" means. It may mean not naming the source or using information only as background. If a person does not want to be quoted, try to get agreement that quotations may be attributed to an unnamed source or worked into the text of a report without attribution.

Conducting the Interview

The goal of the informational interview is to get in-depth and insightful information that only an interviewee can offer. It is essential, then, to get beyond superficial and safe Level 1 interactions to riskier and deeper Level 2 and Level 3 interactions. You must **motivate** an interviewee to disclose beliefs, attitudes, and feelings as well as unknown facts.

Motivating Interviewees

There are many reasons why a person might be reluctant to talk to you or to communicate beyond Level 1 if an interview takes place.[18] An interviewee may have been "burned" in previous interviews such as this one or by interviewers from your organization, by interviewers like you, or by you. Your negative or threatening reputation may precede you. An interviewee may see the interview as posing a risk to self-image, credibility with others, or to a career. Perhaps the interview is seen as an invasion of privacy or posing the danger of opening up areas the interviewee may prefer to remain forgotten or unknown. And the interviewee may not want to be interviewed on any subject. On the other hand, be careful of interviewees who appear to be too eager to take part and reveal secrets. They may be after publicity, exposure, an ego-trip, a chance to sell a product or idea, or to get even with someone or an organization.

Know what motivates each interviewee.

Interviewees are likely to communicate beyond Level 1 if you adhere to simple guidelines that follow the golden rule: *do unto others as you would have them do unto you.* This rule applies to the most difficult of interview situations. A report about interrogation interviews with insurgents in Iraq and Afghanistan noted that "the successful interrogators all had one thing in common in the way they approached their subjects. They were nice to them."[19] Parties are likely to communicate freely and accurately if they trust you to react with understanding and tact, maintain confidences, use the

Trust is essential for informational interviews.

information fairly, and report what they say accurately and completely. Ken Metzler recommends that we avoid the term *interview* and call it a conversation, talk, discussion, or chat. He also advises us to "drop names" of people the interviewee respects that may serve as credibility enhancers and motivators.

Don't have an *attitude.* From the opening until the interview ends, show sincere interest in and enthusiasm for the interviewee, the topic, and answers. Don't state or imply how you feel about answers and issues; be neutral. Control the interview without interrupting and look for natural pauses to probe or to ask primary questions rather than interrupt the interviewee. Ask questions rather than make statements. Be a good listener not only with your ears but your eyes, face, nods, and attentive posture. Metzler writes, "It's not the questions you ask that make for a successful interview but the attention you pay to the answers you receive." Some experienced interviewers recommend listening to the interviewee 100 percent of the time.[20] Avoid tricks, gimmicks, and deceptions.

Asking Questions

Questions are not just the tools of the trade, but are critical in motivating interviewees to provide the information and insights needed. Unfortunately, interviewers tend to ask too many questions, and this limits their opportunities to listen, observe, and think. Too often interviewers are or appear to be arrogant or assume they "are *entitled* to an answer." Raymond and Moen declare, "You aren't, after all, paying for the service. You will earn an answer, if you earn it, by asking a substantial, interesting, and thought-provoking question—one that implicitly contributes to the experience of the community rather than merely passively demanding knowledge from others."

Ask Open-Ended Questions

Listening is as important as asking.

Open questions motivate and encourage interviewees to communicate, particularly in the opening minutes. Thorough answers to open-ended questions allow you to listen appropriately (for comprehension, empathy, evaluation, resolution) and observe the interviewee's mannerisms, appearance, and nonverbal communication. Listening and observing help determine the accuracy and relevance of answers and how the interviewee feels about the situation and the topic. A raised eyebrow or a slight hesitancy of a respondent from another culture, for instance, may signal that you used a slang phrase, colloquialism, or oxymoron with which this person is unfamiliar or that sounds strange.

Make the interviewee the star of the show.

Closed questions result in the interviewer talking more while listening and observing less. If you find yourself asking question after question and doing most of the work in an interview, you are asking too many closed questions and trying to guess information rather than ask for it. Be *patient* and *persistent.* Do not interrupt a respondent unless the person is obviously off target, evading a question, or promises to continue answering forever.

Ask Probing Questions

The flexible nature of the informational interview requires a full range of probing questions. Metzler writes that "probes—followup questions—are essential. Its seldom the first question that gets to the heart of the matter, it's the seventh, or maybe 16th question you didn't know you were going to ask but have chosen to ask because of your careful, thoughtful listening." Use **silent** and **nudging probes** to encourage an interviewee to continue. Respondents tend to state the first thing that comes to mind, or give a short answer and stop. Silence or a head nod, a smile, or a simple verbal nudge such as "uh-huh," "yeah," or "interesting" encourages an interviewee to continue, to elaborate with details, opinions, or feelings. Use **informational probes** when you detect cues in answers or need additional information or explanation. They resolve superficial and suggestive answers. Use **restatement probes** when interviewees do not answer the question you asked. Use **reflective** and **mirror questions** to verify and clarify answers and to check for accuracy and understanding. Use **clearinghouse probes** before proceeding to new topics to be sure you have obtained everything of importance to your story or report. Metzler suggests asking **metaphorical questions,** such as "Governor, do you hope to hit a home run with this legislative proposal?" to motivate interviewees to expand answers in an interesting and understandable manner. You cannot plan for every piece of information or insight an interviewee might have. Some journalists advise that "even if you go into an interview armed with a list of questions, the most important probably will be ones you ask in response to an answer."[21] For instance, if an interviewee says something surprising or reveals a secret, follow this lead to see where it will take you, perhaps asking a series of questions you never thought to ask. Then you can go back to your schedule and continue as planned until the next lead comes along. An inflexible informational interviewer will miss opportunities to gain valuable insights and information.

Be an active listener, not a passive sponge.

When asking questions and probing into answers, be courteous, friendly, tactful, and nonargumentative. Be understanding when delving into sensitive or personal areas. Be prepared to back off if an interviewee becomes emotionally upset or angry. There are times when you need to pry into potentially embarrassing areas such as the nature of an illness, marital problems, organizational finances, or an arrest.

Persistent probing is essential in informational interviews, but you must know when to stop. An interviewee may become agitated, confused, or silent if you probe too far. This exchange occurred between an attorney and a physician:[22]

Know when enough is enough.

Attorney: Doctor, before you performed the autopsy, did you check for a pulse?

Physician: No.

Attorney: Did you check for blood pressure?

Physician: No.

Attorney: Did you check for breathing?

Physician: No.

Attorney: So, then it is possible that the patient was alive when you began the autopsy?

Physician: No.

Attorney: How can you be so sure, Doctor?

Physician: Because his brain was sitting on my desk in a jar.

Attorney: But could the patient have still been alive nevertheless?

Physician: It is possible that he could be alive practicing law somewhere.

Be persistent and patient, but know when to stop. Listen, observe, and think.

Because informational interviews necessitate creating many questions on the spot, you may fall easily into common question pitfalls discussed in Chapter 3. Review these carefully: the bipolar trap, the tell me everything, the open-to-closed switch, the double-barreled inquisition, the leading push, the guessing game, the yes (no) response, the curious probe, the quiz show, the don't ask, don't tell, and complexity vs. simplicity. Remember the rules: (1) think before asking, (2) stop when you've asked a good question, and (3) use bipolar or leading questions sparingly and for specific purposes. Know the pitfalls well enough that you can catch yourself before stumbling into one. The following good and bad examples will sharpen question skills.

Even the most seasoned interviewer can stumble into a pitfall when unaware.

- The bipolar trap:

  Bad: Do you think the new General Motors will be more successful than the old General Motors?

  Good: How successful do you think the new General Motors will be compared to the old?

- The tell me everything:

  Bad: Tell me about your internship in Australia this past summer.

  Good: Tell me about your major duties during the internship in Australia this past summer.

- The open-to-closed switch:

  Bad: How has your leg injury affected your plans for graduation this year? Has it delayed them?

  Good: How has your leg injury affected your plans for graduation this year?

- The double-barreled inquisition:

  Bad: What are your travel plans for this summer and fall?

  Good: What are your travel plans for this summer?

- The leading push:

  Bad: You're going to change stock brokers, aren't you?

  Good: What are your thoughts about changing stock brokers?

- The guessing game:

  Bad: Did you go in for a physical checkup because you were concerned about your blood pressure?

  Good: Why did you go in for a physical checkup?

- The yes (no) response:

  Bad: Do you want to have a heart attack?

  Good: What are you doing to prevent a heart attack?

- The curious probe:

  Bad: (in a political survey) How often do you attend a religious service?

  Good: How might your religious beliefs affect your choice of presidential candidate?

- The quiz show:

  Bad: (in a recruiting interview) Our newest hotel property is located in the little town of French Lick, Indiana. Do you know the name of the famous NBA star who grew up there?

  Good: What do you know about our newest hotel property located in the small town of French Lick, Indiana?

- The don't ask, don't tell:

  Bad: Your father was a great college quarterback, and so were you and your brother Zack. Would you say you were the best quarterback in the family?

  Good: How would you compare your quarterback skills with those of your father and brother?

- Complexity vs. simplicity:

  Bad: (in a congressional hearing) Mr. Henry, it seems like Canada has developed something with the participation of industry. So industry came in and participated in developing the code and practices, as I understand it, that is tailored to the different industry that applies. Did you find that industry's participation made it less burdensome? I mean, that relationship, did that make it palatable for them to take an all-encompassing law? I mean, you might give us just a little . . . (The Interviewee cut in and answered the essence of the question before it became even more complicated and confusing.)[23]

  Good: How did industry's participation in the process improve privacy legislation in Canada?

Work on the phrasing of each question, including unplanned probing questions, to make each brief and to the point while avoiding common question pitfalls. Then give the interviewee your undivided attention.

All rules are made to be broken, but you must know when and how.

Sometimes you must break the rules to get information you want. It may be necessary to ask an obvious question even when you know the answer in advance, such as "I see you like to hike" when it is listed on an application form. Seemingly obvious questions can relax respondents by getting them to talk about things that are well known and easy to talk about and by showing interest in topics important to interviewees. A leading push such as "Come on, surely you don't believe that?" may provoke a respondent into an exciting and revealing interchange. Be cautious when asking leading questions of children. Several studies have shown that children are susceptible to such questions because they "are very attuned to taking cues from adults and tailoring their answers based on the way questions are worded."[24] You may ask a double-barreled question at a press conference to get two or three answers because it may be the only question you get to ask. A bipolar question will produce a yes or no for the record, a common need in medical interviews.

Know what you are doing and why.

Phrase questions carefully to avoid confusion. The following interaction between a patient and a physician illustrates the dangers of jargon and sound-alike words:

Physician: Have you ever had a history of cardiac arrest in your family?

Patient: We never had no trouble with the police.

Some interviewees will answer questions about which they have no knowledge, faking it rather than admitting ignorance. Others are experts on everything and nothing. Listen to call-in programs on radio to hear people make incredibly uninformed or misinformed claims, accusations, and observations. Sometimes interviewees will play funny games, such as this exchange that took place during an election campaign in New Hampshire:

Reporter: How are you going to vote on Tuesday?

Resident: How am I going to vote? Oh, the usual way. I'm going to take the form they hand me and put x's in the appropriate boxes (laughing).

Reporter: (pause) Who are you going to vote for on Tuesday?

Think before asking.

Listen to answers to avoid embarrassments such as the following exchange between an attorney and a witness:

Attorney: Now, Mrs. Johnson, how was your first marriage terminated?

Witness: By death.

Attorney: And by whose death was it terminated?

Think before asking probing questions that you have not prepared in advance. For instance, Ken Metzler recommends avoiding the "how do you feel about that" question because "It's the most trite, overused question in American journalism and sources begin to hate it after time." Interviewees often respond with brief answers such as "Okay," "Not bad," or "As good as might be expected" that tell you nothing. It's a vague answer to a routine question.[25] Metzler suggests substituting "What were you thinking when . . . ?" for the "feel" question.

Weigh carefully the pros and cons of note taking prior to the interview.

Note Taking and Recording

Although experts on informational interviewing disagree on the extent of note taking and the use of electronic recorders because each can be intrusive and unreliable, it is wise to use the means best suited to you, the interviewee, the situation, and the report

Effective note taking entails maintaining eye contact as much as possible.

you will prepare. Be aware that extensive note taking and recording may inhibit the free and accurate flow of information but also that lack of note taking or recording may make it impossible to recall figures, dates, names, times, and details and to reproduce quotations accurately. Only a recorder can provide a complete record of *how, when, and what* answers were given.

Note Taking

Note taking has three advantages. *First,* note taking increases your attention to what is being said and how. This enhanced attention shows respondents you are interested in what they are saying and are concerned about accuracy. William Zinsser writes that this direct involvement allows the interviewee to see you working and doing your job.[26] *Second,* when taking notes, you do not have to worry about a machine breaking down, running out of space, or batteries going dead at a critical moment. *Third,* listening to entire recordings of interviews to pick out important bits of information is time-consuming, and transcriptions are costly in time and money. On the other hand, if you take notes according to the structure of the interview, you have your notes clearly organized when the interview ends.

Note taking should not threaten the interviewee.

Note taking also has disadvantages. You can rarely take notes fast enough to record exactly what was said. Respondents often speak rapidly. It is difficult to concentrate on questions and answers and to maintain eye contact while writing notes, so you may fail to hear or probe into an answer because you are busy writing rather than listening. Note taking may hamper the flow of information because interviewees may become fearful or curious about what you are writing. Often people are reluctant to talk while you are writing or feel a break in communication while you are focusing on your pad instead of them.

In an in-depth interview with a newspaper publisher, one of our students discovered that whenever she began to write, the interviewee would stop answering until she stopped writing, apparently to let her catch up. Before long, he arranged his chair so he could see what she was writing. Follow these guidelines when taking notes during interviews.

- Preserve communication by taking notes as inconspicuously as possible.
- Maintain eye contact with the interviewee.
- Use abbreviations or a form of professional or personal shorthand so you do not have to write full words and sentences.

- Write down only important information, perhaps key words, to reduce the amount of note taking.
- Do not signal what you think is critically important or a "bombshell" quotation by taking notes frantically during a particular interaction. Wait until the interviewee is answering another question—perhaps a less important or "throwaway" question—before recording the answer or your reactions.

Maintain communication while taking notes.

- If the interviewee is speaking more rapidly than you can take accurate notes, ask the interviewee tactfully to slow down, repeat answers, or use "stalling questions" such as "Tell me more about" that will provide time to get caught up.[27]
- Reduce interviewee curiosity or concern by asking permission to take notes, explaining why notes are necessary for both parties, and showing your notes occasionally to check accuracy. Eric Nalder says this tactic also allows interviewees to fill in blanks and volunteer information.
- Ensure accuracy of your notes by reviewing them immediately after the interview to fill in the gaps, complete abbreviations, and translate your handwriting and shorthand.

Recording

Recording allows interviewers to listen and probe more effectively.

Recording also has advantages. *First,* a recorder enables you to relax, concentrate on what is being said and implied, and then create effective probing questions. *Second,* you can hear or watch what was said and how it was said hours or days afterward. For example, the authors began to record student interviews in class because they discovered they had often missed important questions and answers while they were taking notes and filling out critique forms. *Third,* a recorder may pick up answers that were inaudible at the time. *Fourth,* a recorder gives you an accurate record of the content of the interview.

A recorder may add an intrusive element to the interview.

Ask permission before using a recorder.

Recording has a number of disadvantages. *First,* recorders can malfunction or prove tricky to use. Batteries can go dead at the wrong time, and disks can be defective. A number of our students have used recorders during lengthy interviews for class projects only to discover disks or memory sticks were blank when they tried to review them later. *Second,* some people view recorders as intruders in intimate interviewing situations. *Third,* recordings provide permanent, undeniable records that threaten people with unknown future consequences. Some interviewers such as police officers and insurance claims investigators are required to record interviews. *Fourth,* it takes a great deal of time to review a lengthy recording to locate facts, reactions, and ideal quotes while it may take only seconds to locate the same material in written notes.

Follow these guidelines when recording interviews.[28]

- Reduce interviewee fears and objections by explaining why the recorder is advantageous to the interviewee, telling why you want or need to use a recorder and how the recording will be used, and offering to turn off the recorder when desired.
- Reduce mechanical difficulties by testing the recorder prior to the interview and taking extra batteries disks, or sticks.

- Be thoroughly familiar with the recorder and practice with it in a simulated interview before the real things.
- Research appropriate state laws before using a hidden recorder or recording interviews over the telephone. The law generally allows one party to record a second party (no third parties) without permission, but 12 states prohibit the recording of conversations without the consent of both parties, including California, Connecticut, Florida, Illinois, Maryland, Massachusetts, Michigan, Montana, Nevada, New Hampshire, Pennsylvania, and Washington.[29] If you are interviewing over the telephone, be aware of which states are involved; you, the other party, or both may be in one of the 12 states with restrictive laws. An excellent source on legal aspects of interviewing is a guide published by the *Reporters Committee for Freedom of the Press* (http://www.rcip.org).
- It is always wise to ask permission before recording an interview to avoid possible lawsuits and to establish and maintain goodwill.

Handling Difficult Situations

You will encounter many difficult and unexpected interviewing situations, but you can manage these situations if you plan in advance.

A Sanitized vs. a Real Setting

It is easier to interview persons in pleasant surroundings such as private offices, homes, parks, and restaurants than in real-life settings where the action is. The field interview, however, is often essential to understanding an event, problem, or persons. Most memorable interviews take place at the scenes of hurricanes, terrorist bombings, fires, plant accidents, building sites, commencements, and labor strikes. Interviewers go into prisons, hospitals, nursing homes, factories, stadiums, and neighborhoods or ride along with police officers, taxi drivers, EMTs, and salespersons to experience as well as interview. Eric Nalder claims that it is essential to interview people "at the place where they are doing the thing that you are writing about." It is important not only to *hear* answers but to *see* and get the *feel* of things. When Nalder was writing a book on oil tankers, for instance, a member of a crew told him he could not understand crews and oil tankers unless he was on board in the Gulf of Alaska during the violent seas of January "puking your guts out." He took this advice and got the most insightful interviews and feelings for his book because of his experiences and relationships with a crew.

You may need to feel and experience before you can ask meaningful questions.

In **unsanitized settings,** prepare for human suffering, emotional outbursts or reticence, destruction, filthy settings, and threats to health and safety. Be flexible in structure. Be sensitive in questions and actions. Too often reporters, insurance investigators, and representatives of government agencies intrude into medical emergencies, catastrophes, and people's lives. Know where the interviewee's right to privacy and dignity begins and ends.

Use good sense and good judgment in probing interviews.

The Press Conference or Group Interview

The **press conference** or **group interview** limits interviewer control over the situation. The interviewee may announce when and where the interview will take place and impose ground rules such as length and topics allowed. Protocol may enable the

The interviewee usually controls the press conference.

The broadcast interview presents unique problems for both parties.

interviewee or a staff member to end the interview without warning, perhaps to avoid or escape a difficult exchange. You may or may not get to ask prepared questions or have an opportunity to probe into answers. Listen carefully to answers other interviewers receive because they might provide valuable information and suggest questions to ask.

Your relationship with the interviewee at a press conference is critical. If the interviewee likes, respects, and trusts you, you may be picked from among several interviewers to ask questions. If a relationship is hostile, an interviewee may refuse to recognize you or give a vague, superficial, or hostile answer and turn quickly to another interviewer to evade follow-up questions. It may be necessary to ask a double-barreled question because it may be your only question opportunity.

The Broadcast Interview

The media interview presents unique problems. Being on real or figurative stages may cause one or both parties to be extremely nervous or to engage in performing for audiences, cameras, and microphones. Become familiar with the physical setting, including possible seating for interviewer and the interviewee, audio and video equipment, technicians, and program format and purpose. Pay close attention to the briefing concerning time limits, beginning and closing signals, and microphone use, levels, and locations. Adequate preparation reduces nervousness and enhances efficiency and performance. By being on the air, in newspapers, or on the Internet, there is an outside force, a third party, in broadcast interviews. This force or party is the viewer, listener, or reader, and some sources claim this makes the broadcast interview a "three-way interaction" because both interviewer and interviewee are aware of this party and may adapt questions and answers to it.[30]

In most broadcast interviews, you will need to obtain answers, statements, reactions, sound, and pictures that will replay well over the air. Some sources recommend that you use a headset so you can determine sound quality more accurately and be aware of unwanted background noises such as traffic, ringing telephones, heating and cooling systems, bells in clock towers, and nearby interactions. Position the microphone approximately seven to nine inches from the interviewee's mouth and to the side so it is less obtrusive for the interviewee and the recording avoids a "mugging" quality. Nudging probes should be head nods rather than oral utterances such as "uh huh," "ummm," and "I see." In oral history interviews and many investigative interviews, begin by stating your name, the interviewee's name, place, time, and date of the interview.[31]

Being familiar with the physical setting can eliminate many surprises.

Deadlines and time limitations require questions that are direct, to the point, and moderately open. You may normally have several minutes, an hour, or more to discuss a problem with a source, customer, or employee, but a broadcast interaction may last no longer than seconds or a few minutes. Fred Fedler warns that "the live [broadcast] interview usually lasts just a few minutes and allows little chance to ask challenging questions."[32] Know questions well enough to ask them from memory or from a few small cards because forms or lists of questions may make noise or cast an awkward, amateurish, unprepared appearance. If you want the interview to be spontaneous, do not provide questions prior to the broadcast.

Spontaneous questions generate spontaneous answers.

Some utterances and actions cannot be broadcast or may be embarrassing, such as profanities, obscene gestures, poor grammar, too many "uhs," "you knows," "know what I means," and excessive "blood and gore." Some newspaper reporters, when being crowded out by cameras and microphones, shout obscenities to shut down their electronic counterparts and get closer to the action. A state legislator told one of the authors that he would purposely insert profanities into answers to prevent reporters from using them on the air.

Those involved in broadcast interviews must be aware of and skilled in "staging" interviews. For instance, framing shots is important, so the interviewer (or director) will decide whether the interviewer and interviewee will face the camera left or right, whether shots will be mid-shot or medium close-ups, and whether to select a sequence of shots. At the same time, the interview parties must make decisions about lighting, props, backgrounds, eyelines (interviewee's eyes level with the interviewer's), and studio setting. All of these decisions make the broadcast interview more complex than a simple face-to-face interview.[33]

The Videoconference Interview

As mentioned in Chapter 1, the videoconference interview is becoming increasingly common as a means of communicating long distances quickly, efficiently, and inexpensively. Unfortunately, few interviewers or interviewees have training or experience in using or being subjected to video cameras. Videoconferences share similarities with face-to-face interviews, but there are differences you need to understand and practice. A Boston College Web site offers these suggestions for video interviewing.[34]

- **Hesitate slightly** before asking or answering questions because there is typically a slight delay in receiving the audio and video.
- **Look straight into the monitor** so you appear to be looking into the interviewer's or interviewee's eyes.
- **Focus on the interviewer or interviewee** so you can become comfortable with the video interview situation.
- **Avoid excessive motion or stiffness** so you appear relaxed and enjoying a pleasant conversation.
- **Speak naturally** without shouting because the microphone will pick up your voice, and you need not lean into the microphone to be heard.
- **Show energy and enthusiasm** through your voice and face (including smiling) because you will appear as a "talking head," no more than from the waist up.

Other suggestions include wearing solid and neutral color clothing. Both cameras and interview parties have problems focusing on the interview when parties are wearing plaids, stripes, or white shirts and jackets. Avoid noises that are particularly distracting in videoconferences, such as tapping on a desk, moving papers, or jewelry that makes audible sounds. Glittery jewelry may catch light and be distracting to interview parties. Remember to smile because the videoconference enables you to talk face-to-face.[35]

Handling Difficult Interviewees

Informational interviews delve into feelings, attitudes, and reasons for actions, so they may hit raw nerves and evoke reactions ranging from tears and hostility to an interviewee stopping the interview. The settings of disasters, crimes, election defeats, losses in sporting events, memorial ceremonies, deaths, and scandals are tense, emotional, and embarrassing. Be prepared to handle difficult interviewees in difficult situations. As journalist Bob Steele warns, "If we aren't proficient at asking the right questions at the right time, we'll miss on accuracy, fall short on context, and stumble on fairness."

Emotional Interviewees

Silence is often better than talk with emotional interviewees.

Respondents may burst into tears during interviews. The problem is not helped when others exclaim, "Oh, God!" or "Now, stop that!" or when interviewers blurt out, "I know just how you feel." Reactions such as the following may help if they are tactful and sincere.

It's okay to cry.
Take your time.
Do you need a few minutes?

Remain silent until a person regains composure and is ready to continue. If you have a close relationship with an interviewee, you may hold the person's hand or place an arm across the shoulders as comforting gestures.

Treat others as you would like to be treated.

Be sensitive to people who have experienced tragedies and do not invade their privacy merely for pictures or tearful comments for news broadcast, data, or curiosity. How we broach a sensitive topic at a sensitive time is a serious ethical issue in journalistic and other informational interviews.[36] Reporters are notorious for asking thoughtless questions such as, "How do you feel about your child's death?" or "Is the family devastated by this tragedy?" John and Denise Bittner suggest that you ask only direct and necessary questions at such times. "Remember, people in crisis situations are under a great deal of stress," they write. "A prolonged interview won't provide additional information; it will only upset people."[37] The dangers of insensitive interviewing were illustrated when a CNN interviewer grilled the mother of a missing boy on national television. She challenged her alibi, demanding to know where she was at the time, what she was doing, and why she wasn't providing specifics about stores she visited and items she purchased. Shortly after the interview, the mother committed suicide. Local media speculated that the CNN interviewer had "pushed her over the edge."[38]

Hostile Interviewees

If you detect hostility, determine if it is real or imagined. If it is real, discover why. A person may feel angry, depressed, helpless, or frightened because of circumstances beyond his or her control, and you become a convenient target for releasing feelings. Hostility may be toward you, your organization, your position or profession, or the way information may be used. Bad experiences with similar interviewers or ones from your organization may lead an interviewee to expect the worst from you. The person may simply be having a bad day because of traffic, a headache, a computer glitch, a late appointment.

A *nondirective interviewing approach* such as the following might reveal the source or cause of hostility.

You appear to be very angry this morning.
You seem very upset; would you like to talk about it?
Do I detect hostility toward your attorney?

Large male interviewers often appear threatening to interviewees.

You may avoid hostility by *not* making unwarranted demands, invading a person's territory or personal space, or allowing your physical presence and manner to appear threatening. You can reduce or avoid creating hostility during interviews.

- Do not intentionally or unintentionally mislead the interviewee about who you are, what you want, why you want it, how you will use it, and whether the interviewee will be identified in your story or report.
- Substitute better sounding words for potentially antagonizing ones: aides for handlers, damage control for spin doctoring, negative campaigning for mudslinging.
- Use neutral, open-ended questions.
- Remain silent to allow the interviewee to explain in depth and perhaps to blow off some steam.
- Proceed to a new topic.

Phillip Ault and Edwin Emery offer a simple rule: "Treat the average person with respect, and he [she] will do the same."[39]

Reticent Interviewees

Be prepared for the "silent types."

If a person seems unwilling or unable to talk, discover why. The person may be inhibited by you or your position, the situation, the topic, the surroundings, or other people nearby. Many people are reticent around authority figures, supervisors, investigators, and journalists. Lack of privacy inhibits communication. Think of a time when you went to a professor or supervisor with a personal problem and the setting was a small cubicle or open area in which other persons could easily overhear. Reticence may be a family or personal trait that has nothing to do with the interview and cannot be altered during the interview.

When communicating with reticent persons, use conversation starters by asking about pictures, awards, or arrangement of furnishings in the room, and begin with easy-to-answer questions about nonthreatening topics. Change your style from formal to informal. If open questions do not generate in-depth answers, substitute closed questions (an inverted question sequence) until the party is warmed up and more ready to talk. Use silent and nudging probes to encourage the interviewee to talk. Realize that no tactic can get some reticent people to talk openly and freely. Some people simply do not talk much.

Talkative Interviewees

Controlling talkative persons may be more difficult than getting reticent ones to open up.

If you think a *reticent interviewee* is difficult to deal with, meet the *talkative interviewee.* Some people love to talk and can do so for many minutes, often without taking a breath. They will give lengthy answers to highly closed questions and seemingly unending answers to open questions. They want to be helpful to a fault.

Use highly targeted, closed questions that give talkative interviewees less verbal maneuverability and more direction. Look for natural openings or slight pauses to insert a question or redirect the interview such as:

I'm glad you mentioned that. Tell me about . . .

Speaking of budget cuts, what are your plans for . . .

That's really interesting. Now, what about . . .

Thanks for clarifying that. Let's turn our attention to . . .

Be tactful and sensitive in using nonverbal signals.

Avoid awkward or insolent interruptions by using nonverbal actions to signal that you need to move on: look at your notes, lean forward, nod your head as if to say "That's enough," stop note taking, or glance at your watch. Telephone and other electronic interviews pose unique problems because you have few nonverbal signals to halt answers, so interviewees tend to give long, rambling answers.

Evasive Interviewees

Discover why a person may be evasive.

Interviewees may evade questions that ask them to reveal feelings or prejudices, make them take stands or give specific information, or may incriminate them in some way. Evasive strategies include humor, fake hostility, counter questions, ambiguous language, or rambling answers that never get to the point. Interviewees may quibble over the wording of questions or the definitions of key words. A common tactic is to counter a question with a question, perhaps revolving the question onto the interviewer:

Well, how would *you* answer that?
What do *you* think we should do?
Tell me about *your* private life.

Be patient and persistent.

Interviewees may answer a question not asked but one they want to answer. You can deal with evasive interviewees by being prepared and persistent in questioning. For instance:

- Repeat or slightly rephrase a question.
- Laugh and continue with your questions.

- Go to other questions and come back to this one later.
- Resort to leading or loaded questions to evoke meaningful responses.

An evasive interviewee may be dishonest. Listen carefully to answers to determine if they square with the facts from your research and previous interviews. Observe nonverbal cues to detect dishonesty but be aware that clever respondents know how to *appear* honest, including excellent eye contact. Pat Stith writes that when an interviewee "says 'to be honest' or 'to be perfectly candid' the hair ought to stand up on the back of your neck. Almost always these phrases are followed by fibs."[40]

Two experienced FBI agents, Joe Navarro and John R. Schafer, offer detailed suggestions on how to detect dishonesty during interviews but warn that "lie detection" is a "50/50 proposition even for experienced investigators."[41] They recommend that interviewers look for "clusters of behavior, which cumulatively reinforce deceptive behaviors unique to the person being interviewed." Nonverbal behaviors include fidgeting feet, increased eye contact, rapidly blinking eyes, leaning away, irregular breathing, folding arms or interlocking legs to use less space, and lack of gesturing or finger pointing. Verbal cues include what Navarro and Schafer call "text bridges" such as "I don't remember," "The next thing I knew," and "After that." Stalling tactics may include asking an interviewer to repeat a question or phrases such as "It depends on what you mean by," "Where did you hear that," and "Could you be more specific?" As an informational interviewer, you must strike a balance between being overly gullible and overly suspicious.

Confused Interviewees

Respondents may become confused by a topic, question, or a tense situation. Be prepared to handle confused persons without embarrassing them or creating hostility. Restate or rephrase a question tactfully. Return to the question later in the interview. Be conscious of jargon and similar sounding words. This exchange took place between an attorney and a witness.[42]

Be understanding, helpful, and adaptive to confused interviewees.

Attorney: Is your appearance here this morning pursuant to a deposition notice which I sent to your attorney?

Witness: No, this is how I dress when I go to work.

Be careful of your nonverbal reactions. Broadcast journalists who get strange responses rarely exhibit a smile or shock when that happens. They go on to the next question or topic as if nothing embarrassing has happened.

Gender and cultural characteristics are generalities and may not apply to a particular interviewee.

Dissimilar Interviewees

Adapt carefully to interviewees who are dissimilar to you. Journalist Wendell Cochran asks us, "How do you deal fairly with someone whose views are anathema to you?"[43] Observe interviews in the media (CNN, for instance) to see how interviewers deal with interviewees they clearly do not like such as a person convicted of shooting children at a school, a captured terrorist, a CEO who deceived workers and investors, or one with very different political, social, or religious beliefs.

Previous chapters have identified important communicative characteristics unique to males and females and different cultures. Gender differences are important in informational interviews. For example, men tend to talk more, monopolize conversations, make more direct statements ("beat around the bush" less often), answer questions with declarations (while women tend to answer questions with questions), get to the point sooner in answers, and respond to questions with minimal responses (yeah, nope, fine, okay, sure). Elderly respondents may be less trusting because of experiences and insecurity, but are often communication starved and may be *very* talkative in interviews.

Interviewers may stereotype ethnic groups such as Irish-Americans, Asian-Americans, African-Americans, Arab-Americans, and Hispanic-Americans and expect them to act in certain ways during interviews. They in turn may have developed solidarity through in-group codes, symbols, expectations, and enemies that outsiders neither share nor understand. Research indicates that African-Americans prefer indirect questions, consider extensive probing to be intrusive, and prefer more frequent and equal turn taking. Mexican-American respondents rely more on emotion, intuition, and feeling than midwestern European-Americans. Persons of rural backgrounds value personal know-how, skills, practicality, simplicity, and self-sufficiency more than those of urban backgrounds. Adapt your questions and structure to different interviewees and be aware of gender and cultural differences that may motivate interviewees and explain the answers you, receive.

Closing the Interview

Close the interview when you have the information you need or your allotted time runs out. If the interviewee has agreed to a 15-minute interview, for instance, complete the interview within this time or prepare to close the interview. Do not ignore a time limit or press the interviewee for additional time. The **interviewee** may grant additional minutes when you signal that your time is up or you obviously need only a few more minutes. If the interviewee appears reluctant to expand the time, close the interview positively and try to arrange for another appointment. Respect the interviewee's time constraints and wishes.

Review the closing guidelines and techniques discussed in Chapter 4, particularly the use of clearinghouse probes. It is wise to begin a closing with a clearinghouse question—such as "Is there anything else you would like to add?" or "What have I not asked that you think is important?"—to be sure you have not failed to ask for important information in your prepared questions. Even the most thoroughly prepared interview may miss something important that did not occur to you before or during the interview. Express appreciation for the interviewee's assistance. Make the closing a dialogue with the interviewee, not a monologue in which you recite a prepared closing statement. **The interviewee must be an active party from opening through closing.**

Be sure you understand the information you have obtained; can reproduce names; position titles, dates, quotations, facts, and statistics accurately; and can interpret attitudes, feelings, and beliefs as meant by the interviewee. Remember that the interview is not really over until both parties are out of sight and sound of one another. An interviewee may relax and be less on guard when the interview appears to be coming to an end and reveal important information, insights, and feelings, some of which may alter your understandings and impressions established during the body of the interview. Journalist Pat Stith writes that "some of the best stuff you're going to get will come in the last few minutes, when you're wrapping up the interview, packing your stuff, and getting ready to, leave."[44] Observe and listen.

Preparing the Report or Story

The final stage in the informational interview is to prepare the necessary **report** or **story.** Review the information and observations obtained through one or more interviews to see if you have obtained the information necessary to satisfy your purpose. This means remembering interchanges, reading notes, and listening or viewing recordings. Sift through hundreds or thousands of words, statements, facts, opinions, and impressions to locate what is most important to include in a report or story. Check answers with other sources, especially if there is reason to suspect an interviewee gave inaccurate information.

Make it a habit to check all sources.

Once you know what you have obtained from the interview stage, editing begins. If the report is a verbatim interview for publication or dissemination, determine if grammatical errors, mispronounced words, expletives, slang, and vocalized pauses such as "uh," "and uh," and "you know" should remain. What about repetitious statements, long and rambling explanations, and simple, unintentional errors? Readers and listeners may enjoy the account with all of the warts showing, but both interview parties may be embarrassed and lose credibility, and the relationship may be damaged beyond repair and place future interviews in jeopardy.

Be honest, accurate, and fair in reporting interview results.

Preface answers and questions so readers and listeners will have a clear understanding of each. Edit questions to make answers more pointed and meaningful. When quoting from notes or memory, strive for accuracy. Do not put words into an interviewee's mouth. Be sure proper qualifiers are included. Do not understate or overstate an interviewee's opinions, attitudes, intentions, or commitments. Be sure both questions and answers are reported in proper context.

The technical steps of report or story preparation are beyond the scope of this book (see the resources at the end of this chapter), but here are a few precautions.

- Remember the ground rules agreed to and what information is "off the record."
- Be careful of assumptions.
- Strive for accuracy and fairness in every fact and interpretation.
- Check carefully all sources and reports.
- Arrange information in order of importance.
- Use quotations to enliven and support the story or report.
- Include several points of view to achieve balance.

A few years ago Ted Mann, the former sports publicist for Duke University, picked up the morning paper and discovered to his surprise that he was dead. It had all started when a friend of a reporter who worked for a rescue squad told the reporter Mann had died. The reporter called the Mann home to verify the report, and the woman who answered the phone said, "Mr. Mann's not here. He's gone." The reporter assumed this phrase was a euphemism for dead and that the woman had verified Mann's death. He wrote an obituary on this false assumption.[45]

The Interviewee in the Probing Interview

Attention in interviewing books typically focuses on the interviewer because most readers and students are concerned with learning how to conduct interviews effectively. But all of us are interviewees at least as often as we are interviewers. Let's turn our attention, then, to becoming a more effective respondent in interviews.

Doing Homework

Get to know the interviewer as well as the interviewer knows you.

Before taking part in an informational interview, become thoroughly briefed on topics that might come up, including recent events, accidents, controversies, innovations, decisions, and laws. Have you played roles in any of these? Check organizations to be sure you understand organizational policies, positions, and involvements and what authority you have to speak for the organization or a subunit of that organization. Is there a more knowledgeable or authoritative person who should be the interviewee?

Learn everything available about the interviewer, including age, gender, ethnic group, education and training, special interests, and experiences. What are the interviewer's attitudes toward you, your organization, your profession, and the topic: friendly or hostile, trusting or suspicious, interested or disinterested. Do not assume the interviewer has little expertise in an area. Some reporters, for instance, have engineering, management, economics, or science degrees or have developed a high level of expertise on topics such as energy, stem cell research, or foreign policy. A mother of a hyperactive child may have become an expert on hyperactivity. A member of the clergy may have been an Air Force pilot before attending theology school. What is the interviewer's reputation for fairness and honesty? What questioning techniques does the interviewer usually employ?

Interviews often take place without warning. A person may call, stop by your office, appear at your front door, or approach you on the street. When this happens, be sure the opening reveals the identity of the interviewer, the interviewer's organization, length of the interview, information desired, and how the information will be used. A thorough opening, including small talk, orients you about the topic, purpose, and relationship and gives you time to think and prepare answers strategically.

Understanding the Relationship

Appreciate the impact of upward and downward communication in interviews.

The relationship between interviewer and interviewee is a major concern in informational interviews because one or the other is likely to be in a superior position: a young accountant interviewing the CFO or the president of the university interviewing a young assistant professor. This upward and downward communication may lead either party to be overawed by the other. Feelings of subordination, obligation, or flattery may lead you to answer any question asked, particularly in the presence of cameras, microphones, technicians, or audiences. Determine whether to speak to a particular person at a particular time. Realize that refusals of interviews may lead interviewers to state ominously at a later date that "Margaret Adams was unavailable for comment" or "refused to talk to us." Such statements imply guilt, but may be preferable to foolish comments that become headlines.

Assess the relationship between parties prior to the interview for indicators of what might take place during the interview.

Understand the relationship prior to the interview.

- What is the relational history?
- How similar are the parties?
- How willing and eager are both parties to take part?
- How much control will you have?
- Do the parties perceive one another to be trustworthy, reliable, and safe?

Awareness of the Situation

Consider the situational variables that are likely to affect the interview. When will the interview take place? How might events prior to and afterward affect the interview? Should you defer an interview until you are better informed and ready to manage difficult questions? Where will the interview take place? What is the physical setting? Will an audience be present? If the interview will be broadcast, review the discussion presented earlier in this chapter. What outside influences must you take into account?

Assess the many situational variables that will impact the interview.

Consider establishing ground rules such as time, place, length, which topics are off limits or off the record, and the identity of the interviewer. Be realistic in demands. If you demand that all important topics be off limits, there is no interview. Occasionally you may require that questions be submitted in advance to prepare well-thought-out answers with accurate and substantial data. If Diane Sawyer of ABC wants to interview you, you would be foolish to demand a different interviewer. How much control you have depends upon your importance as a source, your relationship with the interviewer, the situation, and how eager you are to serve as an interviewee.

Anticipating Questions

Be as prepared to answer as the interviewer is prepared to ask.

Anticipate questions and think through possible responses. What might be the most important information to divulge or conceal? How should you qualify answers? What evidence can you provide for assertions and claims? How might you reply to questions you cannot answer because of lack of information, need for secrecy, protection of sources, legal consequences, or organizational policies and constraints?

In this age of litigation and media involvement in every issue, increasing numbers of interviewees are undergoing training in how to handle questions. For instance, prosecutors, attorneys, and aides prepare witnesses and clients (including presidents of the United States and CEOs) to answer questions in court, congressional hearings, board meetings, and press conferences. Seek help if you are facing a difficult encounter with a trained and experienced interviewer.

Listening to Questions

While listening carefully to each question, follow several guidelines for responding effectively.

Listen and Think before Answering

Fully engage the brain before opening the mouth.

At scenes of accidents, crimes, or controversies, persons make statements they soon regret. African-Americans and Hispanic-Americans are often accused of crimes they did not commit because interviewees claimed to see a black or Hispanic man in the area where a crime took place. False statements and reports may lead to lawsuits, reprimands, or embarrassment. *Listen* carefully to what is being asked. Listen for words you do not know or may misinterpret. Listen for verbal and nonverbal cues that reveal feelings as well as facts.

Be Patient

Do not assume to know what a question is before it is completed. React only after fully hearing and understanding each question. Do not interrupt an interviewer because what the questioner is saying may help you understand the question and determine an answer.

Focus Attention on the Question of the Moment

Do not continue to replay a previous answer that is history or anticipate a future question because you will end up not hearing the current question.

Concentrate on Both the Interviewer and the Question

Watch for nonverbal signals that complement the verbal and reveal the interviewer's feelings, attitudes, and beliefs. Focus eyes and ears on the interviewer. This is particularly important in broadcast interviews that involve several persons, studios, cameras, monitors, and microphones and field interviews that involve spectators, noise, traffic, and distracting objects.

Do Not Dismiss a Question Too Quickly as Irrelevant or Stupid

The interviewer may have a very good reason for asking a question, and it may be one in a series leading up to a highly important question. An icebreaker question, for instance, may not add much to the content of the interview but a great deal to the interaction between parties. An interviewer may be using an inverted funnel sequence, and you will get an opportunity to respond at length later.

Answering Strategically

Design answers carefully. A good answer is concise, precise, carefully organized, clearly worded, logical, well supported, and to the point. There are many strategies for responding to questions. Learn to use them as effectively as the question strategies we introduced in Chapters 3 and 4.

Becoming hostile reduces you to the level of the interviewer.

- Avoid defensiveness or hostility.
  —Give answers not sermons.
  —Give reasons and explanations rather than excuses.
  —Be polite and tactful in words and manner.

—Use tasteful, appropriate humor.

—Do not reply in kind to a hostile question or interruption.

- Share control of the interview.

—Insist on adequate time to answer questions.

—Do not allow the interviewer to "put words in your mouth."

—Challenge the content of questions that contain unsupported assertions or inaccurate data or quotations.

—If a question is multiple-choice, be sure the choices are fair and include all reasonable options.

—Ask the interviewer to rephrase or repeat long, complicated, or unclear questions.

—Answer a question with a question.

—Search reflective and mirror questions for accuracy and completeness.

- Explain what you are doing and why.

—Preface a lengthy answer by explaining why it must be so.

—Preface an answer by explaining why a question is tough or tricky.

—Provide a substantial explanation why you must refuse to answer a question or simply say "No comment."

—Rephrase a question: "If what you're asking is . . ." or "You seem to be implying that . . ."

- Take advantage of question pitfalls,

—Reply to the portion of a double-barreled question you remember and can answer most effectively.

—Answer a bipolar question with a simple yes or no.

—Reply to the open or closed portion of an open-to-closed switch question that is to your advantage.

- Avoid common question traps.

—If a question is leading, such as "Don't you agree that . . . ," do not be led to the suggested answer.

—If a question is loaded, such as "Are you still cheating on your taxes," be aware that either a yes or a no will make you guilty.

—If an apparent bipolar question offers two disagreeable choices, such as "Did you go into medicine for the prestige or for the money," answer with a third option.

—Watch for the yes-no pitfall, such as "Do you want to die," and answer or refuse to answer politely.

- Support your answers.

—Use stories and examples to illustrate points.

—Use analogies and metaphors to explain unknown or complicated things, procedures, and concepts.
—Organize long answers like mini-speeches with an introduction, body, and conclusion.

- Open your answers positively rather than negatively. The authors of *Journalistic Interviews: Theories of the Interview* offer these examples of interviewee responses:[46]

Negative	**Positive**
You failed to notice	May I point out
You neglected to mention	We can also consider x, y, z
You overlooked the fact	One additional fact to consider
You missed the point	From another perspective

Summary

The informational interview is the most common type of interview because it is used daily by persons ranging from journalists, police officers, and health care professionals to students, teachers, and parents. Length and formality vary, but the purpose and method are the same: to get needed information as accurately and completely as possible in the shortest amount of time. The means are careful questioning, listening, observing, and probing. Although preparation of an interview guide or schedule is important, the interviewer must remain flexible and adapt to each interviewee, situation, and response. This chapter has presented guidelines for structured informational interviews that call for thorough preparation and flexibility. The nature of each stage will depend upon the situation and the relationship between the interviewer and interviewee.

Interviewees need not be passive participants in informational interviews. When given advance notice, interviewees should prepare thoroughly. They should share control with the interviewer and not submit meekly to whatever is asked or demanded. And they should know the principles and strategies of effective answers. Good listening is essential. The result will be a better interview for both parties.

Key Terms and Concepts

The online learning center for this text features FLASHCARDS and CROSSWORD PUZZLES for studying based on these terms and concepts.

Broadcast interview
Confused interviewees
Dishonesty
Dissimilar interviewees
Emotional interviewees
Evasive interviewees
False assumptions
Hostile interviewees
Icebreaker questions
Key informants
Metaphorical questions
Off the record
Press conference
Research
Reticent interviewees
Sources
Status difference
Strategic answers
Talkative interviewees
Unsanitized setting
Videoconference

A Probing Interview for Review and Analysis

The interviewer is a student in an oral history class that is conducting a research project on the "home front" during World War II. Her assignment is to interview people who were children during the war to learn their perspectives on the war. This evening she is interviewing a person who was five years old when the United States entered the war and nine years old when it ended in 1945.

As you review this informational interview, ask such questions as, How satisfactory is the opening, including involvement of the interviewee? How well does the interviewer avoid common question pitfalls? How effectively does the interviewer listen and detect clues in answers? What areas of potentially valuable information does the interviewer discover and fail to discover? How satisfactory is the closing, including involvement of the interviewee? Which answer strategies does the *interviewee* employ and how effectively does the *interviewer* deal with them? How well does she manage to share control during the interview?

1. **Interviewer:** Hi. I'm Marilyn O'Malley who called you a few days ago about the project we're doing in my oral history class.
2. **Interviewee:** Oh hi. Won't you come in? What exactly is this project?
3. **Interviewer:** History 476 is an oral history class, and students taking the course have focused the last few semesters on various aspects of World War II.
4. **Interviewee:** That sounds interesting. I read a lot about World War II and have dozens of books in my library. How long will the interview take?
5. **Interviewer:** The interview should take about 15 to 20 minutes. I'm going to tape the interview; is that okay with you?
6. **Interviewee:** I guess so. What will you do with the tape?
7. **Interviewer:** We will keep the tapes in our oral history library, but their immediate use will be to have an accurate account of the interview.
8. **Interviewee:** Okay.
9. **Interviewer:** Tell me what you remember about World War II.
10. **Interviewee:** I was just a kid. Why do you want to interview me about World War II?
11. **Interviewer:** Well, as I mentioned over the telephone, we're studying how people on the "home front" remembered the war. I've been assigned to interview those who were children at the time to get their perspective.
12. **Interviewee:** Okay, but I don't remember much.
13. **Interviewer:** I'll bet things will come to mind as we talk. How old were you when the war started?
14. **Interviewee:** I was about five-and-a-half.
15. **Interviewer:** Do you recall the bombing of Pearl Harbor?
16. **Interviewee:** Yes, sort of.

17. **Interviewer:** Did you hear about it on the radio?

18. **Interviewee:** No.

19. **Interviewer:** Did you read about it in the newspaper?

20. **Interviewee:** No. (laughing) I was only five and didn't know how to read.

21. **Interviewer:** Tell me about what you recall.

22. **Interviewee:** Well, that was a Sunday, and we went down to my uncle's cabin on the Wabash River after church. It was a beautiful cabin high on a hill with a great view of the river. I went fishing with my dad after lunch and we caught several catfish. You have to be very careful getting them off the hook. As I recall, it was a beautiful late fall day. And after we went fishing, we . . .

23. **Interviewer:** (cutting in) When did you hear about Pearl Harbor?

24. **Interviewee:** Oh, that was in the evening.

25. **Interviewer:** Tell me about that.

26. **Interviewee:** We were driving home and came into the downtown area. Boys were in the streets yelling "Extra! Extra! Read all about it." My dad stopped the car and bought a paper. He and Mom talked in low voices as we drove home, and my sister and I could not tell what had happened—but we knew it was something really bad. Neither Mom nor Dad said much when we got home. We didn't have a phone, so we couldn't call family or friends to see what they were feeling.

27. **Interviewer:** As the war went on, how did it affect your life as a child?

28. **Interviewee:** A lot of my memories center on food, particularly sweets. Mom and Dad had rationing stamps that would allow them to buy small amounts of scarce items. I still remember Mom taking these stamps out at the grocery store so she could buy milk, eggs, bread, and other stuff. I remember Dad trying to roll his own cigarettes because he could not buy packages of them.

29. **Interviewer:** Tell me about that.

30. **Interviewee:** About what?

31. **Interviewer:** About the rationing and scarcity of common items.

32. **Interviewee:** Well . . . sugar was difficult to buy, so my mom would save up our sugar allotment for months to have enough to make cookies and candy for Christmas. We rarely had fresh fruit such as oranges and bananas. I can remember times when the word would spread in school that the local drugstore had a box of Hershey bars. We would run all the way there after school in hopes of getting a candy bar. The bigger kids would usually get there first and all the bars would be gone. I remember dreaming about candy bars and bubble gum.

33. **Interviewer:** Uh huh. What did you miss most?

34. **Interviewee:** Well I love chocolate and soft drinks, and it was difficult to find either for most of the war.

35. **Interviewer:** As a young child, what did you do for the war effort?

36. **Interviewee:** Our big effort, apart from giving up fruits and sweets for the troops, was to collect flattened tin cans and newspapers. It seemed like we were always

having a paper or can drive at school. We would go around the neighborhood from door to door with our wagons and pick up stuff and take it to school. I heard later that most of this stuff was thrown away; it was merely a way to make us feel like we were helping the war effort.

37. **Interviewer:** Anything else?

38. **Interviewee:** Oh, and each Friday we would take our War Bond books to school and purchase 10-cent stamps to stick into them. When we got enough, we would get a $25 war bond. I guess this effort by millions of kids helped fund the war.

39. **Interviewer:** Were you ever afraid?

40 **Interviewee:** Oh yeah. We had a huge military depot about a mile from my home, so we were afraid of air raids even though we were in the middle of the country.

41. **Interviewer:** How did the government prepare you for possible attacks?

42. **Interviewee:** I remember there were signs posted on light poles telling people what to do in case of an attack and how to react during air raids.

43. **Interviewer:** Did you have air raids?

44. **Interviewee:** Oh yeah. Well, they were practice air raids. We now know that the Japanese and German planes could not reach the Midwest.

45. **Interviewer:** Um hmm.

46. **Interviewee:** The sirens would go off (I remember once I was in the middle of taking a bath) and we had to turn out all of the lights and pull down the blinds. Men in white helmets patrolled the streets to make sure everyone followed the rules. If you left a light on, they would blow a whistle and pound on your door. We always obeyed because you never knew when it might be the real thing.

47. **Interviewer:** Were members of your family in the military?

48. **Interviewee:** My dad and most of my uncles were too old for the draft, but two of my cousins were in the service, one in the Army and one in the Navy.

49. **Interviewer:** Did they make it home safely?

50. **Interviewee:** One did.

51. **Interviewer:** Which one?

52. **Interviewee:** My cousin Eugene in the Navy didn't make it.

53. **Interviewer:** What happened to him?

54. **Interviewee:** He was shot down off the coast of France patrolling in a big float plane for German submarines. Nothing was ever found. They didn't have a chance against German fighters.

55. **Interviewer:** I guess that was pretty rough, huh?

56. **Interviewee:** Yeah. I remember seeing his picture in the paper with a "Missing in Action" heading.

57. **Interviewer:** How did it affect your family?

58. **Interviewee:** We hoped for a long time that he might be in a prisoner of war camp, but he wasn't. My aunt never got over it, and I now have his medals, the burial flag sent by Navy, even though there was never a funeral, and the dreaded telegram sent

to my aunt informing her that Eugene was missing in action. Eugene was, and still is, my hero.

59. Interviewer: Well, our time's up. I've enjoyed talking to you. Could we make another appointment?

60. Interviewee: Sure. I'd like to see your report when it's done.

61. Interviewer: Okay. Thanks.

Probing Role-Playing Cases

Cash for Clunkers Revisited

A government "cash for clunkers" program in the summer of 2009 was designed to stimulate the sales and production of automobiles and to replace older "gas guzzlers" with higher mileage vehicles. At the time it appeared to be a huge success with many dealers almost running out of vehicles to sell and producers ramping up production. You are now interviewing car dealers to assess the long-term effects of the cash for clunkers program on sales, particularly now that the severe economic crisis is past. Your interviews are taking place with managers at new car dealers who sell both vehicles made in the United States and those made in other countries.

A Veteran from the War in Afghanistan

You are a psychology student in a class focusing on the long-term effects of fighting on military personnel who have spent at least a year in active combat. You have been assigned to interview a local resident who spent 14 months fighting in the mountains of Afghanistan. He returned home to his wife and three children and, after a one-month leave and a brief stay at a VA hospital, resumed his military career. The interview will take place at a local Starbucks.

A Candidate for University President

You are a reporter for your campus student daily newspaper and have arranged an interview with the vice president for Academic Affairs who is a finalist for the presidency of a large university. Your purposes are to discover why she aspires to be a university president and how she feels her current administrative position at your university has prepared her for the top position at another university. You have interacted with her on a number of occasions, social and professional, and have found her easy to talk to. A major concern is how formal your interview should be.

A Mission Trip to Haiti

You are a junior in college and have had a long interest in religious missions to so-called third world nations. An item in the campus newspaper on a midyear student mission trip to Haiti caught your attention, and you have made an appointment to meet with a senior who took part in a mission trip to Haiti when he was a junior. Your goal is to discover more about the particulars of this year's trip to Haiti, including the type of work the mission will do, what it is like traveling in Haiti, how Haitians feel about Americans in general and college students in particular, living arrangements, and cost.

Student Activities

1. Compare and contrast the sample attitude survey in Chapter 6 with the informational interview in this chapter. How are the openings similar and different? How are questions similar and different? What are the apparent question sequences? What schedules are used? How are the closings similar and different? What interviewing skills are required for the participants of each interview?
2. Interview a newspaper journalist and a broadcast journalist about their interviewing experiences and techniques. How does the nature of the medium affect interviewers and interviewees? How does the medium affect interview structure, questioning techniques, and note taking? What advice do they give about note taking and tape recording interviews? How do the end products differ? What constraints does each medium place on interviewers?
3. Record a televised press conference in which one person is answering questions from several interviewers. How is this situation similar to and different from one-on-one interviews? What stated or implied rules governed this interview? What skills are required of interviewers and interviewee? How did the interviewee recognize interviewers? What answering strategies did the interviewee use? What questioning strategies did interviewers use?
4. A growing number of interviewers are turning to the Internet to conduct probing interviews. Develop a moderately scheduled 20-minute interview on a topic that will require fairly lengthy answers and then conduct one face-to-face interview and one over the Internet. Identify the advantages and disadvantages of each with respect to relationship building, communication interactions, depth of answers, self-disclosure, probing questions, spontaneity, and ability or inability to observe and hear the interviewee's answers.

Notes

1. Bob Steele, "Interviewing: The Ignored Skill," http://www.poynter.org/column.asp?id=36&aid=37661, accessed September 25, 2006.
2. Lori Voth (Revezbelle), "Tips for Journalist: How to Conduct an Interview," June 14, 2006, http://www.associatedcontent.com/article/37333/tips_for_journalist_how_to_conduct.html, accessed May 22, 2009.
3. Eric Nalder, *Newspaper Interviewing Techniques,* Regional Reporters Association meeting at the National Press Club, March 28, 1994, The C-SPAN Networks (West Lafayette, IN: Public Affairs Video Archives, 1994).
4. Steele.
5. Ken Metzler, Tips for Interviewing," http://darkwing.uoregon.edu/~sponder/cj641/interview.htm, accessed September 26, 2006.
6. Beverley J. Pitts, Tendayi S. Kumbula, Mark N. Popovich, and Debra L. Reed, *The Process of Media Writing* (Boston: Allyn and Bacon, 1997), p. 66.

7. Eric Steven Raymond and Rick Moen, "How to Ask Questions the Smart Way," http://www.catb.org/~esr/faqs/smart-questions.html, accessed September 26, 2006.
8. R. Thomas Berner, *The Process of Writing News* (Boston: Allyn and Bacon, 1992), p. 123.
9. Pitts, Kumbula, Popovich, and Reed, p. 64.
10. Raymond L. Gorden, *Interviewing: Strategy, Techniques, and Tactics* (Homewood, IL: Dorsey Press, 1980), p. 235.
11. Fred Fedler, John R. Bender, Lucinda Davenport, and Paul E. Kostyu, *Reporting for the Media* (Fort Worth, TX: Harcourt Brace, 1997), p. 227.
12. Eugene C. Webb and Jerry R. Salancik, "The Interview or the Only Wheel in Town," *Journalism Monographs* 2 (1966), p. 18.
13. Metzler.
14. Robert Ogles is a professor of mass communication at Purdue University.
15. Carole Rich, *Writing and Reporting News: A Coaching Method* (Belmont, CA: Thomson/Wadsworth, 2005), p. 124; Berner, p. 127; The Missouri Group, *Telling the Story: Writing for Print Broadcast, and Online Media* (Boston: Bedford/St. Martin's, 2001), p. 51; Melvin Mencher, *Basic Media Writing* (Madison, WI: Brown & Benchmark, 1996), p. 231.
16. Henry Schulte and Michael P. Dufreshe, *Getting the Story* (New York: Macmillan, 1994), p. 24.
17. Metzler.
18. "Journalistic Interviews," http://www.uwgh.edu/clampitp/Interviewing/Interviewing%20lectures/Journalistic%20Interviews.ppt., accessed October 4, 2006.
19. Stephen Budiansky, "Truth Extraction," *The Atlantic Monthly,* June 2005, 32.
20. Tamar Weinberg, "Tips for Asking Questions During Journalistic Interviews," http://lifehacker.com/351399?tips-for-asking-questions-during-journalistic-interviews, accessed May 22, 2009.
21. Missouri Group, p. 58.
22. Originally cited in "The Point of View," a publication of the Alameda District Attorney's Office.
23. "The EU Protection Directive: Implications for the U.S. Privacy Debate," Subcommittee on Commerce, Trade, and Consumer Protection, March 8, 2001, http://www.access.gpo.gov/congress/house.
24. "Leading Questions," http://www.mediacollege.com/journalism/interviews/leading-questions.html, accessed October 4, 2006.
25. "Open-Ended Questions," http://www.mediacollege.com/journalism/interviews/open-endedquestions.html, accessed October 4, 2006.
26. William Zinsser, *On Writing Well* (New York: Harper Perennial, 1994), p. 70.
27. Missouri Group, p. 58.
28. "Oral History Project: Guidelines for Recording an Interview," *Alberta Online Encyclopedia,* http://www.youthsource.ab.ca/teacher_resources?oral_interview.html,

accessed July 14, 2009; "How to Record Interviews," *Transcriptionlive,* http://www.transcriptionlive.com, accessed July 14, 2009.

29. Carole Rich, *Writing and Reporting News: A Coaching Method* (Belmont, CA: Wadsworth, 1997), p. 110; "A Practical Guide to Taping Phone Calls and In-Person Conversations in the 50 States and D.C.," The Reporters Committee for the Freedom of the Press, 2008, http://www.rcfp.org/taping/, accessed July 14, 2009; "Recording interviews: Legal issues," Knight Citizen News Network, http://www.kcnn.org/interviewing/resources_recording, accessed July 14, 2009.

30. "Interview Structure," http://www.mediacollege.com/video/interviews/structure.html, accessed October 4, 2006.

31. "Interview Tips & Resources," Veterans History Project, American Folklife Center, Library of Congress, http://www.loc.gov/vets/moreresources.html, accessed July 14, 2009.

32. Fedler, Bender, Davenport, and Kostyu, p. 224.

33. "Framing Interview Shots," http://www.mediacollege.com/video/interviews/framing.html, accessed October 4, 2006; "Composing Interview Shots," http://www.mediacollege.com/video/interviews/composition.html, accessed October 4, 2006; "Studio Interview Settings," http://www.mediacollege.com/video/interviews/studio.html, accessed October 4, 2006.

34. "Video Interviewing: Tips for Interviews Using Video Cameras," http://www.bc.edu/offices/careers/skills/intrerview/video/, accessed September 30, 2006.

35. "Videoconference Interview Tips," Career Development and Experiential Learning, Memorial University, http://www.mun.ca/cdel/career_students/videoconference_interviewtips.php, accessed July 15, 2009.

36. Reporter and editor Wendell Cochran in Steele.

37. John R. Bittner and Denise A. Bittner, *Radio Journalism* (Englewood Cliffs, NJ: Prentice Hall, 1977), p. 53.

38. Travis Reed, "Did TV Interview Lead Woman to Kill Herself?" http://www.suntimes.com/news/nation/52533,CST-NWS-grace14.article, September 14, 2006.

39. Phillip H. Alt and Edwin Emery, *Reporting the News* (New York: Dodd, Mead, & Co., 1959), p. 125.

40. Stith, p. 2.

41. Joe Navarro and John R. Schafer, "Detecting Deception," *FBI Law Enforcement Bulletin,* July 2001, pp. 9–13, accessed on the Internet, July 20, 2009.

42. William T. G. Litant, "And, Were You Present When Your Picture Was Taken?" *Lawyer's Journal* (Massachusetts Bar Association), May 1996.

43. Steele.

44. Pat Stith, *Getting Good Stories: Interviewing with Finesse* (ProQuest Research Library, April 24, 2004), p. 2.

45. "Man Reads His Obituary in Paper," Lafayette, Indiana *Journal & Courier,* June 13, 1985, p. D4.

46. "EE's Perspective," http://www.uwgb.edu/clampitp/interviewing/interviewing%20Lectures/Journalistic%20Interviewsppt, accessed October 4, 2006.

Resources

Adams, Sally, and Wynford Hicks. *Interviewing for Journalists.* Florence, KY: Routledge, 2001.

Heritage, John. "Designing Questions and Setting Agendas in the News Interview," in *Studies in Language and Social Interaction,* Philip Glenn, Curtis LeBarob, and Jenny Mandelbaum, eds. Mahwah, NJ: Lawrence Erlbaum, 2002.

Metzler, Ken. "Tips for Interviewing," http://darkwing.uoregon.edu~sponder/j641/Interview.htm.

Rich, Carole. *Writing and Reporting News: A Coaching Method.* Belmont, CA: Thomson/Wadsworth, 2005.

Steele, Bob. "Interviewing: The Ignored Skill," http://www.poynter.org/column.asp?id=36&aid=37661.

"Videoconference Interview Tips." Newfoundland and Labrador, Canada: Memorial University of Newfoundland, 2009.

CHAPTER 6 The Survey Interview

"Surveys reach out and touch everyone."

If you seem to encounter surveys and polls every day, you are not imagining things. Groups and individuals conduct over 30 million surveys each year for governmental agencies, political parties and candidates, religious bodies, schools and colleges, special interest groups, social organizations, communities, and the media, to name a few.[1] "Let's do a survey" is a frequent proposal at all types of meetings. The ensuing interviews may take place face-to-face, over the telephone, or through the Internet and occur nearly everywhere, including malls, streets, offices, homes, businesses, sporting events, and hospitals.

Survey interviews are neither flexible nor adaptable.

Unlike the informational interview discussed in Chapter 5 that could range from a simple guide to a moderate schedule of questions, the survey interview is meticulously planned and highly structured. Whereas **flexibility** and **adaptability** characterize the informational interview, **reliability** (assurance that the same types of information are collected each time in repeated interviews) and **replicability** (the duplication of interviews regardless of interviewer, interviewee, and setting) characterize the survey interview.

Purpose and Research

Begin preparation of your survey by determining precisely what facts, opinions, and attitudes are needed and why. Your purpose and the background research you conduct will then determine topic areas, structure, types of questions and question strategies you will employ, the number and characteristics of interviewees, who will conduct the interviews, and the degree of precision required of results.

Determining Purpose

Survey interviews have multiple purposes.

Social science researchers Leslie Baxter and Earl Babbie identify a number of goals for surveys, including the interviewee's level and kind of knowledge, beliefs and perceptions, positive and negative feelings, past behaviors, and personal traits or characteristics.[2] You may have one or more of these goals in mind, and which you select will depend upon the following:

- The types of information you need: opinions, attitudes, facts, or statistics.
- How you will use the information.
- Your short- and long-range goals.

- What your research reveals
- Whether you are making predictions of the future or assessing the past.

Longitudinal studies reveal trends and changes over time.

Many survey interviews are brief, four or five minutes, but longer interviews cover more areas and are more reliable. A **cross-sectional survey** takes a slice of what is felt, thought, or known during a narrow time span and is used when you need to determine how interviewees are reacting at present. A **longitudinal survey** determines trends in feeling, thought, or knowledge over time.

Conducting Research

Don't assume adequate knowledge of a topic.

When you have a clearly defined purpose, investigate all aspects of the topic. Explore its past, present, and future as well as proposed and attempted solutions. Check resources such as organizational files and archives, correspondence and interviews with knowledgeable people, government documents, professional journals, books, previous surveys on this topic, the Internet, news magazines, and newspapers. Talk to people who have studied this topic or have been involved.

Don't waste time learning what you already know.

Research reveals information already available in other sources that need not be gathered in a survey. Become an expert on the topic, particularly unique terminology and technical concepts. If you are going to deal with concepts such as stem cell research, third wave feminism, or variable rate mortgages, you must specify the meaning of these terms to the satisfaction of interviewees and users of the survey results. Research will reveal past attitudes and opinions and speculations about current attitudes and opinions. A thorough knowledge of the topic provides insights into the topical areas you need to explore, the complexities of the issue, and potential intentional and unintentional inaccuracies in answers during interviews.

Structuring the Interview

Once you have determined a precise purpose and conducted necessary research, develop a thoroughly structured interview.

ON THE WEB

Select a current international issue and do background research through the Internet. Use at least three different search engines, such as the United Nations (http://www.un.org), International Forum on Globalism (http://www.ifg.org/), global engineering (http://news.foodonline.com/pehanich/fpso11598.html). What types of information did you discover? What information is unavailable on the Internet? What does the search suggest for a survey on this issue: subtopics, areas of conflict, differing views of experts, public opinion, history of the issue, current developments?

Interview Guide and Schedule

An interview guide is essential for survey interviews because the guide dictates the topics and subtopics to be covered and all primary and probing questions to be asked. Review carefully the suggestions for creating interview guides in Chapter 4.

A detailed guide is easily transformed into a scheduled format.

Begin an **interview guide** by listing major areas. For example, if you are planning to survey residents about the need to alter the public school calendar, major topics might include respondent experiences with and attitudes toward the current school calendar instituted 10 years ago, experiences with and attitudes toward other school calendars in different geographical locations, and attitudes toward a number of alternative school calendars such as starting classes later in August or after the Labor Day holiday and ending classes later in May or the first or second week of June. If you are conducting a **qualitative survey,** in which you will present your "findings in textual form—usually words" you may develop a highly scheduled interview that includes open-ended questions, planned probes, and the possibility of unplanned probes that depend upon interviewee responses.[3] There is a degree of flexibility in questioning because you are more concerned about depth of information than with statistical compilation of data. The traditional interview guide (who, what, when, where, how, and why) may be adaptable to qualitative surveys, but surveys often require a more detailed guide and schedule that ensures complete coverage of a topic or issue and the manner of organizing, reporting, and interpreting answers.

Standardization is essential for surveys.

The **quantitative survey,** in which you will present your "findings in numerical form—frequencies, averages, and so forth," is the most common because it enables many interviewers (1) to control hundreds of interviews with diverse interviewees in various settings and (2) to elicit answers that are easy to record, tabulate, and analyze.[4] The flexibility and adaptability of the qualitative survey may lead to difficulties in coding and tabulation of results, so interviewers rely on a highly scheduled, standardized format for quantitative surveys that ensures replicability of interviews and accurate compilation of findings.

The Opening

Although "each interview is unique, like a small work of art . . . with its own ebb and flow . . . , a mini-drama that involves real lives in real time,"[5] each respondent must go through as identical an interview as possible. Write out the opening that typically includes a greeting, name of the interviewer, the organization conducting the survey, subject matter of the interview, purpose, amount of time the survey will take, and assurance of confidentiality. Encourage interviewers to give this opening verbatim without reading it or sounding stilted. To make the opening sound more natural, you may allow interviewers to create their own openings as long as each opening includes all of the elements you have stipulated. The following is a standardized opening for a survey and includes a qualifier question.

> Good evening, I'm __________. I'm helping the school board conduct a survey of parents with children in the Springfield public school system to determine how they feel about the current school calendar that starts in mid-August and ends the first week of June and possible changes to this calendar. The survey will take

about 10 minutes and your answers will be strictly confidential. (GO TO THE FIRST QUESTION.)

1. Are you a resident of Springfield? (IF YES, PLACE AN X BY THE ANSWER AND GO TO Q. 2. IF NO, TERMINATE THE INTERVIEW.)

   Yes ___1-1
   No ___1-2

2. Do you have children currently enrolled or who were enrolled in the past five years in the Springfield public schools? (IF YES, PLACE AN X BY THE ANSWER AND GO TO Q. 3. IF NO, TERMINATE THE INTERVIEW.)

   Yes ___2-1
   No ___2-2

There are no icebreaker questions or small talk in surveys.

This opening identifies the interviewer and organization and states a general purpose and length of the interview. Notice that the interviewee is not asked to respond. The interviewer moves smoothly and quickly from orientation to the first question without giving the respondent an opportunity to refuse to take part. The first two questions are employed to determine the interviewee's qualifications: a resident of Springfield and parent of current or former students (within five years) in the Springfield public schools. The survey schedule provides instructions for each interviewer to follow and has precoded each question for ease of tabulating results when the survey is completed.

In some surveys, the opening will not identify the group that is paying for it (a political candidate, a pharmaceutical company, special interest group, for instance) or the specific purpose (to determine which strategies to employ during a political, advertising, or lobbying campaign) because such information might influence how interviewees respond. When a newspaper such as the *New York Times* or the *Washington Post*, a cable or television network such as CBS or CNN, or a well-known polling group such as Harris or Gallup conducts a survey, the organization's name is used to enhance the prestige of the poll and the interviewer, to reduce suspicion that a candidate or corporation is behind the survey, and to motivate respondents to cooperate. In some surveys, interviewers must show identification badges or letters that introduce them and establish their legitimacy as survey takers.

Simple incentives reduce rejections.

If a survey deals with sensitive matters and information, provide effective assurances of confidentiality in the opening to improve the chances of accurate and complete responses. One study indicated that a simple prepaid, nonmonetary incentive (such as a ballpoint pen) made during the opening can increase response rates and result in greater completeness in answers during the early portion of survey interviews.[6]

The Closing

The closing is usually brief and expresses appreciation for the time and effort expended to aid the survey. For example:

> That's all of the questions I have. Thank you very much for your help.

If the survey organizer wants a respondent's telephone number to verify that a valid interview took place, the closing might be:

> That's all the questions I have. May I have your telephone number so my supervisor can check to see if this interview was conducted in the prescribed manner? (gets the number) Thank you very much for your help.

If you can provide respondents with results of a survey, a common practice in research interviews, the closing might be:

> That's all the questions I have. Thank you for your help, and if you'll give me your address, I'll be sure that you receive a copy of the results of this study. (gets the address) Thanks again for your help.

Interviewees prefer anonymity.

Some interviewees are reluctant to give their telephone numbers or addresses to strangers. Be prepared to back off from either request if the interviewee appears anxious, suspicious, or very reluctant. Do not sacrifice the rapport and goodwill you created during the interview. When one of the authors was conducting polls for a political party, he discovered that many respondents did not want to give their telephone numbers for fear they would be deluged with calls from candidates during the campaign. With permission from the party, he stopped asking for telephone numbers, and closings went smoother.

Respondents may be curious about a survey or very interested in the topic and want to discuss it. This can be a good relationship builder and motivator for taking part in future surveys, but do so only if (1) time permits, (2) the interviewee will have no opportunity to talk to future interviewees, and (3) the survey organization has no objections.

Survey Questions

Interviewers cannot make on-the-spot adjustments.

Create each question with great care because you cannot rephrase, explain, or expand on questions during interviews without risking the ability to replicate interviews, an essential element of surveys. In quantitative surveys, all question phrasing and strategic decisions are made in the planning stage; none on the spot. In qualitative surveys, all primary questions and most probing questions are planned ahead of time.

Phrasing Questions

Every word in every question may influence results.

All interviewees must hear the same questions asked in the same manner; phrasing and nonverbal emphasis are critical. A slight change in wording or vocal emphasis on a word can generate different answers. For example, in a religious survey, interviewers asked one set of respondents, "Is it okay to smoke while praying?" Over 90 percent responded "No." When they asked another set of respondents, "Is it okay to pray while smoking?" over 90 percent replied "Yes." Although these questions appear to be the same, respondents interpreted them differently. The first sounded sacrilegious, lighting up while praying. The second sounded like a good idea, maybe even necessary. Recall the discussion of *why questions* in Chapter 3 that showed how emphasis may change the focus and meaning of simple questions. This is critical in surveys in which you are striving for replicability.

A single word might alter significantly how people respond to a question, thereby altering the results of a survey. Researchers asked the following question to one group of respondents:

> "Do you think the United States should allow public speeches against democracy?"

The results were "should allow" 21 percent and "should not allow" 62 percent. Then these researchers substituted a single word and asked respondents:

"Do you think the United States should forbid public speeches against democracy?"

The results were "should not forbid" 39 percent and "should forbid" 46 percent.[7] Respondents obviously viewed the word "forbid" as a much stronger and more dangerous action than "not allow"—perhaps un-American—even though the effect of the governmental policy would be the same.

Adapt phrasing to all members of a target population.

Make each question clear, relevant, appropriate to the respondent's level of knowledge, neither too complex nor too simple, and socially and psychologically accessible. This is not a simple task when respondents may be of both genders and differ widely in culture, age, income level, education, intelligence, occupation, geographical area, and experiences. The increasing diversity of the American population may result in your target population representing widely diverse continents, cultures, and nations. Be careful of using formal names or acronyms for persons or organizations with which your interviewees may not be familiar. Persons of different cultures may be fluent in English but be confounded with colloquialisms, aphorisms, jargon, euphemisms, and slang. Avoid ambiguous words and phrases such as a lot, often, much, large school, or recently discovered that have many and vague meanings.

Be wary of negatively phrased questions.

Survey researchers warn against phrasing questions negatively because they can be misleading and confusing. For instance, Jack Edwards and Marie Thomas note that "a negative answer to a negatively worded statement may not be equivalent to the positive answer to a positively worded statement."[8] Even the explanation sounds confusing. They give this example: "Disagreeing with the statement 'My work is not meaningful' does not necessarily mean that the same individual would have agreed with the statement 'My work is meaningful.' " Forcing a respondent to disagree with a negative statement can be confusing. Think of the difficulties you've had with negatively phrased multiple-choice questions in examinations. Babbie warns that many respondents will fail to hear the word not in a question during an interview so those in favor of a statement such as "The U.S. should not establish diplomatic relations with Iran." And those who disagree may answer the same way.[9] "And," Edwards and Thomas warn, "you may never know which is which."

Sample Question Development

Questions may evolve as you develop a schedule, particularly for a quantitative survey. Here is how what appears to be a simple question concerning gun regulations might evolve during preparation.

How do you feel about the university-imposed rule against students and faculty carrying firearms on campus?

Keep recording of answers in mind when phrasing questions.

Take a closer look at this seemingly neutral question. "University-imposed" may bias results because it may sound tyrannical and unconstitutional to some respondents. The openness of the question and the ambiguity of the word "feel" may result in a wide range of answers, some positive ("It makes me feel safer," "I'm generally for it," and "Whatever it takes to reduce violence on campus") and some negative ("It's another effort of antigun groups to violate my constitutional rights," "Angry," and "Fearful for my safety"). Others may give lengthy answers for and against the new restriction that will create recording and coding nightmares.

Try a second version that closes up the question and eliminates "*university-imposed.*"

> Are you for, against, or have no feelings about the university's rule against students and faculty carrying firearms on campus?
>
> For ________
> Against ________
> No feelings ________

This version eliminates the potential bias of the first (and resolves recording and coding problems), but it may be too closed for qualitative and quantitative purposes. Interviewees may not be simply for or against the rule or believe there should be exceptions or qualifications, perhaps allowing unconcealed pistols. Intensity of feelings is not accounted for. The "No feelings" answer option may generate a great many undecided and don't know answers and either necessitate a lot of probing or reduce the impact of the question.

Develop a third version that allows for degree of feelings and includes important notes on the extent of the restrictions.

> Do you strongly agree, agree, disagree, or strongly disagree with the university's rule against students and faculty carrying firearms of any type on campus?
>
> Strongly agree ________
> Agree ________
> Disagree ________
> Strongly disagree ________
> Undecided ________ (DO NOT PROVIDE UNLESS REQUESTED.)
> Why? ________________________________
> (ASK ONLY OF RESPONDENTS CHOOSING STRONGLY AGREE OR STRONGLY DISAGREE.)

This third option assesses intensity of feelings, is easy to record and code, leaves undecided as an unstated option, provides instructions for interviewers, and includes a built-in secondary "*Why*" question to discover reasons for strong approval or strong disapproval. The authors have discovered that those with moderate responses tend not to have ready explanations for agreeing or disagreeing, approving or disapproving, liking or disliking. They just have that general feeling.

Build in secondary questions for reasons, knowledge, level, and qualifiers.

Work with each question until it satisfies phrasing criteria and is designed to obtain the information needed. Careful phrasing avoids confusion and inaccurate results. Later we will address the pretesting of surveys to detect potential problems with questions.

Probing Questions

Although probing questions are less frequent and more planned in survey interviews than in informational interviews, they play important roles. For instance, if a respondent gives an unclear answer, you might ask, "What do you mean by that?" "How do you mean that?" or "What I hear you saying is . . . ; is this what you meant to say?" If a respondent provides a very brief answer or appears reluctant to elaborate, you might use a silent probe, a nudging probe such as "Uh-huh," or an informational probe such as, "Tell me more about. . . ." If you are unsure a respondent has told you everything of relevance to a question, use a clearinghouse probe such as, "Anything else?" or "Is there anything else you would like to add?" Remember that you must record probing questions and the answers they elicit carefully, clearly, and accurately for later tabulation and analysis.[10]

The goal is to perform nearly identical survey interviews over and over. On-the-spot probing may result in interviewer bias if some interviewers are phrasing questions verbally and nonverbally in ways that suggest the answers they prefer or lead different respondents to provide different answers. If some interviewers ask frequent probing questions and others do not, the amount and type of information attained will be different from one interview to the next. The result will be unreliable data or data that is impossible to tabulate and analyze with any degree of confidence.

Question Strategies

There are five question strategies that enable interviewers to assess knowledge level, honesty, and consistency; reduce undecided answers; prevent order bias; and incorporate probing questions.

Filter Strategy

The **filter strategy** enables you to determine interviewee knowledge of a topic. For example:

Interviewer: Are you familiar with the changes in the laws pertaining to credit card interest rates?

Interviewee: Yes, I am.

Interviewer: What are these changes?

If an interviewee says no, you go to the next topic. If the interviewee says yes, you ask the interviewee to reveal the extent and accuracy of knowledge. This follow-up question may discover that the respondent is confused or is misinformed. Many interviewees will say yes to bipolar questions, even when they have no idea what the interviewer is talking about, to avoid appearing uninformed.

Don't take "yes" as the final answer.

Repeat Strategy

The **repeat strategy** enables you to determine if an interviewee is consistent in responses on a topic, particularly a controversial one. You may ask the same question several minutes apart and later compare answers for consistency. A variation of this strategy is to disguise the question by rephrasing it.

5. Do you supervise your employees' use of the Internet?
12. Do you give your employees free access to the Internet?

Another example of a repeat strategy is to go from a moderately closed to a highly closed question, such as:

11. How often do you fly on business?

____

Repeat questions must be essentially the same to determine consistency in answers.

18. I am going to read a list of frequencies of flying on business trips. Stop me when I read the frequency that best describes your business air travel.

At least once a week ______
At least once a month ______
At least once every few months ______
At least once a year ______
Less than once a year ______

Do not make the repetition too obvious or near the initial question and be sure the rewording does not change the intent of the initial question.

Leaning Question Strategy

Respondents may be reluctant to take stands or make decisions, often because they do not want to reveal their feelings or intentions. Employ a *leaning* question, not to be confused with a *leading* question, to reduce the number of "undecided" and "don't know" answers. The following is a typical **leaning question strategy.**

7a. Which of these city council candidates do you plan to vote for in the primary? (IF UNDECIDED, ASK Q. 7b.)
Kristine Wallace ______
Dale Francis ______
Wally Kahn ______
Juan Hernandez ______
Undecided ______

7b. Well, which of the city council candidates do you lean toward today?
Kristine Wallace ______
Dale Francis ______
Wally Kahn ______
Juan Hernandez ______
Undecided ______

Leaning questions urge respondents to take a stand or make a decision.

The "undecided" option remains in question 7b because an interviewee may be truly undecided at the moment. A variation of the leaning question is, "Well, if you had to choose today, how would you vote?" Clearly stated "undecided" and "don't know" options may invite large percentages of these answers, particularly when a question asks for criticism of people, organizations, or products. However, some sources recommend that you always include "don't know" or "not applicable" answer options in all questions, unless all interviewees will have a definite answer, to reduce interviewee frustration and provide the most honest and accurate answers.[11]

Shuffle Strategy

The order of options in questions may affect interviewee selection. Research indicates that last choices in questions tend to get negative or superficial evaluations because interviewees get tired or bored and that interviewees also tend to select an option because it is the first mentioned or the last heard. The **shuffle strategy** varies the order of questions or answer options from one interview to the next to prevent **order bias.** The method of rotation is carefully explained when training interviewers. Notice the built-in instructions to interviewers in the following example:

> Now I'm going to read you a list of soft drinks, and I want you to tell me if you have a highly favorable, favorable, neutral, unfavorable, or highly unfavorable attitude toward each. (ROTATE THE ORDER OF THE SOFT DRINKS FROM INTERVIEW TO INTERVIEW. ENCIRCLE ANSWERS RECEIVED.)

	Highly Favorable	Favorable	Neutral	Unfavorable	Highly Unfavorable
Colas	5	4	3	2	1
Root beer	5	4	3	2	1
Cream soda	5	4	3	2	1
Ginger ale	5	4	3	2	1
Lemon-lime	5	4	3	2	1

Order bias is both fact and myth.

Potential order bias has resulted in strange events in political, persuasive, and advertising surveys. A political candidate in Indiana changed his name legally so it would begin with A. This placed him at the top of the ballot on election day, the belief being that voters select the top names in lists of candidates. He lost, but his and similar actions have led states to shuffle names on ballots.

Chain or Contingency Strategy

Highly standardized and highly scheduled formats allow for preplanned questions that enable you to probe into answers. This **chain or contingency strategy** is illustrated in the following series from a market survey. Notice the built-in instructions and precoding for ease of recording answers and tabulating data.

All probing questions in surveys are included in the schedule.

1a. During the past month, have you received any free samples of hair shampoo? (PLACE AN X BY THE ANSWER RECEIVED.)

Yes _____ 1—ASK Q. 1b.
No _____ 2—ASK Q. 2a.

1b. Which shampoo did you receive?

Worthington Big Hair ____ 1
Head & Shoulders ____ 2
Pantene Pro-V ____ 3
Suave ____ 4

Garnier Fructis ____ 5
Aussie ____ 6
Other ____________ 7 (*Please specify.*)

1c. (ASK ONLY IF PANTENE PRO-V IS NOT MENTIONED IN Q. 1b; OTHERWISE SKIP TO Q. 1d.)

Did you receive a free sample of Pantene Pro-V?

Yes ____ 1—ASK Q. 1d.
No ____ 2—SKIP to Q. 2a.

1d. Did you use the free sample of Pantene Pro-V?

Yes ____ 1—SKIP to Q. 2a.
No ____ 2—ASK Q. 1e.

1e. Why didn't you use the free sample of Pantene Pro-V?

____

____

Replicability means to reproduce interviews.

The chain or contingency strategy enables you to probe into answers while maintaining control of the process and ensuring that each interview is as identical as possible.

Question Scales

A variety of scale questions allow you to delve more deeply into topics and feelings than bipolar questions and to record and tabulate data more easily.

Interval Scales

Likert scales provide a range of feelings, attitudes, or opinions.

Interval scales provide distances between measures. For example, **evaluative interval scales** (often called **Likert scales**) ask respondents to make judgments about persons, places, things, or ideas. The scale may range from five to nine answer options (five is most common) with opposite poles such as "strongly like . . . strongly dislike," "strongly agree . . . strongly disagree," or "very important . . . not important at all." Here is an example of an evaluative interval scale:

Do you strongly agree, agree, have no opinion, disagree, or strongly disagree with the methods used to select the two teams for the bowl game that determines the Division I national collegiate football champion?

5 Strongly agree ______
4 Agree ______
3 Neutral ______
2 Disagree ______
1 Strongly disagree ______

Provide aids for interviewee recall of answer options.

You may provide respondents with cards (color-coded to tell them apart) for complex questions or ones with many choices or options. A card eliminates the faulty-recall problem that respondents experience. They can study the answers or objects they are evaluating, rating, or ranking without trying to remember all of the options given orally.

Here is an example of card use:

Please use the phrases on this card to tell me how the recent television ads for the new television reality show *On the Brink* has affected your intent to watch it when it debuts on September 22.

5 Increases my interest a lot ________
4 Increases my interest a little ________
3 Will not affect my interest ________
2 Decreases my interest a little ________
1 Decreases my interest a lot ________

Frequency scales deal with number of times.

Frequency interval scales ask respondents to select a number that most accurately reflects how often they do something or use something. For example:

How frequently do you eat pizza?

More than once a week ________
Once each week ________
Every other week ________
Once or twice a month ________
Less than once a month ________
Rarely ________

Numerical scales deal with ranges.

Numerical interval scales ask respondents to select a range or level that accurately reflects their age, income, educational level, or rank in an organization. For example:

I am going to read several age groupings. Please stop me when I read the one that applies to you.

18–24 ________
25–34 ________
35–49 ________
50–64 ________
65 and over ________

Nominal Scales

Nominal scales deal with naming and selecting.

Nominal scales provide mutually exclusive variables and ask respondents to name the most appropriate variable. These are self-reports and do *not* ask respondents to rate or rank choices or to pick a choice along an evaluative, numerical, or frequency continuum. Choices may be in any order. For example, you might ask:

Do you consider yourself to be a:

Democrat ________
Republican ________
Libertarian ________
Independent ________
Other ________

When you last cooked on an outdoor grill, did you cook:

Beef _____
Pork _____
Lamb _____
Poultry _____
Fish _____
Vegetable _____
Other ____________________ (PLEASE WRITE NAME.)

In nominal questions, the options are mutually exclusive and include most likely options from which to choose. "Other" is the final option because the respondent must be able to choose one of the named options or provide an option.

Ordinal Scales

Ordinal scales ask for ratings or rankings.

Ordinal questions ask respondents to rate or rank the options in their *implied* or *stated* relationship to one another. They do not name the most applicable option as in interval and nominal scales.

The following is a **rating ordinal scale:**

During the past 10 years, you have rented cars from several agencies. Please rate each of the *applicable* rental agencies as excellent, above average, average, below average, and poor.

Hertz	Ex.	Abv. Av.	Av.	Bel. Av.	Poor	N/A
Avis	Ex.	Abv. Av.	Av.	Bel. Av.	Poor	N/A
Alamo	Ex.	Abv. Av.	Av.	Bel. Av.	Poor	N/A
Enterprise	Ex.	Abv. Av.	Av.	Bel. Av.	Poor	N/A
National	Ex.	Abv. Av.	Av.	Bel. Av.	Poor	N/A
Thrifty	Ex.	Abv. Av.	Av.	Bel. Av.	Poor	N/A

Note that this rating scale generates six responses, including not applicable for an unused agency, and respondents will consciously compare the six auto rental agencies while developing their answers. You might ask interviewees to rank order options. The following is a **ranking ordinal scale:**

On this card are the names of 10 automobile manufacturers. Rank order them in terms of quality and dependability of their products.

Corporation	Rank	Corporation	Rank
General Motors	____	VW	____
Ford	____	Chrysler	____
Honda	____	Mazda	____
Toyota	____	Subaru	____
Kia	____	Hundai	____

The following ordinal question asks respondents to select from among and rank order options.

On this card are several reasons cited frequently for granting school vouchers to poor grade school and high school students. Pick the three you think are most important and rank them in order of importance to you.

____ Fairness	____ Reduction of union power
____ Competition	____ Higher quality education
____ Cost	____ Reduced government control
____ Parental involvement	

Bogardus Social Distance Scale

Bogardus scales measure effect of relational distances.

The **Bogardus Social Distance Scale** determines how people feel about social relationships and distances from them. You want to know if a person's attitude or feeling changes as the issue comes closer to home. This scale usually moves progressively from remote to close relationships and distances to detect changes as proximity narrows. For example, you might use the following Bogardus Social Distance Scale to determine how interviewees feel about the development of wind farms.

1. Do you favor the development of wind farms in the United States? ______ Yes ______ No
2. Do you favor the development of wind farms in the Midwest? ______ Yes ______ No
3. Do you favor the development of wind farms in your state? ______ Yes ______ No
4. Do you favor the development of wind farms in your county? ______ Yes ______ No
5. Do you favor the development of a wind farm on your property? ______ Yes ______ No

In many questions, respondents are safely removed from the attitude or feeling they are expressing about a product, issue, action, or person. The Bogardus Social Distance Scale brings an issue ever closer to home so it is no longer something impersonal or that affects others "over there."

Minimize guessing in surveys.

Question scales are designed to obtain a range of results and Level 2 and 3 disclosures, but respondents may try to "out psyche" survey takers. Students do this when taking standardized tests. For instance, respondents may try to pick "normal" answers in nominal and ordinal scales and safe, moderate, or middle options in interval scales. Rather than admit they do not know the correct answer, even when there is no correct answer, respondents may pick the option that stands out, such as the second in a list that includes 10 percent, 15 percent, 20 percent, 30 percent, and 40 percent. Respondents who first agree that a certain activity would make most people uneasy are less likely then to admit ever engaging in that activity and may attempt to change the subject.[12]

Anticipate confusion in scale questions.

Phrase scale questions carefully to avoid game playing, guessing, and confusion. Listen and observe reactions during pretesting interviews to detect patterns of responses, levels of interviewee comprehension, and hesitancy in responding. Long scales, complicated rating or ranking procedures, and lengthy explanations may confuse respondents, perhaps without either party realizing it at the time.

Question Sequences

Question sequences complement question strategies.

Use the question sequences discussed in Chapter 4 for survey interviews. The tunnel sequence is common in surveys when no strategic lineup of questions is needed. Gallup's quintamensional design sequence, or a variation of it, is appropriate when exploring intensity of attitudes and opinions. Funnel, inverted funnel, hourglass, and diamond sequences include open-ended questions, so answers may be difficult to record, code, and tabulate. This is taken into consideration for those doing qualitative surveys, because the wealth of information interviewers obtain from open questions is worth the problems involved. A study of the effects of question order suggests that general questions should come first followed by more specific questions. This is a funnel sequence.[13]

Selecting Interviewees

Select interviewees carefully because they are the sources of your data. The best schedule of questions will be of little help if you talk to the wrong people at the wrong time and in the wrong place.

Defining the Population

The first step in selecting interviewees is to define the **population** you wish to study. The population may be as small and similar as members of a baseball team or as large and diverse as those who attend sporting events on a regular basis. You may be interested in a subset of a larger population such as all veterans on a baseball team or all adults from ages 21 to 45 who attend sporting events on a regular basis. The identified population should include all persons who are able and qualified to respond to your questions and about whom you want to draw conclusions.

If a target population is small (members of a fitness club or faculty of a history department), you may interview all of them. Most surveys, however, deal with populations that far exceed time, financial, and personal limitations—the 35,000 undergraduate students at a university or residents over the age of 18 in a city of 250,000. Dozens of interviewers could not reach, let alone interview, all of these people. Since you may be unable to interview all persons in a target population, interview a sample of them and extend findings to all of them.

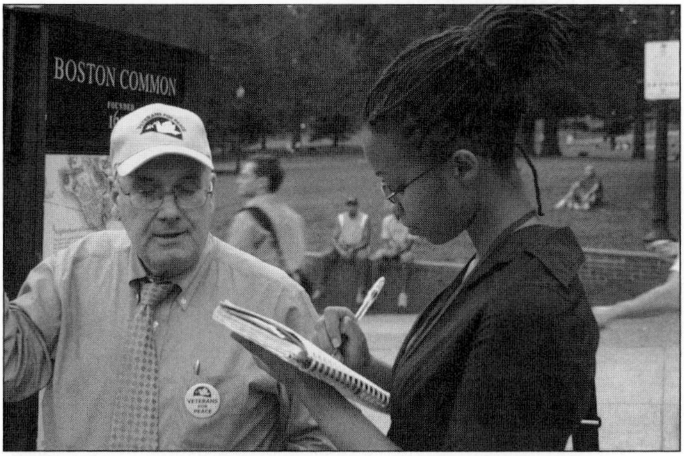

The first step in selecting interviewees is to define the population or target group you wish to study.

Sampling Principles

The fundamental principle is that a sample must accurately represent the population or target group under study. Old-time watermelon sellers practiced this principle when they carefully cut out a triangular plug from a watermelon. This plug represented the entire watermelon.

Each potential respondent from a defined population must have an equal opportunity of being selected. You must determine, then, the probability that each person might be selected to decide upon an acceptable **margin of error.** The precision of a survey is the "degree of similarity between sample results and the results from a 100 percent count obtained in an identical manner."[14] Most surveys attain a 95 percent **level of confidence,** the mathematical probability that 95 out of 100 interviewees would give results within 5 percentage points (margin of error) either way of the figures you would have obtained if you had interviewed the entire targeted population. Survey results reported in the media routinely state that a survey had a margin of error of 4 percent. This means that if 42 percent of respondents approve of the way congress is doing its job, the real figure might be as low as 38 percent or as high as 46 percent.

A sample is a miniature version of the whole.

A tolerable margin of error depends on the use of survey results. If you want to predict the outcome of an election or the effects of a new medical treatment, strive for a small margin of error, 3 percent or less. If you are conducting a survey to determine how employees feel about a new recreation facility, a higher margin of error is acceptable, 4 or 5 percent.

Margin of error determines the worth of a survey.

A sample is the actual number of persons interviewed.

Determine **sample size** by the size of the population and the acceptable margin of error. Some survey organizations produce accurate national surveys with a margin of error in the 3 percent range from a sample of 1,500. Standard formulas reveal that as a population increases in size, the percentage of the population necessary for a sample declines rapidly. In other words, you have to interview a larger percentage of 5,000 people than of 50,000 people to attain equally accurate results. Formulas also reveal that you must increase greatly the size of a sample to reduce the margin of error from 5 percent to 4 percent to 3 percent. The small reduction in the margin of error may not be worth the added cost of conducting significantly more interviews. Philip Meyer offers the following table that shows the sample sizes of various populations necessary for a 5 percent margin of error and a 95 percent level of confidence.[15]

Population Size	Sample Size
Infinity	384
500,000	384
100,000	383
50,000	381
10,000	370
5,000	357
3,000	341
2,000	322
1,000	278

Creative Research Systems offers a sample size calculator as a public service.[16] You may employ its calculator once you know the confidence interval (margin of error of 3, 4, or 5 points), the confidence level (percentage of sureness you have in results such as 95 percent), and your target population size.

Sampling Techniques

Size of sample is important, but how you select the sample is of utmost importance to the validity of a survey. As W. Charles Redding warned years ago, "a bad survey is worse than no survey."[17]

Random Sampling

Random sampling is like "drawing names from a hat."

Random sampling is the simplest method of selecting a representative sampling. For example, if you have a complete roster of all persons in a population, you place all names in a container, mix them thoroughly, and draw out one name at a time until you have a sample.

Table of Random Numbers

A more complicated random sampling method is to assign a number to each potential respondent and create or purchase a **table of random numbers.** With eyes closed, place a finger on a number and read a combination up, down, across to left or right, or diagonally. Select this number as part of the sample or decide to read the last digit of the number touched (46) and the first digit of the numeral to the right (29) and thus contact respondent number 62. Repeat this process until you have the sample you need.

In skip interval you select every *n*th name from a list.

Skip Interval or Random Digit

In a **skip interval** or **random digit sampling,** you choose every 10th number in a telephone book, every fifth name in a roster of clients, or every other person who walks into a supermarket. The Random Digital Dialing system now in wide use for conducting surveys "randomly generates telephone numbers in target area-code and prefix areas," "gives every telephone number in the area an equal chance of being called," and ensures anonymity because no interviewee names are used.[18] This common sampling technique may have some built-in flaws. For instance, a growing percentage of the population has unlisted phone numbers or relies on cell phones. A voter, customer, or membership roster might be outdated. Time of day, day of the week, and location may determine the types of persons available for interviews.

Stratified Random Sample

A stratified sample most closely represents the whole.

Random sampling procedures may not provide adequate representation of subgroups within a population. If a population has clearly definable groups (males and females; ages; education levels; income levels; and diverse cultural groups), employ a **stratified random sampling method.** This method allows you to include a minimum number of respondents from each group, typically the percentage of the group in the target population. For instance, if a targeted population consists of 30 percent first-year students, 25 percent sophomores, 20 percent juniors, 20 percent seniors, and 5 percent graduate students, your sample would represent these percentages.

A sample point is usually a geographical area.

Sample Point

A sample point represents a geographical area (a square block or mile, for instance) that contains specific types of persons (grain farmers or retired persons, for instance). Instructions may tell interviewers to skip corner houses (corner houses are often more expensive) and then try every other house on the outside of the four-block area until they have obtained two interviews with males and two with females. The U.S. Department of Agriculture uses aerial photographs of farm areas and crops to determine which farmers to interview to determine the amounts of various crops planted and possible yields of these crops each year. The **sample point** or **block sample** gives the survey designer control over selection of interviewees without resorting to lists of names, random digits, or telephone numbers.

Self-Selection

Self-selection is the least representative of sampling methods.

The most inaccurate sampling method is **self-selection.** You see this method used nearly every day in radio and television talk shows, newscasts, and on the Internet. Who is most likely to call C-SPAN, Rush Limbaugh, Larry King Live, or a television station? You guessed it—those who are very angry or most opposed to/most in favor of an action. Moderates rarely call or write. It is easy to predict how self-reporting surveys on gun control, health care reform, and labor unions will turn out. Randomness and representation of diverse elements of a population disappear in self-selected and "convenience samples" in which interviewers interview people when and where it is convenient for them such as in the evening, at lunchtime, or near their homes or businesses.[19]

Selecting and Training Interviewers

Creating a survey instrument and developing a careful sample of interviewees are critical, but so is selecting interviewers and training them to conduct the interviews properly.

Number Needed

You can rarely do it all by yourself.

If you plan to interview a small number of persons and the interviews will be brief, one interviewer may be sufficient. Most often you will need several interviewers, particularly when interviews will be lengthy, the sample is large, time allotted for completing the survey is short, and interviewees are scattered over a large geographical area. Large and difficult interviewing assignments result in serious interviewer fatigue and decline in motivation;[20] both will reduce the quality of interviews and the data received.

Qualifications

Interviewers must follow the rules.

A highly scheduled, standardized interview does not require the interviewer to be an expert on the topic or skilled in phrasing questions and probing into answers. It does require a person who can learn and follow guidelines, read the questions verbatim and effectively, and record answers quickly and accurately. If you are using a highly scheduled interview format that requires skillful probing into answers, interviewers must have the ability to think on their feet, adapt to different interviewees, handle unanticipated interviewee objections and concerns, and react effectively and calmly to strange answers. In this type of interview, professionally trained interviewers are more efficient and produce more accurate results.[21]

Interviewer credibility is critical in surveys.

Personal Characteristics

Interviewers who are older, have a nonthreatening demeanor, and have an optimistic outlook get better response rates and cooperation, regardless of their experiences. Age generates credibility and self-confidence, and optimism motivates interviewees to cooperate.[22] One study discovered that personality and attitude of the interviewer are the most important elements in shaping interviewee attitudes toward surveys.[23]

Interviewee Skepticism

Nearly one-third of respondents believe that answering survey questions will neither benefit them nor influence decisions, that there are too many surveys, that surveys are too long, and that interviewers ask too many personal questions. Some 36 percent of respondents in one study said they had been asked to take part in "false surveys," sales or political campaign interviews disguised as informational surveys. Clearly, survey interviewers must be aware of relational dimensions such as warmth, involvement, dominance, and trust and make every effort to establish a positive relationship with each respondent by appearing to be friendly, relaxed, and trustworthy.

Interviewees are increasingly wary of surveys.

Similarity of Interviewer and Interviewee

Similarity is an important relational dimension in survey interviews. You should dress similar to interviewees because if interviewers *look like me,* I am more likely to cooperate and answer appropriately. An in-group relationship with the interviewee (black to black, senior citizen to senior citizen, Hispanic-American to Hispanic-American) may avoid cultural and communication barriers and enhance trust because the interviewer is perceived to be safe, capable of understanding, and sympathetic. It may be essential that interviewers can speak to interviewees in their own language, including dialects or regional differences.[24]

Similarity, but not a mirror image, may be important.

Training Interviewers

Conduct training sessions with carefully written instructions for all interviewers, regardless of experience. Training results in greater use of appropriate probing questions, feedback, and giving instructions.[25]

During training sessions and developing written guidelines, discuss common interviewee criticisms of surveys and stress the importance of following the question schedule exactly as printed. Explain complex questions and recording methods. Be certain interviewers understand the sampling techniques employed. Emphasize the need to replicate interviews to enhance reliability and attain an acceptable margin of error and level of confidence. Be sure to describe the entire process and purpose, particularly if it is a research study. Discuss the nature and danger of interviewer bias. You may need to assist interviewers in reading maps and identifying households. Rehearse the interview, including the opening, asking questions and recording answers—critical if probing questions are included or interviewers will need to create them on the spot, and closing the interview.[26] The following are typical instructions for interviewers.

Poor execution can undo thorough preparation.

Preparing for the Interview

Study the question schedule and answer options thoroughly so you can ask rather than read questions and record answers quickly and accurately. Dress appropriately, and be neat and well groomed. Do not wear buttons or insignia that will identify you with a particular group or position on the issue to avoid biased responses. Choose an appropriate time of week and day.

Guard against interviewer bias.

Conducting the Interview

Be friendly, businesslike, and interested in the topic. Speak clearly, at a good pace, and loudly enough to be heard easily. Maintain eye contact and don't be afraid to smile. Ask all questions clearly, without hesitation, and neutrally. Adopt an informal speaking manner that avoids the appearance of reading or reciting openings, questions, and closings.

Opening the Interview

You must motivate the interviewee from the moment the interview commences. State your name, identify your organization, and present your credentials if appropriate. Explain the purpose, length, nature, and importance of the study; then move to your first question without appearing to pressure the interviewee to take part.

Asking Questions

No question can be altered in any way.

Ask all questions, including answer options, exactly as worded. You may repeat a question but not rephrase it or define words. Do not change the order of questions or answer options unless instructed to do so. If you are doing a qualitative study, probe carefully into answers to obtain insightful and thorough answers free of ambiguities and vague references.

Receiving and Recording Answers

Maintain a pleasant "poker face" throughout.

Give respondents adequate time to reply, and then record answers as prescribed in your training and on the schedule. Write or print answers carefully. Remain neutral at all times, reacting neither positively nor negatively to responses.

Closing the Interview

When you have obtained the answer to the last question, thank the interviewee for cooperating and excuse yourself without being abrupt. Be polite and sensitive, making it clear that the interviewee has been most helpful. Do not discuss the survey with the interviewee.

Conducting Survey Interviews

With all preparation completed, it is essential to **pretest the interview** with a portion of the targeted sample to detect potential problems with questions and answer options.

Pretesting the Interview

Lack of pretesting invites disaster.

The best plans on paper may not work during real interviews. Try out the opening, questions, recording answers, and closing.

Leave nothing to chance. For instance, in a political poll conducted by one of our classes, students deleted the question "What do you like or dislike about your major?" because it took too much time, generated little useful data, and posed a coding nightmare because of diverse replies. When interviewees were handed a list of political candidates during another project and asked, "What do you like or dislike about . . . ?" many became embarrassed or gave vague answers because they did not know some of the candidates. This question was replaced with a Likert scale from "strongly like" to "strongly dislike," including a "don't know" option, and interviewers probed into reasons for liking or disliking only for candidates ranked in the extreme positions on the scale. Respondents tended to know something about candidates they strongly liked or strongly disliked. In a survey of mudslinging during political campaigns, one of the authors discovered that scale questions tended to confuse elderly respondents, so he added special explanations to complex questions.

Here are typical questions to ask when pretesting survey interviews:

Leave nothing unquestioned.

- Did interviewees seem to understand what was wanted and why?
- Did interviewees react hesitantly or negatively to any questions?
- Did questions elicit the kind of information desired?
- Were there problems recording answers?
- Could answers be tabulated easily and meaningfully?

Once you have studied the pretest results and made alterations in procedures, questions, and answer options, you are ready to conduct the full survey.

Interviewing Face-to-Face

Ideally, the survey interview would be conducted face-to-face, a "personal" interview. It obtains a good response rate because of the personal touch and interviewees can see and hear the interviewer and feel, touch, experience, and perhaps taste products. The face-to-face interview has a number of advantages over other forms of survey taking.[27]

- The interviewer can establish credibility through physical appearance, dress, voice, eye contact, and presentation of credentials.
- Respondents will take part in longer interviews.
- Interviewers can ask more complex questions on complex issues.
- Interviewers can focus on in-depth attitudes and information by probing into answers.
- Respondents are more likely to provide self-generated answers.
- Respondents may provide more accurate answers because of the "naturalness" of the interview.
- Interviewers can observe attitudes and reactions through face, eye contact, gestures, and posture.
- Interviewers can interview specific respondents, in specific places, and at specific times.
- Interviewers can reach and obtain respondents from "marginalized populations."

While the face-to-face interview has many advantages, it also has some significant disadvantages. It is expensive, time-consuming, and slow. It requires a considerable number of thoroughly trained interviewers who may or may not interview the representative sample the survey requires. It may be impossible to do face-to-face interviews over a wide geographical area.

Interviewing by Telephone

Telephone interviews may be inexpensive in money but costly in results.

Because of the disadvantages of the face-to-face survey interview, the telephone interview is now the dominant approach. A single face-to-face interview may cost $100 or more, and with changes in society—particularly fewer homemakers at home during the day and flexible working hours—it has become difficult to predict when respondents might be available.

While some studies indicate that telephone and face-to-face interviews produce similar results, many researchers urge caution when selecting interviewing methods. One study discovered that many interviewers do not like telephone interviews, an attitude that may affect responses. Another found that fewer interviewees (particularly older ones) prefer the telephone. There is a lower degree of cooperation in telephone interviews.[28] People feel uneasy about discussing sensitive issues with strangers they cannot see, and it is difficult for interviewers to make convincing confidentiality guarantees when they are not face-to-face with respondents.[29] Add to these problems the growing number of persons with unlisted telephone numbers and cell phones and those using answering machines, answering services, and call identifiers to filter out unwanted calls, including surveys.[30]

Regardless of the potential problems with telephone survey interviews, they have become dominant because of significant advantages.[31]

- Telephone interviews are less expensive and provide faster results, literally overnight in many instances.
- There are fewer interviewer effects, including interviewer bias.
- Respondents provide fewer socially acceptable answers.
- There is increased interviewer uniformity in manner, delivery, and standardization of the interview.
- Interviewers feel safer on the telephone than venturing into dangerous neighborhoods, particularly at night.
- Respondents prefer the anonymity of the telephone when answering controversial and personal questions.
- Respondents prefer the safety of the telephone that does not require them to admit strangers to their homes or places of business.

Since the telephone survey interview has become so dominant today, here are some guidelines for conducting interviews over the telephone.

Opening the Telephone Interview

Most refusals in telephone surveys occur prior to the first substantive question: one-third in the opening seconds, one-third during the orientation, and one-third at the point of listing household members.

Speaking skills (pitch, vocal variety, loudness, rate, and distinct enunciation), particularly during the opening, are more important than content. One study concluded, "Respondents react to cues communicated by the interviewer's voice and may grant or refuse an interview on that basis."[32] Telephone interviewers must establish trust through vocal and verbal analogs to the personal appearance, credentials, and survey materials

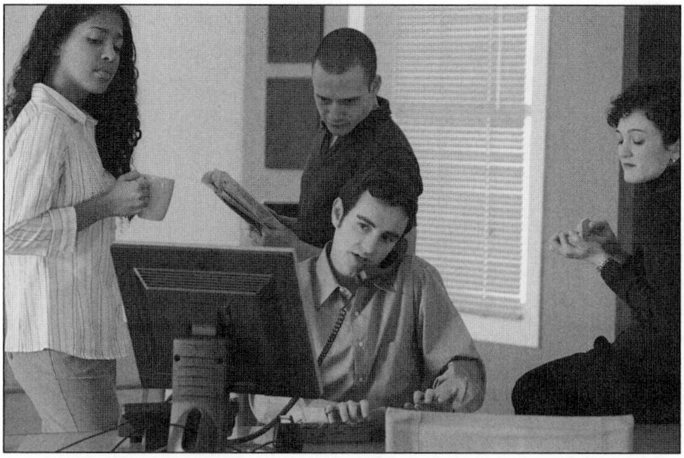
photo by Comstock/Punch Stock

A growing number of interviewers are turning to the telephone for easier and less expensive means of conducting surveys and polls.

that enhance trust in face-to-face interviews.

How to Use the Telephone

The literature on survey interviewing contains important advice for would-be telephone interviewers. These guidelines are equally relevant to face-to-face interviews.

Opening the telephone interview is critical.

Do nothing but ask and listen during telephone interviews.

- *Do not give a person a reason or opportunity to hang up.* Develop an informal but professional style that is courteous (not demanding) and friendly (not defensive). Get the interviewee involved as quickly as possible in answering questions because active involvement motivates people to take part and cooperate.
- *Listen carefully and actively.* Give your undivided attention to what the interviewee is saying by not drinking, eating, sorting papers, or playing with objects on your desk. Don't communicate nonverbally with others in the room, and say nothing you do not want the interviewee to hear even if you believe you have the mouthpiece covered. Explain any pauses or long silences of more than a few seconds or signal you are listening with cues such as "Uh huh," "Yes," "Okay."
- *Use your voice effectively.* Talk directly into the mouthpiece. Speak loud enough, slowly, clearly, and distinctly because the interviewee must rely solely on your voice. State each answer option distinctly with vocal emphasis on important words and pause between each option to aid in comprehension and recall.
- *Use a computer-assisted telephone interview system* that enables you to dial random numbers quickly and to compile results within minutes of completing interviews.

Interviewing through the Internet

An increasing number of survey interviews are taking place through the Internet—e-mail, Web pages, and computer direct.[33] They are substantially less expensive and faster than either face-to-face or telephone interviews. A survey posted on a popular Web site may generate thousands of responses within hours.[34] Because they are highly flexible, Internet surveys can target large populations over great distances. A major problem of survey interviews—interviewees attempting to give socially acceptable answers—is lessened because of the anonymity and perceived safety of the Internet interview. Respondents give more honest answers to sensitive topics. Unlike paper-and-pencil surveys, and even some face-to-face and telephone surveys, interviewees tend to provide more detail in answers to open-ended questions, perhaps because it is easy and quick to type lengthy answers on a keyboard and they can reply when it suits them.

On the other hand, the critical nonverbal communication that aids face-to-face and telephone interviews is lost when you use the Internet. Response rates may suffer because it is more difficult to establish the credibility of the survey and its source or to distinguish the survey interview from a slick telemarketer sales interview. While the Internet gives respondents time to think through answers, it may lose the spontaneity of interactions in face-to-face and telephone interviews; they are essentially electronic bulletin boards. However, "real-time chat" software can ensure spontaneity. It's nearly impossible to probe into answers or employ question strategies such as shuffle, leaning, and repeat. Evidence indicates that completion rates are lower for lengthy surveys; respondents grow tired of the process and simply log off.

It is extremely difficult to target specific audiences you wish to sample in wide-ranging, Internet surveys, and you may not know who in a family, corporation, school, or state replied to your survey. Your sample, and thus your results, may be highly questionable. Those who feel most strongly about an issue, usually with negative attitudes, may overwhelm the results in self-selected Internet surveys. This has led researchers Chris Mann and Fiona Stewart to warn, "There is no doubt that the unrepresentativeness of current Internet access remains the greatest problem for data collection on-line."[35]

Coding, Tabulation, and Analysis

Once all interviews are completed, the final phase of the survey begins. This phase involves coding, tabulation, and analysis of the information received.

Coding and Tabulation

Begin the final phase of the survey by **coding** all answers that were not precoded, usually the open-ended questions. For instance, if question 20 is "You say you oppose a government-run health care option. Why do you oppose such an option?" a wide variety of answers are possible. If question 20 is coded #20, each answer can be coded 20 plus, 1, 2, 3, 4, etc., such as the following:

20-1 It would be far too expensive.

20-2 The government messes up everything it tries to run.

20-3 It would run private health care plans out of business.

20-4 It would be a major step toward socialized medicine such as in Canada and Great Britain.

20-5 It would add trillions of dollars to the national debt.

20-6 It is another step toward socialism.

20-7 It would interfere with the physician's right to prescribe the most effective treatment I might need. I could die because of the government's interference.

Record answers to open-ended questions with great care.

Answers to open-ended questions may require analysis and structuring before developing a coding system. For example, in a study of voter perception of mudslinging in political campaigns, the interviewer asked, "What three or four words would you use to describe a politician who uses mudslinging as a tactic?" Answers included more than 100 different words, but analysis revealed that most words tended to fit into five categories: untrustworthy, incompetent, unlikable, insecure, and immature.[36] A sixth category, "other," received words that did not fit into the five categories. All words were placed into one of these six categories and coded from one to six.

Analysis

Analysis is making sense of your data.

Once all answers are coded and the results tabulated, the **analysis** phase begins. This task can be overwhelming. One of the authors surveyed 354 clergy from 32 Protestant, Catholic, and Jewish groups to assess the interview training they had received during college and seminary and since entering the ministry.[37] The 48 questions in the survey times 354 respondents provided 16,992 bits of information.

How can the survey interviewer handle massive amounts of information generated in most surveys? The late Charles Redding offered several helpful suggestions.[38]

- *Be selective.* Ask "What findings are likely to be most useful?" and "What will I do with this information once I get it?" If you have no idea, do not ask for it.
- *Capitalize on the potential of data.* Subject data to comparative breakdowns to discover differences between demographic subgroups.
- *Dig for the gold.* What is the really important stuff hidden within raw data and simple tabulations? For instance, in polls of registered voter attitudes, interviewers often discover that female respondents favor a candidate far less than male respondents and that Americans who have recently become citizens are likely to have very different views toward immigration than third or fourth generation Americans.
- *Look for what is missing.* What you do not find may be more important than what you do find. What information did you not obtain?

Know the limitations of your survey.

During analysis of data, ask a number of questions. What conclusions can you draw and with what certainty? For what segment of a target population can you generalize? What are the constraints imposed by the sample, schedule of questions, the interviewing process, and the interviewers? Why did people respond in specific ways to specific questions? What unexpected events or changes have occurred since the completion of the survey that might make this survey dated or suspect? What should be done with the "undecided" and "don't know" answers or blanks on survey forms?

Be careful in using survey results.

Caution is essential for all survey takers. For example, journalists must be cautious when writing headlines and making predictions. Organizations must be cautious when basing policy decisions on survey results. Voters must be cautious when casting votes according to candidate-preference polls. You might subject data to a statistical analysis designed to test reliability and significance of data. Babbie and other research methodologists (see resources) provide detailed guidelines for conducting sophisticated statistical analyses.

When the analysis of data is complete, determine if the purpose and objectives of your survey are achieved. If so, what are the best means of reporting the results?

The Respondent in Survey Interviews

The ever-growing number of surveys conducted throughout the world each day by government agents and agencies, political candidates and parties, advertisers and marketing representatives, special interest groups and activists, charities and religious organizations, colleges and students ensures your involvement in these highly structured interviews. They are rarely compulsory, so you are free to "just say no," but when you do, you may forfeit an opportunity to influence important decisions that affect you, your family, your field of work, and your community. Don't walk away, close the door, hang up the phone, or hit the delete button too hastily, but approach all survey requests cautiously and with a healthy skepticism.

The Opening

Understand what a survey is all about before participating.

Take an active part in the opening and discover through observing, listening, and asking questions (1) the identity of the interviewer, (2) the interviewer's credentials, (3) the organization sponsoring the survey, (4) the purpose of the survey, (5) why and how you were selected to participate, (6) the length of the interview, (7) how the information you give will be used, and (8) the confidentiality of your answers and your identity. The goal is to become thoroughly oriented prior to answering questions. If the interviewer does not provide important information, ask for it. When one of the authors was visiting his daughter and her family in Vancouver, Washington, more than 2,000 miles from home, he was approached in a shopping mall by a market researcher. The researcher explained who she was, what she was doing, and why she was doing it. She did not state that he had to be a local resident. When asked if it made any difference that he was visiting from the Midwest, the interviewer said she wanted only those who regularly visited the mall. The interview ended.

The opening minutes enable you to determine if the interview is really part of a survey or a slick persuasive interview under the guise of a survey and whether or not you want to take part. For example, is it a nonpartisan political survey being conducted by a nationally known and reputable polling organization or part of a political campaign for a specific candidate or party? When one of the authors responded to the doorbell at his home, a college-age person announced that she was conducting a survey of families with children for a summer internship. A few questions revealed that she was selling child-oriented magazines for a summer job, not an internship sponsored by her college as implied in her opening.

The Question Phase

Listen perceptively.

Listen carefully to each question, particularly to answer options in interval, nominal, and ordinal questions. If a question or option is difficult to recall, ask the interviewer to repeat the question slowly. If a question is unclear, explain why and ask for clarification. Avoid replays of earlier answers, especially if you think you "goofed." Do not try to guess what a question is going to be from the interviewer's first words. You might guess wrong and become confused, give a stupid answer, or needlessly force the interviewer to restate a perfectly clear question.

Think before answering.

Think through each answer to respond clearly and precisely. Give the answer that best represents your beliefs, attitudes, or actions. Do not permit interviewer bias to lead you toward an answer you think the interviewer wants to hear or how other respondents might answer.

You have rights as a respondent. You can refuse to answer poorly constructed or leading questions or to give data that seem irrelevant or an invasion of privacy. For instance, an interviewer recently asked one of the authors, "Do you favor boutique solutions to our energy needs such as wind farms or environmentally friendly nuclear power plants that can supply electricity to major industries and cities?" The word "boutique" clearly revealed the bias and agenda of the interviewer. Expect and demand tactful, sensitive, and polite treatment from interviewers. Insist on adequate time to answer questions. If you have agreed to a 10-minute interview and the interview is still going strong at the 10-minute mark, remind the interviewer of the agreement and proceed to close the interview unless only a few more seconds are required. Survey interviews can be fun, interesting, and informative if both parties treat one another fairly.

Summary

The survey interview is the most meticulously planned and executed of interviews. Planning begins with determining a clearly defined purpose and conducting research. The purpose of all survey interviews is to establish a solid base of fact from which to draw conclusions, make interpretations, and determine future courses of action. Only then does the survey creator structure the interview and develop questions with appropriate strategies, scales, sequences, coding, and recording methods. Selecting interviewees not only involves delineating a target population to survey, but also involves choosing a sample of this population that represents the whole. The creator of the survey chooses sampling methods, determines the size of the sample, and plans for an acceptable margin of error. Each choice has advantages and disadvantages because there is no one correct way to handle all survey situations.

Survey respondents must determine the nature of the survey and its purposes before deciding whether to take part. If the decision is to participate, respondents have a responsibility to listen carefully to each question and answer it accurately. Be sure you understand each question and its answer options. Demand enough time to think through answers. Feel free to refuse to answer obviously leading or poorly phrased questions that require a biased answer or choosing among options that do not include how you feel and what you prefer.

Key Terms and Concepts

The online learning center for this text features FLASHCARDS and CROSSWORD PUZZLES for studying based on these terms and concepts.

Bogardus Social Distance Scale
Chain or contingency strategy
Convenience sample
Cross-sectional survey
Evaluative interval scale
Face-to-face interview
Filter strategy
Frequency interval scale
Internet interview
Interval scale
Leaning question strategy
Level of confidence
Likert scale
Longitudinal survey
Margin of error
Marginalized respondent
Nominal scale
Numerical interval scale
Ordinal scale
Personal interview
Population
Qualitative survey
Quantitative survey
Precision journalism
Random digital dialing
Random sampling
Ranking ordinal scale
Rating ordinal scale
Reliability
Repeat strategy
Replicability
Sample point
Sampling principles
Self-selection
Shuffle strategy
Skip interval scale
Stratified random sample
Table of random numbers
Web survey

A Survey Interview for Review and Analysis

The purpose of the following survey is to discover how parents with school-age children (kindergarten through 12th grade) perceive the problems their children are encountering in their daily lives, both inside and outside the school setting, what should be done to assist their children in meeting these problems, and who should assist them.

As you read through this survey schedule, notice the parts of the opening, including the opening and qualifying questions. Identify the question strategies, question scales, and question sequences. How are the built-in probing questions, instructions for interviewers, and precoded answers designed to aid the interviewer and ensure accuracy and replicability of the survey being conducted by many interviewers? What is included in the brief, planned closing?

How might the opening be improved, including the order and placement of demographic and qualifying questions? As a potential interviewee, what questions might you have for the interviewer before proceeding with the interview? Which questions could have been phrased more effectively? What problems might the open-ended questions pose for interviewers and interviewees? How well do the questions cover the areas of concern in this research survey? How might answer options have been precoded for ease of tabulation? How adequate is the closing?

Problems School-Age Children Are Encountering Today

Speak to any parent of school-age children (KINDERGARTEN THROUGH 12TH GRADE) *residing in the household.* Hello, my name is ______________, a graduate student in educational psychology at California State at Long Beach. I'm assisting with a national study of how parents of school-age children perceive the problems their children are encountering in today's society. The results will be published in professional journals and released to the press. The interview will only take a few minutes.

1. I'm going to read you several age ranges. Stop me when I read the one that includes your age.

   18–24 ________
   25–34 ________
   35–49 ________
   50 and over ________

2. What was the last grade level of your formal education?

   8–11 years ________
   12–15 years ________
   High school graduate ________
   College graduate ________
   Postgraduate work ________

3. Are you a parent of a school-age child, kindergarten through 12th grade? (IF NO, ASK IF SUCH A PARENT RESIDES IN THE HOUSEHOLD. IF NO PARENT RESIDES IN THE HOUSEHOLD, TERMINATE THE INTERVIEW. IF YES, PROCEED TO Q. 3a).

3a. How many school-age children do you have?

1–2 ________ 5–6 ________

3–4 ________ 7 or more ________

3b. What are their ages?

5–7 ________ 14–16 ________

8–10 ________ 17–19 ________

11–13 ________

4a. When you think of a serious problem facing your school-age children (child) today, which problem comes to mind first?

____

4b. What do you see as the major cause of this problem?

____

4c. What are other possible causes of this problem?

____

____

____

5. Many parents tell us that the use of drugs is the greatest problem facing their school-age children (child) today. How would you rate the job parents are doing in addressing this drug problem? (CIRCLE ANSWERS IN THE SCALES PROVIDED AT THE END OF Q. 7.)

6. How would you rate the job the schools are doing in addressing the drug problem? (CIRCLE ANSWERS IN THE SCALES PROVIDED AT THE END OF Q. 7.)

7. How would you rate the job law enforcement is doing in addressing this drug problem? (CIRCLE ANSWERS IN THE SCALES LISTED BELOW.)

	Parents	**Schools**	**Law Enforcement**
Excellent	1	1	1
Good	2	2	2
Average	3	3	3
Not so good	4	4	4
Poor	5	5	5

8. Do (Does) your children (child) have free access to a computer at home?

Yes ________

No ________

9. Here is a card (HAND CARD TO INTERVIEWEE.) that lists some of the problems parents identify as major problems facing their school-age children. (ROTATE THE ORDER FROM ONE INTERVIEW TO THE NEXT.) Which one do you think is likely to address these problems most effectively: parents, schools, law enforcement, or the government?

	Parents	Schools	Law Enforcement	Government
Drugs	1	2	3	4
Alcohol	1	2	3	4
Assault	1	2	3	4
Robbery	1	2	3	4
Gun violence	1	2	3	4
Rape	1	2	3	4
Sexual predators	1	2	3	4
Bullying	1	2	3	4
Suicide	1	2	3	4

10. Many parents of school-age children tell us they are concerned about the availability of drugs for school-age children. This card (HAND CARD TO THE INTERVIEWEE.) lists several possible solutions to the drug availability problem. Which one do you believe would be the most effective deterrent?

More law enforcement in and near schools.	1
Stiffer mandatory sentences for those who **sell** drugs to school-age children.	2
Stiffer mandatory sentences for those who **supply** drugs to school-age children, including parents.	3
A law that requires teachers and principals to report all suspected drug use by students.	4
Permanent expulsion of any student caught supplying drugs to other students.	5

11. Many parents we talk to feel that the United States has become a more violent society since they were in school. This card (HAND CARD TO THE INTERVIEWEE.) gives often-cited causes of violence facing our school-age children today. Which one of these causes do you feel is the greatest cause? (RECORD ANSWER.) Which is the next greatest cause? (RECORD ANSWER.) Which would be the next cause? RECORD ANSWER. And which would be the next cause? (RECORD ANSWER.)

	First	Second	Third	Fourth
Guns	1	2	3	4
Gangs	1	2	3	4
Television	1	2	3	4
The Internet	1	2	3	4
Electronic games	1	2	3	4
Drugs	1	2	3	4
Lack of discipline in the home	1	2	3	4
Poverty	1	2	3	4
Violence in the home	1	2	3	4

12. Some sources claim that the only way to reduce the problems facing school-age children today is to strengthen the traditional family in the United States. Tell me whether you strongly agree, agree, disagree, or strongly disagree with each of these recommended ways to strengthen the traditional family. (RECORD ANSWERS IN THE SPACES BELOW AND ROTATE THE ORDER IN WHICH THE STATEMENTS ARE GIVEN FROM INTERVIEW TO INTERVIEW.)

a. Physical abuse should be the only grounds for divorce.
b. Abortion should be illegal.
c. A constitutional amendment should forbid same-sex marriages.
d. New income tax deductions should enable more women to remain at home with their children.
e. Adultery should be a felony.
f. The minimum wage should provide an adequate income for every family.

	a	**b**	**c**	**d**	**e**	**f**
Strongly agree	1	1	1	1	1	1
Agree	2	2	2	2	2	2
Don't know	3	3	3	3	3	3
Disagree	4	4	4	4	4	4
Strongly disagree	5	5	5	5	5	5

13a. Are you familiar with the No Child Left Behind Act?

Yes _____ (IF YES, ASK Q. 12b.*)*
No _____

13b. What do you know about the No Child Left Behind Act?

____

____

14. Do you control your children's (child's) access to a computer at home?

Yes ________
No ________

15a. Educational psychologists claim that bullying is one of the major problems facing school-age children today. Do you approve or disapprove of making bullying an illegal act that might lead to arrest and incarceration?

Approve ________
Disapprove ________

15b. Why do you feel this way?

____

____

15c. How strongly do you feel about this?

Strongly ________
Very strongly ________
Something about which you will never change your mind ________

16. With a growing concern for juvenile crime and the arrest of significant numbers of preteens and teenagers for adult crimes such as assault, robbery, rape, burglary, and the use of firearms in committing these crimes, many communities are building juvenile detention centers to house these young offenders.

    a. Would you be in favor of building such centers in your state?
    Yes ________ No ________
    b. Would you be in favor of building such a center in your county?
    Yes ________ No ________
    c. Would you be in favor of building such a center in your city?
    Yes ________ No ________
    d. Would you be in favor of building such a center in your neighborhood?
    Yes ________ No ________

That's all the questions I have. The survey results should be made public within five to six weeks.

Now I would like to ask you some personal questions so we can see how people with different backgrounds feel about the problems facing their school-age children today.

17. Do you generally consider yourself to be a conservative, liberal, centrist, or other?

    Conservative ________
    Liberal ________
    Centrist ________
    Other ________

18. Do your children attend public schools, private schools, or are they homeschooled?

    Public schools ________
    Private schools ________
    Homeschooled ________

19. I'm going to read several household income ranges. Stop me when I read the range that includes your current annual family income.

    0 through $14,999 ________
    $15,000 through $24,999 ________
    $25,000 through $49,999 ________
    $50,000 through $74,999 ________
    $75,000 through $99,999 ________
    Over $100,000 ________

That's all the questions I have. Thank you very much for participating in this important survey. The results should be made public within six months.

Survey Role-Playing Cases

Safety on Campus

Safety on your college campus is a growing concern with increasing numbers of assaults and shootings, particularly at off-campus housing and drinking establishments. The interviewer is chairing the Student Affairs Committee that has taken on the task of creating a survey to interview a cross section of faculty and students to discover their experiences with safety issues on campus, their fears and concerns for their safety and that of others, and suggestions for making the campus safer in perception and reality.

Rising Health Care Costs

In spite of efforts by Congress to establish health care reform in the past few years, costs for health care have continued to rise much faster than inflation. The recession that gripped the country from 2008 to 2010 resulted in many employers discontinuing health care coverage for employees or greatly reducing their contributions to employee health care. A group of medical, governmental, and religious leaders has banded together to assess the problems, concerns, and attitudes of a cross section of adults (anyone 18 years or older) to guide their discussions and proposals for further health care reforms.

Need for a 24–7 Child Care Facility

You and four friends with experiences in local child care feel that there is a need for a facility that would provide 24–7 child care in your community. All local facilities open at 6:00 a.m. and close at 6 p.m., but a growing number of parents, including single parents, are working 4:00 p.m. to midnight and midnight to 8:00 a.m. shifts and need day care during these evening and nighttime periods. The five of you are considering building and staffing a 24–7 day care facility but need to assess the number of clients and children you might serve to make it financially feasible. You are both creating a survey instrument and trying to determine your target population.

A Run for the School Board

You have been unhappy with the actions of the local board for a number of years, and a professional acquaintance has decided to run for the school board in the fall election. He faces stiff competition from current board members and two other well-known members of the community who have decided to run. Your goals early in the campaign are to determine your acquaintance's name recognition, degree of satisfaction with the current makeup of the school board, and potential roles of social and political organizations that support specific educational philosophies.

Student Activities

1. Serve as a volunteer interviewer for a survey being conducted on your campus or community. What instructions and training did you receive? How were interviewees determined? What problems did you encounter in locating suitable and cooperative interviewees? What problems did you have with the survey schedule? What is the most important thing you have learned from this experience? What advice would you give the organization you volunteered to serve?
2. Try a simple interviewer bias experiment. Conduct 10 short opinion interviews on a current issue, using an identical question schedule for all interviews. During five of them, wear a conspicuous T-shirt, button, or badge that identifies membership in or support of an organization that supports one side of the issue: a Republican

elephant, or Democratic donkey, a crucifix or a Star of David, an organization's logo or a product slogan. Compare results to see if and how your identification with an organization on one side of the issue affected answers to identical questions.

3. Obtain a number of market survey schedules used in face-to-face, telephone, and Internet surveys. Compare and contrast these schedules. How are the openings similar and different? How are schedules and sequences similar and different? How are question strategies and question scales similar and different? How are closings similar and different? What surprises did you discover in your comparisons?

4. Interview a person experienced in survey interviews. How does this person (or the person's organization) conduct background research? Create and pretest survey schedules? Determine the size of sample and sampling methods? Determine acceptable margins or error? Select and train interviewers? Use face-to-face, telephone, and Internet methods?

Notes

1. Paul Rosenfeld, Jack E. Edwards, and Marie D. Thomas, "Improving Organizational Surveys," *American Behavioral Scientist* 36 (1993), p. 414.
2. Leslie A. Baxter and Earl Babbie, *The Basics of Communication Research* (Belmont, CA: Wadsworth/Thomson, 2004), p. 167.
3. Baxter and Babbie, p. 22.
4. Baxter and Babbie, p. 22.
5. http://www.socialresearchmethods.net/kb/interview.htm, accessed September 29, 2006.
6. Diane K. Willimack, Howard Schuman, Beth-Ellen Pennell, and James M. Lepkowski, "Effects of a Prepaid Nonmonetary Incentive on Response Rates and Response Quality in Face-to-Face Survey," *Public Opinion Quarterly* 59 (1995), pp. 78–92.
7. Stanley L. Payne, *The Art of Asking Questions* (Princeton, NJ: Princeton University Press, 1980), p. 57.
8. Jack E. Edwards and Marie D. Thomas, "The Organizational Survey Process," *American Behavioral Scientist* 36 (1993), pp. 425–426.
9. Earl Babbie, *The Practice of Social Research* (Belmont, CA: Wadsworth/Thomson, 1995), p. 145.
10. "Survey Interviewing," http://www.audiencedialogue.net/kya4c.html, accessed August 10, 2009; Jennifer Dewey, NCREL, "Guidelines for Survey Interviewing," accessed September 14, 2000; "Interviews," http://www.socialresearchmethods.net/kb/interview.php, accessed July 16, 2009.
11. Creative Research Systems, "The Survey System," file://C:DOCUME~1\stewart\LOCALS\Temp\G2BBVAF.htm, accessed September 29, 2006.
12. Norman M. Bradburn, Seymour Sudman, Ed Blair, and Carol Stocking, "Question Threat and Response Bias," *Public Opinion Quarterly* 42 (1978), pp. 221–234.
13. Sam G. McFarland, "Effects of Question Order on Survey Responses," *Public Opinion Quarterly* 45 (1981), pp. 208–215.

14. Morris James Slonim, *Sampling in a Nutshell* (New York: Simon and Schuster, 1960), p. 23; W. Charles Redding, *How to Conduct a Readership Survey: A Guide for Organizational Editors and Communication Managers* (Chicago: Lawrence Ragan Communications, 1982), pp. 27–28.

15. Philip Meyer, *Precision Journalism* (Bloomington: Indiana University Press, 1979), p. 123; Redding, pp. 31–36.

16. "Sample Size Calculator," http://www.surveysystem.com/sscalc.htm, accessed August 14, 2009.

17. Redding, p. 1.

18. "Designing the Survey Instrument and Process," http://www.airhealthwatch.com/mdph_instrument.htm, accessed September 29, 2006.

19. "Sampling (Statistics)," http://en.wikipedia.org/wiki/sampling_%28statistics29, accessed August 14, 2009.

20. Eleanor Singer, Martin R. Frankel, and Marc B. Glassman, "The Effect of Interviewer Characteristics and Expectations on Response," *Public Opinion Quarterly* 47 (1983), pp. 68–83.

21. Robin T. Peterson, "How Efficient Are Salespeople in Surveys of Buyer Intentions," *Journal of Business Forecasting* 7 (1988), pp. 11–12.

22. Singer, Frankel, and Glassman, pp. 68–83.

23. Stephan Schleifer, "Trends in Attitudes toward and Participation in Survey Research," *Public Opinion Quarterly* 50 (1986), pp. 17–26.

24. "Evaluation Tools for Racial Equity: Tip Sheets," http://www.Evaluationtoolsforracialequity.org/, accessed September 29, 2006.

25. Jacques Billiet and Geert Loosveldt, "Improvement of the Quality of Responses to Factual Survey Questions by Interviewer Training," *Public Opinion Quarterly* 52 (1988), pp. 190–211.

26. "Interviews," http://www.socialresearchmethods.net/kb/interview.php, accessed July 16, 2009.

27. Roger W. Shuy, "In-Person versus Telephone Interviewing," in *Inside Interviewing: New Lenses, New Concerns,* James A. Holstein and Jaber F. Gubrium, eds. (Thousand Oaks, CA: Sage, 2003), pp. 175–183.

28. Lawrence A. Jordan, Alfred C. Marcus, and Leo G. Reeder, "Response Style in Telephone and Household Interviewing," *Public Opinion Quarterly* 44 (1980), pp. 210–222; Peter V. Miller and Charles F. Cannell, "A Study of Experimental Techniques in Telephoning Interviewing," *Public Opinion Quarterly* 46 (1982), pp. 250–269.

29. William S. Aquilino, "Interview Mode Effects in Surveys on Drug and Alcohol Use," *Public Opinion Quarterly* 58 (1994), pp. 210–240.

30. Michael W. Link and Robert W. Oldendick, "Call Screening: Is It Really a Problem for Survey Research?" *Public Opinion Quarterly* 63 (Winter 1999), pp. 577–589.

31. Theresa F. Rogers, "Interviews by Telephone and in Person: Quality of Responses and Field Performance," *Public Opinion Quarterly* 39 (1976), pp. 51–65; Stephen Kegeles,

Clifton F. Frank, and John P. Kirscht, "Interviewing a National Sample by Long-Distance Telephone," *Public Opinion Quarterly* 33 (1969–1970), pp. 412–419.

32. Lois Okenberg, Lerita Coleman, and Charles F. Cannell, "Interviewers' Voices and Refusal Rates in Telephone Surveys," *Public Opinion Quarterly* 50 (1986), pp. 97–111.

33. "Personal Surveys vs. Web Surveys: A Comparison," http://knowledge-base.supersurvey.com/in-person-vs-web-surveys.htm, accessed September 29, 2006; Creative Research Systems, "The Survey System."

34. "Personal Interviews vs. Web Surveys: A Comparison," http://knowledge-base.supersurvey.com/in-person-vs-web-surveys.htm, accessed August 10, 2009.

35. Chris Mann and Fiona Stewart, "Internet Interviewing," in Holstein and Gubrium, p. 243.

36. Charles J. Stewart, "Voter Perception of Mudslinging in Political Communication," *Central States Speech Journal* 26 (1975), pp. 279–286.

37. Charles J. Stewart, "The Interview and the Clergy: A Survey of Training, Experiences, and Needs," *Religious Communication Today* 3 (1980), pp. 19–22.

38. Redding, pp. 119–123.

Resources

Baxter, Leslie A., and Earl Babbie. *The Basics of Communication Research*. Belmont, CA: Wadsworth/Thomson, 2004.

Conrad, Frederick G., and Michael F. Schober, eds. *Envisioning the Survey Interview of the Future.* San Francisco: Wiley-Interscience, 2007.

Fink, Arlene. *How to Conduct Surveys: A Step-by-Step Guide.* Thousand Oaks, CA: Sage, 2009.

Gwartney, Patricia A. *The Telephone Interviewer's Handbook.* San Francisco: Jossey-Bass, 2007.

Holstein, James A., and Jaber F. Gubrium, eds. *Inside Interviewing: New Lenses, New Concerns.* Newbury Park, CA: Sage, 2003.

Meyer, Philip. *Precision Journalism.* Lanham, MD: Rowman & Littlefield, 2002.

CHAPTER 7 The Recruiting Interview

The primary reason you may be reading this textbook, and taking a course in interviewing, may be to learn how to be a successful applicant and land a great position that starts a successful career. Why, then, does this chapter focus on the recruiter in the employment interview and precede the chapter that focuses on the applicant? We do so for two important reasons. First, you can play the role of applicant more effectively if you have a clear understanding of what and why recruiters do what they do in interviews and the selection process. In a way, you are on a scouting expedition. Second, although few of you may be heading toward careers in Human Resources (HR), all of you will be involved on a regular basis in assisting your organizations in hiring quality employees, your colleagues. We have seen many of our students return to our campuses as recruiters within a year after graduation because their employers felt they could identify readily with student recruits, particularly those at their alma mater. Knowing how to assist in the recruiting process makes you a valuable asset to your employer.

Recruiting new employees is a never-ending and critical task for every organization because their futures depend on it. Tom Peters, in his book titled *Re-Imagine,* writes that today "talent rules," so management must be obsessed with attracting and retaining new talent.[1] Others echo Peters's predictions. William Lewis writes that finding talent at a reasonable cost and developing that talent is the ultimate difference between success and failure.[2] A senior manager told the authors, "Anyone can buy technology, but the critical element in competing globally is the *people!*"

Recruiting is expensive and complex.

The task of recruiting high-quality people is neither easy nor inexpensive, however. A search firm executive told the authors, "You can't know enough, learn enough, or experience enough" in a single interview. The process often entails multiple contacts with several staff members at different locations. It is an elaborate courtship process fraught with all sorts of interpersonal problems between two complex parties and susceptible to bias and distortion. In spite of such problems, the interview remains a critical component of the selection process because recruiters must become keenly aware of and probe into the skills, attitudes, behaviors, and abilities that may make an applicant an ideal **fit** for the **organization** and **position.**[3]

Where to Find Good Applicants

There are numerous sources available to locate good applicants. The Internet provides sources in virtually all fields from college graduates to senior citizens. Every university and college has its own Web site. Churches, senior citizen clubs, for-hire agencies, and placement services are readily available, most with Web sites.

Merely publishing an opening is not sufficient.

Web sites have not replaced personal contacts.

Don't overlook traditional sources. Use your social and professional networks. Keep a file of "potentials" you can refer to when necessary. College career centers and those of professional societies and ethnic organizations are excellent sources. Attend job fairs on campuses, at malls, and those coinciding with professional meetings and conferences.

The job or career fair, typically held on college campuses, is an excellent way to make or improve a name for your organization and to attract excellent students who are interested in internships and full-time positions. Focus on key schools where your recruiting has been successful in the past. Interns with your organization are excellent recruiters because they will sing your praises and college-age students can readily identify with them. If you are not currently hiring, be honest with students. Be sure to make follow-up contacts with those who give you a resume and express interest and everyone you interview.

Many organizations, particularly in retail, have in-store terminals and kiosks to attract people who might not apply otherwise. This allows them to establish and update "a prospective database every minute the store is open" and to sort through applications to locate the most qualified applicants.[4]

There are literally hundreds of Internet and electronic sources available to locate quality applicants. Here are a few key sources:

- Job Search (http://www.jobsearch.com)
- HeadHunter.net (http://www.headhunter.net)
- MonsterTrak (http://www.monstertrak.com)
- Kennedy's Directory of Executive Recruiters (http://www.kennedyinfo.com/db/db_der_bas.html)
- P.A.C.E., founded in 1992 to serve contract professionals, is good for older workers (http://www.pace.pros.com)
- Yahoo search engine (http://www.yahoo.com)
- Wall Street Journal search engine (http://wsj.com)
- Monster board career search (http://www.monster.com)
- Hot Jobs (http://www.hotjobs.com)

Most organizations are striving to diversify their workforces, particularly among ethnic groups. Joyce Gioia suggests that you advertise in ethnic media (such as alternate language newspapers, magazines, Web sites, radio, and television) and in movie theaters that attract a highly diverse clientele.[5] Think globally, Gioia writes, because recruiting employees from diverse ethnic groups "holds opportunities for companies beyond their wildest dreams."

Don't overlook your Web site because the majority of prospective applicants will check this site to determine if your organization is attractive and a good fit. One study revealed that one in two potential applicants consider the employer's Web site to be "important" and that one in four would reject a potential employer on the basis of a poor Web site.[6] Your site should be easy to read, interesting, and sophisticated. A simple reality check is to log onto your site *as a potential employee* to see if it meets these criteria.

Preparing the Recruiting Effort

Since the recruiting interview remains the central component of attracting and selecting employees, recruiters must approach the process systematically and learn how to prepare for, participate in, and evaluate it. Professionally conducted interviews not only select better employees but also present good impressions of organizations.[7]

Reviewing EEO Laws

Start the recruiting process by carefully reviewing **equal employment opportunity (EEO)** laws, including those of the states in which you will be recruiting that may be more stringent than federal laws. Although such laws (and executive orders) can be traced back to the Civil Rights Act of 1866, you must know six laws thoroughly.[8]

Unintentional violations are still violations.

- The Equal Pay Act of 1963 requires equal pay for men and women performing work that involves similar skill, effort, responsibility, and working conditions.
- The Civil Rights Act of 1964, particularly Title VII, prohibits the selection of employees based on race, color, gender, religion, or national origin, and requires employers to discover discriminatory practices and eliminate them.
- The Age Discrimination in Employment Act of 1967 prohibits employers of 25 or more persons from discriminating against persons because of age.
- The Rehabilitation Act of 1973 (Sections 501 and 505) orders federal contractors to hire persons with disabilities, including alcoholism, asthma, rheumatoid arthritis, and epilepsy.
- The Civil Rights Act of 1991 (often referred to as the 1992 Civil Rights Act) caps compensation and punitive damages for employers, provides for jury trial, and created a commission to investigate the "glass ceiling" for minorities and women and reward organizations that advance opportunities for minorities and women.
- The Americans with Disabilities Act of 1990 (effective July 25, 1992), Title I and Title V, prohibits discrimination against persons with physical and mental impairments that substantially limit or restrict the condition, manner, or duration under which they can perform one or more life activities and requires reasonable accommodation by employers.

© Digital Vision
Review EEO laws carefully.

Understanding and complying with EEO laws is good for business. Aging baby boomers and senior citizens, rather than being a drag on organizations as previously thought, bring valuable experiences to positions; know what they can and cannot do; are willing to take the initiative; are loyal; exhibit a willingness to learn, adjust, and adapt as they have for many years; show patience and a willingness to "hang in there" when facing difficult situations and relationships; are good listeners; and have the ability to get the job done.[9] Not hiring these people in the first place because of age is not only unlawful but may deprive your organization of valuable resources.

Compliance with EEO Laws

Although EEO laws have been in effect for decades, interviewers continue to violate them knowingly and unknowingly. One study reported that 70 percent of 200 recruiters for Fortune 500 companies thought at least 5 of 12 unlawful questions were "safe to ask."[10] Another study found that 12 percent thought it was acceptable to ask questions about political beliefs, 27 percent about family background, 30 percent about the candidate's spouse, and 45 percent about the candidate's personal life.[11] Job discrimination cases rose to an all-time high (more than 95,000) during the recession of 2008–2010 due in large part to mass layoffs and scarce hiring. The leading charges were race, gender, age, and disability discrimination.[12]

Numerous EEO laws would seem to complicate the employee recruiting/selecting process, but complying with them is rather simple. Be sure that everything you do, say, or ask during the selection process pertains to **bona fide occupational qualifications (BFOQs),** requirements essential for performing a particular job. BFOQs usually *include* work experiences, training, education, skills, conviction records, physical attributes, and personality traits that have a direct bearing on one's ability to perform a job effectively. BFOQs usually *exclude* gender, age, race, religion, marital status, physical appearance, disabilities, citizenship, place of birth, and ethnic group that have no bearing on one's ability to perform a job effectively.

BFOQs are the keys to non-discriminatory hiring.

Exceptions to laws and orders are made when an employer can demonstrate that one or more normally unlawful traits are essential for a position. For example, appearance may be a BFOQ for a modeling position, religion for a pastoral position, age for performing certain tasks (serving alcohol, operating dangerous equipment), and physical abilities such as eyesight and manual dexterity for pilots.

EEO violations are easy to avoid.

You can avoid EEO violations, and possible lawsuits for your employer, if you take advantage of the training your organization offers, review sources readily available in professional journals and on the Internet, and take an online course designed to help you comply with EEO laws and guidelines.[13] These sources, for example, can help you avoid asking discriminatory questions, such as the following, of applicants with disabilities.

- How did you become disabled?
- How severe is your disability?
- How will you be able to get to work?
- How often have you been hospitalized?
- Have you undergone treatment for a mental condition?

They offer practical suggestions such as shaking hands with a person who is disabled, not pushing a wheelchair unless asked, identifying yourself and others involved in the interview if the applicant is blind, and using physical signals, facial expressions, and note passing if an applicant has a hearing impairment.[14] Sources can also help you keep up-to-date in laws and situations. For instance, a number of our students from the military reserve and active military units that were called to duty in the wars in Iraq and Afghanistan have informed us that recruiters have asked them about the type of military discharge they received. This is an unlawful question because it is not a job-related question and may delve into an applicant's medical record or disability.[15]

Focus on the positive, not the negative.

Treat applicants as you would want to be treated.

A few simple guidelines will help you avoid most EEO violations and lawsuits.[16] First, meet the **test of job relatedness** by establishing legally defensible selection criteria. Second, be sure *all questions* are related to these selection criteria. Third, standardize the interview by asking the *same questions* for all applicants for a position. If you ask certain questions only of applicants who are female, disabled, older, or minority, you are undoubtedly asking unlawful questions. Fourth, be cautious when probing into answers because a significant number of EEO violations occur in these created-on-the-spot questions. Fifth, be cautious of innocent chit-chat during the informal parts of interviews, usually the opening and closing or the minutes following the formal interview. This is when you are most likely to ask or comment about family, marital status, ethnic background, and nonprofessional memberships. Sixth, focus questions on what an applicant *can do* rather than on what an applicant *cannot do.* Seventh, if an applicant begins to volunteer unlawful information, tactfully steer the person back to job-related areas.

Exercise #1—Testing Your Knowledge of EEO Laws

Test your knowledge of EEO laws and selection interviews by rating each question below as *lawful* (can be asked), *depends* (may be asked under certain circumstances), or *unlawful* (cannot be asked). Explain why it is lawful, unlawful, or depends.

	Lawful	Unlawful	Depends
1. Are you a U.S. citizen?			
2. How did you lose the three fingers on your left hand?			
3. I see you were in the Marine Corps from 2001 to 2008. What kind of discharge did you receive?			
4. Any marriage plans in the offing?			
5. What will you do if your husband gets transferred?			
6. How fluent are you in Spanish?			
7. Mind if I call you Candy?			
8. Do you smoke?			
9. Which computer programs have you used?			

	Lawful	Unlawful	Depends
10. Who will take care of your children when they are ill?			
11. Were you ever arrested when you were in college?			
12. How long would you plan to work for us?			
13. What is your native language?			
14. What clubs do you belong to?			
15. Do you prefer Miss, Ms., or Mrs.?			

Keep these final rules in mind when recruiting.

- Federal laws supersede state laws unless the state laws are more restrictive.
- The Equal Employment Opportunity Commission (EEOC) and the courts are not concerned with *intent* but with *effect.*
- Advertise each position where all qualified applicants have a reasonable opportunity to learn about the opening.
- Your organization is liable if unlawful information is maintained or used even if you did not ask for it.
- Do not write or take notes on the application form. Doodling on an application form may appear to be a discriminatory code.
- Three recent concerns have arisen in the law: domestic partners, same-sex marriage, and hearing as a disability. An appropriate response is, "We hire persons based on what they know and how well they can do the job, not on personal preferences or disabilities." Organizations should be prepared to enhance volumes on phones and computers.
- EEO laws generally pertain to all employers of 15 or more people.

Accepting or keeping unlawful information creates liability for the company even if the information was not requested.

Developing an Applicant Profile

The profile must be a composite of BFOQs.

The profile is the ideal by which all applicants are measured.

With EEO laws in mind, conduct a thorough analysis to develop a **competency-based applicant profile** for the position for which you are recruiting. This profile of the ideal employee typically includes specific skills, abilities, education, training, experiences, knowledge levels, personal characteristics, and interpersonal relationships that enable a person to fulfill a position with a high degree of excellence.[17] The intent is to measure all applicants against this profile to ensure that recruiting efforts meet EEO laws, are as objective as possible, encourage all interviewers to cover the same topics and traits, and eliminate (or at least minimize) the **birds of a feather syndrome** in which recruiters favor applicants who are most like themselves—traditionally this has favored male applicants.

Over the past 15 years, a rapidly growing number of organizations are employing a **behavior-based** selection technique to ensure that each interviewer asks questions that match each applicant with the applicant profile. Behavior-based interviewing rests on two interrelated principles: that past behavior in specific job-related situations

Is past performance the best predictor of future performance?

is the best predictor of future behavior and that past performance is the best predictor of future performance. Interviewers ask interviewees to describe situations in which they have exhibited specific skills and abilities.[18] The behavior-based techniques begin with a needs and position analysis to determine which behaviors are essential for performing a particular position. Other organizations have modified this approach into a **trait-based** or **talent-based** system in which specific traits or talents rather than behaviors are identified in a position analysis. For instance, traits might include the following:

achievement	dependability	oral communication
ambition	initiative	people-oriented
assertiveness	listening	responsibility
competitiveness	motivation	responsiveness

Can nondominant group applicants match your profile?

Regardless of the means you use, check each profile trait carefully. Is each trait essential for excellent job performance? Is leadership necessary for an entry-level position? Can you measure the trait? Are you expecting recruiters to act as psychologists? Will some targeted traits adversely affect your organization's diversity efforts and discriminate unintentionally? For example, traits such as competitiveness, aggressiveness, direct eye contact, forcefulness, and oral communication skills may run counter to the upbringing and culture of many nondominant groups.[19] Traits being sought must be position-related—BFOQs—and clearly defined so that all interviewers are looking for the same ones.

Once you have developed an applicant profile, write a clear description that "encapsulates requirements for a given position." Karen O'Keefe writes, "Ultimately, the job description is the inspiration for any subsequent interview so defining the position up front will make finding the right person for the job much easier."[20] Being underprepared is the biggest mistake you can make.

Assessing What Applicants Want

Times and people are changing.

Since recruiting interviews are as much about attracting as selecting outstanding employees, it is imperative that you understand the targets of your search.

What Do Applicants Desire in a Position and Career?

Young, college-educated applicants are very different from those of 10 or 20 years ago. While they are interested in career paths and steady employment, the thought of remaining with one organization until receiving the gold watch is unrealistic to most. Applicants are more interested in strong reputations than in brand name.

Salary and benefits are no longer the key factors in job attraction. Young applicants are more interested in stress training programs, mentoring, supervision, tuition assistance, and career development opportunities.[21] They want extensive information about positions and organizations prior to interviews.

Applicants are increasingly information-driven.

The new workforce fully understands that diversity is reality. They expect and welcome working with a range of educations, ages, races, and ethnic groups. Political and geographical boundaries pose few obstacles since many have traveled, studied, or worked abroad.

What Do Applicants Desire in an Interviewer?

Today's applicants have clear preferences in interviewers. Applicant decisions are significantly affected by their satisfaction with the communication that takes place, and their attraction to the interviewer is the strongest predictor of their attraction to an organization.[22] They view the recruiter's behavior as a model of what to expect from the employer, so a negative experience may eliminate an organization from further consideration.

The recruiter is the organization in the applicant's eyes.

Applicants expect interviewers to be friendly, attentive, sensitive, warm, honest, enthusiastic, straightforward, personable, and genuinely interested in them. They do not want to be pressured or interrupted. They prefer interviewers to act and talk naturally without reading questions, being stuck to a schedule, or giving canned presentations.

Select recruiters with applicant traits in mind.

Applicants want interviewers to be professionals who know what they are talking about. In one survey, 93 percent reported they like to meet with and learn the experiences of relatively new employees rather than veteran representatives determined to sell their organizations.[23] Nondominant group applicants (women, minorities, lower class) report they are more comfortable and communicate more openly with and feel better understood and evaluated by interviewers more like them. On the other hand, this openness and relief may turn to confusion, anger, and guarded interactions if they feel scrutinized by "one of their own."[24]

Applicants want interviewers to ask them relevant, open questions and give them opportunities for self-expression. They like interviewers to offer limited self-disclosures to avoid shifting the focus away from the applicant.[25] And applicants want detailed information that is relevant to the position and organization.

Obtaining and Reviewing Information on Applicants

With planning completed and the recruitment under way, gather as much information as possible about each applicant through application forms, resumes, letters of recommendation, and objective tests.

Application Forms

Modify application forms to fit the applicant profile.

Design **application forms** with EEO laws and the applicant profile in mind. Avoid traditional categories that violate EEO guidelines such as gender, age, race, ethnicity, national origin, marital status, physical characteristics, arrest records, type of military discharge, and request for a picture. Include a few open-ended questions similar to ones you will ask during the interview. Be sure to provide adequate space for applicants to answer all questions thoroughly. Look for what is and is not reported on the form, how applicants respond to open-ended questions, and gaps in dates of employment and education.

Resumes

Review each resume carefully in advance. Patricia Buhler writes that "reading the resume for the first time in front of the applicant sends a clear message about a lack of preparedness and a lack of importance."[26] Delete unlawful information from the resume (picture, age, marital status, religious organizations, and so on) before any person involved in the recruitment effort can see it. If you keep this information (even though you did not request it), you can be held liable for possible discrimination.

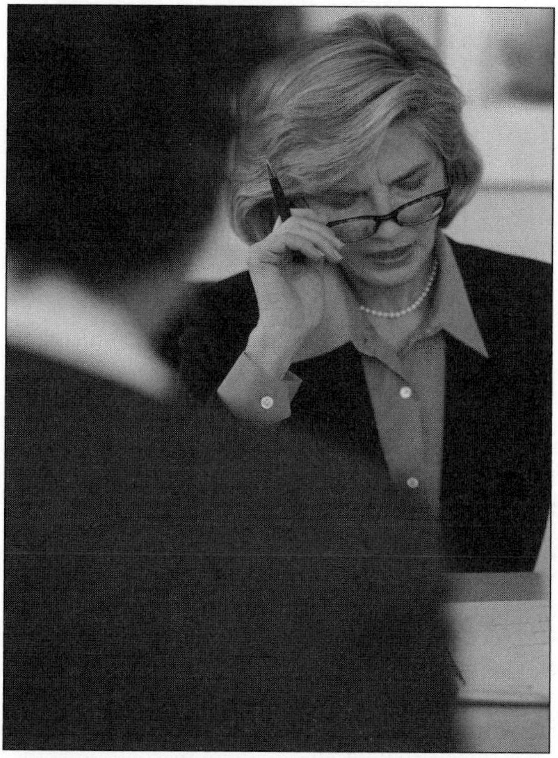

Ryan McVay/Getty Images

Review the applicant's credentials prior to the interview so you can devote full attention to the applicant during the interview.

Note how well the applicant's career objective meets the applicant profile. If it does, assess how well the applicant's education, training, and experiences complement the stated career objective and the applicant profile. Look for what *is* and *is not* included on the resume.

Be aware that many applicants exaggerate their qualifications and experiences on resumes. In a survey on Careershop.com, 73 percent of applicants admitted that they lied on their resumes. Common deceits were inflating job titles, years of work, experiences, education, and current salary. The most common, however, was leaving out items that might appear unfavorable to a recruiter.[27]

If your organization receives large volumes of resumes for positions or is hiring a large number of workers, a scanning system may be worth the cost. Resume scanning systems sort out applicants based on key words or skills listed in the system by a hiring manager or human resources department. A scanning system can save time, sort through and store a large volume of resumes, and enable you to scan the pool again if the need arises.

Some applicants do not match their resumes.

Consider a scanner if you attract hundreds of applicants.

There are disadvantages to using scanning systems. For example, if an excellent candidate uses "personnel" instead of "human resources" or "purchasing" instead of "procurement/materials management," the candidate may be eliminated from the system and sent a rejection letter. The result is the same if an applicant's degree abbreviations do not match those in the system. Your system may identify candidates who know the system or operable key terms or jargon rather than the best qualified. Include key scannable terms in your advertisements and recruiting literature so all candidates are playing on the same field.

Cover Letters

The cover letter is often your first opportunity to "see" an applicant.

Review each **cover letter** carefully. What does it reveal about career goals and qualifications? How well is it adapted to your position and organization, or is it a "To Whom It May Concern" all-purpose letter? Does it reveal interest in the position and your organization? Is it written professionally? Is it free of spelling, grammatical, and punctuation errors?

Letters of Recommendation and References

Review **letters of recommendation** with skepticism because they are written by friends or admirers. They rarely contain negative information. Letters do reveal people an applicant knows who will write letters and add bits of information about how well the applicant fits the profile.

References are usually persons applicants choose carefully to guarantee a favorable recommendation. Calls to references, however, allow you to ask open-ended questions and probe into answers to get beyond the superficial or guarded words and phrases of a letter. Unfortunately, fears of lawsuits have led many organizations to formulate policies that allow them to give you nothing more than the dates on which the applicant attended school or was employed. Organizations may require interviewers to get permission from applicants before contacting letter writers or references. Bob Ayrer recommends calling references once a short list is determined and picking out those with a medium range relationship to the applicant—"not close enough to lie for them, but close enough to have an opinion" of the applicant's worth.[28]

Fears of lawsuits are hampering reference checks.

Tests

A growing number of organizations are using testing as a supplement in the recruiting process. Some sources claim that the behavioral interview is more effective "when combined with employment tests, many of which are now administered online."[29] All tests must be job-related, validated on a cross-section of the population, and nondiscriminatory. If a test screens out one group more than another (more women than men, more black Americans than white Americans, more Hispanic than European-Americans, more older applicants than younger applicants), do not use it.[30]

All tests must be carefully pretested.

Basic Skills Tests

Basic skills tests measure mathematics, measurement, and reading or spelling skills. Poor reading and spelling skills pose major problems when individuals or teams are asked to write up problems on their machines or with their groups. Some tests describe a basic problem and ask the applicant to write five to seven sentences describing the problem. Examiners or test monitors look for spelling, sentence structure, verb tense, and readability using a common formula.

Basic skills appear to be declining when they are more important than ever.

Personality Tests

Personality tests attempt to assess the people skills, personality traits, and personality types of applicants. Standard tests such as the Myers-Briggs and the Wilson Analogy may help you identify personality type and thinking skills of applicants when these are important for the position.[31]

Assessing Honesty

Some sources reveal that 38 percent of applicants ranging from college students to poet laureates, big-time football coaches, and CEOs are dishonest on their resumes and application forms.[32] Julia Levashina and Michael Campion, developers of the Interview Faking Behavior (IFB) scale, discovered that 90 percent of undergraduate job candidates were guilty of "faking" (intentionally distorting answers) ranging from exaggerations, embellishments, omissions, and concealments to outright lies that included colleges attended, fictitious degrees, job titles, previous salaries, experiences, responsibilities, and employment dates.[33] CNN/Careerbuilder.com provided a list of "whoppers" told by applicants such as claiming to be a member of the Kennedy family,

Hispanic rather than 100 percent Caucasian, a member of the military before being born, a professional baseball player, and a CEO when an hourly worker.[34] The truth can best be determined, first, through a thorough analysis and comparison of factual information about the applicant prior to the interview.[35]

Honesty Tests

Honesty tests may appear intrusive, but they are here to stay.

Second, consider paper and pencil honesty tests designed to assess ethics, honesty, and integrity in both the selection process and at the workplace. When we ask our students how many have taken honesty tests, the majority who reply "Yes" were applying for jobs at fast-food restaurants in which they would handle money. A task force of the American Psychological Association reviewed over 200 studies pertaining to honesty tests and concluded that they identify individuals with a *high propensity* for stealing in the workplace, but this finding left others wondering about applicants who fall in the *moderate* to *low* ranges.[36] Robert Fitzpatrick, a Washington attorney who specializes in employment law, warns, "While they [honesty tests] might screen out some undesirable job candidates, they also screen out [like the old polygraph tests] a tremendous percentage of perfectly honest, upstanding citizens."[37] If you use honesty tests, be sure they have been thoroughly validated on a cross-section of the American population to avoid charges of discrimination.

Interviews

Third, employ a thorough probing interview in which you attempt to "read" the applicant's verbal and nonverbal reactions to questions to help separate the truth from deception. Do not accept an initial answer and move on—listen, observe, think, and then probe. In the spring semester of 2009, Dana Olen, a recruiter for Stryker (a Fortune 500 company that employs a behaviorally based interviewing approach) made a presentation at Purdue University explaining this approach in detail. When asked what she would do if an applicant provided a suspicious answer to a behavior-based question, she immediately provided six probing questions that would determine the truthfulness and completeness of the answer: "Who did you work with on this project?" If a company-sponsored project: "What company was this?" and "How did that company's structure integrate into this project?" If a class project: "Describe this class project for me." "How many people were you working with?" Unfortunately, extensive probing is not without pitfalls. In their studies of applicant faking behavior, Levashina and Campion discovered that "follow-up questioning increased faking in both situational and past behavioral structured interviews." During informal debriefing, participants revealed that standardized follow-up questions (e.g., "Could you please elaborate?") were perceived as cues signaling that the requested information was important for the interviewer and prompting more detailed answers that encouraged respondents to fake."[38] Before you shy away from probing, however, these researchers also discovered that "past behavioral interviews with no follow-up questioning were the most resilient to faking."

Probing deeply into answers is essential in assessing honesty.

Some organizations use **integrity interviews** to assess the honesty or integrity of prospective employees.[39] Truthful applicants tend to acknowledge the probability of employee theft, reply without hesitation, reject the idea of leniency for dishonesty, and expect favorable test results. Interviewers have reported a strange phenomenon called *outguessing* in which applicants cheerfully admit to unethical activities because

ON THE WEB

Integrity interviews are becoming more common during the selection process as employers attempt to assess the integrity of potential employees in an age when honesty often seems the exception rather than the norm. Many employers and researchers are raising serious questions about the accuracy and value of honesty tests in the employment selection setting. Search the Internet for discussions of the uses and concerns raised by written and oral honesty tests. These sources should get you started on your search: Infoseek (http://www.infoseek.com), PsycInfo (http://www.psycinfo.com), The Monster Board (http://www.monster.com/), CareerBuilder (http://www.careerbuilder.com/), and PsychLit (http://www.psychlit.com/).

they believe they are normal and "everyone does it."[40] Two formats are used most frequently. The first consists of highly structured interviews that focus on ethics and integrity by delving into previous work experience directly related to the position available. Work-related questions result in applicants having positive feelings toward the integrity interview and the organization. Second, if previous work experience is unavailable, the interviewer poses situational questions using specific dimensions of ethical and honest behavior. Donna Pawlowski and John Hollwitz have developed a structured situational interview "based on the assumption that intentions predict behaviors."[41] Interviewers ask interviewees to respond to hypothetical scenarios and employ a 5-point scale with an agreed upon definition of the dimension. Other dimensions are relationship manipulation, interpersonal deception (lying), security violation (giving out trade secrets), and sexual harassment (telling dirty jokes or displaying nude pictures).

Focus on real or hypothetical work situations.

Benefits of Previewing Applicants

Previewing information on the applicant gives you a clear notion of your relationship with the applicant by revealing how much each of you wants to take part in the interview, the degree of interest, and how control is likely to be shared. It is your first opportunity to determine how well the applicant fits your organization's unique culture.[42] The preview also reveals areas to probe during the interview, perhaps comparing oral and written answers to similar questions. Fredric Jablin and Vernon Miller discovered that employers who review applicant credentials thoroughly ask more questions, a wider variety of questions, and probe more into answers.[43] The result is a better determination of how well each applicant fits the position.

Doing your homework leads to more effective interviews.

Structuring the Interview

Once you have obtained extensive information on applicants, focus attention on structuring the interview.

The Opening

As stated often in this book, the opening is a critical part of each interview. It sets the tone for the interview and creates the all-important first impression of you and your organization.

Involve the applicant in the opening.

Establishing Rapport

Begin the recruiting interview by greeting the applicant by name in a warm, friendly voice and with a firm but not crushing handshake to create **rapport.** Introduce yourself and your position with the organization. Do not ask the applicant to call you by first name if this is a first interview because few applicants will feel comfortable doing so.

Rapport building is particularly important in cross-cultural interviews. Establish a relationship "that is based on trust, understanding, and acceptance" from the first moments of the interview, and bear in mind "that speaking the same language does mean sharing the same culture."[44]

Do not delay the inevitable.

Engage in a bit of small talk about a noncontroversial issue, but do not prolong casual conversation or fall into overworn questions such as "What do you think of this weather?" and "How was your trip?" that elicit few meaningful responses and add nothing to your rapport with the applicant. Prolonged idle chatting may heighten tension by creating anxiety and suspense.

Orientation

Proceed to the orientation phase of the opening in which you tell the applicant how the interview will proceed. Traditionally this has meant:

- Questions from the recruiter.
- Information about the position and the organization.
- Questions from the applicant.

Be systematic and creative.

Giving information first delays active involvement of the applicant in the interview and may communicate that the recruiter intends to dominate the interview. You might tell the applicant how long the interview will take and approximately how long you will devote to each part. If the interview is taking place during an on-site or plant trip, provide the applicant with an agenda for the visit and the names and positions of people who will be involved in the selection process.

Share control with the applicant.

While the traditional approach has been interviewer-controlled, some recruiters are recommending an interviewee-controlled approach. For instance, Bob Ayrer, who specializes in hiring salespersons, recommends an extensive orientation period. "At this point SHUT UP!" he writes. "Allow the prospective salesperson to take control (that is what you are hiring them to do in the field, isn't it?)"[45]

The Opening Question

The **opening question** serves as a transition to the body of the interview. This open-ended, easy-to-answer first question gets the applicant talking about a familiar subject (education, experiences, background, recent internship.) It sets the proper tone for the interview—the applicant talking and the recruiter listening and observing.

Begin with an open question, but not too open.

Plan the opening question carefully, and avoid always starting with the same question. Adapt it to what you have learned in previewing information. The most common opening question, "Tell me about yourself," is so open that applicants often do not know where to begin or how much information to give. Do they start with birth, grade school, high school, college, or current/recent positions? Do they talk about hobbies, education, work experiences, major events? This highly open, generic question neither relaxes the applicant nor gets the applicant talking about meaningful subjects. A better opening question is "Tell me about your duties (or responsibilities) in your current position."

Do not set up the applicant for an early failure.

Do not put the applicant on the spot too early because interviewers tend to put more weight on negative information, and the earlier it comes in the interview, the more devastating it may be. Pose an easy-to-answer, reasonably open question to get the applicant ready and able to answer more difficult questions.

The Body of the Interview

Unstructured interviews do not recruit top-quality applicants.

Sources differ on how structured the body of the recruiting interview ought to be, but research indicates that the validity of recruiting highly qualified applicants is most successful when organizations utilize highly structured formats.[46] The old "seat of the pants," "off the top of the head," and "my gut tells me" interviews lead to numerous hazards. An unstructured, rambling, unfocused interview tells the interviewer almost nothing about job candidates."[47] For instance, interviewers talk more than applicants in unstructured interviews rather than the 80 percent for applicants to 20 percent for recruiters rule of thumb. Interviewers tend to make their decisions within the first four minutes, long before answers to critical and thought-provoking questions, to cover factual and biographical information that is readily available on application forms and resumes, are more susceptible to stereotyping and biases, and more likely to ask questions that violate EEO laws.

Highly Structured Interviews

Highly structured interviews are more reliable but less flexible and adaptable.

A growing number of recruiters advocate highly scheduled interviews in which all questions are prepared and tested ahead of time and posed to each applicant without variation. Highly structured interviews are more reliable because all applicants are asked the same or very similar questions and recruiters must pay close attention throughout the interview instead of the first few minutes. Organizations may employ a highly structured interview centered on specific traits in the applicant profile (interpersonal skills, computer expertise, team experience) or an interview guide (can the person do the job, will the person do the job, will the person fit into the organization).

Fit with the position and organization is critical because well-qualified applicants who do not match the organization's culture result in poor performance and high turnover rate. Some interviews cover topics such as company environment, management influence, and co-workers.

Behavior-based methods focus on job-related skills.

Behavior-based recruiting is very common. An organization develops a highly structured interview that provides for skillful patterning and selecting of questions, recording of responses, and rating of applicants on behaviorally defined dimensions. In the following example, the interviewer employs a five-point scale to rate answers according to the degree to which it exhibits or gives information about one or more behaviors: 5 = strongly present and 1 = minimally present.

Rating	Behavior	Question
_______	Initiative	Give me an example of when you have resolved conflicts between employees.
_______	Energy	How many times have you done this?
_______	General intelligence	What was the outcome?
_______	Decisiveness	How did you feel about the results you got?
_______	Adaptability	When faced with intransigence, what did you do?

Build in insightful secondary questions.

While listening to the answer to the first question, for example, look for the kinds of conflicts the applicant has addressed and their complexity. Preplanned probing questions probe deeper into the experience, including methods used, and success the applicant had in resolving them. The answer may reveal a number of other characteristics such as communication ability, sensitivity, fairness, and ability to follow prescribed procedures.

Highly scheduled interviews have significant limitations.

While the highly scheduled interview may lessen the influence of stereotypes, recruiter-applicant dissimilarity, and the possibility of lawsuits for EEO violations, it has several shortcomings:[48] It enhances recruiter control and may be detrimental to underrepresented group members. The applicant may have little opportunity to introduce job-related information. Recruiters have little opportunity to adapt to specific applicants, to probe into answers, or to share information when thought necessary. The organization dominates what should be a mutual activity between recruiter and candidate.

Place the applicant in realistic work settings.

William Kirkwood and Steven Ralston argue that the highly structured interview bears little resemblance to situations applicants will face on the job. Thus, the interviewee is unable to demonstrate and the recruiter is unable to observe the applicant's skills in realistic settings.[49] Any process that stifles the recruiter's ability to probe into answers is likely to result in fewer insights into the applicant as a person and potential employee. We recommend a moderately scheduled interview that allows both parties the flexibility necessary for meaningful interactions and a maximum of self-disclosure.

Question Sequences

Get the applicant talking as quickly as possible.

Select one or more **question sequences** appropriate for the interview and the applicant; normally this means funnel, inverted funnel, or tunnel sequences. Interviewers tend to use the inverted funnel sequence by asking closed primary questions during the early minutes of the interview and open-ended probing questions in the later minutes.[50] The inverted sequence enables recruiters to test applicants and then switch to a funnel sequence with applicants they perceive to be most qualified. Since applicants tend to give short answers to closed questions while they feel out the interviewer and longer answers and more information to open questions, interviewers may make snap judgments within the first few minutes of interviews based on very little information. Also, the best way to relax an applicant is to get the person talking. Begin with a funnel or tunnel sequence to get the interviewee talking, relaxed, and giving maximum information.

Closing the Interview

The closing must sustain the positive tone of the interview.

If you have the authority to hire on the spot (rare in most interviews), either offer the position or terminate further consideration. If you do not have hiring authority or do not want to make an immediate decision, explain specifically what the applicant can expect after the completion of the interview. For example:

> Jackie, I've enjoyed talking with you this morning. (pause to let the applicant talk) We are recruiting on several midwestern campuses for this position at our Kansas City facility. We plan to invite four or five candidates to Kansas City for additional interviews within a few weeks. You will be hearing from us within the next 10 days about whether you will be invited for these interviews. Do you have any final questions for me? (pause to let the applicant talk) If you need to contact me or you have additional questions, here is my card with my cell phone and office telephone numbers and e-mail address.

Do not encourage or discourage applicants needlessly.

Be honest and candid with applicants. If you have many excellent applicants for a position, do not give each the impression that he or she is at the top of the list. If you know an applicant will not be considered further, do not "string the person along" with false hope. Let the individual down gently.

Watch what you do, say, and ask following the formal closing as you walk with the person to the door or to the parking lot, or escort the person to meet another member of your organization. These informal times can lead to EEO violations. Do not do or say anything that adversely affects the relationship you have developed carefully during the interview.

Make decisions and notify all applicants as soon as possible.

Follow up on all prospects. If possible, have all letters signed by you or your representative. A personal touch, even when rejecting an applicant, can maintain a feeling of goodwill toward you and your organization.

Conducting the Interview

Establish an environment that is conducive to sharing information and disclosure of feelings and attitudes. It should be a comfortable, quiet, and private location. Prevent interruptions. Turn off telephones, cell phones, computers, and beepers. Close office doors. Provide seating that maximizes interpersonal communication.

Approach each interview in a positive manner, realizing that it is likely to be a major event in the applicant's life (even if routine for you) and a critical part of attracting and selecting productive employees. Patricia Buhler writes: "The interview is a two-way street. While the interviewer is screening applicants for fit with the organization and the position, the applicant is 'interviewing' the company for fit as well. The interview, then, should also be viewed as a public relations tool." She warns that "Bad publicity travels quickly."[51] Give the impression that this interview is your day's top priority.

You are your organization.

Applicants make no distinction between you and your organization. They are more likely to accept offers if you are perceived to be a good representative of your organization; you are recruiting as well as selecting applicants. Be open and honest. Give a realistic picture of the position and organization. Practice a **conscious transparency** in which you share information with applicants, explain the purpose of questions, provide a supportive climate, and promote dialogue.[52]

Nontraditional Interviewing Approaches

Applicants and recruiters prefer the traditional one-on-one interview.

Some organizations are using nontraditional approaches. For instance, a **team, panel,** or **board** of two to five persons interview an applicant at the same time. In some situations, panel members divide up the applicant's resume and application form with one member asking about previous work experiences, a second asking about education and training, a third asking about technical knowledge, and a fourth asking about job-related skills. Some research indicates that the panel is more effective in predicting job performance than the traditional one-on-one interview, but applicants and interviewers prefer the traditional approach.[53] A panel or team would be advisable when conducting cross-cultural interviews to enhance communication and understanding and to eliminate possible bias.

In a **chain format** one person may take 20 minutes getting a general impression of the applicant's skills and then pass the applicant on to another person who probes into technical knowledge. This person passes the applicant to a third person who probes into specific job skills. The chain format is common in "plant trips" or determinate interviews that follow the initial screening process. The series of interviews may last more than one day and include meals with various staff members.

Stifle any signs of competition in seminar interviews.

A **seminar format,** in which one or more recruiters interview several applicants at the same time, is subject to the pitfalls of individual interviews (if only one interviewer is present), but it takes less time, allows the organization to see several applicants at the same time, and may provide valuable insights into how applicants work with one another in a team effort. If conducted with skill, applicants will not see the interview as a competition but as an opportunity to build upon others' comments and reveal their experiences and qualifications.

Asking Questions

Questions are your primary tools for obtaining information, assessing how well the applicant matches the applicant profile, determining fit with your organization, and discovering what the applicant knows about the position and organization.

Keep your questions open-ended.

Use open-ended, neutral, insightful, and job-specific questions. Open-ended questions encourage applicants to talk while you listen, observe, and formulate effective probing questions. Applicants give longer answers to open-ended questions and feel greater satisfaction with interviews that are dominated by open-ended primary and probing questions.[54]

Common Question Pitfalls

Recruiters create or rephrase questions to detect relevant behaviors and probe for details, clarity, and implied meanings. This spontaneity makes the interview a lively and insightful conversation but makes it susceptible to common question pitfalls identified in Chapters 3 and 5.

- Bipolar trap

  Have you used a Mac?

- Open-to-closed switch

  Tell me about your internship at Chrysler. Did you work in teams?
- Double-barreled inquisition

  What about your supervisory and finance experiences?
- Leading push

  You're willing to work in any area of the country, aren't you?
- Guessing game

  Did you attend DePaul University because some of your family went there?
- Yes (no) response

  Do you think you're qualified for this position?
- Curious probe

  What was the population of your hometown?
- Quiz show

  Do you know how many employees we have in other countries?
- Don't ask, don't tell

  How much debt have you taken on while in college?

Be on guard for pitfalls in primary and probing questions.

There are three question pitfalls that are particularly relevant to the recruiting interview. Recognize and avoid them.

Evaluative responses will lead to safe, superficial answers.

1. *The evaluative response:* The interviewer expresses judgmental feelings about an answer that may bias or skew the next response.

   That was not a good decision, was it?
2. *The EEO violation:* The interviewer asks an unlawful question.

   Which religious holidays do you observe?
3. *The resume or application form question:* The interviewer asks a question that is already answered on the resume or application form.

   Where did you earn your BS in psychology?

Do not ask for information you already have.

Exercise #2—What Are the Pitfalls in These Questions?

Each of the following questions contains one or more common employer question pitfalls: bipolar trap, open-to-closed switch, double-barreled inquisition, leading push, guessing game, curious probe, quiz show, don't ask, don't tell, evaluative response, EEO violation, yes (no) response, and resume-application question. Identify the pitfall in each and rewrite it to make it a good question without stumbling into another pitfall.

1. You like working on teams, don't you?
2. Have you studied abroad?
3. Tell me about your duties at CVS and Macy's.
4. Are you interested in this position?

5. Which internship did you enjoy most? Was it the one at the Indianapolis Motor Speedway?
6. Did you take communication courses as your electives because they were a good fit with your major in English?
7. That was a mistake, wasn't it?
8. Do you know what the average salary of a CEO is in China?
9. How does your prosthetic leg hamper you in traveling by air?
10. Are you interested in the new media?

Traditional Questions

The following are **traditional recruiter questions** that avoid pitfalls and gather important job-related information.

- Interest in the organization

  Why would you like to work for us?
  What materials have you read about our organization?
  What do you know about our products and services?

- Work-related (general)

  Tell me about the position that has given you the most satisfaction.
  How have your previous work experiences prepared you for this position?
  What did you do that was innovative in your last position?

- Work-related (specific)

  Describe a typical strategy you would use to motivate people.
  What criteria do you use when assigning work to others?
  How do you follow up on work assigned to subordinates?

- Teams and teamwork

  How do you feel when your compensation is based in part on team results?
  What does the word *teamwork* mean to you?
  How would you feel about working on cross-functional teams?

- Education and training

  What computer programs do you know?
  What in your education has prepared you for this position?
  If you had your education to do over, what would you do differently?

- Career paths and goals

  If you join us, what would you like to be doing five years from now?
  How do you feel about the way your career has gone so far?
  What are you doing to prepare yourself for advancement?

- Performance

  What do you believe are the most important performance criteria for a project engineer?

All of us have pluses and minuses in our performance. What are some of your pluses (minuses)?
How do you make difficult decisions?

- Salary and benefits

What are your salary expectations?
Which fringe benefits are most important to you?
How does our salary range compare to your last position?

- Career field

What do you think is the greatest challenge facing your field?
What do you think will be the next major breakthrough in your field?
How do you feel about environmental regulations in your field?

The major problem with traditional questions is that applicants are familiar with them and may have scripted answers in advance. Be ready to probe into answers to get beneath surface answers to attain Level 2 and Level 3 answers.

Nontraditional Questions

The trend is toward on-the-job questions.

A variety of question strategies attempt to determine how an applicant has handled or will handle work-related situations. These questions also enable interviewers to counter impression management tactics used by nearly all applicants such as self-promotion (designed "to evoke attributions of competence") and ingratiation (designed "to evoke interpersonal liking and attraction"). Both of these tactics have proven to be "positively related to interviewer evaluations."[55]

Behavior-Based Questions

Interviewers conducting behavioral-based interviews ask questions about past experiences in which applicants have handled situations that are related to the position. For instance, recruiters may ask:[56]

Tell me about an idea of yours that was implemented primarily through your efforts.

How did you handle a past situation when the rules were changed at the last minute?

Tell me about your most difficult relationship with a team member. How did you handle it?

Describe a time when you experienced a setback in a class, in a sport, or on the job. How did you handle it?

Tell me about a situation when you had to handle an irate customer or client.

Give me an example of an unpopular idea you had to sell to fellow workers.

Be prepared for coached applicants.

Unfortunately, applicants have gotten wise to past experience questions and are often coached on how to respond. Even worse, some applicants are making up impressive stories to satisfy recruiters. For instance, when MBAs were asked to tell about a time when they faced a challenge, six gave identical answers about serving on a fund-raising committee. Later investigation revealed that none of the six had been on such a committee.[57] Experienced applicants have a wealth of examples from which to draw, while soon-to-be college graduates and those with little experience have few. Behavioral questions favor those who can tell good stories in a positive and likeable manner. They may measure social skills and storytelling rather than intelligence and ability to perform well on the job.[58]

Some recruiters have become so concerned with dishonest and rehearsed answers to behavioral-based questions that they have resorted to strange questions (many discarded years ago) for which applicants will not have ready-made and perhaps fictitious answers.[59]

If you could be a character in fiction, whom would you be?

If you were a salad, what kind of dressing would you be?

If you were a fruit, what kind of fruit would you like to be?

Do not be too quick to abandon behavior-based questions for such weird questions. Applicants will always try to adapt to new interviewing approaches and questions. "Drill down for details" with insightful probing questions not only to see if an applicant is "faking" or lying but to get important Level 2 and Level 3 details into the applicant and the applicant's experiences. Be prepared to react if you get information you do not want or need and that may violate EEO laws. Rochelle Kaplan relates an incident in which an applicant replied to a question about the greatest challenge in undergraduate studies by stating: "Coming out as a gay male to my friends and family."[60] Other applicants have delved into religion and politics.

Critical Incident Questions

Critical incident questions assess how applicants would handle real work situations.

In **critical incident questions,** recruiters select actual incidents that are occurring or have occurred on the job within their organizations and ask applicants how they would handle or would have handled such incidents. For instance:

We are experiencing a growing problem of waste in our milling operation. How would you handle this if we hired you?

Last year we encountered a lot of strife among our sales staff. If you had been with us, what would you have done?

Like many firms, we are experiencing a decline in sales of our traditional products. What would you suggest we do about it?

We have traditionally faced difficulties in recruiting a diverse staff because most of our plants are located in small cities in rural areas of the west. How would you suggest we improve our recruiting efforts? . . . How might we improve our retention efforts?

Hypothetical Questions

Hypothetical questions are often criticized because they have posed unrealistic, even silly, situations such as, "How would you go about counting all of the golf balls in the United States?"[61] Hypothetical questions, like critical incident questions and case questions, can be valuable tools in the recruiting interview. Justin Menkes writes that questions such as these are useful because they "raise questions and situations that the candidate has never confronted" and for which the candidate cannot be prepared in advance.[62]

In hypothetical questions, a recruiter creates highly realistic but hypothetical situations and asks applicants how they would handle each.

Suppose you are suspicious that some workers are doctoring their time cards. What would you do?

If your company suddenly announced the closing of your facility by January 1, what would you do?

If a female employee came to you claiming sexual harassment, how would you handle it?

A Case Approach

A case approach is the most realistic on-the-job question format.

In a case approach, an applicant is placed into a carefully crafted situation that may take hours to study and resolve. It could be a personnel, management, design, or production problem. Some are elaborate simulations that require role playing and may involve several people, including other applicants.

Closing Thoughts on Use of Questions

All on-the-job questions (behavior-based, critical incident, hypothetical, case) are based on the belief that the best way to assess ability to perform a job is to observe the applicant doing the job. Many applicants can tell you about the theories and principles they would use, but they are unable to put these theories and principles into practice. It is one thing to say how you might confront a hostile employee but quite another to do it.

Do not settle for Level 1 interactions.

Regardless of your questioning methods, design the questioning phase of the interview to explore how well the applicant meets the ideal employee profile and fits into your organization. Probe for specifics; explore suggestions or implications in responses; clarify meanings with reflective probes; and force the applicant to get beyond safe, superficial Level 1 responses to reveal feelings, preferences, knowledge, and expertise.

Use all available tools to get the information necessary to select the best applicants. **Remember there are always two applicants in each interview, the real and the make-believe.** Your task is to determine how much of what you see and hear is a facade and how much is genuine. Get beneath the surface of rehearsed and planned answers to find the real person.

Be responsive without talking.

Listen carefully to all that *is* said and *is not* said. Silent and nudging probes are effective because applicants feel less threatened and more respected when interviewers respond with simple verbal and nonverbal signals and do not interrupt them. Avoid becoming a cheerleader, as many of our student interviewers tend to do, by saying "Great!" "Very good" or "Awesome!" after every answer. Applicants will come to expect the praise and become concerned if it stops. Maintain a pleasant, supportive poker face that never reveals whether you believe an answer is very good, negative, or outrageous.

Giving Information

Giving information is an essential ingredient in successful interviews. Information before and during the interview is a major determinant of applicant satisfaction.

Information is the primary interest of applicants.

Before you begin to give information, however, ask two important transition questions: *"What do you know about this position? What do you know about our organization?"* Answers to these questions show, first, how much homework the applicant has done, revealing the applicant's level of interest and work ethic. Second, they tell you what the applicant already knows about the position and organization so you can begin where the person's knowledge leaves off. This prevents you from wasting valuable interview time giving information the applicant already has or is readily available on your Web site.

Give adequate information to facilitate the **matching process** between the organization and the applicant. Information about your organization's reputation, organizational environment, the position, typical work day, and advancement opportunities are the most important factors in acceptance of job offers. You may compare your organization to your competitors', but do not be negative.

Minimize "you" in the interview.

Sell the advantages of your position and organization. Do not exaggerate, intentionally hide negative aspects of the position or organization, or inflate applicant expectations. These practices result in high rates of employee dissatisfaction and turnover. Avoid gossip. Do not talk too much about yourself, a common turn-off in selection interviews.

Rule #1: Keep your ears open and your mouth shut.

While you want to inform applicants thoroughly, your information giving must not dominate the interview. Studies have found that applicants speak for only 10 minutes in a typical 30-minute screening interview.[63] Reverse this figure. You will learn more about the applicant by listening than by talking. Review the guidelines for information giving in Chapter 13 and follow these suggestions.

- Practice good communication skills because applicants may judge the "authenticity" of information by how it is communicated verbally and nonverbally.
- Encourage applicants to ask questions about information you are giving so you know it is being communicated accurately and effectively.
- Do not overload applicants with information.
- Organize your information systematically and logically.

Evaluating the Interview

Record your impressions and reactions immediately.

Take notes during interviews because note-taking increases recall and judgment accuracy.[64] Review your thoughts and notes carefully, and then record your reactions to each applicant as soon as possible. Build in time between interviews for this purpose. Organizations may provide recruiters with standardized evaluation forms to match applicants with the applicant profile for each position. If the interview is a screening interview, decide whether to invite the applicant for a second round of interviews. If the interview is a determinate interview, decide whether to make an offer or send a rejection letter.

Figure 7.1 *Interview evaluation report*

Interview Evaluation Report

Applicant ______________________ Position ______________________

Interviewer ______________________ Date__________ Location ____________

	Excellent	Very Good	Good	Unsatisfactory
Interest in this position	____	____	____	____
Interest in the company	____	____	____	____
Fit with this position	____	____	____	____
Education and training	____	____	____	____
Experiences	____	____	____	____
Adaptability	____	____	____	____
Analytical ability	____	____	____	____
Self-confidence	____	____	____	____
Enthusiasm	____	____	____	____
Communication skills	____	____	____	____
Professional appearance	____	____	____	____

General comments and reactions: ______________________________________

____

Do you favor an offer? ____ Yes ____ No ____ Undecided

Overall rating: Unfavorable 1 2 3 4 5 6 7 8 9 10 Favorable

The **interview evaluation** often consists of two parts: a set of standardized questions and a set of open questions. See the sample interview evaluation form in Figure 7.1. The standardized part should consist of bona fide occupational qualifications for each position and be extensive enough to allow you to determine how well the applicant matches these qualifications. Focus on the applicant's qualifications, not irrelevant factors. A study at the University of North Texas revealed that recruiters often chose applicants on the basis of voices and regional accents. Those identified with specific regions by accent were less likely to be chosen for "high profile jobs" and more likely to be assigned, if hired, to lower-skilled and lower-contact positions.[65]

The following are typical open-ended questions in postinterview evaluations:

- What are the applicant's strengths for this position?
- What are the applicant's weaknesses for this position?
- How does this applicant compare to other applicants for this position?
- What makes this applicant a good or poor fit with our organization?

Use the evaluation stage to assess your interviewing skills and performance. Ask yourself:

Assess the performance of both interview parties.

- How successfully did I create an informal, relaxed atmosphere?
- How effectively did I encourage the applicant to speak openly and freely?
- How thoroughly did I explore the applicant's qualifications for this position with primary and probing questions?
- How effectively did I listen and observe?
- How adequate was the information I provided on the position and organization?
- Did I reserve adequate time for the applicant to ask questions?
- How well did I respond to the applicant's questions?
- How effectively did I close the interview?

Summary

The recruiting interview can be an effective means of selecting employees, but it takes preparation that includes becoming familiar with state and federal EEO laws, developing an applicant profile, obtaining and reviewing information on applicants, and developing a carefully structured interview. Preparation must be followed by a thoroughly professional interview that includes an effective opening, skillful questioning, probing into answers, thorough information giving, honest and detailed answers to questions, and an effective closing. You must practice effective communication skills that include language selection, nonverbal communication (silence, voice, eye contact, facial expressions, posture, and gestures), listening, and empathy.

When the interview is concluded, conduct evaluations of the applicant and yourself. The first focuses on the applicant's suitability and fit and the second on your effectiveness as recruiter and evaluator.

Key Terms and Concepts

The online learning center for this text features FLASH CARDS and CROSSWORD PUZZLES for studying based on these terms and concepts.

Applicant profile
Basic skills tests
Behavior-based selection
Birds of a feather syndrome
Board interview
Bona fide occupational qualification (BFOQ)
Conscious transparency
Cover letters
Critical incident questions
EEO laws
Honesty tests
Integrity interviews
Interview evaluation
Job fairs
Matching process
Talent-based selection
Trait-based selection

A Recruiting Interview for Review and Analysis

Trent Douglas is applying for an entry-level management position with TBD Electronics that produces parts for several automobile manufacturers. Elizabeth Prohosky, a recent college graduate, is a college recruiter for TBD and is spending the week interviewing management, supervision, and organizational communication majors at California State University at Long Beach.

How satisfactory are the rapport and orientation stages of the opening? How well do the recruiter's questions meet EEO guidelines and avoid common question pitfalls? How effectively does the recruiter *probe into* and *react to* answers? What evidence is there that the employer has an ideal applicant profile in mind? How adequate is the employer's information giving? Does the employer control the interview too much, too little, or about right? How satisfactory is the closing?

1. **Recruiter:** Good afternoon. I'm Elizabeth Prohosky from TBD Electronics.
2. **Applicant:** Hi. I'm Trent Douglas.
3. **Recruiter:** I'm glad we could meet this afternoon. Plaese call me Liz.
4. **Applicant:** Uh, okay.
5. **Recruiter:** How's your semester?
6. **Applicant:** It's been a very difficult semester.
7. **Recruiter:** Uh huh. Well, let's get to it. I'm going to ask you some questions to see how you fit the position we have open in management at TBD; then I will tell you a little bit about TBD; and finally, I'll answer a few questions if you have any. Okay?
8. **Applicant:** Certainly. I've really been looking forward to this interview with TBD.
9. **Recruiter:** Great. First, why did you switch from Cal. State at Fullerton to Cal. State at Long Beach after your first year?
10. **Applicant:** Well, to be honest, it was because my girlfriend was at Long Beach.
11. **Recruiter:** I see. Was that the *only* reason for switching universities?
12. **Applicant:** That was the clincher, but I did look into the management program at Long Beach and it looked pretty good, about the same as Fullerton.
13. **Recruiter:** That's good. How people-oriented are you?
14. **Applicant:** That's one of my strong suits. I've always been people-oriented, joined lots of clubs, been active in my fraternity, served as social secretary for the Future Manager's Club, things like that, you know.
15. **Recruiter:** Good. Good. What experience have you had working on teams?
16. **Applicant:** Well, I have been a three-year member of the speech team and, during my second year, I played on the rugby team. Of course, we work as teams in most of my management courses, particularly strategic management courses. I just seem to gravitate to teams.
17. **Recruiter:** Awesome. How about internships or co-ops or study abroad experiences?
18. **Applicant:** As I put on my resume, I had an internship at a TRW plant back home that made gears for cars and trucks. I spent part of a summer break in Mexico living with a Mexican family to sharpen up my Spanish.

19. **Recruiter:** Very good. Tell me about one of the most difficult problem-solving situations you have been involved with.

20. **Applicant:** Let's see. I guess I would pick a time when the speech team coach asked us to assign research tasks to each team member with the idea that we would put all of this research together so we could prepare for upcoming extemporaneous speaking contests. Two of the team members were not doing their assignments and this was making it impossible to prepare a final resource book.

21. **Recruiter:** What did you do?

22. **Applicant:** I got all of us together in the Union café and said it was to all of our advantages to get the research completed and compiled because it would help or hurt all of us in future tournaments. I guess I also laid a guilt trip on the team members who were not doing their jobs. Other members leaned on them as well, and we got the job done.

23. **Recruiter:** How did your coach react to your involvement in this situation?

24. **Applicant:** He didn't say much but thanked all of us for getting the job done.

25. **Recruiter:** Uh huh. If you were doing this again, what would you do differently?

26. **Applicant:** I've thought about that a lot. I think I would try to meet first with the slackers to encourage them to complete their research before involving all of the team.

27. **Recruiter:** Why would you do that?

28. **Applicant:** Some of the people were embarrassed and took my criticism personally. It did affect our relationship for the remainder of the year.

29. **Recruiter:** I'm sure it did. By the way, where was your next speech tournament?

30. **Applicant:** Let me think. I believe it was at San Diego State . . . or maybe at Concordia. We did okay; I remember that.

31. **Recruiter:** What was the focus of your research?

32. **Applicant:** I think it was . . . uh, it had something to do with controlling investment firms, something like that.

33. **Recruiter:** I see. Tell me, Trent, what interests you most in a management position with TBD Electronics.

34. **Applicant:** Well, I like the locations in the West and I've always been interested in cars and in the auto industry. The job description seems to be what I'm looking for.

35. **Recruiter:** So, Trent, why should we hire you over other applicants?

36. **Applicant:** That's a tricky question. First, I have a good GPA in management from a strong management program. Second, I have a lot of experience working with people. And, third, I'm really interested in the auto industry, and TBD of course.

37. **Recruiter:** Of course. By the way, what is your overall GPA.

38. **Applicant:** My GPA in management courses is a 2.9 on a 4.0 scale.

39. **Recruiter:** And what about your overall GPA.

40. **Applicant:** It's around a 2.1.

41. Recruiter: Okay. What do you know about TBD Electronics?

42. Applicant: Let's see. I know you have plants in Denver, Boise, and Seattle—and some others—that make electronic parts for several auto manufactures, both foreign and domestic.

43. Recruiter: Anything else?

44. Applicant: I think I read somewhere that TBD started out making electronics for the military, maybe the Army.

45. Recruiter: Actually we started out making electronics for the Navy and some small aircraft manufacturers. In 1994 we began to switch to the auto industry, focusing on antilock braking and traction control systems. Ford and GM were our first auto customers, and we now work with Chrysler, Honda, Kia, and Hyundai. We have developed revolutionary new ignition and GPS systems. We are headquartered in San Diego because of our early Navy connection. We have some time left for a question or two.

46. Applicant: How has the value of TBD stock fared in the economic downturn?

47. Recruiter: Like most stock of companies dealing with the auto industry, we took a hit early on, particularly when GM made major cuts and Chrysler essentially shut down for a few months. Thanks to government intervention and the sale of Chrysler to Fiat, the improvement in the economy, and pent-up demand for new cars, our stock has rebounded to about where it was before the recession.

48. Applicant: What is most of your research focusing on today?

49. Recruiter: We are working very hard on early warning systems that would alert drivers when they are closing in on another vehicle or another vehicle is closing in on them from the side or rear. A few of these systems will be on some models within a year or two.

50. Applicant: That sounds exciting.

51. Recruiter: Well, Trent, our time's about up. It's been good talking to you. We will get back to you within two weeks. If you've not heard from us by then, call my office or e-mail me at the numbers on this card.

52. Applicant: I'm really looking forward to hearing from you. Thanks for the interview.

53. Recruiter: (shakes hand) I'm glad to hear that and good luck with your job search.

Recruiting Role-Playing Cases

A Public Relations Position

Your public relations firm has created a new area that specializes in repairing the image of individual and corporate clients who have been accused of unlawful, unsocial, injurious, or unethical acts. An increasing number of these clients—companies, politicians, entertainers, sports figures, and charitable organizations—are turning to you to help them defend themselves effectively and thus to repair or maintain their images and credibility. The person you wish to hire must be a college graduate who has taken courses in public relations, persuasion, and image repair strategies and has experience working with clients with image problems.

A Sales Position

Your firm, Global Marketing, Inc., is seeking salespersons to call homeowners about new windows, doors, and siding for several manufacturers. The positions require training and experience in sales, a high level of interpersonal communication skills, and the ability to communicate pleasantly and effectively with a diverse customer base. Since making "cold calls" results in a high percentage of rejections, applicants must be able to handle rejection and keep a positive attitude. A bachelor's degree is preferred but at least two years in college would be acceptable.

A Sportscaster

You are the new owner-manager of radio station WPRZ in a city of 75,000 people. The station has changed owners a number of times during the past 15 years, and a new format has come with each new owner: classic rock, syndicated talk shows, a mixture of everything, and most recently country and western. You want to maintain the current format (country and western) because you feel that it fits the community best, but you also want to hire a sportscaster who would focus on local college and high school teams and begin some live broadcasting for football and basketball games. You want to hire a first-rate, on-air sportscaster who can establish good relations with the community, the college, and the schools in the city and county. Basic requirements are a college degree in broadcasting, at least three years of experience, the ability to identify with a small town and its agricultural surroundings and roots, and good interpersonal skills with coaches, students, schools, and citizens.

Student Activities

1. Many recruiters believe that motivation is critical to a good hire. Contact your campus career center and ask permission to pose two questions to a dozen recruiters: What questions do you ask that pertain to motivation? How do you assess motivation from applicant responses, applicant questions, and applicant credentials?
2. Contact a number of recruiters from different career fields and ask them to discuss the pluses and minuses of hiring recent college graduates. Probe for specifics and illustrations (without names). What changes have they seen in recent college graduates during the past 10 years?
3. Contact a number of recruiters to see how many employ a behavior-, trait-, or talent-based approach to recruiting new employees. If they do not use or have abandoned one of these approaches, what are their reasons for doing so? What differences can you detect among the three approaches? How do recruiters using one or more of these approaches minimize dishonest answers?

4. Do a Web-based search of sources on EEO laws and regulations and the recommendations these sources make to recruiters to ask only lawful questions and to applicants for recognizing and replying to unlawful questions. What changes have affected employment interviews during the past five years? What are the most controversial and often violated EEO laws and regulations? Which state laws tend to be more stringent than federal laws?

Notes

1. Tom Peters, *Re-Imagine: Business Excellence in a Disruptive Age* (London: Dorling Kindersley, 2003), pp. 18 and 81.

2. William W. Lewis, *The Power of Productivity: Wealth, Poverty, and the Threat to Global Stability* (Chicago: University of Chicago Press/McKinsey and Company, 2004).

3. Patricia M. Buhler, "Interviewing Basics: A Critical Competency for All Managers," *Supervision* 66 (March 2005), pp. 20–22; Adam Agard, "Pre-employment Skills Testing: An Important Step in the Hiring Process," *Supervision* 64 (June 2003), pp. 7–8.

4. Roger Herman and Joyce Gioia, "You've Heard of E-Business . . . How About E-Recruiting?" The Workforce Stability Institute, http://www.employee.org/article_you_heard_of_e-business.html, accessed September 14, 2006.

5. Joyce Gioia, "Special Report: Changing the Face(s) in Your Recruiting Efforts," Workforce Stability Institute, http://www.employee.org/article_changing_the_face.html, accessed September 14, 2006.

6. Joyce Gioia, "Are Prospective Applicants Saying 'No'—Based on Your Website?" Workforce Stability Institute, http://www.employee.org/article_prospective_saying_no.html, accessed September 14, 2006.

7. Michael A. McDaniel, Deborah H. Whetzel, Frank L. Schmidt, and Steven D. Mauer, "The Validity of Employment Interviews: A Comprehensive Review and Meta-Analysis," *Journal of Applied Psychology* 79 (1994), pp. 599–616.

8. The U.S. Equal Opportunity Commission, "Federal Laws Prohibiting Job Discrimination Questions and Answers," http://www.eeoc.gov/facts/qanda.html, accessed September 18, 2009.

9. Roger Herman, "Older Workers—A Hidden Treasure," Workforce Stability Institute, http://www.employee.org/article_older_workers_hidden_treasure.html, accessed September 14, 2006; "Old, Smart, Productive," *BusinessWeek Online,* June 27, 2005, http://www.businessweek.com, accessed September 11, 2006.

10. Junda Woo, "Job Interviews Pose Risk to Employers," *The Wall Street Journal,* March 11, 1992, pp. B1 and B5.

11. Clive Fletcher, "Ethics and the Job Interview," *Personnel Management,* March 1992, pp. 36–39.

12. "Job Discrimination Claims Rise to Record Levels," http://www.msnbc.com/id/29554931/, accessed March 13, 2009.

13. "Human Resource Training Curriculum on CD-ROM," http://www.bizhotline.com/html/interviewing_skills_laws_gove.html, accessed September 18, 2009; "EEOC Is Watching You: Recruitment Discrimination Comes to the Forefront," http://www.multicultural/advantage.com/recruit/eeo-employment-law/EEOC-is-watching, accessed September 18, 2009.

14. "Etiquette for Interviewing Candidates with Disabilities," *Personnel Journal* supplement, September 1992, p. 6.

15. Personnel Policy Service, "You Can't Ask That: Application and Interview Pitfalls," http://www.pps.publishers.com/articles/application_interview.htm, accessed September 18 2009; University of Connecticut, Office of Diversity and Equity, "Unlawful Questions," http://Web.uconn/uwode/quest.html, accessed October 18 2007; U.S. Equal Opportunity Commission, "New and Proposed Regulations," http://www.eeoc.gov/policy/regs/index.html, accessed September 18, 2009.

16. Phillip M. Perry, "Your Most Dangerous Legal Traps When Interviewing Job Applicants," *Law Practice Management,* March 1994, pp. 50–56; Stephen Sonnenberg, "Can HR Legally Ask the Questions That Applicants with Disabilities Want to Be Asked?" *Workforce,* August 2002, pp. 42–44; Susanne M. Bruyere, William A. Erickson, and Sara VanLooy, "Comparative Study of Workplace Policy and Practices Contributing to Disability Nondiscrimination," *Rehabilitation Psychology* 49 (2004), pp. 28–38.

17. Kevin Wheeler, "Interviewing Doesn't Work Very Well," *Electronic Recruiting Exchange,* http://www.ere.net, accessed September 14, 2006; West Virginia Bureau of Employment Programs, "Guidelines for Pre-employment Inquiries," http://www.wvbep.org/bep/Bepeeo/empinqu.htm, October 18, 2007.

18. University of Minnesota, College of Liberal Arts, "Behavior-Based Interviewing," http://www/cclc.umn.edu/interviews/behavior.html, accessed February 26, 2009; Katharine Hansen, "Quintessential Careers: Behavior Interviewing Strategies," http://www.quintcareers.com/printable/behavioral_interviewing.html, accessed February 26, 2009; About.com.Job Searching, "Behavioral Interview," http://jobsearch.about.com/cs/interviews/a/behavioral.htm?p=1, accessed February 26, 2009.

19. Patrice M. Buzzanell, "Employment Interviewing Research: Ways We Can Study Underrepresented Group Members' Experiences as Applicants," *Journal of Business Communication* 39 (2002), pp. 257–275; Patrice M. Buzzanell and Rebecca J. Meisenbach, "Gendered Performance and Communication in the Employment Interview," in *Gender and Communication at Work,* Mary Barrett and Marilyn J. Davidson, eds. (Hampshire, England: Ashgate Publishing, 2006), pp. 19–37.

20. Karen O'Keefe, "Five Secrets to Successful Interviewing and Hiring," http://www.writingassist.com, accessed September 14, 2006.

21. Troy Behrens, "How Employers Can Ace Their Campus and Site Interviews," *Journal of Career Planning & Employment,* Winter 2001, pp. 30–32.

22. Steven M. Ralston and Robert Brady, "The Relative Influence of Interview Communication Satisfaction on Applicants' Recruitment Decisions," *Journal of Business Communication* 31 (1994), pp. 61–77; Camille S. DeBell, Marilyn J. Montgomery,

Patricia R. McCarthy, and Richard P. Lanthier, "The Critical Contact: A Study of Recruiter Verbal Behavior during Campus Interviews," *The Journal of Business Communication* 35 (1998), pp. 202–224.

23. Behrens, pp. 30–32.

24. Patrice M. Buzzanell, "Tensions and Burdens in Employment Interviewing Processes: Perspectives of Nondominant Group Applicants," *Journal of Business Communication* 36 (1999), pp. 134–162.

25. DeBell, Montgomery, McCarthy, and Lanthier, pp. 204–224.

26. Buhler.

27. Wayne Tomkins, "Lying on Resumes Is Common; Catching It Can Be Challenging," Lafayette, Indiana *Journal and Courier,* September 1, 2000, p. C7; Landy Chase, "Buyer Beware: How to Spot a Deceptive Sales Resume," *New Orleans City Business,* November 4, 2002, p. 22.

28. Bob Ayrer, "Hiring Salespeople—Getting behind the Mask," *American Salesman,* December 1997, pp. 18–21.

29. Stephanie Clifford, Brian Scudamore, Andy Blumberg, and Jess Levine, "The New Science of Hiring," *Inc* 28 (August 2006), pp. 90–98, http://www.wf2la7.webfeat.org, accessed September 13, 2006.

30. Rochelle Kaplan, "Do Assessment Tests Predict Behavior or Screen Out a Diverse Work Force?" *Journal of Career Planning & Employment,* Spring 1999, pp. 9–12.

31. Patrick H. Raymark, Mark J. Schmit, and Robert M. Guion, "Identifying Potentially Useful Personality Constructs for Employee Selection," *Personnel Psychology* 50 (1997), pp. 723–736.

32. Rosemary Haefner, Careerbuilder.com, "Ten Tall Tales on Resumes," http://www.cnn.com/2008/LIVING/worklife/08/13/cb.lies.on.resumes/, accessed September 22, 2009.

33. Julia Levashina and Michael A. Campion, "Measuring Faking in the Employment Interview: Development and Validation of an Interview Faking Behavior Scale," *Journal of Applied Psychology* 92 (2007), pp. 1638–1656.

34. "Ten Tall Tales Told on Resumes."

35. Anita Gates, "The Secrets of Making a Good Hire," *Working Woman* 17 (1992), pp. 70–72.

36. Wayne J. Camara, "Employee Honesty Testing: Traps and Opportunities," *Boardroom Reports,* December 15, 1991.

37. Carol Kleiman, "From Genetics to Honesty, Firms Expand Employee Tests, Screening," *Chicago Tribune,* February 9, 1992, p. 8–1.

38. Levashina and Campion, pp. 1650–1651.

39. Donna R. Pawlowski and John Hollwitz, "Work Values, Cognitive Strategies, and Applicant Reactions in a Structured Pre-Employment Interview for Ethical Integrity," *The Journal of Business Communication* 37 (2000), pp. 58–75.

40. Pawlowski and Hollwitz, pp. 58–75.

41. Pawlowski and Hollwitz, p. 61.

42. Louis Rovner, "Job Interview or Horror Movie?" *Occupational Health & Safety,* February 2001, p. 22.

43. Fredric M. Jablin and Vernon D. Miller, "Interviewer and Applicant Questioning Behavior in Employment Interviews," *Management Communication Quarterly* 4 (1990), pp. 51–86.

44. Choon-Hwa Lim, Richard Winter, and Christopher C.A. Chan, "Cross-Cultural Interviewing in the Hiring Process: Challenges and Strategies," *The Career Development Quarterly* 54 (March 2006), p. 267.

45. Ayrer, pp. 18–21.

46. Arthur H. Bell, "Gut Feelings Be Damned," *Across the Board,* September 1999, pp. 57–62; Allen I. Huffcutt and Winfred Arthus, "Hunter and Hunter (1984) Revisited: Interview Validity for Entry-Level Jobs," *Journal of Applied Psychology* 79 (1994), pp. 184–190; Karen I. van der Zee, Arnold Bakker, and Paulien Bakker, "Why Are Structured Interviews So Rarely Used in Personnel Selection?" *Journal of Applied Psychology* 87 (2002), pp. 176–184.

47. Clifford, Scudamore, Blumberg, and Levine.

48. Buzzanell, pp. 134–162.

49. William G. Kirkwood and Steven M. Ralston, "Inviting Meaningful Applicant Performances in Employment Interviews," *The Journal of Business Communication* 36 (1999), p. 66.

50. Craig D. Tengler and Fredric M. Jablin, "Effects of Question Type, Orientation, and Sequencing in the Employment Screening Interview," *Communication Monographs* 50 (1983), pp. 245–263.

51. Buhler.

52. Kirkwood and Ralston, pp. 69–71.

53. Marlene Dixon, Sheng Wang, Jennifer Calvin, Brian Dineen, and Edward Tomlinson, "The Panel Interview: A Review of Empirical Research and Guidelines for Practice," *Public Personnel Management* 31 (2002), pp. 397–428.

54. Jablin and Miller, pp. 51–86; Gerald Vinton, "Open versus Closed Questions—an Open Issue?" *Management Decision* 33 (1995), pp. 27–32.

55. Aleksander P. J. Ellis, Bradley J. West, Ann Marie Ryan, and Richard P. DeShon, "The Use of Impression Management Tactics in Structured Interviews: A Function of Question Type," *Journal of Applied Psychology* 87 (2002), pp. 1200–1208.

56. Randy Myers, "Interviewing Techniques from the Pros," *Journal of Accounting* 202 (August 2006), pp. 53–55; "Using Behavioral Interviewing to Help You Hire the Best of the Best," *HR Focus* 81 (August 2006), p. 56; Slippery Rock University, "Behavior Based Interview Questions," http://www.sru.edu/pages/11217.asp, accessed February 26, 2009.

57. Jim Kennedy, "What to Do When Job Applicants Tell . . . Tales of Invented Lives," *Training,* October 1999, pp. 110–114.

58. Justin Menkes, "Hiring for Smarts," *Harvard Business Review* 83 (November 2005), pp. 100–109.

59. Abita Bruzzese, "Prepare for Tough New World of Job Interviews," Lafayette, IN *Journal & Courier,* July 2, 2008, p. D2.

60. Kaplan, pp. 9–12.

61. Myers.

62. Menkes.

63. Thomas Gergmann and M. Susan Taylor, "College Recruitment: What Attracts Students to Organizations?" *Personnel* 61 (1984), pp. 34–36; Fredric M. Jablin, "Organizational Entry, Assimilation, and Exit," *Handbook of Organizational Communication* (Beverly Hills, CA: Sage, 1987).

64. Catherine Houdek Middendorf and Therese Hoff Macan, "Note-Taking in the Employment Interview: Effects on Recall and Judgments," *Journal of Applied Psychology* 87 (2002), pp. 293–303.

65. "If They Say Tomato, and You Say To-Mah-To, What Then?" Workforce Stability Institute, http://www.employee.org/article_tomato.html, accessed September 14, 2006.

Resources

Barrett, Mary, and Marilyn J. Davidson, eds. *Gender and Communication at Work.* Hampshire, England: Ashgate Publishing, 2006.

Farr, Michael. *America's Top 101 Jobs for People without a Four-Year Degree.* Indianapolis: JIST Works, 2005.

Fein, Richard. *Baby Boomers Guide to the New Work Place.* New York: Taylor Trade Publishing, 2006.

Fields, Martha R. A. *Indispensable Employees: How to Hire Them/How to Keep Them.* Franklin Lake, NJ: Career Press, 2001.

Lancaster, Lynn C., and David Stillman. *When Generations Collide: Who They Are, Why They Clash, and How to Solve the Generational Puzzle.* New York: HarperBusiness, 2002.

Miller, Michael. *Googlepedia: The Ultimate Google Resource.* Indianapolis, IN: Que, 2008.

CHAPTER 8 The Employment Interview

Choosing a career and a position that fits you best is a daunting task when recent economic realities have seen millions of jobs disappear and our electronic and global age seemingly creates new and modifies or eliminates old career paths daily. The search for an ideal position is never easy or simple, even in the best of times, and it requires serious effort on your part. There are no formulas or shortcuts. As Lois Einhorn writes, getting a job is "a job in itself."[1] Think of the employment search as a series of steps or stages, beginning with a thorough, insightful, and honest self-analysis.

Analyzing Yourself

You cannot sell you if you don't know you.

You must *know yourself* so you can determine which careers, positions, and organizations are best for you. Since interview questions are aimed at discovering who *you* are, what *you* can do, and how well *you* fit a specific position within an organization, you can answer questions insightfully and persuasively only if you know who you are. In essence, you are the product you are selling in each employment interview, and if you don't know you, you can't sell you to a prospective employer.

Questions to Guide Your Self-Analysis

Self-analysis may be painful because few of us want to probe deeply and honestly into our strengths and weaknesses, successes and failures. No one needs to see your self-analysis but you, so be painfully honest with yourself. The following questions and traits can serve as a preflight checklist prior to launching your job search in earnest.[2]

- What are my *personality* traits?

  ____ Motivated   ____ Willing to take risks
  ____ Open-minded   ____ Assertive
  ____ Adaptive   ____ Able to work under pressure
  ____ Flexible   ____ Open to criticism

- How *trustworthy* am I?

  ____ Honest   ____ Tolerant
  ____ Reliable   ____ Sincere

____ Ethical
____ Fair
____ Self-controlled
____ Even tempered

- What are my *intellectual* strengths and weaknesses?
  ____ Intelligent
  ____ Creative
  ____ Organized
  ____ Planner
  ____ Analytic
  ____ Rational
  ____ Critical

- What are my *communicative* strengths and weaknesses?
  ____ Oral communication skills
  ____ Written communication skills
  ____ New media skills
  ____ Listening skills
  ____ Interpersonal skills
  ____ With diverse people
  ____ With subordinates, co-workers, superiors

- What are my *accomplishments* and *failures?*
  ____ Academic
  ____ Extracurricular activities and interests
  ____ Work
  ____ Professional
  ____ Goals set and met

Focus on strengths and weaknesses.

- What are my *professional* strengths and weaknesses?
  ____ Formal education
  ____ Informal education
  ____ Training
  ____ Experiences
  ____ Skills

- What do I want in a *position?*
  ____ Responsibility
  ____ Independence
  ____ Authority
  ____ Prestige
  ____ Type of work
  ____ Decision making
  ____ Contact with people
  ____ Security
  ____ Variety
  ____ Salary
  ____ Benefits

- What are my most valued *needs?*
  ____ Home and family
  ____ Income
  ____ Possessions
  ____ Geographical location
  ____ Free time
  ____ Recreation opportunities
  ____ Feeling of success and accomplishment

Why and how have you made past decisions?

- What are my *professional* interests?

  ____ Short-range goals ____ Growth

  ____ Long-range goals ____ National/international recognition

  ____ Advancement

By the time you answer these questions thoroughly and honestly, you should know who you are, what you are qualified to do, what you would like to do, and what you want in life. Above all, you will "have identified what sets you apart from other candidates" so you can present your uniqueness through your resume, cover letter, and interviews.[3]

Doing Your Homework

Research your field or fields, the organizations to which you will apply, the positions for which you will apply, current events, and the interviewing process. Knowing too little about a position and organization is a major turnoff for recruiters. Sixty-eight percent of recruiters in one study said "researching the company and position is the most important step in preparing for an interview."[4]

Research Your Field

Knowing your field is essential for selecting organizations and scheduling interviews.

Discover your field's history, developments, trends, areas of specialization, challenges, current and future problems, and employment opportunities. What education, training, and experiences are essential for entering this field? Develop a mature, realistic perception of what your field is like and what people do during typical workdays.

Internships, cooperative arrangements, part-time positions, observational visits, shadowing members of the profession, and volunteer activities enable you to discover what a field is all about. There are numerous published and Internet resources on every major career field from acting and advertising to visual arts and writing that can assist your research. Some sources are:

Career Opportunities and Information Sites (http://topeducationguide.com/directory/career-opportunities.asp)

Career Resources, Career Guide, Online Education and Degree Directory (http://www.careers.org)

Searching: Careers (https://elgg.leeds.ac.uk/tag/careers)

Peterson's Job Opportunities (http://www.nmt.edu/~nmtlib/subject/jobs.html)

Industry Web Sites (http://careerweb.georgetown.edu/jobs/search/7307.html)

Occupational Outlook Handbook (http://www.bls.gov/search/ooh.asp?ct=OOH)

WetFeet.com (http://www.wetfeet.com)

Vault.com (http://www.vault.com)

Employers expect you to be acquainted with organizational life and have positive attitudes toward whatever career you choose. They expect you to know why you want to enter a field.

Research enables you to answer and ask questions insightfully.

Research Organizations

Learn everything you can about each organization you contact. Focus on its leaders and staff, products and services (old and new), geographical locations, expansion or downsizing plans, potential mergers, competitors, and financial status. Discover the organization's reputation in the field.

Only through careful research can you answer a critical interview question, *Why do you want to work for us?* And only through research can you determine if your personality and interests are a good fit with the organization's culture.

You can discover information about organizations by talking to current and former employees, clients, professors, and friends. Read the organization's publications, Web site, recruiting literature, and annual reports. Look for a mission statement or strategic plan. Current employees can identify the kinds of persons and the specific skill sets their employers are looking for. Check the library for sources such as the following:

Information is available if you know where to look.

Dictionary of Professional Trade Organizations
Encyclopedia of Business Information Sources
Open the Book: How to Research a Corporation
Standard and Poor's Corporation Records
Thomas Register of American Manufacturers
Ward's Directory of Public and Private Corporations

Do not overlook the growing number of databases, many on CD-ROM, such as American Business Disc, Dun's Electronic Business Directory, and Dun's Million Dollar CD-ROM Collection.[5] The article "50 Places to Launch a Career" by Lindsey Gerdes identifies the best places for new college graduates.[6]

Research the Recruiter

When possible, get to know the interviewer ahead of time.

If you are able to identify the recruiter ahead of time, talk to friends, associates, professors, career center personnel, and members of the interviewer's organization to discover the interviewer's position, professional background, organizations to which the interviewer belongs, personality, and interviewing characteristics. An interviewer may have a dry sense of humor, come from a different culture, or be "all business." It helps to know the person ahead of time.

Research the Position

Learn everything you can about the position for which you are applying, including responsibilities, duties, necessary skills, required education, training, experiences, type of supervision, advancement potential, amount of travel involved, locations,

Figure 8.1 *The Cash-Stewart search model*

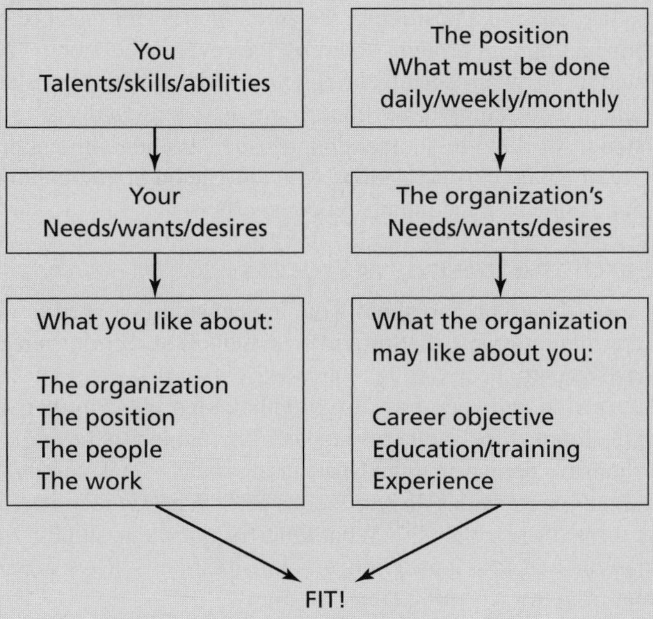

How closely do you and the position fit?

organizational culture and climate, job security, fringe benefits, training programs, salary and commissions, relocation possibilities and policies, rate of turnover, co-workers, and starting date. A thorough knowledge of the position prepares you to answer questions effectively, ask meaningful questions, and determine if you, the position, and the organization are a good *fit*. See Figure 8.1. Besides the usual research sources, arrive for the interview a few minutes early to determine "how well a potential employer fits" your "work style and career goals."[7] Observe the dress of employees, office interiors (including whether employees are allowed to decorate their offices), whether there is a break room and how it is outfitted, how employees interact with one another and supervisors, the makeup of the workforce, level of technology, and if senior managers are located near their staff.

Research Current Events

Keep abreast of what is happening in the world and in your field.

Keep up to date with what is going on in the world. *Newsweek, Time, BusinessWeek, Fortune, The Wall Street Journal,* and online news sources are excellent for current developments. Employers expect mature applicants to be aware of what is going on around them and in the world—local, state, national, international—and to have formed intelligent, rational positions on important issues.

Know about current trends, changes, developments, research, and mergers that are affecting the organization to which you are applying, your field, and your profession. If you are interested in a position in the auto industry, for instance, you need to be aware of the major changes brought about by the severe recession of 2007–2010. If you are interested in the pharmaceutical field, you need to be aware of new products, promising research, and controversies concerning new drugs and cost to consumers. If you are interested in working in another country such as China, India, or Poland, you need to be aware of the country's relations with the United States, cultural differences, cost of living, and policies affecting noncitizen workers.

Research the Interview Process

Learn everything you can about what happens during interviews. Read Chapter 7 on the recruiting interview that provides insights into recruiter practices. Talk to people who have recently been through the interviewing process, professors who are involved in interviewing and keep track of what is taking place in their fields, and recruiters. Check the Internet for numerous resources pertaining to the employment interview and suggestions for preparing to take part in interviews. Seek answers to questions such as: "What kinds of questions do recruiters ask?" "What do recruiters look for in answers?" "What turns off recruiters?" "What kinds of questions should you ask?" "How likely is it that you will face a panel or seminar situation?" "How are subsequent interviews different from the screening interview?"

Rely on no single source about employment interviews.

There is no single or standard means of conducting interviews, so talking to one person, even a highly skilled corporate recruiter, will give you only one view of the process. That is why we seldom bring a recruiter to class to "show how it is done." There is no single source that can speak for the hundreds of variations in selection interviews. Some employ behavior-based or talent-based interviews and others do not. Some employ highly structured interviews, and others employ moderately scheduled or unstructured interviews. Some probe extensively into answers and others rely on a list of prepared questions. Some focus on past success as the best predictor of future success and others focus on your future when you are no longer a student. Some provide extensive information and reserve several minutes for your questions, and others do not.

Telephone interviews are a common means of screening applicants.

Some companies employ video- or telephone conferencing so several representatives of the organization can talk with you at the same time[8] and others rely on the traditional one-on-one interview. Some put applicants through a series of interviews and others rely on two: a **screening interview** and a **determinate** (decision-making) **interview.** Some will ask you to take a drug test and others will not.

Expect a variety of tests in many fields.

The one consistent concern of recruiters is to determine the **honesty** of applicants. A highly educated, trained, and skilled employee without honesty, morals, and sincerity will quickly become a detriment to the organization. A recruiter may ask you to take a written and/or oral honesty test designed to determine degrees of honesty or conduct (taking a pencil or some paper home versus taking expensive printer cartridges or a laptop home). A recruiter may conduct an **integrity interview** or incorporate questions into an interview to assess honesty. An important rule is to be honest in

Integrity is essential for all positions.

all of your preinterview materials (application form, cover letter, resume) and in every answer during an interview. Any hint of dishonesty or evasiveness will likely result in a rejection notice.

Expect the unexpected.

Your research into the interview process may produce surprising results. For example, recent studies reveal that 50 percent of "speech acts" in sample interviews were declarative statements rather than questions and answers. Most interviewers have no training in interviewing. In a study of 49 interviews, 10 interviewers did not give applicants opportunities to ask questions. Recruiters are increasingly viewing the interview as a *work sample* and look for relevant job behaviors from applicants: can you do the job, will you do the job, and how well will you *fit* into the organization?

Conducting the Search

Choose a range of positions for which you are qualified and would be happy. For instance, instead of being set on a position as a cost accountant, public relations director, or editorial writer, try for a position with a good firm or newspaper, with the hope of moving into cost accounting or a director's or op-ed position.

You may have to start at the bottom to get to the top.

The changing labor market may prompt you to consider a part-time or temp position in which to gain experience and work your way into a full-time position. Some teachers serve as substitute teachers or time-share in which they teach a class for a half-day while another teacher teaches the other half. This arrangement may evolve into full-time positions.

As you begin your search, do not overlook any source that may get you an interview and eventually a position in which you can grow and prosper. Do not assume this must be an electronic or career center process.

Networking

Networking remains a major source for locating positions. Fifty-seven percent of human resources executives report they rely on networking to locate qualified applicants.[9] You may use internships to start your network, and a summer internship may serve as entry into a full-time position.

Leave no potential source off your network tree.

Begin your network by taking a sheet of paper and starting a **network tree** with names on one side and addresses and telephone numbers on the other. Start your tree with the most readily available sources: friends, acquaintances, relatives, family connections, former employers, alumni, internship directors, and professors. Your primary contacts may be as many as 50, but you can never have too many. Call the person in slot number one and say you are looking for a *career opportunity,* never a *job*. The word *job* signals the impression that you are looking for anything that pays money. If this contact gives you a lead, write it down under this individual's name so you can recall who made the suggestion. The *who* may be the major factor in a lead's willingness and enthusiasm to help you. Be sure to record the lead's full name, position, and telephone number. If this contact has no opportunities, ask for three or four names of persons who might know of career possibilities. Everyone knows at least three possible leads if they think a bit.

Knocking on Doors

One of the most effective search techniques is literally knocking on doors of organizations for which you would like to work and may have positions for which you are uniquely qualified. Identify companies with positions that may be hundreds or thousands of miles from where you live. Tell them what you have to offer, why you are interested in working for them, and when you might be in the area for an interview.

The personnel office is not the starting point for salaried and professional positions.

Newspapers and Newsletters

Newspaper classified sections are good places to locate positions because if organizations advertise there, their opening will meet the EEO test of making it known to all who are interested and qualified. *The Wall Street Journal* is an excellent source for openings around the country. Check organizational bulletin boards and printed materials that announce personnel openings. Subscribe to professional publications such as *The Chronicle of Higher Education* that include ads for a variety of positions.

The Placement Agency or Service

Your campus career center does more than schedule interviews.

The **placement agency** or service may be a source. A perusal of the Internet will enable you to select from a variety of agencies, services, and centers. Every college and university has a free center for students and alumni that provide contacts for on-campus interviews and offer counseling services that will help you analyze yourself (including the careers you seem most interested in and qualified for), discover career fields, obtain information on organizations and positions, develop resumes, and write cover letters. Other placement services are associated with professional organizations or specific career areas. Check into specialized resources for health care professionals, teachers, management majors, communication majors, civil engineering majors, and so on.

Percentage agencies will help place you for a fee, often a percentage of your first year's salary, payable upon assuming a position they helped you obtain. Most of these agencies have **fee-paid positions,** which means that an organization has retained them on a fee basis to locate quality applicants. You pay nothing. If you use a percentage agency, be aware that they may charge a registration fee to process your credentials. Most agencies are ethical and want to find excellent positions for their clients, but use reasoned skepticism. If they want a great deal of money in advance just to process your resume or make claims of placing nearly all of their applicants in highpaying positions, go elsewhere. Be careful of agencies that want to produce videotapes and other expensive credentials.

If it sounds too good to be true, it probably is.

The Internet

Learn to use the Internet efficiently and effectively.

The Internet is a major source for positions and tips on how to obtain them. Colleges and other organizations use Web pages to advertise positions and seek quality applicants. Here is a sample of Web sites.

- "Best Job Search Websites," About.com: Job Seeking
- Career One Stop Centers

ON THE WEB

Select a position you will be interested in when you complete your education or training. Search at least three Internet resources to discover the availability of such positions, geographical areas in which they are located, organizations that are seeking to fill them, and the nature of the positions being offered. Check resources such as Job Hunt (http://www.job-hunt.org), CareerBuilder Center (http://www.careerbuilder.com), MonsterTrak (http://www.monstertrak.com). After collecting this information, develop a list of interview questions to which you would need answers before making a decision to accept one of these positions.

- Hot Jobs
- "How to Use the Internet in Your Job Search," The Riley Guide: How to Job Search
- Monster.com
- The Riley Guide
- Yahoo!HotJobs—Thousands of Jobs

Know how to make the most of job fairs.

The Career/Job Fair

Career or job fairs held on your campus, a local mall, or around the country are excellent for meeting several employers at one location, finding out what positions are available, networking, and on-the-spot, face-to-face interviews. Some fairs are designed for specific fields or majors such as health care, the aircraft industry, engineering, agriculture, liberal arts, education, or pharmacy. Large corporations or government agencies may conduct their own fairs.

Prepare carefully and thoroughly for each job fair. Know your career goals, who you want to talk to, and what you are looking for in a career or the interaction will be a waste of time for you and the recruiter. Recruiters expect you to have a clear career focus or objective. Allison Doyle recommends that you prepare a "one minute commercial" that stresses your strong points, goals, and where you would like to go within the company.[10]

When you attend a fair, be professionally dressed and have copies of resumes with you. Scout the terrain by noting who is there, where they are in a crowded maze of tables and organizational banners, and whether they are conducting interviews or merely handing out information.[11] Gather printed information and listen and observe as you walk about and stand in line. Is this an organization for which you would like to work, and are you qualified for the types of positions they are talking about? If not, don't waste both your and the recruiter's time.

When you come face-to-face with a recruiter, be aware that this person is sizing you up quickly by noting your appearance, communication skills, and professionalism. Strive to be assertive, enthusiastic, and calm. The worst question you can ask is "What are you offering/hiring for?" Where is your clear career goal? The worst answer to a question such as "What are you looking for?" is "A job." This might be cute, but it is an immediate turnoff.[12]

Use the Internet to search for positions and conduct research on organizations.

If there are no job fairs in your area or you want to cast a larger net, Web sites can help locate fairs around the country.

- Job Fairs, http://www.employmentguide.com/browse_jobFairs.html
- Job Fairs, http://en.wikipedia.org/wiki/Job_fair
- Job Fairs, http://resources.monster.com/job-fairs
- National Career Fairs, http://www.national/careerfairs.com
- Targeted Job Fairs, http://www.targetedjobfairs.com

If attractive fairs are too far to visit in person, consider virtual job fairs. Don Best of Unisfair writes that "A virtual job fair is just like a regular job fair, with different employer booths and chances to talk to employers about jobs."[13] Prepare for these like you would for a face-to-face interaction even though the conversation is in text form. Be prepared and make an immediate good impression, making certain that grammar and spelling are without error. Answer questions thoroughly and have intelligent, mature questions ready for employers.

Preparing Credentials

Once you have analyzed yourself thoroughly, completed your homework, and searched for positions, it is time to prepare your credentials: resume, portfolio, and cover letter.

Resumes

No single resume is suitable for all positions.

Because so much attention is paid to creating the perfect resume, you may believe it is the magic bullet that will bring on a position and launch your career. In reality, the resume's sole purpose is to get an interview that may lead to more interviews and finally employment of your choosing. With this in mind, realize that you are likely to prepare different versions of resumes for each different position. The **resume** is your *silent sales representative,* and it is most persuasive when it is tailored to the skills and expectations of positions and appears to be highly professional.

Your resume is the first opportunity for a recruiter to *see* you. Since most recruiters will spend only seconds scanning each resume, yours must gain and maintain **positive**

attention if you hope to get beyond the application stage in the selection process. James Campion recommends that you "think like the boss" if you want the job.[14] Would *you* hire *you?*

Content of Resumes

Make it easy for interviewers to locate you.

Although there is disagreement on exactly what resumes should include, exclude, and look like, we will offer suggestions that apply to most situations. Beware of Internet sites and books that claim to offer "award winning resumes" guaranteed to get you hired. Richard Bolles, author of the famous book *What Color Is Your Parachute?*—updated annually—writes that he collects such resumes and shows them to his employer friends. Inevitably they declare that each resume would never get a job for anyone, even though they did.[15] This illustrates how each of us tends to feel about the content and appearance of resumes. Place your *full name* at the top center of the page in bold print. Use no nicknames.

Provide one or two *complete addresses* (with zip codes), telephone numbers (with area codes), and e-mail address so the employer can reach you easily and quickly. If you list a campus telephone, provide a date when it will no longer be operable.

Phrase career objectives with great care.

Your **career objective** usually comes next. This is critical if the employer does not have a cover letter from you or chooses to review resumes alone. The majority of employers will read no further if your career objective does not fit the opening or is unimpressive. Impressive career objectives are:

- Career rather than job oriented.
- Brief and precise.
- Targeted to a specific type of position.
- Not self-centered.

Your educational record is most important for your first position.

If you are just completing your education or training and your work experiences are minimal or unrelated to the position, your educational record usually comes next. In a survey of 188 college recruiters conducted by John Cunningham, 57 percent preferred education to be listed first, even when the college applicant had significant work experiences.[16] List your degrees or training **in reverse chronological order** so the employer can detect quickly what you are *doing now* or recently completed. List degree, diploma, certificate or license, date of graduation or completion, school, location of the school if name is insufficient for accurate identification (many universities have multiple campuses or use the same name), and majors and minors. You might provide a *selective list of courses* relevant to the opening, particularly if you are short on experience. List your grade point average (GPA) if it is a B or better, and indicate the numerical system used at your college, for example: 3.35 (4.0 scale) or 3.35/4.0. Do not use abbreviations for courses, majors, or degrees. An interviewer may not know if Eng. refers to English or engineering.

Relevant experiences can set you apart from the crowd.

After education and training, present your relevant experiences for the specific position for which you are applying. If you title this section "Experiences" you can include more than work or salary earning situations, an advantage if you are young and just completing your education or training. Volunteer activities may be relevant and impressive. One study revealed that recruiters rate the following as *very important* or *above average* in importance in selecting employees:[17]

Job-related work experiences	88%
Leadership roles in student organizations	86%
Paid, job-related experiences	79%
Member of preprofessional organizations	73%
Experience in volunteer community service	58%

Types of Resumes

If you are developing a **chronological format,** the most common form of resume, list your experiences (including internships, co-op arrangements, assistantships, unpaid positions, organizational activities) in *reverse* chronological order so the employer can see quickly what you have been up to most recently. See Figure 8.2 for a sample chronological format resume.[18] List organization, title of your position or positions, dates, and what you did in each position. Emphasize the skills and experiences most relevant for the opening. The primary concern of recruiters is applicant achievement and accomplishment. Avoid meaningless phrases such as "proven track record" and "responsible for" that are turnoffs for recruiters. They prefer action verbs, such as the following, that show you are a *doer:*

Be honest when constructing your resume.

Administered	Facilitated	Oversaw
Advised	Fashioned	Performed
Arbitrated	Formulated	Persuaded
Arranged	Founded	Planned
Built	Generated	Recommended
Budgeted	Improved	Reconfigured
Coached	Increased	Researched
Consulted	Instructed	Sold
Counseled	Led	Solved
Created	Maintained	Supervised
Designed	Managed	Tested
Directed	Modified	Trained
Edited	Negotiated	Updated
Eliminated	Operated	Wrote
Evaluated	Organized	

Action verbs can show you are a doer.

If you are developing a **functional format,** most appropriate for creative positions and those in which writing is important, place your experiences under headings

Figure 8.2 *Chronological resume*

Tyler Wiggins

Campus Address	Permanent Address
3301 North Hudson Avenue	612 Colorado Avenue
Lincoln, NE 68508	Sioux Falls, SD 57108
(402) 547-2066	(605) 334-8841
Email: TWiggins@UNL.edu	

Objective: An advertising sales position with a television station

Education: **University of Nebraska Lincoln**

Bachelor of Arts degree, May 2011
Dual majors: Advertising and marketing
Minor: Sales
GPA: 3.17/4.0 overall and 3.4/4.0 major

Experience: **Advertising sales intern**—summer 2010

KETV (ABC), Omaha, NE

- Shadowed advertising sales representatives
- Researched potential clients
- Assessed the changing advertising needs of clients

Marketing intern—spring 2009

City-TV, Lincoln, NE

- Revised marketing strategies for the Husker Football Shuttle
- Consulted with potential advertisers
- Planned summer marketing strategies

Awards: Hugh Palmer Award for Outstanding Marketing Presentation, 2010
Outstanding Advertising Campaign Award, 2009

Activities: **President**—Advertising Club, 2009–2010

- Planned monthy activities
- Conducted monthly meetings
- Created an internship hotline for members

Marketing Director—Old Masters in Marketing Program, 2008–2009

- Arranged visits for outstanding alumni
- Directed advertising campaigns for Old Masters visits
- Escorted Old Masters visitors to classes

that highlight your qualifications for the position (see Figure 8.3). Typical headings are management, sales, advertising, training, counseling, team building, organizational development, recruiting, finance, teaching, administration, supervision, project manager, and marketing. You can include a variety of experiences from different positions, internships, and organizations under each heading, an advantage when you have had few paying positions or positions directly related to the opening. Use action verbs when identifying your experiences, such as "Wrote press releases for . . ." and "Developed training modules for . . ." Avoid too many headings and subheadings.

Leadership, not membership, impresses interviewers.

If you are using a chronological format, the next section may list relevant organizational memberships and activities, including college, professional, and community. Be selective. High school activities are excluded for college graduates, and college activities will be excluded after a few years in your career. It is a continual updating process. A long list of organizations without leadership roles will give a negative impression. Show you are a doer. Include honorary organizations such as Phi Beta Kappa and Golden Key, and provide brief descriptions of organizations.

If you are using a functional format, list organizations, or include them within various major headings under experience, or blend them within your skills and experiences. Your outside activities may indicate motivation, communication skills, ability to work with people, work ethic, ability to lead, and indicate that you are not a narrow specialist.

Select the resume format best suited to you.

A chronological format, such as the one in Figure 8.2, is easy to write and organize, emphasizes experiences, is most common, and is easy for an employer to scan for relevant experiences.

A functional format, such as the one in Figure 8.3, focuses attention on relevant skills to match the ideal applicant profile, dates are less important, and seemingly unrelated positions and education are not highlighted. A functional resume does not repeat the same skills and experiences under different positions, so it can be tighter and shorter. Many resumes are blends of the two formats.

Exclude items that might lead to EEO violations.

Do not include references; political, religious, or ethnic memberships or activities; a picture; or personal data such as age, marital status, parental status, height, and weight. You do not break any laws if you include these items, but you are providing information apart from bona fide occupational qualifications and assuming that an employer may hire you from unlawful criteria. You may *not* get a position because of this information.

Pay attention to content and appearance.

Regardless of the resume format you select, follow these rules when selecting content: be precise, do not repeat the same information, be persuasive, and—above all—be honest.

It is estimated that one in six college students lie on resumes and application forms, most often claiming experiences they have not had, courses they have not taken, and graduation indexes they have not achieved. Michael Josephson, president of the Josephson Institute of Ethics, warns that "Lies are like potato chips. You can't tell just one."[19]

While some applicants have something to hide, many believe that a little "puffery," a euphemism for lying, will get them a position and advancement. Employers and ethicists agree that this is a **bad idea** with potentially **bad results.** One source warns that "When fitted onto resumes, falsehoods can sit undetected indefinitely. Or, they can detonate at any moment, proving fatal to careers and credibility."[20] Scott Reeves writes

Figure 8.3 *Functional resume*

Megan M. Morgan
1425 Ashland Drive
Beaumont, TX 77705
(409) 213-4971
Email: mmorgan@lu.edu

Objective: Assistant Director

Education: **Lamar University**

Bachelor of Arts, June 2011
Major: Theater
Minor: Dance
GPA: 2.9/4.0 overall, 3.6/4.0 major

Experience:

Acting

- Performed in six major university productions
- Performed in three civic theater productions

Directing

- Directed an experimental version of *The Death of a Salesman*
- Directed a children's production of *Snow White*
- Developed a training program for inexperienced performers

Managing

- Supervised the technical staff for small stage productions
- Developed a budget for scenery in a production of *Macbeth*
- Served as a liaison between faculty directors and student actors

Writing

- Wrote press releases for student productions
- Revised scripts for experimental productions

Work Experience:

Sales Associate May to September 2010
Macy's, St. Louis, MO

Server May to September 2009
Joshua's Steak House, St. Louis, MO

bluntly: "A solid resume will get you in the door. A lie on the resume will get you kicked down the stairs."[21]

Mechanics of Resumes

Make your resume easy to review.

Pay attention to appearance and layout. Print your resume on white, off-white, light gray, or light beige bond paper. Pay attention to how the resume is blocked so it looks neat, attractive, organized, carefully planned, and uncrowded. Employers like white space on resumes, so indent sections carefully, double-space parts, and leave at least one-inch margins all around. Center your name at the top in bold letters so it stands out. Use different printer fonts so headings guide the reader through important information about you. Employers prefer resumes with bullets that separate and call attention to important information because this helps them scan the resume more efficiently. If you provide two addresses, place one on each side under your name. If you provide one address, place it in the center or on the right side away from staples and paper clips. Use perfect grammar, select wording carefully, check spellings and grammar, and proof for errors.

Proofread your resume with great care.

Most employers prefer a single-page resume. A two-page resume is acceptable, however, if it is less crowded and provides valuable information about experiences, skills, awards, and organizational activity and leadership that will not fit on a single page. If you develop a two-page resume, print it front to back on one sheet of paper because a second page may get misplaced or ripped off when your resume is taken from a file or briefcase. Signal with a page number or notation that there is more on the back. Repeat your name at the top on the left and a page number on the top right.

The Electronically Scanned Resume

Some organizations with large numbers of openings that attract large numbers of applicants use electronic systems to scan resumes. The scanner saves time and money.

If one of your resumes is likely to be electronically scanned, follow these basic rules. Use white paper. Employ only one or two print fonts. Do not use underlining. Be sure your resume contains up-to-date terms, labels, and names the scanner is programmed to detect. Some employers scan career objectives to sort resumes into files for different positions, so be sure to have a clearly identifiable career objective. It may be wise to ignore the usual one-page resume rule. Joyce Lain Kennedy, an authority on the electronic job search, recommends, "The more keyword marketing points you present about yourself, the more likely you are to be plucked from an electronic resume database now, in six months, or a year from now."[22]

The following are examples of correct and incorrect terms for scannable resumes:

Terms and labels are critical in scannable resumes.

Yes	No
human resources	personnel
administrative assistant	secretary
sales associate	sales clerk
information systems	data processing
environmental services	housekeeping

accountant	bookkeeper
facilities engineering	maintenance
inside sales	customer relations

Organizations may reject candidates with less than 50 percent of the required skills.

Organizations are now accepting or asking for resumes to be sent electronically to save time and to create electronic files on applicants. Be sure your software system will send your resume in an attractive format. Instructors and students at some universities have reported that organizations have requested all applicant files be sent on CD-ROMs. Paper files are unacceptable. On the other hand, many organizations are being inundated with hundreds of e-resumes from unqualified applicants. They find such resumes to be sloppy, impersonal, and mass-mailed rather than customized for a particular position with a particular organization. Unless told to do otherwise, include a cover letter that clearly identifies the position you are applying for and stresses how you are a good fit. Always bring copies of your cover letters and resumes to the interview.

Online Resumes

With the Internet an integral part of our lives, organizations and entrepreneurs have created online sites for posting resumes and seeking positions. The advantages are that it is easy and you have the potential of reaching a wide variety of potential employers in many career fields worldwide.

Use online services with caution.

Unfortunately, the ease of posting resumes online has made applicants easy prey for unscrupulous Web searchers who act as fake employers to take your money and your identity. Heather Galler of Carnegie Mellon University has developed a computer program called "Identity Angel" that searches online job boards for what she calls the "holy trinity" of information thieves love to attain: name, address, and Social Security number. If it locates such information, it sends a warning to the potential target of online thieves and frauds.

Galler offers these suggestions:[23] First, read the privacy policy carefully to determine how long your resume will be active and how you can delete it. "If there's no privacy policy, forget it." Second, be aware of fake recruiters, particularly if they ask for a driver's license or other personal information under the pretense of needing this for background checks. Ask the "recruiters" for references and check to see if they are members of local or national recruiter's associations. Third, set up an alternative e-mail address, use a cell phone, and provide a P.O. box as your address for job hunting. Fourth, if you want to see if your personal information is online, type in your name and the last four digits of your Social Security number. By providing more information, you may outsmart yourself because thieves can use spyware to get more of your personal information.

The Portfolio

Your portfolio shows you in action.

Portfolios are essential if you are in fields such as photography, advertising, public relations, art and design, journalism, architecture, teaching, and professional writing. Your **portfolio** should be a small yet varied collection of your best work. Organize your portfolio thematically. Make it visually attractive. Have excellent copies of your work—not faded, soiled, marked-up, graded, or wrinkled samples. Employers want to see how well you write, design, photograph, edit, and create, and the well-designed and presented portfolio is the best means of doing this.

If you are going into broadcasting, your portfolio must contain an audio or videorecording of selections that illustrate your best oral and video work. Quality, not quantity, is what sells.

Some colleges and universities are encouraging or requiring students to create electronic portfolios that can include a wide variety of materials in an attractive, compact, and highly usable package. In addition to revealing what a candidate has done and can do, the e-portfolio demonstrates knowledge of and ability to apply new technologies.

The all-purpose form letter is rarely taken seriously.

The Cover Letter

Your **cover letter** may open the employment door by showing *interest* in the position, the organization, and its products or services. Make the recruiter want to read your resume by making a pleasant and professional impression.

Send an *original* cover letter along with each resume to any lead that might prove fruitful. Form cover letters and ones aimed at several positions impress no one. Tailor letters to each position and organization.

Whenever possible, address your letter to a *specific person* who will be actively involved in the selection process. "To whom it may concern" letters rarely get responses. Sending a letter to a person uninvolved in recruiting will, at best, delay reaching the correct person.

Design and target letters to specific positions and organizations.

The letter should be brief, usually three or four paragraphs, and never more than one page. Figure 8.4 illustrates a typical cover letter. As with the resume, the cover letter must be neat, be printed on bond paper, have at least one-inch margins, be phrased in the employer's language, and look professional with no typos, misspellings, grammatical errors, or punctuation errors.

Specify the position in which you are interested and why. Reveal how you discovered the opening and what you know about the organization. Explain how your education and training, experiences, organizational memberships, and activities make you an ideal fit with the applicant profile. You can refer to your resume, but do not merely repeat it. The goal is to persuade the recruiter that you are well suited for *this position* with *this organization* at *this time*.

Show interest and enthusiasm or do not apply.

Emphasize your *enthusiasm* for this position with this organization. Show that you have researched both thoroughly. If you reveal that you know little about the position or organization, your application is dead upon arrival.

Close the cover letter by restating your interest in the position and organization. Ask for an interview and state when you might be available for an interview.

If a position is listed on a Web site or in a newspaper or journal, use the ad's language. Do not merely repeat the words but show you fit the requirements. Use the cover letter to sell the skills, abilities, and experiences you possess that make you a good match for the position. Be positive and to the point.

Figure 8.4 *Sample cover letter*

3379 North Mountain Road
Santa Clara, CA 95052
January 15, 2011

Mr. Lou Gaffney
Motorola Energy Products Division
4412 Industrial Avenue
Mundelein, IL 60019

Dear Mr. Gaffney:

I am writing in response to your advertisement in *The Wall Street Journal* for an industrial engineer with 2–3 years experience and a background in sonic welding. It is my understanding that the Energy Division is a spinoff division of the Cellular Phone Division and supplies batteries to that division.

I am very interested in this position and in Motorola because it is a position for which I feel I am uniquely qualified. My BS degree from the University of California at Davis is in industrial engineering, and I have spent the last three years working at Mattel Toys providing engineering support for its mini-toy division that uses Unitek Sonic Welders. Over the years I have used many Motorola products personally and professionally and have found them to be outstanding. Reports of Motorola's new generation cell phones that are under development sound very exciting.

I look forward to discussing the opportunity that this position affords someone with my background and interests with a representative from Motorola. Enclosed is a resume that provides additional details. Please feel free to contact me at my home telephone number (608-355-4109) or through e-mail (flopez@hotmail.com). I will be in the Chicago area visiting family during the first two weeks of February and would be available for an interview at your convenience.

Sincerely,

Francis Lopez

Enclosure; resume

Personal Web Sites, Pages, and Blogs

Applicants create Web sites for personal use and as a supplement to the standard resume and portfolio. These can be effective means of selling you and your potential if they are done carefully and you follow the guidelines offered in this chapter and elsewhere for creating your credentials. Prepare these with care to present a professional and mature image and to show your creative, technical, and writing abilities.

Your private notes and thoughts are public.

The most potentially dangerous sites to you as an applicant are the highly popular social networking sites such as Facebook, MySpace, TagWorld, Bebo, Blogger, Flickr, Friendster, Orkut, Linkedin, Ryze, and Monster. College students and others, often with humorous and personal intent (a diary to share with family or friends), include pictures of themselves drinking excessively or in sexually explicit poses, profanity, stories of sexual escapades and drunken parties, and threats that may impress someone of their age but not potential employers. Blog users may feel these "social" sites are safe, private, easy to delete, irrelevant to their professional lives, and unknown to potential employers.[24] **Wrong!**

Virtually anyone can access your blog site with a little effort and discover your personal life and, once discovered, it becomes public knowledge and impressions. Students have been dropped as hot job prospects because of what they included in their sites and blogs. Interested parties can access your site even after you have attempted to delete it. One source warns, "The Web may seem ephemeral, but what you casually post one night might just last a digital eternity."[25] Employers are concerned about how applicants will fit into their culture, perform maturely on the job, and present a positive image in the organization, community, and field. Materials on your blog may make you appear to be a dangerous hire.

Recruiters are aware of and do check your sites.

A study by Kimberly Shea and Jill Wesley of Purdue University's Center for Career Opportunities discovered that over a third of recruiters routinely run applicant names through search engines to discover what is "out there." Nearly half use some sort of technology to screen applicants. Some 75 percent of recruiters indicated that what they found did influence their decisions, 50 percent negatively.[26] In spite of these figures, over 50 percent of students believe recruiters do not check such sites as Facebook. Recruiters employ college students and interns to search sites their peers use routinely. Shea and Wesley remind students that "You are responsible for your personal marketing campaign." They ask, "Would you be willing to share your Web site/blog/Facebook profile with your grandparents?"

Creating a Favorable First Impression

As you approach the interview, realize that your **attitudes** are a critical ingredient in your success or failure.[27] Be thoroughly prepared. Anxiety is heightened when you feel you do not know enough about the position or the organization, are unready to answer tough questions, and do not know what questions to ask. If you feel you are not going to do well in an interview, you won't.

Avoid self-fulfilling prophecies.

Approach the employment interview for what it is, a sales process, and you are the product. Know yourself thoroughly. If you cannot sell you to you, how can you sell you to the recruiter? Be *positive* about yourself, current and past employers, associates, professors, and clients. Be professional and ethical throughout the interview. Never bad-mouth others or reveal confidences. One study revealed that good **first impressions** lead interviewers to show positive regard toward applicants, give important job information, sell the organization to them, and spend less time gathering information.[28]

Know how and when to share control of the interview.

If the interview will be over the telephone, avoid common "interruptions" such as flushing toilets, cleaning dishes, barking dogs, and answering e-mail messages.[29] Find a quiet place and give your full attention to the interview interaction. Avoid the cell phone if possible because the signal may fade and it's often difficult to hear clearly on cell phones.

Relationship of the Interview Parties

Understand and adapt to the relationship with the recruiter.

Assess the *relationship* that is likely to exist between you and the interviewer. How will control be shared? Control is often determined by the job market and the organization's need to fill the position. *Successful applicants* dominate interviews but also know when to let the interviewer control the conversation. *Unsuccessful applicants* are submissive or try to dominate when the employer clearly wants to do so.

Do you want to take part in this interview? You may find it difficult to "get fired up" for an interview if you have been turned down a number of times during previous months or you are not really interested in this position or organization. Are you interviewing for a sales position only because you cannot get into management?

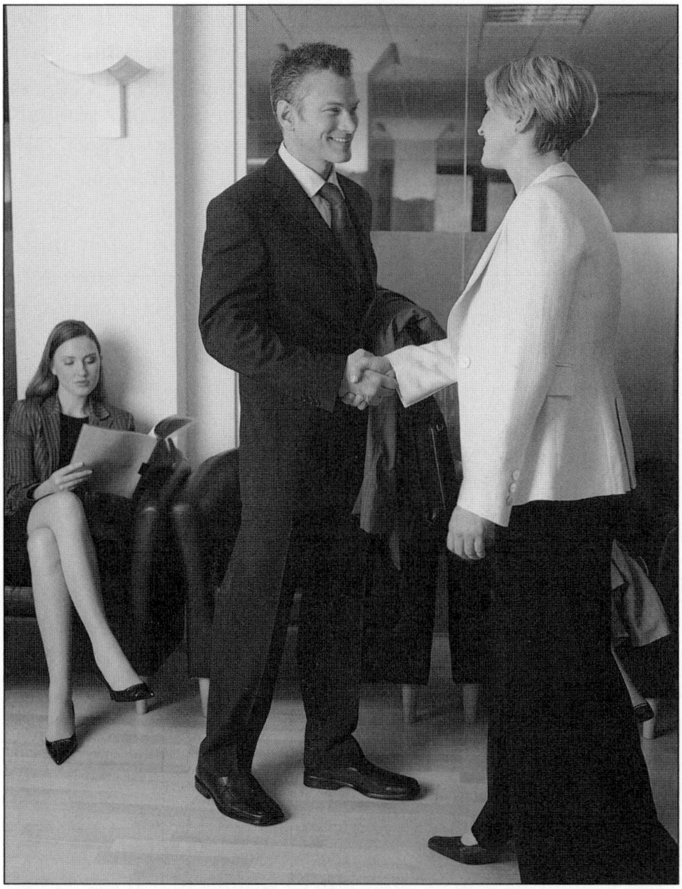
© Digital Vision

Dress appropriately for a professional interview.

What degree of liking (mutual trust, respect, friendship) is there between you and the interviewer as revealed in previous encounters, telephone contacts, and letters? How similar are you to the interviewer in age, gender, race, ethnic group, background, education, and profession? Research reveals that candidates racially similar to interviewers (black and white) receive higher interviewer ratings.[30]

Dress and Appearance

Dress and *appearance* are critical elements in a favorable first impression. In a survey of college recruiters, 95 percent cited professional image as *important* or *very important*.[31] They see clothes and accessories as "making a strong visual statement" that suggest confidence and "gives the interviewee a competitive edge." While many companies are now promoting business casual at the workplace, 81 percent of respondents in this

Dress for a formal business occasion.

survey prefer formal business attire for formal interviews "to see how applicants would present themselves in a business meeting or presentation." Mary Dawne Arden, an executive coach and president of Arden Associates in New York, states that "No one can fault you for being too formal in an interview. But being sloppy, or even too casual, will kill your prospects."[32]

The following are common mistakes men and women make.[33]

Neatness costs nothing and pays dividends.

- Clothing inappropriate for the workplace.
- Dirty and wrinkled clothing that does not fit properly.
- Shirts and blouses that are too tight at the collar or waist.
- Scuffed shoes or shoes inappropriate for clothing or workplace.
- Dirty hands, nails, or hair.
- Dingy teeth.
- Too much or inappropriate jewelry.
- Noticeable perfume, cologne, or aftershave.

Be sure you hair is neatly combed or brushed and trimmed. Beards and mustaches are generally acceptable but should be neat and trimmed. Bonnie Lowe writes that "your goal is to look professional and conservative. This applies to makeup, nail polish, jewelry, body piercings, tattoos, etc. If there's any chance that the Interviewers might not like it, no matter how 'cool' it is, don't let it show."[34] For most interviews, you will want to wear a conservative, solid-color suit, but you must "learn about an industry's fashion culture" because some are more casual than others. When in doubt ask about the preferred dress code when arranging an interview. Kate Wendleton, president and founder of a national career counseling and placement firm, recommends the rule of thumb "that you dress one or two levels higher than the job that you're going for."[35]

Be on the conservative side in dress and appearance.

Advice for Men

Standard interviewing apparel for men is a dark suit (blue, gray, black, charcoal) with a white or pastel solid shirt and a contrasting but not "wild" tie. Wear conservative, professional apparel to the interview, even if the interviewer (who has a job by the way) may be dressed informally.

Try the sit-down test to check for fit. Almost anyone can wear clothes that are a bit too tight when standing, but sitting down quickly reveals if the jacket, waistband, seat, or collar is too tight or the shirt gaps at the waist. Insert one finger into the collar of your shirt. If the collar is too tight, you need a larger shirt; if it is too loose, you need a smaller shirt to avoid the sloppy look of a drooping collar.

Coordinate colors carefully.

Wear dark socks that complement your suit and cover at least half a leg so when you sit down and cross your legs, no skin is visible. Tie size and age depend upon what is in style, but it is always safe to wear a wide stripe, small polka dot, or conservative pattern that is blue, red, gray, or burgundy.

Choose clothing that is appropriate for your body shape: regular, thin or slender, heavy or muscular, and tall or short. For example, a heavy, muscular male should choose dark shades with small pinstripes. For less formal settings, such as dinner

When in doubt, ask for help.

during the interviewing process, you might wear a blue blazer with light gray or tan slacks. A thin or slender male may wear a greater variety of clothing, and some plaids might add size and depth to the physical appearance.

Jewelry for men should be minimal and professional. A gold or silver watch, and a gold or silver ballpoint or fountain pen are impressive. One or more earrings will negatively affect some interviewers. Do you want to take the risk?

Advice for Women

Appearance should not call attention to itself.

Makeup, hairstyle, and clothing are personal decisions that reveal a great deal about your personality—who you are, your self-concept, and what you think of others. Take them seriously. No makeup is probably too little, but if makeup calls attention to itself, it is too much. Recruiters suggest small (not dangling) earrings with one per ear, one ring per hand, and no bracelets. Coloring is essential, and a cosmetic counselor can help determine what is professionally appropriate for you.

Select a conservative business suit or dress in blue, navy, gray, beige, tan, or brown. Skirt or dress "length should be at least to the bottom of the knee."[36] Wear a conservative blouse that matches the suit. Low, comfortable pumps are more appropriate than high heels or flats.

Provocative clothing can end your candidacy.

Try the sit-down and one-finger-in-the-collar tests recommended for men. Avoid "see through" blouses or ones with plunging necklines. Avoid skirts with long slits. If you must tug at your skirt when you sit down, it is too short. Wear clear or plain color stockings appropriate for your outfit. Be neat, clean, comfortable, and professional.

Nonverbal Communication

Nonverbal communication (voice, eye contact, gestures, and posture) are important ingredients throughout selection interviews. Scott Reeves reports a typical example in which an applicant looked very strong on paper but "offered a deadfish handshake, slouched and fidgeted in his chair, failed to make eye contact with the interviewer and mumbled responses to basic questions." He was not hired.[37] Arden cites a study that found "a first impression is based on 7% spoken words, 38% tone of voice and 55% body language."[38] Interviewers react more favorably toward applicants and rate them higher if they smile, have expressive facial expressions, maintain eye contact, and have clear, forceful voices. Technology plays important roles in the employment process, but recruiters interview applicants because they prefer "high touch" to "high tech" when selecting people who will join and influence the futures of their organizations. They want to see, hear, and observe you in action.

Be alive and dynamic.

Dynamism and energy are communicated through the way you shake hands, sit, walk, stand, gesture, and move your body. Use a firm but not crushing handshake. Try to appear (and be) calm and relaxed, but sharp and in control. Avoid nervous gestures, fidgets, movements, and playing with pens or objects on the interviewer's desk. Respond crisply and confidently with no sign of arrogance. When replying to questions, maintain eye contact with the recruiter. If there are two or more recruiters in the room, glance at the others when answering a question but focus primarily on the questioner, particularly as you complete your answer.

Good communication skills are important in all positions.

Speak in a normal conversational tone with vocal variety that exhibits confidence and interpersonal skills. Interviewers prefer standard accents. If English is your second language or you have an accent developed since birth, work on your accent and pronunciation so interviewers can understand you clearly and effectively.

Do not hesitate to pause before answering difficult questions, but frequent pauses may make you appear hesitant, unprepared, or "slow." Interviewers interpret pauses of one second or less as signs of ambition, self-confidence, organization, and intelligence.

Arrival and Opening

Arrive for the interview a few minutes ahead of time. If you are not on time for the interview, will you be on time for work? Is this a sign of the importance you place on this interview? Do not arrive too early. The recruiter may have other tasks to perform or interviews to conduct and does not want to assign staff to entertain you until the scheduled interview. Be courteous to everyone you meet.

Be on time and ready to interact.

Greet the employer pleasantly and dynamically. Do not use the interviewer's first name unless invited to do so. Sit when asked to do so and never sit down before the interviewer does. Be an active participant during the opening. You will become relaxed once you get into the flow of the interview, so respond to opening, icebreaker questions as you would in a normal conversation. How you handle yourself during the first few minutes with a stranger tells the interviewer a great deal about your interpersonal communication and people skills.

Answering Questions

Decisions are made on the total interview.

Dress, appearance, and nonverbal communication are important ingredients in the selection process, but do not overestimate their importance. Studies suggest that the final decision is most often based on a combination of verbal and nonverbal impressions, with a combination of interviewing skills, background, and experiences accounting for most successful searches.[39]

Preparing to Respond

Be ready and eager to answer questions effectively. Nervousness will lessen when you concentrate on answering confidently and thoroughly. Successful applicants are prepared to handle frequently asked questions such as:

Be ready to handle traditional questions.

- Tell me about yourself.
- Why do you want to work for us?
- What are your greatest strengths? Weaknesses?
- What are your short-range career goals? Long-range goals?

- Why did you leave your position with __________?
- What did you like best in your position at __________? Like least?
- Why should we select you over the other applicants for this position?
- What do you know about our organization?

These traditional questions play major roles in selection interviews, particularly during the opening minutes. Interviewers use them to get applicants talking and relaxed, and to learn about them as human beings and budding professionals.

As discussed in Chapter 7, the nature of questioning in employment interviews has changed. Interviewers are asking more challenging questions about your experiences in specific situations (behavior-based questions) and placing applicants in **joblike situations** to see how they might fit in and function as employees. The philosophy is simple: employers can determine best how applicants might operate in specific positions by placing them in these positions during the interview. Task-oriented questions assess thinking and communication abilities and reveal how well you can operate in stressful or surprise situations. Here are common on-the-job question strategies:

Welcome on-the-job questions to show what you can do.

- *Behavior-based questions:*

  "Tell me about a time when you operated as part of a team to solve a vexing technical problem."

- *Current critical incident questions:*

  "We are facing a situation in which we . . . If you were on our team, what would you recommend we do to resolve this situation?"

- *Historical critical incident questions:*

  "Two years ago we had a conflict between . . . If you had been the supervisor in this situation, what would you have done?"

- *Hypothetical questions:*

  "Suppose you had a customer who claimed his computer hardware was damaged in shipment. How would you handle this?"

- *Weird hypothetical questions:*

  "If you were a vegetable, what kind of vegetable would you like to be?"

- *Task-oriented questions:*

  "Here's a sheet of paper. Write a policy statement for the assignment of overtime." Interviewers have been known to take out a ballpoint pen and say, "Sell this to me."

Many employers are requiring would-be teachers to teach, salespersons to sell, engineers to engineer, managers to manage, and designers to design. Job simulations, role-playing, presentations, and day-long case studies challenge applicants to demonstrate their knowledge, skills, experiences, maturity, and integrity.

Responding: Successful Applicants

Listen, think, and then answer.

Successful applicants *listen* carefully to the *whole question* without interrupting or trying to second-guess the interviewer. They *think* before replying, and then give answers that are succinct, specific, and to the point of the question. Many applicants miss the mark of questions, such as in the following example:

1. **Recruiter:** Why would you like to work for Chrysler?
2. **Applicant:** I've been interested in cars all of my life and would love to find a position in the auto industry.

This applicant emphasizes interest in cars, but does not address the question "Why Chrysler?"

Effective answers are long on substance and short on puffery.

Present organized responses with clear arguments, relevant content, good grammar, and action verbs that show you are a doer. Be aware of common words and how to use them correctly. Michael Skube, who teaches journalism, discovered that these simple and common words stumped many college students: impetus, ramshackle, lucid, advocate, derelict, satire, brevity, novel, and afflicted vs. afflict.[40] These "potholes in exchanges" turn off recruiters. Use professional jargon when appropriate. If you are short of actual work experiences, provide relevant illustrations from other experiences. If you are asked a question about working in teams, the recruiter will be listening to the pronouns you use. If you work well in teams, you will speak of *us* and *we;* if you work better alone, you will speak of *I* and *me*.

Any hint of dishonesty, insincerity, unethical behavior, or evasion is fatal. Do not reply with prepared and rehearsed answers to sound good. A skilled recruiter will see through your answer or destroy it with a few, well-placed probing questions:

1. **Recruiter:** Why would you like to work for Lilly?
2. **Applicant:** I believe your research is on the cutting edge in the pharmaceutical industry.
3. **Recruiter:** How so?
4. **Applicant:** Well, you are working in areas such as aids, hypertension, and Alzheimer's.
5. **Recruiter:** Tell me what you know about our Alzheimer's research.

Do not play act; act yourself.

Beware of sources that want to provide you with the correct or most impressive answers to recruiter questions—there is *no single correct answer* to each question. Five different recruiters, even from the same organization, asking an identical question may be looking for somewhat different answers.

Be enthusiastic and dynamic. Be interested in the position and organization and show it. Speak positively about your experiences. Successful applicants demonstrate the characteristics of the organization's ideal applicant profile through communication skills, answers, and actions.

Good recruiters detect phoniness.

Accept responsibilities for past actions. Give reasons, not excuses. Show in everything you do and say that you are a mature man or woman, not an immature boy or girl.

Answer questions thoroughly, but know when to stop talking. This is particularly difficult during telephone interviews because you do not have the usual interviewer nonverbal cues (leaning forward, looking at notes, facial expressions, gestures) present in face-to-face interviews to tell you when to stop.

Successful applicants know when to follow up questions with questions. If you are asked a vague question or one you do not understand, paraphrase it in your own words or ask tactfully for clarification.

Be informed before replying.

If you are asked a difficult behavior-based, critical incident, hypothetical, or task question, think through your answer carefully and consider the ramifications of your response for you and the organization. You might ask for additional details or what authority you would have in this situation. Asking for such information will impress the interviewer with your professionalism and understanding of organizational situations and caution about acting with haste. Ralston, Kirkwood, and Burant write that behavioral questions require applicants to tell stories, and these stories are critical to successful interviews. They list a number of criteria for good stories.[41] Is the story internally consistent? Is it consistent with the facts the recruiter holds to be true? Is it relevant to the question and the applicant's claim? Does it provide details that support the claim? How does it reflect the applicant's beliefs and values?

Responding: Unsuccessful Applicants

Unsuccessful applicants play passive, limited roles in openings and closings. They seem unable to identify with the needs and interests of the employer, perhaps because they know little about either. They appear uncertain about the kinds of positions they want and where they hope to be in 5 or 10 years. They fail to show interest in and their qualifications for the position. At the end, they do not ask for the position.

Unsuccessful applicants are evasive and use less active, concrete, and positive language and technical jargon that exhibit experiences and knowledge of the field and position. Their brief answers are nonassertive, including the following.

Poor applicants are passive and cautious.

- *Qualifiers* such as "perhaps" and "maybe."
- *Meaningless slang* such as "you know," "know what I'm sayin," and "know what I mean."
- *Nonfluencies* such as "ummm" or "uhh."
- *Vagueness* such as "and stuff like that" or "and that sort of thing."

A Marist College poll, released to the media in October 2009, discovered that some of these words and phrases, along with "Whatever," "It is what it is," and "At the end of the day," are among the most annoying and irritating to Americans. Imagine how recruiters might react to them.

Unsuccessful applicants answer before thinking. For instance, when asked "Why should I hire you?" one applicant answered that he could be a great asset to the company softball team while another replied that he was bored watching TV.[42] Some applicants seem to volunteer interview ending comments. For example:[43]

- "Sorry for yawning, I usually sleep until my soap operas are on."
- "I am quitting my job because I hate to work hard."
- "My resume might make it look like I am a job hopper. But I want you to know that I never left any of those jobs voluntarily."

Avoid doing weird or impolite things during interviews. Here are a few real-life examples.

- An applicant put his feet on the recruiter's desk.
- An applicant stretched out on the floor to fill out the application form.
- An applicant wore an iPod and said she could multitask during the interview.
- An applicant said she had not had lunch and proceeded to eat a hamburger and fries during the interview.
- When a recruiter asked an applicant to tell him about his hobbies, the applicant stood up and danced around the office.
- An alarm clock went off in an applicant's briefcase. He shut it off, and asked the recruiter to hurry with his questions because he had to leave for another interview.
- An applicant for a high-level academic administrative position started crying when relating a story about a person who had been influential in his life.

You may not be guilty of such interview improprieties, but you may commit common ones. In a survey of 188 college recruiters, John Cunningham discovered a number of ways applicants can "slip up" during interviews.[44] Notice how they summarize (in a negative way) the suggestions presented in this chapter.

Know what not to do during interviews, and then do not do it.

1. Lacking in awareness about the company and position.
2. Showing no interest or enthusiasm.
3. Lying or telling the recruiter what you think he or she wants to hear.
4. Exhibiting poor communication skills.
5. Being too money oriented.
6. Having unclear or unrealistic goals.
7. Not having relevant experience.
8. Having no campus involvement.
9. Presenting a poor appearance.
10. Not having any questions to ask.
11. Exhibiting a bad attitude.
12. Being inflexible.
13. Arriving late for the interview.
14. Having poor listening skills.
15. Being arrogant or cocky.

Unlawful Questions

Do not be surprised by unlawful questions.

Applicants, particularly women, are still asked unlawful questions even though federal and state laws have existed for decades and most organizations train employees to follow EEO guidelines. Violations range from mild infractions such as "What does your husband do?" to sexual harassment. Some are accidental during informal chatting with applicants and some are due to curiosity, tradition, lack of training, or ignorance of the laws.

Unlawful questions pose dilemmas for applicants. If you answer an unlawful question honestly and directly, you may lose the position. If you refuse to answer an unlawful question (almost impossible to do graciously), you may lose a position because you are uncooperative, evasive, or "one of those."

Review EEO laws and your rights.

Be prepared to answer unlawful questions tactfully and effectively. First, review the EEO laws and exercise in Chapter 7 so you can determine when a question is unlawful.

Exercise #1—Which Questions Are Unlawful and Why?

If you are a Hispanic, female college graduate interviewing for a management position for a national retail chain, which of these questions would be unlawful? Why? How might you reply?

1. Where are you from?
____
2. Any marriage plans?
____
3. Tell me about your management position at Macy's.
____
4. Where do you hope to be in your career in five years?
____
5. How long would you expect to work for us?
____
6. How well do you speak Spanish?
____
7. Which religious holidays do you observe?
____
8. Do you have a significant other?
____
9. What do you do after work?
____
10. I see you have a hearing aid; how might that affect your work with us?
____

Second, be aware of tricks recruiters use to get unlawful information without appearing to ask for it.[45] For example, a low-level clerk may ask you which health insurance plan you would choose if hired; your answer may reveal that you are married and have children, that you are a single parent, or that you have a serious medical problem. During lunch or dinner or a tour of the organization's facilities when you are least expecting serious questions, an employer, perhaps a female, may probe into child care under the guise of talking about her own problems: "What a day! My daughter Emily woke up this

Beware of recruiter tricks to get unlawful information.

morning with a fever, my husband is out of town, and I had an eight o'clock conference downtown. Do you ever have days like this?" You may begin to tell problems you have had with your children or family members and, in the process, reveal a great deal of irrelevant, unlawful, and perhaps damaging information without knowing it. Employers have learned how to get unlawful information through lawful questions. Instead of asking, "Do you have children?" an employer asks, "Is there any limit on your ability to work overtime (evenings, weekends, holidays)?" Others use coded questions and comments.

- "Our employees put a lot into their work" means "Older workers like you don't have much energy."
- "We have a very young staff" means "You won't fit in."
- "I'm sure your former company had its own corporate culture, just as we do here" means "Hispanics need not apply."
- "We are a very traditional company" means "We don't hire women beyond clerical staff."

Consider your needs and desires before responding.

Third, determine how important the position is for you. Your primary goal is to get a good position, and if you are hired, you may be able to change organizational attitudes and recruiters' practices. You can do nothing from the outside. If questions are gross violations, consider reporting the recruiter to his or her superior or to the career center.[46] If this person is typical of the organization or a person you would report to if hired, you might be wise to look elsewhere.

Fourth, practice using a variety of answer tactics. For example, try a tactful refusal that is more than a simple "I will not answer that question because it is unlawful."

Be tactful!

1. **Interviewer:** How old are you?

   Interviewee: I don't think age is important if you are well qualified for a position.

2. **Interviewer:** Do you plan to have children?

   Interviewee: My plans to have a family will not interfere with my ability to perform the requirements of this position.

Use a *direct, brief* answer, hoping the interviewer will move on to relevant, lawful questions.

1. **Interviewer:** What does your wife do?

   Interviewee: She's a pharmacist.

2. **Interviewer:** Do you attend church regularly?

   Interviewee: Yes, I do / No, I don't.

Pose a *tactful inquiry* such as the following that skirts the question and attempts to guide the recruiter away from the unlawful inquiry with a job-related question.

1. **Interviewer:** What does your husband do?

   Interviewee: He's in construction. Why do you ask?

2. **Interviewer:** You seem confined to a wheelchair; how might this affect your work performance?

   Interviewee: I am quite mobile in my chair. How is my disability relevant for a position as a computer software designer?

Try to *neutralize* the recruiter's obvious concern.

1. **Interviewer:** Do you plan on having a family?

   Interviewee: Yes, I do. I'm looking forward to the challenges of both family and career. I've observed many of my women professors and fellow workers handling both quite satisfactorily.

2. **Interviewer:** What happens if your husband gets transferred or needs to relocate?

   Interviewee: The same that would happen if I would get transferred or asked to relocate. We would discuss location moves that either of us might have to consider and make the best decision.

Make unlawful questions work for you.

Try to *take advantage* of the question to support your candidacy.

1. **Interviewer:** Where were you born?

   Interviewee: I am quite proud that my background is __________ because it has helped me work effectively with people of diverse backgrounds.

2. **Interviewer:** Are you married?

   Interviewee: Yes, I am, and I believe that is a plus. As you know, studies show that married employees are more stable and dependable than unmarried employees.

You might try what Bernice Sandler, an authority on discrimination in hiring, calls a **tongue-in-cheek test response** that sends an unmistakable signal to the recruiter that he or she has asked an unlawful question. This tactic must be accompanied by appropriate nonverbal signals to avoid offending the interviewer.

Be careful when being clever.

1. **Interviewer:** Who will take care of your children?

   Interviewee: (smiling, pleasant tone of voice) Are you trying to see if I can recognize an unlawful question in the selection process?

2. **Interviewer:** How long do you expect to work for us?

   Interviewee: (smiling, pleasant tone of voice) Is this a test to see how I might reply to an unlawful question?

Asking Questions

While applicants pore over lists of recruiter questions and formulate appropriate answers, too few spend time planning questions *they* will ask. Most recruiters will give you an opportunity to ask questions.

Guidelines for Asking Questions

Asking good questions results in more than information.

Your questions are critical, not only to get information to make an important life decision but also to reveal preparation, maturity, professionalism, interests, motivation, and values. You control this part of the interview; make the most of it.

A major mistake is not having any or too few questions to ask. Your questions can convince the recruiter that you are the ideal person for a position and organization or destroy the favorable impression you made during the opening and while answering questions.

Ask insightful and mature questions.

If you have a number of questions prepared but the interviewer answers all of them during the information-giving stage of the interview, do not ask a question merely to ask a question. There is a good likelihood it will be a poor one because you have not considered it carefully.

Successful applicants ask probing questions.

Successful applicants ask more questions than unsuccessful applicants. And the questions of successful applicants are open-ended and probe into the position, organization, and recruiter's opinions to get complete and insightful answers.

In addition to the guidelines presented in Chapter 3 for effective questions, here are specific guidelines for employment questions.

Ask your most important question first.

- Avoid the "me . . . me . . . me . . ." syndrome in which all of your questions inquire as to what you will get, how much you will get, and when you will get it.
- Avoid questions about salary, promotion, vacation, and retirement during screening interviews and never pose them as your first questions.
- Do not waste time asking for information that is readily available on the organization's Web site or in the library.

Question Pitfalls

When asking questions, you are acting as an informational interviewer, and you may be prone to tumble into the common question pitfalls discussed in previous chapters: double-barreled, curious probe, leading, yes/no response, bipolar, guessing game, and open-to-closed switch.

In addition to common question pitfalls, applicants have some pitfalls of their own. These are centered on common wording that can produce a negative impression at a critical time late in the interview.

Exercise #2—Applicant Pitfalls

Rephrase each bad question below to make it a good question.

Prepare a schedule to avoid question pitfalls.

1. *The have to question* may sound like you will be an unhappy and uncooperative employee.

   Bad: Would I have to travel much?
   Good:

2. *The typology question* focuses on type rather than explanation that is desired.

   Bad: What type of training program do you have?
   Good:

3. *The pleading question* (often a series of them) seems to beg for answers.

   Bad: Could you please tell me about your expansion plans?
   Good:

4. *The little bitty question* may indicate lack of interest in detailed information, perhaps asking a question merely to ask a question.

   Bad: Tell me a little bit about your facility in Atlanta.
   Good:

5. *The uninformed question* may exhibit lack of maturity or background study prior to the interview.

   Bad: Tell me about benefits and stuff like that.
   Good:

How you ask may be more important than what you ask.

Prepare a moderate schedule of questions so you have questions phrased effectively. Order them according to importance because you may not get the opportunity to ask five or six questions in a 20- to 25-minute interview, particularly if your questions are open-ended and you probe into answers. Also, the recruiter will assume that you will ask your most important questions first or second and if these are salary and benefits, this is a major turnoff.

Sample Applicant Questions

The following sample applicant questions show interest in the position and the organization, are not overly self-centered, and meet question guidelines:

Adapt your questions to each position and organization.

- Describe your ideal employee for me.
- Tell me about the culture of your organization.
- How does your organization encourage employees to come up with new ideas?
- How much choice would I have in selecting geographical location?
- What is a typical workday for this position?
- What is the possibility of flexible working hours?
- How does your organization evaluate employees?
- What characteristics are you looking for in applicants for this position?
- How might your organization support me if I wanted to pursue an MBA?
- How often would I be working as part of a team?
- What, in your estimation, is the most unique characteristic of your organization?
- How might an advanced degree affect my position in your organization?
- Tell me about where other persons who have held this position have advanced within the organization.
- What do you like most about working for this organization?
- Tell me about the merger with TelEx.
- I noticed in *The Wall Street Journal* last week that your stock has risen almost 4 percent during this economic recession. What explains this increase?

- Tell me about the people I would be working with.
- Tell me about your training program.
- What major departmental changes do you anticipate during the next five years?
- What is the most important criterion for selecting a person for this position?

The following questions may help with a variety of positions in new and startup organizations:

- Which of your products are most in demand?
- Who are your major competitors?
- How much collective experience do your top officers have in the field?
- What are your plans for going public?
- Who are the major regulators of your business?

The Closing

Be aware of everything you say and do.

The closing stage of the employment interview is usually brief. Do not say or do anything that will detract from an impressive performance. Play an active role in the closing. Express your interest in the position and organization. And discover what will happen next, when, and whom you should contact and how if you need to get in touch about the position.

The interview "Is not over 'til it's over." If a member of the organization walks you to the outer office, the elevator, or the parking lot, the interview is not over. If a person takes you on a tour of the organization or the area, it is not over. If a person takes you to lunch or dinner, it is not over. The employer will note everything you do and say. Positions are lost because of the way applicants react during a tour, converse informally, meet other people, eat dinner, or handle alcoholic beverages.

Evaluation and Follow-Up

Debrief yourself immediately following each interview. Jot down your answers to tough questions, information the recruiter provided, and the recruiter's answers to your questions. Make a list of pros and cons of the position and organization and what you don't know that would be critical in making a decision. Do you think you did well or not so well? Be careful not to overreact. Your perceptions of what took place during the interview may be greatly exaggerated toward the positive or the negative.

Ask questions such as these during your postinterview debriefing:

Remember: the interview is more art than science.

- How adequate was my preparation?
- How effective was I during the opening?
- How appropriate were my dress and appearance?
- What opportunities to sell myself did I hit and miss?
- How thorough and to the point were my answers?

Be thorough in your debriefing.

- How well did I adapt my questions to this organization and position?
- How effectively did I show interest in this organization and position?
- Did I obtain enough information on this position and organization to make a good career decision?

Quality applicants write thank-you notes.

Follow up the interview with a brief, professional letter thanking the interviewer for the time given you. Promptness is less important than content. Avoid firing off letters with little thought. Lisa Ryan, managing director for recruiting at Heyman Associates of New York, tells the story of walking a person to the elevator and finding an e-mail thank-you note waiting for her when she returned to her office moments later. The candidate had e-mailed her from the elevator. She recommends that you "put some substance into your thank-you note."[47] Emphasize your interest in this position and organization. The thank-you letter provides an excuse to contact the interviewer, keeps your name alive, and includes additional information that might help the organization decide in your favor.

Handling Rejection

Every applicant will face rejection, even when he or she feels an interview went well. Potential employers reject applicants for a variety of reasons, often because of fit or because another applicant has a valued experience or skill. They may interview dozens of people for a single position and must make difficult choices. You will never hear from some recruiters.

How you handle rejections influences your attitudes, attitudes that may lead to further rejections. One writer warns: "**Don't be a victim.** The worst thing tired and frustrated job seekers can do is to conclude that employer reps and hiring managers are out to get them, that the job search process is out of their control, and that they're the victims of some evil, monolithic power."[48]

Learn from rejections.

Use each interview as a learning process. Ask what you might do differently in the next interview. How did you handle behavioral-based and critical incident questions? What was the nature of the questions you asked? How might you have prepared more thoroughly? What did you do that might have turned off the recruiter? Was this a position for which you were highly qualified, or was it a stretch?

Summary

Technology has allowed us to communicate instantly and to send and check information immediately. The scanning of resumes and the use of the Internet as sources for positions and resume storage are changing the face of searching for positions. Personality, integrity, and drug tests are adding a new dimension to the process.

We have become a part of the global economy and are undergoing a second industrial revolution moving from a manufacturing to a service- and information-oriented society. The best positions in the future will go to those who understand and are prepared for the selection process. You must know yourself, the position, and the organization to persuade an employer to select you from hundreds of other applicants. The job search must be extensive and rely more on networking and hard work than merely appearing at your college career center for an interview. Your resumes and cover letters must be thorough, professional, attractive, adapted to specific positions with specific organizations, and persuasive.

Interviewing skills are increasingly important because employers are looking for employees with communication, interpersonal, and people skills. You can exhibit these best during the interview. Take an active part in the opening, answer questions thoroughly and to the point, and ask carefully phrased questions about the position and the organization. Take an active part in the closing, and be sure the interviewer knows you want this position. Close on a high note.

Follow up the interview with a carefully crafted thank-you letter that expresses again your interest in this position and organization. And do an insightful postinterview evaluation that addresses strengths and weaknesses with future interviews in mind.

Key Terms and Concepts

The online learning center for this text features FLASHCARDS and CROSSWORD PUZZLES for studying based on these terms and concepts.

Appearance
Arrival
Attitudes
Behavior-based
Career/job fair
Career objective
Chronological format resume
Cover letter
Determinate interview
Electronically scanned
Fee-paid positions
First impression
Follow-up
Functional format resume
Honesty tests
Integrity interview
Joblike situations
Network tree
Networking
Nonverbal communication
Percentage agencies
Placement agency
Portfolio
Relationship
Research
Resume
Screening interview
Self-analysis
Successful applicants
Talent-based
Universal attitudes
Universal skills
Unsuccessful applicants

An Employment Interview for Review and Analysis

This interview is between a senior in computer technology and a college recruiter for Software Specialties, Inc., a firm that creates computer software for the aircraft industry. SS has been growing rapidly as more sophisticated aircraft have come on line and security against terrorism has become a critical concern since 9/11.

How active and effective is the applicant during the opening? What image does the applicant present during the interview? How appropriate, thorough, to the point, and persuasive are the applicant's answers? Has the applicant done adequate homework? How persuasively does the applicant demonstrate an interest in and fit for the position as a production supervisor for SS? How well do the applicant's questions meet the criteria presented in this chapter? How active and effective is the applicant during the closing?

1. **Recruiter:** Good afternoon, Carolyn. (shaking hands) Please be seated.
2. **Applicant:** Thanks.

3. **Recruiter:** I hope you have had a chance to meet some of our people here at the computer science job fair.
4. **Applicant:** Yes, I have.
5. **Recruiter:** Good. And you've had an opportunity to look through some of our materials?
6. **Applicant:** Yes.
7. **Recruiter:** Good. I want to talk to you for about 20 to 25 minutes. Let me begin by asking why you chose computer science at Texas Tech.
8. **Applicant:** I've always been a Tech fan, and I wanted to go to a large university close to home.
9. **Recruiter:** And why computer technology?
10. **Applicant:** Well, during my first year, I realized that I was both hands-on and theory-oriented. The computer technology program is very hands-on. After taking some CS classes and talking to students and faculty, I decided to switch majors.
11. **Recruiter:** Describe what you would consider to be an ideal position for you.
12. **Applicant:** I guess it would be like my internship with Microsoft. It would give me an opportunity to work on interesting projects, do some troubleshooting, and stuff like that.
13. **Recruiter:** What do you include in "stuff like that"?
14. **Applicant:** Well, you know, interesting stuff like handheld computers and working on problems with new software.
15. **Recruiter:** Tell me about the most difficult situation you have ever faced.
16. **Applicant:** It was when my father had a heart attack during my second year.
17. **Recruiter:** How did you handle it?
18. **Applicant:** I leaned sort of on my mom and my older sisters.
19. **Recruiter:** How did you lean on them?
20. **Applicant:** I talked to them a lot, hung out with them more often, and asked for help.
21. **Recruiter:** How did you help them deal with your father's health?
22. **Applicant:** Well, like I said, I talked it out with them and we formed a bond that we had not had before. I guess we acted sort of as a team and helped each other.
23. **Recruiter:** I see.
24. **Applicant:** Dad got better and we have been closer than ever.
25. **Recruiter:** How about geographical location?
26. **Applicant:** I like to travel and find people very friendly everywhere. Know what I mean?
27. **Recruiter:** Are you saying that you have no geographical preferences?
28. **Applicant:** Pretty much. I guess I would prefer a warm climate.
29. **Recruiter:** What experience have you had working with teams?
30. **Applicant:** Quite a bit actually.
31. **Recruiter:** Tell me about some of these experiences.

32. **Applicant:** I was involved in teams and group work in most of my CT classes. And I worked with teams quite often during my internship.
33. **Recruiter:** How often was that?
34. **Applicant:** Oh, I'd say a couple of times a week; sometimes more often than that.
35. **Recruiter:** Tell me about a difficult team project.
36. **Applicant:** Well, that was in a design class, and the group was not getting the job done. I had to step in and take charge by calling meetings, assigning specific tasks, and things like that.
37. **Recruiter:** And then?
38. **Applicant:** I managed to meet the deadline and get an A– on the project.
39. **Recruiter:** So this ended up being your project rather than a team project.
40. **Applicant:** Oh no. I kind of served as leader and instigator, but we all did our parts.
41. **Recruiter:** Why would you like to work for SS?
42. **Applicant:** Well, everything I have read indicates that you are one of the fastest growing computer software companies, and I'm really interested in developing software for aircraft and national security.
43. **Recruiter:** Anything else?
44. **Applicant:** Yes. You're located in Georgia near some great beaches.
45. **Recruiter:** That's true. Why should we hire you for this position?
46. **Applicant:** Well, I have received an excellent education at Tech, and I think my experiences have prepared me for this job.
47. **Recruiter:** What do you know about SS?
48. **Applicant:** Not much. You were originally started by Robert Cabrini. You went public in the early 90s and formed Software Specialties, Inc. You now have facilities in Oregon, Washington, and Nevada.
49. **Recruiter:** We have nearly 1,500 employees. We have facilities in the states you named and have plans for a facility near Boston. What questions do you have?
50. **Applicant:** What is the salary range for this position?
51. **Recruiter:** It would depend upon the location, but we are very competitive with the industry.
52. **Applicant:** Tell me a little bit about the stock-sharing plan mentioned in one of your brochures.
53. **Recruiter:** After you've been with us for six months, you are eligible to purchase stock in the company. We believe this is a good way for all of us to have a stake in what we do.
54. **Applicant:** Would I have to relocate often?
55. **Recruiter:** Not often.
56. **Applicant:** Tell me about the culture of SS. Do you have a diverse research staff?
57. **Recruiter:** Yes we do. In fact, our research staff includes people from 12 different countries. Any other questions?

58. **Applicant:** Not right now.

59. **Recruiter:** Good. We hope to make a decision in about two or three weeks. It's been good talking with you and getting acquainted.

60. **Applicant:** Thanks for the interview.

61. **Recruiter:** You're welcome. We'll be in touch.

Employment Role-Playing Cases

A Career in Computer Games Technology

You are a recent graduate with a degree in computer science and media technology and design. Although you are confined to a wheelchair because of a swimming accident while in high school, you have managed to get around a large university campus for four years and played in a wheelchair basketball league. Your interest is in computer games design and technology, and you are applying for a position that would require you to travel to a variety of locations in the United States and Japan to confer with other designers and check out technological developments.

Managing a Corporate Farm

You grew up on a 700-acre grain farm in eastern Kansas and will graduate this spring in the animal science department at Kansas State University. Since there is no opportunity to manage the family farm and your interests are in livestock rather than grain, you are interviewing recruiters for corporate farms. You have an appointment with a recruiter for Prairie Farms, a corporation that owns both grain and livestock farms through the Midwest and Southwest. The opening is for a manager of Bar Y farms in South Dakota that includes herds of beef cattle and bison. It is a major supplier for specialty steak restaurants in the Midwest, particularly Omaha, Kansas City, Minneapolis, and Chicago.

A New-Car Salesperson

You are in your late 20s and have worked for six years as a salesperson of women's clothing in a major department store. You have a very good record, and many of your customers seek you out for help with purchases. After becoming dissatisfied with your salary and no opportunity for advancement, you have decided to interview for a position as a new-car salesperson. You have an interview with the owner of a large dealership that includes Pontiac and BMW brands.

A Public Relations Position

You recently graduated from college with a major in general communication rather than a specialty because you weren't sure what you wanted to do. The position you are applying for is with a public relations and advertising agency. Its advertisement specified a degree and experience in public relations. While you only took one introduction to public relations course in college, you have worked with local politicians on their campaigns and with the intercollegiate communications office. You helped write press releases and organize events.

Student Activities

1. Contact five college recruiters from different corporations of diverse sizes. See if they use a behavior-based, talent-based, or trait-based system. If so, why do they use this system and how have they modified it over time to suit their specific needs? If they do not use such a system, why have they decided not to do so? If they have abandoned one of these systems after trying it for a few years, why did they abandon it?
2. Visit your college career center to discover the services and materials they offer. How do they counsel students who are trying to determine careers they might be interested in and qualified for? How can they help you arrange and prepare for interviews?
3. Take the Myers-Briggs Personality Indicator. How do the results compare to your self-perceptions? How might these results help determine career paths and positions?
4. Interview five recent college graduates with your major. How large were their networks, and how did they use these networks to locate positions? Who on their networks proved most helpful? How many interviews were involved in the hiring process for their current positions? Did they experience panel interviews as well as traditional one-on-one interviews? How did screening interviews differ from determinate interviews? What were the most critical questions they were asked? What were the most critical questions they asked?

Notes

1. Lois Einhorn, *Interviewing . . . A Job in Itself* (Bloomington, IN: The Career Center, 1977).
2. Charles J. Stewart, *Interviewing Principles and Practices: Applications and Exercises* (Dubuque, IA: Kendall/Hunt, 2007); Lois J. Einhorn, Patricia Hayes Bradley, and John E. Baird, *Effective Employment Interviewing: Unlocking Human Potential* (Glenview, IL: Scott, Foresman, 1981).
3. J. Craig Honaman, "Differentiating Yourself in the Job Market," *Healthcare Executive,* July–August 2003, p. 66.
4. John R. Cunningham, *The Inside Scoop: Recruiters Tell College Students Their Secrets for Success in the Job Search* (New York: McGraw-Hill, 1998), p. 120.
5. Reid Goldsborough, "Job Hunting on the Internet," *Link-Up,* November–December 2000, p. 23.
6. Lindsey Gerdes, "50 Places to Launch a Career," *BusinessWeek,* September 18, 2006, p. 64.
7. Chuck Paustian, "What's Not Said Makes a Difference," *Marketing News,* April 2001, p. 13.
8. Rene Jackson, "Nailing the Interview," *Nursing Management,* October 2003, pp. 6–8.
9. Catherine Smith MacDermott, "Networking and Interviewing: An Art in Effective Communication," *Business Communication Quarterly,* December 1995, pp. 58–59.

10. Allison Doyle, "Job Fair Participation Tips," http://jobsearch.about.com/od/jobfairs/a/jobfairs.htm?p=1, accessed October 2, 2009.
11. "The Walkabout Technique," College Grad.com, http://www.collegegrad.com/job-search/Job-Fair-Success/The-Walkabout-Technique, accessed October 2, 2009.
12. "Job Fair Success," College Grad.com, http://www.collegegrad.com/jobsearch/Job-Fair-Success/, accessed October 2, 2009.
13. Anita Bruzzese, "Virtual Job Fairs Expand Search Options for Those Seeking Work," Lafayette, IN, *Journal & Courier*, July 30, 2008, p. D2.
14. "Extra Touches Help Resume Dazzle," Lafayette, IN, *Journal & Courier,* May 21, 1995, p. C3.
15. Richard N. Bolles, *What Color Is Your Parachute? 2010* (Berkeley, CA: Ten Speed Press, 2010), p. 53.
16. Cunningham, p. 68.
17. Robert Reardon, Janet Lenz, and Byron Folsom, "Employer Ratings of Student Participation in Non-Classroom-Based Activities: Findings from a Campus Survey," *Journal of Career Planning and Employment,* Summer 1998, pp. 37–39.
18. We wish to thank Rebecca Parker, Department of Communication, Western Illinois University, for assisting us with the sample chronological and functional resumes included in Figures 8.2 and 8.3.
19. Kris Frieswick, "Liar, Liar—Grapevine—Lying on Resumes," *CFO: Magazine for Senior Financial Executives,* http://www.findarticles.com, accessed October 2, 2006.
20. "Lying on Resumes: Why Some Can't Resist," *Dallas Morning News,* The Integrity Center, http://www.integctr.com, accessed October 2, 2006.
21. Scott Reeves, "The Truth About Lies," http://www.forbes.com, accessed October 2, 2006.
22. "The New Electronic Job Search Phenomenon," an Interview with Joyce Lain Kennedy, Wiley, http://archives.obs-us.com/obs/german/books/kennedy/JLKInterview.html, accessed December 2, 2008.
23. Annette Bruzzeze, "Online Resumes Can Trigger Identity Theft," Lafayette, IN, *Journal & Courier*, August 30, 2006, p. D3.
24. Justin Pope, "Colleges Add Net Behavior to Orientation," Lafayette, IN, *Journal & Courier*, August 3, 2006, p. A4.
25. Brad Stone, "Web of Risks," *Newsweek,* August 28, 2006, p. 77.
26. Kimberly Shea and Jill Wesley, "FaceBook, and Friendster, and Blogging—Oh My! Helping Students to Develop a Positive Internet Presence," Center for Career Opportunities, Purdue University, unpublished manuscript, 2006.
27. Benjamin Ellis, "The Four A's of the Successful Job Search," *Black Collegian,* October 2000, p. 50.
28. Thomas W. Dougherty, Daniel B. Turban, and John C. Callender, "Confirming First Impressions in the Employment Interview: A Field Study of Interviewer Behavior," *Journal of Applied Psychology* 79 (1994), pp. 659–665.

29. Sarah E. Needleman, "Four Tips for Acing Interviews by Phone," *The Wall Street Journal,* http://www.career;journal.com, accessed September 11, 2006.

30. Amelia J. Prewett-Livingston, Hubert S. Field, John G. Veres III, and Philip M. Lewis, "Effects of Race on Interview Ratings in a Situational Panel Interview," *Journal of Applied Psychology* 81 (1996), pp. 178–186.

31. Karol A. D. Johansen and Markell Steele, "Keeping Up Appearances," *Journal of Career Planning & Employment,* Summer 1999, pp. 45–50.

32. Scott Reeves, "Is Your Body Betraying You in Job Interviews?" http://www.forbes.com, accessed October 20, 2006.

33. Richard J. Ilkka, "Applicant Appearance and Selection Decision Making: Revitalizing Employment Interview Education," *Business Communication Quarterly,* September 1995, pp. 11–18.

34. Bonnie Lowe, "Job Interviews: Plan Your Appearance to Make a Great First Impression," Ezine Articles, http://ezinearticles.com/?Job-Interview:-Plan-Your-Appearance-to-Make-a-Great-First-Impression, accessed October 2, 2009.

35. Thad Peterson, "Dress Appropriately for Interviews," http://career-advice.monster.com/job-interview/Interview-Appearance/Appropriate-Interviews, accessed October 2, 2009.

36. "How to Dress for an Interview," http://www.123getajob.com/jobsearch2.html, accessed October 2, 2009.

37. Reeves, "Is Your Body Betraying You in Job Interviews?"

38. Reeves, "Is Your Body Betraying You in Job Interviews?"

39. Ann Perry and Caren Goldberg, "Who Gets Hired: Interviewing Skills Are a Prehire Variable," *Journal of Career Planning & Employment,* Winter 1998, pp. 48–52.

40. Michael Skube, "College Students Lack Familiarity with Language, Ideas," Lafayette, IN, *Journal & Courier*, August 30, 2006, p. A5.

41. Steven M. Ralston, William G. Kirkwood, and Patricia A. Burant, "Helping Interviewees Tell Their Stories," *Business Communication Quarterly,* September 2003, pp. 8–22.

42. "Why Should I Hire You?" *Afp Exchange,* November–December 2003, p. 8.

43. "Run That One by Me Again: You Did What at Your Last Job?" *Barron's,* January 13, 2003, p. 12.

44. Cunningham, p. 184.

45. William Poundstone, "Why Are Manhole Covers Round (and How to Deal with Other Trick Interview Questions)," *Business,* July 2003, p. 14.

46. Kris Maher, "The Jungle: Focus on Recruitment, Pay and Getting Ahead," *The Wall Street Journal,* January 26, 2003, p. B6.

47. Kris Maher, "The Jungle: Focus on Recruitment, Pay and Getting Ahead," *The Wall Street Journal,* January 14, 2003, p. B10.

48. "Job Seekers, Take Heart—and Control," *BusinessWeek Online,* http://www.businessweek.com, accessed September 11, 2006.

Resources

Bolles, Richard N. *What Color Is Your Parachute? 2010: A Practical Manual for Job-Hunters and Career-Changers.* Berkeley, CA: Ten Speed Press, 2010.

Enelow, Wendy S., and Shelly Goldman. *Insider's Guide to Finding a Job*. Indianapolis, IN: JIST Works, 2005.

Martin, Carole. *Perfect Phrases for the Perfect Interview*. New York: McGraw-Hill, 2005.

Wall, Janet E. *Jobseekers Online Goldmine*. Indianapolis, IN: JIST Works, 2006.

Yate, Martin. *Knock 'Em Dead: The Ultimate Job Seekers Guide*. Adam, MA: Adam Media Corp., 2006.

CHAPTER 9 The Performance Interview

Assumptions about workers and work have changed.

The world of work has changed immensely since the 1970s when manufacturing dominated and performance expectations and measures that determined salary, benefits, and promotions were simple and straightforward, often stipulated by union contracts. Today the complex and flexible nature of positions, the widespread use of teams, the pervasiveness of technology, elimination of layers of management, and emphasis on brain over brawn have greatly influenced performance expectations and the performance interview. Compensation methods previously reserved for top management—stock options, bonuses, profit-sharing, and contributions to 401K programs—are now available to nearly all employees. The organization's strategic plan and objectives are often the basis of compensation.

The goal is to achieve a balance among all facets of the organization.

To adapt to these changes in the workplace and the prevalence of strategic plans, many organizations are turning to a **balanced scorecard approach** that is best illustrated in Robert Kaplan and David Norton's book titled *The Strategy-Focused Organization*. The basic framework from which the scorecard flows is seen in the Kaplan-Norton model in Figure 9.1.[1] With fewer management levels, increased competition, and rapid technological development that make changes in products and services continuous, the use of separate programming structures no longer makes sense. A balance must be struck between an organization's performance, products, processes, customers, and finances. Performance and its measurement are keys at every level. Figure 9.2 portrays five paths to this balance presented in Katzenbach's book *Peak Performance*.[2]

Performance is the key to new thinking.

One realization has reverberated throughout organizations in both economic upturns and downturns: people's performance makes the difference. A senior executive from a major high-tech organization told one of the authors that "Today everyone has the same computers, technology, and buildings, so the major difference is people and their creative contribution. My job is to attract, develop, empower, and retain the best minds and creative spirits that I can find." How can you develop, empower, and retain these minds and creative spirits?

Development rather than judgment is key to the performance review.

A new vision for organizations and emphasis on development has been accompanied by a new vision for the performance interview, what management consultant Garold L. Markle calls "catalytic coaching." Catalytic coaching is:

> A comprehensive, integrated performance management system built on a paradigm of development. Its purpose is to enable individuals to improve their production capabilities and rise to their potential, ultimately causing organizations to generate

Figure 9.1 *The balanced scorecard as a strategic framework for action*

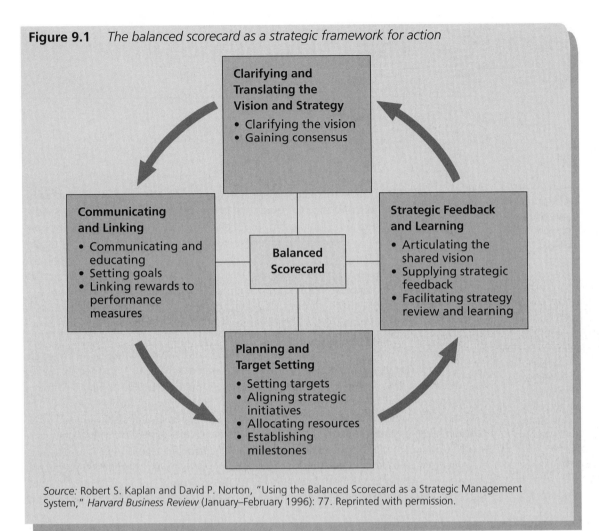

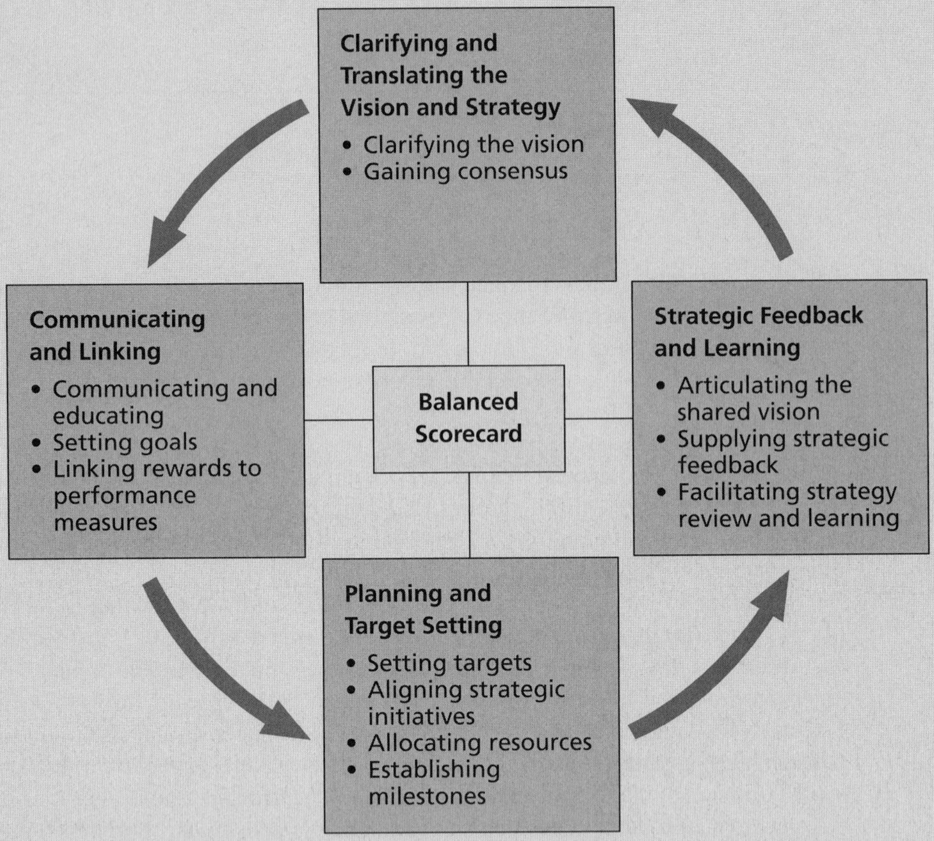

Source: Robert S. Kaplan and David P. Norton, "Using the Balanced Scorecard as a Strategic Management System," *Harvard Business Review* (January–February 1996): 77. Reprinted with permission.

> better business results. It features clearly defined infrastructure, methodology and skill sets. It assigns responsibility for career development to employees and establishes the boss as developmental coach.[3]

Catalytic coaching is *future* rather than *past* centered, places responsibility on the employee rather than the superviser, and deals with salary indirectly. The supervisor is a coach rather than evaluator. Markle declares that this approach spells "the end of the performance review" as we have known it.

Later in this chapter, we review several processes designed to develop employees and enhance performance, and the notion of coaching is a centerpiece of each. The amount of time, the number of individuals involved, and the depth of data and feedback

Figure 9.2 *Characteristics of the five balanced paths*

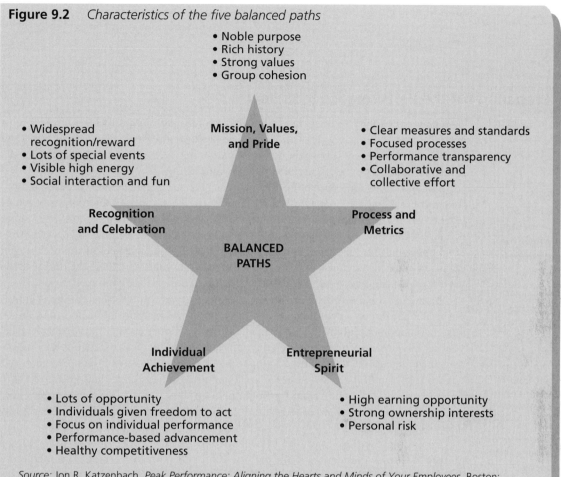

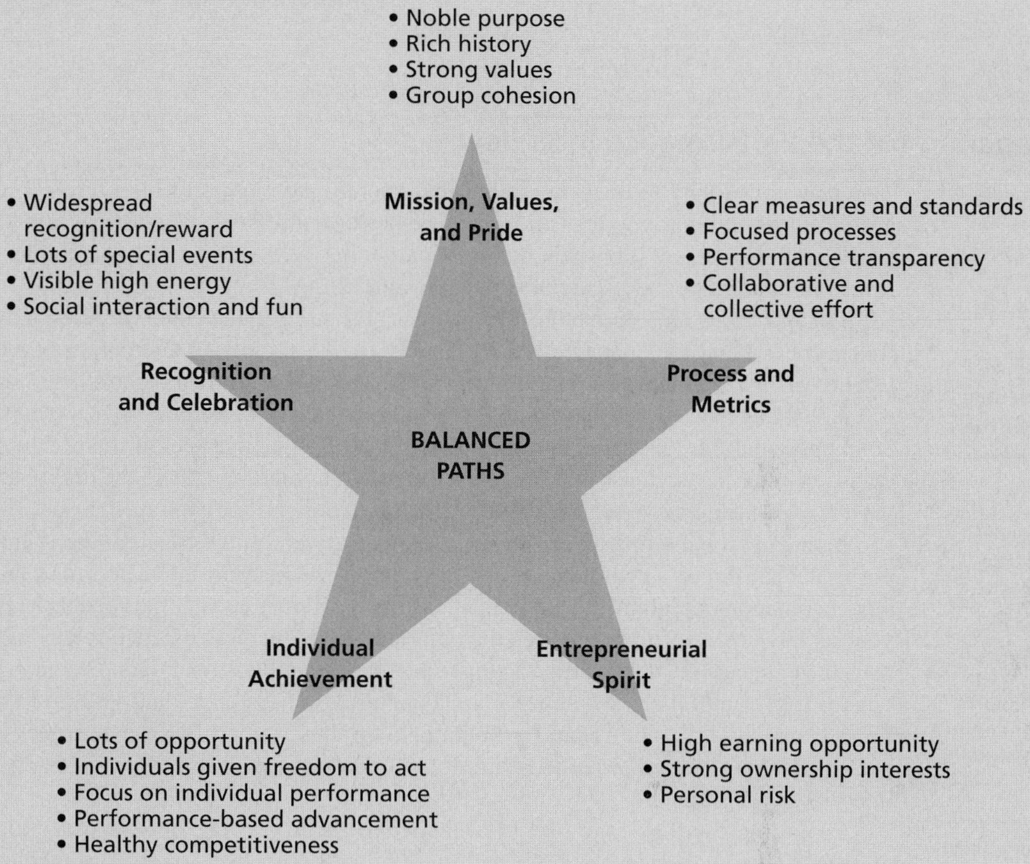

Source: Jon R. Katzenbach. *Peak Performance: Aligning the Hearts and Minds of Your Employees.* Boston: Harvard Business School Press, 2000. Reprinted with permission.

vary widely, but employee review-development processes are aimed at improving individual performance. Former pro-football coach Don Shula and player Ken Blanchard offer a set of basic principles that appropriately spell out coach.[4]

- Conviction driven—Never compromise your beliefs.
- Overlearning—Practice until it's perfect.
- Audible ready—Respond predictably to performance.
- Consistency of leadership—Consistency in performance.
- Honesty based—Walk the talk.

Markle and the Shula-Blanchard duo emphasize the importance of commitment to excellence, honesty, responsibility, and teamwork that result in a high level of performance.

Preparing for the Performance Interview

This new philosophy of coaching rather than merely judging performance has heightened the need for more frequent and improved performance interviews, discussions, and coaching/development. Frequent communication between supervisors and employees results in more favorable job-related performance ratings.[5]

Create a supportive climate that involves the interviewee.

Organizations are conducting various forms of performance interviews on a more frequent basis and are connecting them closely to developmental and coaching plans. Employees prefer a **supportive climate** that includes mutual trust, subordinate input, and a planning and review process. They want to be treated sensitively by a supportive, nonjudgmental interviewer. They want to contribute to each aspect of the review, get credit for their ideas, know what to expect during the interview, have the ability to do what is expected, receive regular feedback, and be rewarded for a job well done.

Attack the problem, not the person.

"Too seldom" is a common complaint.

You can create a relaxed, positive, and supportive climate by continually monitoring the employee's progress, offering psychological support in the forms of praise and encouragement, helping correct mistakes, and offering substantial feedback. Base your review on performance, not on the individual. Provide performance-related information and measure performance against specific standards agreed upon during previous reviews. Employees see supervisors as helpful, constructive, and willing to help them solve performance-related problems when these supervisors encourage them to express their ideas and feelings and to participate equally in performance review interviews.[6]

Training and effectiveness are inseparable.

Providing feedback on a regular basis can avoid formal, once-a-year "tooth-pulling" reviews dreaded by both parties. Evaluate poor performance immediately before damage to the organization and the employee is irreparable. Avoid surprises during the interview caused by withholding criticisms until the formal review session. Conduct as many sessions as necessary to do the job right.

Be careful of judging what you cannot measure.

Training is essential for successful reviews. You must know how to create a genuine dialogue with the interviewee. Be a good listener by not talking when the other wants to talk and by encouraging the employee to speak freely and openly.[7] Be an active listener by asking appropriate and tactful questions, not a passive listener who lets the other party talk with little guidance or support. Playing the role of evaluator reduces the two-way communication process and negatively affects your relationship. Interviewees perceive interviewers who know how to handle performance-related information, assign goals, and give feedback to be equitable, accurate, and clear during performance interviews.

Changing demographics have led to changes in methods and assumptions.

Reviewing Rules, Laws, and Regulations

The rapidly changing demographics of the workplace require a keen familiarity with EEO laws and guidelines, particularly Title VII of the 1964 Civil Rights Act as amended, The

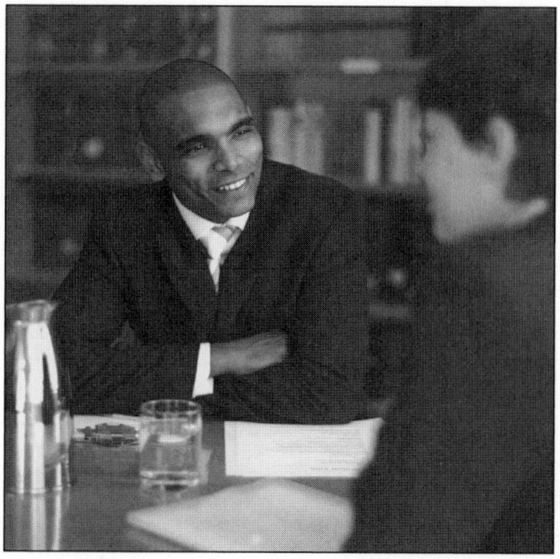

Supervisors at all levels have found it useful to talk periodically with each subordinate about personal and work-related issues.

Age Discrimination in Employment Act of 1967, and the Americans with Disabilities Act of 1990 that forbid discrimination based on age, race, color, gender, religion, national origin, and physical and mental impairments. All elements of the employment process are covered by civil rights laws and EEO guidelines, including hiring, training, compensating, promoting, transferring, and discharging. Be careful of assessing traits such as honesty, integrity, appearance, initiative, leadership, attitude, and loyalty that are difficult to judge objectively and fairly. "Using unreliable and unvalidated performance appraisal" systems may cause serious legal problems because personal preferences, prejudices, and first impressions may lead to intentionally inflating or deflating performance ratings to get even, punish employees, or promote them to another department.[8]

Laws do not require performance reviews, but ones conducted must be standardized in form and administration, measure work performance, and be applied equally to all employees. Goodall, Wilson, and Waagen warn that communication between "superiors" and "inferiors" in the review process leads to ritual forms of address "that are guided by commonly understood cultural and social stereotypes, traditional etiquette, and gender-specific rules."[9] If this is so, do not be surprised if you violate EEO laws and guidelines. The American workforce is increasingly older, and age discrimination is becoming the most prominent area of litigation even though older workers perform better than younger workers.[10]

Age will play an ever-greater role as baby boomers turn 50 and 60 in ever-greater numbers.

Selecting an Appropriate Review Model

Theorists and organizations have developed several performance review models to meet EEO laws and to conduct fair and objective performance-centered interviews applicable to different types of positions and organizations. They share common purposes: to establish competencies, set goals and expectations, monitor performance, and provide meaningful feedback.[11] Each has strengths and weaknesses.

Behaviorally Anchored Rating Scales (BARS) Model

The BARS model focuses on skills.

In the **behaviorally anchored rating scales** (BARS) model, skills essential to a specific position are identified through a position analysis and standards are set, often with the aid of industrial engineers. Typical jobs for which behaviors have been identified and standards set include telephone survey takers (at so many telephone calls per hour), meter readers for utility companies (at so many meters per hour), and data entry staff or programmers (at so many lines of entry per hour). Job analysts identify specific skills and weigh their relative worth and usage. Each job has specific measurable skills that eliminate game-playing or subjective interpretation by interviewers.

Employees report high levels of review satisfaction with the BARS model because they feel they have greater impact upon the process and see interviewers as supportive.[12] They know what skills they are expected to have, their relative worth to the organization, and how their performance will be measured. However, not every job has measurable or easily identifiable skills, and arguments often arise over when, how, and by whom specific standards are set.

Management by Objectives (MBO) Model

The **management by objectives** model involves a supervisor and an employee in a mutual (50-50) setting of results-oriented goals rather than activities to be performed. Advocates of the MBO model contend that behaviorally based measures can:

The MBO model focuses on goals.

- Account for more job complexity.
- Be rated more directly to what the employee actually does.
- Minimize irrelevant factors not under the employee's control.
- Encompass cost-related measures.
- Be less ambiguous and subjective than person-based measures.
- Reduce employee role ambiguity by making clear what behaviors are required in a given job.
- Facilitate explicit performance feedback and goal setting by encouraging meaningful employer-employee discussions regarding the employee's strengths and weaknesses.

The MBO model applies four criteria to each position: quality, quantity, time, and cost.

The MBO model classifies all work in terms of four major elements: inputs, activities, outputs, and feedback.[13] Inputs include equipment, tools, materials, money, and staff needed to do the work. Activities refer to the actual work performed: typing, writing, drawing, calculating, selling, writing, shipping. Outputs are results, end products, dollars, reports prepared, or services rendered. Feedback refers to subsequent supervisor reaction (or lack of it) to the output. If you serve as a performance review interviewer using an MBO model, keep several principles in mind.

1. Always consider quality, quantity, time, and cost. The more of these criteria you use, the greater the chances that the measurement will be accurate.
2. State results in terms of ranges rather than absolutes. Whether you use minimum, maximum, or achievable, or five- or seven-point scales, allow for freedom of movement and adjustment.
3. Keep the number of objectives few and set a mutual environment. If you are measuring a year's performance with quarterly or semiannual reviews, measure no more than six to eight major or critical aspects of performance.
4. Try for trade-offs between mutually exclusive aims and measures. An objective that is too complex may be self-defeating. For example, if you attempt to reduce labor and decrease cost at the same time, you may create more problems than you solve.
5. When the value of the performance is abstract, initiate practices that make it measurable. Measuring may be difficult.

Do not consider too many objectives.

Beware of setting complex objectives.

Anyone or anything that works can be measured.

6. If you cannot predict conditions on which performance success depends, use a floating or gliding goal. As one part of the target grows or moves, the other part does the same.

Universal Performance Interviewing Model

William Cash developed **universal performance interviewing model** and tested it in more than 40 organizations. This model begins with four basic questions that are followed by six important words.

1. What is not being done that should be?
2. What expectations are not being met at what standard?
3. Could the person do it if he or she really wanted to?
4. Does the individual have the skills to perform as needed?

The UPI model focuses on performance and work requirements.

Personality clashes, prejudices, or politics may result in unfair interviews that lead to termination. If an interviewer says, "I cannot put my finger on it, but he is just not doing . . . ," the four questions set up in columns on a blank piece of paper can serve as guidelines for fairness and comparisons of one employee to another. The interviewer must be able to specify what is missing or not being done well. This feedback can lead to change.

Understand why performance is lagging.

Narrow each problem to a coachable answer. Maybe no one has emphasized that getting 100 percent of customers' numbers at the beginning of calls is critical because the customer number drives the system and makes it easier to access billing or other pieces of information under that number. Maybe the employee knows the customer's number by heart and intends to place it in the correct position on the screen after the customer hangs up. The observation judgment dilemma has always been a problem for performance reviewers.

The four questions in conjunction with six key words shown in Figure 9.3 allow interviewers to make a number of observations about performance. This model can be employed with others (such as the popular 360-degree review process) or with separate

Figure 9.3 *Six key words in the universal performance interviewing model*

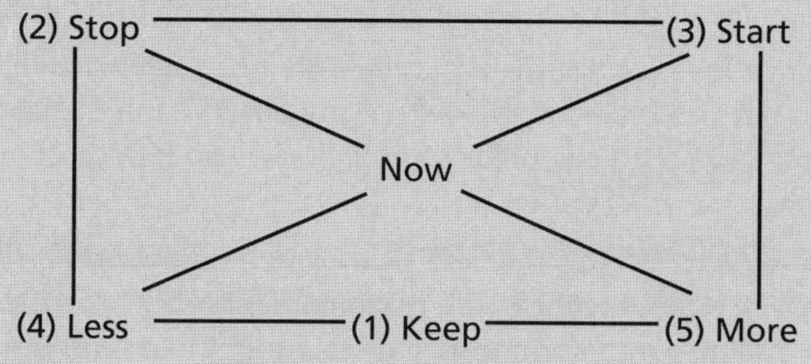

observations by supervisors, peers, and customers (internal and external) that can be compared to one another for consistency, trends, and rater reliability.

Use UPI in conjunction with other models.

An 11-by-14 sheet of paper with the four questions in columns can provide the bases for quarterly or annual reviews or brief coaching sessions. Organizations are eliminating the annual performance review and replacing it with a coaching process that takes place weekly for production workers and monthly for professionals. A summary session may be done quarterly with an annual review to set goals for the coming year, review progress, and look at developmental needs.[14]

Reviews must recognize excellence as well as problems.

Once you have answered the four basic questions, start on the model with *keep.* When an employee is doing something well, make sure the person knows you appreciate a job well done. Then go to *stop,* followed by *start, less, more,* and finishing with a time frame for improving performance. The word *now* emphasizes the importance of making appropriate changes immediately. Define *now* in terms of weeks or perhaps months. Be specific.

Play the role of coach rather than evaluator or disciplinarian.

The universal performance interviewing model enables you as coach to start with positive behavior you wish the employee to maintain, followed immediately by behaviors you wish corrected now. This begins the interview on a positive note. Your *stop* list should be the shortest and reserved for behaviors that are qualitatively and procedurally incorrect, place an employee at risk, or are destructive to others in the workplace.

You can present each of the four questions and the six words at different verbal and nonverbal levels, including hints, suggestions, and corrections. For example, you might say:

I want you to stop doing . . .	You must do more of . . .
I want you to start doing . . . now	You must do less of . . .

Many interviewers spend too much time on the analytical end and too little time on specific behavior to be altered and how. If you cannot provide a specific alternative behavior, there is no need for a performance review.

Don't turn a mole hill problem into a mountain.

Let's use the customer service representative mentioned earlier as an example. Assume that the representative knows many customer numbers because of the frequency of calls from them and has the numbers memorized. She thinks it is unnecessary to log each number into the system until she has finished discussing specific problems with customers. Use one of the following styles to present the problem without making it a bigger problem.

Hint and suggest before correcting.

- *Hint:* (smiling pleasantly) I noticed you were busy this morning when I stopped by to observe you. I just thought it might be easier for you to record each customer's number at the beginning of your conversation.
- *Suggestion:* (neutral facial expression and matter-of-fact vocal inflections) Just one idea came to mind from my observation this morning. I'd like to see you record each customer's number early so it doesn't get lost in the shuffle of answers to other callers.
- *Correction:* (stern voice and face) Based on my observation this morning, you must be sure to record each customer's number before you do anything else on the system for that number. This number drives our entire system, and problems result when it is not recorded immediately.

Think before commenting.

The purpose of every performance interview is to provide accurate feedback to the employee about what must be altered, changed, or eliminated and when. Most employees want to do a good job, and the performance mentor or coach must provide direction. "Feedback" must identify the problem and provide suggestions for resolving the problem.

Vague comments and suggestions may harm relationships and fail to improve performance.

Another part of the model, crucial in performance interviews, are the two Ss—*specific* and *several*. Performance interviews must not be guessing games. The two Ss enable interviewers to provide specific examples to show the problem is not a one-time incident but a trend.

Figure 9.4 includes all parts of the universal performance interviewing model. It allows you to measure or observe on-the-job behavior and either compare it to goals or quickly correct the smallest error.

The 360-Degree Approach

The 360-degree approach involves multiple observers.

The **360-degree approach** to performance review has gained widespread acceptance, particularly among Fortune 500 companies. It "enables organizational members to receive feedback on their performance, usually anonymously, from all major constituencies they serve": supervisors, peers, subordinates, subcontractors, customers, and so on.[15]

The interviewee plays a role in selecting evaluators.

Each firm employs a somewhat unique 360-degree process, questionnaires, and interview schedules, but we can describe the typical process. An employee works with a supervisor to select a number of evaluators, such as a direct supervisor, staff at the same level as the employee, colleagues, and individuals from departments the employee interacts with on a regular basis. The 360-degree model requires team and interpersonal skills. Questionnaires covering skills, knowledge, and style are sent to each of the evaluators. The completed questionnaires are summarized and, in some cases, scores are displayed on a spreadsheet. The manager selects individuals from the original group to serve as a panel to conduct a feedback interview. The interviewer/facilitator may take the raw data from the questionnaires and interview the evaluators. The employee receives the data in advance of the meeting. Each participant comes with coaching or behavior change input. The purpose is not to attack, blame, or hurt the employee but to provide objective, behavior-based feedback with suggestions where

Figure 9.4 *The universal performance interviewing model*

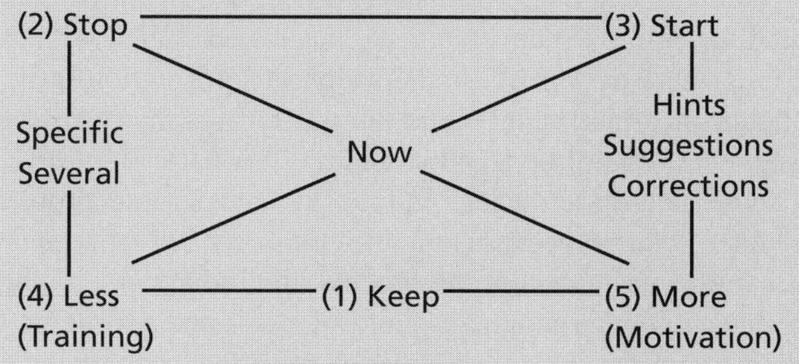

The 360-approach uses a group feedback interview.

necessary for improvement. The employee may not need much improvement, so compliments are acceptable.

The interviewer/facilitator may ask the employee to start the meeting with reactions to the data, then ask open questions with neutral probes. For example:

- Tell me about your responsibilities in R&D.
  - Tell me more.
  - Explain it to me.
  - Describe your frustrations with the consultants' training manual.

Employ open questions and probe into answers.

- If you were going to take on a similar project, what would you do more or less of?
- When you identified people in accounting as "bean-counters" what did you mean?
  - How did they behave?
  - What did they say?
  - What did they do?

A plan for improvement is essential.

Once the feedback session is completed, both parties formulate a plan for improvement.

The use of **multisource feedback** for employee development works best in organizations that use a goal-setting process from the top down.[16] The 360-degree approach has a number of advantages.

Be aware of pluses and minuses of each review model.

- The single process is useful for improvement and development.
- Questionnaires and interviews provide objective data and the feedback needed for employee development.
- Feedback emanates from multiple sources such as supervisors, peers, subordinates, and customers rather than a single supervisor.
- The employee has control over who gives feedback.
- The employee reads, hears, and discusses the data, so data are more than numbers on a form.
- The process provides documentation for dealing with performance problems.

Although the 360-degree approach is widely popular, it is not without its critics. Jai Ghorpade writes that it is fraught with five significant paradoxes.[17] (1) Although it is designed for employee development, "it gets entangled with the appraisal process." (2) Multiple raters may increase the scope of information provided to the employee but not better information. (3) Anonymous ratings may be inaccurate, incompetent, and biased. (4) "Quantitative and structured feedback on generic behaviors is easy to acquire, score, and disseminate," but it may have serious problems of accuracy, fairness, and interpretation because it is difficult to control rater tendencies. (5) "Involving persons in authority may taint the process and reduce its credibility." Angelo DeNisi and Avraham Kluger recognize many of the same problems with the 360-degree feedback approach and write that although most feedback reviews lead to improvement in performance, 38 percent of effects are negative.[18] They offer several suggestions

ON THE WEB

As you begin to think seriously about specific careers and organizations, investigate how organizations assess the performance of employees. Use the Internet to discover the types of performance review models used by employers in which you have a career interest. Access two types of resources. First, research employers through general resources such as CareerBuilder (http://www.careerbuilder.com), MonsterTrak (http://www.monstertrak.com/), and Monster (http://www.monster.com/). Second, check the Web sites of specific organizations such as Pricewaterhousecoopers (http://www.pwc.com), Ford (http://www.ford.com/), and Electronic Data Systems (http://www.eds.com).

for improving the 360-degree system, including: (1) Use this system for development rather than decision-making purposes, (2) help employees interpret and react to ratings, (3) minimize the amount of information given to employees, (4) do not have performance review team members evaluate employees in all areas, and (5) use the 360-degree system on a regular basis rather than once or occasionally. Vernon Miller and Fredric Jablin cite different scores from raters, including the employee, the involvement of untrained raters or ones with inexperience in areas they are rating, and the assumption that increasing the number of raters results in feedback quality.[19]

Garold Markle writes that the 360-degree approach is highly inefficient because it is enormously time-consuming on the part of both interviewer and interviewee and takes weeks or months in turnaround time. This delay may result in both parties forgetting what they had to say during the process.[20]

The critics of the 360-degree approach recognize its strengths as well as its deficiencies and recommend solutions to make it a more efficient and reliable method of reviewing and enhancing performance.[21]

- Use the 360-degree approach for decision making only.
- Do not employ the 360-degree approach as the "primary mechanism for delivering downward feedback."
- Do not assume that using more raters results in quality feedback.
- Provide training and guidance for all raters.
- Emphasize objectivity in ratings to lessen potential bias.
- Limit raters to their areas of experience and expertise.
- Minimize the amount of data to avoid overloading employees.
- Use the 360-degree approach as a regular part of performance reviews.

Conducting the Performance Interview

Do your homework.

Regardless of the review model you select, do your homework. Study the employee's past record and recent performance reviews. Review the employee's self-evaluation. Understand the nature of the employee's position and work. Pay particular attention to the fit between the employee, the position, and the organization. Identify in advance the primary purpose of the interview, especially if it is one of several with an employee. Prepare possible questions and forms you will use pertaining to measurable goals.

Select and understand the perspective of the interview.

Know yourself and the employee as persons. Are you aware of your potential biases and how you can minimize or eliminate them in your review? Will you approach the interview from an appraisal or a developmental perspective? From an **appraisal perspective,** you see the interview as required and scheduled by the organization, superior-conducted and directed, top-down controlled, results-based, past-oriented, concerned with *what* rather than *how,* and organizationally satisfying. By contrast, from a **developmental perspective,** the interview is initiated by individuals whenever needed, subordinate-conducted and directed, bottom-up controlled, skill-based, now- and future-oriented, concerned with *how,* cooperative, and self-satisfying.[22] Select a developmental approach, Markle's "catalytic coaching," rather than an appraisal approach.

Relationship influences both parties and the nature of the interview.

Understand the relationship likely to exist between you and the employee. What is your relational history? Are you the best person for the interviewer role, or would the interviewee prefer someone else? How motivated is each party to take part in the process? How will control be shared? Research reveals that two or more reviewers often evaluate the same employee differently because their relationships differ.

Schedule the interview several days in advance so that both parties can prepare and it is not a spur-of-the-moment crisis or problem interview. Prepare a possible action plan to be implemented following the interview.

Opening the Interview

Climate and atmosphere are critical.

Put the interviewee at ease with a pleasant, friendly greeting. Get the person seated in an arrangement that is nonthreatening and not superior-subordinate. Fear of what performance interviews might yield interferes with communication between parties and keeps the review process from achieving its full potential."[23]

Be prepared but flexible in opening the interview.

Establish rapport by supporting the employee and engaging in a few minutes of small talk. Orient the employee by giving a brief outline of how you want to conduct the interview. If there is something the employee would rather talk about first, do so. An alteration of your interview plan is worth the improved communication climate. Encourage the employee to ask questions, bring up topics, and participate actively throughout the interview.

Discussing Performance

Use all of your listening skills.

Communication skills are critical to successful performance interviews. Be aware of your own nonverbal cues and observe those emanating from the interviewee. It is often not so much *what* is said but *how* it is said. Listen carefully to the interviewee and adapt your listening approach to the changing needs of the interview, listening for comprehension when you need to understand, for evaluation when you must appraise, with empathy when you must show sensitivity and understanding, and for resolution when developing courses of action to enhance performance.

"Be an active listener" is good advice and common sense, but Goodall, Wilson, and Waagen warn that interviewers must know *why* they are listening actively: "Motives may include a desire to exhibit efficient appraisal behavior, to show a concern for the interviewee's well-being, or to collect evidence of talk that may be used for or against the subordinate at a later date."[24] The first two are positive, but the third may be detrimental both to the interview and future interactions.

Feedback is central in performance interviews.

Maintain an atmosphere that ensures two-way communication beyond Level 1 by being sensitive, providing feedback and positive reinforcement, reflecting feelings, and exchanging information. Feedback may be your most important skill. Use a team of interviewers rather than a single interviewer. Research indicates that the panel approach produces higher judgment validation, better developmental action planning, greater compliance with EEO laws, more realistic promotion expectations, and reduced perception of favoritism.

Develop a true dialogue with the interviewee.

Make the discussion full and open between both parties with the goal of improving individual and organizational performance. Keys to the success are your abilities to communicate information effectively and encourage open dialogue. Strive to be a coach in career management and development.

Discuss the interviewee's total performance, not just one event. Begin with areas of excellence so you can focus on the person's strengths. Strive for an objective, positive integration of work and results. Cover standards that are met and encourage the interviewee to identify strengths. Communicate factual, performance-related information and give specific examples.

Excessive and prolonged praise may create anxiety and distrust because employees expect and desire to discuss performance weaknesses. An employee who receives no negative feedback or suggestions of ways to improve will not know which behavior to change. Discuss needed improvements in terms of specific expected behaviors in a constructive, nondirective, problem-solving manner. Employees are likely to know what they are not doing, but unlikely to know what they should be doing. Let the employee provide input. Probe tactfully and sensitively for causes of problems.

Strive for a balance between praise and criticism.

Do not heap criticism upon the employee. The more you point out shortcomings, the more threatened, anxious, and defensive the employee will become. As the perceived threat grows, so will the person's negative attitude toward you and the review process. It is often not what is intended that counts but what the other party believes is intended.

Terry Lowe identifies seven ways to ruin a performance review.[25] The **halo effect** occurs when you give favorable ratings to all duties when the interviewee excels in only one. The **pitchfork effect** leads to negative ratings for all facets of performance because of a particular trait you dislike in others. The **central tendency** causes you to refrain from assigning extreme ratings to facets of performance. The **recency error** occurs when you rely too heavily on the most recent events or performance levels. The length of service of an interviewee may lead you to assume that present performance is high because post-performance was high. The **loose rater** is reluctant to point out weak areas and dwells on the average or better areas of performance. The **tight rater** believes that no one can perform at the necessary standards. And **competitive raters** believe no one can perform higher than their levels of performance.

Know how to conduct performance interviews.

Use question tools to gain and verify information.

Summarize the performance discussion and make sure that the employee has had ample opportunity to ask questions and make comments before establishing goals. Use reflective probes and mirror questions to verify information received and feedback given. Use clearinghouse questions to be sure the employee has no further concerns or comments.

Setting New Goals and a Plan of Action

Focus on the future and not the past.

Goal-setting is the key to successful performance reviews and should constitute 75 percent of the interview. Focus on future performance and career development. Be a coach rather than a judge. Hill writes that "Although it is important to evaluate on the basis of past performance, it is just as important to anticipate future growth, set goals, and establish career paths."[26]

Follow these guidelines when discussing and setting goals.

The interviewee must be an active participant.

- Review the last period's goals before going on to new ones.
- Avoid either/or statements, demands, and ultimatums.
- Make goals few in number, specific, well-defined, practical, and measurable.
- Feedback combined with clear goal-setting produces the highest employee satisfaction.
- Never intentionally or unintentionally impose goals.
- Avoid ambiguous language in goals such as teamwork, cooperation, unity, and group effectiveness.
- Set goals that are neither too easy nor too difficult.
- Encourage the employee to suggest and agree on means of improvement.
- Decide upon follow-up procedures and how they will be implemented.
- Both parties must be able to determine when goals have been accomplished and why.

Closing the Interview

Close with the perception that the interview has been valuable for both parties.

Do not rush the closing. Be sure the interviewee understands all that has transpired. Conclude on a note of trust and open communication. End with the feeling that this has been an important session for interviewee, interviewer, and the organization. If you have filled out a form such as the one in Figure 9.5, sign off the agreements. If organizational policy allows, permit interviewees to put notes by items they feel strongly about. Provide a copy of the signed form as a record of the plan for the coming performance period.

The Employee in the Performance Review

Do a self-evaluation before the interview.

As an employee, maintain complete, detailed, accurate, and verifiable records of your career activities, initiatives, accomplishments, successes, and problem areas.[27] Make a list of goals set during the last performance review and how you took on these goals and met or exceeded them. Keep letters and e-mails that contain positive and unsolicited comments from supervisors, co-workers, subordinates, clients, customers, and management. Analyze your strengths and weaknesses and be prepared for corrective actions with ideas to improve on your own. Self-criticism often softens criticism from others.

Figure 9.5 *Performance appraisal review form*

Name: ______________________	**Date of Appraisal:** ____________
Performance Expectations	Performance Accomplishments
Employee Signature ______________	Employee Signature ______________
Supervisor Signature ______________	Supervisor Signature ______________
Manager Review ______________	Manager Review ______________

Understand your relationship with the interviewer and his or her performance review style. Check into the interviewer's mood prior to the interview. Be aware that sexual harassment occurs in organizations and that employees who have submitted to it tend to be judged more harshly than those who have resisted when such cases come to trial.

Approach the interview with a positive attitude.

At least half of the responsibility for making the interview a success rests with you. Approach the performance interview as a valuable source of information on prospects for advancement, a chance to get meaningful feedback about how the organization views your performance and future, and an opportunity to display your strengths and accomplishments. Be prepared to give concrete examples of how you have met or exceeded expectations. Prepare intelligent, well-thought-out questions. Be ready to discuss career goals.

Avoid unnecessary defensiveness.

Maintain a productive, positive relationship with the interviewer and do not become defensive unless there is something to become defensive about. If you are put on the defensive, maintain direct eye contact and clarify the facts before answering charges. Ask, "How did this information come to your attention?" or "What are the exact production figures for the third quarter?" This gives you time to formulate thorough and reasonable responses based on complete understanding of the situation. Answer all questions thoroughly. Ask for clarification of questions you do not understand. Offer explanations, not excuses. Assess your performance and abilities reasonably, and be honest with yourself and your supervisor. Realize that what you are, what you think you are, what others think you are, and what you would like to be may describe different people.

A good offense is better than a good defense.

The performance review interview is not a time to be shy or self-effacing. Mention achievements such as special or extra projects, help you have given other employees, and community involvement on behalf of the organization. Be honest about challenges or problems you expect to encounter in the future. Correct any of the interviewer's false impressions or mistaken assumptions. Do not be afraid to ask for help.

Leave your temper at the door.

If you are confronted with a serious problem, discover how much time is available to solve it. Suggest or request ways to solve your differences as soon as possible. The interviewer is not out to humiliate you, but to help you grow for your own sake and that of the organization. Keep your temper cool. Telling off your supervisor may give you a brief sense of satisfaction, but after the blast, the person will still be your supervisor and the problem will be worse. Do not try to improve everything at once. Set priorities with both short- and long-range goals.

As the closing approaches, do not be in a hurry. Summarize or restate problems, solutions, and new goals in your own words. Be sure you understand all that has taken place and the agreements for the next review period. Be certain that the rewards fit your performance.[28] Close on a positive note with a determination to meet the new goals.

The Performance Problem Interview

When an employer has problems with an employee, the situation today is handled as a performance problem that requires coaching. The negative connotation and implication of discipline implies guilt, and organizations are reluctant to imply guilt.

Determining Just Cause

Just cause means fair and equitable treatment of each employee. Many organizations use behavioral selection interview processes and behavioral performance reviews to provide documentation in case a performance problem arises. This typically involves a team that provides more and better insights, and spreads the blame among several members of the organization.

The following tests of just cause come from union contracts and attorneys involved in termination cases.

Know what constitutes a just cause.

- *Did the employee violate reasonable rules or orders?*

  For instance, if an employee has been working on a specific machine, his or her supervisor may request the employee to move to a similar piece of equipment until the current one undergoes needed repairs.

- *Was the employee given clear and unambiguous notice?*

If an employee has been with your organization for six months to a year, follow an oral warning with a written warning within a short time.

Treat all employees fairly and equally.

- *Was the investigation timely?*

  Timely usually means within one to three days. If there is a refusal to work or a confrontation, the supervisor or manager may want to have a witness present and obtain a written statement from this witness.

- *Was the investigation conducted fairly?*

  Did the supervisor interview all parties involved and obtain all necessary documentation?

- *Were all employees given equal treatment?*

  "Equal treatment under the law" means that each organizational investigation of performance problems is conducted in exactly the same manner.

- *Is there proof and documentation that a performance problem has occurred?*

  Most failures are due to a supervisor's unwillingness to take the time to write down the problem and obtain necessary records before arranging a performance problem review.

The punishment must fit the infraction.

- *Is the penalty fair?*

  If an offense is minor, a written warning may be appropriate. Penalties should be progressive rather than regressive.

Preparing for the Interview

Practice before conducting the real thing.

Prepare for performance problem interviews by taking part in realistic role-playing cases. These rehearsals can lessen anxiety and help you anticipate employee reactions, questions, and rebuttals. The variety of situations and interviewees encountered can help you refine your case-making, questioning, and responding while sticking to the facts and documenting all claims with solid evidence.

Role-playing cases, literature reviews on performance problem situations, and discussions with experienced interviewers will help you learn what to expect. For example, Monroe, Borzi, and DiSalvo discovered four common responses from subjects occurred in 93 percent of incidents.[29]

Be prepared for common reactions and responses.

1. *Apparent compliance:* overpoliteness and deference, apologies, promises, or statements of good intentions followed by the same old problem behaviors.
2. *Relational leverage:* statements that they have been with the organization longer than the interviewer and therefore know best, that they are the best and you can't fire or discipline them, reference to friends or relatives within the organization, or reference to your close relationship to them.
3. *Alibis:* claims of tiredness, sickness, being overworked, budget cuts, family problems, it's someone else's fault, or poor instructions or information.
4. *Avoidance:* disappearing on sick leave or vacation, failure to respond to memos or phone calls, or failure to make an appointment.

What evidence do you have of the infraction?

Review *how* you know the employee has committed an infraction that warrants an interview. Did you see the infraction directly, as in the case of absenteeism, poor workmanship, intoxication, harassing another employee, or insubordination? Did you find out indirectly through a third party or by observing the results (such as lateness of a report, poor quality products, or goals unmet)? Were you anticipating an infraction because of a previous incident, behavior, or stereotype? For example, African-Americans and other minorities are often watched more closely than others because supervisors believe they are more likely to violate rules. On the other hand, supervisors tend to be lenient with persons they perceive as likable, similar to themselves, or possessing high status or exceptional talent. Supervisors may avoid confronting persons they know will "explode" if confronted. Not confronting is the easy way out.

Distinguish between the severity of infractions.

Next, decide whether the perceived problem warrants a review. Absenteeism and low performance are generally considered more serious than tardiness and horseplay. Determine the cause of the infraction because this will affect how you conduct the interview and what action to take.

Learn why an infraction has occurred.

Review the employee's past performance and history. Two basic reasons for action are poor performance or a troubled employee. When a person's performance gradually or suddenly declines, the cause may be motivational, personal, work-related, or supervisory. Drops in performance may be indicated by swings in the employee's behavior. Keep an eye on performance indicators such as attendance, quality or quantity of work, willingness to take instructions, and cooperation.

A troubled employee may have an alcohol or drug dependency, a marital disturbance, problem with a child, or an emotional problem such as depression. An employee may be stealing from your organization to support a gambling habit, drug or alcohol addiction, or a boyfriend or girlfriend. These employees need professional counseling.

Relational dimensions are critical in performance problem interviews.

For principles applicable to the performance problem interview, see the performance portion of this chapter and Chapter 12 on the counseling interview. Consider the relational dimensions discussed in Chapter 2. Often neither party wants to take part, and as supervisor, you may have delayed the interview until there is no other recourse and multiple problems have piled up. As a specific problem comes to a head, you and the employee may come to dislike and mistrust one another, even to the point of verbal and nonverbal abuse. Trust, cooperation, and disclosure are difficult to attain in a threatening environment.

Keeping Self and the Situation under Control

Uncontrolled anger can destroy an interaction.

While you want to head off a problem before it becomes critical, do not conduct a performance problem interview when you are angry. You will be unable to control the interview if you are unable to control yourself.

When one or both parties may have difficulty containing their anger or animosity, follow these suggestions.

Timing of the interview is important.

- *Hold the interview in a private location.* Meet where you and the employee can discuss the problem freely and openly.
- *When severe problems arise, consider delaying a confrontation and obtaining assistance.* Let all tempers cool down. Depending on the situation, you may want to consult a counselor or call security before acting.

- *Include a witness or union representative.* The witness should be another supervisor because using one employee as a witness against another employee is dangerous for all parties involved. Be sure to follow to the letter all procedures spelled out in the union contract and organizational policies.

Focusing on the Problem

Deal with facts rather than impressions and opinions.

Deal in specific *facts,* such as absences, witnesses, departmental records, and previous disciplinary actions. Do not allow the situation to become a trading contest: "Well, look at all the times I have been on time" or "How come others get away with it?"

- *Record all available facts.* Unions, EEOC, and attorneys often require complete and accurate records. Take detailed notes, record the time and date on all material that might be used later, and obtain the interviewee's signature or initials for legal protection. A **paper trail** may be critical for future interactions.

Avoid unsupported accusations.

- *Try not to be accusatory.* Avoid words and statements such as troublemaker, drunk, thief, and liar. You cannot make medical diagnoses of alcoholism or drug addiction, so avoid these terms.
- *Preface remarks carefully.* You may begin comments with phrases such as "According to your attendance report . . . ," "As I understand it . . . ," and "I have observed . . ." These force you to be factual and avoid accusing an employee of being guilty until proven innocent.

Ask questions that draw out the interviewee.

- *Ask questions that allow the person to express feelings and explain behavior.* Begin questions with "Tell me what happened . . . ," "When he said that, what did you . . . ," "Why do you feel that . . . ?" Open-ended questions allow you to get facts as well as feelings and explanations from the employee.

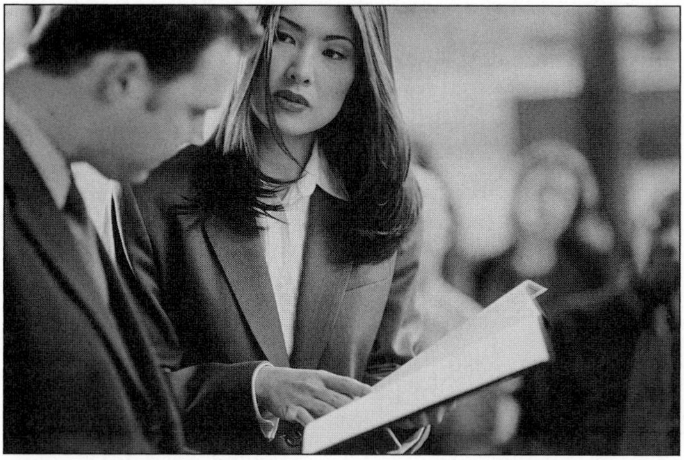
© Digital Vision

Never conduct a performance review interview when you are angry, and conduct the interview in a private location.

Avoiding Conclusions during the Interview

A hastily drawn conclusion may create more problems than it solves. Some organizations train supervisors to use standard statements under particular circumstances. If you are sending an employee off the job, you may say:

> "I do not believe you are in a condition to work, so I am sending you home. Report to me tomorrow at . . ."

Be slow to draw conclusions.

"I want you to go to medical services and have a test made; bring me a slip from the physician when you return to my office."

"I'm sending you off the job. Call me tomorrow morning at nine, and we can discuss what action I will take."

These statements give you time to talk to others, think about possible actions, and provide a cooling-off period for all concerned.

Closing the Interview

Conclude the interview in neutral. If discipline is appropriate, do it. Realize, however, that delaying action may enable you to think more clearly about the incident. Be consistent with organizational policies, the union contract, and all employees. Refer to your organization's prescribed disciplinary actions for specific offenses.

Summary

Review an employee's performance on the basis of standards mutually agreed upon ahead of time. Apply the same objectives equally to all employees performing a specific position. Research and good sense dictate that performance, promotion, and problem issues are discussed in separate interview sessions. Performance review interviews should occur at least semiannually, while promotion, salary, and performance problem interviews usually take place when needed. Deal with performance problems before they disrupt the employee's work or association with your organization. Select a performance review model most appropriate for your organization, employees, and positions.

For both employer and employee, flexibility and open-mindedness are important keys in successful performance review interviews. Flexibility should be tempered with understanding and tolerance of individual differences. The performance process must be ongoing, with no particular beginning or end. Supervisors and subordinates are constantly judged by the people around them. By gaining insights into their own behavior and how it affects others, both parties can become better persons and organization members.

Key Terms and Concepts

The online learning center for this text features FLASHCARDS and CROSSWORD PUZZLES for studying based on these terms and concepts.

360-degree approach
Balanced scorecard approach
Behavior-based feedback
Behaviorally anchored rating scales
Catalytic coaching
Central tendency
Competitive rater
Halo effect
Just cause
Loose rater
Management by objectives
Multisource feedback
Pitchfork effect
Recency error
Supportive climate
Tight rater
Universal performance interviewing model

A Performance Interview for Review and Analysis

Med-Tech manufactures a variety of electronic monitors and diagnostic tools used in hospitals and clinics throughout the United States. It has grown in 10 years from a staff of 10 to more than 150, many of whom are engaged in assembling the complicated monitors and tools that rely heavily on microchips and tiny circuits. Peter McBride is the manager of production, and Cindy Tiller is a production supervisor who has worked at Med-Tech for three years.

How effective is the opening in rapport building and orientation? Is the climate supportive or defensive? How effectively do manager and production supervisor deal with positive aspects of performance before getting to negative aspects? Does either party dominate a specific phase of the interview? How effectively do the parties set goals for the next review period? How effectively is the interview closed? How skilled is the manager, as a coach?

1. **Interviewer:** Good morning, Cindy. Come in and have a seat.
2. **Interviewee:** Thanks. It's a beautiful spring day, and the grounds around our complex are really attractive this year.
3. **Interviewer:** Yes they are. I think the new lawn care people are doing a great job. How's the family?
4. **Interviewee:** They're doing well. We got the sailboat out on the lake for the first time on Saturday, and the kids are learning to handle it quite well.
5. **Interviewer:** Good. I've always wanted to learn to sail. Do you have any questions or concerns before we get started?
6. **Interviewee:** Things are going well, but I'm wondering when the new models will be coming to us from R&D? I'd like to get some training done so we can move full-speed ahead with production.
7. **Interviewer:** I believe the target date for release to production is May 25, but there have been a few minor delays. I'm glad you feel things are going well in your department. Let's review where we were when we set objectives for this quarter.
8. **Interviewee:** Okay. I believe we have met them fairly well.
9. **Interviewer:** The goals were to enhance training for new associates, quality improvement, and meeting production quotas.
10. **Interviewee:** That's what I remember.
11. **Interviewer:** As I look over my notes and figures, you have instituted a training program for new and transfer associates and this has improved quality considerably. Our customer complaints are down by 22 percent and returns are down by 57 percent. Great job.
12. **Interviewee:** Thanks for supporting the training program we instituted. Several of my colleagues have proven to be good teachers, and their teaching has improved their own quality.
13. **Interviewer:** I like to help when I can. I'm very pleased with the training and quality improvement.
14. **Interviewee:** I thought you would be. I'm pleased with these areas.
15. **Interviewer:** I am concerned with one goal, however. Production has not increased as much as I thought it would by this time.

16. **Interviewee:** That's true, but you may remember that I warned you about this happening when we eliminated 15 positions during this severe recession.
17. **Interviewer:** Yes, I recall your concern. In spite of this, you have met your deadlines rather well. My concern is your overtime budget that is up 12 percent this quarter.
18. **Interviewee:** Since you cut my staff, I've had to give overtime to several associates from time to time to meet specific deadlines.
19. **Interviewer:** Couldn't you simply speed up the production lines a bit and eliminate some of this overtime?
20. **Interviewee:** We could if we become less concerned about quality. Increased speed and higher quality do not go together. One's going to suffer.
21. **Interviewer:** Uh huh.
22. **Interviewee:** I think we've done very well with the new micro circuits and products and fewer staff. I also think overtime is less expensive than hiring more staff with full benefits.
23. **Interviewer:** What about hiring a few temps to help out?
24. **Interviewee:** They might help some, but they will need extensive training and supervision to make sure they keep up the quality we all want.
25. **Interviewer:** Uh huh. Are there any problems with your staff?
26. **Interviewee:** Only one. I think you know April Proctor.
27. **Interviewer:** What is April's problem? Have you trained her to increase her speed and efficiency?
28. **Interviewee:** Yes, but that's not the problem.
29. **Interviewer:** And the problem is . . . ?
30. **Interviewee:** She's getting rather severe arthritis in her hands and fingers and is having difficulty maneuvering elements, particularly in the new monitors.
31. **Interviewer:** Have you reported this to the HR department? It seems to me that either she can do the job assigned or not.
32. **Interviewee:** I understand that, but she's been a loyal employee since Med-Tech was founded and her husband has been laid off for nearly a year.
33. **Interviewer:** Well, I certainly don't want to appear hard-hearted, but we're not a charity. How about the three of us meeting on Wednesday morning at around 9:00 to evaluate her situation. Perhaps we could transfer her to another position that would pay about the same.
34. **Interviewee:** That sounds good. I'll talk to her this afternoon.
35. **Interviewer:** I appreciate your wanting to protect a loyal employee, but these situations cannot continue when there's no way to improve them. Since everything else seems to be in order, let's continue with the same goals for the next quarter. Keep up the good work.
36. **Interviewee:** Thanks. I'll see you on Wednesday.

Performance Review Role-Playing Cases

A Sales Representative

The interviewer is the sales manager for WYMO located in western Connecticut. She is conducting a semiannual performance review with an assistant sales manager who joined the station four years ago. He has been very successful in attracting new accounts, particularly for the early morning news program than runs from 6:00 to 8:00 a.m. and the noon news update that runs from 12:00 to 1:00 p.m. While she was reviewing the interviewee's sales records and comparing them to other assistants, she noticed a surprising trend over the past half-year. The interviewee is attracting new accounts but losing a number of long-time accounts. She wants to address this trend with the interviewee.

A Gymnastics Coach

The interviewer is the owner of Twisters Gymnastics Club and reviews the performance goals of each coach prior to the start of meets in January and at end of the season in May. The interviewee is the coach of the Level 5 girl's team and has been with the club for nearly four years. This is the preseason review and expectations are high because of success last season when many of the girls excelled at Level 4. This review will focus on goals set for the team in all events and on individual members who appear to be very good in events such as floor or bars. The Level 5 team's performance was very good this past season but a bit disappointing at major meets.

A Troubleshooter

The interviewer is the vice president of a large paper products manufacturer that has plants throughout the United States and in several other countries. He oversees plant managers and engineering troubleshooters who travel weekly to different plants to resolve production problems, set up and troubleshoot new computer systems, and train personnel in operating new production equipment. The interviewee, a former plant manager, is an excellent troubleshooter, but he is becoming unhappy with the constant travel and being away from his family. This performance interview is aimed at keeping the interviewee happy and on the job as well as reviewing performance.

A Borderline Performer

The interviewer is the manager of a women's clothing department in a major department store. The interviewee is a young married employee with two small children. When she is at work, she does an excellent job. She anticipates problems, thinks of various solutions, and is professional in dress and manner. However, about every three or four weeks, she has what is laughably called in the department a "mommy problem." Reasons or excuses abound: one of her children is sick, the babysitter is late, her husband is out of town, and so on. She is late so often by several hours that five months into the year she has used up all of her sick days and four vacation days. She obviously needs coaching. The interviewer must determine how he can make her aware that her tardiness violates company policy, is adversely affecting her co-workers, and is seriously jeopardizing her position. He wants to set goals with her for reducing tardiness by at least 50 percent during the next quarter.

Student Activities

1. Interview a human resources director at a medium to large organization about performance reviews. Ask questions such as: Which performance review system or model do you employ? Why did you select this system? How did you adapt this model to your organization? How do you train interviewers to be coaches rather than judges? How do you address potential bias in performance reviews?
2. Compare and contrast Garold Markle's "catalytic coaching" approach to performance review with the traditional balanced scorecard approach, the behaviorally anchored rating scales model, the management by objectives model, and the universal performance interviewing model. How might the catalytic coaching approach alter each and improve each?
3. Contact supervisors at three different types of organizations: industrial, academic, and religious. Ask about the types and severity of behavioral problems they have encountered among employees during the past three years. What were the causes of these problems? How did they use performance interviews to address these problems? Who were involved in these interviews? How were interviews adapted to type and severity of behavioral problems? How effective were the interviews in resolving the problems short of dismissal?
4. Contact 3 to 5 organizations (for-profit and not-for-profit) and ask them for their philosophy of performance review and the resulting methods of compensation. Do they use individuals, groups, or both as a means of rewarding and paying for performance? Do they use profit sharing, stock options, direct cash payments, or other forms of compensations?

Notes

1. Reprinted with permission from Robert S. Kaplan and David P. Norton, "Using the Balanced Scorecard as a Strategic Management System," *Harvard Business Review,* January–February 1996, p. 77.
2. Reprinted by permission from Jon R. Katzenbach, *Peak Performance: Aligning the Hearts and Minds of Your Employees* (Boston: Harvard Business School Press, 2000).
3. Garold L. Markle, *Catalytic Coaching: The End of the Performance Review* (Westport, CT: Quorum Books, 2000), p. 4.
4. Taken from *Everyone's a Coach* by Don Shula and Ken Blanchard. Copyright 1995 by Shula Enterprises and Blanchard Family Partnership. Used by permission of Zondervan Publishing House (http://www.zondervan.com).
5. K. Michele Kacmar, L. A. Witt, Suzanne Zivnuska, and Stanley M. Gully, "The Interactive Effect of Leader-Member Exchange and Communication Frequency on Performance Ratings," *Journal of Applied Psychology* 88 (2003), pp. 764–772.

6. Ronald J. Burke, William F. Weitzell, and Tamara Weir, "Characteristics of Effective Employee Performance Review and Development Interviews: One More Time," *Psychological Reports* 47 (1980), pp. 683–695; H. Kent Baker and Philip I. Morgan, "Two Goals in Every Performance Appraisal," *Personnel Journal* 63 (1984), pp. 74–78.
7. "Guidelines for Conducting the Performance Interview," http://www.lcms.org, accessed December 19, 2006.
8. "Performance Appraisal," Answer.com, http://www.answers.com/topic/performance-appraisal?&print=true, accessed October 9, 2009.
9. H. Lloyd Goodall, Jr., Gerald L. Wilson, and Christopher F. Waagen, "The Performance Appraisal Interview: An Interpretive Reassessment," *Quarterly Journal of Speech* 72 (1986), pp. 74–75.
10. Gerald R. Ferris and Thomas R. King, "The Politics of Age Discrimination in Organizations," *Journal of Business Ethics* 11 (1992), pp. 342–350.
11. David Martone, "A Guide to Developing a Competency-Based Performance-Management System," *Employment Relations Today* 30 (2003), pp. 23–32.
12. Stanley Silverman and Kenneth N. Wexley, "Reaction of Employees to Performance Appraisal Interviews as a Function of Their Participation in Rating Scale Development," *Personnel Psychology* 37 (1984), pp. 703–710.
13. This explanation comes from a booklet prepared by Baxter/Travenol Laboratories titled *Performance Measurement Guide*. The model and system were developed by William B. Cash, Jr., Chris Janiak, and Sandy Mauch.
14. Jack Zigon, "Making Performance Appraisals Work for Teams," *Training,* June 1994, pp. 58–63.
15. Jai Ghorpade, "Managing Five Paradoxes of 360-Degree Feedback," *The Academy of Management Executive* 14 (1993), p. 140.
16. Anthony T. Dalession, "Multi-Source Feedback for Employee Development and Personnel Decisions," in *Performance Appraisal: State of the Art in Practice,* James W. Smitter, ed. (San Francisco: Jossey-Bass, 1998).
17. Ghorpade, pp. 140–150.
18. Angelo S. DeNisi and Avraham N. Kluger, "Feedback Effectiveness: Can 360-Degree Appraisals Be Improved?" *The Academy of Management Executive* 14 (1993), pp. 129–139.
19. Vernon D. Miller and Fredric M. Jablin, "Maximizing Employees' Performance Appraisal Interviews: A Research and Training Agenda," paper presented at the 2003 annual meeting of the National Communication Association at Miami Beach; correspondence with Vernon Miller, December 12, 2008.
20. Markle, pp. 76, 78.
21. Miller and Jablin; DeNisi and Kluger, pp. 136–137; Ghorpade, pp. 144–147; Markle, p. 79.

22. From a speech to a client briefing on September 30, 1983, in San Francisco by Buck Blessing of Blessing and White, Inc., a leading international career development company.

23. Goodall, Wilson, and Waagen, pp. 74–87; Arthur Pell, "Benefiting from the Performance Appraisal," *Bottomline* 3 (1996), pp. 51–52.

24. Goodall, Wilson, and Waagen, p. 76.

25. Terry R. Lowe, "Eight Ways to Ruin a Performance Review," *Personnel Journal* 65 (1986), pp. 60–62.

26. Hill, p. 7.

27. "Powering Up Your Annual Performance Reviews," July 23, 2009, *Executive Career Insights,* http://www.executivecareerinsights.com/my_weblog/performance-reviews/, accessed October 8, 2009.

28. Tanya N. Ballard, "Performance Pay Pitfalls," *Government Executive,* December 2003, p. 16.

29. Craig Monroe, Mark G. Borzi, and Vincent DiSalvo, "Conflict Behaviors of Difficult Subordinates," *Southern Communication Journal* 54 (1989), pp. 311–329.

Resources

Fletcher, Clive. *Appraisal, Feedback, and Development: Making Performance Work.* New York: Routledge, 2008.

Harvard Business Review Staff. *Harvard Business Review on Appraising Employee Performance.* Cambridge, MA: Harvard Business School Press, 2005.

Markle, Garold L. *Catalytic Coaching: The End of the Performance Review.* Westport, CT: Quorum Books, 2000.

Shepard, Glenn. *How to Be the Employee Your Company Can't Live Without.* New York: John Wiley, 2006.

Thaler, Linda Kaplan, and Robin Koval. *The Power of Nice.* New York: Currency Doubleday, 2006.

Winter, Graham. *The Man Who Cured the Performance Review.* New York: John Wiley, 2009.

CHAPTER 10 The Persuasive Interview: The Persuader

This chapter and the next focus on interviews in which the essential purpose is to influence how an interviewee *thinks, feels,* and/or *acts*—the persuasive interview. When you think of a persuasive interaction, a car, insurance, clothing, condo, or credit card sales representative may come to mind immediately. You may not be planning on a career in sales, but you are a persuader when you attempt to recruit a person for your sorority, raise funds for a hunger hike, convince a professor to give you a few more days to turn in an assignment, try to convince a team member to do his or her part on a class project, or urge a roommate to join your church. Such situations are endless, and you are involved in them every day. The pervasiveness of persuasion in our lives leads Roderick Hart, dean of the College of Communication at the University of Texas, to write, "one must only breathe to need to know something about persuasion."[1]

We cannot avoid persuasion in our society.

This chapter focuses on your role as a persuasive interviewer and will begin with a fundamental concern of persuasion theorists and practitioners—ethics. Isocrates wrote in ancient Greece more than 2400 years ago that it is not enough to learn the mere techniques of persuasion, you must also be aware of moral responsibilities when attempting to alter or reinforce the behavior of others.[2]

The Ethics of Persuasion

Ethics is a growing concern in society.

Concern over ethics in general and persuasion in particular remains as strong in the twenty-first century as it was in the fifth century BC of Isocrates. A recent survey revealed that 78 percent of college students admitted that they had cheated on some form of assignment.[3] Virtually every profession has published codes of ethics, but they are violated so often that skepticism abounds in our society. Surveys have indicated that we see car salespeople as least trustworthy (as low as 6 percent approval in some surveys), followed closely by talk back announcers, journalists, politicians, lawyers, business leaders, and accountants. Health care professionals reside at the top.[4] This skepticism and the disturbing reality of rampant dishonesty in our society led political scientist David Callahan to write *The Cheating Culture: Why Most Americans Are Doing Wrong to Get Ahead.*[5] If you are going to be a successful persuader, the interviewee must see you and your persuasive effort as meeting high ethical standards. Let's begin by determining what is meant by ethical.

What Is Ethical?

Richard Johannesen, an authority in the ethics of persuasion, writes that "**Ethical issues** focus on value judgments concerning degrees of right and wrong, virtue and vice, and ethical obligations in human conduct."[6] Notice the word *degrees*. It's easy to agree that a person trying to sell a fraudulent investment scheme or home repair rip-off, particularly to a vulnerable or desperate person, is unethical. Other situations are not so easy. For instance, you may criticize a politician or insurance sales representative for using extreme fear appeals and then use these same appeals to persuade a friend to stop smoking or a child not to get into a car with a stranger. What about a "stealth strategy" in which an "undercover" person pretends to be a tourist, fellow student, or concerned citizen rather than a skilled persuader? Even single, carefully selected words may tip the balance: depression for recession, socialist for government-funded institution, terrorism for all violent acts, excuse for explanation, propaganda for information.

When do we cross ethical boundaries?

Every strategy and tactic discussed in this chapter, even careful analysis and adaptation to the interviewee, may be misused and identified as *manipulative* and, therefore, unethical.

Fundamental Ethical Guidelines

It is difficult to develop a code of ethics applicable to all persuasive situations that we can all agree to, but Gary Woodward and Robert Denton offer us a starting point when they write, "ethical communication should be fair, honest, and designed not to hurt other people."[7]

When you are planning to take part in a persuasive interview, ask these fundamental questions:

Ethics is the foundation of persuasion.

- Who are you: social status, position held, and level of expertise?
- Who is your interviewee, particularly the person's degree of vulnerability?
- How serious are potential negative results?
- How adequate is your content, including fair selection of language and tactics, accurate and adequate evidence, and honest claims?
- How open will you be about your motives, balance of original ideas with adaptation to this person and situation, and belief in what you advocate?
- Are you innocent of violating fundamental ethical standards, including intent to deceive, adherence to agreed upon standards, and willingness to fulfill commitments and promises?

Kenneth Andersen writes that "although we do not wish to force a given system of values or ethical code upon the reader, we do argue that he [she] has a responsibility to form one. We believe that it is desirable both for the immediate practical reasons of self-interest and for more altruistic reasons that a person accept responsibility for what he [she] does in persuasion both as receiver and as source."[8] The age-old "golden rule" remains relevant for your ethical conduct: "Do unto others as you would have them do unto you." Would you want an interviewer to lie, use fictitious evidence, hide ulterior motives, employ racist or sexist language, pretend dangerous consequences are minimal or nonexistent, or play tricks with language?

What are the implications of the golden rule?

If each of us were to treat others as we wish to be treated, few unethical practices would occur in persuasive interviews.

Selecting the Interviewee

You often face persuasive situations in which the interviewee is predetermined: a parent, an instructor, an employer, a member of a team, an acquaintance. This is the only person you must persuade because this person alone can grant a wish, solve a problem, complete a task, or meet a financial need.

In other situations, you must select from among a number of potential interviewees or locate a number of interviewees in your university, community, city, state, or country. Professional persuaders call this **prospecting.** Start with your own network of persons with whom you have had previous connections and have established some sort of relationship. These may be family members, friends, fellow alumni, clients, associates, church members, customers, contributors, and supporters. Contact sources in your network who are not potential interviewees but may help you locate good prospects.

Prospecting is to a certain extent a numbers game because you may need to locate dozens or hundreds of interviewees, but try to avoid **cold calls** in which you contact a list of strangers with no connection to you or one of your sources. Some estimate that only 5 to 10 people in 100 cold calls will listen, two or three may be interested in what you are "selling," and only one will "buy."[9] This rate of failure can be demoralizing. All persuaders face rejection, and you must learn to deal with it. Eric Adams recommends that you "See rejection as a necessary evil in the process and be ready to move on. Or think of it this way; a quick 'no' is often better than uncertainty or delaying tactics that result in a 'no'much later, after you have invested time and money in a proposal."[10] Darrell Zahorsky warns that making an appointment does not mean the prospective interviewee will keep the appointment or be a good prospect. Some people "find it easier to agree to an appointment rather than saying they are not interested."[11]

The next step is to qualify your list of prospects because quality is more important than quantity. Although there is no guarantee of success in any persuasive interview, the possibility of success is increased if your interviewee meets these five criteria.

1. *Your proposal creates or addresses a need, desire, or motive for this interviewee.* If there is no need, desire, or motive, there will be no persuasion.
2. *Your proposal and you (including your profession and organization) are consistent with the interviewee's values, beliefs, and attitudes.* Lack of compatibility, trust, or respect will result in failure to persuade.
3. *Your proposal is feasible, practical, or affordable for this interviewee.* Possibility is critical in persuasion.
4. *Your proposal's advantages outweigh its disadvantages for this interviewee.* You must recognize and neutralize stated and unstated objections.
5. *There is no better course of action for this interviewee.* Your proposal is the best among choices.

Once you have a quality list of prospective interviewees, it's time to prepare for the interview. The next step is to do a thorough analysis of each prospect.

Analyzing the Interviewee

Learn everything you can about the interviewee so you can tailor your message to this specific human being rather than create a generic approach that is "sort of" adapted. Seek answers to four questions.

1. What is the interviewee's makeup?
2. What does the interviewee know?
3. What does the interviewee believe?
4. How does the interviewee feel?

The Interviewee's Physical and Mental Characteristics

Tailoring requires knowing.

Consider potentially relevant demographic characteristics such as age, gender, race, size, health, disabilities, and appearance. Each of these characteristics is shaped by specific and perhaps unique experiences, roles played (past, present, and future), society, and culture, and how they are shaped may be critical to your persuasive effort. A large, young male interviewee, for instance, might be interested in studying early childhood development with the goal of becoming a preschool or kindergarten teacher, a goal you hope to reinforce. But society says this is a role for women who are by nature and experience more able to nurture young children.[12] You need to understand societal stereotypes (all senior citizens are slow and gullible, all blonds are dumb, all Hispanics are illegal aliens, all college students abuse alcohol) and to be open-minded.

Level of intelligence may make interviewees more or less receptive to your message. Research indicates that highly intelligent interviewees are more influenced by evidence and logical arguments but tend to be highly critical and therefore more difficult to persuade.[13]

Socioeconomic Background

Memberships may be powerful outside forces.

Socioeconomic makeup includes the interviewee's memberships because attitudes are strongly influenced by the groups people belong or aspire to. The more committed an interviewee is to various groups, the less likely you are to persuade this person with an effort that appears to conflict with group norms. Charles Larson writes that one of two major determinants of behavior intention is "the normative influence on an individual and its importance to the individual. **Normative influence** is a person's belief that important individuals or groups think it is advisable to perform or not to perform certain behaviors."[14] Know the interviewee's occupation, income, avocations and hobbies, superior/subordinate relationships, marital status, dependents, work experiences, and geographical background because these affect frames of reference—ways of viewing people, places, things, events, and issues.

Culture

You will need to understand cultural differences that may affect the interview. For instance, Western cultures, such as the United States, tend to be "me" centered and stress the importance of individual accomplishment, leadership, and accumulation of awards and things. Others, particularly in Asia, are "we" centered and stress the importance of the group or team and see those who stress self and claim individual achievement as distasteful and offensive. Some cultures consider bribery a normal part of business. Others feel it is necessary to give gifts as part of the process. Bargaining is an essential part of persuasion in many cultures, often preceded by a relationship-building period over dinner or tea. In the United States, "time is money," so Americans expect others to be on time. In Great Britain it is considered "correct" to be 5 to 15 minutes late, and in Italy a person may arrive two hours late and not understand why you are upset.[15]

Values/Beliefs/Attitudes

Each culture has a set of generally accepted **values**—fundamental beliefs about ideal states of existence and modes of behavior that motivate people to think, feel, or act in particular ways.[16] Values, often referred to as "hot buttons" by college recruiters, sales representatives, and politicians, are the foundations of beliefs and attitudes. The following scheme of values includes those central to the American value system, the hot buttons that motivate interviewees to think, feel, or act in certain ways at certain times. You need to determine which ones are most relevant to your interviewee at this time and your persuasive purpose.

Values are the "hot buttons" we push in persuasive interviews.

Survival Values

Peace and tranquility	Preservation of health
Personal attractiveness	Safety and security

Social Values

Affection and popularity	Generosity
Cleanliness	Patriotism and loyalty
Conformity and imitation	Sociality and belonging

Success Values

Accumulation and ownership	Material comfort
Ambition	Pride, prestige, and social recognition
Competition	Sense of accomplishment
Happiness	

Independence Values

Equity and value of the individual	Freedom from restraint
Freedom from authority	Power and authority

(continued)

Progress Values	
Change and advancement	Quantification
Education and knowledge	Science and secular rationality
Efficiency and practicality	

As you review this list of values, recall recent experiences urging you to contribute to the state police program for summer camps, help the children in Haiti, or replace cable with satellite TV. Appeals of these persuaders may have centered on values such as prestige, generosity, considerateness, security, belonging, peace, and salvation. Determine which values are most relevant to this interviewee in this situation, with this issue.

Political, economic, social, historical, and religious **beliefs** emanate from values. You need to determine which of these beliefs relate to a topic and proposal. If equity and value of the individual are important values, an interviewee is likely to support equal rights and opportunities for women, African-Americans, and Hispanics. If education and knowledge are important values, a person is likely to support increased funding for schools, give to college fund-raising campaigns, and be interested in books and computer databases.

Values are the foundations of our belief systems.

Attitudes are relatively enduring combinations of beliefs that predispose people to respond in particular ways to persons, organizations, places, ideas, and issues. If you are a conservative, you are likely to react predictably to things you consider to be liberal. The reverse is true if you are a liberal. Attitudes come from beliefs that come from cherished values. Determine the interviewee's probable attitude toward the need or desire you will develop and the proposal you will make.

Attitudes tend to predict actions.

Consider the other party's probable attitudes along an imaginary scale from 1 to 9 with 1, 2, and 3 indicating strongly positive; 4, 5, and 6 indicating neutrality or ambivalence; and 7, 8, and 9 indicating strongly negative.

Strongly for			**Undecided/neutral**			**Strongly against**		
1	2	3	4	5	6	7	8	9

From what you have learned about the interviewee, where along this scale is this person's attitude likely to rest? If on positions 1 or 2, little persuasive effort may be required. If on positions 8 or 9, persuasion may be impossible beyond a small shift in feeling or thinking. If the attitude is on positions 4, 5, or 6, theoretically you should be able to alter ways of thinking, feeling, or acting with a good persuasive effort. This may not be the case, however, if an interviewee is strongly committed to remaining neutral, undecided, or noncommital.

Know what is possible, likely, and impossible.

Persuasion theorists from Aristotle in ancient Greece to the present day have claimed that the interviewee's attitude toward the interviewer (ethos, credibility, image) is the most important determinant of success.[17] You must assess the interviewee's attitudes toward you, your profession, and the organization you represent. Several dimensions determine your credibility with an interviewee, including *trustworthy/safe* (honest, sincere, reliable, fair), *competent/expert* (intelligent, knowledgeable, good judgment, experienced), *goodwill* (caring, other-centered,

Low credibility may undermine the best effort.

sensitive, understanding), *composure* (poised, relaxed, calm, composed), and *dynamic/energetic* (decisive, strong, industrious, active).[18] Think of your previous experiences with this person. Recall the discussion of attitudes that identified low-credible and high-credible professions. If an interviewee dislikes you, distrusts your organization, or sees your profession as dishonest or untrustworthy, you must alter these attitudes during the interview. To create and maintain high credibility with an interviewee, your appearance, manner, reputation, attainments, personality, and character must communicate trustworthiness, competence, caring, composure, and dynamism. People tend to react more favorably to highly credible interviewers who are similar to them in important ways and appear to share their values, beliefs, and attitudes. While they want interviewers to be similar to them, they also expect them to be wiser, braver, more knowledgeable, more experienced, and more insightful.[19] Consider all of these factors prior to the interview.

Perceived similarities may enhance receptivity.

Emotions

Emotions, sometimes called feelings or passions, significantly influence how people think, feel, and act. Along with values, emotions are "hot buttons" you need to discover and push if you hope to persuade. Some emotions are necessary for *survival* including hate, fear, anger, love, and sexual attraction. Others are necessary for social involvement: pride, shame, guilt, sympathy, pity, humor, joy, and sadness. You must be aware of the other party's mood, why the party feels that way, and how it is likely to affect the interview. With mood of the interviewee in mind along with topic, situation, and purpose, determine which emotions you must appeal to in this interview.

How we feel may determine what we do.

What, then, is the relationship of values, beliefs, attitudes, and emotions in persuasive interviews? As indicated in Figure 10.1, the process begins with values (our fundamental beliefs about existence and behavior), which lead to *specific beliefs* (judgments about what is probably true or believable), which form *attitudes* (organizations of relevant beliefs that predispose us to respond in particular ways), which may result in *judgment or actions* toward persons, places, things, ideas, proposals, and acts. Specific values and emotional appeals serve as triggering devices for judgments and actions. Altering or reinforcing an interviewee's thinking, feeling, or acting is a complex process.

Figure 10.1 *The relationship of values, beliefs, attitudes, and emotions*

Values } Beliefs } Attitudes } Values / Emotions } Judgment/Action } Persons / Places / Things / Ideas / Acts

Analyzing the Situation

The interview situation is a total context of persons, relationships, motives, events, time, place, and objects.

The "why" of the interview may vary significantly between parties.

Atmosphere

Study carefully the atmosphere in which the interview will take place. Know why the interview is occurring at this time: a regularly scheduled event, an emergency, a moment of opportunity, a major event, or a routine interaction. Will the climate be hostile, friendly, ambivalent, or apathetic?

Timing

Timing may be everything.

Timing may be critical. When is an ideal time to conduct the interview? When would be too early or too late? Contacting a potential United Way donor months in advance of the annual campaign may be too early for the interviewee to think about making a commitment. In the fall of 2009, health care workers were contacting parents to convince them to have their children vaccinated for the H1N1 flu virus. A delay of a day could have meant the difference between life and death. What events have preceded this interview such as visits from your competitors? You would not want to be the fourth employee of the day to ask for a raise from an employer who has just discovered a serious financial problem. What events will take place following the interview, such as a competing fund-raiser, an annual sale, or a budget meeting? Certain times of the year (vacation time, tax time, Christmas season) are great for some interviewers and terrible for others.

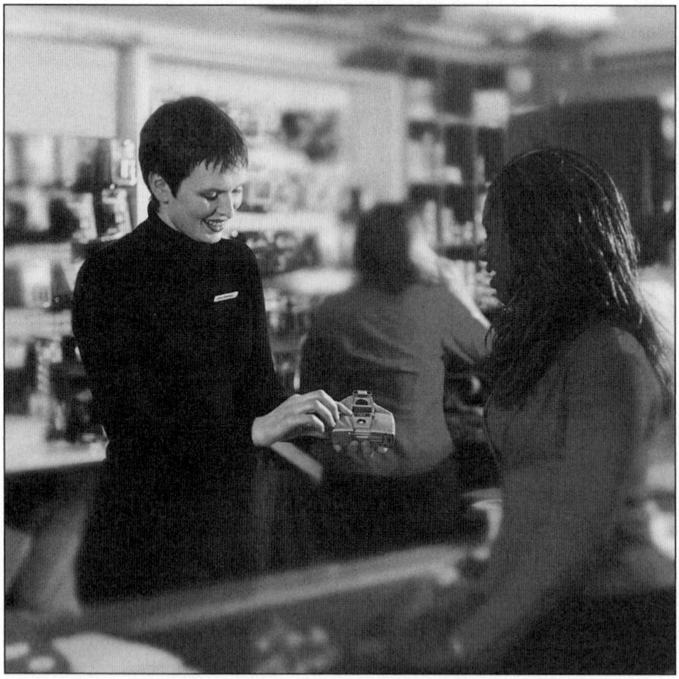

Getty Images/Stockbyte

The persuasive situation is a total context of persons, relationships, events, time, place, and objects.

Physical Setting

Consider carefully the physical setting of the interview. Provide for privacy and control interruptions, especially telephone calls. Make an appointment if it is difficult to guess how much time an interview will take.

Will you be the host (the interview is in your office or residence); a guest (the interview is in the interviewee's place of business or residence); or on neutral ground (a conference room, restaurant, hotel, club)? If you are trying to recruit a student for your university, you might prefer to get the interviewee

On whose turf will the interview take place?

on campus during a beautiful day when everything is green and in bloom, perhaps following a sports victory. If you are selling a life insurance policy, you might want the interview to take place in the interviewee's home surrounded by family members, furnishings, and valued possessions the family would want protected in case of an accident or death.

Outside Forces

Outside influences may wage counter-persuasive efforts.

Consider the influence of **outside forces.** For instance, organizational or professional policies may prescribe what you can and cannot do in a sales interview. You may be trying to convince a friend to attend your college while another college is recruiting this person with a full-ride scholarship. Mom and Dad want the interviewee to attend their alma mater. A significant other may want the interviewee to attend a local college. Awareness of outside influences may determine how you open an interview, select appeals and evidence, develop proposals, and address counterpersuasion.

Researching the Issue

Be the best informed, most authoritative person in each interview. Investigate all aspects of the topic, including events that may have contributed to the problem, reasons for and against change, evidence on all sides of an issue, and possible solutions. Search for solid, up-to-date information to persuade the interviewee that your proposal is the best for a need or desire. You are taking part in a persuasive interview, not giving a speech to an audience of one, so the interviewee can demand support, challenge assumptions, generalizations, and claims, and ask for documentation of a source at any moment during an interview. Parties are impressed with persuaders who reply to inquiries with facts and documentation rather than generalities and evasions. Try to determine what the interviewee knows about an issue and attitudes held toward the issue and possible solutions.

You must have the facts and know how to use them.

Sources

Do not overlook any potentially valuable source of information: the Internet, e-mail, interviews, letters, pamphlets, questionnaires, surveys, unpublished studies, reports, newspapers, periodicals, professional journals, and government documents. Use your own experiences and research. What sources are available to the interviewee?

An overlooked source may be the most important.

Types of Evidence

Search for a variety of evidence to support the need and proposal. Collect *examples,* both factual and hypothetical, that may illustrate your points. People like good *stories* that make problems seem real. Gather *statistics* on relevant areas such as inflation, growth rates, expenses, benefits, insurance coverages, profits and losses, causes and effects. Collect *statements* from acknowledged *authorities* on the topic as well as *testimonials* from those who have joined, attended, purchased, signed, or believed. Look for *comparisons and contrasts* between situations, proposals, products, and services. Locate clear and supportable *definitions* for key terms and concepts.

Gather and use a variety of evidence.

The effect of a well-supported interview lasts longer than a poorly supported one.

Distinguish *opinion* (something that is assumed, usually cannot be observed, can be made at any time, and either is or should be believed tentatively) from *fact* (something that can be or has been observed, is verifiable, and is thought of as securely established). Present your evidence effectively, including thorough documentation of your sources: identifications and backgrounds of authorities or witnesses, when research occurred, and where the evidence was reported. The substance of your persuasive interview enhances the long-term effect of your interview and is particularly important if a decision will not be made for weeks or months.

Planning the Interview

Only after analyzing the interviewee, studying the situation, and researching the topic are you ready to plan the interview. Begin by determining your purpose.

Determining Your Purpose

Be realistic. If you know the interviewee will be a "hard sell" because of a value, belief, and attitude system, then your purpose may be only to influence thinking or feeling in minor ways. Merely getting the interviewee to think about an action or to admit there might be a problem could be a major success for a first interview. Later you might move the interviewee toward a more significant change or action. On the other hand, if an interviewee contacts you and tells you he or she wants to change auto insurance companies, is interested in an investment, or would like to transfer to your major, you may move quickly through need and desire to solutions with a good chance of success.

Be realistic but not defeatist.

Be realistic in the goal you set for an interview. Big changes often come in increments and after a series of interviews. Do not assume after one interview that an interviewee is not interested or will not change. Authorities on sales interviews claim that it typically takes five contacts before a sale is made. Be prepared to be patient.

Selecting Main Points

Do not make the need too complicated.

Select reasons to establish a need or desire. Do not rely on a *single* reason because the interviewee may see little urgency in a problem that is so simple or unidimensional or find it relatively easy to attack or reject *only* one point. Research indicates that more points also enhance the effectiveness of persuasion over time.[20] On the other hand, six or eight points may make an interview too long and superficial as you rush through so many points. An interviewee may become overloaded with information and complex arguments and end up confused or bored.

Know the strength of each point and introduce it strategically.

As you select and develop reasons for a change, ideally three or four, determine the strength of each for this interviewee in this situation. This will help you decide the order in which you present points. Let's assume that you are trying to recruit a top merit scholar for your university and research indicates that this interviewee has three major criteria for choosing a university, ranked in this order: available majors, academic reputation, and financial aid. Studies show that introducing your strongest point first or last (available majors) is about equal in effect. If there's any possibility you might run out of time or be interrupted before you can present all of your points or reasons, start with your strongest point.

Developing Main Points

Develop each point into what the interviewee will see as a valid and acceptable pattern. Effective interviews are a carefully crafted blend of the logical and the psychological. You have choices to make.

Arguing from accepted belief, assumption, or proposition involves three explicitly stated or implied assertions (statements you believe and clearly want others to believe). For instance, a health care interviewer might argue this way:

Your assertions must lead to your conclusion.

Assertion #1: Children under the age of 16 are in a very high risk area for the H1N1 flu.
Assertion #2: Your children are five and seven.
Point: Your children should receive the H1N1 vaccination.

You need not state all three parts of this pattern if the interviewee is likely to provide the missing assertion or conclusion. Regardless, your argument rests on the first assertion that is the critical belief, assumption, or proposition. For instance, you might leave the second assertion unstated and let the interviewee provide it. This involves the interviewee in the process and encourages self-persuasion. This strategy is possible with all patterns of argument.

Assertion #1: Children under the age of 16 are in a very high risk area for the H1N1 flu.
Assertion #2: (left unstated)
Point: Your children should receive the H1N1 vaccination.

You might state your assertions and let the interviewee draw the conclusion.

Assertion #1: Children under the age of 16 are in a very high risk area for the H1N1 flu.
Assertion #2: Your children are five and seven.
Point: (left unstated)

Arguing from condition is based on the assertion that if something does or does not happen, something else will or will not happen. You might reason this way with a student.

Assertion #1: If you miss any more quizzes, you will fail my course.
Assertion #2: Your record indicates that you will miss one or more quizzes by the end of the semester.
Point: You will fail my course.

Weigh conditions carefully and be able to support them effectively. As with arguing from accepted belief, you may invite the interviewee to fill in a missing part or parts.

Arguing from two choices is based on the assertion that there are only two possible proposals or courses of action. You delete one by establishing that it will not work or resolve a problem, and conclude the obvious. For example:

Assertion #1: Your choice of a full-size pickup really comes down to a Ford or a Chevy.
Assertion #2: The Ford has been the leader for many years.
Point: You ought to buy a Ford pickup.

This argument rests, first, on being able to limit the choices and, second, convincing the interviewee that one is unacceptable so yours is the only one remaining. An informed and alert interviewee might well inquire about brands you conveniently left out: GMC, Dodge, Toyota, and Nissan.

Your evidence must warrant your conclusion.

Arguing from example leads to a generalization about a whole class of people, places, things, or ideas from a sample of this class. For instance, an interviewer attempting to "sell" the manager of a city bus service on the advantage of hybrid buses, might argue like this:

> *Sample:* In a recent EPA study of 500 hybrid buses in cities the size of yours, researchers discovered that hybrid buses, although initially more expensive than gasoline-powered buses, saved 29 percent on fuel cost. This savings would make up the difference in costs within two-and-a-half years.
>
> *Point:* Hybrid buses are the best option for replacing your old buses.

The quality of the sample, as in the survey interview, is critical in argument from example.

Arguing from cause-effect is related to example because interviewers often use a sample as proof of a causal relationship. Unlike the argument from example that leads to a generalization, this argument attempts to establish what caused a specific effect. For instance:

Beware of false causes.

> *Evidence:* In a study of 50 muggings of students near campus, it was discovered that 67 percent involved excessive drinking and walking home in the early hours of the morning.
>
> *Point:* Drinking excessively and walking alone early in the morning result in mugging.

You must convince the other party that the evidence leads to the only or major cause of effect.

Arguing from facts reaches a point that explains best a body of facts. This is how detectives and make-believe detectives argue when attempting to prove who committed a crime. For instance:

> *Facts:* Jack Wolfolk was seen walking in the area of the fires in the basement of the theater about 20 minutes before he was the first to report them. He had keys to the areas that are always locked. Almost no one goes in those areas at that time of day. A search of his apartment discovered two propane lighters like those found at the scene. He appears reluctant to talk to authorities.
>
> *Point:* Jack Wolfolk set the fires in the basement of the theater.

Unlike argument from example, the interviewer in this case is arguing from a variety of facts, not a sample of a class of things.

Arguing from analogy occurs when you point out that two things (people, places, objects, proposals, ideas) have important characteristics in common and draw a conclusion based on these similarities. For example, a coach might argue like this:

How similar are the similarities?

> *Points of comparison:* The Waymire Clinic reminds me of the one we used when we were students at Illinois in Champaign. It has excellent state-of-the-art facilities, including a new 297-bed hospital. There are a number of highly trained and very

personable physicians and nurse practitioners in internal medicine, pediatrics, obstetrics, geriatrics, and dermatology. It is highly respected in heart, spinal, and eye surgery. And it staffs several urgent care facilities in different areas of the city.

Point: The Waymire Clinic would be excellent for you and your family.

The number of significant similarities are critical in developing and selling this argument.

Selecting Strategies

When you think theories, think strategies.

Once you have a clear purposes and have chosen main points and developed these points into persuasive patterns, select psychological strategies that will make them persuasive. There are a number of theories that explain how persuasion comes about and prescribes how you might bring about changes in thinking, feeling, and acting. Theories explain complex human activities through careful observation of what happens in the real world and may serve as persuasive strategies.

Identification Theory

Kenneth Burke, arguably the leading rhetorical theorist of the twentieth century, claims that you persuade by identifying with the interviewee. Strive to establish **consubstantiality** (a substantial similarity) with the interviewee. The overlapping circles representing the interview parties in the model developed in Chapter 2 are based on Burke's notion that to communicate or persuade, you must talk the other party's language "with speech, gesture, tonality, order, image, attitude, *identifying*" your ways with theirs.[21]

There are several ways you can identify with a person to establish common ground.[22]

- *Associating* with groups to which you both belong, shared cultural heritage or regional identification, programs you both support.
- *Disassociating* from groups, cultures, regions, or programs the interviewee opposes or is distant from.
- Developing *appearance and visual symbols* that establish identification such as dress, hairstyle, makeup, jewelry, political buttons, or religious symbols.
- Sharing *language* such as jargon, slang, colloquialisms, and in-group words and phrases.
- Employing *content and values* important to the interviewee.

Appearances are important in perceiving common ground.

Strive for real identification, not a fabrication to initiate the change you desire.

Balance or Consistency Theory

Balance and consistency theories are based on the belief that human beings strive for a harmonious existence with self (values, beliefs, and attitudes) and experience psychological discomfort (dissonance) when aspects of existence seem inconsistent or unbalanced.[23] We may experience source-proposition conflict when we like persons but detest their positions on issues or dislike persons but favor their products or services.

Not all interviewees are happy with harmony.

We may experience attitude-attitude conflict when we oppose government involvement in our lives but want the government to outlaw hate speech and require prayer in the public schools. We may experience perception-perception conflict when we see Mexico as a great but dangerous place for vacation. We may experience a behavior-attitude conflict when we believe strongly in law and order but break the speed limit and use fake IDs to get into bars.

An interviewer may create or resolve dissonance.

As a persuader, you may create psychological discomfort (dissonance) by attacking a source or pointing out attitude, perception, and behavioral conflicts. Then you show how the interviewee can bring these inconsistencies into balance by providing changes in sources, attitudes, perceptions, and behaviors. If you detect that an interviewee is experiencing psychological discomfort, you may bring about balance or consistency by helping the interviewee see no inconsistency, perceive the inconsistency to be insignificant, or tolerate inconsistency.

Inoculation Theory

An inoculation strategy immunizes an interviewee from future persuasion.

Inoculation theory is based on the belief that it may be more effective to prevent undesired persuasive effects from occurring than using damage control afterward.[24] For example, a few years ago one of the authors received a telephone call from the state police warning him of solicitors who were claiming to be representatives of a state police sponsored charity for children and relating what solicitors were telling contributors. The caller hoped the preemptive call would prevent the author from being victimized and maintain the credibility of legitimate state police charities.

In this strategy, you forewarn the interviewee, perhaps by exposing the interviewee to small doses of a potential persuader's language, arguments, and evidence so the interviewee can resist the effort. Or you might provide arguments and evidence the interviewee may use to mount an effective countereffort if confronted by an interviewer against whom he or she is being immunized.

Induced Compliance Theory

There are many ways to trigger self-persuasion.

In the **induced compliance theory,** you may change interviewees' thinking, feeling, or acting by inducing them to engage in activities counter to their values, beliefs, and attitudes.[25] Participation in counteractivities may bring about self-persuasion. It is important to apply enough pressure so an interviewee will comply with your request without feeling there is no choice. Feeling coerced may prevent change in thinking, feeling, or acting.

There are a variety of ways to induce compliance. You might induce an interviewee to *espouse* a belief or counterattitude to understand or appreciate the other side of an issue, such as a liberal position on sex education or a conservative position on health care reform. You might induce an interviewee to *take part* in an unaccustomed or unattracted activity, such as going to a religious service or helping at a homeless shelter. You might induce an interviewee to *play an opposite role,* such as a superior instead of a subordinate, teacher instead of a student, parent instead of a child. You might induce a party to act to *receive a reward* or *avoid a punishment,* such as tickets to a concert or a speeding ticket.

Psychological Reactance Theory

Restricting behavior may lead to persuasion or resentment.

According to **psychological reactance theory,** people react negatively when someone threatens to restrict or restricts a behavior they want to engage in.[26] They may come to value the restricted behavior, such as renting R-rated videos, more and want to engage in it more than they normally do. People may devalue alternatives because they feel they are stuck with these alternatives instead of preferring them. Such people may resent the restricting agent.

Organizations produce limited editions of books, stamps, coins, and cars to enhance demand for them. Tickets to the NCAA basketball Final Four become of great value because they are scarce. Interviewees may be in favor of giving to the college development fund or joining their athletic booster clubs until they feel they are being forced to do so.

Whenever possible avoid real or perceived pressure on the other party to think, feel, or act differently. Make your proposal attractive, make scarcity or a deadline known without appearing to threaten, develop a serious need without excessive appeals to fear, and offer choices.

Conducting the Interview

As you approach the interview, remember to be flexible, adaptable, and cautious about assumptions. You are conducting an interview, an interaction between two parties, not writing an essay or giving a speech to one. Plan how you will involve the interviewee from the first seconds of the interview.

Opening the Interview

Do not use routine openings even for routine interviews.

Design your opening to gain attention and interest, establish rapport, and motivate the interviewee to take part. The major advantage of the interview over public or mass persuasion is the opportunity to tailor your message to a single person or party. Adapt the opening to each interviewee and setting. Resist the temptation to rely on a standard or traditional formula that may be inappropriate for a particular interviewee. When insufficient information is available to you or you have no opportunity to study the interviewee ahead of time, use the first few minutes of the interview to discover what you need to adapt to this person.

- *Observe* the interviewee's makeup, appearance, dress, and manner.
- *Ask questions* that reveal background, interests, attitudes, and purpose of this interview.
- *Listen* to what the interviewee says and does not say.
- *Determine* who is the leader of a multiple-person interview party.

If the opening fails, there may be no body or closing.

Some estimate that "roughly 75 percent" of all sales representatives "fail in the attention step."[27] Think of the openings in sales calls made to your home and how you reacted. Persuaders trying to convince you to give to a charity are often trained to recite a prescribed opening regardless of your age, gender, income, background, or level of interest. You may dislike this charity; it makes no difference to the persuader. Little wonder that few of these calls are successful.

Review the opening techniques and principles discussed in Chapter 4. Select one or more techniques suitable for this party and situation. Begin with a warm greeting and use the interviewee's name. If the person is a stranger, do not make your greeting sound like a question: "Good evening, Mrs. Walsh?" This suggests that you are unsure of the person's name or identity, unsure of yourself, and not well prepared.

If you know the interviewee well enough and both the situation and your relationship warrant it, use the person's first name. As a general rule, do not greet a stranger, superior, or person in a formal setting by first name or nickname unless you are asked to do so.

Neither rush nor prolong the opening.

It may be necessary to introduce yourself (name, position, title, background), your organization (name, location, nature, history, products, services), and the purpose of the interview. Orientation is essential when there is no relational history between parties and no appointment or arrangements are made ahead of time. Be brief.

You may begin with a sincere inquiry about family or mutual friends or small talk about the weather, sports, highway construction, or campus facilities. Do not prolong this rapport stage. Be conscious of the interviewee's situation and preferences. If a person replies immediately after the greeting, "What can I do for you?" this signals that the person wants to get down to business.

Reduce reticence by involving the interviewee immediately and often.

Cultures differ in amount of acceptable small talk and socializing. Most Americans want to "get to the point" and "get the job done." Japanese and other cultures desire to get acquainted, to follow "interaction rituals," and to go slower in making commitments and decisions.[28] Do not prolong the rapport stage, and make it appropriate.

Involve all members of the other party from the start so each person will play an active role throughout the interaction. Persuasion is not something you do *to* a person but *with* a person. American persuaders and persuadees, particularly males, tend to take turns unevenly during interactions and to speak at length during each turn. Japanese and others take turns evenly and make shorter statements.

The opening should be a good fit with the whole interview.

The opening should create mutual interest in the interview and establish trust and degree of affection or liking between the parties. Each party should understand the purpose of the interview and how they will share control.

Creating a Need or Desire

Create a need or desire by developing in detail the three or four points you selected in the preparation stage. Introduce them in the order you have determined will be most effective, strongest point first or last with weaker points in the middle.

Develop One Point at a Time

Explain a point thoroughly. Provide sufficient evidence that is factually based, authoritative, recent, and well documented. Use a variety of evidence (examples, stories, authority, statistics, comparisons, definitions) so the interviewee is neither buried under an avalanche of figures nor bored with one story after another. Incorporate the values, beliefs, and attitudes most important to this interviewee.

Encourage Interaction and Interviewee Involvement

Don't lecture; interact.

This is an interview, not a speech. You are more likely to persuade when the interviewee is actively involved. Stress how each point affects this interviewee's needs and desires.

Do not go to your next point until there has been some sort of agreement. With one point developed and agreed upon, move to point two, then three, and so on. Do not rush through a point or jump to the next one if the interviewee raises objections or poses questions. Move on when the interviewee seems ready to do so. Be patient and persistent.

Using Questions Strategically

Questions play unique roles in persuasive interviews.

Although you will rarely come to a persuasive interview with a schedule of questions, questions do serve a variety of functions in persuasive interviews. Never *tell* when you can *ask* because this involves the interviewee as an active participant rather than a passive recipient. Ask and then listen. You cannot plan on a series of questions to get the job done, particularly when an interviewee sees no need, has no desire, or is unaware of options. There are a number of question strategies that serve important functions in persuasive interviews.

Information-Gathering Questions

Use questions to analyze the interviewee.

Ask questions to determine knowledge level and to draw out concerns and objections. Listen carefully to responses and probe for accuracy and details. For example:

- Tell me your concerns about your current liability insurance coverage.
- What do you know about the compensation programs for installing windmills on your property?
- How frequently do you travel between Pittsburgh and Philadelphia?

Verification Questions

Questions can clarify and verify interactions.

Use reflective, mirror, and clearinghouse probing questions to check the accuracy of assumptions, impressions, and information obtained before and during an interview. For instance, you may assume you have answered an objection satisfactorily or gotten an agreement when you have not. Be certain an interviewee understands what you are saying and grasps the significance of your evidence and points. Silence on the interviewee's part can indicate confusion or disagreement as well as understanding and agreement. For example:

- Does that answer your concerns about the length of time for our MBA program in strategic management?
- You seem to be most concerned about scholarship money available for your daughter.
- Are we in agreement that a desktop computer would serve your needs and financial situation better than a laptop?

Encouraging Interaction Questions

Questions can stimulate interactions.

Use questions early in interviews to serve as a warm-up and tone-setting phase so that questioning, talking, and answering become natural for the interviewee. Encourage the interviewee to play an active role in the interview. Interviewees will feel freer to ask questions and provide meaningful feedback once they play an active part in the process and understand that you want them to. Employ questions to discover how a quiet or noncommittal interviewee is reacting. For example:

- What do you think of our new nanotechnology labs?
- What are your thoughts about purchasing the hybrid model?
- How was your tour of the new airport terminal?

Attention and Interest Questions

Questions can sustain attention and interest.

Use questions to keep interviewees tuned in and alert to what you are saying. They may be busy or preoccupied with other concerns and their minds may wander. Interesting, challenging, and thought-provoking questions maintain interest and attention. For example:

- What would you do if someone stole your identity?
- Remember your experience a few years ago when Peachtree Creek flooded your home for three days?
- How would you feel if you knew the pilot and copilot of your plane were playing with their laptops in the cockpit?

Agreement Questions

Questions can attain agreements and commitments.

Employ questions to obtain small agreements that will lead to bigger agreements. Getting agreement after each point leads to agreement at the end of the need so you can move effectively to establishing criteria for solutions. Do not ask for agreement or commitment before you have developed or supported a point thoroughly. A barrage of generalizations and claims will not prove a point or establish a need. Use a yes-response question (often in the form of a statement) to control the interview and lead to agreement after thoroughly developing of one or more points and small agreements. For example:

- With the market about to rebound, this seems to be a great time to invest, don't you agree?
- I know you understand that limiting bonuses this year is the best way to meet the recession.
- Do you want to risk your child getting the H1N1 virus?

Objection Questions

Do not try to substitute questions for substance.

Use questions to respond tactfully to objections and to draw out unstated questions and objections. Get them on the table at the proper time. Questions can also discover what an interviewee knows about an issue and reveal the importance or reasons behind objections. For example:

- You say cost is a major concern in purchasing a hybrid SUV, but what would you pay over the next five years for gasoline in a nonhybrid SUV?
- You seem hesitant about this trip to Egypt; what is your major concern?
- What information do you need to remove your doubts about this proposal?

Questions are valuable tools in persuasive interviews if asked tactfully and strategically. Don't ask questions prematurely that call for agreements when you have established nothing upon which to agree. Use leading and loaded questions sparingly because interviewees are turned off by high-pressure tactics. A series of questions are unlikely to persuade; you must present good reasons supported by information and evidence.

Adapting to the Interviewee

Tailor each part of the persuasive interview to the values, beliefs, and attitudes of the interviewee. Determine the probable disposition of the interviewee, and select appropriate tactics and strategies.

Indecisive, Uninterested Interviewees

The interviewee may see no personal need or relevance.

If an interviewee is indecisive, uninterested, or uncertain, educate the person to see the reality and urgency of the problem, issue, or need. Use opening techniques to get the interviewee's attention and generate interest in the seriousness of the situation. Then lead off with your strongest point and provide a variety of evidence that informs, persuades, and shows why the issue is of critical importance to this interviewee at this time. Use questions to draw out feelings and perceptions, and involve the interviewee in the interaction.

Avoid real or perceived pressure, but emphasize the urgency of the problem and the necessity of acting *now.* Use moderate fear appeals to awaken the interviewee to dangers to self, family, or friends. Appeal to values such as preservation of health, safety and security, freedom from restraint, ownership, and value of the individual. Show *how* the interviewee can make a difference in solving or reducing a problem or danger.

Hostile Interviewees

Do not assume there will be hostility.

If an interviewee may be hostile, be sure your anticipation or impression is accurate. Do not mistake legitimate concerns or objections or a gruff demeanor for hostility. If a person is truly hostile, determine why; then consider a common ground approach.

- A **yes-but approach** begins with areas of agreement and similarity and gradually leads into points of disagreement to lessen hostility and disagreement later by establishing common ground early on.
- A **yes-yes approach** gets an interviewee in the habit of agreeing when you reach apparent disagreements.
- An **implicative approach** withholds an explicit statement of purpose or intent to avoid a knee-jerk negative reaction from the interviewee. You hope interviewees will see the implications of what you are saying, perhaps feeling they came up with the concerns and solutions.

You must get to the point in a reasonable amount of time.

Regardless of the common ground approach, listen, be polite, and avoid defensiveness or anger when working with hostile interviewees. Hostility often results from lack of information, misinformation, or rumors. Respond with facts, expert testimony, examples, stories, and comparisons that clarify, prove, and resolve issues between parties. Be willing to accept minor points of disagreement and to admit your proposal is not perfect; no proposal is. Employ **shock-absorber** phrases that reduce the sting of critical questions: "Many residents I talk to feel that way, however . . ." "That's an excellent question, but when you consider . . ." "I'm glad you thought of that because. . . ."

Closed-Minded and Authoritarian Interviewees

Select evidence most appropriate for each party.

A **closed-minded or authoritarian interviewee** relies on trusted authorities and is more concerned about who supports a proposal than the proposal itself. Facts alone, particularly statistics, will not do the job. Show that the interviewee's accepted authorities support your persuasive efforts. The closed-minded and authoritarian person has strong, unchangeable central values and beliefs, and you must be able to identify yourself and your proposal with these values and beliefs.

Do not bypass hierarchical channels or alter prescribed methods. Authoritarians react negatively to interviewers who don't belong or appear to be out of line, and may demand censure or punishment for appearing to violate accepted and valued norms.[29]

Skeptical Interviewees

Image or credibility may be the major cause of failure.

The interviewee may be skeptical. Begin the interview by expressing some views the interviewee holds—a yes-but or yes-yes approach. Maintain positive nonverbal cues such as a firm handshake, good eye contact, a warm and friendly manner, and appropriate appearance and dress. If the interviewee feels you are young and inexperienced, allude tactfully to your qualifications, experiences, and training and provide substantial and authoritative evidence. Be well prepared and experienced without bragging. Avoid undue informality and a cocky attitude. If the interviewee sees you as argumentative, avoid confrontations, attacks on the person's position, and demands. If the interviewee thinks you are a know-it-all, be careful when referring to your qualifications, experiences, and achievements. If the interviewee has concerns about your organization, you might withhold its name until you have created personal credibility with the interviewee. If the name must come out early in the interview, try to improve its image by countering common misperceptions, relating how it has changed, or identifying its strengths. You may have to distance yourself from some elements or past practices of your organization.

Shopping-Around Interviewees

Be prepared for interviewees facing counter-persuasion.

Many interviewees shop around before making a major purchase or decision and will face **counterpersuasion** from other interviewers. When meeting with a shopper or an undecided interviewee, forewarn and prepare the interviewee. Provide the interviewee with supportive arguments, evidence, and responses to questions or points likely to be raised in encounters with others. Give small doses of the opposition's case (inoculation theory of persuasion) to show the strengths and weaknesses of both sides. Develop a positive, factual, nonemotional approach that addresses the competition when necessary but dwells primarily on the strengths of *your* position and proposal.

Intelligent, Educated Interviewees

The highly **intelligent or educated interviewee** tends to be less persuasible because of knowledge level, critical ability, and faculty for seeing the implications behind arguments and proposals. Research indicates that such interviewees "are more likely to attend to and comprehend the message position but are less likely to yield to it."[30] For example, they are likely to see through the good guy–bad guy approach used in many sales situations.

A two-sided approach addresses but does not advocate each side.

When working with highly intelligent and educated interviewees, support all of your ideas thoroughly, develop arguments logically, and present a two-sided approach that weighs both sides of issues. Minimize emotional appeals, particularly if the interviewee is neutral or initially disagrees with your position and proposal. Encourage the interviewee to ask questions, raise objections, and be an active participant.

If an interviewee is of low intelligence or education, develop a simple, one-sided approach to minimize confusion and maximize comprehension. A complex, two-sided approach and intricate arguments supported by a variety of evidence may confuse the interviewee. Use examples, stories, and comparisons rather than expert testimony and statistics.

Presenting the Solution

When you have developed the need, summarized your main points, and gotten important agreements, you are ready to consider solutions.

Establishing Criteria

Begin the solution phase by establishing criteria (requirements, standards, rules, norms, principles) that any solution should meet. If the interviewee is obviously ready to move into this phase of the interview before you have presented all of your points, move on.

Establishing criteria is natural but often unconscious.

Establish a set of criteria *with the interviewee* for evaluating all possible solutions to the need that you have agreed upon. This process is natural to us. For example, when selecting a college major, you may have considered courses, core requirements, specialties, careers, faculty, availability of internships, and marketability when you graduate. In simple decisions such as selecting a place to eat, you have criteria in mind, such as type of food and beverage, cost, distance, location, atmosphere, music, availability of large screen television for watching a football game, and preferences of others. Use this natural process in persuasive interviews.

All criteria are not created equally.

As you think of criteria prior to the interview and develop them with the interviewee during the interview, realize that not all criteria are of equal importance. For example, admissions directors at state universities have found that quality of school is the most important criterion for out-of-state applicants while cost is number 1 and quality is number 2 for in-state students. The situation can influence criteria. For instance, cost may override all other criteria during economic recessions.

Criteria are designed to evaluate and to persuade.

Establishing a set of criteria with the interviewee involves the interviewee in the process; shows that you are attempting to tailor your proposal to his or her needs, desires, and capabilities; provides a smooth transition from the need to the solution; and reduces the impression that you are overly eager to sell your point. Agreed-upon criteria enable you to build on a foundation of agreements, provide an effective means of comparing and assessing solutions, and deal with objections.

Considering the Solution

Seeing is believing.

Present your solution in detail. Do not assume the interviewee will understand the details and nature of the solution you have in mind unless this has become clear during your preinterview research or earlier in the interview. It's best to err on the side of too much information rather than too little.

If you consider more than one solution, deal with one at a time. Explain a solution in detail and use whatever visual aids might be available and appropriate: booklets and brochures, drawings and diagrams, graphs, letters, pictures, slides, computer printouts, sketch pads, swatches of materials, objects, and models. Some sources claim that interviewees remember only about 10 percent of *what they hear* but 50 percent of *what they do* and 90 percent of *what they both see and do.*[31]

Approach the solution positively, constructively, and enthusiastically. Believe in what you are presenting and show it. Emphasize the strengths and benefits of your proposal rather than the weaknesses of the competition. Avoid **negative selling** unless the competition forces you to do so as a matter of self-defense. The interviewee is likely to be more interested in the advantages of your proposal than the disadvantages of another.

Help interviewees make decisions that are best for them. Encourage questions and active involvement. Use repetition, what one writer calls the "heart of selling," to enhance understanding, aid memory, gain and maintain attention, and make the interviewee aware of what is most important.[32] Educate interviewees about options, requirements, time constraints, and new features.

Handling Objections

You cannot address an objection you do not hear.

Nothing is more threatening to an interviewer than the thought of an interviewee raising unexpected or difficult objections. Encourage the interviewee to do so because objections voice the need for more information or clarification and reveal the interviewee's concerns, fears, misunderstandings, and misinformation.

Do not assume agreement because an interviewee does not raise questions or objections. Watch for nonverbal clues such as restlessness, fidgeting, poor eye contact, raised eyebrows, confused expressions, signs of boredom, or silences. Find out what is happening within.

Objections are numerous and often issue, goal, situation, or interviewee specific.

Anticipate common objections.

- *Procrastination: Never do today what you can put off until tomorrow.*
  Let me think about it.
  I've still got three weeks before that paper is due.
  My old truck is doing fine, so I'll wait awhile.
- *Cost: That's a lot of money.*
  That copier model is too expensive for us.
  I didn't expect remodeling to cost that much.
  That's pretty expensive for a week on the beach.
- *Tradition: We've always done it this way.*
  We've always done business that way.

We've always had our reunions in Eagle River.
My grandfather chose that line of clothing when he opened the business in 1924.

- *Uncertain future: Who knows what tomorrow will bring.*
  My job is rather iffy right now.
  The economy is struggling, so I'm reluctant to hire new staff.
  At my age, I don't buy green bananas.
- *Need: What's the problem?*
  We've got good investments, so we don't need life insurance.
  The current no-smoking policy enacted just three years ago is working just fine.
  We don't have much crime around here, so we don't need a gun in the home.

How to Approach Objections

Anticipate objections to eliminate surprises, and think about handling each objection as a series of steps.

Meeting objections requires thought, understanding, tact, and substance.

Plan how to respond to reduce surprizes.

Listen carefully, completely, and objectively, never assuming you understand the other person's point or concern until you have heard it.

Clarify the objection, making sure you understand exactly what it is and its importance before you respond.

Respond appropriately, diplomatically, tactfully, and professionally. Never treat an objection as if it is frivolous. *If it is serious to the interviewee, it is serious.*

Minimize the Objection

Reduce the importance of the objection.

There are four common strategies for handling objections. Minimize an objection by restating it to make it less important or by comparing it to other weightier matters. Provide evidence to reduce the importance of the objection, as in the following example:

1. **Interviewee:** We've always thought it would be great to live downtown in a loft like this, but we're afraid of the crime rate in downtown areas.
2. **Interviewer:** That was true a few years ago, but crime is declining in the centers of cities and spreading to outlying areas where there are fewer police officers. For example, in this area during the past three years, robberies and theft have declined by 23 percent, assaults by 43 percent, and shootings have all but disappeared. At the same time, in the outlying areas of this city, robberies and theft have increased by 27 percent, assaults by 12 percent, and shootings by 15 percent.

Capitalize on the Objection

Take advantage of the objection.

Capitalize on an objection by using it to *clarify* your own points, *review* the proposal's advantages, *offer* more evidence, or *isolate* the motive behind the objection. Convert a perceived disadvantage into an advantage. For example:

1. **Interviewee:** We'd like to purchase a house instead of continuing to pay rent on an apartment, but the housing market seems really bad with all the foreclosures and banks being reluctant to make home loans right now.

2. **Interviewer:** Actually, this is a great time to purchase a home. The mortgage rates are the lowest in almost 50 years; the market is flooded with excellent homes in all price ranges; and the government has special programs for first-time home buyers. All of this will change within the next few months as the recession comes to an end and more buyers enter the market.

Deny an Objection

If you deny it, you must prove it isn't so.

Deny an objection *directly* or *indirectly* by offering new or more accurate information or by introducing new features of a proposal. You cannot deny an objection by merely denying it; *prove it.* Here is an example of denying an objection.

1. **Interviewee:** I've heard the Citizen's Action Coalition is tied in with anti-gun groups and plans to raise property taxes.
2. **Interviewer:** We're not involved in the gun or property tax issues. In fact, many of our members are hunters and gun collectors. Three are actively involved in competitive skeet and trap shooting. You may have seen Karen McBride's name in the sports pages last fall as state champion in skeet shooting. Our concerns are with clean air and water and we want citizens like you to pressure Congress to toughen and enforce laws that will enable us to breathe easier and live longer. We are on public record, published in *The Herald Times* just last week, opposing any increase in property taxes.

Confirm an Objection

Do not try to deny the undeniable.

Confirm an objection by agreeing with the interviewee. It is better to be honest and admit problems than to offer weak defenses. Here is a confirmation tactic:

1. **Interviewee:** Why should I pay $89.95 for the new edition of the textbook when I can buy the last edition on eBay for $19.95?
2. **Interviewer:** You're right; the old edition is much less expensive and some things are about the same. But take a good look at the new edition. It has more up-to-date case studies, new study questions, the most recent research studies, more extensive explanations of old topics, and new topics in nearly every chapter. It will be very difficult to prepare for class discussions and exams if you do not have the latest edition.

Closing the Interview

Both parties may fear the closing.

Approach the closing positively and confidently by not pressuring the interviewee or appearing too eager. Interviewers often hesitate to close, fearing they may fail to persuade, while interviewees fear they will make a wrong decision. Sales professionals, for instance, cite hesitation to ask for a sale as the major cause of failure to sell.[33]

The closing usually consists of three stages: (1) trial closing, (2) filling out the contract or agreement, and (3) leave-taking.

Trial Closing

Close as soon as possible and don't continue talking if the interviewee is sold on your proposal. You may talk yourself out of an agreement.

As you approach the end of the solution phase, watch and listen for verbal and nonverbal cues that the interviewee is moving toward a decision. Verbal cues include questions and statements such as "How soon will the new software be available?" "The idea appears sound." "This looks like a great resort." Nonverbal cues include enthusiastic vocal expressions, head nods, and smiles. Two interviewees may exchange glances at one another as if to verify interest or agreement or begin handling brochures, pictures, or written reports.

Know when to stop talking.

Yes-response and leading questions verify that the interviewee is ready to close: "I'm sure you can see this is the best way to go." "You want this internship, don't you?" "Do you want to face a lawsuit?" After you ask a trial closing question, *be quiet!* Give the interviewee time to think and self-persuade. Silence communicates confidence and gives the interviewee an opportunity to raise unanswered questions and objections. An interviewee may need reassurance that he or she is doing the right thing.

Probe insightfully and cautiously into negative responses.

If you get a no to your trial closing question, ask why. You may need to review the criteria, compare advantages and disadvantages of acting now, or provide more information. An interviewee may not be ready to act. Fear of possible consequences and how others may react (outside forces) may overcome a need or desire.

If you get a yes to your trial closing question, lead into the contract or agreement stage: "We can sign off on this today." "We can have this equipment installed within two weeks." "It would be a relief to have this decision made."

Contract or Agreement

After a successful trial closing, move to the contract or agreement stage. This is a critical time because the interviewee knows the closing and a commitment are coming. Be natural and pleasant. Maintain good communication. A variety of closing techniques are appropriate for this stage.

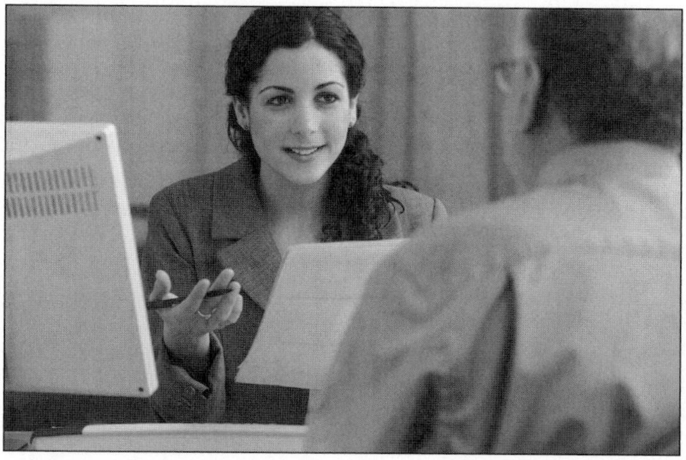

Jose Luis Pelaez, Inc./Getty Images

The contract or agreement stage is critical because the interviewee knows a commitment is imminent.

- An *assumptive close* addresses part of the agreement with a phrase, such as "I assume that you prefer . . ."
- A *summary close* summarizes agreements made as a basis for decisions.
- An *elimination of a single objection close* responds to the single objection that stands in the way of an agreement.
- An *either-or close* limits the interviewee's choices, then shows that the solution you advocate has the most advantages and the fewest disadvantages.

Select closing techniques most appropriate for this interview and interviewee.

- An *I'll think it over close* acknowledges the interviewee's desire to think about a decision, but tries to discover the level of interest and why the interviewee is hesitating.
- A *sense of urgency close* stresses why an interviewee should act now.
- A *price close* emphasizes the savings possible or the bottom line of the offer.

Leave-Taking

Leave-taking should reinforce all you have accomplished.

When the contract or agreement is completed, no agreement or contract can be reached, or another interview is necessary, conclude pleasantly and positively. Do not let the **leave-taking** phase be **abrupt** or **curt.** You may undo the rapport and trust you worked so hard to establish.

The verbal and nonverbal leave-taking techniques discussed in Chapter 4 may be adapted or combined to suit each interview. Be sincere and honest in this final closing phase, and make no promises you cannot or will not keep because of personal or authority limitations, organizational policies, laws, or time constraints.

Summary Outline

This outline summarizes the elements in the structure of a persuasive interview that covers need/desire and solution.

I. Opening the interview
  A. Select the most appropriate techniques from Chapter 4.
  B. Establish rapport according to relationship and situation.
  C. Provide appropriate orientation.

II. Creating a need or desire
  A. Provide an appropriate statement of purpose.
  B. Develop a need point-by-point with maximum involvement of and careful adaptation to the other party.
    1. Use appropriate argument patterns
    2. Provide a variety of evidence.
    3. Employ effective strategies.
    4. Appeal to important values and emotions.
    5. Obtain overt agreements as you proceed, being sure to point out how the interviewee party is involved or must be concerned.
  C. Summarize the need or problem and attain overt agreements from the interviewee.

III. Establishing criteria
  A. Present the criteria you have in mind, explaining briefly the rationale and importance of each criterion.
  B. Encourage the interviewee to add criteria.
  C. Involve the interviewee in the discussion of criteria.
  D. Summarize and get agreement on all criteria.

IV. Presenting the solution
  A. Present one solution at a time.

1. Explain the solution in detail using visual aids when possible.
2. Evaluate the solution using agreed-upon criteria.

B. Respond to anticipated and vocalized objections.

C. Get agreement on the appropriateness, quality, and feasibility of the preferred solution.

V. Closing the interview

A. Begin a trial closing as soon as it seems appropriate to do so.

B. When the trial closing is successful, move to a contract or agreement with the interviewee.

C. Use appropriate leave-taking techniques discussed in this chapter and Chapter 4.

There is no set pattern for all persuasive interviews.

You will not develop all parts of this outline in every interview. If an interviewee agrees with the need or problem prior to the interview, merely summarize the need in the opening and move directly to criteria. An interviewee may see the need but not agree with your proposed solution. Or an interviewee may feel any move now is impossible because of constraints. Feasibility is the central concern in this interview, not need or a specific proposal. The interviewee may like your proposal but see no need to act at this time.

ON THE WEB

Assume you are going to purchase a new car upon graduation. You want to be thoroughly informed and prepared when you contact sales representatives so you can make an intelligent decision and get a good deal. Use the World Wide Web to access information on brands, models, features, comparative prices, and assessments by automotive experts. Sample manufacturer sites are Toyota (http://www.toyota.com), Acura (http://www.acura.com), Mazda (http://mazdausa.com), Buick (http://www.parkavenue.com), and Chrysler (http://www.chryslercars.com). What information is readily available on the Internet, and why is this so? What information is not included on the Internet, and why is this so? What are common persuasive tactics used on the Internet? What questions does your research suggest you pursue during interviews?

Summary

Good persuasive interviews are ones in which both parties are actively involved, not speeches given to an audience of one but interpersonal interactions in which both parties must speak and listen effectively. The guiding principle is that persuasion is *done with* not *done to* another party.

Good persuasive interviews are honest endeavors conducted according to fundamental ethical guidelines. They are not games in which the end justifies the means or *buyer beware* is a guiding principle. The appeal should be to the head and the heart rather than relying on emotional hot buttons that will override critical thought and decision making.

Good persuasive interviews are carefully researched, planned, and structured, yet they remain flexible enough to meet unforeseen reactions, objections, and arguments. Adapt the persuasive effort to *this persuadee.* The persuader develops, supports, and documents important reasons for a change in thinking, feeling, or acting and presents a detailed solution that meets criteria agreed upon by both parties. Persuasion often entails several contacts in which the persuader and persuadee reach incremental agreements.

Key Terms and Concepts

The online learning center for this text features FLASHCARDS and CROSSWORD PUZZLES for studying based on these terms and concepts.

- Agreement questions
- Analyzing the interviewee
- Arguing from accepted belief
- Arguing from analogy
- Arguing from cause-effect
- Arguing from condition
- Arguing from example
- Arguing from facts
- Arguing from two choices
- Atmosphere
- Attention and interest questions
- Attitude-attitude conflict
- Attitudes
- Balance or consistency theory
- Behavior-attitude conflict
- Beliefs
- Closed-minded or authoritarian interviewee
- Closing
- Cold calls
- Consubstantiality
- Contract or agreement closing
- Criteria
- Culture
- Dissonance
- Encouraging interaction questions
- Ethics
- Evidence
- Hostile interviewee
- Identification theory
- Implicative approach
- Indecisive interviewee
- Induced compliance theory
- Information-gathering questions
- Intelligent interviewee
- Interrelated conditions
- Leave-taking
- Motives
- Normative influence
- Objection questions
- Objections
- One-sided approach
- Opening
- Outside forces
- Physical and mental characteristics
- Physical setting
- Prospecting
- Psychological discomfort
- Psychological reactance theory
- Shock-absorber phrases
- Shopping-around interviewee
- Situation
- Skeptical interviewee
- Socioeconomic background
- Solution
- Source-perception conflict
- Structure
- Timing
- Trial closing
- Two-sided approach
- Values
- Verification questions
- Yes-but approach
- Yes-yes approach

A Persuasive Interview for Review and Analysis

This interview is between Josh Molinsky, a member of the County Council, and Susan Dawson, president of the Chamber of Commerce, in which Josh will attempt to convince Susan of the need to implement a highly controversial Local Option Highway User Tax, better known as a wheel tax. Susan has expressed concerns about the need for such a tax and the potential negative impact of this tax on businesses located or doing business in the county, particularly if surrounding counties do not adopt a wheel tax. Josh feels that Susan's support is critical in selling the idea of a user tax to other segments of the community and hopes this interview will be a first step in changing her mind. No action is desired.

How thoroughly has the interviewer done his homework, including analyzing the persuadee? How does the relationship of the parties affect the interview? How satisfactory are the opening, need, and closing? How satisfactory is the evidence in support of reasons for a change? How effectively does the persuader respond to objections and questions?

1. **Interviewer:** Good morning, Susan. (cheerful and smiling) How are the kids?
2. **Interviewee:** Hi, Josh. They're fine, thanks. (shakes his hand) Jamie will graduate from high school in a few weeks.
3. **Interviewer:** That's great. My kids are doing well, too. The twins are in eighth grade and Julie is in fifth. Didn't I see you at the Chamber of Commerce Convention in Nashville a couple of weeks ago?
4. **Interviewee:** Yes. It was a great opportunity to share ideas on what is impacting businesses, particularly small ones like mine.
5. **Interviewer:** I always find the sharing of ideas and concerns at conventions to be helpful. Just to discover you're all in the same boat helps at times.
6. **Interviewee:** That's true. (looks at her watch) What can I do for you?
7. **Interviewer:** Did the Local Option Highway User Tax come up during any of your meetings?
8. **Interviewee:** Yes, it did. (frowning) It's not very popular among Chamber members or their communities. Is that what you want to talk to me about? I know the County Council is considering it.
9. **Interviewer:** Yes, that's why I'm here this morning. I'm well aware of the unpopularity of the so-called wheel tax. Letters to the *Constitution* and call-ins on local radio shows are running 3 to 1 opposed to the idea. As you know, several of us on the County Council feel it's the lesser of two evils.
10. **Interviewee:** Uh huh. And what does that have to do with me or the Chamber of Commerce?
11. **Interviewer:** Well . . . frankly . . . we feel it is essential to have you aboard on this issue if we're going to sell it to business leaders and employers.
12. **Interviewee:** That's not going to happen until our members change their minds, which is unlikely. You see . . .
13. **Interviewer:** (cuts in) I'd like to explain why we've changed our minds during the past year and maybe why you ought to reconsider it.
14. **Interviewee:** I find this need for new money rather curious since you were the leader of the faction that opposed taking any of the federal economic stimulus money specifically designated for road repair and building projects. Other communities have taken advantage of this money while we are looking for new taxes.
15. **Interviewer:** Well, as they say, that's water under the bridge and we are facing some big decisions.
16. **Interviewee:** Well, as they also say, that's money over the dam that might have prevented some of these big decisions.

17. **Interviewer:** I hear you, but I'm still against taking any so-called stimulus money from the feds. It's a matter of principle.
18. **Interviewee:** I also think not adding a new tax is a matter of principle.
19. **Interviewer:** At the time, we hoped the state legislature would provide supplemental appropriations and perhaps a small increase in the gas tax to provide needed highway funding. Because of opposition to raising taxes of any kind and then the catastrophic recession this past year, the legislature cut funding. We're now in a bind with new projects and necessary repairs far exceeding the funds available.
20. **Interviewee:** I think, in times like this, all agencies must live within their means. Even if that seems painful to some.
21. **Interviewer:** I guess it depends upon who's feeling the pain, or "whose ox is being gored" so to speak.
22. **Interviewee:** I don't follow that metaphor at all. All of us were gored during the recession and all of us felt the pain of budget cuts.
23. **Interviewer:** Well, the Chamber has been pushing the county to make Karber Road four lanes instead of two because of the rapidly growing development on the south side. The cost of this improvement, with necessary curbs, sidewalks, and storm sewers, will be more than $1 million per lane per mile. This limits us to a quarter-mile of a four-lane Karber Road per year. That's a long time to complete this much-needed five-mile stretch of road.
24. **Interviewee:** The federal stimulus money was designed for projects like this that would have employed dozens, maybe hundreds, of workers, most of them unemployed. We in the county must live with the past principled actions of its leaders. I think it's time to prioritize projects. Those of us in *business* (vocal emphasis) have to do that all the time.
25. **Interviewer:** And so do those of us in government positions. The problem is that many projects seem to be at the top of the priority list. For instance, the Karber Road project is highly important, but so are the replacement costs of 15 bridges in the area that the state is demanding we repair or replace. The cost is more than a million a bridge just for repair work.
26. **Interviewee:** A lot of the stimulus money was earmarked for bridge repair and replacement, particularly after the disaster in Minneapolis. Those could have been at the top of the county's list.
27. **Interviewer:** (sounds exasperated) Susan . . . The past is past, and debating past decisions will not solve any of our problems. The average life for a paved road is about 15 years, and a great many new roads built in the county in the booming 1990s are reaching that age. Do you know what it costs just to repave a road?
28. **Interviewee:** No (laughing), but you're going to tell me.
29. **Interviewer:** That's right. (not smiling) Last year it cost $50,000 to resurface a mile of road that required no other repairs. Since we rely primarily on asphalt that is oil based, the cost this year with the rise in oil prices is likely to exceed $55,000 a mile, not including gas price increases for running our equipment.

30. **Interviewee:** I can appreciate this fact, but you'll just have to delay some resurfacing until the economy and tax revenue improve.

31. **Interviewer:** That *sounds* (vocal emphasis) like a good idea until you figure in the added cost of a deteriorated road that requires more than resurfacing. The cost could jump to $75,000 a mile. We have over $650 million invested in county roads.

32. **Interviewee:** Josh, it's priority again. Prioritize the important projects and reduce or eliminate other costs.

33. **Interviewer:** Okay, that sounds like *good business* (vocal emphasis). We can do this by eliminating culvert repairs, guardrail improvements, signage, snow plowing, salting of icy roads, mowing during the summer, picking up dead animals, and patching of potholes. Would you and county residents be in favor of this after the first snowfall or severe damage to tires and suspensions because of potholes and ruts?

34. **Interviewee:** I'm not proposing the elimination of these *essentials* (vocal emphasis).

35. **Interviewer:** I see. Then what are top priority items?

36. **Interviewee:** I see some of what you're saying. There seem to be a lot of high priority items. But a wheel tax would burden our county residents but not those driving in from surrounding counties.

37. **Interviewer:** (sounding incredulous) You're president of the Chamber of Commerce, and you're concerned about those who bring their business and their money into this county?

38. **Interviewee:** Of course not (sounds a bit testy). We have many programs designed to encourage working and shopping here. I'm just concerned about fairness. When we all but begged you and the council to accept stimulus money, you told us you could not and would not sacrifice your principles. Well, my principle is no new taxes, and now you're begging me to sacrifice my principles to make up for the problems largely caused by your principles.

39. **Interviewer:** I hear you and can appreciate what you're saying, but short of tollbooths on every road, there is no way to charge a road tax on those coming in, and we both agree we want them to continue coming in.

40. **Interviewee:** That's not what I had in mind. It's ridiculous.

41. **Interviewer:** Real or imagined tollbooths won't be necessary because I suspect that surrounding counties will soon have a Local Option Highway User Tax of their own. In fact, Jefferson and Henry counties to our west will institute such a tax this fall. Like us, they see no other choice.

42. **Interviewee:** Well, you've made some good points. I'm not sold on the idea of a new tax yet, but I will think about it and then talk to you about the nature of the tax plan you would initiate, such as a sunset provision that would end it after three years.

43. **Interviewer:** That's all I wanted to do this morning, to encourage you to think about the idea and the problems we face. Can we meet on Thursday morning around 9:00?

44. **Interviewee:** That time is open on my calendar, but I'd like to see a breakdown of the highway budget for this year before then to see where our road money is going.

45. **Interviewer:** The County Council committee on option taxes is meeting Wednesday night, and I might have some ideas to share the next morning. I'll get you a copy of the budget.

46. **Interviewee:** Okay. See you then. We do pay a price for our principles, don't we?

47. **Interviewer:** Yes, we do, but what else do we have to live by?

Persuasion Role-Playing Cases

Acquiring a Commuter Airline Service

The interviewer is the manager of a university-operated airport that had provided commercial passenger service to the area since the 1950s. Unfortunately, the convenience and limo service every two hours to an international airport just 65 miles away and the cost of commuter airline tickets resulted in several airlines coming and going over the years because of lack of passengers. Nighthawk Air is the only airline continuing to serve the airport with two morning and two afternoon flights to Detroit. It has announced that it will discontinue service on December 1. The interviewer is scheduling interviews with several commuter airlines in an effort to persuade them to begin service in December.

The interviewee is chief of operations for Eastern-Southern, a four-year-old commuter airline serving Delaware, Maryland, Virginia, and North Carolina. Its long-range plans are to extend service to Pennsylvania and Ohio. Competition from large airlines, a steep rise in fuel bills, and a severe economic recession have made these plans tenuous at best. She is willing to listen to the interviewer from a service area that might be in the airline's future, but she is well aware of the number of airlines that have come and gone from his airport. There would have to be guarantees of reasonable passenger numbers and some financial incentives. The interviewer has a good background in the aviation industry but little management experience or success in selling commuter service to his campus and community.

Development of Three Resort Complexes

The interviewer is one of several people who have formed Resorts Unlimited to develop resorts in the Upper Peninsula (UP) of Michigan, which has suffered severe economic problems and unemployment since the copper and iron ore mines closed during the 1970s and 1980s. Resorts Unlimited wants to create several resorts in the hills and along the lakes of the UP that have remained undeveloped and populated by people who prefer the solitude of the area and the pristine condition of the lakes. Fishing and hunting are excellent because few tourists have invaded the area. The interviewer is trying to convince three families—the Lindbergs, Petersens, and Johnsons—to join the consortium or to sell their land to the consortium so it can build three resorts that will attract year-round tourists who enjoy hunting, fishing, and winter sports.

The interviewees (one each from the Lindberg, Petersen, and Johnson families) want the area to stay as it has in the five generations they have lived on their property or in the area. They are aware of the economic problems of the area but feel efforts should be directed toward restarting the mines or attracting companies willing to build on the old mine sites. They fear that resorts will permanently destroy the area as they have known it for generations. They think the interviewer is more interested in the profit from hoards of tourists at resorts than in resolving the area's economic plight. Most of the new jobs created would be low-paying service positions. Above all, the interviewer is from the Lower Peninsula, an outsider who does not appreciate the unique history and characteristics of the UP.

Adoption of the New Line of Clothing

The interviewer is 24 years old and is the assistant manager of Abbey's, a women's clothing store in a shopping mall close to a college campus. The three lines of clothing and the selection of jewelry clearly appeal to "mature" women in their late 30s and older, not the college customer but her mother. The interviewer wants to persuade the owner–manager to eliminate at least one line of clothing and replace it with one or ones that will attract the teenage and young adult clientele. The selection of jewelry would be mixed in appeal. The interview is taking place in the interviewee's office at 8:00 a.m. before the shop opens at 9:30.

The interviewee has owned Abbey's for nearly 20 years and has been satisfied with sales and the number of repeat customers she attracts. Ego involvement is high because the interviewee personally selected the shop's brands and jewelry and travels to Chicago, San Francisco, and New York to make stock selections. She sees Abbey's as offering a distinct alternative, one of the very few remaining in the area, to all of the "teeny-bopper" stores that populate the local mall that have nothing for women over 30. The interviewer is seen as a very hard worker with excellent communication skills but highly interested in her own tastes in clothing and jewelry. She is part of her generation, but this does not prevent her from interacting with and selling to women several years older.

A Vacation Home in the Poconos

The interviewer is a real estate sales representative for Mountain View Realty in the Pocono Mountains a few hours north of Philadelphia. During the past several months, he has been working with the Kabara family, who are looking for a vacation home in the area, preferably on or near a large lake. The Kabaras have four children, ages 6 to 12, and are eager to purchase a home so all of their children will have years to enjoy it. Unfortunately, they have been unable to locate a suitable home. Mountain View Realty has recently purchased several two-acre lots in a heavily wooded area with access to a nearby lake. He wants to persuade the Kabara family to build a log home on one of these lots.

The interviewees have not given much thought to building a home, particularly since they still have less than fond memories of building their current home eight years ago. The wife manages a restaurant, and the husband is a chemical engineer for a pharmaceutical company. Their combined income should make the investment of nearly $400,000 feasible if they encounter no financial difficulties. Two of their children have been diagnosed with learning disabilities and recently enrolled in expensive private schools in Philadelphia. They would like to find a house they can move into without the building headaches. They like the realtor but see him as too eager at times to make a sale.

Student Activities

1. Locate a professional (sales representative, recruiter, fund-raiser) who conducts persuasive interviews on a regular basis and spend a day on the job with this person. Observe how this person prepares for each interview, selects strategies, opens interviews, develops needs and solutions, closes interviews, and adapts to interviewees.
2. Visit two different establishments (such as a department store, car dealer, travel agent, or real estate representative) with persons who wish to make persuasive transactions. Observe a persuasive interview in each establishment. How much information about the person did the interviewer get before making a presentation or suggestion? How did the person's personal characteristics such as age, gender, race, culture, dress, physical appearance, and apparent degree of wealth seem to affect these interactions? Which values and emotions did the interviewers appeal to?
3. Interview two college coaches, one for the men's and one for the women's basketball teams, who are actively involved in recruiting high school and junior college players. How are their persuasive efforts adapted to the students' characteristics: age, gender, race, national origin, academic goals, professional goals, and geographical region? Probe specifically into how the coaches adapt to each recruit's needs and desires. What kinds of information do the coaches provide? What "hot buttons" does each coach try to push, and how do the coaches determine these are the ones to push? How does the coach handle objections? When and how does the coach try to close persuasive efforts?
4. Select three persons in different career fields (e.g., sales, medicine, athletics, lobbying, recruiting, advocacy) who have extensive experience in persuasive interviewing. Probe into how they prepare for and try to persuade three of the following types of interviewees: indecisive, hostile, closed-minded, skeptical, shopping around, highly educated. Which do they find most difficult? What are their most effective strategies for each? Which value and emotional appeals do they use most often and why?

Notes

1. Roderick P. Hart, "Teaching Persuasion," in *Teaching Communication: Theory, Research, and Methods,* John A. Daly, Gustav W. Friedrich, and Anita L. Vangelisti, eds.
(Hillsdale, NJ: Lawrence Erlbaum, 1999), p. 133.
2. Isocrates, "Against the Sophists," in *The Rhetorical Tradition: Readings from Classical Times to the Present,* Patricia Bizzell and Bruce Herzberg, eds. (New York: Bedford/St. Martins, 2001), pp. 72–75.
3. Melanie Butler, Tiffani Ridley, and Mary Allen, "The Demographics of Cheating in College Students," http://www.psich.org/pubs/articles/article_324.asp, accessed October 21, 2006.
4. Morgan Poll, http://roymorgan.com/news/polls/2005/3938, accessed October 21, 2006; "Public Still Regards Doctors as the Most Trustworthy Group," http://www.ipos-mori.com/researchpublications/researcharchive/poll.aspx?oItemId=1469, accessed October 16, 2009; Allison Schiff, "Public Opinion of Accountants on the

Rise," *The Trusted Professional*, http://www.nysscpa.org/trustedprof/1006a/tp9.htm, accessed October 16, 2009; David Rood, "Car Salesmen Get Lemon Rating," *The Age*, http://www.theage.com-au/articles/2002/12/19/1040174345151.html, accessed October 16, 2009.

5. David Callahan, *The Cheating Culture: Why More Americans Are Doing Wrong to Get Ahead* (New York: Harcourt, 2004).

6. Richard L. Johannesen, "Perspectives on Ethics in Persuasion," in Charles U. Larson, *Persuasion: Reception and Responsibility* (Belmont, CA: Thomson/Wadsworth, 2007), p. 27.

7. Gary C. Woodward and Robert E. Denton, Jr., *Persuasion and Influence in American Life* (Long Grove, IL: Waveland Press, 2004), p. 339.

8. Kenneth E. Andersen, *Persuasion: Theory and Practice* (Boston: Allyn and Bacon, 1971), p. 327.

9. Charlie Lang, "Making Cold Calls Enjoyable . . . Impossible?" *Articlebase,* http://www.articlebase.com/business-articles/making-cold-calls-enjoyable-impossible-46, accessed October 17, 2009.

10. Eric J. Adams, "The Art of Business: Client Prospecting for Creative Pros Who Hate Prospecting," http://www.creative pro.com/article/the-art-of-business-client-prospecting-for-creative-pros, accessed October 15, 2009.

11. Darrell Zahorsky, "Myths of Sales Prospecting," *About.com,* http://sginformation.about-com/cs/sales/a/prospect.htm?p=1, accessed October 15, 2009.

12. Daniel M. Dunn and Lisa A. Goodnight, *Communication: Embracing Difference* (Boston: Pearson, 2008), pp. 237–239.

13. Deirdre Johnston, *The Art and Science of Persuasion* (Madison, WI: Brown & Benchmark, 1994), p. 185; Sharon Shavitt and Timothy Brock, *Persuasion: Psychological Insights and Perspectives* (Boston: Allyn and Bacon, 1994), pp. 152–153.

14. Larson, p. 91.

15. Michael Argyle, "Intercultural Communication," in *Intercultural Communication: A Reader,* Larry A. Samovar and Richard E. Porter, eds. (Belmont, CA: Wadsworth, 1988), pp. 35–36.

16. Milton Rokeach, *Beliefs, Attitudes, and Values* (San Francisco: Jossey-Bass, 1968), p. 124.

17. Aristotle, *Rhetoric,* W. Rhys Roberts, trans. (New York: The Modern Library, 1954), Bk. I, Chap. 2, p. 25.

18. Robert H. Glass and John S. Seiter, *Persuasion, Social Influence, and Compliance Gaining* (Boston: Pearson, 2007), p. 77; Charles U. Larson, *Persuasion: Reception and Responsibility* (Belmont, CA: Thomson/Wadsworth, 2007), pp. 276–277.

19. Gray C. Woodward and Robert E. Denton, Jr., *Persuasion and Influence in American Life* (Long Grove, IL: Waveland Press, 2009), pp. 114–117; Omar Swartz, *Persuasion as a Critical Activity* (Dubuque, IA: Kendall/Hunt, 2009), p. 207.

20. Daniel J. O'Keefe, *Persuasion: Theory and Practice* (Newbury Park, CA: Sage, 1990), p. 186.

21. Kenneth Burke, *A Rhetoric of Motives* (Berkeley: University of California Press, 1969), p. 55.

22. Burke, pp. 21–45; Charles J. Stewart, Craig Allen Smith, and Robert E. Denton, Jr., *Persuasion and Social Movements* (Prospect Heights, IL: Waveland Press, 2007), pp. 160–163.

23. Woodward and Denton (2009), pp. 143–146; Larson, pp. 90–93.

24. Kathleen Kelley Reardon, *Persuasion in Practice* (Newbury Park, CA: Sage, 1991), pp. 54–55; Daniel J. O'Keefe, *Persuasion: Theory and Practice* (Newbury Park, CA: Sage, 1990), pp. 179–181; Erin Alison Szabo and Michael Pfau, "Nuances of Inoculation: Theory and Applications," in *The Persuasion Handbook: Development in Theory and Practice,* James Price Dillard and Michael Pfau, eds. (Thousand Oaks, CA: Sage, 2002), pp. 233–258.

25. O'Keefe, pp. 71–77.

26. Michael Burgoon, Eusebio Alvaro, Joseph Grandpre, and Michael Voulodekis, "Revisiting the Theory of Psychological Reactance," in *The Persuasion Handbook: Development in Theory and Practice,* James Price Dillard and Michael Pfau, eds. (Thousand Oaks, CA: Sage, 2002), pp. 213–232.

27. James F. Roberson, H. Lee Mathews, and Carl G. Stevens, *Selling* (Homewood, IL: Richard D. Irwin, 1978), p. 109.

28. William B. Gudykunst and Tsukasa Nishida, *Bridging Japanese/North American Differences* (Thousand Oaks, CA: Sage, 1994), pp. 68–73.

29. Stewart, Smith, and Denton, pp. 136–138; Robert N. Bostrom, *Persuasion* (Englewood Cliffs, NJ: Prentice Hall, 1983), pp. 181–182.

30. Shavitt and Brock, pp. 152–153.

31. Larson, p. 295.

32. Tom Hopkins, *How to Master the Art of Selling* (Scottsdale, AZ: Champion Press, 1982).

33. Lee Iacocca, *Iacocca: An Autobiography* (New York: Bantam Books, 1984), p. 34.

Resources

Dillard, James Price, and Michael Pfau, eds. *The Persuasion Handbook: Developments in Theory and Practice*. Thousand Oaks, CA: Sage, 2002.

Glass, Robert H., and John S. Seiter. *Persuasion, Social Influence, and Compliance Gaining*. Boston: Pearson, 2007.

Johannesen, Richard L. *Ethics in Human Communication.* Long Grove, IL: Waveland Press, 2002.

Larson, Charles U. *Persuasion: Reception and Responsibility*. Belmont, CA: Thomson/Wadsworth, 2007.

Swartz, Omar. *Persuasion as a Critical Activity: Application and Engagement.* Dubuque, IA: Kendall/Hunt, 2009.

Woodward, Gary C., and Robert E. Denton. *Persuasion and Influence in American Life.* Long Grove, IL: Waveland Press, 2009.

CHAPTER 11 The Persuasive Interview: The Persuadee

In the previous chapter, we emphasized that persuasion is *done with* not *to* another, a mutual activity in which both parties should play active and critical roles. Unless you are on a deserted island with no cell phone, you take part in persuasive interviews every day as customer, client, student, child, parent, recruit, or voter. This list could go on. You cannot afford to be a passive participant or ignorant of the complex persuasive process because most of the persuaders you encounter will be neither. And persuasive interviews may affect your feeling, thinking, and acting in positive and negative ways. The goals of this chapter, along with Chapter 10, are to help you understand the process and to be a responsible, informed, active, and critical interviewee.

Be an active participant.

Ethics and the Persuadee

Both parties share ethical responsibilities.

Since the persuasive interview is a mutual activity, both parties share ethical responsibilities. Richard Johannesen writes that "As receivers and senders of persuasion, we have the responsibility to uphold appropriate ethical standards for persuasion."[1] Herbert Simons suggests, "In your role as communicator and recipient of persuasive messages, ask yourself: What ethical standards should guide my conduct in this particular case? What should I expect of others?"[2] There are few universally accepted ethical standards applicable to all persuasive interviews that deal in degrees of right and wrong, good and bad, but there are fundamental ethical standards that may serve as guidelines when you are a persuadee.

Be Honest

We know when we are being honest.

Most of us feel we are basically honest and rarely tell lies or cheat even though we might "fib" a bit for missing class, "exaggerate" a little to get sympathy, or "fudge" on a desire or motive. After all, what harm does it do to tell a telemarketer that your roommate (sitting across the room) is not home, a sales associate you are "just browsing" when you are actively shopping, a caller for a charity that you "gave at the office," or claim you are a vegetarian to a person selling beef door-to-door? Simons suggests that we ask two questions to assess our honesty: "How will I feel about myself after this communicative act? Could I justify my act publicly if called on to do so?"[3] Some suggest a simpler, more personal question: "Would I be willing to report this behavior to my mother or grandmother?"

Be Fair

Relationships can grow or wither during interviews.

If you follow the golden rule, "Do unto others as you would have them do unto you," fairness will not be a problem. Ask real and fair questions. Avoid stockpiling grievances and objections until late in an interview and then dumping them on the persuader. Don't drag in irrelevant, trivial, or far-fetched ideas or arguments that detract from the quality of the interview and disadvantage the other party.[4] Strong and emotional disagreements are common in persuasive interviews, but avoid name-calling and other tactics that may negatively impact not only this interaction but also your long-term relationship with this interviewer.

Be skeptical but open to change and actions.

Be Skeptical

Don't be gullible. Every con artist depends on it. Have a healthy skepticism of the messages that bombard you.[5] Scams work because we are willing accomplices usually driven by greed. Be wary of assertions, claims, promises, and solutions that offer quick fixes, really good deals, and something for nothing. As the wise old saying goes, "If it sounds too good to be true, it probably is." Bernie Madoff, the Ponzi scheme operator during the years before the 2008–2009 recession who bilked thousands of investors (including family and friends) out of more than $50 billion, ensnared well-known investors, celebrities, and those seeking the fortune and prestige of being one of his investors. They asked few questions, did no research, and refused to listen to the few who tried to raise red flags. The "buyer beware" notion of ethics places the burden of proof on the persuadee. Accept it.

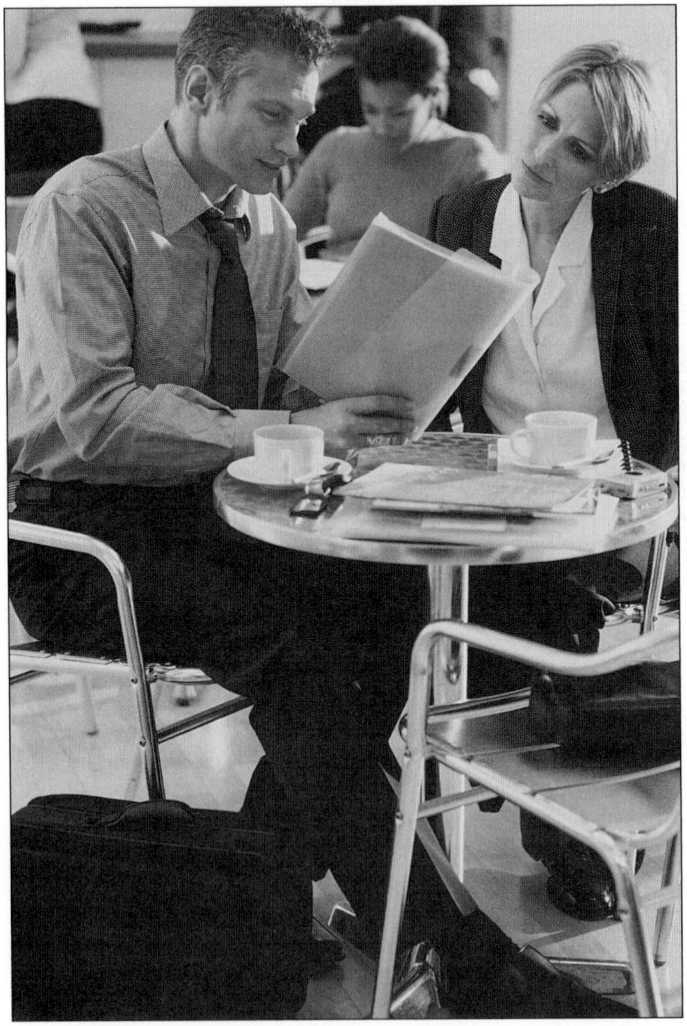
© Digital Vision

Listen, question, analyze, and synthesize before acting.

Be Thoughtful and Deliberate in Judgment

Listen, question, analyze, synthesize, and then decide whether to accept or reject a person, idea, or proposal.[6] Raise critical objections and demand responses backed by solid evidence. Research indicates that we are frequently more interested in appearances than substance.

Listen, question, and analyze.

If we like the interviewer, who looks like us, talks like us, sounds like us, and appears to have the right connections, we assume the proposal is logical and acceptable.[7] The appearance of logic or reasoning may be more important than the substance of it. Many see no difference between biased and unbiased sources or sources such as supermarket tabloids and *The Wall Street Journal* as long as they agree with their predetermined beliefs, attitudes, and values and support biases and prejudices. Johannesen claims that "an essential element of responsible communication, for both sender and receiver, is the exercise of thoughtful and deliberate judgment."[8]

Be Open-Minded

Open-mindedness is not gullibility.

Having an open mind does not mean that you have no strong values, beliefs, or attitudes or commitments to positions and organizations. It does mean that you do not automatically assume that persuaders, because of profession, political party, religion, race, gender, or culture, are trustworthy/untrustworthy, competent/incompetent, caring/uncaring—a kind of "persuader profiling." Likewise, do not automatically accept or reject proposals because they challenge the way things have always been done/should be done or the persons, professions, or organizations that offer them. "Be open to dissent and opinions of others."[9]

Be Responsive

Feedback is essential to the process.

Provide thorough verbal and nonverbal feedback to interviewers so they understand your needs, limitations, and perceptions of what is taking place and being agreed to. Reveal what you are thinking and how you are reacting. Be actively involved in the interview from opening through closing. Johannesen writes that "persuasion can be seen as a transaction in which both persuaders and persuadees bear mutual responsibility to participate actively in the process."[10]

Be an Informed Participant

Interviewers are often highly experienced and trained in the art and science of persuasion and understand how changes in the ways of thinking, feeling, and acting are produced. On the other hand, interviewees, the consumers of persuasion, tend to have little training and learn difficult lessons from failed encounters. You need to know some of the *tricks of the trade* to prepare yourself, in a way to inoculate yourself, from unwanted persuasive effects.

Psychological Strategies

We may act automatically during persuasive interviews.

Interviewers use strategies designed to create psychological discomfort—dissonance—that leads you to alter ways of thinking, feeling, and/or acting.[11] For instance, **standard/learned principles** may automatically guide an action or decision. You may believe, for example, that:

You get what you pay for.

If it's expensive, it's got to be good.

Sales save money.

If an expert says so, it must be true.

If it's in print, it's true.

If it meets industry standards, it's safe.

Upscale retailers depend on these standard/learned principles to move expensive, high-quality items ranging from jewelry to automobiles. One of the authors remembers working at a supermarket while in college. The manager wanted to move bunches of radishes late one Saturday, so he raised the price from 2 for 19 cents to 10 cents a bunch with a sale sign. They sold out in a matter of minutes because customers thought 10 cents was a real bargain.

Look for real differences.

In the **contrast principle,** interviewers know that if a second item is fairly different from the first in attractiveness, cost, or size, it seems *more different* than it actually is. If I want to rent you an apartment, I may show you a run-down one first and then a somewhat better apartment. You may see the second apartment as substantially rather than minimally or moderately better. The same strategy works with persons: introduce an ugly or obnoxious person first and a somewhat homely person next. If I can sell you an expensive suit first, then expensive ties, shirts, and belts seem inexpensive in comparison. The same principle applies to automobiles and expensive accessories. If you pay $30,000 for an SUV, a $350 towing package doesn't sound too bad.

We feel obligated to return favors.

The **rule of reciprocation** instills in you a sense of obligation to repay in kind what another provides. For instance, if a person gives you a free soft drink and then asks you to buy a raffle ticket, you feel obligated to buy the ticket even though it may cost more than the soft drink. This process is at work every time you open your mail and discover yet another packet of personalized address labels. You are likely to send in a donation or not use the labels even though you did not request them. If you use the labels and do not send in a donation or accept the coke and then decline the request to purchase a raffle ticket, you may experience psychological discomfort and fear shame or disapproval if someone discovers your action.

One concession deserves another, or not.

In a **reciprocal concessions** strategy, you may feel a sense of obligation to make a concession in response to a concession. Parties employ this psychological strategy in labor–management negotiations when one party, for example, concedes on health care and the other then feels obligated to concede on retirement benefits. It is common in legal interviews, sales transactions, and recruiting. You encounter this strategy in everyday interactions such as when a roommate agrees not to come in late on weekdays and you then offer to limit the amount of time a friend spends in the room. A time-honored concession takes place on high school and college campuses when one person offers to provide the car and the other feels obligated to pay for the gas.

Persuaders may ask for a lot and settle for less.

A **rejection then retreat** strategy begins with a proposal that may make a second more acceptable. The idea is that after you reject the first you will feel both obligated and somewhat relieved to agree to the second. One study discovered that if Boy Scouts asked persons to purchase $5 circus tickets and were turned down, the same persons were likely to say yes to a second proposal of a $1 chocolate bar. The Boy Scouts gained either way, and the persuadees felt good about helping out for a lesser amount. One of the authors experienced this strategy recently when he received a call from his alma mater. The student caller asked, "Can we put you down for a $500 donation this year?" When the answer was a stunned "No," the student then asked, "Can we put you down for the $100 you gave last year?" The answer was a relieved "Yes," and the caller got a donation. Sales persons often start with the top of the line and then retreat to a fallback position *if* necessary.

In **undercover** or **stealth marketing,** an interviewer party of two or more persons pretends to be a friendly, disinterested party and not a sales representative. For example, two people appearing to be tourists or visitors ask a person passing by if she will take their picture. The cooperative passerby agrees and just happens to notice that the couple has a very interesting and attractive digital camera. She asks about it and the party, who just happen to be undercover sales reps for this camera company gladly comply. The persuadee has no idea that a sales interview is taking place.

Be a Critical Participant

You must be a critical participant in every persuasive interview. Silence is not enough. Be ethical, knowledgeable, and critical. Challenge language strategies and the substance of interviews, including the logical strategies and evidence interviewers employ to alter or strengthen the way you think, feel, and act. Let's turn first to language strategies.

Language Strategies

Seek the meanings of symbols.

Woodward and Denton write that language "is far more than a collection of words and rules for proper usage. Language is the instrument and vehicle of human action and expression."[12] Skilled interviewers are keenly aware of the power and manipulation of verbal symbols, but too many of us see these symbols as merely words and rules. Larson warns that "as receivers, we need to get to the bottom of persuasive meanings; carefully analyzing the symbols used or misused by persuaders can help us get there."[13] An important first step in this analysis is to identify common language strategies.[14]

Framing and Reframing

Jargon is not harmless.

Persuaders use language to frame or construct the way you see people, places, things, and objects. For instance, **jargon** (sometimes called bureaucratese because bureaucrats rely upon it frequently) substitutes peculiar words for common words. While some jargon seems harmless enough (schedule irregularity for airline flight delay), others can hide the truth (culturally deprived environment for slum or terminological inexactitude for lie), make something sound more technical than it is (wood interdental stimulator for toothpick or emergency exit light for a flashlight), more valuable than it is (garment management system for one hook and two hangers), or less severe (collateral damage for the killing of civilians during military actions). Woodward and Denton warn that jargon may "require special interpretations and make us dependent on attorneys [physicians, engineers, professors, consultants] for help, advice, and action."[15]

Ambiguities say little but sound like a lot.

Strategic ambiguities are words with multiple or vague meanings. Persuaders may assume you will interpret the words according to their specific needs or perceptions without asking embarrassing, negative, or insightful questions. If a politician claims to be a conservative or moderate, what exactly is this person? What is a lifetime guarantee or a limited warranty? What is an affordable apartment or a top salary? What is free-range poultry or poultry raised the old-fashioned way? What is a natural food bar or low-carb ice cream? Studies show that we will pay a premium price for lite, diet, natural, and low-carb products without knowing how these differ from ones that are not and the positive or negative effects they may produce.

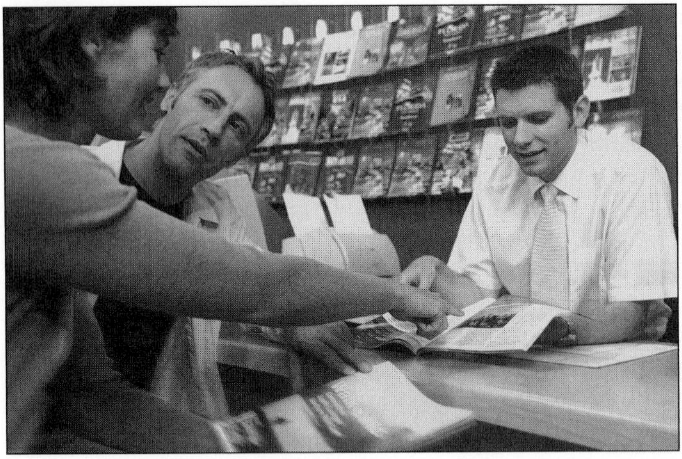

Image Source/Getty Images

Look beyond words and pictures in weighing alternatives.

Imagery substitutes for experiences.

Persuaders employ **imagery**—word pictures—that contains multisensory words to color what you have experienced, will experience, may experience, or experience indirectly. A representative of a travel agency, with the aid of leaflets, posters, and Web sites, will help you visualize skiing in the mountains of Switzerland, visiting the Aztec ruins in Mexico, surfing on the beaches of Hawaii, seeing the wildlife of Kenya, or enjoying the theater in New York. On the other hand, an interviewer might employ the same tactics to paint a negative picture complete with apocalyptic images and dire predictions if you vote for a political opponent, purchase a competing product, join a different religious group, accept a golf scholarship with another school, or travel to Egypt instead of Kenya.

Euphemisms replace substance with sound.

Euphemisms substitute *better sounding* words for common words. Cadillac was the first to substitute preowned for used cars, emphasizing ownership rather than use. You might find an inexpensive interview suit but not a cheap one and purchase it from a sales associate rather than a clerk. A lifelike Christmas tree sounds better than a fake or artificial one. Women's sizes is a common substitution for large sizes, and you will not find petite sizes in a men's department. You might order a lite beer at your favorite campus hangout, but would you order a diet beer? You are attracted by pleasant sounding words, names, and labels. Powder room *sounds better* than toilet or john.

Words may alter reality.

Differentiation is not an attempt to find a better sounding word but to alter how you see *reality*. For example, when an animal rights advocate wants you to become an animal guardian instead of an animal owner, this person wants to alter how you see your relationship with your pet. Calling female members of an organization women is not "political correctness"—a euphemism—but an effort to change perceptions of the abilities, capabilities, and maturity of women compared to girls. When President George W. Bush called suicide bombers in the Middle East homicide bombers, White House spokesperson Ari Fleischer explained to reporters that "these are not suicide bombings. These are not people who just kill themselves. . . . These are people who deliberately go to murder others, with no regard to the values of their own life. These are murderers."[16] The purposes of euphemisms and differentiation are very different; the first wants something to *sound better* while the second seeks to change your *visions of reality*.

Appealing to the People

For many of us, the majority rules.

Interviewers often appeal to your historic faith in the rule and wisdom of "the people," following Lincoln's adage that you can fool all of the people some of the time and some of the people all of the time, but you can't fool all of the people all of the time." The ***ad populum*** tactic claims to speak on behalf of the people—the alleged majority—such as voters, students, employees, college athletes, consumers, and small business owners. It's the "common folk," of course, not the elite, the government, the administration, or the executives. When, for instance, an attorney claims that he's "here for the people," who are these people? If a college dean advocates for the "students," who are these students?

The **bandwagon** tactic urges you to follow the crowd, to do what everyone else is allegedly doing, buying, wearing, attending, or voting. It appeals to your desire to belong and conform, often accompanied by a note of urgency: "My course is filling up very quickly," "The concert tickets are being snapped up," "This is the most sought after toy this Christmas."

Have an inquiring mind.

Listen for important qualifiers such as nearly, probably, almost, and majority. Ask for numbers or names of those who have signed a petition, agreed to a change, or joined an organization. Be cautious of phrases such as experienced investors, people in the know, and those who are on the move that are designed to pressure and flatter.

Simplifying the Complex

Interviewers may attempt to reduce complex problems, issues, controversies, and situations to their simplest elements. The **thin entering wedge,** also known as the **domino effect** or the **slippery slope,** claims that one decision, action, or law after another is leading toward disastrous consequences. Talk to a person who is against censorship, gun control, or same-sex marriages and you are likely to hear how censorship of books in public schools is one more step toward censoring all reading materials, how the registration of handguns is yet another step toward outlawing and confiscating all guns, and how same-sex marriage is a slippery slope toward the destruction of the home and the family. Look for evidence of a related, intentional string of actions that are tipping dominos, producing wedges, or sliding down a dangerous slope.

Fear of chain reactions may stifle any action.

Slogans are clever phrases and more.

Slogans and **tabloid thinking** are clever words or phrases that encapsulate positions, stands, or goals. They are typically vague but powerful ways to alter the way you think, feel, or act because they are catchy and entice you to fill in the meaning—to self-persuade. A politician may campaign for hope, change, freedom, or midwestern values with few specifics or clear definitions and intentions. Organizations rely on slogans to attract customers, recruits, contributors, and loyalty and may change them to communicate different messages. For instance, when Purdue University changed its slogan from "Touching tomorrow today" and then "Discover Purdue" with "Purdue: It's Happening Here," President Martin Jischke explained that "there is a tremendous amount of excitement around campus. . . . I think this theme is just trying to capture that sense of energy, momentum and pride that we have at Purdue."[17] Ask what slogans mean and if they truly represent a person, organization, campaign, or solution.

Polarizing limits our choices and our thinking.

An interviewer may **polarize** people, organizations, positions, or courses of action by claiming that you have only a choice of two: conservative or liberal, friend or foe, Chevy or Ford, wind power or nuclear power, for gun control or against gun control. It's a simplistic, but often persuasive, view of the world. A few years ago, Marine Corps recruiters on campus divided all students into two types: dreamers who think of nothing else but getting their degrees and realists who think of taking exciting college credits that will enable them to achieve a good job and good life. Do all college students fit into these neat categories? Are you either conservative or liberal or some of each?

Dodging the Issue

Attacking a source does not address the issue.

Interviewers may attempt to dodge critical issues, questions, or objections. ***Ad hominem*** (getting personal) dodges undesired challenges by discrediting a source because of age, culture, gender, race, affiliation, or past positions, statements, or claims. A parent may tell a child to "just consider the source" when called a name or has a belief challenged. An acquaintance may urge you to ignore research conducted by a known conservative or liberal, government agency or corporate association, religious or secular organization. Insist that the interviewer address the issue, point, or substance of the research.

Sharing guilt does not remove guilt.

You have used the ***tu quoque*** tactic since childhood to dodge an issue or objection by revolving it upon the challenger or questioner: "You're one too," "It takes one to know one," or "So do you." These are classic *tu quoque* responses. If you question a political candidate about taking money from special interests, the person may reply, "All politicians take money from special interests" or "Your candidate has accepted money from labor unions and trial lawyers."

Blaming others is an attempt to dodge responsibility.

Interviewers may dodge issues by **transferring guilt** to others, making the accuser, victim, or questioner the guilty party. Cheating on an exam is the professor's fault; failing to report all income on a tax report is the IRS's fault; parking illegally is the college's fault for not providing enough parking places. Defense attorneys turn victims of crimes into the guilty parties, particularly in rape or abuse cases. Do not allow attribution of guilt to others without addressing questions, concerns, and objections.

Logical Strategies

The logical and psychological are inseparable.

As pointed out in Chapter 10, persuaders develop reasons into what you may see as valid and acceptable patterns. It is important to recognize and challenge common logical patterns, the ways persuaders attempt to *reason* with you.[18]

Always check the sample from which generalizations come.

Reasoning from example or generalization is a statement about the distribution of some characteristic among the members of a whole class of people, places, or things. It's based on a sample of this class. For instance, a college basketball recruiter might tell a high school student and his parents that 8 out of 10 student athletes complete their degrees within five years, so this is the place to play sports and succeed academically. This ratio consists of a sample of athletes from different sports, and the coach generalizes to all basketball players. If you recognize this pattern, ask:

- What is the total amount of this sample?
- What is the nature of this sample?
- When was the sample taken?
- What is the interviewer asserting from this sample?

Be careful of coincidences seen as causes.

Beware of a *hasty generalization* in which the persuader generalizes to a whole group of people, places, or things from one or a few examples. For instance, a friend may warn you against dining at a particular restaurant because he had a bad meal there once.

Reasoning from cause-to-effect addresses what caused an effect. For instance, an interviewer might argue that a study of 300 students who had left campus during their first semester found the majority had lived alone in a residence hall or apartment. Therefore, living alone is the cause of college dropouts. Ask questions such as:

- Was this cause able to generate this effect?
- Was this cause the only possible cause?
- Was this cause the major cause?
- What evidence is offered to establish this causal link?
- Is a coincidence mistaken for the cause?

Just because B followed A, it does not mean that A caused B.

Beware of the ***post hoc*** or **scrambling cause-effect** fallacy that argues simply because B followed A, A must have caused B. For instance, I got the flu the day after I got that flu shot, so the shot gave me the flu.

Be a super-sleuth when encountering hypotheses.

Reasoning from fact or hypothesis offers the best accounting or explanation for a body of facts and is the type of reasoning sleuths use in murder mysteries—the "whodunits" of television and book fame. For instance, a construction manager might reason that the new intersection will be completed before classes begin in August because the lanes have been poured, the curbs are in, sidewalks are well under way, landscaping is progressing because of the good weather, and signage will be delivered within a week. Ask these questions during an interview when hearing an argument from fact:

- How frequently is this hypothesis accurate with these facts?
- Is the body of facts sufficient?
- What facts would make the claim more or less convincing?
- How simple or complex is the hypothesis?

A sign may have many meanings or no meanings.

Reasoning from sign is a claim that two or more variables are related in such a way that the presence or absence of one may be taken as an indication of the presence or absence of the other. For example, you may note that the flag on the post office is at half-mast and reason that someone of importance has died. A few years ago one of the authors noted a large number of people standing outside of the arena during a basketball game and thought there must be a bomb scare. The answer was simpler. The university had instituted a no-smoking policy for the arena and hundreds of people were smoking outside the arena during halftime. Ask these questions when hearing an argument from the sign:

- What is the relationship between the variables?
- Is the presence or absence verifiable?
- What is the believability or reliability of the sign?

Look for important differences as well as important similarities.

Reasoning from analogy or comparison is based on the assumption that if two people, places, or things have a number of similarities they also share significant others. For instance, a salesperson might argue that since a moderately priced SUV has many of the same features as a luxury SUV (V8 engine, room for six adults, equal cargo space, video system for rear seat occupants, leather seating, and four-wheel drive), you should lease the less expensive SUV because it is of the same quality. Ask these questions:

- How similar are the similarities?
- Are enough similarities provided?
- Are the similarities critical to the claim?

Identify the major assertion upon which the argument rests.

Reasoning from accepted belief, assumption, or proposition is based on a statement that is thought to be accepted or proven. The remainder of the argument follows from this assertion, such as: Smoking causes cancer. You are a smoker. Therefore you will get cancer. Ask these questions:

- Do you accept the foundational assertion?
- Do the other assertions follow logically from this assertion?
- Does the claim necessarily follow from these assertions?

Beware of argument based on alleged **self-evident truths** that cannot be questioned or disputed because they are "fact."

"If" arguments may ignore obvious or unpredictable conditions.

In reasoning from condition, an interviewer asserts that if something does or does not happen, something else will or will not happen. The central focus is the word *if.* Ask these questions:

- Is the condition acceptable?
- Is this the only condition?
- Is this the major condition?

Evidence

Look closely at the evidence an interviewer offers (or does not offer) to gain attention and interest, establish credibility and legitimacy, support arguments, develop a need, and present a solution.[19] Evidence may include examples, stories, authorities or witnesses, comparisons and contrasts, statistics, and key definitions. Use these questions to assess the acceptability of the interviewer's evidence.

Assess the reliability and expertise of sources.

- *Is the evidence trustworthy?* Are the persuader and the persons and organizations being cited unbiased and reliable? Are the sources of the evidence (newspapers, reports, Internet, publications) unbiased and reliable?
- *Is the evidence authoritative?* What are the training, experience, and reputation of the authorities or witnesses being cited? Were they in positions to have observed the facts, events, or data?
- *Is the evidence recent?* Is it the most recent available? Are newer statistics or findings available? Have authorities changed their minds?
- *Is the evidence documented sufficiently?* Do you know where and how the statistics or results were determined? Who determined them? Where and when were they reported?

- *Is the evidence communicated accurately?* Can you detect alterations or deletions in quotations, statistics, or documentation? Is the evidence cited in context?

Insist on both quantity and quality of evidence.

- *Is the evidence sufficient in quantity?* Are enough authorities cited? Enough examples given? Enough points of comparison made? Adequate facts revealed?
- *Is the evidence sufficient in quality?* Are opinions stated as facts? How satisfactory is the sample used for generalizations and causal arguments? Does proof evidence (factual illustrations, statistics, authority, detailed comparisons) outweigh clarifying evidence (hypothetical illustrations, paid testimonials, figurative analogies, and metaphors)?

Be an Active Participant

Be an active and critical player in the interview.

Play an active role in the interview. Each interview has the potential of altering or reinforcing the way you think, feel, or act, including the money you spend, the votes you cast, the relationships you establish or maintain, the possessions you protect, the work you do, and the life you lead.

Use a variety of questions during each of the interview stages. Informational questions enable you to obtain information and explanations, probe into vague and ambiguous words and comments, and reveal feelings and attitudes that may lie hidden or merely suggested. Reflective, mirror, and restatement questions enable you to be certain about what the other party is saying, what you and the other party are agreeing to, and what commitments each party is making. There are no foolish questions, only questions you foolishly fail to ask.

The Opening

Play an active role in the opening because it initiates the persuasive process.

Be alert and active from the first moments of each interview. If the interview is a "cold call" in which you have no time to prepare, use carefully phrased questions to discover the identity, position, and qualifications of the interviewer. Discover the real purpose and intent of the interview. Use the opening to "level the playing field" so you can play an active, critical, and informed role in the interview. It starts with the opening.

Too many persuadees play passive roles during openings. Here is a typical example from a recent interview in one of our classes. The persuadee is head of surgery at this hospital, believes in following strict hierarchies with surgeons at the top, feels physicians rather than nurses will detect and address any real problems, and is all business.

Persuader: Dr. Smalley, I'm Lilly McDowell, one of the surgical nurse supervisors.

Persuadee: Hi Lilly, have a seat.

Persuader: I'd like to talk to you about the problems we are having with surgical patients after they leave the hospital and a solution to this problem.

Persuadee: Okay.

Persuader: Well, we have discovered that . . .

The interviewee does not exhibit personality or attitudes and learns little about the purpose of this interview, how long it will take, or the nature of the problem. He allows the interviewer to launch into the need without question even though the interviewee appears to be encroaching on his authority and status, his area of expertise and responsibility, and does not explain the nature of the problem or how it was determined.

Creating a Need or Desire

Ask questions, challenge arguments, and demand solid evidence.

If an interviewer attempts to conduct an unstructured interview without a clear purpose and in which the need is a collection of generalizations and ambiguous claims, insist on a point-by-point development with each point crafted carefully and logically, supported with adequate evidence, and adapted to *your* values, beliefs, and attitudes. Beware of fallacies and tactics that dodge your questions and objections. An interviewer may attempt to introduce another point rather than address your concerns about a point. Insist on answers to your questions and objections and get agreements before delving into another point.

Weigh evidence carefully and be on guard against psychological strategies designed to manipulate your reactions and make you feel obligated to reply in kind. Do not tolerate innuendos or half-truths aimed at the competition, what is often called negative selling or mudslinging. Insist on getting agreements on the need before going into criteria or a solution.

Establishing Criteria

Criteria enable you to weigh solutions.

Establishing criteria with the interviewer that any solution should meet is a critical part of the persuasion process. An interviewer may come to an interview with a list of criteria, and this helps the process and shows planning. Regardless, take an active part in establishing criteria. Are the criteria clear? Do you wish to modify some criteria? Which are the most important criteria? Are there criteria you wish to add?

Presenting the Solution

Be sure the solution meets the need and is the best available.

An interviewer may claim there is only *one* obvious solution to the need or desire agreed upon. There is rarely only one solution to any problem. Insist upon a detailed presentation of each possible solution. Ask questions and raise objections. Be sure the criteria are applied equally to each solution to determine which is best for you in this situation. Ask for clarifications of terminology. If possible, insist on seeing, feeling, hearing, or experiencing the product or proposal.

When you have agreed upon a solution or course of action, beware of qualifiers or "add-ons" such as guarantees, rebates, accessories, processing fees, and commitments. What exactly is a "lifetime" warranty or guarantee? The persuader may hope that since you have made the *big* decision, you will agree to *small* decisions—the contrast principle discussed earlier. What are you getting that's "free"?

Take your time when making a final decision.

The Closing

Do not be rushed into making a decision or commitment. You have little to gain and much to lose through haste. A common tactic is to create a psychological reaction by claiming the possibility of censorship or the scarcity of a product. An organization may produce a limited number of books, coins, cars, or positions to make them more in demand. You must act quickly before it is too late or an agency steps in to prevent you from acting.

Do not hesitate to take time to think about a decision; sleep on it. Be sure all of your questions and objections are answered satisfactorily. Be aware of the possible ramifications of your decision. Consider getting a second or third opinion. Talk to persons who have relevant expertise or experiences. Check out competing products, candidates, offers, and programs. For instance, when coming to a new community, check out several neighborhoods before buying a home or renting an apartment. Visit several universities before deciding where to pursue a graduate or professional degree, try out several laptops before deciding which to purchase.

Summary

Good persuasive interviews involve the interviewee as a responsible, informed, critical, and active participant who plays a central role, not a passive recipient of a persuasive effort. It is a mutual activity in which both parties must play active and critical roles. Interviews are interactions in which interviewees act ethically, listen critically, ask insightful questions, raise important objections, challenge evidence and arguments, recognize common tactics for what they are, and weigh proposals according to agreed upon criteria.

Key Terms and Concepts

The online learning center for this text features FLASHCARDS and CROSSWORD PUZZLES for studying based on these terms and concepts.

Ad hominem
Ad populum
Attitudes
Bandwagon tactic
Beliefs
Bureaucratese
Buyer beware
Contrast principle
Differentiation
Dissonance
Domino effect
Ethics
Euphemisms
Evidence
Fairness
False dichotomy
Framing and reframing
Hasty generalization
Honesty
Imagery
Jargon
Language strategies
Logical strategies
Name-calling
Open-minded
Polarization
Post hoc fallacy
Psychological discomfort
Psychological strategies
Reasoning from accepted belief, assumption, or proposition
Reasoning from analogy or comparison
Reasoning from cause-to-effect
Reasoning from condition
Reasoning from example or generalization
Reasoning from fact or hypothesis
Reasoning from sign
Reciprocal concessions
Rejection then retreat
Rule of reciprocation
Scrambling cause-effect
Self-evident truths
Slippery slope
Slogans
Standard/learned principles
Stealth marketing
Strategic ambiguities
Symbols
Tabloid thinking
Thin entering edge
Transferring guilt
Tu quoque
Undercover marketing
Values

A Persuasive Interview for Review and Analysis

This interview is between Marci Overmeyer representing the Environmental League of America and Darrell Roloff. It is taking place at the front door of the Roloff home in Trout Lake, a city of approximately 30,000 in upstate New York. Marci is going door-to-door introducing people to the ELA and trying to persuade them to sign a petition to be sent to the state assembly and to make a "significant" contribution. Darrell is concerned about environmental issues but feels hounded by charities and special interest groups asking for money. He is reluctant to sign his name to any document unless he feels the organization is both legitimate and effective.

Since persuasion is done with and not to an interviewee, how mutual is this interview? How active and critical is the interviewee in the opening, the need step, establishing a set of criteria, analyzing evidence, and weighing the proposed solution?

1. **Interviewer:** Good evening, my name's Marci Overmeyer with the Environmental League of America. How are you this evening?
2. **Interviewee:** Fine thanks. We're just beginning to watch the evening news. What can I do for you?
3. **Interviewer:** I'm one of several volunteers going door-to-door in Trout Lake on behalf of the important work the Environmental League of America is doing to protect our environment through projects and close contacts with the members of the New York Assembly.
4. **Interviewee:** Does volunteer mean that you are unpaid for your efforts?
5. **Interviewer:** Yes it does. We do not use paid or professional representatives, only citizens such as you.
6. **Interviewee:** Do you have some credentials I might see?
7. **Interviewer:** Of course. Here is my name badge and number.
8. **Interviewee:** I see. What can I do for you this evening?
9. **Interviewer:** Well, I mainly want to tell you a little bit about the ELA, the work we do, and how citizens like you can help us.
10. **Interviewee:** Okay, but I only have a few minutes.
11. **Interviewer:** That's fine. The ELA is one of the oldest environmental advocacy groups in the United States. We were first formed as Citizens for the Environment in 1961 in the Upper Peninsula of Michigan because of environmental hazards posed by the abandoned copper mines. Since then, we have organized groups in all 50 states. We changed our name to the ELA about 10 years ago.
12. **Interviewee:** What exactly does the ELA do besides organize?
13. **Interviewer:** Well, let me ask you, do you think we face an environmental crisis?
14. **Interviewee:** I think we face a lot of environmental problems, but I'm not sure it's a crisis.
15. **Interviewer:** We see a crisis when there is evidence of serious global warming, rain forests are disappearing by millions of acres each year, the oceans have enormous

areas of floating garbage, and our lakes and rivers are polluted. That's a crisis, don't you agree?

16. **Interviewee:** Yes, I think that's true. But what does ELA do? What are its effects?
17. **Interviewer:** Well, let me give one important example. I'm sure you've seen some of the large wind farms, many with hundreds of windmills, just north of this city.
18. **Interviewee:** Yes, they're impressive in size and number.
19. **Interviewer:** If it were not for the ELA, those probably would not be there. The companies such as BP were set on building more coal-fired power plants, some of the worst polluters in the world. We petitioned the companies, the state, and the federal government and, largely through our efforts, the wind farms came online instead of power plants. This may be our biggest achievement in the past 20 years.
20. **Interviewee:** What proof do you have that your petitions did all of this?
21. **Interviewer:** Some of these companies tried to counter our efforts through the media and lobbying efforts at the state and national levels. We were their number one target. Now that they have accepted our solution, wind farms, they have privately told us that we turned the tide, so to speak.
22. **Interviewee:** That's interesting. I read a story covering the phenomenal rise of wind farms in this area that claimed that BP and some of the power companies had been targeting this area for several years and were only waiting on technology from Europe.
23. **Interviewer:** I think a lot of that was face-saving propaganda. They acted because the handwriting was on the wall, so to speak, with a lot of pressure coming from Washington and grassroots movements such as ours.
24. **Interviewee:** Then you agree that ELA did not bring about wind farms all by itself.
25. **Interviewer:** Of course. I didn't mean to say we did it alone, but we were a major player.
26. **Interviewee:** What other environmental issue is ELA targeting at present?
27. **Interviewer:** In this part of the country, we have been working with farmers to reduce the amount of fertilizers and herbicides they use to reduce the serious pollution of our creeks and rivers. During this past year alone, the amount of fertilizers and herbicides used on corn and soybean fields has dropped by 18 percent. And that's just a start.
28. **Interviewee:** I read in the paper that the use of fertilizers and herbicides had dropped this year, but one national agricultural analyst attributed this drop to the economic recession. Farmers were forced to cut back to reduce costs. Why do you think ELA was the main cause?
29. **Interviewer:** We've had many recessions over the years, but this is the first significant decline in fertilizer and herbicide use in almost 30 years. We have put a lot of our time and money into this problem and solution. I think we both agree that we have significant environmental problems that must be addressed now. Only the people can demand changes that will address these problems.
30. **Interviewee:** Yes, I think I can agree with that. I don't doubt the power of the people when they get behind something, but I do question simple cause-effect claims when many forces are at work.

31. **Interviewer:** I understand. It's just that ELA has been in the trenches for a long time, and it's great to see the fruits of its labor.

32. **Interviewee:** What are you trying to do this evening—while I'm missing the news?

33. **Interviewer:** I have a petition that, as you can see, many of your neighbors have already signed, that is aimed at supporting legislation in the state that would require all coal-burning power plants to install the new technology that greatly reduces the carbon emissions of these plants. Can I have your signature along with your neighbors'?

34. **Interviewee:** I take signing a document very seriously. If my signature is on something, I want to be able to stand behind it.

35. **Interviewer:** I feel the same way.

36. **Interviewee:** I will need some literature that explains the nature of the ELA and documents what it has done. Signing a petition at my door after a few minutes of discussion is not a wise thing to do.

37. **Interviewer:** I can appreciate that, and we would be happy to send you some materials that prove we are an effective guardian of the environment. Mailing such materials is expensive of course. Would you consider a donation to our cause that would cover such materials and further our cause?

38. **Interviewee:** What did you have in mind?

39. **Interviewer:** We usually ask for a minimum donation of $50.

40. **Interviewee:** That's a lot of money for a few pieces of literature.

41. **Interviewer:** It sounds like a lot until you figure in the cost of postage, handling, materials, and organizational items we automatically include such as a tee shirt, calendar, and note pad. These help get our message across and name better known.

42. **Interviewee:** I'm not very interested in a tee shirt. All I want is some simple literature that shows why I should support the ELA instead of some other group. If your case is as impressive as you suggest, I will be happy to send a donation that more than covers your expenses and materials.

43. **Interviewer:** I'm sure you will, but organizational policy dictates that a mailing can only follow a minimal donation. Fifty dollars is not a lot of money.

44. **Interviewee:** Fifty dollars does not sound like a lot unless you factor in all of the other worthwhile groups that seem to be constantly asking for donations. We seem bombarded with them; all arguing for good causes.

45. **Interviewer:** I understand. I'm sure I get many of the same requests. Perhaps you can weigh the seriousness of the environmental crisis with other needs of a less urgent nature.

46. **Interviewee:** They all claim great need and are accompanied by fear appeals and pictures of starving or suffering people.

47. **Interviewer:** Let me have your name and address, and I will try to get some materials to you that report what we do with signatures and funds and what we have accomplished over the years.

48. **Interviewee:** That sounds good to me. Here is my business card with name and address.
49. **Interviewer:** Thank you very much—Mr. Roloff. I really appreciate you talking to me and your interest in our mission.

Persuasion Role-Playing Cases

A Home Security System

The interviewer's grandparents are in their 80s and live in an old, established neighborhood in Atlanta. Until recently, robberies and home break-ins rarely happened in this historic district and many people did not lock their doors. Robberies and break-ins are now becoming commonplace with elderly people being prime targets. These elderly victims are often attacked physically even when they do not put up any resistance. She believes her grandparents should have a security system installed immediately before they become victims and has been shopping around to locate the best systems.

The interviewees have always been independent and are in good physical condition. They see their granddaughter as a worrier and feel the problem is a fad that will soon disappear after the police apprehend a few troublemakers. Although they are now locking their doors and have installed dawn-to-dusk lights in the front and back yards, at their granddaughter's insistence, they feel installing a security system is both too expensive and unnecessary. After all, they have loaded handguns in the house and know how to use them. The grandfather, a former Marine, has remarked, "Let them try to break in here. It will be their last."

A New Type of Seed Corn

The interviewer is a sales representative for Harvest Gold Hybrids that has a new type of seed corn on the market that has proved in tests to be quite effective in fighting wireworms. The intent of this new hybrid seed is to prevent wireworms from getting into seed in the field before it has a chance to sprout. He first met the interviewee, a farmer-owner of a 2000-acre grain farm in western Ohio, when he was a college intern with Harvest Gold Hybrids. He's now in his second year as a sales representative for Harvest Gold and knows wireworms are a problem in this area.

The interviewee used Harvest Gold Hybrids in the past but switched to Premium Hybrids three years ago to fight wireworms more effectively. He remembers the interviewer and knows he is young and new to the seed market and sales. Although he is willing to talk about the new hybrid, he is planning to switch rather than fight the problem by planting soybeans and wheat instead of corn. A friend of his in eastern Indiana made the switch two years ago and is pleased with the results.

Preserve a Historical Home

The Cable home was built in the country in the early 1850s, some 10 miles from St. Charles, Missouri. Many of the imported materials were shipped from Italy, Germany, and Switzerland, transported up the Mississippi River, and then carried by wagon to the home site. It remained in the Cable family until the 1960s when the last of the family died. Since then, several people have owned the home, the most recent owner turning it into a bed and breakfast that went out of business in 1998. Since then it has remained empty and in growing disrepair. The roof leaks; the ornate porch is sagging; the original plaster walls are cracking; and both electrical and plumbing systems are in serious need of updating to meet county codes. The interviewer purchased the home for $70,000 but needs at least $250,000 to restore it to its glory days. She is contacting the director of the State Department of Historic Preservation to obtain a grant to initiate restoration work.

The director of the State Department of Historic Preservation has read the persuader's prospectus for the Cable home and is sympathetic. However, the director is swamped with proposals to preserve old homes in the state and has limited funds to support only a few projects each year. The director is curious about how much money the new owner is willing to invest in this historic home.

Need for Additional Staff

The interviewer is the production manager of BJO Automotive, a small supplier of parts to several American and Japanese auto manufacturers. During the severe recession of 2008–2009 when automotive sales declined sharply and two clients, GM and Chrysler, faced bankruptcy, his staff of 575 was reduced to a mere 250. This worked during the height of the recession, but now several auto manufacturers are experiencing double-digit percentage gains in sales from the past two years and are ramping up production of new, more fuel-efficient models. The upper management's response is to give overtime to the current staff and work them six or seven days a week. This is taking a toll on workers and is still not enough to get parts to manufacturers "on time." She is proposing the hiring of 100 additional production workers.

The CEO is aware of the overtime problems, including cost, and rising complaints from some auto companies. At the same time, he is concerned that these rising sales figures may be a bubble that will burst when things settle down in a few months. In particular, he believes that the government's "cash for clunkers" program produced an artificial sales bump when inventories of autos were in need of replenishing. He wants to wait to see what happens over the next 12 months.

Student Activities

1. Go with a person who is in the process of making a major purchase: auto, home, boat, piano, jewelry. See if you can detect the use of psychological strategies by the persuader: standard/learned principles, the contrast principle, the rule of reciprocation, reciprocal concessions, and rejection then retreat.
2. Every family has a member who is famous for driving hard bargains and getting better deals than anyone else. Identify such a person in your family and go with this person to a persuasive interview; it need not be a sales situation. Observe the roles the person plays in the opening, how the person handles the need or desire the persuader is trying to create, the information the person obtains and the objections and questions raised about the solution, and how the person negotiates a final decision. If the person threatens to leave or go to a competitor, how does the persuader react?

3. Go to the Internet and observe the use of language strategies designed to entice you to purchase products and services. How do they communicate urgency and scarcity? What functions do jargon, euphemisms, and strategic ambiguities play? How do they make complex problems, issues, and decisions appear simple? Which logical strategies are most common, and how can you explain this?
4. Over a two-week period, keep a log of telephone and e-mail solicitations you receive. How well are these adapted to your demographic characteristics, needs, motives, and desires? Which values and emotions do they use as triggering devices? Which types of evidence do they employ? Do they employ ethically questionable tactics? How do they react when you raise objections? How do they close interviews?

Notes

1. Richard L. Johannesen, "Perspectives on Ethics in Persuasion," in *Persuasion: Reception and Responsibility* by Charles U. Larson (Belmont, CA: Thomson/Wadsworth, 2004), p. 27.
2. Herbert W. Simons, *Persuasion in Society* (Thousand Oaks, CA: Sage, 2001), p. 374.
3. Simons, p. 374.
4. Johannesen, p. 32.
5. Omar Swartz, *Persuasion as a Critical Activity: Application and Engagement* (Dubuque, IA: Kendall/Hunt, 2009), pp. 321–322.
6. Gary C. Woodward and Robert E. Denton, Jr., *Persuasion and Influence in American Life* (Long Grove, IL: Waveland Press, 2004), p. 348.
7. James Price Dillard and Michael Pfau, eds., *The Persuasion Handbook: Developments in Theory and Practice* (Thousand Oaks, CA: Sage, 2002), pp. 4–14.
8. Johannesen, p. 28.
9. Woodward and Denton, p. 348.
10. Johannesen, p. 31.
11. Kelton V. Rhoads and Robert B. Cialdini, "The Business of Influence: Principles That Lead to Success in Commercial Settings," in *The Persuasion Handbook: Developments in Theory and Practice,* James Price Dillard and Michael Pfau, eds. (Thousand Oaks, CA: Sage, 2002), pp. 514–517; Robert B. Cialdini, *Influence: Science and Practice* (New York: HarperCollins, 1993), pp. 19–44.
12. Gary C. Woodward and Robert E. Denton, Jr., *Persuasion and Influence in American Life* (Long Grove, IL: Waveland Press, 2009), p. 30.
13. Larson, pp. 103–104.
14. See Woodward and Denton (2009), pp. 69–73; Larson, pp. 118–146; Swartz, pp. 273–291.

15. Woodward and Denton (2009), p. 72.
16. Lafayette, IN, *Journal & Courier*, April 13, 2002, p. A4.
17. West Lafayette, IN, *The Exponent*, August 22, 2003, p. B1.
18. See Woodward and Denton (2009), pp. 85–95; Larson, pp. 184–215.
19. See Simons, pp. 167–171.

Resources

Cialdini, Robert B. *Influence: Science and Practice*. Boston: Allyn and Bacon, 2000.

Dillard, James Price, and Michael Pfau, eds. *The Persuasion Handbook: Developments in Theory and Practice*. Thousand Oaks, CA: Sage, 2002.

Larson, Charles U. *Persuasion: Reception and Responsibility.* Belmont, CA: Thomson/Wadsworth, 2007.

Seiter, John S., and Robert H. Gass, eds. *Perspectives on Persuasion, Social Influence, and Compliance Gaining.* Boston: Pearson Education, 2007.

Woodward, Gary C., and Robert E. Denton, Jr. *Persuasion and Influence in American Life.* Long Grove, IL: Waveland Press, 2009.

CHAPTER 12 The Counseling Interview

This chapter introduces you to the counseling interview, perhaps the most sensitive of interviews because it occurs when persons feel incapable or unsure of themselves and how to address a *personal* problem—work performance, grades, finances, relationship, health. Merely asking for assistance may be a blow to a person's ego and pride because we are taught to be independent, to "stand on our own two feet," to be a man or woman, and to solve our own problems. The goal of the counseling interview is to *assist* another person in gaining insight into and coping with a problem; it is not to *resolve* the problem for this person. That is why many prefer to call it the *helping interview*.

Trust may overcome lack of expertise.

The counseling or helping interview is an everyday activity for each of us as coworkers, friends, family members, students, club members, or neighbors approach us with a problem, need for advice, or a bit of help. Your training in counseling may range from none to a few hours, even in your position as clergy, physician, teacher, student, lawyer, or manager. Some experts in crisis management point out that in a time of crisis, "Everyone is a resource."[1] Fortunately, the *lay counselor* has proven to be quite successful. People seeking help trust persons similar to them who appear to be open, caring, and willing to listen.[2] Nearly every state has a CASA (Court Appointed Special Advocate for children) program in which carefully screened volunteers from the community undergo several weeks of training and then become advocates for children who are abused and neglected. They work closely with children to get to know them and their situations and serve as the children's "voice in court." The result is better outcomes for children who become involved in the social and legal systems.

Be a helper, not a problem solver.

This chapter introduces you to the basic principles of the counseling interview so you can help those who turn to you for assistance with day-to-day problems in their personal and work lives. **It does not prepare you to be a psychotherapist or to handle critical problems such as drug or alcohol abuse, severe psychological problems, or legal issues.**

Preparing for the Counseling Interview

Start preparing for a counseling interview with a thorough and insightful analysis of the interview parties, focusing first on you as the interviewer–helper.

Do not stray beyond your level of expertise.

Analyzing Self

You will find it difficult to help others if you do not know yourself. Cormier, Nurius, and Osborn write that "Self-awareness is an important aspect of competence and involves a balanced assessment of our strengths and limitations."[3] You bring your entire self to each counseling interview, including your personality, values, attitudes, culture, and experiences.

Strengths and Limitations

Be realistic about your counseling skills. Do not try to handle situations for which you have neither the experience nor the training. Know when to refer the interviewee to a professional with greater skills and expertise. A teacher, for instance, must know when a student needs psychological or medical rather than academic help. Ask yourself questions such as these: Are you an active listener? Are you people-centered rather than problem-centered? Can you be sensitive to others' needs? Are you able to communicate understanding, warmth, comfort, and reassurance? Can you give your undivided and focused attention? Can you provide appropriate nonverbal and verbal responses? Can you guide the direction and flow of the interview without ordering, prescribing, or persuading? Can you restrain your personal needs and beliefs?

Be aware of the dangers in trying to help others. You may give bad advice. You may get blamed for outcomes or lack of them. You may get emotionally involved. Some sources warn that you may become sexually involved. Thousands of men and women helped families, friends, and co-workers following the tragedy of September 11, 2001. In some cases, the helpers became emotionally and sexually involved to the extent that they destroyed their own families while trying to help other families.

Personality Characteristics

Research indicates that qualities intrinsic to the personalities, attitudes, and nonverbal behavior of interviewers—rather than gender or ethnic group membership—largely account for counseling effectiveness.[4] Review your personality traits. Good counselors are open-minded, optimistic, self-assured, relaxed, flexible, and patient. They are good listeners. Jeffrey Kottler, author of *A Brief Primer of Helping Skills,* writes, "I'll say that again: *Listening is the most crucial helping skill.*"[5] They are not argumentative or defensive. How comfortable are you in disclosing your motives, feelings, and beliefs? Some sources claim that an interviewer's self-disclosure of personal experiences and background helps the interviewee gain insights and new perspectives for making changes because of an equalized relationship and reassurance.[6] Others warn, however, that while sharing personal stories may be very powerful, such sharing may appear to be self-indulgent to the interviewee and detract from the interviewee's own experience.[7]

How comfortable are you when people reveal embarrassing problems and incidents or express intense feelings such as sorrow, fear, and anger? Society provides us with all sorts of euphemisms for vagina, breasts, penis, buttocks, masturbation, rape, and intercourse. How comfortable are you with using technical terms and proper names for conditions, actions, and body parts? How comfortable are you when others use the proper terms?

Values

Be aware of the importance of the values you hold and how they compare to those of the interviewee. The values held by the two parties may affect all aspects of counseling interactions, and Helen Cameron warns, "Anyone who feels they can operate from a *value neutral* perspective is deeply mistaken."[8] You transmit your values through dress, appearance, eye contact, words, and manner. Although it is impossible to be value neutral or free, you must strive to understand and respect the interviewee's values that may be very different from your own. For instance, a college friend who is struggling academically may turn to you for help. You cherish values such as education, dependability, punctuality, close relationship with your professors, and a high GPA. Your roommate sees education as an unpleasant interlude to getting a job, goes to class occasionally, is late to team project meetings, misses most deadlines for assignments, sees no need to develop relationships with professors, and is satisfied with the lowest GPA that will allow him to graduate. Can you "set aside" your values or "suspend judgment" so you can help your roommate?

Cultural Awareness

Culture and cultural differences between the parties may have a variety of effects on counseling interviews, and being culturally unaware is unacceptable. Paul Pedersen claims, "Culture controls our lives and defines reality for each of us, with or without our permission and/or intentional awareness."[9] When you think of culture, the usual categories come to mind: age, gender, race, ethnicity, and national origin, but Cormier, Nurius, and Osborn "recommend that helpers regard *all* conversations with clients as 'cross-cultural.'"[10] Along with the usual categories you should include sexual orientation, socioeconomic class, geographical area, religion or spirituality, physical and mental abilities, and family form.

Research indicates that culture may determine the extent of self-disclosure in counseling interviews.

Self-disclosure varies from person to person.

Females tend to disclose significantly more about themselves and their problems than do males, especially on intimate topics such as sex, and a person's self-disclosure history often affects disclosure in other interviews.[11] Males often have psychological defenses to protect themselves from feelings of weakness and to restrict emotional reactions.[12] A study of African-Americans engaging in counseling at a community health agency discovered that African-Americans in this setting "engaged in an ongoing assessing process. Initially, they assessed client-therapist match [white or black], which was influenced by three factors: salience of Black identity, court involvement, and ideology similarity between client and therapist. These clients then assessed their safety in therapy and their counselor's effectiveness simultaneously." They used this information to "monitor and manage their degree of self-disclosing along a continuum."[13] Another study supported the importance of counselor self-disclosure in cross-cultural counseling—particularly their reactions to and experiences of racism or oppression. Such counselor self-disclosure typically improved the counseling relationship and made clients feel more understood.[14]

Other research reveals how different cultures see the authority of counselors. In some Eastern cultures, people see counselors as authority figures and may find a nondirective interviewing approach unsettling because the authority has turned the interview over to them to control.[15]

If you feel you are inadequately prepared for cross-cultural helping sessions, training will help.

A study of white racial identity in counseling interviews recommended that counselors "who are racially unaware must obtain sufficient training to aid them in becoming multiculturally competent." This training should "emphasize racial and cultural self-awareness, knowledge about other racial and cultural groups in the context of interpersonal interactions (e.g., counseling relationships), and skill development in terms of intervening with clients in a culturally appropriate manner."[16] Refer to resources contained at the end of this chapter. Improve your cultural awareness by avoiding generalizations such as all Asian students are high achievers, all Hispanics are illegal immigrants, all poor people are lazy, and all women are nurturing. There is diversity within diversity. Be open-minded by avoiding stereotypes. Try to meet people where they are, not where you think they ought to be. Don't assume the best or correct values belong to your culture exclusively. Employ culturally appropriate nonverbal and verbal messages. Don't impose your gender-based values.

Relationship

Be aware of past, present, and future events.

Think very carefully about your relationship with the interviewee because it is crucial to every counseling interview. Sherry Cormier and her colleagues write, "The potential value of a sound relationship base cannot be overlooked because the relationship is the specific part of the process that conveys the counselor's interest in and acceptance of the client as a unique and worthwhile person and builds sufficient trust for eventual self-disclosure and self-revelation to occur."[17] Review the critical dimensions of relationships discussed in Chapter 1: similarity, inclusion/involvement, affection/liking, control/dominance, and trust. Of all these dimensions, trust/safety may be the most important. Some call it the "core trait" or the essential element of the helping interview.[18] Without trust, an interview with you is unlikely to take place.

What social or professional relations do you have in common? What values, beliefs, and attitudes do you share? Under what circumstances and how effectively have you counseled this person before? How much do you trust one another? How will control be shared? One study found that those not yet contemplating change (compared to those who were contemplating change, already engaged in change, or maintaining previous changes) have significantly lower expectations of help and the interviewer's acceptance, genuineness, and trustworthiness.[19] Other studies have shown that when there is a match of worldviews between interviewer and interviewee, particularly agreement on the causes of problems, good working relationships are established and interviewees feel more understood. On the other hand, a mismatch may hinder the relationship, particularly when counseling Asian-Americans.[20]

Analyzing the Interviewee

A thorough analysis of the interviewee prior to the interview will enable you to focus the interview on the *person* rather than *gathering information.*

Information Gathering

Be aware of potentially relevant information such as gender, age, ethnicity, socioeconomic status, education, work history, family background, memberships, medical and psychological histories, test results, and past problems and courses of action. If you have been in a helping relationship with this person in the past, what were the problems and outcomes? Talk to people who know the interviewee well (instructors, employers, counselors, family members, friends, and fellow workers) to gain insights into the person and why the person may be coming to you at this time.

Review information from other sources carefully. Think of when you formed a negative, defensive, or wary attitude toward a person because of what other people had told you, only to discover the opposite seemed true when you interacted with the person. Do not allow preconceptions (yours or others') to prejudice the interview, to prejudge the interviewee, or to formulate a defensive or antagonistic approach. This is particularly important when working with children.

Anticipating Questions and Responses

If you know an interviewee thoroughly prior to the interview, you may anticipate and respond effectively to common questions and comments such as the following:

Be prepared for rejections of offers to counsel.

If I need help, I'll let you know.

I can take care of myself.

I need to get back to work.

Why should I discuss my personal problems with you?

You wouldn't understand.

Don't tell Mom and Dad.

Just tell me what I should do.

No one knows how I feel.

You don't know what it's like being a student (parent, patient, teenager).

Get off my back.

I can't afford to take time off.

The more thoroughly you have analyzed the interviewee, the more likely you are to know *why* a person is reacting in a particular way and how you might reply effectively.

Listen rather than talk.

If an interviewee asks for help without notice or explanation and you have no relational history with this person, rely on your training and experiences to discover what is bothering the person and how you might help. Do not assume you know why a person is calling, showing up at your door, or bringing up a topic. Ask a few open-ended questions that enable the interviewee to explain the purpose of the interview and listen carefully for information and insights that will enable you to help this person.

Considering Interviewing Approaches

After carefully analyzing yourself and the interviewee, consider appropriate interviewing approaches. Chapter 2 introduced you to two fundamental approaches, *directive* and *nondirective* and their advantages and disadvantages. The sensitive and potentially explosive nature of the counseling interview necessitates a careful selection of approach.

Directive Approach

When using a **directive approach,** you control the structure of the interview, subject matter attended to and avoided, pace of interactions, and length of the interview. You collect and share information, define and analyze problems, suggest and evaluate solutions, and provide guidelines for actions. In brief, you serve as an expert or consultant who analyzes problems and provides guidelines for actions.

Know when to maintain control and when to let go.

The interviewee is more of a reactor and recipient than an equal or major player in the interaction. The directive approach is based on the assumption that you know more about the problem than the interviewee and are better suited to analyze it and recommend solutions. The accuracy of this assumption, of course, depends upon you, the interviewee, and the situation.

Nondirective Approach

Is the interviewee capable of or willing to take control?

In the **nondirective approach,** the interviewee controls the structure of the interview, determines the topics, decides when and how they will be discussed, and sets the pace and length of the interview. You assist the interviewee in obtaining information, gaining insights, defining and analyzing problems, and discovering and evaluating solutions. You listen, observe, and encourage but do not impose ideas. Most sources prefer a nondirective approach to counseling and emphasize the interviewer's role as engaging, exploring, encouraging, listening, understanding, affirming, reassuring, and validating rather than ordering, confronting, directing, warning, threatening, cautioning, and judging.[21]

The nondirective approach is based on the assumption that the interviewee is more capable than you of analyzing problems, assessing solutions, and making correct decisions. After all, the interviewee must implement recommendations and solutions.

The accuracy of this assumption, like the directive assumption, depends on you, the interviewee, and the situation. The interviewee may know nothing about the problem or potential solutions, or worse, may be misinformed about both.

Do not assume the problem is lack of information.

The interviewee's problem may not be lack of information or misinformation but the inability to visualize a current or future problem or make sound decisions. The person may be hopelessly confused about what to do or how to do it. You serve as an objective, neutral referee, presenting pros and cons of specific courses of action. Distinguish between when you are serving as expert advisor and when, perhaps subtly and unintentionally, you are imposing personal preferences.

On the other hand, the interviewee may prefer a directive (highly structured) approach. A study of Asian-American students discovered that when career counselors used a directive approach, students saw them as more empathetic, culturally competent, and providing concrete guidance that produced immediate benefits.[22]

Combination of Approaches

Be flexible in choosing and changing approaches.

Many counseling interviewers employ a combination of directive and nondirective approaches. You may, for instance, begin with a nondirective approach to encourage the interviewee to talk and reveal the problem and its causes. Then you may switch to a more directive approach when discussing possible solutions or courses of action. A directive approach is best for obtaining facts, giving information, and making diagnoses, while a nondirective approach tends to open up large areas and bring out a great deal of spontaneous information.

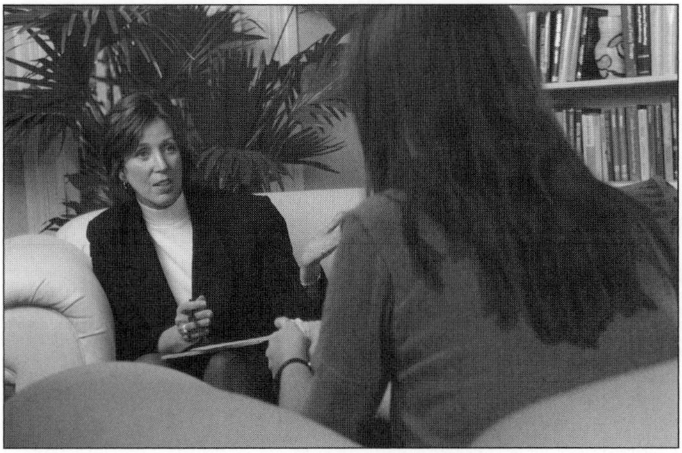

Provide a climate conducive to effective counseling, which is a quiet, comfortable, private location, free of interruptions.

Selecting the Setting

Consider carefully the climate and tone of the interview. Both will affect the levels of communication that will take place and the willingness of both parties to disclose feelings and attitudes.

Provide a climate conducive to good counseling—a quiet, comfortable, private location, free of interruptions. You cannot expect an interviewee to be open and honest if other employees, students, workers, or clients can overhear the conversation. Select a neutral location such as a restaurant, lounge, park, or organization's cafeteria where the interviewee might feel less threatened and more relaxed. Some interviewees feel comfortable or safe only on their own turf, so consider meeting in the person's room, home, office, or place of business.

Do not underestimate the importance of location and seating.

When possible, arrange the seating so that both interviewer and interviewee are able to communicate freely. You may want to sit on the floor with a child, perhaps playing a game or looking at a book or favorite toy. Studies suggest that the **situation** is the most important variable in determining level of self-disclosure and that an optimal interpersonal distance is 3.5 feet. Many students comment that an interviewer behind a desk makes them ill at ease, as though the "mighty one" is sitting in judgment. They prefer to sit in a chair at the end of the desk—at a right angle to the interviewer—or in chairs facing one another with no desk in between.

A round table is a traditional arrangement for problem solving.

Arrangements of furniture can contribute to or detract from the informal, conversational atmosphere so important in counseling sessions. Many counseling interviewers are discovering that a round table, similar to a dining room or kitchen table, is preferred by interviewees because it includes no power or leader position. Interviewees seem to like this arrangement because they have often handled family matters around the dining or kitchen table.

Conducting the Interview

As you approach the interview, keep important principles in mind. Realize that you are "investing in people" and that people can change, grow, and improve. You must be able to accept the person as the person is, so don't approach the interview as an opportunity to remodel an individual to your liking. The interview is a learning process for both parties and is unlikely to be a one-shot effort.[23]

The Opening

Want to help and show it.

The first minutes of a counseling session set the verbal and psychological tone for the remainder. Greet the interviewee by name in a warm, friendly manner, being natural and sincere. Show you want to be involved and to help. Do not be condescending or patronizing. You might want to say, "It's about time you showed up!" or "What have you done this time?" Stifle your frustration or irritation. Accept the interviewee as he or she is and try to understand "the client's world from inside the client's frame of reference."[24]

Initial Comments and Reactions

Do not try to second-guess the interviewee's reason for making an appointment or dropping by. It is natural and tempting to make statements such as:

Are you still fighting with your roommate?

I assume you want to be excused from class again.

I suppose this is about money.

I know why you're here.

A person may not have initiated this interview for any of these reasons but may feel threatened or angry by your comment and attitude. At the least, your interruption and comment may ruin an opening the interviewee has prepared that would have revealed why the interviewee has turned to you for help.

Be tactful and neutral but not indifferent.

Avoid tactless and leading reactions all too common in interactions with family members, children, friends, and associates. All of us have been on the receiving end of such statements as:

Why did you pierce your tongue?

You look awful.

You've been turning work in on time, haven't you?

Looks like you've put on a few pounds.

When did you get red hair?

Such comments and questions can destroy the climate and tone necessary for a successful counseling interview and destroy the interviewee's self-confidence and self-esteem.

Rapport and Orientation

Accept seemingly irrelevant opening comments.

The counseling interview may consume considerable time getting acquainted and establishing a working relationship, even when your relationship with the interviewee has a long history. This relational history may be positive or negative because both parties monitor previous interactions and enter a new exchange with high or low expectations. It may be a critical factor in self-disclosure. The counseling interview is often more threatening than other interactions. An interviewee may begin by talking about the building, your office, books on the shelves, pictures on the walls, the view out the window, the weather, or sports unrelated to the interview topic and purpose. Be patient. The interviewee is sizing up you, the situation, and the setting and is, perhaps, building up the nerve to introduce the issue of concern.

The **rapport** stage, in which you establish a feeling of goodwill with the interviewee, is your chance to show attention, interest, fairness, willingness to listen, and ability to maintain confidences. You can discover the interviewee's expectations and apprehensions about the interview and attitudes toward you, your position, your organization, and counseling sessions in general.

When rapport and orientation are completed, let the interviewee begin with what seems to be of most interest or concern. This is the first step toward the precise nature of the problem that the interviewee has been unable to face or resolve. Do not rush this process; be patient. The person's nonverbal cues may reveal inner feelings and their intensity.

Encouraging Self-Disclosure

Disclosure of beliefs, attitudes, concerns, and feelings determines the success of the counseling interview and is a major factor in the interviewee's decision to seek or not seek help.[25] Studies reveal that "self-disclosing is a very complex process that involves intricate decision making."[26] The climate conducive for this disclosure begins during the opening minutes of the interaction. If positive, it creates a trusting relationship and engenders "feelings of safety, pride, and authenticity." The interviewee may come to see that keeping secrets inhibits" the helping process "whereas disclosing produces a sense of relief from physical as well as emotional tension."[27] During this early stage, focus attention on strengths and achievements rather than weaknesses and failures and on what is most in need of attention. This approach builds confidence and a feeling that it is safe to disclose beliefs, attitudes, and feelings with you.

You may encourage interviewee disclosure by disclosing your feelings and attitudes, ensuring confidentiality, and using appropriate humor.[28] Although full self-disclosure is a desirable goal, an interviewee may be less tense and more willing to talk to you by hiding some undesirable facets of themselves.[29]

Work within a known time frame.

If you initiate the counseling session, state clearly and honestly what you want to talk about. If there is a specific amount of time allotted for the interview, make this known so you can work within it. The interviewee will be more at ease knowing how much time is available. Quality is more important than the length of time spent with an interviewee.[30] Attire and role behavior significantly affect the interviewee's perceptions of attractiveness and level of expertise and determine how closely the person will be drawn to you and the level of self-disclosure.

Although you will play many roles in each counseling interview, four dominate: listening, observing, questioning, and responding.

Listening

Focus on the interviewee and the interviewee's problem.

Listening is the most important skill to master. Listen for empathy so you can reassure, comfort, express warmth, and try to place yourself in the interviewee's situation and world. Listen for comprehension so you can be patient, receive, understand, and recall interactions accurately and completely. Avoid listening for evaluation that judges and may openly criticize. Directly or indirectly moralizing, blaming, questioning, and disagreeing are major roadblocks to effective counseling.[31] To get to the heart of a problem, you must give undivided attention to the interviewee's words and their implications and to what is intentionally or unintentionally left unmentioned. Be genuinely interested in what the person is saying.

Do not interrupt or take over the conversation. Beware of interjecting personal opinions, experiences, or problems. Too often, a person may want to talk about a serious illness of a father or mother, but the counselor takes over with a story about his or her own family illness.

If the interviewee pauses or stops talking for a few moments, do not chatter to fill in the silence. Use silence to encourage the interviewee to continue talking. Rebecca Leonard suggests several nonverbal behaviors that communicate a willingness to listen: lean toward and face the other person squarely, maintain good eye contact, and reflect attention through facial expressions.[32] Interviewees tend to interpret smiles, attentive body postures, and gestures as evidence of warmth and enthusiasm.

Observing

Look for nonverbal signals but interpret them cautiously.

Observe how the interviewee sits, gestures, fidgets, and maintains eye contact. Pay attention to the voice for loudness, timidity, evidence of tenseness, and changes. These observations provide clues about the seriousness of the problem and the interviewee's state of mind. Deceptive answers may be lengthier, more hesitant, and characterized by longer pauses. People maintain eye contact longer when they lie.

If you are going to take notes or record the interview, explain why, and stop if you detect that either activity is affecting the interview adversely. Many people are hesitant to leave a recording that others might hear. They are willing to confide in you, not others.

Questioning

Do not ask too many questions.

Questions play important roles in counseling interviews, but asking too many questions is a common mistake. Questions may interrupt the interviewee, change topics prematurely, and break the flow of self-disclosure. Numerous questions reduce the interviewee to a mere respondent and may stifle the interviewee's own questions.

Keep your questions open-ended.

Open-ended questions encourage interviewees to talk and express emotions. Both are very important for encouraging, reflecting, and questioning about feelings and restating and probing for information.[33] Ask one question at a time because double-barreled questions result in ambiguous answers with neither portion answered clearly and thoroughly. Use encouragement probes such as:

And?	I see.
Uh-huh?	Go on.
Then what happened?	And then?

Use *informational probes* for clarification, explanation, and in-depth information. For example:

Tell me why you think that happened.

How exactly did she react to your comments?

What do you mean he "overreacted" during this incident?

Tell me more about your confrontation with Professor Barger.

The *clearinghouse probe* can ensure that you have obtained all necessary information about an incident or problem. For instance:

What if anything happened after that?

Have you given me all of the important details?

Is there anything else you would like to talk about?

Have I answered all of your questions about a communication major?

Some questions can help interviewees *make meanings* of situations. Steele and Echterling provide these examples:

What worries you most right now?

What do you think you can learn from this?

What scares you most now?

They also provide examples of what they call *getting through* questions that help interviewees manage their emotions.[34] For example:

How did you get through that?

How are you finding it possible to get through this family crisis?

What did you do to feel better about this?

Avoid **curious probes** into feelings and embarrassing incidents, especially if the interviewee seems hesitant to elaborate. Beware of questions that communicate disapproval, displeasure, or mistrust and make the interviewee less open and trusting. Avoid leading questions except under *unusual* circumstances. Counselors working with children may go through intensive training in programs such as "Finding Words" that stress the use of nonleading questions. Avoid *why* questions that appear to demand explanations and justifications and put the interviewee on the defensive. Imagine how an interviewee might react to questions such as, *Why* weren't you on time? *Why* did you do that? *Why* confront Doug? *Why* do you think that?

Phrase all questions with care.

Responding

Selecting appropriate responses to questions and information requests may be difficult. The emphasis in this chapter is on a client-centered approach to the counseling or helping interview in which the interviewer focuses on the interviewee, what the interviewee is saying verbally and nonverbally, and what the interviewee is feeling. This approach suggests appropriate responses to elicit and identify feelings about self, feelings about the problem, and feelings of trust in the interviewer.[35]

A client-centered approach focuses the interview on the interviewee.

Interviewers may respond to interviewee information, questions, comments, and feelings in a variety of ways. These responses may be placed along a continuum from highly nondirective to nondirective, directive, and highly directive.

Center the interview on this interviewee, no one else.

Highly Nondirective Reactions and Responses

Highly nondirective reactions and responses encourage interviewees to continue commenting, analyze ideas and solutions, and be self-reliant. The interviewer offers

Highly nondirective reactions give total control to the interviewee.

no information, assistance, or evaluation of the interviewee, the interviewee's ideas, or possible courses of action.

Remain silent to encourage interviewees to continue or to answer their own questions, as in the following example:

1. **Interviewee:** I'm thinking of quitting the team.
2. **Interviewer:** (silence)
3. **Interviewee:** I'm not getting much playing time and the long practices make it difficult for me to study at night.

Encourage interviewees to continue speaking by employing semi-verbal phrases, such as the following:

1. **Interviewee:** Nothing I do seems to make my supervisor happy.
2. **Interviewer:** Um-hmm.
3. **Interviewee:** She's always on my case even when I'm on time and don't visit with my friends much.

When reacting and responding in a highly nondirective manner, be aware of your *nonverbal behaviors*. Face, tone of voice, speaking rate, and gestures must express sincere interest and reveal empathy. Show you are listening. Interviewees look for subtle signs of approval or disapproval, interest or disinterest. Ruth Purtilo discusses five kinds of smiles, each of which may send a message you do not intend to send: I know something you don't know; poor, poor you; don't tell me; I'm smarter than you; and I don't like you either.[36]

Holding one's hand or a simple touch may reassure a person and show caring and understanding.

Simple nonverbal reactions such as rolling your eyes, raising an eyebrow, crossing your arms, and sitting forward on your chair may adversely affect an interview. Do not prolong silence until it becomes awkward for both parties. If an interviewee seems unable to continue or to go it alone, switch to a different response.

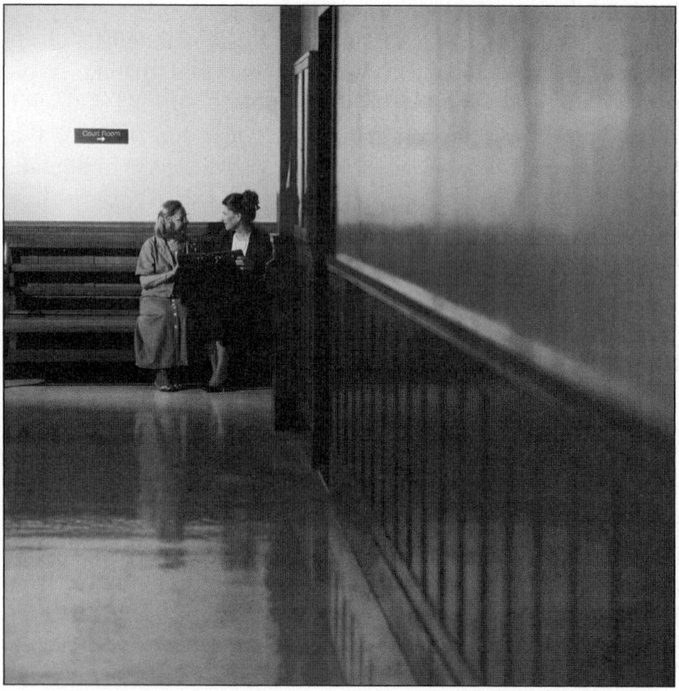

Brand X Pictures

Review the interviewee's file prior to the interview so you can devote full attention during the interview.

A variety of question techniques serve as highly nondirective responses. Silent, nudging, and clearinghouse probes are quite useful. You may restate or repeat an interviewee's question or statement instead of providing answers or volunteering information, ideas, evaluations, or solutions. The goal is to urge the person to elaborate or come up with ideas.

You may *return* a question rather than answer it. The purpose is to encourage the interviewee to analyze problems and select from among possible solutions. A return question looks like this:

Use questions that force the interviewee to formulate answers and solutions.

1. **Interviewee:** Should I ask to be reinstated?
2. **Interviewer:** How do *you* feel about that?

Do not continue to push a decision back if you detect that the individual has insufficient information or is confused, misinformed, genuinely undecided, or unable to make a choice.

Invite the interviewee to discuss a problem or idea. The following is a typical invitation question in counseling interviews:

1. **Interviewee:** I'm beginning to doubt that I can handle this.
2. **Interviewer:** Want to talk about it?

The invitational question asks if the person is *willing* or *interested* in discussing, explaining, or revealing. The interviewer does not intrude with more demanding questions such as, "Tell me about it" or "Such as?" Avoid a *why* question that may communicate criticism or impatience.

Reflective and mirror questions are valuable techniques to make sure you understand what the interviewee has just said or agreed to. They are designed to *clarify* and *verify* questions and statements, not to lead a person toward a preferred point of view. Here is a reflective response:

Use questions to determine what a person is and is not saying.

1. **Interviewee:** I think our relationship is souring.
2. **Interviewer:** Are you saying you are not enjoying your times with Emily as much as you were during the spring?

Reflective questions often begin with phrases such as: "Is it accurate to say . . . ?" "I feel you are saying . . . ?" "If I understand what you're saying, you're . . . ?" and "Let me see if I understand what you're saying . . . ?" They require careful listening and a concerted verbal and nonverbal effort not to lead the interviewee.

Nondirective Reactions and Responses

Nondirective reactions and responses inform and encourage with no imposition of either intended. The following is an example of information giving:

Be an informer rather than a persuader.

1. **Interviewee:** What are my options?
2. **Interviewer:** The university offers you two options at this point of the semester. You may take my course pass/fail so you need to earn only a C grade or you can withdraw from the course by midsemester with a passing grade.

Be specific in answers. If you do not have the information, say so and promise to get it or refer the interviewee to a better-qualified source. Encourage and reassure the interviewee by noting that certain feelings, reactions, or symptoms are normal and to be expected, such as the following:

1. **Interviewee:** I've been back from Afghanistan for six months, and I still duck or drop to the ground when I hear a loud sound. My family gets embarrassed, particularly when it happens in public.
2. **Interviewer:** I know what you are experiencing. It happened to me when I returned from two years in Iraq. It will take you some time, but you will gradually adjust and recognize these for what they are.

A thoughtless comment or two can damage a relationship.

There are quick ways to lose the trust and respect of an interviewee facing a difficult situation. You may give unrealistic assurances such as, "There's nothing to worry about," "I'm sure everything will be just fine," or "Everything works for the best." You may preach to the person with "in the old days" comments such as, "You think you have it tough? When I was your age, I had to . . ." or "When we were first married, we faced . . ." Avoid clichés "like the plague."

Every cloud has a silver lining.

We all have to go sometime.

It's always darkest before the dawn.

It could have been worse.

No pain, no gain.

Be careful of falling into the *we* trap. Think of when you experienced common *we'isms* from counselors, teachers, health care providers, parents, and others.

How are *we* doing this afternoon?

We can handle it.

Let's take it one day at a time.

Are *we* ready for the exam?

You may have felt like shouting, "What do you mean *we*? I'm the one taking the test (getting the shot, undergoing therapy, overcoming grief)!"

Directive Reactions and Responses

Directive reactions and responses go beyond encouragement and information to mild advice and evaluations or judgments. In the following interchange, the interviewer supports the interviewee's ideas and urges action:

Directive responses advise and evaluate but do not dictate.

1. **Interviewee:** I'm terrible at math and don't think I can handle the required course in quantitative research methods.
2. **Interviewer:** I understand your concern, but why don't you try the 200 level course first and see how it goes?

A directive response may mildly question the interviewee's comments or ideas. Be tactful and cautious.

1. **Interviewee:** My supervisor is talking about scheduling me to work on weekends, and that would keep me from visiting my grandmother who raised me.
2. **Interviewer:** Why don't you talk to her about it?

The interviewer may provide information and personal preference when asked, such as:

1. **Interviewee:** If you were in my shoes, what would you do?
2. **Interviewer:** I would work on completing my high school education and then take some courses at the local community college to prepare me for today's workforce.

Directive reactions and responses may challenge an interviewee's actions, ideas, or judgments, or urge the person to pursue a specific course or to accept information or ideas. They are mild, however. Employ directive responses only if nondirective responses do not work.

Highly Directive Reactions and Responses

Reserve **highly directive reactions** and responses for special circumstances. Suggestions and mild advice are replaced with ultimatums and strong advice. The following are examples of highly directive responses and reactions:

Exhaust all less directive means first.

1. **Interviewee:** I don't think I can stop drinking; maybe cut back a bit but not go cold turkey.
2. **Interviewer:** Then how do you expect to get your children back?
3. **Interviewee:** I can be a good mother and drink a bit less.
4. **Interviewer:** You've proven several times that you cannot do both. Your only option is to join an AA group and stop drinking. Otherwise, you'll never get your children back.

Highly directive responses are most appropriate for simple behavioral problems and least appropriate for complex ones that are based on long-time habits or firmly held beliefs and attitudes. Be a helper, not a dictator. The change or solution must come from the interviewee. You can rarely force people to comply with instructions and regimens, even when you have the authority or power to punish them.

Interviewer reactions and responses enhance self-disclosure during interviews, so select appropriate ones.

Know when to become more or less directive.

- Use highly directive responses only after you have established a close relationship with the interviewee.
- Do not be shocked by what you hear.
- Prepare carefully to reduce surprises and make extreme reactions less likely to shock you.
- Do not try to dodge unpleasant facts.

- Be honest and tactful.
- Let your voice, facial expressions, eye contact, and gestures communicate a relaxed, unhurried, confident, warm, and caring image.
- Create a good working relationship with the interviewee.
- Release tensions with tasteful and tactful humor.
- Talk as little as possible.
- Do not interrupt the interviewee.
- Listen empathically.

Research reveals that interviewees who receive positive feedback comply more with the interviewer's requests and recommendations, return more often for counseling, and arrive earlier. These findings led the researcher to conclude that "How interviewers respond seems to make a crucial difference."[37] Interviewees are more likely to implement interviewer recommendations when there is a good match between the recommendation and the problem, the recommendation is not too difficult to implement, and the recommendation is built on the interviewee's strengths.[38]

Closing the Interview

Closing the counseling interview is critical. If interviewees feel they have imposed on you or been pushed out the door as though on an assembly line, progress made during the interview may be erased, including the relationship fostered so carefully throughout.

Involve the interviewee as an active participant in the closing.

The verbal and nonverbal leave-taking actions discussed in Chapter 4 explain how interviews are closed both consciously and unconsciously. Decide which means or combination of means best suits you and the other party.

The interviewee should be able to tell when the closing is commencing. Don't begin new topics or raise new questions. Don't expect to meet all expectations or finish with a neat solution. Be content that you have stirred thought and enabled the interviewee to discuss problems and express feelings. Leave the door open for further interactions.

Evaluating the Interview

Think carefully and critically about the counseling interviews in which you take part. Only through perceptive analysis will you improve your helping interactions with others. Be realistic. They are interactions between complex human beings, at least one of whom has a problem and may not know or admit it.

Review all you did and did not do and accomplish.

Your perceptions of how the interview went and how the interviewee reacted may be exaggerated or incorrect. You will be greatly surprised by your successes and your failures in attempting to help others. Some of each are short-lived.

The following questions serve as guides for your postinterview evaluations.

Preinterview Preparation

How prepared were you for this interaction?

How thoroughly did I review available materials concerning the interviewee?

How effectively did I assess how I communicate and come across with this party?

How thoroughly did I review questions I might ask?

How thoroughly did I review questions the interviewee might ask?

How successfully did I prepare a climate and setting in which openness and disclosure would be fostered?

Structuring the Interview

How effective was the opening?

How effectively did I blend directive and nondirective approaches?

How effectively did I explain all options?

How effective was the closing?

Interviewing Skills

How skillful were my question techniques?

How appropriate were my responses and reactions?

How was the pace of the interview—too fast or too slow?

How effectively did I motivate the interviewee to communicate at Levels 2 and 3?

How effectively did I listen for comprehension, empathy, evaluation, and resolution?

Which skills need more work?

Counseling Skills

How well did I adapt to this party and situation?

How effectively did I help the interviewee gain insights and make decisions?

How effectively did I discover the real problem?

Did I make promises I will not be able to keep?

Did I agree with the interviewee when I should have disagreed?

How did my responses, feedback, and presentation of recommendations enhance the likelihood of interviewee compliance?

The Telephone Interview

Many counseling interviews take place over the telephone, perhaps a cell phone while one or both parties are walking to class, driving to work, having dinner, working in an office, or relaxing after class or during a vacation. Crisis centers have used telephones effectively for many years.

Telephone interviews are common because they are inexpensive, convenient, allow for anonymity (may be "safer" than a face-to-face interaction), can give one a sense of control (you can hang up at any time), and can take place over long distances and at any time of the day or night. Unfortunately, telephone interviews may come at very inconvenient times when a counselor is too busy to talk, is in a different time zone, or is counseling another person. This often happens during office hours. The telephone invites "multitasking" because a party can do other things while "listening" to you.

A recent study of telephone counseling revealed that respondents found "telephone counseling was helpful for both global and specific improvement and that they were satisfied with the counseling they received. Respondents also rated the counseling relationship and level of interpersonal influence similar to face-to-face counseling studies measuring the same attributes."[39] The authors of this study noted the absence of visual contact between interview parties and recommended training for counselors to use their voices as substitutes for place, clothes, nonverbal cues such as eye contact and gestures, and physical appearance.

ON THE WEB

Selecting counseling approaches and responses most appropriate for a particular interviewee and problem may be critical to the outcome of the interview. Philosophies and practices differ among counselors and counseling agencies. Use the Internet to explore the interviewing approaches currently advocated and illustrated by researchers, practitioners, and agencies when dealing with a variety of clients and problems. Useful sources are the Pamphlet Page (http://uhs.uchicago.edu/scrs/vpc/virtulets.html), the Counseling Center Village (http://ub-counseling.buffalo.edu/ccv.html), and Counseling and Psychological Services at Purdue University (http://www.purdue.edu/caps).

Summary

You take part in a counseling interview whenever you try to help a person gain insight into a physical, career, emotional, or social problem and discover ways to cope. The counseling interview may be the most sensitive of interview settings because it usually does not occur until a person feels incapable of handling a problem or a counselor decides that a helping session is needed.

Preparation helps to determine how to listen, question, inform, explain, respond, and relate to each interviewee. No two interviews are identical because no two interviewees and situations are identical. Thus, many suggestions but few rules are available for selecting interview approaches, responses, questions, and structures.

Key Terms and Concepts

The online learning center for this text features FLASHCARDS and CROSSWORD PUZZLES for studying based on these terms and concepts.

Client-centered approach	Directive approach	Highly directive reactions
Cognitive phase	Directive reactions	Nondirective approach
Compliance	Expressed feelings	Lay counselor
Curious probes	Getting through questions	Make meaning questions

A Counseling Interview for Review and Analysis

This interview is between Katy Downey and Ruth Rhodes, lifelong friends and co-workers at Staying Fit Health Club. They are both married with two children under the age of 10 and have graduate degrees in health and exercise physiology. Their husbands are high school teachers and each earns about $50,000 a year. Katy and her husband are having serious financial problems brought on by a recent recession that reduced the value of their investments and the 4000-square-foot, two-story home they purchased three years ago. Her husband had been earning several thousand dollars each year by making custom furniture in his workshop, but the market for expensive, custom-made furniture nearly disappeared during the recession. In addition, Katy's hours have been cut back at Staying

Fit. Katy is coming to Ruth for advice because Ruth and her husband seem to be doing well financially.

Which counseling approach(es) does the interviewer employ? How would you assess the relationship between the parties from this interview? Does the interviewer focus more on feelings than information? See if you can locate highly nondirective, nondirective, directive, and highly directive responses. What types of questions does the interviewer use and how effectively? Which types of listening dominate the interview and how effectively?

1. **Interviewer:** Hi Katy, come in and let's relax with a cup of coffee.
2. **Interviewee:** That sounds great. It's been a very hectic week at the club.
3. **Interviewer:** You mentioned the other day that you and Bob are getting away by yourselves this weekend, someplace in the Ozarks?
4. **Interviewee:** That's right. We've found a great place in Arkansas with log cabins, fireplaces, hiking trails, and a lake with kayaks. We need to escape from the kids and some problems for a few days.
5. **Interviewer:** Wow!That sounds like fun. Dave and I need to get away sometime, but, as you know, money is tight right now.
6. **Interviewee:** Yes, money is a problem for most of us right now. This recession just seems to hang on. Bob's woodworking business has all but died.
7. **Interviewer:** I'm sorry to hear about that. I know you rely on that income for the extras.
8. **Interviewee:** Yes, we do, more than we thought, as a matter of fact. That's sort of why I want to talk to you this afternoon.
9. **Interviewer:** Oh?
10. **Interviewee:** Well, you and Dave seem to be doing okay, in spite of this recession. I wish we could say the same.
11. **Interviewer:** Um-hmm.
12. **Interviewee:** We're really struggling right now, and I'm really concerned about this next year.
13. **Interviewer:** How bad is it?
14. **Interviewee:** Well . . . frankly, we're concerned about keeping our house. Now don't tell Dave I told you this.
15. **Interviewer:** I won't if you don't want me to.
16. **Interviewee:** Bob would be upset if he knew I was talking to you about our finances. He's old school you know, wants to keep family problems within the family.
17. **Interviewer:** I can understand that. My parents were that way, and us kids had no idea what our finances were like, only that they would tell us sometimes that we could not afford a vacation, a new car, or parochial schools.
18. **Interviewee:** You can understand, then, why we must keep this talk between ourselves.
19. **Interviewer:** Of course.
20. **Interviewee:** Well, you know that we have been sending our kids to the McShane Academy, one of the best private schools in Colorado.

21. **Interviewer:** Yes, I knew Marybeth and Jake were attending the McShane Academy. We had thought about it ourselves, but it was too pricey for us.
22. **Interviewee:** I think you were wise to make that decision even though our kids are thriving at McShane. In a good year, Bob was bringing in about $15,000 in his custom furniture business, and that kept us in good shape.
23. **Interviewer:** How much has it dropped?
24. **Interviewee:** It's mid-November and Bob's total income from that is less than $2,000.
25. **Interviewer:** That is a big drop, and I can understand how that would pose a big problem for you.
26. **Interviewee:** But Bob doesn't seem to accept the problem this is causing. Just this week, he went to Sears and bought a top-of-line laser drill press for nearly $700. And he doesn't even have an order on which to use this.
27. **Interviewer:** Have you two talked about this?
28. **Interviewee:** I've tried, but he gets angry, and blames me for arranging the Ozark weekend. He says it will cost more than the drill press and won't bring in any money.
29. **Interviewer:** Didn't you two talk about this weekend before you agreed to it?
30. **Interviewee:** Yes, sort of.
31. **Interviewer:** What do you mean "sort of"?
32. **Interviewee:** I said I had found a really neat place that was really reasonable.
33. **Interviewer:** Is it?
34. **Interviewee:** Well. . . . It would have been when things were better financially. I thought we could put it on a credit card and pay it off over time.
35. **Interviewer:** Uh-huh.
36. **Interviewee:** We can't do that now.
37. **Interviewer:** Why not?
38. **Interviewee:** Our credit cards are maxed out.
39. **Interviewer:** How many credit cards do you have?
40. **Interviewee:** Nine.
41. **Interviewer:** Nine credit cards!
42. **Interviewee:** Yeah, we just seemed to get them over the years, at the gas station, at a few department stores, you know.
43. **Interviewer:** No wonder you're having problems with the high interest rates charged by nine credit cards and, I assume, pretty hefty house payments on that beautiful home you bought a few years ago.
44. **Interviewee:** You're right. What do think we ought to do?
45. **Interviewer:** What do you think you ought to do?
46. **Interviewee:** I don't know; that's why I came to you. You seem to have things under control.

47. Interviewer: We're making ends meet, but we're not able to put much into our savings.

48. Interviewee: I wish we had some savings. Those are long gone.

49. Interviewer: Have you considered making an appointment with a financial counselor? They can give you some very good professional advice.

50. Interviewee: Bob would never go for that. He doesn't like to share our private matters with anyone. In fact, he'd say that paying a financial counselor would just get us more in debt.

51. Interviewer: Many churches and nonprofit groups have free financial counseling. In fact, I think your church has such a service.

52. Interviewee: Bob would never go for that. We know these people.

53. Interviewer: I can appreciate his feelings, but you need help fast so you don't lose your home and get beyond help. At least think about seeing a financial counselor, maybe one connected with our school. The State Teachers Association might have someone.

54. Interviewee: I suppose you're right, but it's going to be a hard sell. I've got to get going; Bob will be home soon.

55. Interviewer: I'm glad you stopped by. Sometimes it helps just to talk to someone.

56. Interviewee: You're right again. Thanks for listening and, remember, not a word to Dave about any of this. Bob would really get angry.

57. Interviewer: It's just between us. Take care and come talk when you need to.

58. Interviewee: Thanks Ruth. You're a good listener and good friend.

Counseling Role-Playing Cases

Theft of Rings

The interviewer, Jake Hauser, and his wife Barbara employed Josey Ditmer for a number of years to clean their home and considers her to be a "member of the family." Josey has a key to the interviewer's home and often comes when neither the interviewer nor his wife are home. A few weeks ago Josey started bringing her teenage daughter Lizzy to help clean the home. Almost immediately Barbara noticed some rings missing. At first, she thought she had either lost or misplaced them. Then, when Jake came home and started to put a ring into his jewelry box, he discovered that a diamond ring Barbara had given him for their anniversary some years before was missing. He immediately called Josey and told her about the missing rings.

The interviewee, Josey, immediately confronted her daughter, and her daughter admitted that she had taken the rings and had already sold the anniversary ring. Josey called the jeweler who had purchased the ring and retrieved it from him. Barbara's rings are long gone. Josey called Jake and returned the ring without a word about the other rings and what punishment her daughter would receive for her theft. The interviewer has asked to meet with Josey to discuss the situation but is not interested in getting the police involved. He believes Josey's daughter needs help immediately before her stealing really gets her into trouble.

Dating and Religion

The interviewee is 24 years old and a graduate student at the University of South Dakota. She has been dating a classmate from South Dakota State University for several months, and both are beginning to get serious about a future together. She is Catholic and he is Jewish, and their religious faiths are very important to them. While neither sees religion as a major problem, neither of them is willing to change faiths or to commit themselves to raising future children in the other's religious tradition. They have talked about attending each other's worship services "on occasion."

The interviewee has decided to meet with a neighbor back home, Sheri Prohofsky, during Thanksgiving break to get some suggestions. Sheri is married with three children, and her husband is Jewish. She and her husband have seemed to work out their religious differences quite well with each remaining active in their church and temple. They have allowed their children to decide which faith tradition they will follow, if any.

A Graduate School Decision

The interviewee is a first semester senior in college and has been planning to enter the job market in human resources. Because she has a 3.85/4.0 grade point average and has worked on research projects with two faculty members, friends and family members are urging her to consider going to graduate school after she graduates, particularly with a job market that is very weak for college graduates. Some are pushing an MBA while others are suggesting an MS as preparation for work toward the PhD and perhaps a college teaching career. She doesn't know what to do and wonders whether she should work for a few years before considering a graduate program.

The interviewer is a professor of management and has taught the interviewee in two human resources courses. He has both an MBA and PhD and worked in industry before and after the master's degree. The last time he talked to the interviewee she was excited about job fairs being held on campus in the fall.

A Child in a Foster Home

The interviewer is a newly sworn-in Child Advocate and has been assigned a case involving 10-year-old Joey Spitzer who was taken away from his mother two years ago because of her drug addiction problem that caused her to disappear on several occasions from the apartment she shared with her boyfriend and Joey. The interviewer has reviewed documents on the case and is meeting Joey and his foster parents for the first time.

Joey has never met his father and has now been in three foster homes, having been removed from the previous two because of altercations with the foster parents. A month ago he ran away from his third foster home and was found by police three days later. Things seem to be going better, and his foster parents, the owners of a large dairy farm, have tried to make him comfortable in a rural setting. Joey had never seen a dairy operation until moving in with this third set of foster parents, and he is fascinated by the machinery and computer-driven milking operation. The purpose of this interview is to get acquainted with Joey and to explain the relationship between Child Advocates and their assigned children. The interviewer is particularly interested in discovering how Joey feels about his living situation and foster parents.

Student Activities

1. Visit a crisis center in your community or on your campus. Talk with counselors about their training techniques and self-evaluations. Observe how volunteer counselors handle telephone counseling. How does telephone counseling differ from face-to-face counseling? What types of persons call the crisis center most often? How often are callers repeat callers? What are typical crises? What kinds of help can crisis counselors offer?
2. Interview three different types of counselors, such as a marriage counselor, a student counselor, a financial counselor, or a legal counselor. How are their approaches and techniques similar and different? What kinds of training have they had? How much training do they consider essential? In their estimation, what makes a "successful" counselor?
3. Pick one of the counseling role-playing cases and develop a complete approach to the case, beginning with setting and furniture arrangement. How would you begin the interview? What questions would you ask? How much would you disclose about yourself—training, background, experiences, and so on? What kinds of reactions and responses would you use? What solution would you suggest? What would you do and not do to aid interviewee compliance? How would you close the interview?
4. Interview an experienced CASA (Court Appointed Special Advocate for children). Explore the training that is required to become a CASA. What kinds of cases has this volunteer handled? Which have proven to be the most difficult? How do CASAs attempt to establish relationships with their assigned children? What may threaten the relationships they establish? How do they communicate with different-age children? How do they adapt to children from cultures very different from their own? What is the most important skill they have learned about counseling?

Notes

1. William Steele, "Crisis Intervention: The First Few Days—Summary of Dr. Lennis Echterling's Presentation," reprinted from *Trauma And Loss: Research and Interventions* V4 N2 2004, http://www.tlcinst.org/crisisint.html, accessed July 5, 2010.
2. Donald R. Atkinson, Francisco Q. Ponce, and Francine M. Martinez, "Effects of Ethnic, Sex, and Attitude Similarity on Counselor Credibility," *Journal of Counseling Psychology* 31 (1984), pp. 589–591.
3. Sherry Cormier, Paula S. Nurius, and Cynthia J. Osborn, *Interviewing and Change Strategies for Helpers: Fundamental Skills and Cognitive Behavioral Interventions* (Belmont, CA: Brooks/Cole, 2009), p. 17.
4. Barbara Goldberg and Romeria Tidwell, "Ethnicity and Gender Similarity: The Effectiveness of Counseling for Adolescents," *Journal of Youth and Adolescents* 19 (1990), pp. 589–603.
5. Jeffrey A. Kottler, *A Brief Primer of Helping Skills* (Thousand Oaks, CA: Sage, 2008), p. 73.

6. Sarah Knox, Shirley A. Hess, David A. Petersen, and Clara E. Hill, "A Qualitative Analysis of Client Perceptions of the Effects of Helpful Therapist Self-Disclosure in Long-Term Therapy," *Journal of Counseling Psychology* 44 (1997), pp. 274–283.

7. Kottler, p. 58.

8. Helen Cameron, *The Counseling Interview: A Guide for the Helping Professions* (New York: Palgrave Macmillan, 2008), p. 14.

9. Paul B. Pedersen, "Ethics, Competence, and Professional Issues in Cross-Cultural Counseling," in *Counseling Across Cultures*, Paul B. Pedersen, Juris G. Draguns, Walter J. Lonner, and Joseph E. Trimble, eds. (Thousand Oaks, CA: Sage), p. 5.

10. Cormier, Nurius, and Osborn, p. 25.

11. Timothy P. Johnson, James G. Hougland, and Robert W. Moore, "Sex Differences in Reporting Sensitive Behavior: A Comparison of Interview Methods," *Sex Roles* 24 (1991), pp. 669–680; Judy Cornelia Pearson, Richard L. West, and Lynn H. Turner, *Gender and Communication* (Madison, WI: Brown & Benchmark, 1995), pp. 149–152.

12. James R. Mahalik, Robert J. Cournoyer, William DeFranc, Marcus Cherry, and Jeffrey M. Napolitano, "Men's Gender Role Conflict and Use of Psychological Defenses," *Journal of Counseling Psychology* 45 (1998), pp. 247–255.

13. Ward, p. 471.

14. Alan W. Burkard, Sarah Knox, Michael Groen, Maria Perez, and Shirley A. Hess, "European American Therapist Self-Disclosure in Cross-Cultural Counseling," *Journal of Counseling Psychology* 53 (2006), p. 15.

15. Cormier, Nurius, and Osborn, p. 73.

16. Madonna G. Constantine, Anika K. Warren, and Marie L. Miville, "White Racial Identity Dyadic Interactions in Supervision: Implications for Supervisees' Multicultural Counseling Competence," *Journal of Counseling Psychology* 52 (2005), p. 495.

17. Cormier, Nurius, and Osborn, p. 5.

18. Cormier, Nurius, and Osborn, p. 82; Cameron, p. 23; Kottler, p. 53.

19. William A. Satterfield, Sidne A. Buelow, William J. Lyddon, and J. T. Johnson, "Client Stages of Change and Expectations about Counseling," *Journal of Counseling Psychology* 42 (1995), pp. 476–478.

20. Bryan S. K. Kim, Gladys F. Ng, and Annie J. Ahn, "Effects of Client Expectation for Counseling Success, Client-Counselor Worldview Match, and Client Adherence to Asian and European American Cultural Values on Counseling Process with Asian Americans," *Journal of Counseling Psychology* 52 (2005), pp. 67–76.

21. Steele and Echterling; Cameron, pp. 2, 45–49; Kottler, pp. 40, 57.

22. Lisa C. Li and Bryan S. K. Kim, "Effects of Counseling Style and Client Adherence to Asian Cultural Values on Counseling Process with Asian American College Students," *Journal of Counseling Psychology* 51 (2004), pp. 158–167.

23. "Effective Counseling," http://www2.ku.edu/~coms/virtual_assistant/via/counsel.html, accessed October 12, 2006; "Counseling Interviews," http://www.uwgb.edu/clampit/

interviewing/interviewing%20lectures/counseling%Interviews%.html, accessed October 12, 2006.

24. Cameron, p. 23.

25. David L. Vogel and Stephen R. Wester, "To Seek Help or Not to Seek Help: The Risks of Self-Disclosure," *Journal of Counseling Psychology* 50 (2003), pp. 351–361.

26. Earlise C. Ward, "Keeping It Real: A Grounded Theory Study of African American Clients Engaging in Counseling at a Community Mental Health Agency," *Journal of Counseling Psychology* 52 (2005), p. 479.

27. Barry A. Farber, Kathryn C. Berano, and Joseph A. Capobianco, "Client's Perceptions of the Process and Consequences of Self-Disclosure in Psychotherapy," *Journal of Counseling Psychology* 51 (2004), pp. 340–346.

28. Bryan S. K. Kim, Clara E. Hill, Charles J. Gelso, Melissa K. Goates, Penelope A. Asay, and James M. Harbin, "Counselor Self-Disclosure, East Asian American Client Adherence to Asian Cultural Values, and Counseling Process," *Journal of Counseling Psychology* 50 (2003), pp. 324–332.

29. Anita E. Kelly, "Clients' Secret Keeping in Outpatient Therapy," *Journal of Counseling Psychology* 45 (1998), pp. 50–57.

30. Paul R. Turner, Mary Valtierra, Tammy R. Talken, Vivian I. Miller, and Jose R. DeAnda, "Effect of Session Length on Treatment Outcome for College Students in Brief Therapy," *Journal of Counseling Psychology* 43 (1996), pp. 228–232.

31. Cameron, pp. 45–49.

32. Rebecca Leonard, "Attending: Letting the Patient Know You Are Listening," *Journal of Practical Nursing* 33 (1983), pp. 28–29; Ginger Schafer Wlody, "Effective Communication Techniques," *Nursing Management,* October 1981, pp. 19–23.

33. Lennis G. Echterling, Don M. Hartsough, and H. Zarle, "Testing a Model for the Process of Telephone Crisis Intervention," *American Journal of Community Psychiatrists 8* (1980), pp. 715–725.

34. Steele and Echterling.

35. Sherry Cormier and Harold Hackney, *Counseling Strategies and Interventions* (Boston: Pearson, 2008), pp. 136–141; Cameron, pp. 51–58; Kottler, pp. 86–89.

36. Ruth Purtilo, *The Allied Health Professional and the Patient: Techniques of Effective Interaction* (Philadelphia: Saunders, 1973), pp. 96–97.

37. Peter Chang, "Effects of Interviewer Questions and Response Type on Compliance: An Analogue Study," *Journal of Counseling Psychology* 41 (1994), pp. 74–82.

38. Collie W. Conoley, Marjorie A. Padula, Darryl S. Payton, and Jeffrey A. Daniels, "Predictors of Client Implementation of Counselor Recommendations: Match with Problem, Difficulty Level, and Building on Client Strengths," *Journal of Counseling Psychology* 41 (1994), pp. 3–7.

39. Robert J. Reese, Collie W. Conoley, and Daniel F. Brossart, "Effectiveness of Telephone Counseling: A Field-Based Investigation," *Journal of Counseling Psychology* 49 (2002), pp. 233–242.

Resources

Cameron, Helen. *The Counseling Interview: A Guide for the Helping Professions.* New York: Palgrave Macmillan, 2008.

Cormier, Sherry, and Harold Hackney. *Counseling Strategies and Interventions.* Boston: Pearson, 2008.

Cormier, Sherry, Paula S. Nurius, and Cynthia J. Osborn. *Interviewing and Change Strategies for Helpers: Fundamental Skills and Cognitive Behavioral Interventions.* Belmont, CA: Brooks/Cole, 2009.

Hill, Clara E. *The Helping Skills: Facilitating Exploration, Insight, and Action.* Washington, DC: American Psychological Association, 2009.

Kottler, Jeffrey A. *A Brief Primer of Helping Skills.* Thousand Oaks, CA: Sage, 2008.

Pedersen, Paul B., Juris G. Draguns, Walter J. Lonner, and Joseph E. Trimble, eds. *Counseling Across Cultures.* Thousand Oaks, CA: Sage, 2008.

CHAPTER 13 The Health Care Interview

Whether or not you are planning a career in health care, you will take part in health care interviews throughout your life, particularly with the growing emphasis on preventive care. Interviews will range from routine checkups to major surgery. An interview may be a single, brief consultation with a patient or physician or one of numerous interactions that establish a relationship with a long history.

Health care interviews deal with the ordinary and the extra-ordinary.

This chapter starts with a discussion of how providers and patients can establish a productive relationship that promotes a collaborative effort to diagnose and treat health problems. It then addresses behaviors critical to patients' perceptions of providers' communication competence: opening the interview, gathering information, sharing information, discovering and reaching agreement on problems and courses of action, and closing the interview.[1]

Creating a Collaborative Relationship

Perceptions of health care are undergoing rapid change in the twenty-first century, as health care educators and providers see and espouse the importance of a collaborative partnership, a mutual participation in health care. The emphasis is on patients and providers as "coagents in a problem-solving context."[2] Advocates of co-agency contend that when patients are more actively involved as partners, rather than passive bystanders, they are more satisfied with their care, receive more patient-centered care such as information and support, are more committed to treatment regimens and managing health issues, have a stronger sense of control over their health, and experience better health.[3]

Collaboration is critical in health care.

The goal of the health care interaction is to "develop a reciprocal relationship, where the exchange of information, identification of problems, and development of solutions is an interactive process," a reciprocal rather than an authoritative relationship.[4] Researchers claim that "the physician–patient relationship is the most critical component of the health care delivery process."[5] Establishing a partnership tends "to ensure that potential health decisions respect patients' wants, needs, and preferences, and that patients have the education and support they need to make decisions effectively and participate in their own care."[6] "How a patient perceives his/her relationship with a doctor may influence the manner in which s/he talks to a doctor."[7]

How can this collaborative relationship be established, maintained, and adjusted through interactions? Although it takes two parties to form a productive relationship, providers and patients continue to believe the provider has the burden to make the

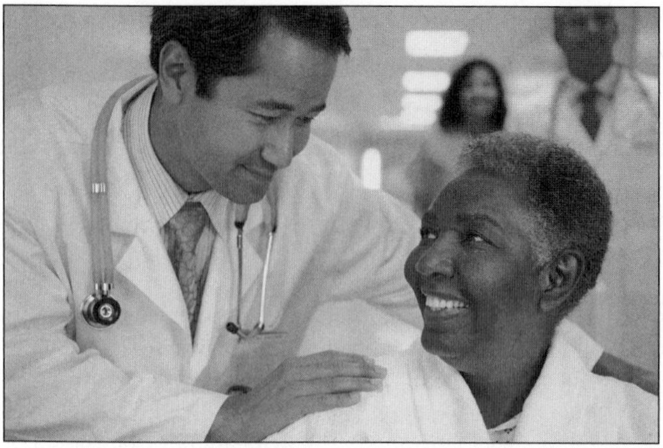

The development of positive relationships between health care providers and receivers is essential for effective communication and health care.

relationship work.[8] This finding leads Hullman and Daily to conclude that the health care provider's "ability to be flexible and adaptable is extremely important in medical encounters."[9]

Sharing Control

A sharing of control is the first step in forming a collaborative relationship. Traditionally, power and authority have been lopsided in the health care interview. The provider is highly trained, sees the situation as routine, speaks in scientific terms and acronyms few patients understand, appears to be in control of self and the situation, is emotionally uninvolved, and is fully clothed in a suit or uniform. Control gravitates to the provider because this party chooses and controls the setting, timing, and structure of the interview. Closed questions, limited reactions, changing of topics, and interruptions signal who is in charge. When patients challenge this situation, providers may quickly reassert their "authorial presence" or ignore the challenge.[10] A recent study of patients' presentation of Internet research findings during health care interviews reveals that physicians may dismiss such research as "face threatening" and to assert their authority. Male patients in particular perceived that physicians "felt a loss of control" when they mentioned Internet research, perhaps because they feared they would be proven wrong or didn't know enough.[11]

Both parties must share control.

On the other hand, the patient is typically uninformed, sees the situation as a crisis, is emotionally involved, has little medical knowledge, has little control over what happens in an unfamiliar and threatening environment, and may be partially nude, highly medicated, or in severe pain. Patients are partly to blame for the parent–child relationship that may exist in the interview by dutifully taking on a subordinate role in the relationship and remaining compliant.[12] While a majority of patients, particularly younger ones, want to be actively involved in the process, some prefer a "paternalistic model of health care" in which the provider maintains control.[13] They may fail to ask questions at critical times during interviews. A patient may appear to be compliant while employing subtle control strategies, such as changing topics, asking numerous questions, giving short, unrevealing answers to open questions, withholding vital information, or talking incessantly. A person may demonstrate relational power through silence rather than conversational dominance or agree with a provider during an interview and then ignore prescriptions, regimens, and advice afterward.

Patients must be active and responsive.

While there is considerable agreement on what constitutes competent physician communication, there is little evidence of what constitutes competent patient communication. One study revealed that "From the physician's perspective, the communicatively competent patient is well prepared," "gives prior thought to medical concerns," educates himself or herself about the illness, comes to the interview with an agenda (and remains focused on it), provides "detailed information about his or her medical history, symptoms, and other relevant matters," and seeks information by asking questions about the diagnosis and treatment.[14] The patients' perspective in this study mirrored the physicians'. While these results are encouraging, this study also discovered that there was not "a significant correlation between perceptions of competence and patients' actual discourse, that "perceptions of communication in a medical interview do not necessarily match what is actually said." What physicians and patients think they see and hear often does not match reality.

Both parties in the health care interview must negotiate and share control "as partners striving for a common goal."[15] As a provider, develop positive relational climates by showing interest in the patient's lifestyle, nonmedical concerns, and overall well-being. Supportive talk that includes statements of reassurance, support, and empathy demonstrates interpersonal sensitivity and sincere interest in the patient as a person.

Empathy is "an essential element of the physician-patient relationship," and a showing of empathy increases patient satisfaction and reduces time and expense. Carma Bylund and Gregory Makoul write that "Empathy is not just something that is 'given' from physician to patient. Instead, a transactional communication perspective informs us that the physician and patient mutually influence each other during the interaction."[15a] They discovered that while some patients provided repeated opportunities for empathic responses, others provided little or none. When patients did so, physicians in their study "had a clear tendency for acknowledging, pursuing, and confirming patients' empathic opportunities." This is a positive trend in physician–patient interactions.

It takes two to form an effective relationship.

As a provider, encourage the patient to express ideas, expectations, fears, and feelings about the medical problem and value the patient's expertise. The goal is to treat one another as equals. As a patient, come to the interview well informed about the health problem and ready to provide detailed information as honestly and accurately as possible, express concerns, respond effectively to the provider's questions, and state your opinions, suggestions, and preferences.

Reducing Relational Distance

Dwell on similarities, not differences.

Patient-centered care (PCC), in which patient "needs, preferences, and beliefs are respected at all times," is a growing movement in the United States[16] that can advance if both parties share control and actively seek to reduce relational distance. While both parties are unique in some ways, they share many perceptions, needs, values, beliefs, attitudes, and experiences. Both are real persons, not medical magicians or miracle workers and not disease carriers or chronic whiners. Both strive to maintain dignity, privacy, self-respect, and comfort. Provider and patient can build relationships by working to understand and identify with one another.

While medical personnel can reduce relational distance by not hiding behind uniforms, expertise, and policies, patients can do the same by not hiding behind hospital gowns, ignorance, and their medical conditions. Neither party should push the relationship too quickly, but each can reduce emotional distance by encouraging

Enhance relationships through understanding.

two-way dialogues about feelings. They must make efforts to know and understand one another. Mutual understanding reduces relational distance. Providers and patients may enhance relationships by trying to be relaxed, confident, and comfortable; showing interest in one another as individuals; maintaining objectivity; being sincere and honest; treating one another with respect; paying attention to verbal and nonverbal channels; maintaining flexibility; and maintaining appropriate control during the interaction.[16a]

Appreciating Diversity

Diversity among patients and providers is a reality both parties must recognize and address. We understand intuitively that patients, particularly those from other cultures, experience and react differently to health care interviews, but few of us are aware that providers also experience stress and anxiety when dealing with different types of patients and those from other cultures.[17]

Gender

Age and sex influence communication and treatment.

Women tend to be more concerned about health than men and are more verbal during interactions. This may be a learned difference because more health care information in the media is aimed at women than men. Women spend more communication time with providers and are more active communicators during these visits, but their providers take their concerns less seriously. On the other hand, male patients tend to be more domineering than females regardless of the gender of the provider.[18] A by-product of more females entering the fields of obstetrics and gynecology is the significant percentage of women patients choosing female physicians. This has led male physicians to work on improving their interpersonal communication skills.[19]

Age

Age is a growing factor as life expectancy increases and the baby boomer generation reaches retirement age. Older patients are more reluctant to "challenge the physician's authority" than younger patients, often with good reason. Providers who are mostly under 55 are "significantly less egalitarian, less patient, and less respectful with older patients," perhaps reflecting society's changing attitudes toward "aging" and the wisdom of our elders. Providers are "less likely to raise psychological issues with" older patients.[20] Younger patients are more comfortable with "bothering" health care providers and less awed by authority and credentials. If a patient is incapacitated, often because of age, it may be wise to involve a surrogate (spouse or child) or a health care proxy who may have important information to share with the physician and be able to collaborate about the patient's care.[21]

Culture

Health communication differs in the global village.

There are approximately 47 million people in the United States who speak a language other than English at home, and this does not include the millions of international travelers who come to the United States each year.[22]

Globalization and its accompanying cultural differences affect interpersonal communication in many ways. African-American and Puerto Rican patients have indicated that their race, ethnicity, and lower economic status impacted negatively on their information seeking (particularly HIV-related information) and health care.[23] Patients of a lower social class may be openly reluctant to challenge physicians so they attempt to control the relationship.[24] Arab cultures practice close proximity and kissing among men; both actions may be seen as offensive in American or European health care interactions. Native American and Asian cultures prize nonverbal communication, while American and German cultures prize verbal communication. Latinas are a good fit with patient-centered health care providers because they value interactions with physicians more than European- and African-Americans.[25] Many societies, particularly Asian, are less assertive.

Kreps and Thornton identify the differences in medical philosophies in different countries and suggest the difficulties these might pose for nonnative health care providers and patients:[26]

- French physicians tend to discount statistics and emphasize logic.
- German physicians tend to be authoritarian romantics.
- English physicians tend to be paternalistic.
- American physicians tend to be aggressive and want to "do something."

These differences affect communicative roles and control sharing in medical interviews. Providers must be culturally sensitive to differences in reporting pain, understanding informed consent, using appropriate language, and disclosing information that may rely on cultural knowledge, modesty, and comfort. Alice Chen, in an article titled "Doctoring Across the Language Divide," relates an instance when she was treating a Muslim woman and ordered an X ray to assess for arthritis. A male X-ray technician wanted to lift up the horrified woman's hijab so he could position the equipment properly. Chen referred her to a different facility with a notation that the patient needed a female technician.[27]

Stereotypes

"Good" patients get better health care.

Stereotypes affect the way providers see and treat patients. Provider perception of the patient as childlike is revealed in condescending attitudes and baby talk with adults. One study indicated that 20 percent of staff interactions in nursing homes qualifies as *baby talk,* a speech style common when speaking to infants that has a "slower rate, exaggerated intonation, elevated pitch and volume, greater repetition, and simpler vocabulary and grammar.[28] Other health care providers use *elderspeak* when addressing older adults. Examples include "Hi *sweetie*. It's time for *our* exercise," "Good girl. You ate all of your dinner," and "Good morning *big guy.* Are *we* ready for *our* bath?" The results of such "inappropriately intimate and childish" baby talk and elderspeak are "decreased self-esteem, depression, withdrawal, and the assumption of dependent behaviors congruent with stereotypes of frail elders." Providers have traditionally had positive attitudes toward middle-aged patients and negative attitudes toward others such as adolescents.

The stereotypical *good patient* is cooperative, quiet, obedient, grateful, unaggressive, considerate, and dispassionate. *Good patients* tend to get better treatment than *bad patients*. Patients seen as lower class tend to get more pessimistic diagnoses and prognoses. Overweight patients are deemed *less* likable, seductive, well educated, in need of help, or likely to benefit from help and *more* emotional, defensive, warm, and likely to have continuing problems.

Creating and Maintaining Trust

Trust is critical in health care interactions because they deal with intimate and sensitive personal information and must maximize self-disclosure. Trust comes about when both parties "see one another as legitimate agents of knowledge and perception."[29] Breaches of confidentiality, a fundamental right of patients, may lead to discrimination, economic devastation, or social stigma. Trust is destroyed and with it any hope of building or maintaining a productive relationship. Breaches of confidentiality may be intentional or unintentional and occur in many places: elevators, hallways, cafeterias, providers' offices, hospital rooms, cocktail parties, or over the telephone, particularly the ubiquitous cell phone. Maria Brann and Marifran Mattson relate an instance in which a patient tried to keep the reason for her appointment confidential by handing the provider a written note; the provider insisted that the patient read the note aloud. In another situation, a patient tried to answer confidential questions quietly; the provider proceeded to ask questions about her situation in a loud voice.[30] Solutions include talking and answering questions in soft tones, exchanging information only with providers who have a need to know, and conducting interactions in private, audibly secure locations.

Confidentiality and trust go hand in hand.

Trust is established in the early minutes of interviews when each party is determining if this is a person he or she can trust. It is further negotiated as both parties "enact behaviors" that construct "shared expectations of a trusting relationship."[31] Humor, for instance, can "facilitate positive patient–provider interactions" and "create a patient-centered environment" that affects "patients' positive attitude and happiness."[32] The results are positive perceptions of caregivers that enhance trustworthiness and lead to better health outcomes, increased compliance with providers' advice, and fewer malpractice suits.[33] Spontaneous humor is most effective. Health care providers can enhance trust through supportive talk that increases patient participation in interviews and by eliciting full disclosure of information, clarifying information, and assessing social and psychological factors involved in illness.[34]

Providers and patients co-create trust.

Opening the Interview

The opening of the health care interview, when and where it takes place, and who initiates it have significant impact on the remainder of the interview. Neither party should see it as routine.

Enhancing the Climate

The opening sets the tone for the entire interview.

The provider should create an atmosphere in which the patient feels free to express opinions, feelings, and attitudes. Both parties rely heavily on interviews to get and give information. The process is often taken for granted and parties fail to realize that cooperation is essential for sharing information and attitudes toward courses of action.

True collaboration leads to information exchange, greater patient satisfaction, and compliance with instructions.

Location and setting promote collaborative interactions.

Select a comfortable, attractive, quiet, nonthreatening, and private location free of interruptions in which interactions will remain confidential. Check out a typical pediatrics area and one for adults of all ages and conditions. The first is designed thoughtfully in every detail (pictures, aquarium, toys, plants, books) for the young patient and parents to minimize fear and anxiety and maximize cooperation and communication. The second is likely to be a stark treatment room that contains a variety of medical gadgets and a few magazines. This is not a setting likely to decrease anxiety and tension.

Being Sensitive and Personal

Employ individualized opening approaches. In a study of provider–patient satisfaction, Mohan Dutta-Bergman discovered that "open physician-patient communicative style is not the universal solution to patient needs. Instead, the fundamental message that emerges from this research is the need for tailoring the health care providers' communicative styles depending on the needs of the patient."[35]

Use the opening to reduce apprehension.

Open the interview with a pleasant greeting and by introducing yourself and position if you are unacquainted with the patient or family. If you address the patient by first name (Hi Sally) while you address yourself by title (I'm Dr. Percifield), you create a superior-to-subordinate relationship from the start. If you are acquainted with the patient, open with a personal greeting that acknowledges your relationship. As a patient, return the greeting and take an active part in the opening.

Neither rush nor drag out the opening.

Establish rapport through small talk, humor, or self-disclosure to relax the patient, show interest, increase trust, and enrich the relationship. This patient-centered approach enhances patient satisfaction.[36] Reduce apprehension by carefully explaining procedures, being attentive and relaxed, treating patients as equals, and talking to them in their street clothes rather than hospital gowns. Rapport building and orientation are strengthened if the provider reviews the patient's file before entering the examination room so the interview can begin on a personal and knowledgeable level. Neither rush nor prolong the opening unless trust is low because both parties prefer to get to the point after establishing a personal connection.

If a patient has been waiting for some time because you are behind schedule, apologize for the inconvenience and explain the reason for it. Simple politeness and courtesy—treating people the way you want to be treated—can defuse an angry or impatient interviewee or interviewer and show you value each person's time and are sensitive to perceptions and needs. Judith Spiers has shown the relevance of *politeness theory* and how it can improve communication in the health care interaction. She writes that:

Politeness breeds politeness.

> Politeness is used primarily to ease social interaction by providing a ritualistic form of verbal interaction that cushions the stark nature of many interactions such as requests, commands, or questioning. Politeness provides a means for covering embarrassment, anger, or fear in situations in which it would not be to one's advantage to show these emotions either as a reflection of one's self or because of the reaction of the other.[37]

This is excellent advice for helping health care receivers "save face" in a threatening situation over which they have little control.

Adapting the Opening

The content of the opening after greeting and a brief pleasantry depends on who initiated the interview and how much information has been exchanged prior to the interview. When a patient initiates an interview without explanation, the provider's opening question is most likely to be a "general-inquiry" such as, "What brings you in this morning?" "What seems to be the problem?" or "What can I do for you today?" If a patient has mentioned a reason when making an appointment or told the physician's assistant or nurse about a problem, the provider's opening question is likely to be a "confirmatory" question such as, "I understand you're having some sinus problems today?" "What kind of difficulties are you having with your knee?" or "Tell me about the stress you are experiencing." Some health care providers are using electronic interviews with patients prior to in-person visits. Patients select from a list of medical complaints and then reply to a series of questions phrased in language they will understand. When the provider enters the treatment room for the face-to-face interview, he or she has reviewed the information and both provider and patient are ready to begin the interview. One physician relates, "My total focus is on the patient, and it's unusual for me to need to look at the computer."[38]

A second type of confirmatory question focuses on specific symptoms, such as, "Is the pain mainly on the left side of your head?" or "Does the dizziness occur most often when you focus rapidly on near and far objects and then near objects again?" John Heritage and Jeffrey Robinson discovered that general-inquiry questions elicit longer problem presentations, including more current symptoms. More restrictive closed questions, a second form of confirmatory question, constitutes "a method for initiating problem presentation and distinctively communicates physicians' readiness to initiate, and enforce the initiation, of the next phase of the visit: information gathering."[39] The physician takes control and dictates where the interview is heading.

Orient the patient.

If the provider initiates the interview, the opening question may be open-ended, such as "How has your health been during the past year?" or specific such as "Have you experienced any side effects from the medication for your cholesterol?" What takes place after the opening question depends upon the reason for the visit. If it is an annual routine checkup, the provider is likely to orient the patient as to what will take place and then launch into the body of the interview with questions and examinations. If it is a follow-up session, the provider may move to the body of the interview with a series of questions directed toward a specific problem or results of a previous treatment.

Getting Information

Health care providers and patients devote significant portions of interview time seeking information about problems, causes, treatments, and changes in lifestyle. Information exchange is a major component of competence in provider–patient interactions. This is not an easy task, so we begin by identifying barriers to sharing information and then by offering suggestions for gathering information effectively and efficiently.

Barriers to Getting Information

Do not assume patients will provide accurate information.

Physical and emotional factors may make it difficult for patients to recall or articulate information accurately and completely. Their concern is why they are ill rather than what they can do about it. Frightened and anxious patients leave out significant parts of their medical histories or intentionally minimize symptoms to get a good diagnosis. When patients feel ashamed or embarrassed, they may camouflage the real problem and make allegorical statements such as, "You know how teenagers are." Patients say they don't want a lecture or to be judged about smoking, weight, or over-the-counter drugs, so they tell "harmless little white lies" and are not particularly concerned about the potential consequences.[40] Some overestimate the risk of a problem. For instance, research indicates that "many women overestimate their percentage risk of breast cancer, even after they have received careful estimates from health care professionals." They resist the information received.[41] One way to reduce this problem appears to be a "social comparison strategy" in which patients are asked to compare their risk to others. However, even after using this strategy, women continued to see their risk as "50 percent when the actual risk was closer to 14 percent."[42] Mothers recall only about half of their children's major illnesses.

Ask obviously relevant questions as soon as possible.

Self-disclosure will remain shallow if the patient does not trust the provider or strict confidentiality is impossible. A patient may give short answers to end uncomfortable questions, or give answers they think providers want to hear to please them or avoid bad news.

The traditional history-taking portion of interviews is often longer than discussions of diagnostic and prognostic issues. The manner tends to be impersonal, with many questions having little or nothing to do with the patient's current problem or concern. One patient remarked, "He spent so long on things not wrong with me—two pages of lists—that it made me feel the interview had nothing to do with my illness at all."[43] Patients in great pain or psychological discomfort may become angry or numbed by endless, closed questions, what one researcher calls "negative weakening." One of the authors witnessed this wearing down process while visiting a family member in a nursing home in Florida. An elderly, ill, confused, and angry patient had just been admitted to the same room as the author's mother-in-law. Two medical personnel entered soon thereafter and began to ask a lengthy list of questions. Many would have taxed a medically fit person, and it did not take long before the patient was exhausted and obviously confused. The interview droned on, even though one of the questioners remarked to the other, "I don't know why we don't do this over two or three days. It's not like she's going anywhere." The interview continued with diminishing returns.

Weigh the ability of patients to respond.

Provider dominance deadens interactions.

A series of rapid-fire closed questions (sometimes referred to as the Spanish inquisition approach) clearly sets the tone for the relationship: the provider is in charge, wants short answers, is in a hurry, and is not interested in explanations. One study revealed that 87 percent of questions were closed or moderately closed and that 80 percent of answers provided only solicited information with no volunteering.[44] Providers control interactions through closed questions, content selection, and changing of topics. Providers routinely ask questions such as: Do you have regular bowel movements? Do you feel tired? Are you ever short of breath? Any chest pains? What does *regular* mean? Who doesn't feel *tired*? Who hasn't been *short of breath* from time to time or experienced an occasional *chest pain*? What does a yes or no answer to any of these questions tell the health care provider?

Explain medical terms and procedures.

Many health care providers assume familiarity with medical *jargon* and *acronyms* that are useful only for interactions with other medical professionals.

Ask focused, explicit questions.

One study discovered that 20 percent or more of respondents did not know the meaning of such common terms as abscess, sutures, tumor, and cervix, and the percentages escalated with more uncommon words such as edema and triglyceride. Persons over 65 are less knowledgeable than ones between 45 and 64, and more educated respondents are most familiar with medical terms.[45] Patients seldom ask for clarification or repetition of questions or terminology. They feel it is the provider's responsibility as the expert and one in charge.[46]

Ways to Improve Information Getting

Both parties can improve information getting in health care interviews. The key is to find ways to foster exchanges that create a collaborative effort. Providers should promote turn-taking so patients will feel free to ask questions, provide more details, and react to what they are saying. Simple techniques can do this: pauses, eye contact, head nods, and verbal signals to invite interactions instead of monologues. Be careful of verbal routines that give patients false cues for turn-taking. These include "Okay?" "Right?" and "Uh-huh" that only appear to invite reactions. Patients see them as false cues that invite agreement rather than questions or competing notions.

Encourage turn-taking.

Research indicates that patients who take an active part in medical interviews provide more details about their symptoms and medical history, get more thorough answers to their questions, and prompt health care providers to volunteer more information and use "significantly more supportive utterances."[47] Donald Cegala and his colleagues believe that high patient participation "helps the physician to more accurately understand the patient's goals, interests, and concerns, thus allowing the physician to better align his or her communication with the patient's agenda."[48]

Asking and Answering Questions

Use a funnel sequence that begins with open questions to communicate interest, encourage lengthy, revealing responses, and show trust in the patient as a collaborator to provide important information, including information you might not think to ask for. Open questions that are free of interviewer bias and invite rather than demand answers give patients a greater feeling of control.

The funnel sequence gives a sense of sharing control.

Use an inverted funnel sequence with caution because closed questions asked early in an interview may set a superior-to-subordinate tone and communicate the desire of the provider to seek brief answers while maintaining control. Patients will give short answers that reveal little information and hide fears, feelings, and symptoms. Patients may be unable or unwilling to adjust to open-ended questions that come later in the inverted sequence.

Vary listening approaches.

Listen carefully and actively for hidden as well as obvious requests and responses. Listen for evidence of confusion, hesitation, apprehension, or uncertainty. Patients should prepare lists of questions prior to interviews when they can think about concerns without the pressure of interactions with providers. Don't hesitate to ask the other party to repeat or rephrase an unclear question. You cannot reply sufficiently if you do not understand what is being asked. Dr. Nancy Jasper, a clinical professor at Columbia University's College of Physicians and Surgeons, illustrates the need to probe into answers, particularly when patients are "fudging with the truth."

> I always ask my patients whether they smoke. . . . A lot of women will say, "No but I am a social smoker." And I say, "You'll have to define that for me because I have no idea what that means." They'll say they only smoke on the weekends. But you start to uncover more when you ask: "How many cigarettes do you smoke in a week?"[49]

Both patient and provider must listen carefully and be certain they understand what one another is really saying before proceeding with the interview.

Telling Stories

What patients want most is an opportunity to tell their stories, and these narratives are "essential to the diagnostic process" and the most efficient approach to eliciting necessary information.[50] Gary Kreps and Barbara Thornton write:

> Stories are used by consumers of health care to explain to their doctors or nurses what their ailments are and how they feel about these health problems. . . . By listening to the stories a person tells about his or her health condition, the provider can learn a great deal about the person's cultural orientation, health belief system, and psychological orientation toward the condition.[51]

Encourage storytelling and listen.

Susan Eggly writes that both parties must cocreate the illness narrative so they can influence one another and shape the narrative as it is told.[52] She identifies three types of stories: "narratives that emerge through the co-constructed chronology of key events, the co-constructed repetition and elaboration of key events, and the co-constructed interpretation of the meaning of key events." Collaboration in storytelling is critical because patients routinely omit valuable information from narratives they think is unimportant, do not feel safe in revealing, or assume the provider would not be interested.[53]

The less you talk, the more you may say.

Avoid unnecessary interruptions during narratives and answers, especially when patients become overwhelmed with emotion. The success of the interview may be due to the number of words the provider does *not say* or the numbers of questions *not asked*. Some researchers use the phrase "empathic opportunity terminator" to identify interactions that redirect interviews and cut off further revelations of patients' emotional concerns.[54] In the first interaction below, the physician changes the subject.

Patient: I'm in the process of retiring . . .

Physician: You are?

Patient: Yeah. I'll be 73 in February.

Physician: How's your back?

In this interaction, the physician retreats to an earlier, less emotional concern.

Patient: And right now I'm real nauseous and sick. I lost 10 pounds in six days.

Physician: Okay. You lost 10 pounds.

Patient: And I'm getting, and I'm getting worse. I'm not getting any better.

Physician: Okay . . . and right now you are not able to eat anything, you said?

Older patients tend to give significantly longer presentations and narratives than younger patients, but they do not reveal more current symptoms. They do offer more information about a symptom, "engage in more painful self-disclosure," and disclose more about seemingly irrelevant matters such as family finances.[55] Providers need to be patient and to probe for relevant specifics and explanations. Caplan, Haslett, and Burleson write that "It is particularly critical to understand how communication processes change and how older adults communicate their concerns and feelings."[56] They discovered that when older patients discussed a loss in later life, they "shifted from a primarily factual mode (what the loss was, how the loss occurred, etc.) to a focus on the impact of this loss on their lives (e.g., handling new tasks and expressions of emotions)."

Listening, Observing, and Talking

Be patient and persistent.

As a provider, be patient and use nudging probes to encourage patients to continue with a narrative or answer. Avoid irritating interjections such as *right, fine, okay,* and *good.* Avoid guessing games. Ask, "When does your back hurt?" not "Does it hurt when you first get up? When you stand a lot? When you sit for a while?" Avoid double-barreled questions such as "And in your family, has there been high blood pressure or strokes? Diabetes or cancer?" What would a yes or no answer mean? Employ reflective and mirror questions to check for accuracy and understanding. Listen for important cues in answers, what patients are suggesting or implying verbally and nonverbally. You may have to make it clear to parents, spouses, relatives, or friends present that the patient must answer questions if physically and mentally able to do so.

Use leading questions with caution.

Leading questions such as "You're staying on your diet, aren't you?" signal that you want agreement, a yes answer, and that is likely what you will get even if it's false. At times, however, you may need to use leading questions to persuade patients to follow regimens and take medicines properly. Annette Harres discusses the importance of "tag questions" to elicit information, summarize and confirm information, express empathy, and provide positive feedback.[57] Examples are "You can bend your knee, can't you?" "You've been here before, haven't you?" "I'm sure it's been a very difficult adjustment since your husband Paul died."

Addressing the Language Barrier

Health care professionals have long recognized that "**communication** breakdowns are the most common root cause of **health errors** that harm patients," and this problem is exacerbated by an estimated "95 million people" who "do not have the fundamental literacy skills in English to understand even the most basic" health information such as how and when to take medication.[58] Nearly half of this number have little or no command of the English language. The misinterpretation of a single word, such as "irritate," may lead to delayed care and medical errors.

Providers have tried a variety of solutions, some successful and some not. For example, family and friends may speak the patient's native language or be more fluent in English, but they may not repeat all of a provider's questions or explanations or be able to translate or explain medical terms accurately into the patient's native language or at the patient's level of understanding.[59] Children as interpreters pose problems because their command of the parents' native language may be minimal, "their understanding of medical concepts tends to be simplistic at best," and "parents can be embarrassed or reluctant to disclose important symptoms and details to their child."[60]

Successful programs have included comprehensive interpreter services in a language such as Spanish, creation of a course to teach Spanish to health care professionals, and use of specific phrases in Spanish to assess acute pain. They are limited, of course, to a single language. Some large medical facilities include a number of interpreters who are fluent in languages they encounter most often. A national system of interpreters fluent in many languages and trained in health care, similar to the one operated by the Australian government on a 24/7 basis, would be ideal.

Giving Information

Giving information is essential for the provider and patient. Patients provide information when they answer questions and tell stories that explain their medical conditions. Providers explain the nature and causes of medical problems, prescribe medications, and detail regimens that must be followed carefully to resolve problems without causing others.

Patients remember little and follow less.

Giving information is a deceptively difficult process. One study revealed that within 10 to 80 minutes, less than 25 percent of patients remembered everything they were told, and patients who remembered most had received only two items of information. Another discovered that within a short time, 10 patients showed significant distortions of information received and 4 showed minimum distortions.[61]

Causes for Loss and Distortion of Information

There are three root causes for failure to give and to recall information accurately: attitudes of medical providers, problems of patients, and ineffective transmission methods.

Attitudes of Providers

Both parties contribute to loss and distortion.

Health care providers place greater emphasis on getting information than giving it even though the strongest predictor of patient satisfaction is how much information is given on a condition and treatment. In a typical 20-minute interview, less than 2 minutes is devoted to information giving. Providers may be reluctant to provide information because they do not want to get involved, fear patients' reactions, feel they (particularly nonphysicians) are not allowed to give information, or fear giving incorrect information. Nurses, for instance, are often uncertain about what a physician wants the patient to know or has told the patient.

Beware of faulty assumptions.

Providers underestimate the patient's need or desire for information and overestimate the amount of information they give. On the other hand, patients cite insufficient information as a major failure of health care and are turning to the Internet in rapidly increasing numbers.[62] A study of cancer patients revealed that barely over 50 percent of those who wanted a *quantitative* prognosis got one and over 60 percent of those who did not want a *qualitative* prognosis got one.[63] Many providers assume patients understand what they tell them, including subtle recommendations and information laced with medical jargon and acronyms.[64] Metaphors such as "We're turning a corner," "There's light at the end of the tunnel," and "The Central Hospital family is here to help" require patients to complete the implied comparison, and the result may be confusion and anxiety rather than comfort and reassurance. Providers tend to give more information and elaborate explanations to educated, older, and female patients.

As patients turn increasingly to the Internet for information, health care professionals are disturbed that 72 percent of patients believe all or most of what they read on the Internet, regardless of source.[65] This is particularly true for so-called seeker patients with higher educations and incomes, who are younger, and who are actively involved in interpersonal networks. They are "health conscious" and like the active "involvement in the processing of information."[66] It is less true for so-called nonseeker patients who are older, have less education, and come from lowincome groups. They "intentionally avoid information that may cause them anxiety or stress."[67]

Problems with Patients

Patients may hear what they want to hear.

Patients may protect themselves from unpleasant experiences by refusing to listen, or they may interpret information and instructions according to their personalities. For instance, if a provider says, "You have six months to a year to live," a pessimist may tell friends, "I have less than six months to live," while an optimist may relate cheerfully, "The doctor says I might live for years."

Use acronyms cautiously.

Patients may not understand or comprehend information because they are untrained or inexperienced in medical situations. Patients can be confused by conflicting reports, studies, and the media. For instance, in the fall of 2009, the U.S. Preventive Services Task Force recommended that women over 40 should undergo screening mammography only every two years instead of the traditional every-year testing. This created a major controversy among health professionals and organizations with many stating their conflicting opinions through the media. Such controversies pose particular problems for older patients who have less knowledge and understanding of medical situations and greater difficulties in giving information.[68] Patients are bombarded with unfamiliar acronyms (IV, EKG, D & C) and jargon (adhesions, contusions, nodules, cysts, benign tumors). The names of pharmaceuticals are nearly impossible to pronounce, let alone understand. A study by Hagihara, Tarumi, and Nobutomo investigated the common phenomenon in which physicians' and patients' understanding and evaluation of medical test results and diagnoses differ markedly. They recommend that "To avoid either a failure on the part of the patient to understand the explanation, or a patient misunderstanding the physician's explanation, physicians should pay more attention both to the topic under discussion and to their patients' questions and attitudes."[69]

Authority and setting may stifle collaboration.

The aura of authority may inhibit patients from seeking clarification or explanation. A woman who did not understand what *nodule* meant did not ask questions "because they all seem so busy, I really did not want to be a nuisance . . . and anyway she [nurse] behaved as though she expected me to know and I did not want to upset her."[70] The hope for a favorable prognosis leads patients to oversimplify complex situations or misinterpret information. Others are afraid they will appear stupid if they ask questions about words, explanations, problems, or procedures. For a variety of reasons, "patients routinely pass up, or actively 'withhold,' an opportunity to" ask about "the nature of the illness, its relative seriousness or the course it is likely to follow."[71]

A little knowledge can be dangerous.

Many of us rely on **lay theories** to communicate and interpret health problems. Common "theories" include: All *natural* products are healthful. If I no longer feel bad, I do not need to take my medicine. If a little of this medicine helps, a lot will do more good. If this medication helped me, it will help you. And radiation and chemicals are bad for you. Katherine Rowan and Michele Hoover write that "scientific notions that contradict these and other powerful lay theories are often difficult for patients to understand because patients' own lay alternatives seem irrefutably commonsensical."[72]

Ineffective Methods

Information is lost or distorted because of ineffective transmission methods. For instance, providers may rely on a single medium, such as oral information giving, but research reveals that about one-third of patients remember oral diagnoses while 70 percent recall written diagnoses.[73] Oral exchanges are often so brief and ambiguous that they are confusing or meaningless. A provider made this comment: "Now, Mr. Brown, you will find that for some weeks you will tire easily, but you must get plenty of exercise."[74] How long is "some weeks"; what does "tire easily" mean; and how much is "plenty of exercise"? Health care professionals routinely prescribe medications to be taken four times a day without telling the patient what that means: every six hours, every four hours with a maximum of four doses within 24 hours, or as needed, not to exceed four a day. Health care providers *overload* patients with data, details, and explanations far beyond their abilities to comprehend and recall. Ley discovered that within a few hours 82 percent of patients could recall two items of information, but the percentage dropped to 36 percent for three or four items, 12 percent for five or six items, and 3 percent for seven or more items.[75]

Employ more than one medium.

Avoid information overload.

Giving Information More Effectively

When giving information orally, place vocal emphasis on important words, dates, figures, warnings, and instructions. This is a substitute for the underlining, bold lettering, highlighting, and italicizing you employ in printed materials to indicate what is most important.

If you detect patients adhering to one of the lay theories mentioned earlier, help them recognize their theory and its apparent reasonableness and show its fallacies and potentially dangerous results. Encourage patients to ask questions by building in pauses and inviting inquiries, not at the end of a lengthy one-sided presentation. A silent patient may feel intimidated, hopelessly confused, or believe it is the provider's responsibility to provide adequate and clear information. Both parties must work to get and give information effectively and resolve inadequacies and confusions in an open exchange. Ask patients to repeat or explain what you have said and look for distortions, missing pieces, and misunderstandings.

An inquisitive patient is an informed patient.

Avoid overloading patients with information. Discover what they know and proceed from that point. Eliminate unnecessary materials. Reduce explanations and information to common and simple terms. Define technical terms and procedures or translate them into words and experiences patients understand. Present information

Discover what the patient knows.

in two or more interviews instead of one lengthy interview. As a rule, provide only enough clearly relevant information to satisfy the patient and the situation.

Involve a number of sources in the process. Include family members and friends so they can help retain and interpret information and aid in compliance with instructions. A common practice is for the attending physician to fill out a prescription order and explain what it is, what it is for, how it should be taken, and its potential side effects. Then the pharmacist who fills the prescription repeats the same information. Other important sources in this process are nurses, technicians, patient representatives, and receptionists. Make sure all participants in the organizational hierarchy are thoroughly informed about the patient so each is aware of what the patient knows, needs to know, and can be told.

The more heads, the better.

Organize information systematically to aid recall. Present important instructions first so they do not get lost in reactions to a diagnosis. Repeat important items strategically two or more times during the interaction so they are highlighted and easy to recall.

Use a variety of media, including pamphlets, leaflets, charts, pictures, slides, DVDs, models, and recordings. Dentists, for example, use models of teeth and jaws to explain dental problems and DVDs to show the benefits of flossing and brushing frequently. Emergency medical technicians use mannequins to teach CPR. Never hand a pamphlet or leaflet to a patient and say, "This will answer all of your questions." Patients report they are helpful but admit they seldom read them.

Employ a variety of resources.

The telephone, particularly with the widespread use of cell phones, accounts for nearly 25 percent of all patient–provider interactions.[76] Nurse call centers that integrate assessment, advice, and appointment systems are increasing rapidly and have transitioned from "nurse advice" to "telephone risk assessment." If nurses and other practitioners can satisfy patients and physicians that they are effective information conduits as part of a health care triad, the result will be timeliness, accuracy, quantity, and usefulness of information. Perceptions of accuracy and reliability—trust—are best when the telephone provider is seen as a reinforcer.[77] The telephone provider must note time, date, information, and recommendations for the file and pass on information to other providers in the triad.

The telephone accounts for one-fourth of health care interviews.

Counseling and Persuading

Most health care providers are *task oriented* and expect patients to follow their recommendations because they have the authority, expertise, and training. Unfortunately, patient compliance has been notoriously low, as low as 20 percent for prescribed drugs and as high as 50 percent for long-term treatment plans. With these compliance problems and the ever-greater emphasis on treating the whole person, providers must be more than information conduits. They must also act as **counselors** to help patients understand and deal with problems and **persuaders** to convince patients to follow recommendations accurately and faithfully.

Information giving does not ensure compliance.

Barriers to Effective Counseling and Persuading

Patients may make the health care interaction difficult by remaining silent, withdrawing, or complaining about a physical problem rather than admitting a psychological one.

Watch for hints and clues about real problems.

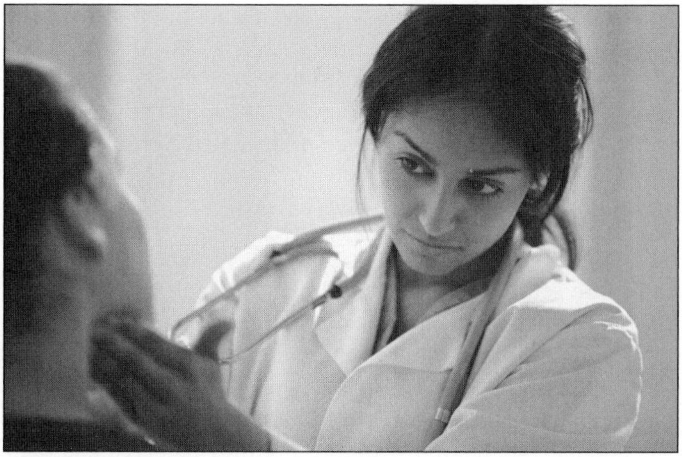

Health care professionals may spend little time talking with patients because they are task oriented rather than people oriented.

One of our students reported that she had missed an examination and several class sessions because she had cancer. Only later did we learn through a third party that the student had long suffered from severe depression and suicidal tendencies. She felt it was more acceptable to have a physical than a mental problem. A provider may dismiss a patient with a diagnosis of stress, nerves, or overactive imagination.

A health care provider may spend little time talking with a patient because there are many tasks to perform and talking is a social rather than a medical activity. Predictably, providers may fail to detect subtle cues and hints that a patient wants to talk about a different and more serious medical issue.

Providers may try to dodge unpleasant exchanges.

A health care provider may employ any of several **blocking tactics** to avoid counseling and persuading. Researchers and practitioners have identified these as all too common tactics:

- Using humor to dodge the issue.
- Denying the seriousness of a problem.
- Pursuing a less threatening line of conversation.
- Dismissing a medical concern by rejecting the patient's source of information such as the Internet or popular magazines.
- Providing minimal encouragement.
- Ignoring a patient's comment or question, perhaps by pretending not to hear.
- Becoming engrossed in a physical task.
- Changing the subject.
- Pretending to have a lack of information.
- Hiding behind hospital rules.
- Passing the buck to the physician, registered nurse, or specialist.
- Running away by leaving the room.

The nurse in the following exchange exhibits common blocking tactics.[78]

Nurse: There you are dear. Okay? (gives a tablet to the patient)

Patient: Thank you. Do you know, I can't feel anything at all with my fingers nowadays?

Nurse: Can't you? (minimal encouragement)

Patient: No, I go to pick up a knife and take my hand away and it's not there anymore.

Nurse: Oh, I broke my pencil! (walks away)

The patient desperately wants to talk to the nurse about a frightening and worsening condition, but the nurse is determined not to get involved or discuss the problem.

Effective Counseling and Persuading

Review the principles and guidelines presented in Chapters 10, 11, and 12. These are highly relevant to the health care setting. Parties should plan for each interview with five relational factors in mind: empathy, trust, honesty, mutual respect, and caring. Source credibility has long been recognized as a key ingredient in the counseling and persuasion process, and a study by Paulsel, McCroskey, and Richmond discovered that "perceptions of physician, nurse, and support staff competence and caring were positively correlated with patients' satisfaction with the care they received and their physician."[79]

Selecting an Appropriate Interviewing Approach

Tradition is not always best.

Providers have traditionally tried two approaches. The first is a paternalistic approach in which the provider assumes the patient will see the wisdom of advice provided and alter attitudes and behavior accordingly. The second is an advise and educate approach that explains the medical reasons why and hopes for the best. Neither approach, has produced results beyond 50 percent compliance. Telling patients what to do when they don't want to do it does not motivate them to act, and repeating unwanted advice may alienate them and produce resistance. Deborah Grandinetti advises that "change isn't an event; it's a process."[80] Let's focus on the process.

No approach is useful all of the time.

Select an approach that is collaborative and best suited to this patient at this time. Barbara Sharf and Suzanne Poirier use a theoretical framework that psychiatrists Szasz and Hollender developed to teach medical students how to select appropriate interview approaches.[81]

- An active (directive approach) is recommended when a patient is passive and unable to participate.
- An advisory (nondirective) approach is recommended when a patient is compliant because of acute illness and thus not at full capacity.
- A mutual participation (combination directive-nondirective) is recommended when gathering data, solving problems, and managing an illness of a patient who can participate fully.

Work for a team effort.

Regardless of approach, strive for **collaboration** during the interview by showing respect for the patient's agenda and encouraging mutual sensitivity. Adherence to medication and instructions is most likely when communication is optimal. Patients often have logical reasons for not complying: too embarrassing, painful, costly, dangerous side effects, ineffectiveness, or time-consuming. Discover this logic, present good counter-reasons, and employ tactful refutation to improve compliance.

Providing an Appropriate Climate

The patient should set the pace of the interaction. Significant changes come about over time and through a series of stages. Do not try to rush ahead or skip stages before either party is ready. A smoker, drinker, or overweight person is unlikely to change in one giant step. Be aware of how your voice and manner may influence a patient or provider.

Humor is an effective facilitator.

A researcher discovered, for instance, that when one physician emphasized the danger of swallowing medication for a canker sore in a direct and dire manner, the patient did not get the prescription filled. Another physician employed self-deprecating humor and a lighter tone when prescribing acne medication, and it was filled.[82] The effects of humor are well documented. Humor facilitates an open, personal, and caring climate; helps patients lose their patient role; and enables parties to convey thoughts and feelings in a nonthreatening and productive manner. If humor is insensitive or used ineffectively, it may embarrass, hurt, or mock the other party.

Encouraging Interaction

Sharing and caring are essential.

Encourage patients to talk. If you share your experiences and feelings, the patient is more likely to confide in you. This promotes self-disclosure beyond Level 1 interactions. Employ nonverbal communication (smiles, head nods, touches, and eye contact) to show that you care and want to listen. Listen with comprehension so that you understand what the patient is saying and implying. Listen with empathy so you can see the situation as the patient does. Don't ask too many questions. Richard Botelho uses question sequences such as the following to get the interviewee talking about a problem and its seriousness.[83]

Make each question count.

Interviewer: If you developed a complication from smoking, say lung disease, do you think you would quit smoking?

Interviewee: Yes, I think so.

Interviewer: Do you want to wait until you get a complication to decide to change?

Interviewee: No, I don't think so.

Interviewer: Why wait?

Use a range of responses and reactions (from highly nondirective to highly directive). Give advice only when the patient lacks information, is misinformed, does not react to less directive means, or challenges information and recommendations. Avoid blaming or judging that may create an adversarial relationship. Fear appeals may lead to patient denial or avoidance of regimens, medications, and checkups. Offer praise for past performance and compliance.

Considering Solutions

Approach a solution when the patient is ready to listen and comply. One survey revealed that only 10 percent of providers feel they are successful in "helping patients change any health-related" behavior.[84] Compliance is low "when instructions are 'preventive,' when patients are without symptoms, and when the treatment regimen lasts for a long period of time."[85]

Collaborate to achieve incremental changes.

Provider and patient should jointly construct a plan of action that recognizes social, psychological, and financial constraints. Present strategies in the context of the patient's life; share the logic behind health care decisions; enable patients to create their own narratives about their health; encourage patients to assume accountability for their decisions; identify short-term goals; and collaborate in naming resources and examining alternative options.[86] Similarly, Lisa Maher writes that providers should "have patients voice their own reasons for change. The patient—not the physician—must articulate the reasons for making—or not making—a change."[87] These recommendations promote **self-persuasion**.

The patient must follow through on commitments.

Present specific instructions and demonstrate how easy they are to follow. Express hope and recall challenges the patient has met in the past. The goals are to encourage patients, give them hope, and provide good reasons for complying with *mutually* agreed upon recommendations. You may have to persuade the patient they will work, are doable, and are effective. You cannot resolve the patient's problem; only the patient can do that.

Closing the Interview

The closing must be a collaborative effort.

When closing the health care interview both parties need to understand completely and clearly what they have discussed, the information they have exchanged, the recommendations made, and agreements reached. Clearinghouse probing questions are essential as an initial closing device: "Is there anything else you wanted to discuss today?" "Are there any other concerns we haven't addressed?"

Important questions and revelations occur during the closing.

The opening may focus on a single concern, so it seems reasonable to conclude the interview once this concern is addressed. However, patients may hold back information or a concern until the closing minutes of the interview. They may ask questions during the final minutes when the provider is busy writing out prescriptions, information, or regimens and is paying less attention. The real purpose of the patient's visit gets lost in the closing.

The summary phase of the interview "must not only make sense to the patient, but also must make sense in terms of the medical care the physician can offer."[88] Make it thorough but not overwhelming with too much information. Ask questions to be certain the patient understands what has taken place, what has been agreed to, and what will happen next, particularly the patient's responsibilities and tasks. Ask patients to tell you these in their words to reveal confusions, misunderstandings, intentions, and successful information exchange.

Close the interaction on a positive and productive note that communicates understanding, empathy, trust, and caring. How each party closes the interview will enhance or detract from the relationship and influence the nature of the next interaction and whether or not there will be a next interaction. A recent study revealed that "Patients' postvisit satisfaction with physicians' communication is important because it is positively associated with objective measures of physician's task proficiency, patients' adherence to medical recommendations, and patients' continuity of care."[89]

Summary

The health care interview is common, difficult, and complex. Situations vary from routine to life-threatening and the perceptions of both parties influence the nature and success of interviews. For a health care interview to be successful, it must be a collaborative effort between provider and patient, and this requires a relationship based on trust, respect, sharing of control, equality of treatment, and understanding. A collaborative and productive relationship will reduce the anxiety, fear, hostility, and reticence that often accompany health care interviews. Provider and patient must strive to be effective information getters, information givers, and counselor–persuaders.

Providers (from receptionist to physician) and patients (including families and friends) must realize that good communication is essential in health care interviews and that communication skills do not come naturally or with experience. Skills require training and practice. Each party must learn how to listen as well as speak, understand as well as inform, commit to as well as seek resolutions to problems. Communication without commitment is fruitless. Both parties must follow through with agreements and prescribed regimens and medications.

Key Terms and Concepts

The online learning center for this text features FLASH CARDS and CROSSWORD PUZZLES for studying based on these terms and concepts.

Assumptions
Baby talk
Blocking tactics
Climate
Co-agency
Collaboration
Confirmatory questions
Counselors
Elderspeak
Face threatening
General inquiry questions
Information overload
Jargon
Lay theories
Patient-centered care
Persuaders
Politeness theory
Relational distance
Self-persuasion
Stereotypes
Stories/narratives
Task oriented
Trust

A Health Care Interview for Review and Analysis

This interview is between a nurse practitioner and a 19-year-old student who ran into a city bus on campus as he hurried to an 8:00 a.m. class on his skateboard. A friend riding near him helped him to the emergency room of the university health center. The patient is bruised and has a large bump on his forehead but does not appear to have any broken bones. He has a number of aches and pains and has been admitted to a treating room.

Assess the relationship between provider and patient. How collaborative is this interaction? How effectively do provider and patient get and give information? How effectively does the provider counsel and persuade the patient? How appropriate is the blend of directive and nondirective reactions and responses? How effectively do provider and patient use questions? How does the friend of the patient help and hinder the interview process?

1. **Provider:** Sean Crider?
2. **Patient:** Yes.
3. **Provider:** Are you a student?
4. **Patient:** Yes.
5. **Provider:** What's your student ID?
6. **Patient:** 379-267-495.
7. **Provider:** Did this happen on campus?
8. **Patient's friend:** Yes, just down the street.
9. **Provider:** Where was that?
10. **Patient's friend:** About the corner of University and Stadium.
11. **Provider:** You were riding a bike?
12. **Patient's friend:** He has a really bad bump on his head and may have some broken ribs.
13. **Provider:** Are you unable to reply to my questions?
14. **Patient:** No, I can do that, but I'm really hurting on my right side.
15. **Provider:** You were riding a bike?
16. **Patient's friend:** No. He ran right into a city bus full of students.
17. **Provider:** I see. Were you running too fast or just in a hurry, Sean?
18. **Patient:** No. I was on my skateboard. Dopey here turned off my alarm.
19. **Provider:** A skateboard.
20. **Patient:** Yeah.
21. **Patient's friend:** They're safer than bikes.
22. **Provider:** Uh-huh. Do you have a headache?
23. **Patient:** Yeah.
24. **Provider:** Are you nauseous?
25. **Patient:** I don't think so.
26. **Provider:** Okay. First, let's take a look at that bump on your head. It's a nasty one. Have you experienced any blurred vision or dizziness since this happened?
27. **Patient:** I was a little light-headed right after it happened.
28. **Patient's friend:** Yeah, he was staggering around like it was Saturday night.
29. **Provider:** You hadn't been drinking, had you?
30. **Patient:** No. Not that early in the morning.
31. **Patient's friend:** He usually waits until at least 9:00.
32. **Provider:** Uh-huh. How do you feel now? Are you disoriented?
33. **Patient:** Maybe.
34. **Provider:** You're not sure? I'll clean that bump and cut for you.
35. **Patient:** Will I need stitches?

36. **Provider:** Maybe a couple. Does that bother you?
37. **Patient:** A little. I've never had a stitch before.
38. **Provider:** It's nothing; you'll hardly feel it.
39. **Patient's friend:** Hey, man, I've had a lot of stitches. It's not fun . . .
40. **Provider:** (to the friend) Why don't you have a seat in the waiting room? Sean will be out soon.
41. **Patient's friend:** Thanks, but I want to stay with my buddy.
42. **Provider:** Okay. Are you allergic to any medications?
43. **Patient:** I'm not sure.
44. **Provider:** Okay. I'll prescribe a painkiller that I want you to take four times a day.
45. **Patient:** Whenever I need to take one?
46. **Provider:** No. Take one every four to six hours. I want you to place an ice pack on your head for the next couple of hours.
47. **Patient:** I live off campus a couple of miles. And I've got to get to my history exam at 10:00.
48. **Patient's friend:** He could come over to my chem lab. We've got ice there.
49. **Provider:** I would like him to remain here for an hour or so until we know he is okay. We need to do some X rays to see if you have any broken ribs. Take a deep breath and let me know how that feels.
50. **Patient:** Oww! That hurts a lot about here.
51. **Provider:** Okay, I want one of our staff to take you down to the X-ray department. Then, he will bring you back up here so we can give you an ice pack and wait on the X-ray results.
52. **Patient:** I can walk okay.
53. **Patient's friend:** Yeah. He walked over here.
54. **Provider:** I'm sure you feel you can, but we don't want to take any chances on your falling. Take this form with you to the X-ray area, and I'll see you soon.
55. **Patient's friend:** That's good because both of his parents are attorneys.
56. **Provider:** Uh-huh. See you in a few minutes. You won't need an attorney, just your X-ray form.

Health Care Role-Playing Cases

A First Visit

The patient recently moved to Salt Lake City after graduating from Montana State University and is meeting for the first time with a primary care physician she never met. She is in good health but wants a checkup and a chance to establish a relationship with a physician near her apartment in Salt Lake City. After making an appointment with the physician, she asked her former primary care physician in Helena, Montana, to send her medical records to her new physician for review prior to her appointment.

A Gunshot Victim

The patient was hunting rabbits with a friend, and the friend spun around trying to get a good shot at a rabbit. He didn't see his companion who was walking about 25 yards to his left. The patient's face was struck by at least a dozen shot, one in his left eye. While his wounds are being cleaned and the shot removed from his face before surgery on his eye, a nurse must get her medical history and determine if he is allergic to any medications or anesthesia. The patient is in a great deal of pain and wants to get on with the surgery.

First Aid at a Football Game

The patient was attending the Green Bay Packers and Chicago Bears football game at Soldier Field in Chicago when he became very dizzy and had trouble focusing. His brother and sister who were accompanying him called 911 and first aid workers employed by Soldier Field rushed to his aid. They helped him from the stands to the nearest first aid station and are in the process of checking his vital signs and learning about his medical history. They have requested that a physician join them as soon as possible, and an ambulance crew is standing by. The patient seems disoriented.

An Annual Checkup

The patient, age 48, has scheduled an annual checkup with his long-time primary caregiver. They were college roommates and kept in touch as the patient became a well-known aeronautical engineer and the caregiver a widely recognized specialist in internal medicine. The patient's family has a history of heart problems; his father and two uncles died of heart attacks in their early fifties. The physician has been urging the patient to exercise more and lose weight for a number of years. The stress caused by the increasing difficulty of securing government grants for aerospace projects is beginning to take a toll on the patient.

Student Activities

1. Nurse practitioners are becoming ever more common in health care, often seeing patients instead of physicians. Interview an experienced nurse practitioner and discuss with this caregiver how she establishes and maintains relationships with patients and other members of her health care organization: receptionists, technicians, nurses, and physicians. How does the nurse practitioner deal with patients who clearly expect to see a physician rather than a "nurse"? How does she deal with physicians who see her as encroaching on their turf?
2. Interview three physicians about problems they have encountered when giving information to patients. Probe into how these physicians have addressed these problems successfully and unsuccessfully. How do they approach giving information to patients of different cultures, ages, genders, levels of education, and health status? What kinds of information tend to get lost or misinterpreted most often? Why does this happen?
3. Visit a pediatric ward of a hospital. Observe how physicians, nurses, technicians, child-life specialists, and other providers address and interact with young patients.

Talk with some of these providers about their training in communication with small children. What communication problems do they experience that are unique to different ages of children?

4. Your campus, like most in the United States, is likely to have students and families from many different countries. Visit the campus health center or a local hospital and discuss how they interact effectively with patients who speak little or no English. What types of interpreters have they used: family, hospital, volunteer, or telephone interpreters? Which do they use most often? What problems have they encountered with interpreters?

Notes

1. Gwen A. Hullman and Mary Daily, "Evaluating Physician Communication Competence Scales: A Replication and Extension," *Communication Research Reports* 25 (November 2008), p. 316.
2. Amanda Young and Linda Flower, "Patients as Partners, Patients as Problem-Solvers," *Health Communication* 14 (2001), p. 76.
3. Richard L. Street, Jr., and Bradford Millay, "Analyzing Patient Participation in Medical Encounters," *Health Communication* 13 (2001), p. 61; Christina M. Sabee, Carma L. Bylund, Rebecca S. Imes, Amy A. Sanford, and Ian S. Rice, "Patients' Attributions for Health-Care Provider Responses to Patients' Presentation of Internet Health Research," *Southern Communication Journal* 72 (July–September 2007), pp. 265–266.
4. Young and Flower, p. 71.
5. Laura L. Cardello, Eileen Berlin Ray, and Gary R. Pettey, "The Relationship of Perceived Physician Communicator Style to Patient Satisfaction," *Communication Reports* 8 (1995), p. 27; Rubin, p. 107.
6. Kami J. Silk, Catherine Kingsley Westerman, Renee Strom, and Kyle R. Andrews, "The Role of Patient-Centeredness in Predicting Compliance with Mammogram Recommendations: An Analysis of the Health Information National Trends Survey," *Communication Research Reports* 25 (May 2008), p. 132.
7. Chas D. Koermer and Meghan Kilbane, "Physician Sociality Communication and Its Effects on Patient Satisfaction," *Communication Quarterly* 56 (February 2008), p. 81.
8. Diana Louise Carter, "Doctors, Patients Need to Communicate," Lafayette, IN *Journal & Courier,* February 22, 2004, p. E5.
9. Hullman and Daily, p. 321.
10. Kandi L. Walker, Christa L. Arnold, Michelle Miller-Day, and Lynne M. Webb, "Investigating the Physician-Patient Relationship: Examining Emerging Themes," *Health Communication* 14 (2001), p. 54.
11. Sabee, Bylund, Imes, Sanford, and Rice, pp. 268, 278–282.

12. Walker, Arnold, Miller-Day, and Webb, pp. 51–52; Merlene M. von Friederichs-Fitzwater and John Gilgun, "Relational Control in Physician-Patient Encounters," *Health Communication* 3 (2001), p. 75.

13. Sabee, Bylund, Imes, Sanford, and Rice, p. 266; Silk, Westerman, Strom, and Andrews, p. 139.

14. Donald J. Cegala, Carmin Gade, Stefne Lenzmeier Broz, and Leola McClure, "Physicians' and Patients' Perceptions of Patients' Communication Competence in a Primary Care Medical Interview," *Health Communication* 16 (2004), pp. 289–304.

15. Walker, Arnold, Miller-Day, and Webb, p. 56.

15a. Carma L. Bylund and Gregory Makoul, "Examining Empathy in Medical Encounters: An Observational Study Using the Empathic Communication Coding System," *Health Communication* 18 (2005), pp. 123–140.

16. Bruce L. Lambert, Richard L. Street, Donald J. Cegala, David H. Smith, Suzanne Kurtz, and Theo Schofield, "Provider–Patient Communication, Patient-Centered Care and the Mangle of Practice," *Health Communication* 9 (1997), pp. 27–43; Silk, Westerman, Strom, and Andrews, p. 132.

16a. Marie R. Haug, "The Effects of Physician/Elder Patient Characteristics on Health Communication," *Health Communication* 8 (1996), p. 256; Hullman and Daily, p. 317; Ashley P. Duggan and Ylisabyth S. Bradshaw, "Mutual Influence Processes in Physician-Patient Communication: An Interaction Adaptation Perspective," *Communication Research Reports* 25 (August 2008), p. 221.

17. Kelsy Lin Ulrey and Patricia Amason, "Intercultural Communication between Patients and Health Care Providers: An Exploration of Intercultural Communication Effectiveness, Cultural Sensitivity, Stress, and Anxiety," *Health Communication* 13 (2001), pp. 454 and 460.

18. Haug, pp. 253–254; Anne S. Gabbard-Alley, "Health Communication and Gender," *Health Communication* 7 (1995), pp. 35–54; von Friederichs-Fitzwater and Gilgun, p. 84.

19. Carma Bylund, "Mothers' Involvement in Decision Making During the Birthing Process: A Quantitative Analysis of Women's Online Birth Stories," *Health Communication* 18 (2005), p. 35.

20. Haug, pp. 252–253; Connie J. Conlee, Jane Olvera, and Nancy N. Vagim, "The Relationship among Physician Nonverbal Immediacy and Measures of Patient Satisfaction with Physician Care," *Communication Reports* 6 (1993), p. 26.

21. G. Winzelberg, A. Meier, and L. Hanson, "Identifying Opportunities and Challenges to Improving Physician-Surrogate Communication," *The Gerontologist* 44 (October 2005), p. 1.

22. Michael Greenbaum and Glenn Flores, "Lost in Translation," *Modern Healthcare,* May 3, 2004, p. 21.

23. Karolynn Siegel and Victoria Raveis, "Perceptions of Access to HIV-Related Information, Care, and Services among Infected Minority Men," *Qualitative Health Care* 7 (1997), pp. 9–31.

24. von Friederichs-Fitzwater and Gilgun, p. 84.

25. Silk, Westerman, Strom, and Andrews, p. 140.

26. Gary L. Kreps and Barbara C. Thornton, *Health Communication: Theory and Practice* (Prospects-Heights, IL: Waveland Press, 1992), pp. 157–178. See also Gary L. Kreps, *Effective Communication in Multicultural Health Care Settings* (Thousand Oaks, CA: Sage, 1994).

27. Alice Chen, "Doctoring Across the Language Divide," *Health Affairs,* May/June 2006, p. 810.

28. Kristine Williams, Susan Kemper, and Mary Lee Hummert, "Improving Nursing Home Communication: An Intervention to Reduce Elderspeak," *The Gerentologist,* April 2003, pp. 242–247.

29. Young and Flower, p. 72.

30. Maria Brann and Marifran Mattson, "Toward a Typology of Confidentiality Breaches in Health Care Communication: An Ethic of Care Analysis of Provider Practices and Patient Perceptions," *Health Communication* 16 (2004), pp. 230 and 241.

31. Walker, Arnold, Miller-Day, and Webb, p. 57.

32. Juliann Scholl and Sandra L. Ragan, "The Use of Humor in Promoting Positive Provider–Patient Interaction in a Hospital Rehabilitation Unit," *Health Communication* 15 (2003), pp. 319 and 321.

33. Jason H. Wrench and Melanie Booth-Butterfield, "Increasing Patient Satisfaction and Compliance: An Examination of Physician Humor Orientation, Compliance-Gaining Strategies, and Perceived Credibility," *Communication Quarterly* 51 (2003), pp. 485 and 495.

34. Taya Flores, "Humanistic Medicine: Compassion and Communication Vital to Patients," Lafayette, IN *Journal & Courier*, March 31, 2009, p. D1.

35. Mohan J. Dutta-Bergman, "The Relation Between Health Orientation, Provider–Patient Communication, and Satisfaction: An Individual-Difference Approach," *Health Communication* 18 (2005), p. 300.

36. Koermer and Kilbane, pp. 70–81.

37. Judith Ann Spiers, "The Use of Face Work and Politeness Theory," *Qualitative Health Research* 8 (1998), pp. 25–47.

38. "Improving Care with an Automated Patient History," Online CME from Medscape, *Family Practice Medicine* (2007), pp. 39–43, http://www.medscape.com/viewarticle/561574+3, accessed December 2, 2008.

39. John Heritage and Jeffrey D. Robinson, "The Structure of Patients' Presenting Concerns: Physicians' Opening Questions," *Health Communication* 19 (2006), p. 100.

40. Delthia Ricks, "Study: Women Fudge the Truth with Doctors," *Indianapolis Star*, April 1, 2007, p. A21.

41. Amanda J. Dillard, Kevin D. McCaul, Pamela D. Kelso, and William M. P. Klein, "Resisting Good News: Reactions to Breast Cancer Risk Communication," *Health Communication* 19 (2006), p. 115.

42. Dillard, McCaul, Kelso, and Klein, p. 123.

43. Allen J. Enelow and Scott N. Swisher, *Interviewing and the Patient* (New York: Oxford University Press, 1986), pp. 47–50; A. D. Wright et al., "Patterns of Acquisition of Interview Skills by Medical Students," *The Lancet*, November 1, 1980, pp. 964–966.

44. Kelly S. McNellis, "Assessing Communication Competence in the Primary Care Interview," *Communication Studies* 53 (2002), p. 412.

45. Carol Lynn Thompson and Linda M. Pledger, "Doctor–Patient Communication: Is Patient Knowledge of Medical Terminology Improving?" *Health Communication* 5 (1993), pp. 89–97.

46. Julie W. Scherz, Harold T. Edwards, and Ken J. Kallail, "Communicative Effectiveness of Doctor–Patient Interactions," *Health Communication* 7 (1995), p. 171.

47. Donald J. Cegala, Richard L. Street, Jr., and C. Randall Clinch, "The Impact of Patient Participation on Physician's Information Provision during a Primary Care Interview," *Health Communication* 21 (2007), pp. 177 and 181.

48. Cegala, Street, and Clinch, p. 181.

49. Ricks, p. A21.

50. Susan Eggly, "Physician–Patient Co-Construction of Illness Narratives in the Medical Interview," *Health Communication* 14 (2002), pp. 340 and 358.

51. Kreps and Thornton, p. 37.

52. Eggly, p. 343.

53. Young and Flower, p. 87.

54. Marlene von Friederichs-Fitzwater, Edward D. Callahan, and John Williams, "Relational Control in Physician–Patient Encounters," *Health Communication* 3 (1991), pp. 17–36.

55. Heritage and Robinson, p. 100.

56. Scott E. Caplan, Beth J. Haslett, and Brant R. Burleson, "Telling It Like It Is: The Adaptive Function of Narratives in Coping with Loss in Later Life," *Health Communication* 17 (2005), pp. 233–252.

57. Annette Harres, "'But Basically You're Feeling Well, Are You?': Tag Questions in Medical Consultations," *Health Communication* 10 (1998), pp. 111–123.

58. "American Medical Association Report Provides Guidelines for Improved Patient Communication," *U.S. Newswire,* June 19, 2006, accessed October 25, 2006.

59. Greenbaum and Flores, p. 21.

60. Chen, p. 812.

61. P. Ley, "What the Patient Doesn't Remember," *Medical Opinion Review* 1 (1966), pp. 69–73.

62. Sabee, Bylund, Imes, Sanford, and Rice, pp. 265–284.

63. Stan A. Kaplowitz, Shelly Campo, and Wai Tat Chiu, "Cancer Patients' Desires for Communication of Prognosis Information," *Health Communication* 14 (2002), p. 237.

64. Silk, Westerman, Strom, and Andrews, p. 141.

65. Sabee, Bylund, Imes, Sanford, and Rice, p. 267.

66. Mohan Dutta-Bergman, "Primary Sources of Health Information: Comparisons in the Domain of Health Attitudes, Health Cognitions, and Health Behaviors," *Health Communication* 16 (2004), p. 285.

67. Shoba Ramanadhan and K. Viswanath, "Health and the Information Seeker: A Profile," *Health Communication* 20 (2006), pp. 131–139.

68. S. Deborah Majerovitz, Michele G. Greene, Ronald A. Adelman, George M. Brody, Kathleen Leber, and Susan W. Healy, "Older Patients' Understanding of Medical Information in the Emergency Department," *Health Communication* 9 (1997), pp. 237–251.

69. Akihito Hagihara, Kimio Tarumi, and Koichi Nobutomo, "Physicians' and Patients' Recognition of the Level of the Physician's Explanation in Medical Encounters," *Health Communication* 20 (2006), p. 104.

70. Patricia MacMillan, "What's in a Word?" *Nursing Times*, February 26, 1981, p. 354.

71. Jeffrey D. Robinson, "An Interactional Structure of Medical Activities during Acute Visits and Its Implications for Patients' Participation," *Health Communication* 15 (2003), p. 49.

72. Katherine E. Rowan and D. Michele Hoover, "Communicating Risk to Patients: Diagnosing and Overcoming Lay Theories," in *Communicating Risk to Patients* (Rockville, MD: The U.S. Pharmacopeial Convention, 1995), p. 74.

73. Carter, p. E5.

74. F. S. Hewitt, "Just Words: Talking Our Way through It," *Nursing Times*, February 26, 1981, pp. 5–8.

75. Ley, pp. 69–73.

76. Thomas K. Houston, Daniel Z. Sands, Beth R. Nash, and Daniel E. Ford, "Experiences of Physicians Who Frequently Use E-Mail with Patients," *Health Communication* 15 (2003), p. 516.

77. Gerald R. Ledlow, H. Dan O'Hair, and Scott Moore, "Predictors of Communication Quality: The Patient, Provider, and Nurse Call Center Triad," *Health Communication* 15 (2003), pp. 437 and 457.

78. Jill M. Clark, "Communication in Nursing," *Nursing Times,* January 1, 1981, p. 16.

79. Michelle L. Paulsel, James C. McCroskey, and Virginia P. Richmond, "Perceptions of Health Care Professionals' Credibility as a Predictor of Patients' Satisfaction with Their Health Care and Physician," *Communication Research Reports* 23 (2006), p. 74.

80. Deborah Grandinetti, "Turning No to Yes: How to Motivate the Reluctant Patient," *Medical Economics*, June 15, 1998, pp. 97–111.

81. Barbara F. Sharf and Suzanne Poirier, "Exploring (UN)Common Ground: Communication and Literature in a Health Care Setting," *Communication Education* 37 (1988), pp. 227–229.

82. Roxanne Parrott, "Exploring Family Practitioners' and Patients' Information Exchange about Prescribed Medications: Implications for Practitioners' Interviewing and Patients' Understanding," *Health Communication* 6 (1994), pp. 267–280.

83. Grandinetti, pp. 97–111.

84. Lisa Maher, "Motivational Interviewing: What, When, and Why," *Patient Care*, September 15, 1998, pp. 55–60.

85. Shelley D. Lane, "Communication and Patient Compliance," in *Explorations in Provider and Patient Interaction*, Loyd F. Pettegrew, ed. (Louisville, KY: Humana, 1982), pp. 59–69.

86. Young and Flower, pp. 69–89.

87. Maher, pp. 55–60.

88. Manning and Ray, p. 467.

89. Jeffrey D. Robinson, Janice L. Raup-Krieger, Greg Burke, Valerie Weber, and Brett Oesterling, "The Relative Influence of Patients' Pre-Visit Global Satisfaction with Medical Care on Patients' Post-Visit Satisfaction with Physicians' Communication," *Communication Research Reports* 25 (February 2008), p. 2.

Resources

Kar, Snehendu B. *Health Communication: A Multicultural Perspective.* Thousand Oaks, CA: Sage 2001.

Murero, Monica, and Ronald E. Rice, *The Internet and Health Care: Theory, Research and Practice.* Mahwah, NJ: Lawrence Erlbaum, 2006.

Ray, Eileen Berlin, ed. *Health Communication in Practice: A Case Study Approach.* Mahwah, NJ: Lawrence Erlbaum, 2005.

Thompson, Teresa L., Alicia Dorsey, and Roxanne Parrott, eds. *Handbook of Health Communication.* Mahwah, NJ: Lawrence Erlbaum, 2003.

Wright, Kevin B., and Scott D. Moore, eds. *Applied Health Communication.* Cresskill, NJ: Hampton Press, 2008.

GLOSSARY

Abrupt or curt: short and often rude responses or curtailing of interactions.

Accidental bias: when an interviewer unintentionally leads respondents to give answers they feel the interviewer wants them to give rather than their true feelings, attitudes, or beliefs.

Ad hominem: an effort to dodge an issue or challenge by discrediting the source that raised it.

Ad populum: an appeal to or on behalf of the majority.

Ambiguity: words to which interview parties may assign very different meanings.

Analysis: a careful examination of the nature and content of answers and impressions noted during an interview.

Appearance: how you look to the other party in the interview, including dress and physical appearance.

Applicant profile: the required knowledge, experiences, skills, and personal traits necessary to perform a job satisfactorily.

Application form: a form created by an organization to gather basic information about applicants, including their backgrounds, experiences, education, and career interests.

Appraisal perspective: the performance interview is seen as required, scheduled, superior-conducted and directed, adversarial, evaluative, and past-oriented.

Arguing from accepted belief: argument based on an accepted belief, assumption, or proposition.

Arguing from analogy: argument based on common characteristics of two people, places, objects, proposals, or ideas shared.

Arguing from cause-effect: an argument that attempts to establish a causal relationship.

Arguing from condition: an argument based on the assertion that if something does or does not happen, something else will or will not happen.

Arguing from example: an argument based on a sampling of a given class of people, places, or things.

Arguing from facts: an argument based on a conclusion that best explains a body of facts.

Arguing from two choices: arguing that there are only two possible proposals or courses of action and then eliminating one of the choices.

Arrival: the point at which one interview party encounters the other to initiate an interview.

Assumptions: assuming that something is true or false, is intended or unintended, exists or does not exist, is desired or undesired, will or will not happen.

Attitude: relatively enduring combinations of beliefs that predispose people to respond in particular ways to persons, organizations, places, ideas, and issues.

Baby talk: speaking to elder patients as if they were infants, including slower rate, exaggerated intonation, and simpler vocabulary.

Balance or consistency theory: a theory based on the belief that human beings strive for a harmonious existence with self and others and experience psychological discomfort (dissonance) when they do not.

Balanced scorecard approach: compensation, measurement, and performance are tied to coaching and improved performance.

Bandwagon tactic: a tactic that urges a person to follow the crowd, to do what everyone else is doing.

Basic skills tests: tests that measure mathematics, measurement, reading, and spelling skills.

Behavior-based selection: selection based upon the behaviors desired in a position and behaviors exhibited by applicants.

Behavior-based selection technique: a selection technique that begins with a needs and position analysis to determine which behaviors are essential for performing a particular job and proceeds to match applicants with this analysis.

Behaviorally anchored rating scale (BARS) model: a performance review model that identifies essential skills for a specific job and sets standards through a job analysis.

Belief: the trust or confidence placed in social, political, historic, economic, and religious claims.

Bipolar question: a question that limits the respondent to two polar choices such as yes or no, agree or disagree.

Bipolar trap: a bipolar question phrased to elicit a yes or no response when the questioner wants a detailed answer or specific information.

Birds of a feather syndrome: the selection of employees most similar to interviewers.

Blocking tactics: efforts of interviewers to avoid counseling or getting involved with interviewees, particularly in the health care setting.

Board interview: when two to five persons representing an organization may interview an applicant at the same time.

Bogardus Social Distance scales: questions that determine how respondents feel about social relationships and distances from them.

Bona fide occupational qualifications (BFOQ): requirements essential for performing a particular job.

Broadcast interview: an interview that takes place live over radio or television or will be played all or in part at a later time.

Built-in bias: interviewer bias that is intentionally or unintentionally built into a schedule of questions.

Career/Job fairs: gatherings of organizations and companies, often at malls or on college campuses, during which job seekers may make contacts with representatives and gather information about employment opportunities.

Career objective: a brief, concise statement of a targeted career goal.

Case approach: when an applicant is placed into a carefully crafted situation that takes hours to study and resolve.

Catalytic coaching: a comprehensive, integrated performance management system based on a paradigm of development.

Cause-to-effect sequence: an outline that addresses causes and effects separately but relationally.

Central tendency: when interviewers refrain from assigning extreme ratings to facets of performance.

Chain or contingency strategy: a strategy that allows for preplanned secondary questions in survey interviews.

Chronological format resume: a resume that lists education, training, and experiences in chronological order.

Clearinghouse probe: a question designed to discover whether previous questions have uncovered everything of importance on a topic or issue.

Client-centered approach: a counseling approach that focuses on the client rather than content or situation.

Closed-minded or authoritarian interviewees: parties with unchangeable central beliefs who rely on trusted authorities when making decisions.

Closed question: a question that is narrow in focus and restricts the respondent's freedom to determine the amount and kind of information to offer.

Closing: the portion of an interview that brings it to an end.

Coaching: helping to improve performance rather than judging or criticizing performance.

Cognitive phase: the thinking and assessing phase of a counseling interview.

Cold calls: persuasive interview contacts made without an appointment or prior notice.

Collaboration: a mutual effort by both parties to inform, analyze, and resolve problems.

Collectivist culture: a culture that places high value on group image, group esteem, group reliance, group awareness, and achievement of the group.

Combination schedule: a question schedule that combines two schedules, such as highly scheduled and highly scheduled standardized.

Communication interactions: verbal and nonverbal exchanges that take place during interviews.

Comparison tactic: a person points out a few similarities between two places, people, or things and then draws conclusions from this superficial comparison.

Competitive rater: an interviewer who believes that no one can perform higher than his or her level of performance.

Complement: to complete, support, or repeat.

Complex interpersonal communication process: the assumption that one-to-one communication is simple is belied by the many variables that interact in this process.

Complexity vs. simplicity: questions that are either complex in wording and options or simple in wording and options.

Compliance: when an interviewee follows assessments and courses of action agreed to during a counseling interview.

Confirmatory questions: questions designed to verify understanding of an interviewee's (typically medical patients) concerns, problems, or statements.

Connotations: positive and negative meanings of words.

Conscious transparency: sharing information with applicants, explaining the purpose of questions, providing a supportive climate, and promoting unrestricted dialogue between interview parties.

Consubstantiality: the effort to establish a substantial sameness or similarity between interviewer and interviewee.

Contrast principle: if a second item or choice is fairly different from the first, it seems more different than it actually is.

Control: the extent to which one or both interview parties directs an interview.

Convenience sample: a sample taken when and where it is most convenient for the interviewee.

Conversation: an unstructured interaction between two or more people with no predetermined purpose other than enjoyment of the process.

Counselors: those who help interviewees to gain insights into and to cope with problems.

Counter persuasion: persuasion aimed at an interviewee by a persuader's competitor or antagonist following a persuasive interview.

Cover letter: a letter an applicant sends to a prospective employer that expresses interest in and qualifications for a position.

Critical incident question: a question that asks applicants how they might resolve a current problem the recruiter's organization is facing.

Cross-sectional study: a study that determines what is known, thought, or felt during a narrow time span.

Culture: shared customs, norms, knowledge, attitudes, values, and traits of a racial, religious, social, or corporate group.

Curious probe: a question that is irrelevant to the interviewer's stated purpose.

Defensive climate: a climate that appears threatening to one or both parties in an interview.

Determinate interviews: an interview designed to determine whether or not to make a job offer to an applicant.

Developmental model: the performance interview is initiated by individuals when needed, subordinate-conducted and directed, now and future oriented, cooperative, and self-satisfying.

Dialectical tensions: the result of conflicts over opposing needs and desires or between contrasting "voices" in an interview.

Dialogic listening: a means of focusing on ours rather than mine or yours to resolve a problem or task.

Diamond sequence: a question sequence that places two funnel sequences top to top.

Differentiation: an attempt through language to alter how a person sees reality by renaming it.

Directive approach: an interview in which the interviewer controls subject matter, length of answers, climate, and formality.

Directive reactions: when an interviewer reacts to a client with specific evaluations and advice.

Disclosure: the willingness and ability to reveal feelings, beliefs, attitudes, and information to another party.

Dishonesty: lying to or deceiving another interview party.

Don't ask, don't tell: a question that delves into information or an emotional area that a respondent may be incapable of addressing because of social, psychological, or situational constraints.

Double-barreled inquisition: a question that contains two or more questions.

Downward communication: an interview in which a superior in the organizational hierarchy is attempting to interact as an interviewer with a subordinate in the hierarchy.

Dyadic: an interaction that involves two distinct parties.

EEO laws: state and federal laws that pertain to recruiting and reviewing the performance of employees.

EEO violation question pitfall: when an interviewer asks an unlawful question during a recruiting interview.

Elderspeak: speaking to elder patients as if they were children, including addressing them as sweeties, girl or boy, and honey and employing the collective pronoun *our* (e.g., "it's time for our bath").

Electronic interviews: interviews conducted over the telephone, through conference calls, by video talk-back, or over the Internet.

Electronically scanned resume: a resume designed in format and wording to be scanned electronically by recruiters.

E-mail interviews: interviews conducted through electronic e-mail rather than face-to-face.

Equal Employment Opportunity Commission: the agency assigned the task of overseeing and carrying out EEO laws.

Equal Employment Opportunity (EEO) laws: laws that pertain to employment and performance review interviews.

Ethical issues: issues that focus on value judgments concerning degrees of right and wrong, goodness and badness, in human conduct.

Euphemism: the substitution of a better sounding word for a common one.

Evaluative interval scales: questions that ask respondents to make judgments about persons, places, things, or ideas.

Evaluative response question pitfall: when an interviewer expresses judgmental feelings about an answer that may bias or skew the next answer.

Evasive interviewee: an interviewee who evades questions and gives indirect answers.

Evidence: examples, stories, comparisons, testimony, and statistics that support a claim being made.

Exchanging: a sharing of roles, responsibilities, feelings, beliefs, motives, and information during an interview.

Expressed feelings: feelings an interviewee expresses overtly and openly during a counseling interaction.

Face-to-face interview: an interview in which both parties are present physically in the same space during an interview.

Face threatening: interview interactions in which questions and answers may threaten the power or credibility of the interviewer.

Failed departure: when an interview has come to a close and parties have taken leave of one another only to come in contact accidentally later, often with a degree of communicative awkwardness.

False assumptions: assuming incorrectly that something is true or false, intended or unintended, exists or does not exist, desired or undesired, will or will not happen.

False closing: when verbal and nonverbal messages signal the closing of the interview is commencing but a party introduces a new topic or issue.

Feedback: verbal and nonverbal reactions of an interview party.

Feelings: emotions such as pride, fear, love, anger, and sympathy.

Fee-paid positions: when an organization retains a placement agency to locate qualified applicants and pays fees the agency would normally charge applicants.

Filter strategy: a question strategy that enables the interviewer to determine an interviewee's knowledge of a topic.

First impression: the initial impression one makes on another as a result of appearance, dress, manner, and quality of communication.

Flexibility: the ability to adapt during interviews to unexpected exchanges, answers, information, or attitudes.

Focus group interviews: a small group of people (6 to 12) act as an interviewee party with a highly skilled interviewer who asks a carefully selected set of questions that focus on a specific topic.

Frequency interval scales: questions that ask respondents to select a number that most accurately reflects how often they do or don't use something.

Functional resume format: a resume in which an applicant places experiences under headings that highlight qualifications for a position.

Funnel sequence: a question sequence that begins with a broad, open-ended question and proceeds with ever-more restricted questions.

Gender: how interview parties being female or male affects interview interactions.

General inquiry questions: an opening question that determines why an interviewee (often a medical patient) has initiated an interview.

Generic message: a persuasive message designed for a variety of audiences rather than a specific targeted audience.

Getting through questions: questions in counseling interviews designed to enable interviewees to manage their emotions.

Global relationships: relationships between parties from different countries and cultures.

Goal oriented: an interaction in which the interviewer is goal or task oriented rather than people oriented.

Ground rules: rules governing an interview agreed to by both parties.

Group interview: an interview in which there are multiple interviewers, such as several journalists at a press conference.

Guessing game: when a questioner attempts to guess information instead of asking for it.

Halo effect: when an interviewer gives favorable ratings to all job duties when an interviewee excels in only one.

Hasty generalization tactic: a person generalizes to a whole group of people, places, or things from only one or a few examples.

Highly closed questions: questions that can be answered with a single word or short phrase, most often a yes or no.

Highly directed reactions and responses: when an interviewer offers ultimatums and strong advice.

Highly nondirective reactions and responses: when an interviewer offers no information, assistance, or evaluations but encourages the interviewee to communicate, analyze, and be self-reliant.

Highly scheduled interview: a schedule in which the interviewer prepares all questions and their exact wording prior to an interview.

Highly scheduled standardized interview: a schedule in which the interviewer prepares all questions and their exact wording as well as answer options prior to an interview.

Historical critical incident question: a question that asks applicants how they would have resolved a problem the recruiter's organization faced in the past.

Honesty tests: tests designed to assess the ethics, honesty, and integrity of job applicants.

Hourglass sequence: a question sequence that begins with open questions, proceeds to closed questions, and ends with open questions.

Hyperpersonal revelations: highly personal (perhaps intimate) revelations of a person during an interview that reveals too much information.

Hypothetical question: a hypothetical but realistic question that asks respondents how they would handle a situation or problem.

Identification theory: a theory that persons persuade others by identifying with them in a variety of ways.

Idioms: expressions unique to a culture or nation likely to be misunderstood by a person from a different culture or nation.

Imagery: creating pictures or images in a person's mind through highly descriptive language.

Implicative approach: an approach that withholds an explicit statement of purpose or intent until the interviewee sees the implications and suggests a course of action.

Individualist culture: a culture that places high value on self-image, self-esteem, self-reliance, self-awareness, and individual achievement.

Induced compliance theory: a theory designed to change thinking, feeling, or acting by inducing others to engage in activities counter to their values, beliefs, or attitudes.

Inform: to provide information or knowledge to another party.

Information: stories, illustrations, comparisons, experiences, quotations, statistics, definitions, and explanations that apprise interview parties of problems, solutions, situations, and events.

Information-gathering interviews: interviews designed to obtain facts, opinions, data, feelings, attitudes, beliefs, reactions, advice, or feedback.

Information-giving interview: interviews designed to exchange data, knowledge, direction, instructions, orientation, clarification, or warnings.

Information overload: when interviewees are provided with more information than they can process or recall.

Informational probe: a question designed to obtain additional information when an answer appears to be superficial, vague, or ambiguous or to suggest a feeling or attitude.

Initiating the interview: the process by which an interview is arranged and started.

Inoculation theory: a theory based on the belief that it is often more effective to prevent undesired persuasion from occurring than trying damage control afterward.

Integrity interviews: interviews designed to assess the honesty and integrity of prospective employees.

Intelligent or educated interviewee: an interviewee with high levels of intelligence or informal and formal education.

Interactional: the exchanging or sharing of roles, responsibilities, feelings, beliefs, motives, and information.

Internet interview: an interview that takes place solely through the Internet.

Interpersonal communication process: a complex and often puzzling communication interaction with another party.

Interval scales: survey question scales that provide distances between measures.

Interview: an interactional communication process between two parties, at least one of whom has a predetermined and serious purpose, and involves the asking and answering of questions.

Interview evaluation: the formal or informal process of evaluating applicants following recruiting interviews.

Interview guide: a carefully structured outline of topics and subtopics to be covered during an interview.

Interview schedule: a list of questions an interviewer prepares prior to an interview.

Interviewee: the party who is not in basic control of the interaction, such as a respondent in a survey interview or an applicant in a recruiting interview.

Interviewer bias: when respondents give answers they feel questioners want them to give rather than express their true feelings, attitudes, or beliefs.

Inverted funnel sequence: a sequence that begins with closed questions and proceeds toward open questions.

Jargon: words that organizations or groups alter or create for specialized use.

Job/career fairs: gatherings of recruiters from a variety of organizations on college campuses or malls in which applicants can obtain information, make contacts, and take part in interviews.

Joblike situations: simulated job situations through questions or role playing that enable the recruiter to perceive how an applicant might act on the job.

Joint actions: when interview parties understand that what each does will impact the other and act in the other's party's interest.

Journalist's interview guide: a guide that focuses on who, what, when, where, how, and why.

Just cause: the fair and equitable treatment of each employee in a job class.

Key informant: a person who can supply information on situations, assist in selecting interviewees, and aid in securing interviewee cooperation.

Knowledge workers: workers that create and access information rather than manufacture products and are valued for their knowledge, ability to motivate others, and teamwork.

Law of recency: people tend to recall the last thing said or done in interviews.

Lay counselor: a person with little or no formal training in counseling.

Lay theories: commonsense theories patients hold about health care that often resist scientific notions and research findings.

Leading push: a question that suggests how a person should respond.

Leading question: a question that suggests implicitly or explicitly the expected or desired answer.

Leaning question strategy: a question strategy that enables interviewers to reduce the number of undecided and don't know responses in surveys.

Learning organization: an organization that places high value on knowledge, skills, competencies, opportunities for learning, and employees as intellectual capital.

Leave-taking: the effort to bring an interview to a close.

Length of service error: when an interviewer assumes that present performance is high because past performance was high.

Letters of recommendation: letters sent by references to prospective employers on behalf of persons applying for specific positions.

Level 1 interactions: interactions that are relatively safe and nonthreatening.

Level 2 interactions: interactions that require a moderate degree of trust and may be moderately threatening because of exchange of beliefs, attitudes, values, and positions on issues.

Level 3 interactions: interactions that require a great deal of trust because parties disclose fully their feelings, beliefs, attitudes, and perceptions on intimate and controversial topics.

Level of confidence: the mathematical probability that the survey is within an accepted margin of error.

Level of information: the amount and sophistication of information an interviewee has to offer.

Likert scale: interval scale questions that ask respondents to make judgments about persons, places, things, or ideas.

Listening: the deliberate process of receiving, understanding, evaluating, and retaining what is seen and heard.

Listening for comprehension: receiving, understanding, and remembering messages as accurately as possible.

Listening for empathy: a method of communicating an attitude of genuine concern, understanding, and involvement.

Listening for evaluation: a means of judging what is heard and observed.

Listening for resolution: a means of mutually resolving a problem or task.

Loaded question: a question with strong direction or dictation of the answer desired through the use of name calling or emotionally charged words.

Longitudinal study: a study to determine trends in what is known, thought, or felt over a period of time.

Loose rater: an interviewer who is reluctant to point out weak areas and dwells on the average or better areas of performance.

Make meaning questions: questions in counseling interviews designed to determine what an interviewee is most concerned about in an interview.

Management by objectives (MBO) model: a performance review model that involves a manager and a subordinate in a mutual (50-50) setting of results-oriented goals rather than activities to be performed.

Margin of error: the degree of similarity between sample results and the results from a 100 percent count obtained in an identical manner.

Marginalized respondent: a respondent who is unlikely to be surveyed because of culture, demographics, or lack of a telephone or easily accessed telephone number or residential address.

Matching process: the process of matching an applicant with a specific position and organization.

Meaning making: actions and questions designed to evoke meaning.

Metaphorical questions: questions that include metaphors, such as "establishing a level playing field" or addressing a company as a "family."

Mirror probe: a question that summarizes a series of answers to ensure accurate understanding and retention.

Moderately scheduled interview: a schedule in which the interviewer prepares all major questions with possible probing questions under each prior to an interview.

Motives: values such as security, belonging, freedom, ambition, and preservation of health.

Multisource feedback: feedback from a number of sources.

Mutual product: when the results of interviews depend upon the contributions of both parties.

Naming: the labeling of people, places, or things to make them appear different, to alter perceptions of reality.

Negative face: the desire to be free of imposition or intrusion.

Negative politeness: an effort to protect another person when negative face needs are threatened.

Negative selling: the attempt to persuade by attacking another or another's proposal rather than supporting yourself or your proposal.

Network tree: a listing of names, addresses, and telephone numbers of primary contacts who can provide leads for job openings and additional contacts.

Networking: creating a list of contacts for possible employment positions.

Neutral question: a question that allows a respondent to determine an answer with no overt direction or pressure from the questioner.

Neutralize: any effort to remove an obstacle to making a favorable impression or attaining a position, including recruiter questions that violate EEO laws.

Nexting: verbal and nonverbal signals from one party that it is time for the other party to enter into the interaction or to become silent.

Noise: anything that may interfere with the communication process, such as machinery, ringing telephones, doors opening and closing, others talking, traffic, and music.

Nominal scales: questions that provide mutually exclusive variables and ask respondents to pick or name the most appropriate.

Nondirective approach: an interview in which the interviewee controls subject matter, length of answers, climate, and formality.

Nondirective reaction: when an interviewer reacts to a client without giving advice or specific direction.

Nonscheduled interview: an interview guide of topic and subtopics with no prepared questions prior to an interview.

Nontraditional forms: newer forms of interviewing such as focus groups, videoconferences, e-mail interviews, and virtual interviews.

Nonverbal closing actions: nonverbal actions that signal a closing is commencing, such as leaning forward, uncrossing legs, breaking eye contact, and offering to shake hands.

Nonverbal communication: nonverbal signals such as physical appearance, dress, eye contact, voice, touches, head nods, hand shakes, and posture.

Nonverbal interactions: nonverbal signals such as physical appearance, dress, eye contact, voice, touches, head nods, hand shakes, and posture.

Normative competence: when an interview party understands the parts each party will play in a relationship and develops workable rules and norms.

Normative influence: a person's beliefs of which behaviors important individuals or groups think are advisable or inadvisable to perform.

Nudging probe: a word or brief phrase that urges a respondent to continue answering.

Numerical interview scales: questions that ask respondents to select a range or level that accurately reflects an age, income level, educational level, and so on.

Observing: paying close attention to surroundings, people, dress, appearance, and nonverbal communication.

Off the record: information that cannot be reported following an interview.

Open question: a question that allows the respondent considerable freedom in determining the amount and kind of information to offer.

Open-to-closed switch: when a questioner asks an open question but changes it to a closed question before a respondent can reply.

Opening: the first minutes of an interview in which the interviewer attempts to establish rapport and orient the interviewee.

Opening question: the initial question during the body of an interview.

Opening techniques: verbal and nonverbal signals that establish rapport and orient the interviewee.

Order bias: possible influence on how interviewees respond due to the order of answer options in survey questions.

Ordinal scales: questions that ask respondents to rate or rank options in their implied relationship to one another.

Orientation: the portion of the opening in which the interviewer explains the purpose, length, and nature of the interview.

Outside forces: influential others such as family, friends, employers, and agencies who are not part of the interview but may affect one or both parties before, during, or after an interview.

Overt identification: an attempt to establish a "we are one and the same" perception.

Panel interview: when two to five persons representing an organization may interview an applicant at the same time.

Paper trail: written materials that allow the tracing of an individual or organization's actions or opinions.

Party: the interviewer or interviewee side in an interview.

Patient-centered care (PCC): when a patient's needs, preferences, and beliefs are respected at all times.

Percentage agencies: placement agencies whose fee for finding positions for clients is a specific percentage of the first year's salary.

Perceptions: the ways people see and interpret themselves, other people, places, things, events, and nonverbal signals.

Personal interview: a survey interview that takes place face-to-face.

Personal space: an imaginary bubble around us that we consider almost as private as our body.

Personality tests: tests designed to assess the people skills of applicants.

Persuaders: interviewers who attempt to alter the ways interviewees think, feel, and/or act.

Persuasive interviews: an interview designed to change an interviewee's way of thinking, feeling, and/or acting.

Pitchfork effect: when an interviewer gives negative ratings to all facets of performance because of a particular trait the interviewer dislikes in others.

Placement agency: an agency that provides services such as career counseling, resume preparation, employer contacts, and interview opportunities for those seeking positions.

Placement interviews: interviews designed to assign employees to positions or to move them from one position or location to another.

Polarizing: the attempt to limit choices or positions to polar opposites.

Politeness theory: a theory that claims all humans want to be appreciated, approved, liked, honored, and protected.

Population: all persons able and qualified to respond in a particular survey.

Portfolio: a small and varied collection of an applicant's best work.

Positive attention: attention that generates recruiter interest in an applicant.

Positive face: the desire to be appreciated, approved, liked, and honored.

Positive politeness: an effort to show concern by complimenting and using respectful forms of address.

Post hoc or scrambling cause-effect tactic: basing a cause-effect relationship on coincidence, a minor cause, or a single cause.

Power speech: words that express certainty, challenges, verbal aggression, and metaphors.

Powerless speech: words and nonfluencies that express apologies, disclaimers, excuses, and uncertainty.

Precision journalism: journalistic reports based on survey research data.

Predetermined: planned in advance of an interaction.

Press conference: a setting in which multiple interviewers interview one interviewee.

Pretest: the test of an interview schedule with a small sample of respondents prior to a survey to detect possible problems that might result during the survey.

Primary question: a question that introduces a topic or new area within a topic and can stand alone out of context.

Privacy: freedom from unwanted intrusion into or access to interview interactions.

Probing: the attempt to discover additional information and understanding.

Probing question: a question that attempts to discover additional information following a primary or secondary question and cannot stand alone out of context.

Problems of the interviewee's behavior interviews: interviews designed to review, separate, correct, or counsel interviewees for their behavior.

Problems of the interviewer's behavior interviews: interviews designed to receive complaints, grievances, or suggestions concerning the interviewer's behavior.

Problem-solution sequence: an outline divided into problem and solution phases.

Problem-solving interviews: interviews designed to discuss mutually shared problems, receive suggestions for solutions, or implement solutions.

Process: a dynamic, continuing, ever changing interaction of variables.

Prospecting: a systematic selection of interviewees who are good prospects for persuasive interviews.

Proximity: the physical distance between interview parties.

Psychological reactance theory: a theory based on the claim that people react negatively when someone threatens to restrict or does restrict a behavior they want to engage in.

Purpose: the reason or goal for a party conducting or taking part in an interview.

Qualitative survey: a survey in which findings are presented in textual form, usually words.

Quantitative survey: a survey in which findings are presented in numerical form, such as percentages and frequencies.

Question: any statement or nonverbal act that invites an answer.

Question pitfall: a slight alteration of questions, often unintentional, that changes them from open to closed, primary to secondary, and neutral to leading.

Question sequence: the strategic interconnection of questions.

Quintamensional design sequence: a five-step sequence designed to assess the intensity of a respondent's opinions and attitudes.

Quiz show pitfall: a question above or beneath the respondent's level of knowledge.

Random digit dialing: a system that randomly generates telephone numbers in target area codes and prefix areas for selecting a survey sample.

Random sampling: selecting respondents randomly from a container, a list or group.

Ranking ordinal scale: questions that ask respondents to rank options in their implied relationship to one another.

Rapport: a process of establishing and sustaining a relationship by creating feelings of goodwill and trust.

Rating ordinal scale: questions that ask respondents to rate options in their implied relationship to one another.

Real setting: an interview setting with all of its defects and problems.

Reasoning from accepted belief, assumption, or proposition: reasoning based on the assertion that a belief, assumption, or proposition is true and without question.

Reasoning from analogy: reasoning based on points of similarity that two people, places, or things have in common.

Reasoning from cause-effect: reasoning based on a causal relationship.

Reasoning from condition: reasoning based on the assertion that if something does or does not happen, something else will or will not happen.

Reasoning from example: reasoning based on a generalization about a whole class of people, places, or things from a sampling of the class.

Reasoning from facts: reasoning that offers a conclusion as the best explanation for available evidence.

Reasoning from sign: a claim that two or more variables are related so the presence or absence of one indicates the presence or absence of the other.

Recall: the ability of an interview party to remember and report accurately what took place during an interview, including agreements, information exchanged, attitudes, and climate.

Recency error: when an interviewer relies too heavily on the most recent events or performance levels.

Reciprocal concessions: the effort to instill a sense of obligation in another to make a concession after the other party has made one.

Recording: taking mental or physical note of what is taking place during an interview.

References: names of persons applicants give to prospective employers who can provide assessments of their qualifications for positions.

Reflective probe: a question that reflects the answer received to verify or clarify what the respondent intended to say.

Reinforce: strengthening or making stronger.

Rejection then retreat: the effort to exaggerate a first proposal just enough to make a second appear more acceptable.

Relational: an interpersonal connection between two parties or persons.

Relational dimensions: critical dimensions such as similarity, inclusion, affection, and trust that determine the nature of relationships.

Relational distance: the closeness of the relationship between interview parties.

Relational history: the past, present, and future connections between two parties or persons.

Relational memory: what interview parties remember from previous encounters with one another.

Relational uncertainty: when either party is unaware of the degree of warmth, sharing of control, or level of trust that will exist during an interview.

Relationship: an interpersonal connection between parties that influences their interest in the outcome of the interview.

Reliability: the assurance that the same information can be collected in repeated interviews.

Repeat question strategy: a question strategy that enables the interviewer to determine interviewee consistency in responses on a topic.

Replicability: the ability to duplicate interviews regardless of interviewers, interviewees, and situations.

Report: a formal or informal recording of the information attained during an interview.

Reproducibility: the ability to duplicate interviews regardless of interviewer, interviewee, and situation.

Research: a careful search for background materials, information, facts, and theories pertaining to a subject, person, or organization.

Restatement probe: a question that restates all or part of the original question that remains unanswered.

Resume: a brief accounting of an applicant's career goal, education, training, and experiences.

Resume or application form question pitfall: asking a question that is already answered on the resume or application form.

Reticent interviewee: an interviewee who seems unwilling or unable to talk and respond freely.

Role competence: the ability of an interview party to play the roles of interviewer and interviewee effectively.

Rule of reciprocation: instills in an interviewee a sense of obligation to repay in kind what another provides.

Sample point or block sampling: preassigned numbers and types of respondents are chosen from assigned geographical areas.

Sample size: the number of persons interviewed during a survey when the whole population is too large to interview.

Sampling principles: principles that create a sample that accurately represents the population under study.

Sanitized setting: an interview setting without time constraints, interviewee problems, or situational problems such as noise, interruptions, inappropriate seating, or uncomfortable temperatures.

Screening interviews: interviews designed to select applicants for additional interviews.

Secondary question: a question that attempts to discover additional information following a primary or secondary (probing) question and cannot stand alone out of context.

Selection interview: an interview in which the purpose is to select a person for employment or membership within an organization.

Self: focus of the interviewee on the interviewee during a counseling interview.

Self-analysis: a careful, thorough, and insightful analysis of self an applicant conducts prior to taking part in interviews.

Self-concept: how a person perceives self physically, socially, and psychologically.

Self-disclosure: the willingness and ability to disclose information pertaining to oneself.

Self-esteem: positive and negative feelings a person has of self.

Self-evident truth: a claim that a question or issue is not arguable because it is settled by rule or fact.

Self-fulfilling prophecy: a prediction that comes true because a person expects or predicts it will be so.

Self-identity: how, what, and with whom people identify themselves.

Self-persuasion: a situation in which a persuader encourages a person to persuade self rather than being persuaded by another.

Self-selection: when respondents alone determine if they will be included in a survey sample.

Seminar format: an interview format in which one or more recruiters interview several applicants at the same time.

Sequential phase model: a counseling model that centers on four phases based on affective (emotional) and cognitive (thinking) functions.

Sex: the genders of interview parties.

Shock-absorber phrases: phrases that reduce the sting of critical questions.

Shuffle strategy: a question strategy that enables interviewers to avoid responses based on the order rather than the content of answer options.

Silence: the absence of vocal communication from one or both parties in an interview.

Silent probe: when an interviewer remains silent after an answer and may use nonverbal signals to encourage the respondent to continue answering.

Similarity: characteristics, experiences, interests, beliefs, attitudes, values, and expectations interview parties have in common.

Situation: a total interview context that includes events prior to and after, time, place, and surroundings.

Situational schema: a schema that includes all of the different types of interviews.

Skip interval or random digit sample: a sampling method in which every predetermined number on a list is selected, such as every 10th name in a directory.

Slang: unofficial jargon that groups use.

Slogan or tabloid thinking: a clever phrase that encapsulates a position, stand, or goal of a persuader.

Sound-alikes: words that sound alike but have different meanings.

Space sequence: an outline that arranges topics and subtopics according to spatial divisions such as left to right, north to south.

Standard/learned principle: principles people learn through life that automatically guide actions and decisions.

Status difference: the difference in social or organizational hierarchy between interviewer and interviewee.

Stealth marketing: when a sales representative pretends to be a friendly, disinterested party rather than a sales representative.

Strategic ambiguities: the strategic use of words with multiple or vague meanings to avoid specific definitions or explanations.

Strategic answers: when interviewees answer questions to their advantage.

Stratified random sampling: a sampling method that selects the number of respondents according to their percentages in the target population.

Structure: a predetermined arrangement of parts or stages into a meaningful whole.

Supportive climate: a climate in which there is trust and respect between parties.

System: a degree of structure or organization that guides a planned interaction between two parties.

Table of random numbers: a sample of respondents selected by assigning each respondent a number and using a table of random numbers for picking a sample.

Talent or trait-based selection process: a recruiting interview in which all interviewer questions focus on specific talents or traits included in the applicant profile.

Talkative interviewee: an interviewee who gives overly long answers and talks too freely.

Task oriented: an interviewer who is more concerned with performing a task efficiently and effectively than in communicating effectively with an interviewee.

Team interview: when two to five persons representing an organization may interview an applicant at the same time.

Telephone interview: an interview that is conducted over the telephone rather than face-to-face.

Tell me everything: an extremely open question with no restrictions or guidelines for the respondent.

Territorial markers: an imaginary bubble around us that we consider nearly as private as our body.

Territoriality: the physical and psychological space in which an interview takes place.

Test of job relatedness: effort to meet EEO laws by establishing legally defensible selection criteria, asking questions related to these criteria, asking the same questions of all applicants, being cautious when probing into answers, being cautious during informal chit-chat, focusing questions on what applicants can do, and steering applicants away from volunteering unlawful information.

The 360-degree approach: a performance review model that obtains as many views of a person's performance as possible from observers who interact with the person on a regular basis.

Thin entering wedge (domino effect or slippery slope) tactic: an argument that one decision, action, or law after another is leading toward some sort of danger.

Tight rater: an interviewer who believes that no one can perform at the necessary standards.

Time sequence: an outline that treats topics and subtopics in chronological order.

Tongue-in-cheek test response: a pleasant, perhaps humorous response that sends a signal to a recruiter that he or she has asked an unlawful question.

Topical sequence: an outline sequence that follows the natural divisions of a topic or subtopic.

Traditional forms: standard types of interviews such as informational, survey, employment, performance review, counseling, and health care.

Traditional recruiter questions: common questions generations of recruiters have asked, such as where do you plan to be five years from now.

Transfer interviews: interviews designed to promote employees, to assign them to positions, or to move them from one position or location to another.

Transferring guilt: an effort to dodge an issue by turning the accuser, victim, or questioner into the guilty party.

Trial closing: the attempt to determine if an interviewee is ready to close an interview with an agreement of some sort.

Tunnel sequence: a series of similar questions that are either open or closed.

Tu quoque: an effort to dodge an issue or objection by revolving it upon the challenger or questioner.

Two parties: an interviewer and an interviewee party consisting of one or more persons with distinct roles and purposes such as getting and giving information, counseling and being counseled, persuading and being persuaded, recruiting and being recruited.

Undercover marketing: when a sales representative pretends to be a friendly, disinterested party rather than a sales representative. Also called stealth marketing.

Unipolar question: a question that has only one obvious or desired answer.

Universal performance interviewing model: a performance review that focuses on coaching by starting with positive behavior a manager wants the employee to maintain and then moving to behaviors that need to be corrected.

Unsanitized setting: a real-world interview setting with all of its problems, crises, interruptions, and unexpected happenings.

Upward communication: an interview in which a subordinate in an organizational hierarchy is attempting to interact as interviewer with a superior in the hierarchy.

Values: fundamental beliefs about ideal states of existence and modes of behavior.

Verbal interactions: words (arbitrary connections of letters) that serve as symbols for people, places, things, events, beliefs, and feelings.

Videoconference: technology that enables interview parties to see and hear one another and to interact in real time.

Virtual interview: an electronic interview employed most often for practice and simulation.

Web survey: a survey that is conducted over the Internet rather than face-to-face or over the telephone.

Yes (no) response: a question that has only one obvious answer.

Yes-but approach: an approach that begins with areas of agreement and approaches points of disagreement after goodwill and a supportive climate are established.

Yes-yes approach: the attempt to get another party in the habit of saying yes so agreements may continue.

AUTHOR INDEX

SUBJECT INDEX